Caring for Cultural Heritage

This book explores how cultural heritage and its care are translated in UK law and non-law instruments. It analyses how communities of care look after cultural heritage because they care about it. These communities include the international and national community, national and local governments, courts, professional bodies, institutions such as museums as well as community groups. 'Care' refers to the varied ways in which communities engage with cultural heritage to maintain it, sustain relationships about it and with it, use it and provide access to it, with a view to passing it on to future generations. The book also assesses how far these nested practices of care assist communities of care in providing respectful, empathetic and dialogical care to navigate harm to cultural heritage. It will be of interest to scholars of cultural heritage studies across disciplines, including law, sociology and anthropology, as well as policymakers and practitioners in cultural heritage management.

Charlotte Woodhead is Associate Professor at Warwick Law School, University of Warwick. Charlotte is a recognised expert in the restitution of cultural heritage, having been commissioned in 2018 by the United Kingdom's DCMS and the Spoliation Advisory Panel to write a report on elements of the 2017 London Conference Action Plan. Charlotte has also served as a member of the Museums Association Ethics Committee (2013–2019).

The Law in Context Series

Series Editors
Professor Kenneth Armstrong
University of Cambridge
Professor Maksymilian Del Mar
Queen Mary, University of London
Professor Sally Sheldon
University of Bristol and University of Technology Sydney

Editorial Advisory Board
Professor Bronwen Morgan
University of New South Wales
Emeritus Professor William Twining
University College London

Since 1970, the Law in Context series has been at the forefront of a movement to broaden the study of law. The series is a vehicle for the publication of innovative monographs and texts that treat law and legal phenomena critically in their cultural, social, political, technological, environmental and economic contexts. A contextual approach involves treating legal subjects broadly, using materials from other humanities and social sciences, and from any other discipline that helps to explain the operation in practice of the particular legal field or legal phenomena under investigation. It is intended that this orientation is at once more stimulating and more revealing than the bare exposition of legal rules. The series includes original research monographs, coursebooks and textbooks that foreground contextual approaches and methods. The series includes and welcomes books on the study of law in all its contexts, including domestic legal systems, European and international law, transnational and global legal processes, and comparative law.

Books in the Series
Acosta: *The National versus the Foreigner in South America: 200 Years of Migration and Citizenship Law*
Alaattinoğlu: *Grievance Formation, Rights and Remedies*
Ali: *Modern Challenges to Islamic Law*
Alyagon Darr: *Plausible Crime Stories: The Legal History of Sexual Offences in Mandate Palestine*
Anderson, Schum & Twining: *Analysis of Evidence, 2nd Edition*
Ashworth: *Sentencing and Criminal Justice, 6th Edition*
Barton & Douglas: *Law and Parenthood*
Baxi, McCrudden & Paliwala: *Law's Ethical, Global and Theoretical Contexts: Essays in Honour of William Twining*
Beecher-Monas: *Evaluating Scientific Evidence: An Interdisciplinary Framework for Intellectual Due Process*
Bell: *French Legal Cultures*

Bercusson: *European Labour Law, 2nd Edition*

Birkinshaw: *European Public Law*

Birkinshaw: *Freedom of Information: The Law, the Practice and the Ideal, 4th Edition*

Blick: *Electrified Democracy: The Internet and the United Kingdom Parliament in History*

Broderick & Ferri: *International and European Disability Law and Policy: Text, Cases and Materials*

Brownsword & Goodwin: *Law and the Technologies of the Twenty-First Century: Text and Materials*

Cane & Goudkamp: *Atiyah's Accidents, Compensation and the Law, 9th Edition*

Clarke: *Principles of Property Law*

Clarke & Kohler: *Property Law: Commentary and Materials*

Collins: *The Law of Contract, 4th Edition*

Collins, Ewing & McColgan: *Labour Law, 2nd Edition*

Cowan: *Housing Law and Policy*

Cranston: *Making Commercial Law Through Practice 1830–1970*

Cranston: *Legal Foundations of the Welfare State*

Darian-Smith: *Laws and Societies in Global Contexts: Contemporary Approaches*

Dauvergne: *Making People Illegal: What Globalisation Means for Immigration and Law*

David: *Kinship, Law and Politics: An Anatomy of Belonging*

Davies: *Perspectives on Labour Law, 2nd Edition*

Dembour: *Who Believes in Human Rights?: Reflections on the European Convention*

de Sousa Santos: *Toward a New Legal Common Sense: Law, Globalization, and Emancipation*

Diduck: *Law's Families*

Dowdle: *Transnational Law: A Framework for Analysis*

Dupret: *Positive Law from the Muslim World: Jurisprudence, History, Practices*

Emon: *Jurisdictional Exceptionalisms: Islamic Law, International Law, and Parental Child Abduction*

Estella: *Legal Foundations of EU Economic Governance*

Fortin: *Children's Rights and the Developing Law, 3rd Edition*

Garnsey: *The Justice of Visual Art: Creative State-Building in Times of Political Transition*

Garton, Probert & Bean: *Moffat's Trusts Law: Text and Materials, 7th Edition*

Ghai & Woodman: *Practising Self-Government: A Comparative Study of Autonomous Regions*

Glover-Thomas: *Reconstructing Mental Health Law and Policy*

Gobert & Punch: *Rethinking Corporate Crime*

Goldman: *Globalisation and the Western Legal Tradition: Recurring Patterns of Law and Authority*

Haack: *Evidence Matters: Science, Proof, and Truth in the Law*

Harlow & Rawlings: *Law and Administration, 4th Edition*

Harris: *An Introduction to Law, 8th Edition*

Harris, Campbell & Halson: *Remedies in Contract and Tort, 2nd Edition*

Harvey: *Seeking Asylum in the UK: Problems and Prospects*

Herring: *Law and the Relational Self*

Hervey & McHale: *European Union Health Law: Themes and Implications*

Scott & Black: *Cranston's Consumers and the Law*

Seneviratne: *Ombudsmen: Public Services and Administrative Justice*

Seppänen: *Ideological Conflict and the Rule of Law in Contemporary China: Useful Paradoxes*

Siems: *Comparative Law, 3rd Edition*

Stapleton: *Product Liability*

Stewart: *Gender, Law and Justice in a Global Market*

Tamanaha: *Law as a Means to an End: Threat to the Rule of Law*

Tuori: *Properties of Law: Modern Law and After*

Turpin & Tomkins: *British Government and the Constitution: Text and Materials, 7th Edition*

Twining: *General Jurisprudence: Understanding Law from a Global Perspective*

Twining: *Globalisation and Legal Theory*

Twining: *Human Rights, Southern Voices: Francis Deng, Abdullahi An-Na'im, Yash Ghai and Upendra Baxi*

Twining: *Jurist in Context: A Memoir*

Twining: *Karl Llewellyn and the Realist Movement, 2nd Edition*

Twining: *Rethinking Evidence: Exploratory Essays, 2nd Edition*

Twining & Miers: *How to Do Things with Rules, 5th Edition*

Wan: *Film and Constitutional Controversy: Visualizing Hong Kong Identity in the Age of 'One Country, Two Systems'*

Ward: *A Critical Introduction to European Law, 3rd Edition*

Ward: *Law, Text, Terror*

Ward: *Shakespeare and Legal Imagination*

Watt: *The Making Sense of Politics, Media, and Law: Rhetorical Performance as Invention, Creation, Production*

Wells & Quick: *Lacey, Wells and Quick: Reconstructing Criminal Law: Text and Materials, 4th Edition*

Young: *Turpin and Tomkins' British Government and the Constitution: Text and Materials, 8th Edition*

Zander: *Cases and Materials on the English Legal System, 10th Edition*

Zander: *The Law-Making Process, 6th Edition*

International Journal of Law in Context: A Global Forum for Interdisciplinary Legal Studies

The *International Journal of Law in Context* is the companion journal to the Law in Context book series and provides a forum for interdisciplinary legal studies and offers intellectual space for ground-breaking critical research. It publishes contextual work about law and its relationship with other disciplines including but not limited to science, literature, humanities, philosophy, sociology, psychology, ethics, history and geography. More information about the journal and how to submit an article can be found at http://journals.cambridge.org/ijc

Caring for Cultural Heritage

An Integrated Approach to Legal and Ethical Initiatives in the United Kingdom

CHARLOTTE WOODHEAD

University of Warwick

CAMBRIDGE
UNIVERSITY PRESS

Shaftesbury Road, Cambridge CB2 8EA, United Kingdom

One Liberty Plaza, 20th Floor, New York, NY 10006, USA

477 Williamstown Road, Port Melbourne, VIC 3207, Australia

314–321, 3rd Floor, Plot 3, Splendor Forum, Jasola District Centre, New Delhi – 110025, India

103 Penang Road, #05–06/07, Visioncrest Commercial, Singapore 238467

Cambridge University Press is part of Cambridge University Press & Assessment, a department of the University of Cambridge.

We share the University's mission to contribute to society through the pursuit of education, learning and research at the highest international levels of excellence.

www.cambridge.org
Information on this title: www.cambridge.org/9781108498401

DOI: 10.1017/9781108696463

First published 2024

A catalogue record for this publication is available from the British Library

A Cataloging-in-Publication data record for this book is available from the Library of Congress

ISBN 978-1-108-49840-1 Hardback

IN MEMORIAM
Richard Giles Woodhead (1949–2021),
whose Yorkshire heritage
– infused with a hint of rhythm and blues –
shone through, and lives on . . .

. . . and to Robert, Charlie, Isobel and Susan,
– whom I care *about*, and care *for* –
I dedicate this book.

Contents

Acknowledgements

The story of the evolution of this book is very much tied up with births, death and a global pandemic.

The book evolved from some of the work undertaken for my PhD thesis, supervised by Professor Janet Ulph and Professor Dawn Watkins, to whom I owe thanks. However, the book ultimately took a very different turn. Inspired by conversations with Professor Fiona Smith, who introduced me to the work of James Boyd White, I thought again about how I read legal cases and wanted to explore the communities that they created. With the desire to move beyond preservation and access as an approach to heritage at some stage I thought that 'care' would encompass the varied activities that we do to cultural heritage to look after it. It is with great thanks to Dr Andrzej Jakubowksi, who, in feedback on my book proposal, opened my eyes to the fact that the really interesting thing about my approach was that of care. As the project developed, and as I interrogated the concept of care more fully, I realised just how fundamental care is to both the feeling towards cultural heritage and the processes that we undertake with cultural heritage *because* we care. As I grappled with the concepts of care, I benefited immensely from comments on the early chapters from Professor Ann Stewart and Professor Vanessa Munro. I am so appreciative of Dr Andrzej Jakubowksi reading the first two chapters and his comments on them. Maria Ovens very kindly read two chapters, and her linguistic advice as well as her advice on one particularly thorny issue was invaluable. Professor Rebecca Probert was so generous with her time and care in reading an entire draft of the book; the work benefited significantly from her advice. I would like to thank Behesti Aydogan for his research assistance in chasing elusive references for some of the footnotes. Sincere thanks are due to the editorial and production teams at CUP and Integra.

And finally, thanks to family members who have assisted: thank you to Robert Fear for reading the entire book and for his advice and to Susan Woodhead for also reading the entire book to check for consistency of references. Her careful notes made the final editing all the easier.

Now come the caveats. This book is long, because the legal landscape in the United Kingdom is so vast and fragmented and the extent to which cultural heritage is cared for is extensive. Given the fact that my husband (who works in an unrelated field) required frequent sips of wine to get through reading the book, I was tempted to provide accompanying tasting notes. However, instead I feel that some words to help navigate the book might be of assistance. For those interested in the ethics of care and its application to cultural heritage I recommend reading Chapters 1, 2 and 5. In the case of a particular interest in the ethics of care, as applicable to restitution and repatriation claims, I recommend reading Chapters 2 and 9. Where the reader's interest lies in the UK perspective and how the United Kingdom specifically cares for cultural heritage, I recommend reading Chapters 6, 7 and 8.

Having started my career as a doctrinal private lawyer, I haven't abandoned my roots as seeing the law as a means of facilitating society. Nevertheless, in the context of cultural heritage I see the clear advantages of using a framework of responsibilities rather than rights and recognise how law can act as a community of care, providing care for cultural heritage, albeit not always appropriately. I hope that this book serves as the start of a dialogue about how law and non-law instruments can care directly and indirectly for cultural heritage.

1

Introduction

The global impetus to care for cultural heritage has never been as important as it is today. Cultural heritage as an area of concern – vital as it is for global peace,[1] sustainable development[2] and respecting the identities of peoples[3] – has been recognised by international organisations such as UNESCO since the 1950s. In recent years cultural heritage has had an augmented role on the international political and legal stages; it has been the subject of UN Security Council Resolutions,[4] the first G7 Meeting on Culture took place in 2017,[5] UNESCO's #Unite4Heritage initiative[6] and 2018 saw the EU's European Year of Cultural Heritage.[7]

The need to respond to the modern-day destruction of cultural heritage objects and places during times of conflict and to stop the circulation of decontextualised objects has been a leitmotiv of the twenty-first century. Museums in possession of cultural heritage objects, of which the original owners lost possession during dark historical events, face difficult questions about justice across the generations. In times of austerity, some publicly owned cultural heritage may be at risk of sale to the highest bidder – with an attendant loss to communities for whom it is important. The continued

---

[1] Constitution of the United Nations Educational, Scientific and Cultural Organization (16 November 1945), Preamble and art. 1(1).

[2] United Nations, *Transforming Our World: The 2030 Agenda for Sustainable Development* (A/RES/70/1), Goal 11.4 – 'Strengthen efforts to protect and safeguard the world's cultural and natural heritage'. In the context of Wales, sustainable development includes improving the cultural well-being of Wales: Well-being of Future Generations (Wales) Act 2015, s. 2. Cultural heritage was included in the Final Declaration of the UNESCO World Conference on Cultural Policies and Sustainable Development – MONDIACULT 2022.

[3] E.g. Universal Declaration on Cultural Diversity UNESCO 2001, art. 8, which describes cultural goods and services as 'vectors of identity, values and meaning'.

[4] Both in response to specific problems caused in wartime (UN Security Council Resolution 1483 (2003) and UN Security Council Resolution 2139 (2014) relating to Iraq and Syria respectively) but also more generally (UN Security Council Resolution 2347 (2017)).

[5] *Joint Declaration of the Ministers of Culture of G7 on the Occasion of the Meeting: Culture as an Instrument of Dialogue Among Peoples* (Florence, 30 March 2017): www.g7.utoronto.ca/culture/culture-2017-en.html (last accessed 15 May 2023).

[6] UNESCO, #Unite4heritage.

[7] Decision (EU) 2017/864 of the European Parliament and of the Council of 17 May 2017 on a European Year of Cultural Heritage (2018) OJ 2017 No. L131 20 May 2017, p. 1.

public display of statues commemorating historical figures may harm modern-day communities. These different areas of concern and contestation illustrate just some of the problems with which national and international legal systems must grapple.

As individuals, groups, as a nation or as humanity, there are strong feelings towards cultural heritage due to the links with these communities' history, religion or culture, often because it forms part of their identity. Harm to these objects, places and practices can cause harm to the community for whom they are important. However, harm can also be felt across borders, impacting communities or individuals further afield. International norms provide support for each individual's right to take part in cultural life. However, decisions about the appropriate course of action, particularly where conflicting views exist about why cultural heritage is important to different communities, pose challenges for domestic legal and non-law regulatory initiatives.

This book is not simply about the monumental or the prized possessions of the internationally renowned museum, but rather it is about all types of cultural heritage within the UK, which may be important to communities for often very different reasons.[8] In some circumstances the law seeks to protect cultural heritage from harm, facilitates it being passed down the generations or provides access to it, but on other occasions the law passes by without affecting how it is cared for. Instead, policy guidance from government or non-governmental organisations, ethical obligations agreed by professional bodies and imposed on their members, or other civil society initiatives may ensure that objects, places or practices are cared for, and memories are not forgotten. It is for this reason that this book adopts an integrated approach. It examines the variety of initiatives, nested within each other as practices of care, which deal with cultural heritage. The book thus provides a window on the way in which the UK, as a community, a network of communities and as part of the international community, cares for cultural heritage.

1.1 Scope of Enquiry

Often the very different and difficult questions about cultural heritage are dealt with in disparate ways and form the focus of different enquiries.[9] The way in which the UK cares for cultural heritage through formalised mechanisms has, on occasions, been separated along artificial lines.[10] Yet, at the

---

[8] Cultural heritage is 'based on the diversity of the individual contributions of all human beings': Jukka Jokilehto, 'Human Rights and Cultural Heritage: Observations on the Recognition of Human Rights in the International Doctrine' (2012) 18 *International Journal of Heritage Studies* 226.

[9] In the context of international cultural heritage law, Lixinski has described these as 'sub-niches': Lucas Lixinski, *International Heritage Law for Communities: Exclusion and Re-Imagination* (Oxford: Oxford University Press, 2019), p. 3.

[10] As to which, see Section 1.7.

heart of all of these difficult questions is a desire to care *for* cultural heritage because we care *about* it.[11] By approaching all cultural heritage through the lens of assessing how it is *cared for*, one can see how communities (local, national or international) recognise its importance, how they enjoy it and how they fulfil any responsibilities to current and future generations.

This book will show how, by focusing on the multivocality of decision-making[12] about how cultural heritage is cared for – through the multiple layers of law, formal guidance, ethical principles and civil society solutions representing nested practices of care – it is possible to navigate dissonance, in particular between conflicting viewpoints. By translating cultural heritage and its importance to different people into and out of legal language and engaging with how the instruments and decision-makers create communities of care, one can better understand the extent to which a community cares about cultural heritage and, in turn, cares for it. A central argument of the book is that the most appropriate way to analyse the extent to which cultural heritage is cared for is to focus on how legal and non-law (ethical) initiatives[13] provide the space to hear the different voices of the communities who care about cultural heritage – not only in decision-making in heritage management (following consultation), but also when resolving disputes about cultural heritage (when balancing different viewpoints) and seeking to resolve dissonance. These different activities of care, undertaken by varied communities of care, are analysed to determine whether the care provided by these nested practices of care is appropriate. Here, appropriate care is recognised as empathetic, respectful and dialogic. The book therefore seeks out the translations of the notion of cultural heritage and how its importance is imagined through embedding the human dimension[14] of cultural heritage into decision-making by creating communities of care. This book therefore takes an

---

[11] See Ian Russell, 'Heritage, Identities, and Roots: A Critique of Arborescent Models of Heritage and Identity' in George S. Smith, Phyllis Mauch Messenger and Hilary A. Soderland (eds.), *Heritage Values in Contemporary Society* (Walnut Creek: Left Coast Press, 2010), p. 30 who suggests these as the two aspects of heritage.

[12] As to multivocality, see James Boyd White , 'Law and Literature: "No Manifesto"' (1987–8) 39 *Mercer Law Review* 739, 746.

[13] Use of the phrase 'ethical initiatives' in the title of the book was chosen to indicate the approaches found outside law which do not have a legally binding effect, but which detail how communities *ought* to act. These ethical initiatives can take a variety of different forms, beyond what might traditionally be considered as 'soft law'. Therefore, in addition to guidance and instruments with an obvious ethical basis, such as codes of ethics, the term 'ethical initiatives' also includes civil society initiatives and public participation initiatives (discussed in Section 1.5.3). To distinguish between these different elements, the rather ineloquent terminology of 'non-law instruments' will be used to encompass such guidance, ethical codes and other non-legally binding documents, whereas the terminology of civil society initiatives and public participation initiatives will be used for those more practical measures, as defined in Section 1.5.3.

[14] As to the human dimension of cultural heritage, see Section 1.2.

interdisciplinary approach in the manner entreated by the Council of Europe's Faro Convention on the Value of Cultural Heritage for Society of 2005.[15]

1.1.1 The Centrality of Care

The justifications for approaching cultural heritage through the framework of care are set out in the next chapter, along with the particular definition of care and its central elements. However, here is an opportune place to explain why the concept of care, specifically within the context of the ethics of care, is an appropriate lens through which to examine cultural heritage.

Unlike Continental systems of law, some of which have heritage codes,[16] the UK's system is multi-layered. It comprises commitments made in international law, national law (in the form of legislation, case law and local bye-laws), and statutory and non-statutory codes of conduct and guidance, which all form nested practices of care. However, rather than adopting a regulatory approach investigating how the state and other institutions mandate appropriate treatment of cultural heritage, taking an approach based on care recognises the assumption of responsibility to look after something, particularly when it is at risk of harm. It therefore can take account of how people use the law and non-law processes as instruments to prevent harm to cultural heritage or to continue its use. Care, as an active process, which focuses on relationships and communities assuming responsibilities, provides an invaluable way of drawing together these varied systems.

The terminology of care is frequently used to refer to institutions having cultural heritage in their care.[17] However, the approach to care adopted in this book uses the term more widely to include how different viewpoints and needs are taken into account and how contested areas involving cultural heritage are navigated. These include grappling with issues of justice, memory and historical record, specifically responses to requests for restitution and the way in which cultural heritage is displayed and presented to the public.[18]

---

[15] Council of Europe Framework Convention on the Value of Cultural Heritage for Society (adopted 27 October 2005, Faro, entered into 1 June 2011) CETS 199.

[16] E.g. the French *Code du patrimoine* and the Italian Decreto Legislativo 22 gennaio 2004, m. 42 'Codice dei beni culturali e del paesaggio, ai sensi dell'articolo 10 della legge 6 luglio 2002, n. 137'.

[17] E.g. ICOM, *Code of Ethics for Museums* (revised 2004), in which 'Care of collections' is a sub-heading of principle II: 'Museums that maintain collections hold them in trust for the benefit of society and its development'. The National Trust for Scotland has 'Caring' as the first of its five values: www.nts.org.uk/our-work/our-manifesto-and-values (last accessed 20 December 2022). An early use of 'care' was the *Report of the Trustees and Director of the National Gallery on Requirements as regards the care and exhibition of the pictures and the additional space to be provided in the proposed enlargement of the gallery* (Presented pursuant to an Address of the House of Lords, dated 21 June 1869).

[18] This includes statues of those involved in the slave trade. See Section 9.8.

Care therefore extends beyond preservation, truth and access[19] and provides a dynamic framework which draws on law and other instruments to provide an holistic overview. Rather than pitting one person against another, the framework of communities of care set out here envisages respectful decision-making with participation and empathy, seeking to resolve dissonance.[20]

1.1.2 Cultural Heritage Rather than Cultural Property

'Cultural heritage' is the subject matter of this book, in preference to 'cultural property'. Adopting the terminology of 'cultural heritage' rather than 'cultural property' has several advantages. First, 'cultural property' frequently suggests the monumental[21] – what might be described as 'high culture'[22] – or those objects or places that a nation considers of vital importance.[23] It is infrequently used to refer to practices.[24] By contrast, 'cultural heritage' more fully reflects the varied ways in which cultural heritage is experienced and used. It therefore encompasses a greater variety of categories of objects, places and practices which a community might identify as cultural heritage[25] and which might not naturally fall within the categories of property.[26]

A second advantage of using the language of cultural heritage is that 'heritage' incorporates the notion of inheritance or passing cultural heritage

---

[19] Which is what Merryman identified as the three elements of a cultural property policy: John Henry Merryman, 'The Public Interest in Cultural Property' (1989) 77 *California Law Review* 339, 355.

[20] See Chapter 2.

[21] Certainly in the context of museums, it tends to be 'reserved for things whose loss would be felt most profoundly': Peter H. Welsh, 'The Power of Possessions: The Case Against Property' (1997) 21 *Museum Anthropology* 12, 15.

[22] Katya S. Ziegler, 'Cultural Heritage and Human Rights' in Giuffrè Milano (ed.), *Alberico Gentili: La Salvaguardia Dei Beni Culturali Nel Diritto Internazionale*, Working Paper No. 26/ 2007 (Oxford Legal Studies Research Paper Series, Faculty of Law, University of Oxford, 2007), p. 2: http://ssrn.com/abstract=1002620 (last accessed 20 December 2022).

[23] Lostal suggests that cultural property is used in international conventions to refer to objects important to one state, whereas cultural heritage is used to refer to those things of universal importance (nevertheless usually the importance of cultural property is linked to the 'cultural heritage' of the particular state party (e.g. UNESCO 1970): Marina Lostal, *International Cultural Heritage Law in Armed Conflict* (Cambridge: Cambridge University Press, 2017), p. 60; Sarah Harding, 'Value, Obligation and Cultural Heritage' (1999) 31 *Arizona State Law Journal* 292, 345.

[24] Usually traditional knowledge, traditional practices and genetic knowledge are categorised as intangible cultural heritage: see Noriko Aikawa-Faure, 'From the Proclamation of Masterpieces to the Convention for the Safeguarding of Intangible Cultural Heritage' in Laurajane Smith and Natsuko Akagawa (eds.), *Intangible Cultural Heritage* (Key Issues in Cultural Heritage, London: Routledge, 2009), p. 15.

[25] See Abdulqaqwi Yusef, 'Cult of Cultural Heritage' in Francesco Francioni and Federico Lenzerini (eds.), *The 1972 World Heritage Convention: A Commentary* (Oxford: Oxford University Press, 2008), p. 31.

[26] E.g. folklore: Lyndel V. Prott and Patrick J. O'Keefe, '"Cultural Heritage" or "Cultural Property"?' (1992) 1 *International Journal of Cultural Property* 307, 319.

on to future generations.[27] This is 'central to the force of the term cultural heritage'[28] and is reflected in UNESCO's Declaration on the Responsibilities of the Present Generations Towards Future Generations under which present generations have the responsibility of transmitting our common heritage to future generations[29] and avoiding 'compromising it irreversibly'.[30]

Thirdly, to some people the term 'cultural property' has political connotations[31] which can side-track the debate by focusing on a nation's appropriation of objects, places or practices for its own ends. It also has a strong legal meaning[32] and its incorporation of 'property' demonstrates disciplinary imperialism,[33] often revealing the author to be a lawyer; it is thus a 'synthetic construction'.[34] Cultural heritage objects or places will often have the legal characteristic of being property, but that particular legal characteristic should not define the subject matter. It is putting the cart before the horse to call it cultural *property*. It may be that recourse is had to property rights and often it is difficult to avoid the property characteristic of cultural heritage (particularly when individual property rights are at odds with the public interest or communities' views). Indeed, Lixinski argues that a shift away from property to heritage 'has also had the (unintended) consequence of disassociating communities from heritage they live with or around, and for whose survival they are necessary'.[35] Whilst 'heritage' has a legal etymology in

---

[27] See Section 3.2.

[28] Janet Blake, 'On Defining the Cultural Heritage' (2000) 49 *International and Comparative Law Quarterly* 61, 69.

[29] Declaration on the Responsibilities of the Present Generations Towards Future Generations, UNESCO, Paris, 12 November 1997, art. 7 (Volume 1, Records of the General Conference, 29th session, Paris, 21 October to 12 November 1997). Note Lixinski's observation that whilst the 1997 Declaration focuses on the present and the future generations, it is silent about the past: Lixinski, *International Heritage Law for Communities*, p. 110. As Besterman observes, 'Museums are the custodians of an intergenerational equity which may extend well beyond local or even national boundaries': Tristram Besterman, 'Museum Ethics' in Sharon Macdonald (ed.), *A Companion to Museum Studies* (Oxford: Blackwell, 2006), p. 435; 'heritage should be cared for in order to hand on things that are valued to future generations': Deborah Mattinson, 'The Value of Heritage: What Does the Public Think?' in Kate Clark (ed.), *Capturing the Public Value of Heritage: The Proceedings of the London Conference* (London: English Heritage, 2006), p. 89.

[30] Declaration on the Responsibilities of the Present Generations, art. 8; 'The fundamental policy behind cultural heritage law is protection of the heritage for the enjoyment of present and later generations'. Prott and O'Keefe, '"Cultural Heritage" or "Cultural Property"?', 309.

[31] James Cuno, *Who Owns Antiquity? Museums and the Battle over Our Ancient Heritage* (Oxford: Princeton University Press, 2008), p. 9.

[32] Charlotte Woodhead, 'A Critical Analysis of the Legal and Quasi-Legal Recognition of the Underlying Principles and Norms of Cultural Heritage' (thesis submitted for the degree of Doctor of Philosophy at the University of Leicester, April 2014).

[33] See Section 3.4.2.

[34] Francesco Francioni, 'The Human Dimension of International Cultural Heritage Law: An Introduction' (2011) 22 *European Journal of International Law* 9, 10.

[35] Lixinski, *International Heritage Law for Communities*, p. 27.

terms of inheritance,[36] and is indeed a term used to refer to land in Scots law,[37] the link with inheritance and passing down the generations is more closely aligned to the very characteristic which makes it cultural heritage – its intergenerational nature. It therefore avoids demonstrating a disciplinary imperialism to the same extent that referring to property does.[38] Certainly by using the word 'property' the focus of discussion frequently shifts to ownership, possession and allocation of resources, which can be unhelpful, leading to a dichotomy between, on the one hand, possessing or owning something, and on the other hand, not being able to do so. Cultural heritage, as a term, therefore 'has less ideological baggage in tow'.[39] Labelling something as cultural property can unhelpfully give the impression of possessive individualism,[40] which again has implications where long-term decisions are made where custodians other than the originating communities have possession. Much ill feeling has been caused by institutions relying on their strict legal rights as property owners or lawful possessors to avoid addressing challenges to their continued retention of objects.[41] For that reason it is helpful to refocus attention on the subject matter itself rather than its legal status. It is clear that the notion of property within the concept of 'cultural property' has on occasions been interpreted in a restrictive, and sometimes unhelpful way, without acknowledging the varied types of property relationships that can exist.[42] It should be acknowledged that some works have attempted to focus on the more varied types of property including stewardship and property for personhood[43] (as well as peoplehood[44] and grouphood[45]). Despite these valiant attempts to reframe the subject matter within more creative forms of property rights, the term 'cultural heritage' still provides far more advantages for the reasons given here. The fourth reason for preferring the terminology of

[36] Tim Murphy, 'Legal Fabrications and the Case of "Cultural Property"' in Alain Pottage, Martha Mundy and Chris Arup (eds.), *Law, Anthropology, and the Constitution of the Social: Making Persons and Things* (Cambridge: Cambridge University Press, 2004), p. 132; Derek Gillman, *The Idea of Cultural Heritage* (Revised ed., Cambridge: Cambridge University Press, 2010), pp. 82–3; Ryan Trimm, 'Heritage as Trope: Conceptual Etymologies and Alternative Trajectories' (2018) 24 *International Journal of Heritage Studies* 465, 467.

[37] The Law Society of Scotland, *Laws of Scotland: Stair Memorial Encyclopaedia* (Edinburgh: Butterworths, 1993). col. 18, Pt I, para. 56.

[38] As to disciplinary imperialism, see Section 3.4.2.

[39] Prott and O'Keefe, '"Cultural Heritage" or "Cultural Property"?', 309.

[40] See Michael F Brown, 'Can Culture Be Copyrighted?' (1998) 39 *Current Anthropology* 193, 203.

[41] This is explored in the discussion of areas of contestation in Sections 1.3 and 3.4 in the context of the uneasy relationship between law and heritage and challenges to the *status quo* by claimants.

[42] For a refreshing approach see Kristen A. Carpenter, Sonia K. Katyal and Angela R. Riley, 'In Defense of Property' (2009) 118 *Yale Law Journal* 1022.

[43] Jeffrey Douglas Jones, 'Property and Personhood Revisited' (2011) 1 *Wake Forest Journal of Law & Policy* 93, 120, 135.

[44] John Lie, *Modern Peoplehood* (Cambridge, MA: Harvard University Press, 2004) p. 13; Carpenter et al., 'In Defense of Property', 1028.

[45] See John Moustakas, 'Group Rights in Cultural Property: Justifying Strict Inalienability' (1989) 74 *Cornell Law Review* 1179.

cultural heritage is that it also avoids what has been described as the 'paradox' of cultural property.[46] This refers to the paradox of combining the static nature of property – which assumes that something 'belongs' to a particular group – with the more dynamic nature of culture.[47] This, in turn, results in real difficulties in recognising the diverse nature of those forms of cultural heritage which evolve over time, on occasions with contributions from people from different cultures.[48]

1.1.3 Cultural Heritage Rather than Heritage

At times reference is made to heritage in this book where the particular instrument or academic article uses the term, but the broad scope is concerned with cultural heritage, as distinguished from natural heritage.[49] At times there may be an artificial or indistinguishable difference between natural and cultural heritage, for example in the context of cultural landscapes,[50] but the primary discussion of this book will be cultural heritage and for that reason this terminology will be adopted.

1.2 The Importance of Cultural Heritage

Heritage, in its broader sense, has been described as 'an influential force in society'[51] which is 'deeply entwined with other aspects of our lives whether at an individual or a group level'.[52] It is 'not something to dispose of as a commodity but integral to our lives'.[53] Cultural heritage is something beyond the ordinary. It is acknowledged that at its simplest it may be property – a place,

---

[46] Naomi Mezey, 'Paradoxes of Cultural Property' (2007) 107 *Columbia Law Review* 2004, 2005.

[47] ibid., p. 2005.

[48] ibid., p. 2005; Kwame Anthony Appiah, *Cosmopolitanism: Ethics in a World of Strangers* (London: Penguin, 2006), p. 129. For the problems relating to hybrid works see Fiona Macmillan, 'Copyright, Creativity and Cultural Property Rights: The Case of Arts Festivals', Cultivate Working Paper No. 1 (2010) (HERA Joint Research Programme on Copyrighting Creativity: Creative Values, Cultural Heritage Institutions and Systems of Intellectual Property) 17.

[49] See generally David Lowenthal, 'Natural and Cultural Heritage' (2005) 11 *International Journal of Heritage Studies* 81. Cf. Lixinski, who adopts the terminology of heritage in preference to cultural heritage: Lixinski, *International Heritage Law for Communities*, p. 22.

[50] In the UK St Kilda in the Hebrides, the Blaenavon Industrial Landscape in Wales as well as the English Lake District, the Cornwall and West Devon Mining Landscape and the Royal Botanic Gardens, Kew are examples of cultural landscapes recognised through designation as such on the World Heritage List: https://whc.unesco.org/en/culturallandscape/ (last accessed 22 May 2023).

[51] Marie Louise Stig Sørensen and John Carman, 'Introduction' in Marie Louise Stig Sørensen and John Carman (eds.), *Heritage Studies: Methods and Approaches* (London: Routledge, 2009), p. 3.

[52] ibid., p. 23.

[53] David Lowenthal, 'Stewarding the Past in a Perplexing Present' in Erica Avrami, Randall Mason and Marta de la Torre (eds.), *Values and Heritage Conservation: Research Report* (Los Angeles: The Getty Conservation Institute, 2000), p. 23.

an object – or it may be a practice. Yet, it has characteristics which make it much more difficult to treat it simply as property.[54] It has been described as 'the contents of humanity's social portfolio'.[55] Cultural heritage has a further role, specifically the importance that it represents to certain people.[56] This may be because of its importance for the individual, community, nation or humanity's identity,[57] or there may be a significant link between cultural heritage and a place.[58] Cultural heritage is often said to have a significance which comprises different types of value.[59] It is therefore clear that cultural heritage has a significant human dimension[60] which 'brings to life community aspirations'.[61] The relevant community may be local, national, or international; cultural heritage can have a universal value which is recognised as a common heritage.[62] Even if communities have no first-hand experience of the cultural heritage, there may be a feeling of common concern for the heritage and a feeling of shared loss if that heritage is at risk of harm or is

[54] 'In all, viewing cultural property and cultural heritage as a distinct, more worthy form of property, whose transmission must be assured, is the particular feature that, along with its specific discrete principles, defines the set of international laws concerning cultural heritage as international cultural heritage law and distinguishes it from other branches of international law': Lostal, *Armed Conflict*, p. 63.

[55] Susan B. Bruning, 'Articulating Culture in the Legal Sphere: Heritage Values, Native Americans and the Law' in George S. Smith, Phyllis Mauch Messenger and Hilary A. Soderland (eds.), *Heritage Values in Contemporary Society* (London: Routledge, 2016), p. 223.

[56] See James Leach, 'Owning Creativity: Cultural Property and the Efficacy of Custom on the Rai Coast of Papua New Guinea' (2003) 8 *Journal of Material Culture* 123, 136.

[57] David Lowenthal, *The Past is a Foreign Country* (Cambridge: Cambridge University Press, 1985), p. 41; Bruning, 'Articulating Culture in the Legal Sphere', p. 221; James O. Young, 'The Values of the Past' in Geoffrey Scarre and Robin Coningham (eds.), *Appropriating the Past: Philosophical Perspectives on the Practice of Archaeology* (Cambridge: Cambridge University Press, 2013), p. 34; Fiona Macmillan, 'The Protection of Cultural Heritage: Common Heritage of Mankind, National Cultural "Patrimony" or Private Property?' (2013) 64 *Northern Ireland Legal Quarterly* 351, 363; Blake, 'On Defining the Cultural Heritage', 77; Lisanne Gibson and John Pendlebury, 'Introduction: Valuing Historic Environments' in Lisanne Gibson and John Pendlebury (eds.), *Valuing Historic Environments* (Farnham: Ashgate, 2009), p. 2.

[58] There is also a close link between identity, community and place – see Rosemary Coombe, 'Possessing Culture: Political Economies of Community Subjects and their Properties' in Veronica Strang and Mark Busse (eds.), *Ownership and Appropriation* (Oxford: ASA Monographs, Berg, 2011), p. 111. The relationship between Indigenous Peoples and place is recognised in the United Nations Declaration on the Rights of Indigenous Peoples (adopted 13 September 2007)) 61/295 2008, art. 12.

[59] These are explored at Section 4.3.1.

[60] See generally Francioni, 'The Human Dimension of International Cultural Heritage Law', 9; Francesco Francioni and Lucas Lixinski, 'Opening the Toolbox of International Human Rights Law in the Safeguarding of Cultural Heritage' in Andrea Durbach and Lucas Lixinski (eds.), *Heritage, Culture and Rights: Challenging Legal Discourses* (Oxford: Hart, 2017), p. 17.

[61] Francioni and Lixinski, 'Opening the Toolbox', p. 34.

[62] Christopher C. Joyner, 'Legal Implications of the Concept of the Common Heritage of Mankind' (1986) 35 *International & Comparative Law Quarterly* 190, 199. Note Macmillan's caution that 'History shows us that it is not possible to decouple cultural heritage from particular identities, national, communal or otherwise': Macmillan, 'The Protection of Cultural Heritage', 363.

destroyed.[63] The Nubian campaign of 1959–1980 shows this. The active response from around the world, in an age without rolling news or social media to rally support to save cultural heritage from physical destruction,[64] showed the importance of the cultural heritage to others, even though these places and monuments may never have been viewed first-hand by those stepping forward to help. Due to the strong human dimension, it is therefore essential that the people(s) for whom cultural heritage is important are central to decision-making about cultural heritage.[65] The concern of those who care about and care for cultural heritage (and, in turn, cultural heritage law) is therefore not only the physical *thing* itself (most usually the object or place) but also the practice and the intangible element of cultural heritage.

1.2.1 As an Intangible Concept

Increasingly cultural heritage is treated as an intangible concept[66] in the form of a 'cultural practice, involved in the construction and regulation of a range of values and understandings' rather than something promoting 'a certain set of Western elite cultural values'.[67] It is 'less of an objective, physical existence than the range of associations which accompany an object or monument and which provide the sense of being part of a group'.[68] 'Cultural heritage is value' rather than the object, place or practice. It is thus ' . . . the importance itself'[69] and legal regimes aim to protect this importance. In essence 'it is the significance of the expression in the social life of a community that is, or should be, the policy focus of heritage protection, according to contemporary wisdom'.[70] For it is the human response to objects, places or practices which justifies our particular treatment of them and thus the intangible dimension of them[71] and in particular the desire to protect them from harm, which can be understood as

---

[63] Darvill refers to this as the existence value: Timothy Darvill, 'Value Systems in Archaeology' in Malcolm A. Cooper, Anthony Firth, John Carman and David Wheatley (eds.), *Managing Archaeology* (London: Routledge, 1995), p. 43.

[64] This co-ordinated effort to salvage and to save from physical destruction key elements of the Nubia culture has been hailed as 'a defining example of international solidarity when countries understood the universal nature of heritage and the universal importance of its conservation': UNESCO Press release, *50th Anniversary of Nubia Campaign* (31 March 2009): https://whc .unesco.org/en/news/497/ (last accessed 20 December 2022).

[65] See Section 5.3.   [66] Laurajane Smith, *Uses of Heritage* (London: Routledge, 2008), p. 11.

[67] ibid., p. 11.   [68] Blake, 'On Defining the Cultural Heritage', 84.

[69] Craig Forrest, *International Law and the Protection of Cultural Heritage* (London: Routledge, 2010), p. 3.

[70] Rosemary J. Coombe and Joseph F. Turcotte, 'Indigenous Cultural Heritage in Development and Trade: Perspectives from the Dynamics of Cultural Heritage Law and Policy' in Christopher B. Graber, Karolina Kuprecht and Jessica C. Lai (eds.), *International Trade in Indigenous Cultural Heritage: Legal and Policy Issues* (Cheltenham: Edward Elgar, 2012), p. 275.

[71] Artefacts can 'often provoke memories' and are 'sensed through our bodies': John Urry, 'How Societies Remember the Past' in Sharon Macdonald and Gordon Fyfe (eds.), *Theorizing Museums* (Sociological Review Monograph Series, Blackwell, 1996), p. 50 and 'seeing certain . . . artefacts functions to reawaken repressed desires and thereby to connect past and present': ibid., p. 55.

the adoption of a functionalist approach.[72] Contrastingly, Lixinski suggests that both the tangible and intangible elements of cultural heritage are relevant and advocates an holistic approach, taking account of both the tangible and intangible elements and their interplay.[73]

1.2.1.1 The Centrality of Participation and Communities

Given the recognition of the human dimension to cultural heritage, participation of communities is central to the way in which cultural heritage is cared for. This reflects another shift away from focusing on traditional Western notions of preserving the tangible[74] towards cultural practices. This is recognised in professional codes of ethics in their focus on the participation of stakeholders.[75]

The prevalence of experts in the care of cultural heritage was emphasised by work identifying the authorized heritage discourse.[76] Broader communities are, however, central to the care of cultural heritage. This extends beyond well-meaning amateurs who might assume responsibility for its care, for 'Heritage can play a key role in communities, for example, by encouraging civic pride and in shaping identity. In order to interpret and preserve local history effectively it must be contributed to, contested and explored by the wider community and not kept within an enclave of heritage enthusiasts.'[77]

It is important to have mechanisms which facilitate the communities of discourse surrounding cultural heritage and which permit, through multivocality, the resolution of dissonance relating to cultural heritage, thereby creating effective communities of care.[78] Central to appropriate care for cultural heritage is providing the space for dialogue and for balancing the various viewpoints of the different stakeholders for whom the particular cultural heritage is relevant. Consultation and dialogue are necessary for 'incorporating the multiplicity of interpretations of . . . heritage' and should include marginalised communities.[79]

---

[72] Tolina Loulanski, 'Revising the Concept for Cultural Heritage: The Argument for a Functional Approach' (2006) 13 *International Journal of Cultural Property* 207, 216. With this approach the focus is shifted away from the subject matter towards an appreciation of cultural heritage as a construction, with the care of cultural heritage being for the sake of people.

[73] Lucas Lixinski, *Intangible Cultural Heritage in International Law* (Oxford: Oxford University Press, 2013), p. 2.

[74] Smith, *Uses of Heritage*, pp. 3, 11.

[75] The Museums Association (MA), *Code of Ethics for Museums* (2015), p. 20.

[76] Smith, *Uses of Heritage*, p. 11.

[77] Corinne Perkin, 'Beyond the Rhetoric: Negotiating the Politics and Realising the Potential of Community-Driven Heritage Engagement' (2010) 16 *International Journal of Heritage Studies* 107, 117.

[78] What constitutes appropriate care is explored at Section 2.5.3. Effective communities of care are therefore those communities which provide such appropriate care.

[79] See Karima Bennoune, *Cultural Rights: Report of the Special Rapporteur in the Field of Cultural Rights: Intentional Destruction of Cultural Heritage* (A/71/317 UN), p. 16.

1.2.2 Caring about Cultural Heritage Because of Its Importance

Since cultural heritage is important, communities care *about* it. The concepts of care, more generally, and specifically caring *about* will be explored in Chapter 2. Suffice it to say, for present purposes, because cultural heritage is recognised as important due to its human dimension, communities care *about* it for a variety of reasons, particularly where there is risk of harm to it. This can result in a desire to take direct or indirect action by caring *for* it. However, risk of physical harm is only one of several areas of contestation which are explored in the next section.

Caring about cultural heritage is different from valuing it. Valuing can be undertaken quite objectively, in a non-emotional manner. Caring about something is having a feeling towards it – a disposition – which may result in a need to do something or to care for something, either directly or indirectly. Decision-makers or lawmakers may care about something but their reason for caring about it is different from communities for whom the cultural heritage is part of their identity.

Caring for cultural heritage is a process, in response to caring about it. It differs from merely preserving it, providing access or seeking the truth. Care, in the context of cultural heritage, may involve either action or inaction such as curated decay.[80] It may also require keeping it away from the public rather than giving access where its importance is sacred or secret. Care includes the use of cultural heritage and sustaining people's relationships with it, encouraging and facilitating its use as part of a culture. It may also involve explaining an object's history or dealing with the way in which it is displayed. Care is thus an all-round activity concerning cultural heritage. As part of the process of caring it is necessary to navigate the various areas of contestation in which cultural heritage finds itself.

1.3 Areas of Contestation

Cultural heritage is not neutral, and for some it is inherently dissonant.[81] The previous section has shown the importance of cultural heritage to communities in varied ways which, at times, conflict with each. Rather than talking about 'contested cultural heritage',[82] which implies that the cultural heritage itself is contested, the terminology of areas of contestation is adopted to refer to

---

[80] See generally Caitlin DeSilvey, *Curated Decay: Heritage Beyond Saving* (London: University of Minnesota Press, 2017).

[81] Smith, *Uses of Heritage*, p. 4; Emma Waterton, *Politics, Policy and the Discourses of Heritage in Britain* (Basingstoke: Palgrave Macmillan, 2010), p. 7.

[82] Helaine Silverman, 'Contested Cultural Heritage: A Selective Historiography' in Helaine Silverman (ed.), *Contested Cultural Heritage: Religion, Nationalism, Erasure, and Exclusion in a Global World* (London: Springer, 2011), p. 1.

those instances where different people object to the ways in which cultural heritage is envisaged, used or at risk of harm.[83] Contestation is taken to mean a social activity that 'entails objection to specific issues that matter to people'[84] and this more fully represents the broader way in which cultural heritage exists in communities.

The areas of contestation in the UK identified here fall into three broad categories. The first is how cultural heritage is imagined, translated into and out of law, and designated (including through the medium of listing). The second area is how to navigate the risk of harm or loss to cultural heritage (both to its tangible manifestations and also the intangible element of cultural heritage). The third area relates to the role played by cultural heritage and its communities of care in seeking and providing justice and memory. These areas of contestation contrast with other approaches to what has been described as the 'cultural heritage predicament'.[85] For example, Nafziger and Paterson have identified 'three dimensions' to this – 'conquest, colonialization, and commerce'.[86] These are helpful categories when considering the international framework relating to the care of cultural heritage (and were in fact raised in the context of the UNESCO Conventions).[87] Many of the areas of contestation identified here can be filed under Nafziger and Paterson's three headings, but several elements of contestation at the national level cannot be. The interests of the varied communities, the reasons for which they care about cultural heritage and their desire to actively care for cultural heritage are overlooked in their categorisation. Local communities may be faced with a risk of harm to cultural heritage from a proposed redevelopment without commerce at its heart. The community's concern may also be grounded in community values rather than commercial ones and be focused on seeking a role in the decision-making process relating to the care of cultural heritage. The care of finds of archaeological interest cannot be said to have conquest, colonialisation or commerce at their heart, but a community's concern may be based on the quest for knowledge or on a desire to connect with the past.[88] Cases involving private owners' use of their cultural heritage will not necessarily involve questions of commerce, but rather a balance between public access and private enjoyment of property.

Each area of contestation will be considered in turn.

---

[83] The terminology of contested heritage will be adopted briefly in the specific sense, when discussing symbols of injustice and the cause of pain, Section 9.8.

[84] Antje Wiener, *A Theory of Contestation* (Heidelberg: Springer, 2014), p. 1.

[85] James A. R. Nafziger and Robert Kirkwood Paterson, 'Cultural Heritage Law' in James A. R. Nafziger and Robert Kirkwood Paterson (eds.), *Handbook on the Law of Cultural Heritage and International Trade* (Cheltenham: Edward Elgar, 2014), p. 13.

[86] ibid.   [87] ibid.

[88] E.g. the search for the remains of Richard III which took place in Leicester.

1.3.1 Imagining 'Cultural Heritage': Translation, Designation and Dissonance

It is difficult to provide a concise yet comprehensive definition of cultural heritage. Often one knows heritage when one sees it[89] – for few people would disagree that the ruins at Palmyra represent cultural heritage. Even those who seek to destroy it understand it to be someone's cultural heritage, if not theirs. A certain level of international consensus can be reached about the sorts of objects, places and practices that are our own cultural heritage, or that of other communities. Often it may not be necessary to grapple with definitions or to classify something as cultural heritage until it is at risk. Only then will it be important whether something *ought* to be treated as cultural heritage and receive enhanced levels of care because of its legal status.[90]

Contestation can arise where laws or other devices with a degree of moral enforceability[91] seek to designate cultural heritage as being set apart from other property and worthy of particular care. The first issue is – what is designated? Who makes the decision about what is designated and for whom is that decision made? What are the implications of designation? An essential element of this is the role that communities play in the process. This includes being consulted not only about designation but also about the effect of their views on final designation. Here the themes of consultation and participation play key roles. Certain things may only need a legal designation as cultural heritage or one of its synonyms temporarily – for the purposes of a particular process such as export or being assumed into public ownership.[92]

The act of designation may affect both the communities for whom it is important and the cultural heritage itself. There are both dark and bright sides to formal designation of cultural heritage;[93] designation as a World Heritage

---

[89] ' [I]n most circumstances, the cultural significance of a certain object is self-evident': Andrea Biondi, 'The Merchant, the Thief and the Citizen: The Circulation of Works of Art within the EU' (1997) 34 *Common Market Law Review* 1173, 1180; a problem is that many charters assume heritage is significant: Kate Clark, 'From Significance to Sustainability', in Kate Clark (ed.), *Capturing the Public Value of Heritage: The Proceedings of the London Conference* (London: English Heritage, 2006), p. 59. However, note the criticism of Waterton et al., whose article is a response to what they describe as an often 'uncritical, common-sense understanding of what heritage entails': Emma Waterton, Laurajane Smith and Gary Campbell, 'The Utility of Discourse Analysis to Heritage Studies: The Burra Charter and Social Inclusion' (2006) 12 *International Journal of Heritage Studies* 339, 340.

[90] Value may only be articulated by the public and heritage professionals 'when the existence of places or practices are threatened or celebrated'. Tracey Avery, 'Values Not Shared: The Street Art of Melbourne's City Laneways' in Gibson and Pendlebury, *Valuing Historic Environments*, p. 140; Rodney Harrison, 'What is Heritage?' in Rodney Harrison (ed.), *Understanding the Politics of Heritage* (Manchester: Open University and Manchester University Press, 2010), p. 13; Lowenthal suggests that 'Nothing arouses affection for a legacy as much as the threat of its loss': David Lowenthal, 'Patrons, Populists, Apologists: Crises in Museum Stewardship' in Gibson and Pendlebury, *Valuing Historic Environments*, p. 19. As to care, see Chapter 2.

[91] Such as codes of ethics produced by professional bodies including the International Council of Museums (ICOM) and the UK's MA.

[92] See, for example national treasures at Section 8.1.2.

[93] Lixinski, *International Heritage Law for Communities*, pp. 3, 7.

Site can increase tourism, but at the same time negatively affect the resident communities.[94] For that reason communities need a central role within the selection and designation process.[95]

Cultural heritage is not solely imagined in legal terms through formal legal designation in what has been described as 'official heritage'.[96] How the courts approach cultural heritage and imagine it in case law, particularly when dealing with non-heritage law principles, provides a window on to how the UK cares for cultural heritage. Frequently, cultural heritage disputes involve difficult questions – so-called 'hard cases'.[97] Clear, unproblematic answers to the legal questions may be difficult to find, particularly when applying principles such as private property. Therefore, the observation that in case law it is likely that 'a range of culturally possible results'[98] will arise 'among which choices will have to be made by lawyers and by judges'[99] is particularly relevant. Yet, one should not see such a 'multiplicity of readings' as a weakness, but recognise that it is 'its strength, for it is this that makes room for different voices, and gives a purchase by which culture may be modified in response to the demands of circumstance'.[100] This appreciation of the, at times, messiness of law means that cultural heritage can be translated in many different situations and in many different ways in case law; dualisms such as 'official' and 'unofficial' heritage are therefore difficult to reconcile with this.[101] Furthermore, it is not simply law that acts in an 'official' way; a plethora of guidance and codes is published by government departments, NGOs and other heritage organisations which all contribute to translating and designating cultural heritage with a view to caring for it. These various 'nested practices of care'[102] and the way they use the label of cultural heritage or one of its synonyms are explored in Chapter 4.

1.3.1.1 Difficulties with Cultural Heritage and the Risk of Including Too Much

Cultural heritage, whilst important to communities for a variety of reasons, should not be assumed to be intrinsically good.[103] Objects, places or practices

---

[94] In some circumstances, designation can have a deleterious effect not only on the communities involved but also on the heritage place itself, for example the impact of Machu Picchu by having large numbers of tourists climbing over the historic place.

[95] See Lixinski, *International Heritage Law for Communities*, p. 125.

[96] Harrison distinguishes between official heritage, which is seen as something that has been classified as heritage by inclusion on a heritage list such as the World Heritage List, and unofficial heritage, which is created by '"the bottom-up" relationship between people, objects, places and memories': Harrison, 'What is Heritage?', p. 8.

[97] See generally Ronald Dworkin, *Law's Empire* (Cambridge, MA: Belknap Press, 1986); Matthias Weller, 'Key Elements of Just and Fair Solutions: The Case for a Restatement of Restitution Principles' in Evelien Campfens (ed.), *Fair and Just Solutions?* (The Hague: Eleven International, 2015), p. 201.

[98] James Boyd White , 'Law as Language: Reading Law and Reading Literature' (1981–2) 60 *Texas Law Review* 415, 436.

[99] ibid., 436.   [100] ibid., 444.   [101] See discussion above in this section.   [102] See Section 3.1.

[103] See UN Report of the Special Rapporteur in the field of cultural rights, A/72/155 on fundamentalism and extremism as threats to cultural heritage.

which might qualify as cultural heritage, but for some problematic characteristics, will need to be considered critically, particularly if their initial labelling as cultural heritage or their continued treatment leads to enhanced levels of care which may be offensive or problematic for some communities. Such problematic characteristics might originate from the very nature of objects, places or practices – for example, if they are made of human remains, although this will depend on context. Equally, the prior use of a place as a concentration camp or other places of mass atrocities may be difficult to navigate as cultural heritage places. Where recognising something as cultural heritage gives it an enhanced status in law which may ensure its protection from harm, it is important that objects, places or practices that are, either by their nature or in practice, patriarchal or which infringe human rights[104] are critically analysed before being admitted into the category of cultural heritage.[105] This is irrespective of whether this is by means of hard or soft laws or through other non-law initiatives.[106]

One consequence of taking a broad approach to the designation of cultural heritage, rather than adopting a narrower category of cultural property,[107] is the risk of admitting a great deal into the scope of protection.[108] This potentially leaves too much to care for, which risks an abundance of heritage.[109] Careful collections management is therefore necessary,[110] as is revisiting formal designation of heritage places over time to consider whether the listing is still appropriate, or whether a place should be delisted.[111] A central element of care is revisiting its appropriateness, as well as revisiting the question of who has responsibility for that care.[112] As part of this re-evaluation, the scope of what is cared for and the necessity for the extent of its continued care will be relevant. Ethical issues may also arise where cultural heritage may become associated with a particular organisation or person

---

[104] Article 2(1) of the 2003 UNESCO Convention for the Safeguarding of the Intangible Cultural Heritage which states that 'consideration will be given solely to such intangible cultural heritage as is compatible with existing human rights instruments'. See UN Report of the Special Rapporteur in the field of cultural rights, A/67/287 on rights of women to enjoy cultural heritage on an equal basis to men. See Lixinski, *Intangible Cultural Heritage*, pp. 172–3. This may also extend to animal rights as well – for example, practices such as bear baiting or bull fighting.

[105] See Gillman, *The Idea of Cultural Heritage*, pp. 94–5.   [106] As to which, see Chapter 2.

[107] Which might only include the superlative examples.

[108] Holtorf suggests that there is a potential to include car wrecks as heritage, giving the example of the car cemetery in Sweden which has been protected since the 1990s 'in a state of continuing deterioration': Cornelius Holtorf, 'Perceiving the Past: From Age Value to Pastness' (2017) 24 *International Journal of Cultural Property* 497, 499.

[109] Rodney Harrison, *Heritage: Critical Approaches* (Abingdon: Routledge, 2013), p. 166 and see National Museum Directors Conference, *Too Much Stuff? Disposal from Museums* (2003) which argues for 'careful review and rationalisation of collections', p. 3.

[110] The MA, *Code of Ethics* distinguishes between responsible disposal based on curatorial decisions and financially motived disposal (principles 2.8 and 2.9 respectively).

[111] See Section 7.4.2.

[112] The nature of 'appropriate care' and the elements of it are considered at Section 2.5.3.

through sponsorship of the particular collection of cultural heritage or the institution in which it is held.[113]

1.3.2 Recognising the Communities for Whom Cultural Heritage Is Important

As part of the designation process, it is necessary to focus on the importance of cultural heritage for a range of different communities. At times certain communities may be marginalised and not considered as part of the decision-making about cultural heritage. This can occur where local communities living within a proposed World Heritage Site are not consulted about the decision to designate it as being of universal value. In other cases, if objects were taken during conflict and times of colonisation and have subsequently passed across borders, the communities from which they originated may be located many miles away from a museum where an important cultural heritage object is now housed. Where those communities have changed over time there may be difficulties in not only recognising the place or community from which cultural heritage originated and for whom it is important but also recognising the voices of those communities.

1.3.3 Assuming Responsibility for Care

In addition to the need to involve communities for whom cultural heritage is important, determining who should assume responsibility for the care of cultural heritage in the future is also an area of contestation. This is particularly challenging where cultural heritage objects were acquired by force or through subjugation of communities who now wish to challenge the rights of the current possessors. A significant area of contestation is where care is paternalistic,[114] where the presumption is that experts or the current possessors are the most appropriately placed to provide direct and continued care.

1.3.4 Reacting to Threats of Harm and Loss

A further area of contestation is the need to navigate actual or potential harm and loss of cultural heritage. This includes not only physical harm but also

---

[113] E.g. the debate over the sponsorship by oil companies of museums in the UK or the connection with the Sackler family: see Gareth Harris, '"End BP Sponsorship of British Museum": 90 Heritage Professionals Sign Open Letter Against Oil Giant', *The Art Newspaper*, 11 November 2021 and José da Silva and Christina Ruiz, 'Serpentine Drops Sackler Name Following "Rebranding"', *The Art Newspaper*, 25 March 2021. See MA, *Code of Ethics*, which defines due diligence as ensuring that a museum has taken all reasonable measures to understand 'the full background of a sponsor, lender or funder': p. 23 and states that museums should 'Ensure editorial integrity in programming and interpretation' and should resist any attempts to influence this by donors or funders: principle 1.2.

[114] A concept derived from Uma Narayan, 'Colonialism and Its Others: Considerations on Rights and Care Discourses' (1995) 10 *Hypatia* 133 and discussed at Sections 2.6 and 9.5.1. Such care is where the community with current responsibility for care refuses to engage with dialogue and emphasises their role as the most appropriate provider of care.

intangible harm as experienced by communities, including loss of information or association. When dealing with harm, questions arise about how to navigate the public/private divide. Often assumptions are made that public rather than private ownership of cultural heritage is the most appropriate means of providing care. However, an element of appropriate care, as identified in Chapter 2, is that it is dialogic. Communities are therefore central to decision-making processes to ensure that any shift from the private to the public domain is appropriate in the circumstances.

1.3.4.1 Desire to Pass Cultural Heritage On to Future Generations and Averting Physical Loss or Damage

Irreparable physical harm can occur because of direct damage or destruction, during peacetime or wars. Destruction of cultural heritage during wartime has a long history. Although often entailing outright destruction or physical harm, harm can also involve removal to other places, with attendant loss to the dispossessed community. Suppression of cultural practices is also a significant tool of oppression against communities, often taking place as part of colonialism.[115]

In times of peace, destruction or harm can be intentionally caused to both cultural heritage places and objects. This can include vandalism, theft, unlawful excavations or unlawful work to a building (whether or not by its owner).[116] Destruction can also be accidental, resulting from damage from fires or natural disasters[117] or through deterioration. Damage may also result from poor restoration,[118] including over-cleaning or over-painting, which may even change the work itself. Harm may also be caused by neglect caused by a failure to undertake quotidian care.

Development projects such as major infrastructure programmes also pose a risk of destruction or harm to cultural heritage places and their settings.[119] Harm may therefore be sanctioned in the name of sustainable development; in such circumstances efforts will often be made to mitigate this harm.[120]

---

[115] For example the potlatch ceremony was prohibited in Canada by federal law which came into effect in 1885 (and only repealed in 1951): Catherine E. Bell and Robert K. Paterson, 'Aboriginal Rights to Cultural Property in Canada' (1999) 8 *International Journal of Cultural Property* 167, 200.

[116] See generally Historic England, *Heritage Crime*: https://historicengland.org.uk/advice/caring-for-heritage/heritage-crime/ (last accessed 20 December 2022).

[117] See Section 7.8.3 for examples of this.

[118] There has been criticism of the cleaning methods used on the collection of marbles from the Parthenon in the care of the British Museum. A colloquium was convened on this subject: Ian Jenkins, *Cleaning and Controversy: The Parthenon Sculptures 1811–1939* (British Museum Occasional Paper, 2001). See Elizabeth Pye, *Caring for the Past: Issues in Conservation for Archaeology and Museums* (London: James & James, 2001), p. 65. See Mark Brown, 'Botched Restorations Put England's Church Wall Paintings at Risk', *The Guardian*, 24 September 2019.

[119] For example during the Crossrail works in London a significant number of listed buildings were either altered or demolished: Cross Rail Act 2008, sch. 9.

[120] See Section 7.8.

1.3.4.2 Maintaining Associations between Objects, Places and Practices

Losses also include intangible loss such as loss of context where archaeological objects are unearthed and removed without proper cataloguing of the find site.[121] The illicit trade in cultural heritage objects is of worldwide concern and can fuel looting of cultural heritage places, further harming them. Not only does the loss of information harm the historical record, but there can also be disfigurement of statues and monuments with irreparable physical harm to places.

Intangible loss is also occasioned where an object is removed from its original location, or where objects forming a collection are dispersed. 'Collections' as a concept require caring for on the basis that individual objects have been brought together and now form a coherent whole or a 'new creation'.[122] The collection might represent a unique example of a particular style or period, an encyclopaedic collection, or if they were created by a particular person, demonstrate their collecting habits or a particular period of history. The sale of, or irreparable harm to, an object which is an element of a collection can cause harm to the entire collection. As well as the loss of association and the harm to the communities for whom the cultural heritage collection is important, aesthetic or scholarly consequences may also result from separating a collection, described as 'the aesthetic equivalent of physical dismemberment'.[123] Yet, this needs to be balanced with claims for the return of cultural heritage objects which, whilst being elements of that 'entity', may have been taken from their original owners, or from the community from which they originated and for whom return is important.

1.3.4.3 Avoiding 'Loss' to a Community or Nation: The Threat of Physical Relocation and 'Saving for the Nation'

A further risk of loss at the national level is where a cultural heritage object, considered of importance to a nation or locally, is at risk of export abroad and the public would no longer be able to access it in the UK. The rhetoric surrounding this is usually that of seeking to 'save the object for the nation'[124] even though the object may have previously been privately owned and the public have never before gazed upon it. This area of contestation is not concerned with the potential physical destruction of the object or indeed with the destruction directly of the intangible element of cultural heritage. Rather, the loss of access by the national community to the physical thing is central.

---

[121] See, for example, Simon MacKenzie, Neil Brodie, Donna Yates and Christos Tsirogiannis, *Trafficking Culture: New Directions in Researching the Global Market in Illicit Antiquities* (London: Routledge, 2019).

[122] Patrick J. O'Keefe, 'The Heritage Value of a Private Collection' in Marc-André Rénold and Quentin Byrne-Sutton (eds.), *La libre circulation des collections d'objets d'art* (Zurich: Schulthess Polygraphischer Verlag, 1993), p. 182. This represents the difficulties found at the public-private divide which are analysed in Section 6.6.2.

[123] Paul M. Bator, *International Trade in Art* (London: University of Chicago Press, 1983), p. 22.

[124] See Section 8.1.

The system thus focuses on possession. Similar concerns about the risk of loss may be felt where plans are made to sell a cultural heritage place or to cease using somewhere for a cultural heritage practice or particular industry. In response, efforts may be made to 'save' it from private sale and development and instead to keep it for a community's use.

1.3.5 Justice and Memory

Cultural heritage can be a symbol of injustice if claims to it are unresolved and wrongs unacknowledged. Return of an object, compensation or acknowledgement of past wrongs can be a significant symbol of justice.

Over the years, cultural heritage objects may have been removed from their places of origin. Occasionally there is a clear history setting out the object's journey from creation to its current location. An artwork with a clear provenance (ownership history) recording all transactions from the artist's studio to the current owner represents the ideal situation. However, in some situations the legal history of an object is far less clear. Acquisitions may not have been clearly legal or indeed ethical – either at the time or according to modern mores. Private collectors and museum collections may have been the beneficiaries of wrongdoing, even if not directly responsible for that wrongdoing. When it comes to privately owned objects, particularly where the current possessors have acquired legal title under statutes of limitation, claims will need to be resolved privately between the parties, as the claimants would have no legal claim.[125] Yet, there are views that museums, tasked with ensuring the public trust in their activities,[126] have obligations (regardless of the legal position) to act and to respond ethically to claims made by those previously wronged.

Key areas of contestation involve cultural heritage that was either taken forcibly from persecuted groups during the Nazi era, or where the owners had no choice but to transfer the cultural objects. Where these objects come to light, in sales, private collections or museums, claims may be made against the current possessors. In other claims lineal descent is less obvious, where broader communities rather than families claim objects. During the long and troubling history of British colonialism, objects were seized without permission;[127] such objects are still in the UK both in private and public ownership.[128] Some of

---

[125] These might be brokered by auctions houses or organisations such as the Art Loss Register or Art Recovery International, perhaps with the involvement of the Commission for Looted Art in Europe or other claimant groups.

[126] MA, *Code of Ethics*, principle 3.

[127] They were taken in a variety of different situations. For example, Hicks' 'preliminary series of seven types of takings' which he sets out in the colonial context: Dan Hicks, *The Brutish Museums: The Benin Bronzes, Colonial Violence and Cultural Restitution* (London: Pluto Press, 2020), p. 238.

[128] These include royal collections, Church collections, government collections and both national and non-national museums.

these were acquired during punitive expeditions (for example at Maqdala and the Kingdom of Benin) or during colonial rule and subsequently appeared on the art market[129] or are housed within museums. Other objects of sacred significance to particular communities, including human remains, were bought, stolen or traded, often in the context of unequal power relations. Modern-day claims are important for the identity of communities.[130] Many arguments for return can be made on the grounds of interference with cultural rights.[131] Counter arguments are made about the need to retain universal collections which represent a common heritage. Allegations are also made that repatriation requests may be political in nature and not represent the best long-term response.[132]

Controversy surrounds instances of cultural appropriation,[133] which can take a variety of forms. This may be the misappropriation of a cultural practice which is then appropriated by another community, or used for tourism without the permission of the community from which it originates. Cultural appropriation can include the commercialisation of symbols used by communities for sacred reasons or the incorporation of these into other artworks.

As discussed above, in the context of designation, certain things associated with troubled histories are difficult to navigate in the context of the care of cultural heritage. Contestation surrounds not only designation but also how these objects, places or practices are cared for, including how they are displayed. Particular problems derive from statues of those involved in slavery or other colonial activities[134] whose continued display also involves commemoration or memorialisation and can cause difficulties for present generations.

1.3.5.1 Inherently Dissonant Disputes: Tangible Difficulties

These – often multifarious – claims bring with them the difficulty of balancing competing interests. Seeking to resolve these is no easy task and navigating these often involves taking account of moral as well as legal

---

[129] As well as international sales, objects can also be found at local auction houses: Alex Capon, 'Benin Plaque Withdrawn from Auction after Curator Raises Provenance Questions', *Antiques Trade Gazette*, 8 May 2021, edition 2491.

[130] Johanna Gibson 'dignity, wisdom and continuity of culture and identity' as elements that must be 'developed and encouraged through the protection of traditional and Indigenous knowledge' (Johanna Gibson, *Community Resources: Intellectual Property, International Trade and Protection of Traditional Knowledge* (London: Routledge, 2005), p. 193, 2005); Kalliopi Fouseki, 'Claiming the Parthenon Marbles Back: Whose Claim and on Behalf of Whom?' in Louise Tythacott and Kostas Arvanitis (eds.), *Museums and Restitution: New Practices, New Approaches* (Farnham: Ashgate, 2014), p. 173.

[131] See generally Janet Blake, *Exploring Cultural Rights and Cultural Diversity: An Introduction with Selected Legal Materials* (Builth Wells: Institute of Art and Law, 2014).

[132] E.g. the Declaration on the Importance and Value of Universal Museums [2004] *ICOM News* 4; see generally Tiffany Jenkins, *Keeping Their Marbles: How the Treasures of the Past Ended Up in Museums . . . and Why They Should Stay There* (Oxford: Oxford University Press, 2016).

[133] See Geoffrey Scarre and Robin Coningham, 'Introduction' in *Appropriating the Past*, p. 3, who distinguish between appropriation and expropriation.

[134] This might be the name of a benefactor of a collection or the donor of an object who may have connections with slavery, colonisation or misappropriation.

considerations.[135] Past injustices and differences of opinion can be entrenched and make the task of resolving seemingly incompatible disputes difficult.[136] As Scarre and Coningham observe, it would be naïve to assume that disagreements about cultural heritage can be resolved 'with a modicum of mutual understanding and good-will'.[137] As they rightly point out, it is possible to reach differing conclusions whilst remaining reasonable simply because the parties' starting points are different.[138]

It is important, though, to acknowledge the dissonance involved with cultural heritage and to engage with the various communities of discourse involved to help navigate this.[139] Doing so is essential to the way in which to appropriately care for cultural heritage and those for whom it is important by assuming responsibility for the care of cultural heritage through communities of care. The framework of care is set out in Chapter 2.

1.4 A Word on Methodology

Inspired by James Boyd White's treatment of law as language,[140] which invites us to read law with humility,[141] this book seeks to avoid abstracting single principles from decided cases.[142] Instead, it analyses how legal instruments and decision-makers translate[143] notions of cultural heritage and the need to care for it. By so doing one can assess how a community cares *about* and cares *for* cultural heritage.[144] Where difficult decisions are made about the long-term approach to caring for cultural heritage (essentially its fate) the analysis will consider how decision-makers take into account the range of voices from communities in the decision-making process.

Various authors have analysed heritage through critical discourse analysis (CDA).[145] There are overlaps between the current, rhetorical approach which

---

[135] 'Cultural-property policies are also controversial because they focus on moral duties, and sometimes on religious, cultural and political belief systems that are not universally held': ACCP Editorial Board, 'Conclusion: Museums at the Center of Public Policy' in Kate Fitz Gibbon (ed.), *Who Owns the Past? Cultural Policy, Cultural Property and the Law* (Piscataway: Rutgers University Press, 2005), p. 310.

[136] David Lowenthal, *The Heritage Crusade and the Spoils of History* (Cambridge: Cambridge University Press, 1998), pp. 2–3. '[Heritage's] potential for both good and evil is huge. On the one hand, it offers a rationale for self-respecting stewardship of all we hold dear; on the other, it signals an eclipse of reason and regression to embattled tribalism.'

[137] Scarre and Coningham, 'Introduction', p. 8.   [138] ibid.

[139] Trimm suggests heritage can 'paper over' dissonance: Trimm, 'Heritage as Trope', 467.

[140] Derived from, inter alia White, 'Law as Language', 415.   [141] ibid., 443.

[142] ibid., 420, 433.

[143] Boyd White sees translation as offering 'a way of thinking about the relations we can establish among different discourse systems, and among the different communities they embody': James Boyd White, *Justice as Translation: An Essay in Cultural and Legal Criticism* (London: University of Chicago Press, 1990), p. 225.

[144] The theme of simultaneously caring *about*, and *for*, heritage stems from Russell, 'Heritages, Identities, and Roots', p. 30.

[145] Smith, *Uses of Heritage*; Waterton et al., 'The Utility of Discourse Analysis', 339.

deals with legal instruments and the way in which CDA treats those same instruments. The latter frequently focuses on the power relations involved. As Harrington et al. observe, CDA focuses on how 'cultural forms represent, conceal and reinforce power qualities' and has contributed to a rhetorical analysis.[146] They also point out that CDA has a certain structuralism which looks at the large scale over long periods of time.[147] Contrastingly, adopting an approach which focuses on the way in which language and rhetoric are used on a smaller scale allows a more specific analysis of how cultural heritage is imagined in specific contexts within UK legal and non-law instruments.[148]

Rather than focusing on the link between power relations and discourse[149] and how this serves to perpetuate the authorized heritage discourse,[150] suppressing other voices, the aim of this book is to consider the way in which attempts have been made to construct notions of heritage and to provide rhetorical communities of discourse.[151] This allows one to see how the human dimension of cultural heritage is placed within the legal and non-law devices. This approach helps to untangle when communities of care are created and how they assume responsibility for the care of cultural heritage. As part of this one can appreciate the multivocality[152] involved in the process.

Typically a legal text is a coercive one – compelling or commanding its reader either directly or indirectly.[153] However, by treating law as a language[154] and as a culture of argument and interpretation one can interpret the legal (and non-law) texts in an ethical and relational manner with an appreciation of the cultural context in which they are interpreted,[155] thus linking closely with the act of caring for cultural heritage, which is relational in nature.[156]

1.4.1 Law, Language and Interpretation

Law and literature are closely intertwined[157] and both 'rely on symbols and myths, use rhetoric in a constitutive fashion and shape reality through language'.[158] This closeness is particularly relevant to the law dealing with cultural heritage. Language and linguistic devices play a significant role when

---

[146] John Harrington, Lucy Series and Alexander Ruck-Keene, 'Law and Rhetoric: Critical Possibilities' (2019) 46 *Journal of Law and Society* 302, 305.

[147] ibid.   [148] E.g. looking at words and meanings: ibid.

[149] Waterton et al., 'The Utility of Discourse Analysis', who focus on the Burra Charter: The Australia ICOMOS Charter for Places of Cultural Significance.

[150] A phrase coined in Smith, *Uses of Heritage*, p. 11.   [151] White, 'Law as Language', 441.

[152] White, 'Law and Literature', 746.

[153] Peter Goodrich, *Reading the Law: A Critical Introduction to Legal Method and Techniques* (Oxford: Basil Blackwell, 1986), p. 91. Boyd White invites us to avoid treating law as a set of commands or rules: White, 'Law as Language', 436.

[154] White, 'Law as Language', 415.

[155] ibid., 427. See also White, 'Law and Literature', 739, 751.   [156] See Section 2.4.

[157] With both being a language and both inherently communal: White, 'Law as Language', 415.

[158] Andrea Bianchi, 'International Adjudication, Rhetoric and Storytelling' (2017) 9 *Journal of International Dispute Settlement* 28, 31.

discussing cultural heritage, on occasions stifling meaningful debate and development of the law, specifically surrounding restitution and repatriation claims. These ultimately hamper the appropriate care of cultural heritage. It will be seen in Chapter 9 how the Myth of the Marbles looms over debates about restitution, and rhetoric such as 'rightful owners' and 'saving for the nation' play central roles in the UK's care of cultural heritage.[159] Narratives and analogies, as linguistic devices, also affect how the UK cares for cultural heritage.[160]

Interpretation of any text is no straightforward endeavour, for frequently there will be sufficient 'real ambiguities and uncertainties' to suggest that there is an observable meaning which could be 'demonstrated in some quasi-scientific way'.[161] There is therefore real scope for interpreting instruments in a variety of different ways. One way is to be overly formalistic and literal. An alternative approach – and that adopted here – is to interpret legal (and non-law) materials by focusing on the human element.[162] By this means it will be possible to appreciate the way in which the notion of caring for cultural heritage is expressed and effectuated in the various instruments that form the corpus of discussion, referred to as nested practices of care.[163]

Law can be used as a 'powerful instrument of empire, denying humanity and trivializing human experience'.[164] In a field such as cultural heritage, so affected by empire, it is important to be alert to the way in which law, specifically retentive museum governing statutes, has been used to stifle debates or challenges to the *status quo*. It is also necessary to recognise how the rhetoric of the 'universal museum' is used to justify continued retention of contentious objects.[165] Yet, Boyd White acknowledges that 'on the other [hand], it can be an important way – perhaps our best way – of seeing, recording, resisting empire'.[166] Where claims are made within frameworks of ethical norms, these can act as mechanisms which can resist empire.

1.5 Matters of Terminology

1.5.1 Communities, the UK as a Community and as a Network of Communities

Although there are some disadvantages to adopting the terminology of 'communities' which will be explored further in Chapter 5, it is nevertheless helpful to use this terminology to describe the extremely varied groups of people who care about and care for cultural heritage. Such communities exist at very different levels, from the international communities down to the very small communities of families who care about cultural heritage for quite personal

---

[159] See Sections 9.5.2.5 and 8.1 respectively.   [160] See Sections 9.7.2.1 and 9.3.6, respectively.
[161] White, 'Law as Language', 417.   [162] As Boyd White invites us to do.   [163] See Section 2.2.
[164] James Boyd White , 'Interview with James Boyd White' (2007) 105 *Michigan Law Review* 1403, 1405.
[165] As to which, see Section 9.5.2.3.   [166] White, 'Interview', 1405.

reasons. The focus of this book is on the UK as a community, as a group of four national communities, as a member of the European and international communities.[167] However, the UK comprises smaller communities within the four nations, many of whom care about and care for cultural heritage directly. This book treats communities as a sufficiently wide enough concept to incorporate these varied communities, as well as the communities of Parliament, as lawmakers and developers of policy, but also the courts and other institutions which care about cultural heritage and care for it which act in a similar capacity acting as communities of care.

The approach taken here then is wider than the Faro Convention's definition of heritage communities and wider than approaches which focus on Indigenous or local communities.[168] It takes heed of reservations regarding the adoption of the word community.[169] It does not prioritise any single individual community over another. Instead, it recognises that they exist in all manner of shapes and forms with a certain 'messiness'.[170] By adopting such an approach it is hoped that this makes visible all the different ways in which care is provided for cultural heritage. It shows how these varied groups – forming communities of care – make use of legal and non-law instruments (representing nested practices of care) and assume responsibility for the cultural heritage that they care about.

1.5.2 'Care' in Preference to 'Safeguarding'

Blake has expressed a preference for the terminology of safeguarding rather than protection and points out that rather than focusing on the 'more negative sense of "protection against" . . . safeguarding implies taking positive actions to foster the heritage, its holders, and the context in which it is developed'.[171] However, the concept of care moves beyond the activity and action that need to be taken which are reflected in the term 'safeguarding' – which may well be positive ones – to encompass as well why people have strong feelings about cultural heritage, the use that they make of the cultural heritage as well as the response to this that might need to be taken to ensure that that use is maintained.[172] It also focuses on the element of sustaining relationships

---

[167] The ability to consider the UK as such a network of communities is perhaps helped by what has been described as Britain arguably having 'a weak statist conception of the nation that partly explains the flowering of notions of sub-state "communities"': Stefan Berger, Bella Dicks and Marion Fontaine, '"Community": A Useful Concept in Heritage Studies?' (2019) 26 *International Journal of Heritage Studies* 325, 344.

[168] As to which see Section 5.1.   [169] ibid.

[170] Emma Waterton and Laurajane Smith, 'The Recognition and Misrecognition of Community Heritage' (2010) 16 *International Journal of Heritage Studies* 4, 5 and see Section 5.1.

[171] Janet Blake, *International Cultural Heritage Law* (Oxford: Oxford University Press, 2015), p. 12.

[172] It is acknowledged that 'In this way, the safeguarding of ICH is a more context-dependent approach that takes account of the wider human, social, and cultural contexts in which the enactment of ICH occurs': ibid., p. 12.

about it. Care thus focuses on the entire process rather than the activity that needs to be done (which could be described as the normative response).

Although 'care' of cultural heritage is only occasionally found in legal instruments,[173] nevertheless it permeates many aspects of cultural heritage (as will be discussed in the context of the frequent reference, often without further analysis, to care).[174] By contrast, safeguarding, as a concept, has been found predominantly in the context of intangible cultural heritage.[175]

1.5.3 Civil Society Initiatives and Public Participation Initiatives

'Civil society' has been described as 'the area between citizen and parliament politics'[176] which, by its nature, presumes 'a background of some degree of caring relations rather than of merely competing interests'.[177] Drawing on the UK government's definition of 'civil society', the general term is understood here to mean those organisations, individuals or initiatives which are outside state control but which create social value.[178] The particular social value of interest here relates directly to the care of cultural heritage.[179] Civil society initiatives play an important role in the care of cultural heritage, facilitating communities coming together and actively assuming responsibility for the care of cultural heritage places, objects and practices through making use of legal devices to structure their organisation. This includes the use of charity law. Potentially this is an enormous, unwieldy category of materials to consider even solely within the UK, and so specific focus will be placed on the narrower category of initiatives which link directly (or interweave) with the legal framework of dealing with cultural heritage and which contribute to the way in which cultural heritage is cared for.

It becomes apparent, though, that certain initiatives have a measure of state control through funding and are thus not entirely independent. They would

---

[173] Although it is found in certain governing statutes of national museums (although not defined): see Section 6.4.1.

[174] See Section 2.2.

[175] The similarities between the elements of care identified in Chapter 2 and safeguarding, as recognised in the ethical elements of safeguarding (set out in the UNESCO, *Ethical Principles for Safeguarding Intangible Cultural Heritage*, Decision of the Intergovernmental Committee, 10.COM 15.A), are explored in Section 2.3.

[176] Selma Sevenhuijsen, 'The Place of Care: The Relevance of the Feminist Ethic of Care for Social Policy' (2003) 4 *Feminist Theory* 179, 183.

[177] Virginia Held, *The Ethics of Care: Personal, Political and Global* (Oxford: Oxford University Press, 2006), p. 17.

[178] Civil society as 'individuals and organisations when they act with the primary purpose of creating social value, independent of state control' (HM Government, *Civil Society Strategy: Building a Future that Works for Everyone* (London: Cabinet Office, 2018), p. 12). Social value here means 'enriched lives and a fairer society for all' (*Civil Society Strategy*, p. 12). See generally Jonathan Garton, *The Regulation of Organised Civil Society* (Oxford: Hart, 2009) and Michael Edwards, *Civil Society* (4th ed., Cambridge: Polity, 2020).

[179] Selma Sevenhuijsen, *Citizenship and the Ethics of Care* (tr. Liz Savage) (London: Routledge, 1998), p. 44.

therefore not strictly be considered civil society initiatives,[180] but operate in such a way as to engage communities in participation with cultural heritage. Examples include the Portable Antiquities Scheme, the Enriching the List initiative and the Register of War Memorials, all of which are funded, in part, by central government agencies. Therefore, in the context of this book the alternative term 'public participation initiatives' will be used to refer to initiatives which seek to engage communities in participation in heritage practices, whether this is through active participation and engagement or participation in the decision-making processes and regardless of whether these initiatives are organised by government departments or NGOs.

1.5.4 National and Non-national Museums

Unlike some European countries, UK national museums are not formed of state-owned collections.[181] National museums are those in receipt of direct government funding and usually governed by legislation and a board of trustees.[182] They have a stronger sense of inalienability than non-national collections because the governing statutes of national museums usually include provisions curtailing their powers of deaccessioning objects.[183] On the other hand, the structure of non-national museums are varied, established using a range of legal devices.[184] These include charities, which are subject to charity regulation and need to have a public benefit. Others are established as private trusts. The 821 local authority museums[185] have

---

[180] Under the approach of Salamon and Anheier, who identify non-profit, civil society organisations as being organized, private (in the sense of being separate from government), nonprofit distributing, self-governing and voluntary: Lester M. Salamon and Helmut K. Anheier (eds.), *Defining the Nonprofit Sector: A Cross-National Analysis* (Manchester: Manchester University Press, 1997), pp. 33–4.

[181] Although some museums were initially controlled by government departments, the ownership of the collections and the care of them were transferred to boards of trustees: see e.g. National Heritage Act 1983, s. 4(1), which transferred the Victoria and Albert Museum from the Minister of the Crown to the newly formed board of trustees and made it clear that the property 'shall not be regarded as property of, or held on behalf of, the Crown': sch. 1, para. 2(2).

[182] See DCMS, *Strategic Review of DCMS-Sponsored Museums* (2017). Examples include: the British Museum (British Museum Act 1963), the National Gallery, National Portrait Gallery and the Tate Gallery (Museums and Galleries Act 1992). National museums also include the Wallace Collection, which was gifted to the nation (Museums and Galleries Act 1992). The national museums of Scotland, Wales and Northern Ireland are not directly sponsored by the DCMS in this way. They are also governed by either legislation or Royal Charter: National Museum of Scotland (National Heritage (Scotland) Act 1985) National Museums and Galleries of Northern Ireland (Museums and Galleries (Northern Ireland) Order 1998). The National Museum of Wales was established by Royal Charter in 1907.

[183] See Section 7.3.2.2.

[184] Jeremy Warren (ed.), *The Legal Status of Museum Collections in the United Kingdom* (London: Museums and Galleries Commission, 1996); Janet Ulph, *The Legal and Ethical Status of Museum Collections: Curatorially Motivated Disposals* (London: Museums Association, 2015).

[185] Bethany Rex and Peter Campbell, Report on *Local Authority Investment in Museums after a Decade of Austerity* (London: Museums Association, 2021), p. 7.

differing legal structures, with some collections forming part of the assets of the local authority, which can lead to tensions in times of austerity. University collections may have been established separately as trusts, although others may form part of the assets of the University and are thereby governed by the institutional legal structure.

1.5.5 The Jurisdictions

Some cultural heritage legislation applies across the UK, whilst some applies only to an individual nation. In addition, separate case law will be applicable to Scotland and to Northern Ireland as compared with England and Wales.

Ecclesiastical law applies solely to the Church of England and forms a particularly rich body of jurisprudence caring for cultural heritage. Although few disputes about cultural heritage reach the secular courts, all sales of 'church treasures' and alterations to listed churches are considered by the Church of England's consistory court.[186] Other churches across the nations make decisions about cultural heritage through the ecclesiastical exemption found in the listed building legislation or sales of church treasures, and aspects of these jurisdictions will be analysed. However, many of these decisions are made at the local level and do not form a body of principles as developed as the Church of England ecclesiastical law.

1.6 Adopting a Doubly Integrated Approach to Law

This book does not presume that law is the answer in the search for the most appropriate means of caring for cultural heritage. Regulation in this area of law can be problematic and litigation has been described as a flawed mechanism in the context of cultural heritage disputes.[187] For that reason, this book adopts a doubly integrated approach. First, it treats all cultural heritage on the same basis – regardless of whether it is tangible, intangible or involves places, objects or practices. Preventing harm to cultural heritage places, objects or practices, stolen art, heritage crime, illicit trade in looting, Nazi-looted art, deaccessions and repatriation are dealt with holistically. A community's compunction to care for cultural heritage means that something *ought* to be done – and what may be appropriate to be done (and who has responsibility for doing it) may differ between those contexts. Yet the fact that communities care about cultural heritage and wish to care for it, either directly or indirectly is a common thread throughout these disparate areas. The subsequent chapters analyse how processes that are in place meet the need for such normative responses and provide such care. Thus, the aim is to break down conceptual barriers to look at how decisions about these important objects, places and practices are addressed across the spectrum of cultural heritage.

---

[186] Under the ecclesiastical exemption. Discussed in Section 3.7.3.   [187] See Section 3.4.1.

The second aspect of the integrated approach is that of blurring the line between the legal and non-law initiatives which support communities who care about cultural heritage and provide care for it. This includes how notions of cultural heritage are transformed into the legal sphere and also into those instruments without the force of law, but which serve to care for cultural heritage.[188]

1.6.1 Providing a Complete Window on a Community

The way in which the law treats something can go a long way to demonstrating how a community views it.[189] But that is not the full picture. Whilst the law goes some way to caring for cultural heritage and ensuring that it is not wilfully destroyed, dispersed or diminished, the UK also relies on other non-law instruments which mandate how either a limited category of people (in the case of professional organisations) or a wider group (in the case of formal government guidance) treat cultural heritage.[190] Furthermore, civil society initiatives facilitating public participation in cultural heritage and decision-making about cultural heritage also contribute to the creation of a fuller picture of how the UK cares for cultural heritage.[191] Public participation initiatives organised by government or NGOS with government backing also add to this.

These decision-makers may be at the community or local level or in particular institutions. Museums will be faced with curatorial decisions relating to acquisition, lending and disposal, the placement of cultural heritage (including who possesses it), who has access to it, who decides what happens to it and who participates in the decision-making process. How disputes are dealt with, and how dissonance is navigated (specifically how cultural heritage is translated in these circumstances), is central to a comprehensive understanding of how cultural heritage is cared for by any community – here, the UK. How decision-makers approach the decision (e.g. how they respond to claims for restitution or how they engage with communities and the public more broadly) as well as how they reach their ultimate decisions demonstrate their care for cultural heritage and how the UK, in turn, cares for cultural heritage. Furthermore, an

---

[188] E.g. codes of ethics, recommendations of experts panels and guidance. See Sections 3.7.5 and 3.7.6.

[189] Soderland argues that 'The law provides a lens through which archaeology can be historicized by exploring the voices through which heritage has come to be defined, redefined in law over time as well as how legal classification engages our contemporary understanding of archaeological heritage': Hilary A. Soderland, 'Values and the Evolving Concept of Heritage: The First Century of Archaeology and Law in the United States' in George S. Smith, Phyllis Mauch Messenger and Hilary A. Soderland (eds.), *Heritage Values in Contemporary Society* (Walnut Creek: Left Coast Press, 2010).

[190] 'Policy texts and legal texts are, after all "stories in themselves": they include patterns of dealing with things which are often the result of political compromises and discursive traditions': Sevenhuijsen, *Citizenship and the Ethics of Care*, p. 30.

[191] E.g. the Portable Antiquities Scheme: www.finds.org.uk (last accessed 20 December 2022) or the Enriching the List scheme run by Historic England: https://historicengland.org.uk/listing/enrich-the-list/ (last accessed 20 December 2022).

assessment of the way in which a community cares for cultural heritage also involves analysing how that final decision is justified or audited whether through judicial review or some other mechanism through which to challenge or appeal the decision. Whilst these different non-law instruments and decision-making communities of care do not represent or make use of binding legal principles, these mechanisms do provide an important way to care for cultural heritage, but the authority of these communities and the enforceability of these instruments and decisions will be considered carefully when analysed.

1.7 Conclusion

The integrated approach to caring for cultural heritage adopted in this book avoids taking a myopic view of heritage[192] by focusing on individual areas of contestation. It looks beyond particular groups of interests (such as international, national or community),[193] but instead takes a holistic approach. It considers how communities of care are created and developed, enabling us to understand the way in which a community (here the UK) cares for cultural heritage through law, policy, ethics and practice. Using the framework of caring for cultural heritage, it focuses on developing and sustaining relationships, acknowledging and accepting responsibilities, ensuring mutual respect, trust and empathy, providing the space and willingness to navigate (and resolve) dissonance, providing the space and willingness to respond to actual or threatened harm and facilitating the flourishing of cultural heritage.[194]

As a methodological approach it draws on the work of James Boyd White to analyse the acts of translation of cultural heritage and care into legal language to consider how the UK provides the space to recognise the importance of cultural heritage through meaningful consultation to facilitate consensus. It thus seeks to avoid the authorized heritage discourse and legal disciplinary imperialism, but instead focuses on the communities of care which develop to care for cultural heritage.

---

[192] Fincham has suggested that a 'myopic view' of heritage can result from concentrating on indigenous claims and repatriation at the expense of adopting a more holistic method: Derek Fincham, 'The Distinctiveness of Property and Heritage' (2011) 115 *Penn State Law Review* 641, 643. This should not be interpreted as showing disrespect towards claims that may be made by indigenous groups, but instead the focus here is on cultural heritage, regardless of origin and broadly conceptualised. This can be seen not only in law, but more generally, for as Bienkowski points out, cosmopolitanism discourse in archaeology has unintentionally 'tended to focus on empowering and involving indigenous communities' rather than more broadly on minority communities: Piotr Bienkowski, 'Whose Past? Archaeological Knowledge, Community Knowledge, and the Embracing of Conflict' in Scarre and Coningham, *Appropriating the Past*, p. 57.

[193] It looks beyond the nationalism/internationalism debate to address the human dimension to cultural heritage, including communities, which has been described as a third way of thinking of cultural property: Lucas Lixinski, 'A Third Way of Thinking about Cultural Property' (2019) 44 *Brooklyn Journal of International Law* 563.

[194] This framework of caring for cultural heritage is fully explored in the next chapter.

The book is separated into three parts, each of which represents one of the broad areas of contestation involving cultural heritage identified in this chapter. The individual chapters within each part look at specific areas of contestation relevant to the UK and for each of these areas the key elements of care are considered and the extent to which these are reflected in the legal or non-law initiatives in the UK are analysed.

Part 1 examines how cultural heritage is imagined and translated in the UK. It starts in Chapter 2 by setting out the framework of care adopted in this book and identifying the key elements of appropriate care, being respectful, empathetic and dialogic. In the next chapter, the various legal and non-law instruments and civil society initiatives in the UK, recognised as nested practices of care, are identified and analysed. Chapter 4 considers the various ways in which cultural heritage is directly translated in law and explores how the human dimension to cultural heritage is recognised and helps to establish the UK's overall approach to caring for cultural heritage.

Part II focuses on how the UK cares for cultural heritage through encouraging flourishing of cultural heritage and averting irreparable harm and loss. Chapter 5 explores the way in which communities of care develop and assume responsibilities to care for cultural heritage. Chapter 6 sets out the quotidian care that is provided in respect of cultural heritage, which includes the provisions in law and non-law instruments for looking after cultural heritage on a daily basis, and providing opportunities for communities to use, enjoy and have access to cultural heritage. Chapter 7 analyses the way in which the UK seeks to navigate harm to cultural heritage – both actual or threatened tangible and intangible harm to cultural heritage, focusing on precautionary, preventative and reactive care as well as efforts to mitigate the effect of harm when it cannot be averted. Chapter 8 explores the rhetoric of saving cultural heritage for the nation and averting loss of access on a national level; it seeks to determine whether the export licensing system is focused on caring for cultural heritage or rather the response to a concern that another nation might acquire cultural heritage which the UK is desireth of keeping.

Part III explores the provision of space to resolve dissonance. Chapter 9 considers the space to provide justice and challenge the *status quo*. It analyses whether cultural heritage has an instrumental role, or whether restitution, repatriation, reunification, return or some other remedy are central to caring for others. A central part of the care here is to ensure mutual respect, trust and empathy. To this end, the approaches taken to dealing with challenges to the *status quo* in the form of paternalistic care are compared with dialogic responses which are infused with the ethics of care.

2

Caring for Cultural Heritage
A Conceptual Framework

2.1 Introduction

Assumptions are sometimes made that because a community values cultural heritage it is therefore worthy of preservation and access to it is important.[1] Cultural heritage disputes are frequently framed as disputes about ownership[2] or possession[3] with a view to determining who should have ultimate control. This can be at the cost of the viewpoints of different parties. Such approaches are often unhelpful because they can assume that physical preservation is paramount, or pit one person or group against another (usually against a particular institution). An alternative way of addressing the many ways in which a community interacts with cultural heritage is to consider why a community *cares about* cultural heritage and how it *cares for* it. The approach taken here adopts well-established concepts of care found in academia and applies them to all aspects of cultural heritage in a new way. As part of this venture one must consider the parameters of the care provided through legal and non-law initiatives[4] and identify who makes the day-to-day and longer-term decisions about that care. Involving more people in the decisions about the care of cultural heritage and the setting of parameters of that care both contribute towards a more holistic way of envisaging how a community cares for cultural heritage. Care is adopted here as a wide concept, incorporating all the activities that communities undertake with cultural heritage.

---

[1] Pantazatos provides a criticism of this approach: Andreas Pantazatos, 'The Normative Foundations of Stewardship: Care and Respect' in Tracy Ireland and John Schofield (eds.), *The Ethics of Cultural Heritage* (New York: Springer, 2015), p. 134.

[2] Evident in part from the numerous books with 'Who Owns . . . ?' in the title: Kate Fitz Gibbon (ed.), *Who Owns the Past? Cultural Policy, Cultural Property and the Law* (New Brunswick: Rutgers University Press, 2005); Michael F. Brown, *Who Owns Native Culture?* (London: Harvard University Press, 2003); James Cuno, *Who Owns Antiquity? Museums and the Battle over Our Ancient Heritage* (Oxford: Princeton University Press, 2008); Susan Scafidi, *Who Owns Culture? Appropriation and Authenticity in American Law* (London: Rutgers University Press, 2005); Geoffrey Robertson, *Who Owns History? The Case of Elgin's Loot* (London: Biteback, 2019).

[3] Which can bring with it the challenges of possessive individualism: see Section 1.1.2.

[4] Discussed in Section 2.2 in the context of the nested practices of care.

This chapter begins by defining care and establishing a conceptual framework of caring for cultural heritage. It analyses the process of caring and introduces the nested practices of care for cultural heritage; these comprise the varied legal instruments, non-law instruments, civil society initiatives and public participation initiatives through which care is provided. It then identifies the central elements of caring for cultural heritage, which seek to provide appropriate care – recognised as being respectful, empathetic and dialogic. This takes place within communities of care and within networks of such communities. Appropriate care seeks to encourage the flourishing of cultural heritage, avert harm both to it and to the communities for whom it is important, and aims to pass it on, where appropriate, to future generations. Furthermore, it aims to provide the space and willingness to navigate and resolve dissonance about cultural heritage.

2.2 Defining Care

The approach to care taken in this book draws on the work of Tronto in treating care as being both a disposition, in the sense of being a motivation,[5] based on the strong feeling towards cultural heritage, and a process[6] which reflects the fact that communities may care about cultural heritage and respond to this through caring for it.[7] The term 'care' is used throughout this book to refer to the varied ways in which communities[8] engage with cultural heritage to maintain it, sustain relationships about it and with it, use it as part of cultural practices, provide access to it and navigate dissonance and threats to tangible and intangible harm, with a view to passing it on to future generations.[9] Care is thus taken to be a 'sensitive, responsive and non-discriminatory way of tending to things'.[10] Each of the international bodies, states, lawmakers, decision-makers, advisory bodies, institutions (such as museums), professional bodies, communities from which cultural heritage originated, local groups and organisations involved in caring for cultural

---

[5] Joan C. Tronto, *Caring Democracy: Markets, Equality and Justice* (London: New York University Press, 2013), p. 48.

[6] ibid., p. 21. Care is thus both thought and action: Joan C. Tronto, *Moral Boundaries: A Political Argument for an Ethic of Care* (London: Routledge, 1993), p. 108.

[7] See Ian Russell, 'Heritage, Identities, and Roots: A Critique of Arborescent Models of Heritage and Identity' in George S. Smith, Phyllis Mauch Messenger and Hilary A. Soderland (eds.), *Heritage Values in Contemporary Society* (Walnut Creek: Left Coast Press, 2010), p. 30.

[8] Defined in Chapter 1, Section 1.5.1.

[9] In reaching this approach it was helpful to take as a starting point Fisher and Tronto's definition of care as being '*a species activity that includes everything that we do to maintain, continue, and repair our "world" so that we can live in it as well as possible*': (Berenice Fisher and Joan Tronto, 'Towards a Feminist Theory of Caring' in Emily K. Abel and Margaret K. Nelson (eds.), *Circles of Care: Work and Identity in Women's Lives* (New York: State University of New York Press, 1990), p. 40. Whilst it is a rather broad conception of care, it can be narrowed down, according to context: Tronto, *Caring Democracy*, p. 21.

[10] Bjørnar Olsen, Michael Shanks, Timothy Webmoor and Christopher Witmore, *Archaeology: The Discipline of Things* (London: University of California Press, 2012), p. 20.

heritage are communities – specifically communities of care.[11] The United Kingdom, as the setting of this book, is both a community in its own right and part of the international community, as well as being made up of a network of other communities. All these communities involve themselves in the care of cultural heritage in different ways, including through the nested practices of care[12] – specifically, through the promulgation of legislation; case law; soft law; international, national, regional or local institutional policies, guidance and codes; other civil society initiatives; making claims for cultural heritage and seeking a voice in decision-making. Other communities make use of these structures to enable them to care for cultural heritage.

The language of 'care' or 'caring' in the context of cultural heritage is not uncommon;[13] frequently these terms are used in policies,[14] or in academia. However, their meanings are seldom engaged with in a critical manner,[15]

---

[11]   The terminology of 'communities of care' is explained in Chapter 5.

[12]   See Chapter 3. 'Nested practices' of care is a notion set out by Tronto, *Caring Democracy*, p. 21.

[13]   Although Pantazatos observes that it can be overlooked: Pantazatos, 'The Normative Foundations of Stewardship', p. 134. In some discussions of the way in which approaches to cultural heritage have been conceptualised in international law, the idea of a 'caring and sharing' approach has been mooted as an alternative to adopting the language of ownership of cultural heritage: outlined in International Law Association (ILA) Berlin Conference (2004) Cultural Heritage Law Committee Report – brought into effect by International Law Association Resolution No 4/2006 Cultural Heritage Law 72nd Conference of the International Law Association, Toronto, 4 June 2006. See also Robert K. Paterson, 'The "Caring and Sharing" Alternative: Recent Progress in the International Law Association to Develop Draft Cultural Material Principles' (2005) 12 *International Journal of Cultural Property* 62. Whilst this is a useful shift in emphasis away from ownership, nevertheless it does not really encapsulate the centrality of caring for cultural heritage. As far back as 1905 the term is used in Gerard Baldwin Brown, *The Care of Ancient Monuments* (Cambridge: Cambridge University Press, 1905, online publication 2011), although not specifically defined.

[14]   For example, Culture, Media and Sport Select Committee Sixth Report (2006–2007) *Caring for Our Collections* HC 176–1, 25 June 2007, Department for Culture Media and Sport, *Guidance for the Care of Human Remains in Museums* PP 847 (London: DCMS, 2005) and Historic England, *Protocol for the Care of the Government Historic Estate 2017*: https://historicengland .org.uk/images-books/publications/protocol-for-the-care-of-the-government-historic-estate/ protocol-for-care-of-govt-historic-estate-2017/ (last accessed 20 December 2022).

[15]   As recognised by Russell, 'Heritages, Identities, and Roots', p. 30. Although 'Caring' features in the book's title, the concept is not defined: Elizabeth Pye, *Caring for the Past: Issues in Conservation for Archaeology and Museums* (London: James & James, 2001). Similarly, the nature of care in the 'caring and sharing' approach from the International Law Association (ILA) Cultural Heritage Law Committee is not analysed in Paterson, 'The "Caring and Sharing" Alternative', 62. See also, Valentina Vasile (ed.), *Caring and Sharing: The Cultural Heritage Environment as an Agent for Change* (Cham: Springer International, 2019). An early attempt of mine to grapple with the care of human remains was rather superficial: Charlotte Woodhead, 'Care, Custody and the Display of Human Remains: Legal and Ethical Obligations' in Myra Giesen (ed.), *Curating Human Remains: Caring for the Dead in the United Kingdom* (Heritage Matters Series, Woodbridge: The Boydell Press, 2013), p. 32. Merryman explores the reasons why 'people care a great deal about cultural property' as being 'the expressive value of cultural property', 'the politics and religion of cultural property' and 'the utility of cultural property': John Henry Merryman, 'The Public Interest in Cultural Property' (1989) 77 *California Law Review* 339, 345–55. Prott and O'Keefe recognise that the terminology of heritage 'creates a perception of something handed down; something to be cared for and

although there have been some more recent efforts to conceptualise care in the museum or archaeological contexts.[16] It is important to untangle what is meant by 'caring for cultural heritage'. This avoids taking an essentialist approach[17] which might recognise innate value in cultural heritage rendering it appropriate for preservation,[18] for '[h]eritage does not simply exist. It is something we have to care about and simultaneously care for'.[19] Caring is 'probably the most deeply fundamental value',[20] and caring for heritage is recognised as universal;[21] it is framed as an obligation in the present to care, thus enabling cultural heritage to be handed on to future generations.[22] But it is important to avoid simply assuming that communities care or should care about, and for, cultural heritage (which is 'often found in the conflation of the concepts of heritage and identity').[23] By questioning *why* a community cares about cultural heritage and *how* a community cares for it avoids taking the 'benefits of cultural heritage' as 'a matter of faith'.[24] The *why* has already been addressed in Chapter 1 through consideration of the importance of cultural heritage to different people and its role within communities, demonstrating the reasons for caring *about* cultural heritage.[25] The specific challenges

cherished': Lyndel Prott and Patrick J. O'Keefe, '"Cultural Heritage" or "Cultural Property"?' (1992) 1 *International Journal of Cultural Property* 307, 311.

[16] Olsen et al., *The Discipline of Things*, suggest that care implies 'devotion, nurturing, and thoughtfulness directed towards something' and that it 'looks for the connections among objects, environments, people, and animals, all of which share membership in the dwelt-in world': p. 172. Pantazatos adopts Fisher and Tronto's definition: Pantazatos, 'The Normative Foundations of Stewardship', p. 15, and Woodham and Kelleher, who consider the work of Tronto and Meyer: Anna Woodham and Shane Kelleher, 'What's in a Name? The Ethics of Care and an "Unloved" Collection' in Anna Woodham, Rhianedd Smith and Alison Hess (eds.), *Exploring Emotion, Care, and Enthusiasm in 'Unloved' Collections* (Leeds: Arc Humanities Press, 2020), p. 65.

[17] Which has been attributed to Ruskin and Riegl (William Morris is also likely to fall into this category): Uffe Juul Jensen, 'Cultural Heritage, Liberal Education, and Human Flourishing' in Erica Avrami, Randall Mason and Marta de la Torre (eds.), *Values and Heritage Conservation: Research Report* (Los Angeles: The Getty Conservation Institute, 2000), p. 43.

[18] See generally ibid., p. 43, and also the notion of the authorized heritage discourse expounded by Laurajane Smith, *Uses of Heritage* (London: Routledge, 2008), p. 29.

[19] Russell, 'Heritages, Identities, and Roots', p. 30.

[20] Virginia Held, *The Ethics of Care: Personal, Political and Global* (Oxford: Oxford University Press, 2006), p. 17.

[21] Merryman, in 'The Public Interest', suggests that 'despite cultural variations, people in most (all?) places care in special ways about objects that evoke or embody or express their own and other people's cultures': p. 343. Olsen et al. call for 'an appeal for "collective care," specifically symmetrical care for people and things (and all nonhumans), and the rapports between things, a care that is more responsive to the "wicked problems" characterizing the complexly interdependent circumstances of our contemporaneity': Olsen et al., *The Discipline of Things*, pp. 164–5.

[22] Prott and O'Keefe suggest that there is a 'broad acceptance of a duty to pass [cultural manifestations of cultural heritage] on to our successors . . . ': Prott and O'Keefe, '"Cultural Heritage" or "Cultural Property"?', 311.

[23] See Russell, 'Heritages, Identities, and Roots', p. 30. Heritage and identity are explored at Sections 1.2.1.1 and 1.2.2.

[24] Avrami et al., *Values and Heritage Conservation*, p. 10.   [25] See Section 1.2.2.

faced by cultural heritage within certain areas of contestation in the United Kingdom were also explored in the previous chapter to identify how the United Kingdom should care for cultural heritage, thus identifying the requirements of care needing to be facilitated through law or non-law instruments. The issue of *how* cultural heritage is cared for forms the basis of the subsequent chapters, which analyse the action or inaction that the United Kingdom, as a community and network of communities, takes through those varied instruments which form nested practices of care.

2.3 Adopting Care as a Framework

The notion of care, specifically the ethics of care and its development, owes much to feminist scholarship.[26] Whilst acknowledging a debt to these scholars, the approach to 'care' and 'caring' of cultural heritage adopted in this book is not intended as taking a specific feminist perspective on cultural heritage. The approach is neither to treat 'care' and 'caring' as inherently feminine activities[27] nor to extract any specific features from motherhood.[28] It draws on the work of Tronto, who sees a feminist ethic of care as one in which caring practices are 'nested within one another';[29] however, as Herring observes, 'it certainly is possible to develop an ethic of care which is not "feminist"'.[30] The choice of care as a framework here is to enable the full inclusion of all aspects of the relationship that people have with cultural heritage, the relationship that they have with other people for whom cultural heritage is important and with the people who assume responsibility for cultural heritage (or on whom responsibilities are placed). Humanity cares about, and for, cultural heritage and the approach taken here seeks to recognise and to respect that. As Held observes, the ethics of care focuses on 'what lies between' the 'extremes of "selfish individual" and "humanity"'.[31] In turn, care is a universal concept.[32]

Theories about caring are usually found in the context of caring about, and for, other people (whether in the family home, children, persons with disabilities or vulnerable parties).[33] Nevertheless, it is clear that caring, as a process, can be

---

[26] Often cited is Carol Gilligan, *In a Different Voice* (London: Harvard University Press, 1982). Caring is situated within the subject of social reproduction: Catherine Hoskyns and Shirin M. Rai, 'Recasting the Global Political Economy: Counting Women's Unpaid Work' (2007) 12 *New Political Economy* 297, 299. See generally Jonathan Herring, *Caring and the Law* (Oxford: Hart, 2013), pp. 47–9.

[27] Herring discusses the gender implications of caring: Herring, *Caring and the Law*, pp. 79–81. Cf. Held, *The Ethics of Care*, p. 22.

[28] One of the feminist ideals of caring has been motherhood: Fisher and Tronto, 'Towards a Feminist Theory of Caring', p. 51.

[29] Tronto, *Caring Democracy*, p. 29. The nested practices of care for cultural heritage are explored in Chapter 3.

[30] Herring, *Caring and the Law*, p. 70.   [31] Held, *The Ethics of Care*, p. 13.

[32] Pantazatos, 'The Normative Foundations of Stewardship', p. 136.

[33] For example, Herring in *Caring and the Law* considers care within the context of, inter alia, medical law, family law, situations involving abuse and within the general law.

directed not only towards people but also towards things,[34] including cultural heritage objects and places, and practices. Scholarship about care extends beyond the private sphere to public life[35] and includes how institutions care.[36] The concept is sufficiently broad to encompass how care is provided through democratic processes establishing laws and guidance.[37] For this reason, care provides a powerful analytical framework for dealing with the United Kingdom, comprising as it does of a patchwork of legislation, case law, guidance, professional ethical codes and civil society initiatives. 'Care' and notions of 'caring for' cultural heritage have the capacity to deal with the complexity of the environment in which UK law and practice interact, which rather than being a regulatory, top-down system comprises laws appropriated for the benefit of cultural heritage,[38] community initiatives and, at times arcane, legal principles grappling with the dynamic creature that is cultural heritage (occasionally ignoring its status as such).[39] Care can therefore encompass the way in which the state not only restricts the development of land to avoid adversely affecting the historical character of an area or the significance of a building[40] but also supports practical, self-initiated efforts of local groups that form themselves into communities of care to assume responsibility for local places. This can include raising money to finance the restoration of discovered public artwork.[41]

It should be emphasised that within this context, 'care' should be understood as neither a synonym for stewardship nor a euphemism for paternalism. Stewardship can focus too heavily on the way in which cultural heritage (usually objects) is in the direct care of institutions, or the way in which archaeologists directly care for objects.[42] It does not necessarily incorporate such activities as developing policies or laws which care for cultural heritage, or the professional standards agreed by membership bodies, and does not account for community-led initiatives where the law may be used instrumentally to challenge potential

---

[34] Fisher and Tronto, 'Towards a Feminist Theory of Caring', p. 40; Tronto, *Moral Boundaries*, p. 103. See Olsen et al., *The Discipline of Things*, p. 164.

[35] Tronto, *Caring Democracy*, p. 17. As Tronto points out, it is not always helpful to make such a stark distinction between the private and public aspects to/spheres of caring: Tronto, *Caring Democracy*, p. 33. See also Selma Sevenhuijsen, 'The Place of Care: The Relevance of the Feminist Ethic of Care for Social Policy' (2003) 4 *Feminist Theory* 179, 186.

[36] See generally Joan C. Tronto, 'Creating Caring Institutions: Politics, Plurality, and Purpose' (2010) 4 *Ethics and Social Welfare* 158.

[37] See generally Tronto, *Caring Democracy*.   [38] See Section 3.7.3.

[39] As to which see Chapter 3.

[40] The Planning (Listed Buildings and Conservation Areas) Act (P(LBCA)A) 1990, discussed at Section 7.4.1.

[41] For example, Historic England's crowdfunding campaign relating to Peter Laszlo Peri's *The Sunbathers*, discussed at Section 7.6.1.

[42] For example, ICOM, *Code of Ethics for Museums*, principle 2. Stewardship is often seen as an interchangeable term with guardianship: Janet Marstine, 'The Contingent Nature of the New Museum Ethics' in Janet Marstine (ed.), *The Routledge Companion to Museum Ethics* (London: Routledge, 2011), p. 18, although it has been suggested that guardianship is relevant in the museum context and stewardship in the context of archaeology: Haidy Geismar, 'Cultural Property, Museums, and the Pacific: Reframing Debates' (2008) 15 *International Journal of Cultural Property* 109, 116.

harm to cultural heritage[43] and in some cases to assume responsibility for the direct care of a cultural heritage place or object. Paternalism can assume a need to care and may impose a situation on others or a thing, place or practice without appropriate levels of consideration, respect, empathy or participation from others.[44] For this reason the concept of appropriate care adopted here is firmly rooted in empathy, trust and respect[45] with opportunities for participation and dialogue with those communities for whom the cultural heritage is important.

Care is thus conceptualised to incorporate the multidimensional way in which a community cares about and for cultural heritage. It more fully reflects the nature of relationships with cultural heritage and provides a comprehensive framework capturing a variety of activities and responses beyond preservation,[46] truth[47] and access.[48] By moving beyond concepts of preservation or conservation (each one of which focuses on the outcome of the intervention), one can consider the feeling towards the cultural heritage, the process (which involves action or inaction) as well as the outcome. 'Care' is thus far broader in nature and scope. It makes no assumption about the appropriate or necessary course of action – therefore, unlike preservation or conservation it does not presuppose that the goal is to protect it from (usually physical) harm and does not presume that ownership and control is the only, or optimum, outcome or that public ownership is paramount. It extends beyond concepts such as personhood,[49] peoplehood[50] or grouphood[51] and beyond framing the issue as conflicts over ownership. 'Care' places the people and their relationships at the centre of discussion,[52] which is essential, particularly when needing to navigate disputes involving often contradictory viewpoints. The ethics of care has previously been adopted as one of two normative foundations for stewardship in the context of archaeological ethics[53] and more recently as being 'fundamental to museum participatory practice'.[54] In the context of archaeologies of the heart, it includes 'acknowledging the context within which [archaeologists] work and the power dynamics that flow from it'.[55] However, the approach in this book is to adopt

---

[43] See the discussion of the case of *R (on the application of Save Stonehenge World Heritage Site Ltd) v. Secretary of State for Transport* [2021] EWHC 2161 (Admin) at Section 5.2.8.3.

[44] See the discussion at Section 9.5.1.   [45] As to which, see Section 2.5.4.

[46] Merryman, 'The Public Interest', 355.   [47] ibid., 359.   [48] ibid., 360.

[49] As to which see Margaret Jane Radin, 'Property and Personhood' (1981–2) 34 *Stanford Law Review* 957 and Jeffrey Douglas Jones, 'Property and Personhood Revisited' (2011) 1 *Wake Forest Journal of Law & Policy* 93.

[50] Kristen A. Carpenter, Sonia K. Katyal and Angela R. Riley, 'In Defense of Property' (2009) 118 *Yale Law Journal* 1022, 1028.

[51] John Moustakas, 'Group Rights in Cultural Property: Justifying Strict Inalienability' (1989) 74 *Cornell Law Review* 1179.

[52] As to the human dimension to cultural heritage, see Section 1.2.

[53] Pantazatos, 'The Normative Foundations of Stewardship'. See also Olsen et al., *The Discipline of Things*, p. 11, in the context of archaeology.

[54] Nuala Morse, *The Museum as a Space of Social Care* (London: Routledge, 2020), p. 186.

[55] Lisa Hodgetts and Laura Kelvin, 'At the Heart of the Ikaahuk Archaeology Project' in Kisha Supernant, Jane Eva Baxter, Natasha Lyons and Sonya Atalay (eds.), *Archaeologies of the Heart* (Cham: Springer, 2020), p. 99.

care as a framework of activity for all cultural heritage, expanding the applicability of notions of care beyond stewardship of one category of objects and analysing how cultural heritage, more broadly constituted, is cared for.[56] This framework also incorporates the way in which dissonance is addressed and attempts are made to resolve it. Specifically, by considering what Tronto describes as the intersection between needs and interests,[57] it is possible to ascertain the most appropriate way in which to care for cultural heritage and to involve in that process the people for whom it is important.

Whilst sharing some similarities with the ethical underpinnings of safeguarding,[58] care should not be understood as indicating vulnerability,[59] and does not focus on measures ensuring the viability of intangible cultural heritage.[60] Unlike safeguarding – which arguably presupposes the existence of potential harm which is to be averted – care treats cultural heritage in all it states, including its 'resting position', when it is being used and enjoyed rather than designated or protected from harm or loss. Care is thus a broader and more holistic concept than safeguarding, and does not focus simply on the relationship between the object of heritage and the need to ensure its safety but also on the relational nature of cultural heritage.

2.4 The Process of Caring

Caring has been described as a process[61] or relational practice.[62] The first stage, relevant to cultural heritage, is caring *about* cultural heritage.[63] This includes 'recognizing the need for care'[64] and is essentially 'an attitude of mind'.[65]

---

[56] Thus incorporating objects other than archaeological ones which form part of cultural heritage, as well as places and practices.

[57] Tronto, *Moral Boundaries*, pp. 164, 168.

[58] This includes mutual respect and transparent collaboration with dialogue and consultation with free and informed consent: UNESCO, *Ethical Principles for Safeguarding Intangible Cultural Heritage*, Decision of the Intergovernmental Committee, 10.COM 15.A, Windhoek, 2015, Annex, paras. 3 and 4.

[59] See Pantazados, 'The Normative Foundations of Stewardship', p. 135; see Section 2.5.3.

[60] Which is part of the definition of safeguarding of intangible cultural heritage, art. 2(3).

[61] Fisher and Tronto, 'Towards a Feminist Theory of Caring', p. 40; Selma Sevenhuijsen, *Citizenship and the Ethics of Care* (tr. Liz Savage) (London: Routledge, 1998), p. 82.

[62] Tronto, 'Creating Caring Institutions', 161. It is described as having four 'intertwining phases' (caring about, caring for, care-giving and care-receiving): Fisher and Tronto, 'Towards a Feminist Theory of Caring', p. 40 – now five (caring with): Tronto, *Caring Democracy*, p. 11. Each of these is then assigned an ethical element (attentiveness, responsibility, competence and responsiveness): Tronto, *Moral Boundaries*, p. 127. The fifth ethical element, corresponding to caring with, is plurality, communication, trust and respect: Tronto, *Caring Democracy*, p. 35. Cf. Herring, who identifies four 'markers of care' as meeting needs, respect, responsibility and relationality: Herring, *Caring and the Law*, p. 14. Rather than separating out the five phases and mapping onto these certain ethical elements, the approach taken here is to set out a bespoke process with relevant elements which more fully represents the way in which a community cares for cultural heritage.

[63] See Fisher and Tronto, 'Towards a Feminist Theory of Caring', p. 40.

[64] Tronto, 'Creating Caring Institutions', 160.   [65] Herring, *Caring and the Law*, p. 15.

Caring *about* incorporates a responsibility to meet the needs of and to pay 'attention to our world in such a way that we focus on continuity, maintenance and repair'.[66] The notion of caring *about* cultural heritage is intertwined with the way in which a community values cultural heritage; it thus provides the impetus for action and recognises the value of cultural heritage and its significance to people(s).

Having recognised that a community cares about cultural heritage, the next stage of the process is caring *for*[67] cultural heritage; this stage 'implies the responsibility for initiating and maintaining caring activities'[68] and requires action or, at times, inaction.[69] Often care-giving and care-receiving are recognised as the next stage of the process of care. However, given the frequent absence of single caregivers and receivers in the context of cultural heritage and the often complex network of relationships, *caring for* is taken here to include all of these relationships and how people care together with others for cultural heritage,[70] thus forming communities of care.

2.5 Central Elements of Caring for Cultural Heritage: Developing Communities of Care

Based on the importance of cultural heritage and the various areas of contestation identified in Chapter 1, it appears that the central elements of how communities of care should provide care for cultural heritage are: (a) developing and sustaining relationships; (b) acknowledging and assuming responsibilities; (c) identifying and maintaining the appropriate care in the circumstances and revisiting this regularly.[71] Informing these central elements of care are the need to: ensure mutual respect, trust and empathy; facilitate flourishing of cultural heritage; provide the space and willingness to navigate (and resolve) dissonance; and provide the space and willingness to respond to actual or threatened harm.

---

[66] Fisher and Tronto, 'Towards a Feminist Theory of Caring', p. 40.

[67] Although in setting out the second element of the process of caring Fisher and Tronto use the idea of 'taking care of': ibid., p. 40. The approach taken here is to adopt the terminology of 'caring for' in preference to 'taking care of' because the latter may imply more direct involvement with physical care, whereas the care of cultural heritage may be indirect, through policies or action taken from afar.

[68] ibid, p. 40.

[69] Herring, *Caring and the Law*, p. 15. See also Held, *The Ethics of Care*, p. 15 and Andreas Pantazatos, 'Does Diaspora Test the Limits of Stewardship? Stewardship and the Ethics of Care' (2010) 62 *Museum International* 96, 99.

[70] This aligns with the notion of 'caring with', an idea developed in recent years as a fifth stage of the process by Tronto, drawing on the work of Sevenhuijsen. It recognises the indirect participants in the caring process who take part through democratic processes: Tronto, *Caring Democracy*, Preface.

[71] These draw on approaches to care taken by several academics which are set out in the subsequent sections, but the structure adopted here represents a new method of approaching the relationship between communities (broadly constituted, as to which see Section 2.5.3) and cultural heritage of importance to them.

2.5.1 The Relational Nature of Caring: Developing and Sustaining Relationships through Active Participation

Adopting a framework of 'care' for cultural heritage ensures that the human dimension of cultural heritage is necessarily at the forefront of the discussion;[72] the relational nature of caring for[73] cultural heritage is central to the 'understanding of people as relational because it connects people ... with the past ... and with each other ... and it thus contributes to our identity'.[74] Given that people are at the heart of cultural heritage and that relationships between those people contribute significantly to the act of caring for cultural heritage (whether directly or indirectly)[75] it is important that for relationships to thrive there is a need for both 'sufficient time and proximity'.[76] Participation in accessing and enjoying cultural heritage is important, including for wellbeing,[77] as well as active participation in dialogue and collaboration relating to cultural heritage.[78] Active participation in dialogue is recognised generally as an important element of caring and can empower participants,[79] particularly where there is direct involvement in decision-making. Participation is more than simply providing the infrastructure for participation; communities need to actively engage with this as a process, through listening and acting upon it by directly involving relevant people, which may include local communities as well as other specialist communities of care.[80] Embedded within these concepts is the need to refrain from imposing one person's views on another person or group, or stifling the thing or the people involved. It thus corresponds with the notion of caring *with*,[81] which seeks to ensure that how caring needs are met is 'consistent with democratic commitments to justice, equality, and freedom for all'.[82]

---

[72] This human dimension was considered at Section 1.2.

[73] Held, *The Ethics of Care*, who talks of cultivating caring relationships, p. 15. See generally Herring, *Caring and the Law*, who looks specifically at the concept of caring in law.

[74] Pantazatos, 'Does Diaspora Test the Limits of Stewardship?', pp. 98–9. For as Held observes, relations 'are part of what constitute our identity': Held, *The Ethics of Care*, p. 14.

[75] Pantazatos acknowledges that the relationship is with the object as well: Pantazatos, 'The Normative Foundations of Stewardship', p. 136.

[76] Tronto, *Caring Democracy*, pp. 164–5.

[77] See Daniel Fujiwara and George MacKerron, *Cultural Activities, Artforms and Wellbeing* (London: Arts Council England, 2015); DCMS, *Heritage Statement 2017* (2017), p. 14 and The Heritage Alliance, *Heritage, Health and Wellbeing: A Heritage Alliance Report* (2020).

[78] See Section 5.3.

[79] Held, *The Ethics of Care*, p. 20. In the context of 'caring with', Tronto emphasises the importance of citizens being 'constantly engaged': Tronto, *Caring Democracy*, p. 154.

[80] Sherry Arnstein, 'A Ladder of Citizen Participation' (1969) 35 *Journal of the American Institute of Planners* 216.

[81] Identified by Tronto in *Caring Democracy*, p. 22 as the fifth stage of the process of caring.

[82] ibid, p. 22.

2.5.1.1 Beyond a Bilateral Relationship of Caring towards Multilateral, Multigenerational Relationship: Communities of Care

In practice there is often no straightforward relationship between cultural heritage and a single care-giver.[83] Whilst the relational nature of care is in any event dynamic[84] the relationships surrounding cultural heritage have a heightened dynamism given that the focus of care is intangible,[85] changing frequently over time, from place to place (if an object is moved) or between participants or people.[86] This dynamism can be reflected in the response through the ethics of care.[87] Care can directly or indirectly benefit a multitude of people – some, but not all, of whom might have been in direct contact with the cultural heritage itself. Caring in the context of cultural heritage necessarily extends to the people who care for cultural heritage concurrently (but perhaps in different ways) and consecutively over time. This section begins by analysing concurrent care and then proceeds to explore consecutive care.

2.5.1.2 Concurrent Caring

Traditionally, curators were the principal carers of cultural heritage in museums; indeed, the etymology of 'curator' is from the Latin *curare* – to care. In such circumstances the relationship was primarily a bilateral one – between the curator as care-giver and the object as the cared for. At most the public may have been noted as the beneficiaries of this care on the basis of preserving cultural heritage for future generations. The trope of holding objects 'in trust' for the public is often employed.[88] A traditional approach to care, applied in this way, would fall squarely within the authorized heritage discourse in terms of experts deciding what is the appropriate way to care for cultural heritage,[89] with perhaps little or no consultation. This preoccupation with caring for the objects themselves may have been at the cost of the people

---

[83] Rather than a traditional setting in which care is provided by one individual to another (or others) – for example the carers and the cared-for in a family context – caring in the context of cultural heritage necessarily extends to the many and varied people who care for heritage over time. Tronto highlights the fact that frequently care is perceived as dyadic, but is seldom so: ibid, p. 151. Therefore Tronto's approach to 'caring with' is particularly helpful in the context of cultural heritage.

[84] Herring, *Caring and the Law*, p. 21.

[85] I.e. adopting the approach that cultural heritage is always intangible – a process about an object, place or practice: see Smith, *Uses of Heritage*, p. 2 and also Section 1.2.1.

[86] See Section 1.1.2.

[87] If the way in which the value of cultural heritage to certain people has changed (e.g. a new event in the history of a place has altered the way in which it is viewed by different people) then in response the nature and the extent of the care may need to be altered to reflect this change. E.g. the physical traces left in St Paul's Chapel in New York following its use by rescuers in September 2001: see Randall Mason, 'Theoretical and Practice Arguments for Values-Centered Preservation' (2006) 3 *CRM: The Journal of Heritage Stewardship* 21, 32.

[88] This was included as part of the definition of a museum by the Museums Association in 1998.

[89] Smith, *Uses of Heritage*, p. 29.

for whom they are important and consequently represent a paternalistic form of care without the necessary respect and empathy.[90]

In contrast to traditional forms of care, which may have ignored differing viewpoints when making decisions, the approach to 'caring for' cultural heritage taken here avoids focusing on a single, direct giver of care. Instead, the approach is holistic, incorporating a wide range of care-givers as well as the cared for. It proceeds on the basis that the significant human dimension of cultural heritage[91] warrants the active participation of these varied members of communities. They are the beneficiaries of the care given to a particular object, place or practice and also participate in the provision of its care. The model presupposes a cycle of caring relationships, or a network of communities of care, rather than a linear process. The focus is therefore not only on the physical custodians of cultural heritage but also on all those who concurrently care for cultural heritage, directly and indirectly. This includes those who directly participate in practices with the cultural heritage[92] and those who participate in the decision-making about the long-term care of cultural heritage. However, it also includes those who legislate to care for cultural heritage, those who develop policies either as part of government or professional bodies or communities, and those involved in establishing and maintaining civil society initiatives caring for cultural heritage. All of these people are members of individual communities of care and represent a network of communities of care. Thus, the ethics of care adopted here extends beyond the local, direct communities or institutions caring for cultural heritage to 'states and the international community to promote care too'[93] and is relevant to 'political institutions and how society is organised'.[94] Caring therefore involves the many people across the globe who care about cultural heritage; feasibly this can include third parties who may never have experienced first-hand the cultural heritage but for whom it remains important.[95]

---

[90] As to which see Section 2.5.4.
[91] Francesco Francioni and Lucas Lixinski, 'Opening the Toolbox of International Human Rights Law in the Safeguarding of Cultural Heritage' in Andrea Durbach and Lucas Lixinski (eds.), *Heritage, Culture and Rights: Challenging Legal Discourses* (Oxford: Hart, 2017), p. 17; Francesco Francioni, 'The Human Dimension of International Cultural Heritage Law: An Introduction' (2011) 22 *European Journal of International Law* 9, 10.
[92] Through visiting the cultural heritage object, place or participating or performing in the cultural heritage practice.
[93] Herring, *Caring and the Law*, p. 76.   [94] Held, *The Ethics of Care*, p. 18.
[95] Deborah Mattinson, 'The Value of Heritage: What Does the Public Think?' in Kate Clark (ed.), *Capturing the Public Value of Heritage: The Proceedings of the London Conference* (London: English Heritage, 2006), p. 89; Randall Mason, 'Assessing Values in Conservation Planning: Methodological Issues and Choices' in Marta de la Torre (ed.), *Assessing the Values of Cultural Heritage: A Research Report* (Los Angeles: The Getty Conservation Institute, 2002), p. 23; David Throsby, 'Cultural Capital and Sustainability Concepts in the Economics of Cultural Heritage' in de la Torre, *Assessing the Values of Cultural Heritage*, p. 103. The existence value is the value of cultural heritage to people irrespective of whether they have seen it: Timothy Darvill, 'Value Systems in Archaeology' in Malcolm A. Cooper, Anthony Firth, John Carman and David Wheatley (eds.), *Managing Archaeology* (London: Routledge, 1995), p. 47.

Participation on equal terms is essential in the museums context, in particular where past mistrust of custodians and concerns about the relative power dimensions have adversely affected communities.[96] This interdependency[97] can be seen when considering the contribution of communities to dialogue about the long-term care of cultural heritage as well as interest groups[98] and amenity societies[99] who play a role in the decisions about cultural heritage places.[100] It includes the active participation of groups who respond to potential risks to cultural heritage.[101] These all represent communities of care undertaking care of cultural heritage, directly and indirectly, to differing degrees and in various ways.

2.5.1.3 Consecutive Caring

The notion of consecutive carers reflects the idea that past generations have passed cultural heritage on to present generations who, in turn, want to pass it on to future generations.[102] Yet it also acknowledges that some cultural heritage is created in the present and will be passed to future generations. Focusing on the different carers over time reflects several elements of relevance to the notion of caring for heritage – the present and the future as well as the different actors involved. It focuses on the interdependency of the multiple communities involved but also the notion of heritage passing down the generations, thus reflecting the idea of inheritance inherent in the concept of heritage.[103]

The communities for whom specific cultural heritage is important may change over time but even the current communities providing care for cultural heritage are not static. For some communities there is clearly continuity between one generation and the next, but in other situations the community (whether a local community or a nation) may have changed significantly from

---

[96] As Morse observes, 'In the case of the museum, the logic of care still requires scrutiny of uneven power structures in the museum (historical and contemporary) and the power relations that animate participation work, including the ways in which emotional connections are themselves sites of power': Morse, *The Museum as a Space of Social Care*, p. 190.

[97] In which care is seen to be grounded: Herring, *Caring and the Law*, p. 21; Pantazatos, 'The Normative Foundations of Stewardship', p. 137. Tronto emphasises that interdependence is better than dependence because she sees care as caring for both the receiver and giver of care: Tronto, *Caring Democracy*, p. 28.

[98] See Section 5.2.6.1.

[99] Listed in the Arrangements for Handling Heritage Applications – Notification to Historic England and National Amenity Societies and the Secretary of State (England) Direction 2021, para. 4(b). See further Section 5.2.10.

[100] Specifically in planning law and ecclesiastical law. See Section 5.2.10.

[101] See Section 5.2.13.

[102] Here the terminology of 'future' is preferred over 'fate' since the nature of caring is an ongoing process rather than static in nature and the details of which may be changed in response to dynamic or evolving value of, or concerns about, cultural heritage; future is thus ongoing. Fate on the other hand suggests something that has been predetermined and effectively the object, place or practice's ultimate destiny. The term 'fate' also brings with it connotations of ultimate destruction or doom, which does not reflect the vibrant nature of much heritage.

[103] As to which, see Section 1.1.2.

one generation to the next.[104] Cultural heritage objects can easily be displaced and there are numerous examples of objects of cultural heritage being removed during, or after, wars or conflicts.[105] For that reason, the nature and extent of the care can shift temporally (or inter-generationally) and spatially.

A potential pitfall with recognising this shifting body of 'carers' is the risk of fragmentation of the care itself. This might feasibly result from disparate groups caring for cultural heritage in different ways across time. For that reason, it is necessary to consider how responsibility for care is allocated or assumed in a respectful and empathetic manner.

2.5.2 Acknowledging and Assuming Respectful Responsibilities

Responsibility[106] is conceptualised here as 'a set of implied cultural practices rather than a set of formal rules or series of promises'.[107] Caring focuses on responsibilities[108] rather than on rights.[109] Some caring responsibilities are not freely entered into and are imposed by context. This may be through legal obligations backed by sanction such as listed buildings legislation which make it a criminal offence for anyone to demolish, alter or extend a building in a manner affecting its special architectural or historic interest.[110] This also often applies to the owner of the cultural heritage place itself and represents the state assuming responsibility for the indirect care of the cultural heritage place, and the state imposing responsibilities on the owner, thereby impacting on their use and enjoyment of private property. Caring responsibilities may also be imposed through ethical obligations by which communities have agreed to be bound, albeit with less binding force.[111] These include professional codes of ethics relating to museum practice, archaeology, conservation, archives and metal detecting to name but a few.[112]

It is important to emphasise that the notion of assuming responsibility for care should be interpreted as neither abrogating the need for dialogue nor ignoring the views of others. As already acknowledged, for some the idea of museums assuming responsibilities for cultural heritage originating from their communities is seen as patronising or paternalistic and perpetuates colonial ill-treatment.[113] In such situations, cultural heritage has effectively been 'taken

---

[104] Here, the term 'community' is understood in its wide meaning set out in Section 5.1. This theme is developed in Chapter 9 in the context of seeking justice.

[105] See generally Section 7.3.1.

[106] Responsibility, as the second ethical element of care identified by Tronto, is mapped on to the stage of the process of *taking care of*: Tronto, *Moral Boundaries*, p. 131.

[107] ibid., pp. 131–2. It is thus adopted in preference to obligation, which is seen as something more formalised and would usually require prior binding agreements: ibid., p. 131.

[108] Tronto describes it as a 'central moral category' but acknowledges that it is problematic: ibid.

[109] Herring, *Caring and the Law*, p. 60; Fisher and Tronto, 'Towards a Feminist Theory of Caring', p. 40.

[110] P(LBCA)A 1990, s. 7(1).   [111] The nature of such obligations is explored at Section 3.7.5.2.

[112] Considered at ibid.   [113] Paternalistic care is explored in this context in Section 9.5.1.

into care' against the will of the original custodians.[114] Similarly where monuments have been seen to be taken into care by the state in the past, this can also be problematic.[115] Adopting the language of care is not intended to give the impression that the communities or their cultural heritage should be viewed as being in any subordinate position, or that where a museum is acknowledged as care-giver this means that it is automatically in a position of power justifying it in determining the appropriate care for the cultural heritage. There are real risks that where responsibility is assumed there is paternalism and excessive power. Failing to engage in dialogue can negatively affect the way in which care is provided.[116] The particular problem of paternalistic communities of care found in the context of certain national museums is explored below.[117] A relational approach to care avoids some of these potential perceptions by seeking to place on an equal footing all of those involved, as partners, in a relational dialogue. For this reason, responsibility requires 'constant evaluation'.[118] Caring should not be interpreted here as suggesting that certain groups require others to look after their cultural heritage, or that experts are best placed to care for cultural heritage. The current approach seeks to challenge care in those situations where there is a desire to unquestionably maintain the *status quo*, for example, where museums seek to keep looted or pillaged objects, despite strong claims for their return. Thus, the perpetuation of unequal power relations can be avoided by adopting a relational approach to care and by recognising that when responsibilities are assumed they should be regularly re-evaluated.

Once one acknowledges that responsibilities exist, several important questions follow: first, to whom are those responsibilities directed? This might be to past, present or future generations. Is the current 'holder' of these responsibilities the most appropriate? One should not only question the person, institution, community or state on whom the responsibility lies, but also consider the extent of that responsibility. In particular, it is necessary to question whether it is appropriate for them to be responsible for care – whether others might be better placed to assume or to act on that responsibility. Is responsibility directed towards cultural heritage[119] or towards the people in the relationship?[120] These people could be direct participants as well as those to whom the cultural heritage is also important, but who may never have

---

[114] As Lixinski observes: 'This rhetoric of benevolence [the idea of preserving a dying culture for the benefit of future generations], however well-intentioned, has the effect of perpetuating paternalistic attitudes of the majoritarian society.' Lucas Lixinski, *International Heritage Law for Communities: Exclusion and Re-Imagination* (Oxford: Oxford University Press, 2019), p. 99.

[115] E.g. in the case of the state care of monuments in Northern Ireland.

[116] See Morse, *The Museum as a Space of Social Care*, p. 190.   [117] In Section 9.5.1.

[118] Tronto, *Moral Boundaries*, p. 131.

[119] Pantazatos, 'The Normative Foundations of Stewardship', p. 136.

[120] Olsen et al. call for '"collective care," specifically symmetrical care for people and things': Olsen et al., *The Discipline of Things*, pp. 164–5.

encountered it.[121] They may thus be other members of a community, a national community or humanity more generally. It is clear though that the responsibilities are both inter- and intra-generational – capturing both the present use of cultural heritage as well as the need to pass on the cultural heritage to future generations. As part of this, dialogue is essential. Responsibility should not be assumed simply because of historical events and should not be based on the location of an object where it ultimately ended up. It is important to revisit the *status quo*. Central to this is the need to question the power dynamics at play. Given the relational nature of care, responsibilities are owed between those people in the relationship[122] such that what informs the ethical application of stewardship guided by an ethics of care 'is not the preservation of material heritage but its responsiveness to the needs of the relationship between people and heritage'.[123] As part of this process one must ensure that appropriate mechanisms are in place to reflect on and reconsider who has assumed responsibility, the extent of that responsibility and care, and whether it remains appropriate.[124] Thus the caring process reflects and respects heritage as a process.

2.5.3 Identifying the Appropriate Care in the Circumstances

Being attentive both to the needs of others and to how one addresses those needs[125] is key to caring for something. It is insufficient simply to provide care; it is also necessary to show responsiveness and to 'remain alert to the possibilities for abuse that arise with vulnerability'.[126] Therefore, in the context of cultural heritage it is important to maintain dialogue to ensure that the care provided is the most appropriate for the circumstances and central to this is the integrity of care – the idea that all of the phases of care should 'fit together into a whole'.[127] This ensures that conflict can be addressed and acknowledges that '[c]are as a practice involves more than simply good intentions. It requires a deep and thoughtful knowledge of the situation and of all of the actors, situations, needs and competences.'[128] It is therefore essential that those making decisions about care and providing care are competent[129] and that they provide good care[130] which meets needs.[131] Given the dynamic nature of the different types of value regarding cultural heritage and the interrelationship between different

---

[121] I.e. the existence value – see Section 2.5.1.2.

[122] Paterson points out that there are responsibilities owed by those making requests for the return of cultural heritage as well as by those receiving the requests: Paterson, 'The "Caring and Sharing" Alternative', 71.

[123] Pantazatos, 'Does Diaspora Test the Limits of Stewardship?', p. 99.

[124] Specifically, being alert to the possibility of abuse: Tronto, *Moral Boundaries*, p. 133.

[125] Recognised by Tronto as the ethical element relevant to the first stage of the caring process, *caring about*: ibid, p. 127.

[126] ibid., p. 135.   [127] ibid., p. 136.   [128] ibid., p. 136.   [129] ibid., pp. 133–4.

[130] ibid., p. 131. In Tronto, 'Creating Caring Institutions', 162, Tronto indicates that to care well, organisations need to focus on politics, particularity and plurality, and purposiveness.

[131] Herring identifies the idea of meeting needs as a marker of caring: Herring, *Caring and the Law*, p. 14.

communities and towards cultural heritage, this is particularly important for current purposes. But is competent care, or care which meets needs sufficient? This seems to be too low a threshold rather than a standard which should be aspired to when dealing with something as important as cultural heritage. 'Good care' could be interpreted as a higher standard, and might equate to 'reasonable care', a standard often found in English tort[132] or contract law,[133] yet greater specificity would assist in determining the relevant standard of care to be expected for cultural heritage and against which the care provided can be assessed. Herring suggests that good care is 'enabling and empowering' whilst law is about the enforcement of that.[134] With these sentiments in mind, and with the view to providing a holistic approach for cultural heritage, the notion of appropriate care adopted here is one which aspires to achieve respectful, empathetic and dialogic care within communities of care and within networks of such communities. It seeks to navigate how to deal with harm to the cultural heritage and to the communities for whom it is important. Each of these is equally relevant to developing and sustaining relationships and acknowledging and assuming respectful responsibilities. Having already considered dialogue, the focus will now turn to respect and empathy.

2.5.4 Ensuring Mutual Respect, Trust and Empathy

Respect, trust and empathy are central to caring for cultural heritage. Respect[135] involves listening to, and ensuring consent[136] and is part and parcel of the ethics of care. It is also key to resolving dissonance between conflicting parties. Given that cultural heritage is relational and involves not only caring for the cultural heritage itself, but also for the people for whom it is important, respect is inherent in any true caring relationship; for that reason the approach taken here is to recognise respect as forming an integral part of the caring relationship rather than as a separate element of discussion.[137]

Unlike other contexts involving the ethics of care, respect in the context of the care of cultural heritage is not always about mutual respect of *identifiable* people for whom cultural heritage is important. Instead, the situation is complicated by the wide reach of cultural heritage, which includes people far away who may have a connection with the cultural heritage, but also those across generations. Therefore, respect extends beyond identifiable people, to include 'persons unknown'.[138] For the purposes here, this could include people

---

[132] See Section 6.11.   [133] See ibid.   [134] Herring, *Caring and the Law*, p. 20.

[135] Identified as one of Herring's four markers of care: Herring, *Caring and the Law*, p. 18.

[136] ibid., p. 18.

[137] Cf. Pantazatos, who in his discussion of stewardship and the ethics of care, argues that caring and respect are separate but interrelated or complementary normative foundations of stewardship: Pantazatos, 'The Normative Foundations of Stewardship', pp. 137–9.

[138] A concept found in possession proceedings for trespass, most recently analysed by the Court of Appeal in *Barking and Dagenham London Borough Council* v. *Persons Unknown* [2022] EWCA Civ 13.

who may not yet be born who will ultimately care for the cultural heritage or for whom the importance of the cultural heritage is different from the importance to the present generation. Therefore, mutual respect (like the responsibilities assumed[139]) is both intra- and inter-generational. In some instances such respect might even be interpreted as extending to past generations (even if there are no specific obligations owed to them to care for the cultural heritage inherited from them). For some people time might not be conceptualised as a linear concept of the past, present and future, but is considered as circular in nature;[140] with such an approach, the respect afforded to those who lived before us or after us would be treated equally. Respect may also be for the cultural heritage itself (whether treating it as the intangible process or the subject matter[141]). An element of care, therefore, may be a respect for the archaeological or historical record and for making the provenance or previous difficult histories transparent.[142]

Navigating dissonance and responding to claims for cultural heritage within the context of providing justice was identified in Chapter 1 as a central area of contestation for cultural heritage. The need for sensitivity and empathy is essential when dealing with such claims as is listening to, engaging with and acting upon viewpoints from those for whom cultural heritage is important and who seek involvement in its care. The ethics of care provides a clear parallel here with its major feature of valuing, rather than rejecting emotion,[143] and consequently 'sympathy, empathy, sensitivity and responsiveness' are relevant.[144] Empathy and sympathy are central to stewards acting with an ethics of care approach;[145] but this also extends to all those who care for cultural heritage and in particular for those who have assumed responsibilities for its care, or on whom responsibilities have been placed. In practice, the ethics of care demonstrates sensitivity,[146] thus including '[u]nderstanding situations from the point of view of others should characterize caring when the participants are more distant'.[147] Ensuring mechanisms for meaningful and active participation wards against assuming what particular care is needed. Well-intentioned but ill-placed care or, more concerningly, paternalistic care in which the views of those for whom the cultural heritage is important do not inform the final decision or are even entirely ignored can be harmful if left unchecked. Dialogue can provide such a check. This element of empathy links very closely with the first element of caring for cultural heritage, that of providing appropriate care and revisiting decisions about this care.

---

[139] Discussed at Section 2.5.2.

[140] B. Steve Csaki, 'Coming Around Again: Cyclical and Circular Aspects of Native American Thought' in 11th National American Symposium, Southeastern Oklahoma State University, 2015.

[141] i.e. the objects, places and practices.   [142] This is explored further in Chapter 9.

[143] Held, *The Ethics of Care*, p. 11.   [144] ibid., p. 10.

[145] Pantazatos, 'Does Diaspora Test the Limits of Stewardship?', p. 99.

[146] Held, *The Ethics of Care*, p. 16.   [147] ibid., p. 18.

Another central element of the relational nature of care is trust,[148] which is closely aligned with respect, empathy and sensitivity. Trust can be built up over time in situations based on people showing respect for each other's viewpoints. Yet it is fragile, and may be at risk of being lost, thereby undermining the caring process. Confidence in the decision-making process and assurance that differing viewpoints have been, and will be, taken into account in the future depends on trust; where processes are circumvented or participation is either tokenistic or completely lacking, trust can be lost. In the context of archaeological stewardship, Pantazatos has observed that where stewards act in the light of the ethics of care, they 'are more sensitive to and respond to need … Stewardship is more than following an empty list of abstract obligations. Central to it is the necessity to be sensitive to the relationship between communities and their heritage.'[149] In the context of museums, public trust is fundamental to how they care for cultural heritage for the benefit of the public.[150] For that reason, the trust built up from respectful and empathetic engagement with the people for whom cultural heritage is important is vital for appropriate care for cultural heritage and for the communities for whom it is important. How far it is embedded into cultural heritage's nested practices of care is relevant to determining whether care is appropriate.

2.5.5 Facilitating Flourishing

Care is 'central to our flourishing' as humans.[151] Similarly, 'cultural heritage means something broader than a curriculum, than canonized texts or pieces of art as preconditions for learning and thus for human flourishing'.[152] Cultural heritage is recognised internationally as 'the wellspring of creativity', for 'creation draws on the roots of cultural tradition, but flourishes in contact with other cultures'.[153] The centrality of care to identity and the impact that its destruction can have on communities, particularly when destruction is used as a means of harming communities, means that it is essential to care for cultural heritage. For that reason, it is important to engage with activities which facilitate the flourishing of cultural heritage, thereby enhancing human flourishing; these include access to and enjoyment of cultural heritage, which are recognised as cultural rights.[154] Flourishing should not be understood as

---

[148] See ibid., p. 57 and Pantazatos, 'The Normative Foundations of Stewardship', pp. 135–6.

[149] Pantazatos, 'Does Diaspora Test the Limits of Stewardship?', p. 99.

[150] The importance of maintaining the public trust is evident in the MA, *Code of Ethics* (2015) through principle 3.

[151] Herring, *Caring and the Law*, p. 13. He cites Eva Feder Kittay, although in her second edition she focuses on flourishing as requiring, at times, dependency on others: Eva Feder Kittay, *Love's Labor: Essays on Women, Equality and Dependency* (2nd ed., London: Routledge, 2020), p. 34.

[152] Jensen, 'Cultural Heritage, Liberal Education, and Human Flourishing', p. 40.

[153] UNESCO Declaration on Cultural Diversity (2 November 2001), art. 7.

[154] Report of the independent expert in the field of cultural rights, Farida Shaheed, UN General Assembly Human Rights Council, 17th session, A/HRC/17/38, pp. 15–16.

representing an unquestioning duty to preserve cultural heritage or to provide public access to it. In some situations flourishing is achieved by leaving the subject matter of cultural heritage to the elements, rather than actively preserving it,[155] enjoying it and participating in the creation of it.

2.5.6 The Space and Willingness to Navigate and Resolve Dissonance

Having identified respectful, empathetic and dialogical care as the appropriate standards to aspire to when caring for cultural heritage, it is important that there are opportunities to revisit decisions about the provision of both current and future care by providing spaces for self-reflection.[156] A successful system of appropriate care would create a space for evaluating and reviewing its caring responsibilities.[157] This would include analysing how threats to harm are assessed and mitigated against as well as the long-term care of cultural heritage. Furthermore, given the, at times, contested nature of disputes about cultural heritage (such as tensions surrounding the current possession or display of cultural heritage) it is important to provide the space but also facilitate the willingness to navigate those areas of dissonance and to seek to resolve them. By facing dissonance and seeking to navigate it, this facilitates the active and meaningful participation of all communities of care, not just those who are currently in physical possession of the cultural heritage in dispute.[158] Often dissonance and mistrust will have developed over years and claims are made in the context of seeking just and fair solutions.[159] It is clear that within a 'network of caring relations' one can demand justice,[160] fairness and rights.[161] Yet, rather than focusing excessively on pitting one viewpoint against another, adopting a caring approach can 'foster social bonds and cooperation'.[162] Thus, 'caring relations should form the wider moral framework into which justice should be

---

[155] Such as palliative curation, discussed by Caitlin DeSilvey, *Curated Decay: Heritage Beyond Saving* (London: University of Minnesota Press, 2017), pp. 160–163.

[156] In the context of establishing caring institutions, Tronto identifies the need for a space within which to resolve conflict which is, in effect, a place for self-reflection: Tronto, 'Creating Caring Institutions', 160, 169.

[157] This would fulfil the responsibilities for 'constant evaluation' which Tronto identifies: Tronto, *Moral Boundaries*, p. 131.

[158] As de la Bellacasa observes, 'to effectively care for a thing we cannot cut off those with whom we disagree from the thing's political ecology': Maria Puig de la Bellacasa, 'Matters of Care in Technoscience: Assembling Neglected Things' (2011) 41 *Social Studies of Science* 85, 90.

[159] This is the terminology of the Washington Conference Principles on Nazi Confiscated Art and the basis on which recommendations are made by the UK's Spoliation Advisory Panel.

[160] For Held suggests that care and justice can be integrated in that whilst an assurance of rights is a priority for justice, 'the humane considerations of care should not be absent': Held, *The Ethics of Care*, p. 17. See also Eithne Nightingale and Richard Sandell, 'Introduction' in Richard Sandell and Eithne Nightingale (eds.), *Museums, Equality and Social Justice* (London: Routledge, 2012), p. 2 and Tristram Besterman, 'Cultural Equity in the Sustainable Museum' in Marstine, *The Routledge Companion to Museum Ethics*, p. 252.

[161] Held, *The Ethics of Care*, p. 73.   [162] ibid., p. 15.

fitted'.[163] With this in mind, Chapter 9 explores the role of cultural heritage and care where challenges are made to the *status quo*, often in the quest for justice.

Contestation can arise between communities for whom the use and enjoyment of the physical cultural heritage is central to their identities and other communities concerned with the risk of physical harm to the cultural heritage itself. This represents the, at times, opposing positions involving cultural heritage. On the one hand, cultural heritage is recognised as dynamic and may be 'living' as an active part of a community's life. On the other hand, some view cultural heritage as more static, representative of the past, leading to the desire to preserve the physical object or place itself.[164]

Providing a space in which to navigate these areas of contestation is important. This therefore ensures that the views of communities for whom the use and enjoyment of the cultural heritage is central to their identity or culture are considered and that the community with responsibility for the direct physical care of the cultural heritage recognises the need to navigate around these differing viewpoints and to make available space for the resolution of such dissonance. This is particularly necessary where the communities with direct responsibility for care are different from the communities for whose identity the cultural heritage is important.

2.5.7 The Space and Willingness to Respond to Actual or Threatened Harm

Adopting the notion of care avoids setting cultural heritage within the framework of protection (including safeguarding it and preserving it). Therefore, when dealing with the way in which individuals, institutions or communities navigate harm, or the potential to harm cultural heritage, the approach taken in the subsequent chapters is not to conflate care with simple protection from harm. Care involves 'taking the concerns and needs of the other as the basis for action'[165] whereas '[p]rotection presumes the bad intentions and harm that the other is likely to bring to bear against the self or group, and to require a response to that potential harm'.[166] With regards to cultural heritage it is as important to anticipate potential threats as it is to address existing ones.[167] These threats could include damage by warfare, deterioration caused by the passage of time, or the negative effect of the illicit trade in cultural objects. All of these make Tronto's emphasis on the ongoing connection with care (rather than the approach that protection need not continue over time)[168] so relevant to the current analysis.

---

[163] ibid., p. 71.
[164] This is arguably the approach that is taken in the context of traditional approaches to preservation.
[165] Tronto, *Moral Boundaries*, p. 105.   [166] ibid.
[167] Thus incorporating the precautionary principle, as to which see Section 7.3.
[168] Tronto, *Moral Boundaries*, p. 105.

Within this space the need for respect, empathy, trust and the avoidance of paternalism is key to providing a caring environment in which to respond to threats of harm. As discussed earlier, there may be situations where cultural heritage is at risk of harm because of its use and enjoyment in a cultural heritage practice; yet, this should not automatically lead to action which discontinues that use solely for the purpose of physically preserving it if that use is essential for the identity of the community.

2.6 Beyond an Unquestioning Duty of Care to the Object, Place or Practice

The approach to care adopted here is not about imposing one view on another – instead at times it will be concerned with negotiating the boundaries of a caring relationship about the nature of the care provided (as is true in many relationships). This should not be interpreted as taking a Western approach to cultural heritage which assumes that a museum curator or other possessor of cultural heritage is better placed to know how to care for cultural heritage than a community from which the cultural heritage originated. This approach avoids doing acts which might be patriarchal or contrary to human rights.[169] This can be a particular problem in the context of certain cultural heritage practices,[170] when dealing with cultural heritage places that represent difficult or dark heritage,[171] or the display of statues which commemorate and memorialise difficult events or historical figures.[172]

Given that some of the discourse concerning colonialism has previously been framed as care,[173] throughout the following chapters, caution will be exercised to ensure that the way in which care for cultural heritage is analysed accounts for the potential for paternalism and negative power domination.

2.7 Conclusion: The Promise of Care: Specificity, Individualisation and Context

Rather than assuming that broad principles exist which apply to cultural heritage, or that there is simply one response to all situations involving cultural heritage, adopting the terminology of care permits a responsive approach to individual situations; it is thus 'spontaneous, free and individualised'[174] rather than homogenous.[175] Care, as a framework, is therefore particularly

---

[169] Report of the independent expert in the field of cultural rights, Farida Shaheed, p. 19.
[170] ibid.   [171] E.g. concentration camps and other sites of massacre.   [172] See Section 9.8.
[173] Described as 'paternalistic caring' by Uma Narayan, 'Colonialism and Its Others: Considerations on Rights and Care Discourses' (1995) 10 *Hypatia* 133, 135.
[174] Herring, *Caring and the Law*, p. 81. Held suggests that the ethics of care is skeptical of generalisations: Held, *The Ethics of Care*, p. 11.
[175] Herring, *Caring and the Law*, p. 26. Pantazatos suggests stewardship which is guided by the ethics of care 'is more than following an empty list of abstract obligations': Pantazatos, 'Does Diaspora Test the Limits of Stewardship?', p. 99.

appropriate for dealing with cultural heritage which has varied subject matter, which may hold significance (or importance) to a variety of people for different reasons and is subject to a number of contested issues which may cause dissonance and require different approaches to achieve resolution.[176] Context is therefore key both to care[177] and to cultural heritage.[178] For that reason it is important to be attuned[179] to the situation and to understand the history of the relationship.[180] This is particularly apposite in the context of cultural heritage where there has been a long history of mistrust between the parties, or a feeling that one party is in a position of power, or not listening or responding to the views of another person or group. These problems have arisen in the context of repatriation requests and when concerns are raised about the appropriate way for museums to display objects of importance to a particular community. Perhaps the most important reason for adopting the approach of caring for heritage is that it avoids making an unquestioning assumption that because something is cultural heritage it should *therefore* be protected or preserved at all costs.

Care provides a particularly useful framework to grapple with the fragmented nature of the UK's approach to dealing with cultural heritage. The common law relevant to cultural heritage – through statute and case law – together with the varied mechanisms found in non-law instruments are created by various communities of care, who are then able to use the tools provided by these instruments to assume responsibility for the care of cultural heritage including through civil society initiatives. These varied instruments and mechanisms form nested practices of care, and analysing all of these results in an integrated approach to considering the way in which the UK cares for cultural heritage.

Care is not taken to be a utopian ideal[181] and it is recognised that, at times, there will be challenges where different communities take alternative views about the way in which cultural heritage should be cared for. When analysing the legal framework in the UK it will become apparent that care – as this respectful, empathetic and dialogic ideal – is not always present and that, at times, the law may hinder the achievement of appropriate care, prioritising other interests instead, but in some instances other non-law instruments, civil

---

[176] The particularity of cultural heritage objects is recognised by Jensen, 'Cultural Heritage, Liberal Education, and Human Flourishing', p. 42.

[177] Herring, *Caring and the Law*, p. 62. One should not assume that there are universal principles which are applicable and the effect of changing contexts is very important: Fisher and Tronto, 'Towards a Feminist Theory of Caring', p. 40.

[178] This is particularly important in terms of the relationship between archaeological objects and their find spots; the context of finds provides vitally important information for our understanding.

[179] Herring, *Caring and the Law*, p. 62. In this context Herring was talking about the importance of being 'attuned to the individuals' other caring responsibilities and relationships'. See also Pantazatos, 'The Normative Foundations of Stewardship', p. 136.

[180] Herring, *Caring and the Law*, p. 62.   [181] See Tronto, *Moral Boundaries*, p. 177.

society initiatives or public participation initiatives may step up to the mark and facilitate appropriate care. An important element of ensuring that care is appropriate is for communities of care to revisit their decisions about how caring is undertaken.[182] This approach places the public at the centre of how things are cared for and gives them the overall responsibility for care; in the context of cultural heritage, encouraging public participation in cultural heritage and the decisions about it is central to ensuring appropriate care.

The following chapters analyse the extent to which the UK law and non-law initiatives recognise and support these central elements of caring for cultural heritage within the different thematic contexts of each chapter. By engaging with and facilitating these elements of care, any legal and non-law system creates a network of communities of care within which cultural heritage is imagined and cared for.

---

[182] Tronto, *Caring Democracy*, p. 179. Sevenhuijsen calls for 'a caring citizenship', which she suggests is 'an ideal in which caring is part of collective agency in the public sphere': Sevenhuijsen, 'The Place of Care', 193.

3

Nested Practices of Care for Cultural Heritage

3.1 Introduction

Law can serve a variety of functions in the context of cultural heritage.[1] It can play an instrumental role, facilitating particular policy objectives and designating cultural heritage as official[2] or acting as a legal label. It has also been interpreted as serving a transformative function, transforming archaeology into heritage,[3] adding value[4] and acting as a gate-keeper to the public domain.[5] For others it is but another element of the discourse of cultural heritage.[6] In this chapter, and the following ones, law (in its many forms) is treated as an active participant in the UK's care of cultural heritage.[7] A focus on how the law deals with cultural heritage is also a window on the UK's overall approach to the care of cultural heritage. Thus, the analysis is shifted beyond recognising law as one element of the discourse, to acknowledging its central role in caring for cultural heritage. Whilst at times the law will be decisive in how cultural heritage is cared for, it is also dependent on other initiatives to supplement the strict legal position and contribute to the care of cultural heritage. Law neither exists, nor functions in isolation, and whilst there is a framework of legal principles applicable to cultural heritage, there are always nuances in its application in case law. Some cases arise involving cultural heritage as the

---

[1] Lixinski explores the relationship between law and non-law through the lens of heterodoxy and orthodoxy: Lucas Lixinski, 'Between Orthodoxy and Heterodoxy: The Troubled Relationships between Heritage Studies and Heritage Law' (2015) 21 *International Journal of Heritage Studies* 203; Lucas Lixinski, *International Heritage Law for Communities: Exclusion and Re-Imagination* (Oxford: Oxford University Press, 2019), pp. 6–13.

[2] Rodney Harrison, 'What is Heritage?' in Rodney Harrison (ed.), *Understanding the Politics of Heritage* (Manchester: Open University and Manchester University Press, 2010), p. 8. Smith talks about genre chains: Laurajane Smith, *Uses of Heritage* (London: Routledge, 2008), p. 94.

[3] John Carman, *Valuing Ancient Things: Archaeology and Law* (Leicester: Leicester University Press, 1996), p. 160.

[4] ibid.   [5] ibid., p. 39.

[6] For example, it provides a lens through which to historicise archaeology: Hilary A. Soderland, 'Values and the Evolving Concept of Heritage: The First Century of Archaeology and Law in the United States' in George S. Smith, Phyllis Mauch Messenger and Hilary A. Soderland (eds.), *Heritage Values in Contemporary Society* (Walnut Creek: Left Coast Press, 2010), p. 139.

[7] The multitudinous types of law, and the communities involved in its promulgation and interpretation are explored in Section 3.7.

subject matter of the dispute, yet the applicable legal principles are unrelated to its status as cultural heritage. How courts deal with these issues, when applying traditional property principles, unravelling technical matters of statutory interpretation, or considering the procedural aspects of a decision-maker, show how the court, as a community of care, cares for cultural heritage. In addition, the layers of guidance (whether or not having legal force), codes of ethics supplementing the ethical obligations of institutions towards cultural heritage,[8] together with the recommendations of panels of experts informing decision-makers, institutional policies, civil society initiatives and public participation initiatives, all provide the nested practices of care for cultural heritage.[9] All those people involved in the promulgation, interpretation and application of law and non-law principles – together with those who use and maintain cultural heritage or for whom it is important – form communities of care.[10] It should be emphasised that no assumption is made that the care provided by any of these communities of care is the most appropriate in the circumstances (i.e. respectful, empathetic and dialogic[11]). Instead, the nature and appropriateness of the care provided will be analysed over the course of the following chapters and in some instances may be found wanting.

The relationship between law and cultural heritage has not been an easy one.[12] Rigid legal rules can stifle the care that would otherwise be provided for cultural heritage;[13] yet at times the full force of legal rules which would prevent harm may be lacking.[14] This chapter begins by exploring the difficulties faced by law because of the challenges brought by cultural heritage. It analyses the way in which law has been used (or misused) to deal with cultural heritage and the dominance of applying general legal principles to cultural heritage. The final part of the chapter sets out, and analyses, the UK's nested practices of care, specifically the law and non-law providing direct care for cultural heritage or facilitating that care indirectly. As part of this analysis, particular focus will be placed on the authority of these nested practices and their enforceability in practice.

3.2 Overall Legal Landscape

At a fundamental, etymological, level, cultural heritage and law are inextricably linked; the linguistic entanglement of the two is evident in the word 'heritage' itself, which has a legal origin indicating something capable of

---

[8] Ethical or moral treatment of cultural heritage is part of the 'common themes' of heritage – specifically duty, honour, stewardship, fairness and responsibility and social obligations: George S. Smith, Phyllis Mauch Messenger and Hilary A. Soderland, 'Introduction' in Smith et al., *Heritage Values*, p. 16.

[9] The terminology of 'nested practices' derives from Joan C. Tronto, *Caring Democracy: Markets, Equality and Justice* (London: New York University Press, 2013), p. 21. The nested practices of care for cultural heritage are set out and analysed at Section 3.7.

[10] Explored in Chapter 5.   [11] See Section 2.5.3.

[12] Lixinski, 'Between Orthodoxy and Heterodoxy', 211.   [13] See Section 3.4.1.

[14] E.g. the illicit trade in cultural heritage – see Section 3.4.4.

inheritance[15] and has a close relationship with the entail. The term imports an expectation that heritage will be passed on to future generations based on this very notion of inheritance.[16] But it is not merely a semantic connection, for cultural heritage and law are fully entwined at a practical level – the subject matter of heritage also has a legal life – more often than not as property. The legal instruments which affect how cultural heritage objects, places and practices are cared for are multitudinous.[17] They touch on areas of public international law, conflict of laws, land law,[18] personal property law,[19] planning law,[20] local government law,[21] trusts law,[22] charity law,[23] sale of goods,[24] historic places legislation,[25] tax law,[26] ecclesiastical law,[27] criminal law,[28] treasure law,[29] export control laws,[30] tort law[31] and the law of bailment.[32] On the topic of cultural heritage law, the late Norman Palmer observed that 'There is, perhaps no more interesting area of English law, nor one within which the elements of public and of private law, of municipal and international

---

[15] See Section 1.1.2.

[16] Blake identifies this as one of the common elements of cultural heritage in international law: Janet Blake, 'On Defining the Cultural Heritage' (2000) 49 *International and Comparative Law Quarterly* 61, 83–4. Prott and O'Keefe identify the future interests of different parties: Patrick J. O'Keefe and Lyndel V. Prott, *Law and the Cultural Heritage, Volume 1: Discovery and Excavation* (Oxford: Abingdon, 1984), p. 26. See also Ryan Trimm, 'Heritage as Trope: Conceptual Etymologies and Alternative Trajectories' (2018) 24 *International Journal of Heritage Studies* 465, 467.

[17] In the context of the legal protection of cultural heritage during armed conflict the area has been described as 'afflicted by legislative congestion': Marina Lostal, *International Cultural Heritage Law in Armed Conflict* (Cambridge: Cambridge University Press, 2017), p. 48.

[18] Including fixtures. In the past the sale of heirlooms out of settled land was primarily an issue of property law, yet at the same time many of these objects, located in stately homes, would be considered as cultural heritage, even if not recognised as such in legal terms.

[19] Specifically, relativity of title is of importance both in the context of competing claims for cultural heritage objects, but also in the context of the common law of finding where objects do not meet the definition of treasure under the Treasure Act 1996.

[20] Specifically the relationship between sustainable development and heritage.

[21] Including the provision of museums and the making of byelaws.

[22] Particularly gifts to charities, conditional gifts and co-ownership of property.

[23] In the legal make up of collections and museums.

[24] The art market, including dealers and auctioneers.

[25] Listed buildings, scheduled monuments, conservation areas, historic battlefields and wrecks.

[26] Where cultural heritage is accepted in satisfaction of tax or where objects are conditionally exempt from tax.

[27] Dealing with the sale of church treasures, the ecclesiastical exemption relating to listing of buildings and any alterations to historic buildings owned by the church.

[28] This includes theft, handling of stolen goods, criminal damage, specific criminal offences relating to cultural heritage and the enhanced sentencing for crimes relating to heritage assets.

[29] Dealing with found portable antiquities which are vested in the Crown.

[30] Where licences are required for the export of objects of cultural interest and the granting of licences can be deferred in the case of objects identified as national treasures to allow time for a UK-based buyer to acquire them, thus 'saving' them for the nation.

[31] Specifically claims relating to the wrongful interference with goods including the tort of conversion.

[32] E.g. the loan of artworks between, or to, museums and conservation work on objects.

law, and of civil and criminal law, more vividly coalesce'.[33] In some ways – to use the vernacular – the cultural heritage lawyer has to dabble in many different areas of law. Yet, throughout all these legal meanderings the key task they have in mind is how to unravel the legal principles affecting the cultural heritage in question. Whilst many of the legal principles apply equally to any other personal or real property, when cultural heritage is the subject matter, certain complicating factors can affect the usual application of these principles. In the context of the sale of goods, particular uncertainties may arise about the attribution of a cultural heritage object or doubts may be raised about its authenticity. In this regard the art market deals in opinions rather than facts, whereas the law upholds the truthfulness of facts rather than correctness of opinions.[34] Judges have a difficult task dealing with evidence and avoiding contributing to the academic debate about an object's authenticity.[35] Similarly, there may be strong public feelings towards privately owned cultural heritage which can sit uneasily with individual property rights.[36] In addition to the general law, particular legal principles unique to cultural heritage may also apply.[37] By drawing together these different areas of law with the specialist legal and non-law instruments dealing with cultural heritage it is possible to analyse the different ways in which the UK, as a community and a network of communities,[38] cares for cultural heritage. Whether there exists a specific *body* of law that can be termed 'cultural heritage law' with underlying principles is outside the scope of this work,[39] although this book is certainly concerned with drawing together the various laws (and non-law principles) which care for cultural heritage and subjecting them to analysis.[40] It is hoped that the present endeavour will, nevertheless, contribute

---

[33] Norman Palmer, 'Museums and Cultural Property' in Peter Vergo (ed.), *The New Museology* (London: Reaktion, 1989), p. 173.

[34] *Harlingdon and Leinster Enterprises Ltd.* v. *Christopher Hull Fine Art Ltd.* [1991] 1 QB 564; *Thomson* v. *Christie Manson & Woods Ltd.* [2005] PNLR 38; [2005] EWCA Civ 555; *Drake* v. *Thos. Agnew & Sons* [2002] EWHC 294 (QB), para. 26.

[35] See the discussion about *De Balkany* v. *Christie Manson and Woods* [1995] 16 TR LR 163 at Section 5.2.8.1.

[36] An early example of this can be seen in the litigation surrounding Stonehenge: *Attorney-General* v. *Antrobus* [1905] 2 Ch 188 (Ch).

[37] E.g. listed buildings legislation, which is part of the planning regime; export licensing; those 'pre-eminent' cultural heritage objects may be accepted in satisfaction of certain taxation liabilities; criminal offences relating to cultural heritage objects have been introduced in recent years: see Section 7.4.1.

[38] For a discussion of how community is interpreted see Section 1.5.1.

[39] So too is the question of whether we have achieved the 'fourth estate' which Crewdson invited us to adopt in 1984: Richard Crewdson, 'Cultural Property: A Fourth Estate?' (1984) 18 *Law Society Gazette* 126. See also Steven Wilf, 'What is Property's Fourth Estate? Cultural Property and the Fiduciary Ideal' (2001–2) 16 *Connecticut Journal of International Law* 177.

[40] Although this book focuses on cultural heritage at the national level, in the context of international intangible cultural heritage Lixinski is unconvinced of the existence of a clear body of law – his chief aim has been 'to create a critique-informed body of law from many fragments, as opposed to a critique-orientated analysis of a body of law': Lucas Lixinski, *Intangible Cultural Heritage in International Law* (Oxford: Oxford University Press, 2013), p. 1.

to the wider project of identifying underlying themes and principles of cultural heritage law as a body of law. International cultural heritage law has undergone a far wider taxonomical analysis than UK domestic law has been subjected to.[41] At the international level there has been both a shift in nomenclature,[42] a shift in the fields of concern,[43] with shifts in focus from nation states to humanity, whilst also seeking to recognise communities.[44] It is therefore an opportune time to focus on the national landscape, here in the UK.

3.3 Features and Challenges of the Legal Landscape: Identifying Shortcomings in the Law

Societies ask a lot of heritage,[45] but cultural heritage in turn asks a great deal of the law,[46] in part because of the very nature of cultural heritage, but also because of how communities have dealt with cultural heritage in the past. The varied nature of cultural heritage, the multiple (and, at times, competing) types of value of heritage to different peoples, the dynamism of that value, and the clear tensions between private ownership and the public feeling of having an interest in heritage all make the law's task a difficult one. However, because of its nature – as being important to the identity of peoples – harm to, or appropriation of, cultural heritage has been used as a tool for suppressing nations and communities. For this reason the past social, political and cultural use (or misuse) of heritage may make demands on contemporary law and

---

Blake observed in 2000 that the driver for the international conventions up until then had been 'contemporary concerns and intellectual fashions' which hampered any unifying underlying principles: Blake, 'On Defining the Cultural Heritage', 62. Contrastingly, Lostal has argued that cultural heritage law has developed to form a branch of international law with the principles of 'relative interest'; 'differentiated duties' and 'prevention' underlying the normative area: Lostal, *Armed Conflict*, p. 57. Fincham describes heritage law as 'the loose collection of doctrines and policies which guide courts and lawmakers in these disputes [involving art and objects of cultural significance]': Derek Fincham, 'The Distinctiveness of Property and Heritage' (2011) 115 *Penn State Law Review* 657; and Chechi highlights that the 'ad hoc fashion of dealing with cultural heritage disputes is not without consequences . . . ': Alessandro Chechi, *The Settlement of International Cultural Heritage Disputes* (Cultural Heritage Law and Policy Series, Oxford: Oxford University Press, 2014), p. 2.

[41] See for example, Lixinski, *Intangible Cultural Heritage*; Janet Blake, *International Cultural Heritage Law* (Oxford: Oxford University Press, 2015); and Craig Forrest, *International Law and the Protection of Cultural Heritage* (London: Routledge, 2010).

[42] See generally Yahaya Ahmad, 'The Scope and Definitions of Heritage: From Tangible to Intangible' (2006) 12 *International Journal of Heritage Studies* 292.

[43] Cultural property to cultural heritage, human rights to cultural rights and a shift away from the monumental to the vernacular and the intangible.

[44] See generally Lixinski, *International Heritage Law for Communities*. This approach therefore rejects a straightforward dichotomy between cultural property nationalism and cultural property internationalism as to which, see John Henry Merryman, 'Two Ways of Thinking about Cultural Property' (1986) 80 *American Journal of International Law* 831.

[45] David Lowenthal, *The Heritage Crusade and the Spoils of History* (Cambridge: Cambridge University Press, 1998), p. 227.

[46] See Blake, 'On Defining the Cultural Heritage', 64.

practice to unravel these past wrongs and to provide justice for modern-day claimants.

3.4 The Uneasy Relationship between Law and Cultural Heritage

Law has had an uneasy relationship with cultural heritage for several reasons, each of which will be explored in this section. The first element to be considered will be the nature and substance of law and cultural heritage and the tensions between these that may prevent law from acting fully as a means of providing appropriate care, in particular by not providing justice for claimants. Secondly, the prevalence of the use of legal language and legal concepts will be explored. Thirdly, the use of law as a protective barrier to claims will be outlined. Whilst these elements might suggest that law's presence can be unwelcome, the fourth consideration sits in juxtaposition, as some areas of practice lack much law, with more being needed to appropriately care for cultural heritage.

3.4.1 Tensions between the Nature and Substance of Law and Cultural Heritage: Not Stepping Up to the Justice Mark

The nature of cultural heritage can mean that law is ill-suited to grappling with the areas of contestation faced by cultural heritage.[47] The dynamic nature of heritage, with differing and changing value to different people, means that statutes or case law (which are more static and less dynamic)[48] can struggle to reflect this dynamism, particularly given the need for more frequent reassessment of cultural heritage.[49] Multiple communities and their, at times, competing interests can create dissonance. Furthermore, the law is faced with the challenge of keeping pace with changing threats to cultural heritage, such as

---

[47] As to which see Section 1.3.

[48] This is because of the time needed to legislate and the infrequency with which cases come before the courts. For these reasons, other non-law instruments such as codes of ethics or guidance, acting as living documents, and which can be amended more frequently may be more suitable: see Janet Ulph, 'Markets and Responsibilities: Forgeries and the Sale of Goods Act 1979' [2011] 3 *Journal of Business Law* 261, 280. See generally Manlio Frigo, 'Ethical Rules and Codes of Honor Related to Museum Activities: A Complementary Support to the Private International Law Approach Concerning the Circulation of Cultural Property' (2009) 16 *International Journal of Cultural Property* 49. Blake recognises the difficulties that the 'diverse interests and objectives' of different actors bring to how to 'assign rights and concomitant duties' under international law: Blake, *International Cultural Heritage Law*, p. 21. In the context of UNESCO, Forrest points out the difficulties involved in revising conventions which require all state parties to agree to amendments: Forrest, *International Law and the Protection of Cultural Heritage*, p. 40.

[49] This includes not only revisiting the definition of cultural heritage and the scope of the field of enquiry, but also the changes in value to different people over time. At a practical level, such re-evaluation may also be necessary to avoid an abundance of heritage: Rodney Harrison, *Heritage: Critical Approaches* (Abingdon: Routledge, 2013), p. 166. This also forms part of responsible collections management.

the need to tackle the illicit trade or destruction of cultural heritage during modern conflicts.[50] At times it may be necessary to look ahead and attempt to future-proof the way in which cultural heritage is cared for, to pre-empt future harm that may befall it, upholding the precautionary principle.[51] The law (particularly in the courtroom) can, at times, lack the creativity to deal with complicated issues concerning the care of cultural heritage and its human dimension.[52] Instead, cases can focus on the tangible dimension to cultural heritage[53] or struggle with differing legal concepts from other communities.[54]

Well-known features of cultural heritage are the ease with which cultural heritage objects can pass national borders, the international nature of the art market[55] and the historic displacement of cultural heritage.[56] These factors present challenges for law by raising jurisdictional questions under the conflicts of law rules, meaning that in practice courts within the nations of the UK may need to apply the laws of foreign countries when resolving disputes.[57] But the

---

[50] Iraq and Syria required fast-paced responses by the UN Security Council: see Section 4.3.4.

[51] See Section 7.3.

[52] Law, at times, completely ignores the intangible element because it does not fit in to the existing legal framework such as intellectual property law; attempts have been made over many years to create a traditional knowledge framework through WIPO. See Section 5.2.8.1, which analyses how property law principles have trumped the ability to care appropriately for cultural heritage in legal cases.

[53] Leiboff, in her discussion of *Leaf International Galleries* and citing Douzinas, suggests that the focus of the court tends to be on the material rather than intangible; she calls it the 'truthful substance, the thing, the material, the tangible': Marett Leiboff, 'Clashing Things' (2001) 10 *Griffith Law Review* 294, 313. The lack of adaptability of the law may also be a particular problem in the context of cultural heritage from indigenous communities where reliance on strict legal entitlement to objects based on property rights (either transferred or acquired through the operation of statutes of limitation) may be at odds with the traditional way in which the rights between the cultural heritage and the community from whom it originated are conceptualised: Michael F. Brown, *Who Owns Native Culture?* (London: Harvard University Press, 2003), p. 249; although one should be careful to generalise the views of communities.

[54] E.g. the tensions between individual and collective rights: see Francesco Francioni and Lucas Lixinski, 'Opening the Toolbox of International Human Rights Law in the Safeguarding of Cultural Heritage' in Andrea Durbach and Lucas Lixinski (eds.), *Heritage, Culture and Rights: Challenging Legal Discourses* (Oxford: Hart, 2017), p. 22. Although see the recognition by the English courts of juridical entities found in the legal systems of other countries: *Bumper Development Corp Ltd.* v. *Commissioner of Police of the Metropolis and others (Union of India and others, claimants)* [1991] 4 All ER 638 (CA). See also Patrick William Duff, 'The Personality of an Idol' (1927) 3 *The Cambridge Law Journal* 42.

[55] Fifty years ago, Lord Denning MR observed in *HRH Maharanee Seethadevi Gaekwar of Baroda* v. *Wildenstein* [1972] 2 QB 283, 292–93 that 'The art world is so international in character today that this issue has itself something of an international character. The parties on either side are citizens of the world.'

[56] These include licit and illicit archaeological excavations, some of which were acquired through a process of partage, objects removed by force during conflict including punitive expeditions, the Second World War and more recent conflict zones.

[57] The infamous example which brought this issue into particular focus is the case of *Winkworth* v. *Christie Manson & Woods Ltd.* [1980] Ch 496 where Italian law, as the *lex situs*, applied, resulting in the recognition of the acquisition of stolen property by a good-faith purchaser in Italy, leaving the prior English owner without legal title to the netsuke in question.

intergenerational nature of claims can also pose significant problems.[58] The passage of time may lead to the application of temporal restrictions on legal claims through statutes of limitation[59] meaning that law may have failed to provide justice because these procedural bars prevent otherwise just claims from being heard.[60] Claims may be underscored by historical grievances caused by events that happened during colonialism or by tensions with the museum who may be in a position of authority. They may be seen as perpetuating the injustice by continuing to provide the direct care for the cultural heritage object. At times property rights were used as tools of oppression, making the resolution of claims more difficult. Imposing Western legal notions on communities who hold property in common, or using legal frameworks which perpetuate unequal power relations and which are seen as part of the colonial power structures may be linked with the authorized heritage discourse.[61] But modern-day common law property rights may also be ill-suited to dealing with cultural heritage claims. Where the applicable legal principles are non-heritage ones there may be no space within a judgment for directly caring for cultural heritage, for making arrangements to care for the cultural heritage, for maintaining the associations between the claimant and the cultural heritage object or for fulfilling the need to do justice in the circumstances.[62]

Furthermore, there may be issues of nuanced changing communities and viewpoints that shift overtime. One generation of a community may have different views or social mores from another and the nature and extent of requests for

---

[58] As well as claims for the return of objects of which the original owners or communities were dispossessed, other long-term relationships may be necessary to untangle. For example, objects may have been on long-term loan or bequested to a museum but there is some uncertainty about the terms of the original loan or bequest which now need to be resolved. In such situations the public interest as well may be relevant to consider. See generally Janet Ulph, 'Frozen in Time: Orphans and Uncollected Objects in Museum Collections' (2017) 24 *International Journal of Cultural Property* 3.

[59] Limitation Act 1980 and the Foreign Limitation Periods Act 1984. See for example the difficulties encountered in dealing with evidence by the Spoliation Advisory Panel and other similar committees across Europe which deal with Nazi Era dispossessions; these difficulties are not insurmountable and a general approach of seeking to achieve just and fair solutions with an acknowledgement of the difficulties of the passage of time has been adopted: see generally Charlotte Woodhead, 'Nazi Era Spoliation: Establishing Procedural and Substantive Principles' (2013) 18 *Art Antiquity and Law* 167, 180. In some instances formalised non-law claims processes exist, such as in the context of Nazi-era claims. However, the different committees to hear such claims established in different countries may reach conflicting decisions: see Charlotte Woodhead, *Implementing Recommendation 3 of the 2017 London Conference Action Plan* (October 2019): https://assets.publishing.service.gov.uk/government/uploads/system/uploads/attachment_data/file/862067/Woodhead_Recommendation_3_FINAL_report_October_2019.pdf (last accessed 20 December 2022), which has led to calls for supra-national dispute resolution processes: European Parliament, *Cross-Border Restitution Claims of Art Looted in Armed Conflicts and Wars and Alternatives to Court Litigations: Study for the Juri Committee*, PE 556.947 (2016).

[60] These are 'just' in the sense that both internationally and nationally they have been recognised as claims to which a moral, if not a legal, response is required.

[61] As to a discussion of the AHD, see Section 1.2.1.1.

[62] See, for example, Sections 7.6.1.1 and 9.5.1.

repatriation or redress for past wrongs may change. All these factors mean that legal argumentation can include impassioned arguments.[63] Occasionally, recourse to law can result in uncomfortable legal arguments being advanced which are troubling for the opposing parties when instead empathy is needed.[64]

Individual claimants whose forefathers suffered loss in times of genocide, for example during the Nazi era, may still feel the losses caused many years earlier by persecution and be determined to seek justice. There is juxtaposition of very personal claims which significantly affect individuals, although the losses occurred may years earlier, but which still affect individuals or communities collectively, with legal arguments which are framed in rights discourses (particularly property rights). These differing interests and arguments can cause tensions. This can detract from the telling of narratives and the recognition of past losses, making the achievement of justice difficult in the circumstances. Furthermore, the traditional remedies available in court may be inappropriate, for it has been said that 'Art restitution is a painful exercise for everyone involved and requires creative thinking by all parties and a willingness to craft solutions that at first glance may appear highly unusual'.[65] All of these complicating factors mean that cultural heritage can give rise to what might be described as archetypal hard cases;[66] the disputes may involve seeking to resolve seemingly conflicting positions of multiple communities and multiple claimants with different viewpoints – potentially over multiple generations.

It is therefore understandable that the language and framework of law, and the processes of litigation pitting one party against another, are at odds with these situations where sensitivity, respect and empathy are needed.[67] Therefore, the

---

[63] Paige S. Goodwin, 'Mapping the Limits of Repatriable Cultural Heritage: A Case Study of Stolen Flemish Art in French Museums' (2008) 157 *University of Pennsylvania Law Review* 673, 685.

[64] This has been seen in US litigation involving claims for cultural objects of which the original owners were dispossessed during the Nazi era where, in defending claims, museums have advanced arguments including pointing out how a claimant's father may have been a member of the Nazi Party and why that should invoke the equitable defence of laches: see Nicholas O'Donnell, *A Tragic Fate: Law and Ethics in the Battle over Nazi-Looted Art* (Chicago: American Bar Association, 2017), p. 140 (despite the claimant being the spouse of one of the descendants of the original owner, who was persecuted by the Nazis).

[65] Monica S. Dugot, 'The Holocaust Claims Processing Office: New York State's Approach to Resolving Holocaust Era Art Claims' in Michael J. Bazyler and Roger P. Alford (eds.), *Holocaust Restitution: Perspectives on the Litigation and Its Legacy* (New York: New York University Press, 2006), p. 279.

[66] Norman Palmer, 'The Best We Can Do? Exploring a Collegiate Approach to Holocaust-Related Claims' in Evelien Campfens (ed.), *Fair and Just Solutions? Alternatives to Litigation in Nazi-Looted Art Disputes: Status Quo and New Developments* (The Hague: Eleven Publishing, 2015), p. 7; Kamil Zeidler, *Restitution of Cultural Property* (Gdańsk: Wolters Kluwer, 2016), p. 48.

[67] Lostal, *Armed Conflict*, pp. 55–6 [citing James A. R. Nafziger, 'A Blueprint for Avoiding and Resolving Cultural Heritage Disputes' (2004) 8 *Art Antiquity and Law* 8] and Forrest, *International Law and the Protection of Cultural Heritage*, p. xxi; Nicole Bohe, 'Politics, Leverage, and Beauty: Why the Courtroom is Not the Best Option for Cultural Property Disputes' (2011) 1 *Creighton International & Comparative Law Journal* 100, 110–11; Palmer describes litigation as a 'flawed medium' in the context of Nazi-era dispossessions: Norman Palmer, *Museums and the Holocaust* (Leicester: Institute of Art and Law, 2000), p. 49;

adversarial nature of the law can act as a barrier to the appropriate resolution of disputes, particularly where the nature of the dispute is centred on justice to the original owners or custodians of cultural heritage (or their heirs).[68] For this reason, alternative means of hearing claims provide opportunities for more sensitive approaches to resolving dissonance by providing an opportunity to present a narrative and for those narratives to be listened to and responded to.

3.4.2 Disciplinary Imperialism: The Language of Law

Boyd White warns of the risk of disciplinary imperialism in law and specifically alerts us to the potential for law to exclude some communities from debate.[69] In the field of cultural heritage, lawyers and law have exerted a certain measure of disciplinary imperialism (particularly in the past) by placing discussions within the framework of property rights – specifically ownership and possession[70] – and by using the language of 'cultural property' at the expense of the human dimension to cultural heritage.[71] However, it is perhaps not as closed a discipline as might be assumed. The different people for whom the human dimension to cultural heritage is important may speak for themselves in the discourse, and it has been suggested that at times they employ legal language.[72] Audi suggests that these non-lawyers use 'legal argument bites'[73] and that this has the effect of diminishing the value of various legal concepts which impact on this area. This includes concepts such as statutes of limitation

Cotler suggests that 'the law's capacity to address "thefticide" requires us to banalize the evil [involved in the Nazi era]': Ian Cotler, 'The Holocaust, "Thefticide" and Restitution: A Legal Perspective' (1998) 20 *Cardozo Law Review* 601, 603.

[68] Chechi highlights the advantages of adopting non-adversarial means of dispute resolution: Chechi, *The Settlement of International Cultural Heritage Disputes*, p. 199. See also Carman's comments about the adversarial approach to treasure trove: Carman, *Valuing Ancient Things*, p. 58.

[69] James Boyd White , 'Establishing Relations between Law and Other Forms of Thought and Language' (2008) 1 *Erasmus Law Review* 3, 12.

[70] Daniel Shapiro, '"Response" to Alan Audi' (2007) 14 *International Journal of Cultural Property* 131, 164; Welsh, 'The Power of Possessions', at 13 points out that the Western notion of ownership dominates our understanding of cultural property. Francioni and Lixinski, 'Opening the Toolbox', p. 32 observe: 'Of course, any idea of promoting rights through heritage calls into question what rights are being protected to begin with. Cultural heritage, as an evolution of the idea of "cultural property" seems to still depend largely on ownership for its legal operation.'

[71] Last suggests that property is a restrictive concept: Kathryn Last, 'The Resolution of Cultural Property Disputes: Some Issues of Definition' in *The International Bureau of the Permanent Court of Arbitration, The Resolution of Cultural Property Disputes: Papers Emanating from the Seventh PCA International Law Seminar, 23 May 2003* (Kluwer, 2004), p. 53 and Naomi Mezey, 'Paradoxes of Cultural Property' (2007) 107 *Columbia Law Review* 2004, 2005 opines that there is not much culture left in 'cultural property'. Lixinski suggests that 'the international legal discourse' based on cosmopolitanism has embraced the idea of heritage and its values, whereas when it comes to domestic law, 'the language of property seems to be impervious to or deny those aspirations': Lixinski, *International Heritage Law for Communities*, p. 27.

[72] Alan Audi, 'A Semiotics of Cultural Property Argument' (2007) 14 *International Journal of Cultural Property* 131, 140.

[73] ibid., 139.

and innocent purchaser defences which lawyers would give more weight to because they impact the legal positions of the parties.[74] Audi argues that this debate about 'cultural property' takes place in a variety of fora outside the courtroom, leading to a 'looser, more fluid character', but more often than not 'cloaked' in legal argument.[75] Audi's argument is that these non-lawyers have not been given permission to make use of the legal argument. However, his suggestion of the need to give permission to those outside the legal sphere seems in itself to demonstrate a disciplinary imperialism by lawyers in seeking to exclude certain communities from the debate, or at least to question their authority to speak. It leads to a further question about who exactly has the authority to give permission and why they are the ones clothed with such authority, and from where does it derive. The main issue really appears to be the incorrect or less nuanced use of legal argumentation by non-lawyers including not fully appreciating the binding nature of the instruments and without employing the necessary specificity or precision of legal terms.[76] Such use of law can hinder and, at times, stifle the debate about the appropriateness of legal principles. Often criticism is mounted at the restrictive nature of such laws without concrete efforts being made to try to shift the views of policymakers and enable reform of the laws.[77] In seeking to avoid the notion of giving permission to others to employ legal language the approach taken in this book aims to deepen the awareness of concrete legal principles but beyond the purely doctrinal. In doing this it provides a fuller appreciation of the role that legal principles play, but at the same time recognises that these act in tandem with other non-law instruments – all of which demonstrate how the UK cares for cultural heritage.

3.4.3 Hiding behind Legal Barriers: Using Law as a Means of Maintaining the *Status Quo*

In the UK, one clear instance of mistrust of the law relating to cultural heritage has been the active use of law as a barrier to dealing justly with claims, or even to considering them at all. A very particular example of this has been reliance by national museums, in particular the British Museum, on the legal

---

[74] ibid., 139. Lixinski has also remarked about the passing reference of non-lawyers (often incorrectly) to law in the context of cultural heritage: Lixinski, *International Heritage Law for Communities*, p. 7.

[75] Audi, 'A Semiotics', 141.

[76] As identified by Lixinski, *International Heritage Law for Communities*, p. 12; Lixinski, 'Between Orthodoxy and Heterodoxy', 206.

[77] Lixinski observes the problematic nature of a doctrinal approach in which 'the law acts as the humble servant or the deferential enforcer of a series of heritage studies and management considerations made in the past' given that 'it prevents the law from keeping up with changes to the field of heritage, and, even in more legal theoretical work, leads to generalizations about practices within heritage management and studies . . .': Lixinski, *International Heritage Law for Communities*, p. 10.

restrictions on the circumstances in which the trustees can transfer objects from their collections.[78] Transfer is not permitted where a claim is made for the repatriation of an object, other than human remains[79] or where the Spoliation Advisory Panel has recommended that a Nazi-era spoliated object is returned.[80] The arguments about whether this statutory provision should be amended have been framed within the context of the Parthenon Marbles and both the legal protection given to the trustees and the trope of the legal prison have been employed in Parliamentary debates about proposals to develop the law.[81] The way in which the metaphor of the marbles has affected the potential care of cultural heritage by hindering attempts to reform the law on transfers from national museums is analysed in Chapter 9.

3.4.4 Too Little Law?

Whilst the prohibitory statutes discussed in the preceding section could be cited as examples of too much law applicable to cultural heritage stifling the ability to resolve claims appropriately,[82] in other situations there may be said to be insufficient law in place. It became clear that the intangible cultural heritage of Harris Tweed (handwoven in the Outer Hebrides) could not be effectively safeguarded[83] by a company limited by guarantee with registered trade marks. For that reason a statutory body was established which could bring proceedings against people who falsely represented material as Harris Tweed.[84] Similarly, both the National Trust and the National Trust for Scotland originally took the form of not-for-profit associations under the relevant Companies Act, but were given statutory footing with the National Trust Act 1907 and the National Trust for Scotland Order Confirmation Act 1935. This was clearly for the purpose of furthering their objectives of 'obtaining and preserving lands and buildings ... for the permanent holding and maintenance thereof and for the preventing as far as possible their destruction or disfigurement and for promoting the permanent preservation of buildings places or property having historic associations or being celebrated for their natural beauty'.[85] The negative effect of a continuing lack of law can be seen in the context of the illicit trade where strong arguments are made that rather than relying on autoregulation[86] additional legislation supported by legal

---

[78] See Chapter 9.   [79] Under the Human Tissue Act 2004, s. 47.

[80] Specifically, under the Holocaust (Return of Cultural Objects) Act 2009, s. 2, where the Secretary of State has also approved the transfer.

[81] See Section 9.5.2.2.

[82] This can be seen in the context of attempts to liberalise the prohibitions on deaccessioning for museum collections which are often stifled by arguments related to the Parthenon Marbles. See Section 9.5.1.

[83] This was the terminology used in the Harris Tweed Act 1993, Preamble.   [84] ibid.

[85] Preamble to both Acts.

[86] Terminology used by Neil Brodie, 'Provenance and Price: Autoregulation of the Antiquities Market?' (2014) 20 *European Journal on Criminal Policy and Research* 427, 428; see generally

sanctions could more effectively stem the illicit trade in cultural heritage objects.[87] As Audi observes, 'In many ways, cultural property is a prototypical example of a conflict- and gap-filled area of the law'.[88]

3.5 The Need for an Integrated Approach: Nested Practices of Care

Law is but one aspect of the care provided in the UK for cultural heritage. The approach here is, like Fincham's, to treat law as a 'multigenerational mechanism' to 'make better informed judgments and predictions about the direction this body of law may be taking'.[89] Through the concept of nested practices,[90] it is possible to see the integrated way in which the UK cares for cultural heritage[91] and ultimately the way in which it creates communities of care, or how communities of care make use of the law. The law's inaction is as important as its action. If non-law initiatives are sufficiently effective in caring for cultural heritage then there is not necessarily a need to legislate. Furthermore, whilst the UK at the national level may not take action to care for certain cultural heritage, international law may nevertheless impact the way in which cultural heritage is cared for in the UK through the principle of complementarity. Here, an international body may only intervene in the absence of action by the UK and is thus a secondary or complementary jurisdiction.[92]

3.6 The Nature and Status of Nested Practices of Care

Caring practices are nested[93] and here are taken to comprise legal instruments and the wide-ranging ethical initiatives that exist. These ethical initiatives include the non-law instruments that prescribe the responsibilities on those who provide care as well as those instruments and initiatives which facilitate the efforts of those who wish to proactively assume responsibility for the care of cultural heritage, including civil society and public participation initiatives. These communities assume responsibility because they care about it – either because it originates from their community, is important for their identity and

---

Simon MacKenzie, Neil Brodie, Donna Yates and Christos Tsirogiannis, *Trafficking Culture: New Directions in Researching the Global Market in Illicit Antiquities* (London: Routledge, 2019).

[87] The recent Council of Europe Convention on Offences Relating to Cultural Property, Nicosia (19 May 2017) CETS No 221 has been considered as a 'gap-filling initiative' regarding regulation in the field of the illicit trade in cultural heritage objects: Derek Fincham, 'The Blood Antiquities Convention as a Paradigm for Cultural Property Crime Reduction' (2019) 37 *Cardozo Arts & Entertainment Law Journal* 299, 321.

[88] Alan Audi, 'Rejoinder' (2007) 14 *International Journal of Cultural Property* 131, 165.

[89] Fincham, 'The Distinctiveness of Property and Heritage', 641, 658.   [90] See Chapter 2.

[91] Although using the language of regulation, as Frigo suggests, the law and ethical codes can combine 'to create a complete, if not homogenous, regulation': Frigo, 'Ethical Rules', 50.

[92] E.g. the ICC would only have jurisdiction in the event that a state failed to prosecute a particular crime: Rome Statute of the International Criminal Court, 17 July 1998, art. 17(1).

[93] Tronto, *Caring Democracy*, p. 21.

community or because it is at risk of harm. These nested practices of care thus represent the complex inter-relationships that exist between the varied people who care for cultural heritage. This approach therefore accords with approaches to heritage, such as treating it as social action.[94] Care is provided in a variety of forms and the nature of the care, and the way in which it is provided, may, at times, conflict with how another community views the nature of appropriate care. For that reason, there need to be frequent opportunities to assess and revisit questions about the nature and extent of appropriate care and to re-evaluate on whom the responsibility to provide appropriate care falls. In this way, care then becomes a plural and democratic process,[95] allowing the views of a varied number of people to be taken into account as part of the process. The following section analyses the nature of nested practices dealing with cultural heritage and the authority of these.

The nature of the instruments and initiatives that form the nested practices of care fall into different categories according to their legal status, enforceability and authority. It is important, from the perspective of the rule of law, to recognise the reach of these instruments and their legal 'bite', if any.[96] During the following analysis, this status and the authority of these instruments will be emphasised, but the structure of this section will first consider those nested practices of care which deal specifically with cultural heritage (thus dealing with cultural heritage frameworks, using law, non-law and participatory initiatives). The second part will analyse the way in which case law, applying non-heritage law principles, may provide nested practices of care in response to the particular dispute at hand. Thirdly, the attention will turn to the way in which committees and groups make instrumental use of law, policies and other processes (including civil society initiatives) to care for cultural heritage, even where those instruments may not have been designed with cultural heritage in mind.

3.7 Nested Practices of Care in a Cultural Heritage Framework

Particular nested practices of care are found within a framework directly relating to cultural heritage. These include formalised laws promulgated internationally, nationally or locally which are specifically designed to deal with cultural heritage. The drafting of these may have been the subject of debate at international meetings or in Parliament[97] and in some cases may have been

---

[94] Denis Byrne, 'Heritage as Social Action' in Graham Fairclough, Rodney Harrison, John H. Jameson Jr and John Schofield (eds.), *The Heritage Reader* (London: Routledge, 2008), p. 149.

[95] See Tronto, *Caring Democracy*, p. 14.

[96] Cf. the often muddied distinction in England between legal regulations and guidance affecting civil liberties during the COVID-19 pandemic – in particular situations where necessary public health measures were presented as mandatory despite in law only being advisory.

[97] Or in the Scottish Parliament, Welsh Parliament or Northern Ireland Assembly – although would not necessarily be in the case of statutory instruments.

subjected to a process of public and professional consultation. These may therefore have specific caring goals in mind, for example, the need to avert harm to cultural heritage,[98] to care for cultural heritage during armed conflict,[99] to stem the illicit trade in cultural heritage,[100] or to safeguard intangible cultural heritage practices.[101] However, as society has changed, including devolution within the UK, these legislative provisions may be riddled with amendments and at times lead to confusion.[102] These frameworks are developed and function at the international, national, regional, municipal, local community, professional body and institutional levels. Some laws and policies have been appropriated for the purposes of caring for cultural heritage[103] but others may have evolved over time to care for cultural heritage.[104] Further nested practices in the form of expert communities which advise decision-makers and non-law instruments providing guidance and ethical principles relevant to the care of cultural heritage exist. Each of these, at times, overlapping categories of instruments and initiatives will be analysed.

3.7.1 International Law and Soft Law

International legal norms provide the first, overarching practice of care; these are obligations reached by consensus with significant input from expert communities of care.[105] Included here are not only legally binding norms in treaties but also customary law and relevant international soft law. Treaties dealing with the care of cultural heritage and other legal instruments are frequently drafted in response to particular concerns about cultural heritage recognised

---

[98] E.g. European Convention on the Protection of the Archaeological Heritage (Revised) Council of Europe, Valetta (adopted 16 January 1992, entered into force 25 May 1995) CETS 14 and Convention on the Protection of the Underwater Cultural Heritage UNESCO, Paris (adopted 2 November 2001, entered into force 2 January 2009) 41 ILM 40.

[99] Convention for the Protection of Cultural Property in the Event of Armed Conflict UNESCO, The Hague (adopted 14 May 1954, entered into force 7 August 1956) 249 UNTS 240.

[100] E.g. Convention on the Means of Prohibiting and Preventing the Illicit Import, Export and Transfer of Ownership of Cultural Property UNESCO, Paris (adopted 14 November 1970, entered into force 24 April 1972 823) UNTS 231, the Convention on Stolen or Illegally Exported Cultural Objects, UNIDROIT (adopted 24 June 1995, entered into force 1 July 1998) 34 ILM 1322 and the Council of Europe Convention on Offences Relating to Cultural Property (19 May 2017) CETS No 221.

[101] 2003 UNESCO Intangible Cultural Heritage Convention.

[102] The Welsh Government has committed to undertaking a legislative consolidation programme of historic environment legislation because it is a 'bewildering jumble of repeatedly amended provisions that even lawyers find confusing': Cadw, *New Legislation*: https://cadw.gov.wales/advice-support/new-legislation (last accessed 20 December 2022).

[103] Carman, *Valuing Ancient Things*, p. 45.

[104] Ecclesiastical case law has developed to take on an enhanced caring role, as guardians of the national heritage. See Section 5.2.8.2.

[105] As to the discussion of expert communities of care, see Section 5.2.10. Lixinski explores the role of experts in international heritage law and the promulgation of treaties: Lixinski, *International Heritage Law for Communities*, pp. 71–84.

by the international community as needing addressing. Frequently these instruments are created reactively to deal with problems,[106] rather than pro-actively in the sense of furthering the precautionary principle.[107] Cultural heritage treaty-making[108] organisations are UNESCO, the United Nations (including through covenants and Security Council Resolutions), the Council of Europe and the European Union. Some of these conventions, such as the World Heritage Convention, rather than 'imposing rules or norms of conduct' are 'constitutive' in nature meaning that they 'create international cooperative schemes and are concerned in the main with how the schemes are to function'.[109] For that reason the focus may be on educative initiatives and systems.[110]

Given the need to ratify treaties and implement them under national law (because of the UK's dualist system), not all of the international conventions concerning cultural heritage are binding on the UK. Whilst in some cases specific legislation is required to satisfy treaty obligations,[111] in others these can be met through policies[112] or it may be concluded that all obligations are already met through domestic laws and other initiatives.[113]

3.7.1.1 The Status of Unratified International Conventions

UNESCO's constitution provides for the representatives of state parties to present copies of treaties and recommendations passed by the General Conference to their national competent authorities within one year.[114] Although it is the act of ratification of a convention which formally brings it into the national law of a state party, nevertheless this requirement of present-ing copies is seen as placing an obligation on state parties to follow the principles of the Convention, or more specifically, not to act in a way which would directly contravene the provisions of the particular treaty.[115]

---

[106] See Forrest, *International Law and the Protection of Cultural Heritage*, p. 31.

[107] As to which see Section 7.3.   [108] Specifically, conventions, covenants and charters.

[109] Forrest, *International Law and the Protection of Cultural Heritage*, p. 49.

[110] See, for example, the 1970 UNESCO Convention, arts. 5(f), 10, 17.

[111] E.g. the Cultural Property (Armed Conflicts) Act 2017 implemented the Hague Convention 1954 and its Protocols.

[112] The UK's commitments under the 1972 World Heritage Convention are met through plan-ning policy and site-specific statements.

[113] E.g. the 1970 UNESCO Convention, which was ratified by the UK in 2002 subject to certain reservations, some of which have now been withdrawn: Convention on the Means of Prohibiting and Preventing the Illicit Import, Export and Transfer of Ownership of Cultural Property (Paris, 14 November 1970) – withdrawal of declaration and reservation by the United Kingdom of Great Britain and Northern Ireland, LA/DEP/2021/006. The conclusions of the Report of the Illicit Trade Advisory Panel (December 2000) were that no specific legislation was needed to meet the obligations set out in the 1970 Convention. See Kevin Chamberlain, 'UK Accession to the 1970 UNESCO Convention' (2002) 7 *Art Antiquity and Law* 231.

[114] UNESCO Constitution, 16 November 1945, art. IV(B)(4).

[115] Malcolm N. Shaw, *International Law* (8th ed., Cambridge: Cambridge University Press, 2017), p. 691. Although in *Kingdom of Spain* v. *Christie Manson and Woods Ltd.* [1986] 1 WLR 1120, 1123 (Ch) Sir Nicholas Browne-Wilkinson V-C observed that because the UK had not acceded to the 1970 UNESCO Convention 'That Convention in no way forms

Some professional codes of ethics require that their members adhere to the principles set out in various international conventions, regardless of whether or not the conventions have been ratified by their governments.[116] Therefore, even before the UK ratified the 1970 UNESCO Convention, the UK museum community was expected to follow its principles. Similarly, the 1994 Unidroit Convention – with an important notion of due diligence – whilst unratified, is still seen as a guiding principle of the ICOM Code.[117] Furthermore, at the national governmental level, the importance of having signed treaties is evident in a document published by Highways England[118] concerning the management of cultural assets, using the terminology of 'care of the cultural heritage'. It indicates that the UK is 'committed' to this by being a *signatory* to several international conventions (rather than simply those that it has ratified).[119] Thus, the document cites the 2005 Faro Convention promulgated by the Council of Europe as well as UNESCO's 2001 Underwater Cultural Heritage Convention, neither of which has been formally incorporated into UK law through ratification.[120] In the Trust Deed entered into between the Secretary of State for Defence and the Maritime Heritage Foundation on the transfer of the wreck of HMS Victory (1744), specific reference was made to the Advisory Group (that was established to provide advice to the Foundation) to advise about their consistency with the archaeological principles set out in Annex A to the 2001 Convention, which has not been ratified by the UK but which has been signed.[121]

3.7.1.2 Customary Law

Customary international law is much more difficult to comprehensively pin down, but has been described as 'a dynamic source of law'.[122] It represents one of the sources of international law developed from state practice and the *opinio*

---

any part of the law of the United Kingdom'. Historic England explains that whilst international treaties may not be law and have direct force in planning decisions, 'signing a treaty is effectively a promise by the UK Government to adhere to the treaty's principles, doing so, if necessary, by making laws or policies that bring principles to bear on life in the UK': Historic England, *International Heritage Conventions, Treaties and Charters*: https://historicengland .org.uk/advice/hpg/coventionstreatiesandcharters/#(2) (last accessed 20 December 2022). A treaty which has been signed but not ratified may be 'deployed for the purpose of the resolution of an ambiguity in English primary or subordinate legislation': *R.* v. *Secretary of State for the Home Department (ex parte Brind and others)* [1991] 1 AC 696, 76.

[116] MA, *Code of Ethics: Additional Guidance*, para. 2(g): www.museumsassociation.org/cam paigns/ethics/code-of-ethics/# (last accessed 20 December 2022).

[117] ICOM, *Code of Ethics for Museums*, principle 7.2.

[118] And its Scottish, Welsh and Northern Irish counterparts.

[119] Highways England, Transport Scotland, Welsh Government and Department for Infrastructure (NI) Design, *Manual for Roads and Bridges: Sustainability and Environmental Appraisal LA116 Cultural Heritage Asset Management Plans* (2019), p. 4.

[120] ibid.

[121] Secretary of State for Defence and The Maritime Heritage Foundation (12 January 2012): https://assets.publishing.service.gov.uk/government/uploads/system/uploads/attachment_ data/file/27932/victory_1744_deed.pdf (last accessed 20 December 2022).

[122] Malcolm N. Shaw, *International Law* (9th ed., Cambridge: Cambridge University Press, 2020), p. 61.

juris of the state;[123] it is set out as one element of international law that is applied by the International Court of Justice.[124] The nature of customary law is that states do certain acts that are considered 'settled practice', but there is an additional subjective element to this in that they do these acts on the basis that they feel as if they are under a legal obligation to do so (hence the *opinio juris* element).[125] Suggestions have been made that such principles exist in the context of the resolution of disputes about cultural property as a form of *lex culturalis*.[126] Whilst this establishes broad norms, it will have less direct application to domestic law than ratified treaties.

3.7.1.3 Soft Law

Nested within binding international norms is the category of international soft law principles developed by institutions including UNESCO, the UN and the Council of Europe.[127] These instruments are standard-setting and lack the binding force of conventions,[128] and include resolutions and recommendations adopted by the General Assembly.[129] Other instruments from the UN and UNESCO include declarations, charters or similar standard-setting instruments.[130] The choice of one device over another may depend on the nature of its subject matter and its provisions – for example, the terminology of declarations is seen as demonstrating a solemnity[131] when dealing with matters such as human rights[132] or the rights of indigenous peoples.[133] In some cases these instruments, rather than introducing new rights and obligations, act as a consolidation of pre-existing recognised international norms.[134] Although the standard-setting instruments other than conventions are not subject to ratification, nevertheless, 'the mere fact that they have been adopted entails obligations even for those Member States that neither voted for it nor approved it'.[135] Furthermore, it is recognised that in some cases despite the instruments having a normative, rather than legally binding effect, this

---

[123] *North Sea Continental Shelf Cases* [1969] ICJ Rep 3, 44.

[124] Statute of the International Court of Justice, art. 38(1)(b).

[125] *North Sea Continental Shelf Cases*, 44.

[126] Chechi, *The Settlement of International Cultural Heritage Disputes*, p. 246.

[127] Soft law has been described as 'a paradoxical term for defining an ambiguous phenomenon' – paradoxical because law gives the sense of enforceable obligations (that is to say, hard rather than soft in nature) and yet ambiguous because soft law is often difficult to discern in practice: Pierre-Marie Dupuy, 'Soft Law and the International Law of the Environment' (1991) 12 *Michigan Journal of International Law* 420.

[128] See Forrest, *International Law and the Protection of Cultural Heritage*, p. 54.

[129] UNESCO Constitution, art. IV(B)(4).   [130] See its constitution p. 118

[131] General introduction to the standard-setting instruments of UNESCO: www.unesco.org/en/legal-affairs/standard-setting/overview (last accessed 20 December 2022).

[132] Universal Declaration of Human Rights, General Assembly Resolution 217 A (III) 1948 (adopted 10 December 1948).

[133] United Nations Declaration on the Rights of Indigenous Peoples 61/295 2008 (adopted 13 September 2007).

[134] ibid.

[135] 'General introduction to the standard-setting instruments'. The same applies to conventions accepted at the General Conference.

'does not detract from their potential for driving cultural and political transform-ations, which often run deeper than legal change'.[136]

It is helpful to take an approach that avoids adopting a binary distinction between hard and soft law, but which instead recognises a continuum from hard law to soft law 'through varied forms of soft law, each with its individual mix of characteristics, to situations of negligible legalization'.[137] By doing this, instruments from NGOs and other organisations, including professional asso-ciations, can be classified as being soft law, despite not being promulgated by a traditional law making institution. It is to these instruments that the discus-sion now turns.

3.7.1.4 Instruments by Non-law making International Bodies: Soft Law?

Other international instruments of a non-legally binding nature include codes of ethics from the International Council of Museums (ICOM), charters from the International Council on Monuments and Sites (ICOMOS) and the International Centre for the Study of the Preservation and Restoration of Cultural Property (ICCROM). These could also be considered as soft law instruments, for it is clear that soft law principles even where these are established by private actors rather than state parties, can, nevertheless, 'assume an important role in fixing international standards'.[138]

Some instruments which are relevant to practice, such as the Venice Charter, promulgated by ICOMOS are frequently cited in a way that implies that they have legal force *per se*.[139] These non-law instruments govern practice and provide a window on how communities care for cultural heritage; they assist communities in developing the principles through which they care for cultural heritage.[140]

Where principles deriving from non-law instruments are used in claims processes it is easier to justify treating these as a form of soft law, given that they affect matters of title[141] to cultural heritage. Therefore, in the context of claims for cultural objects relating to losses during the Nazi era, the Washington Conference Principles, adopted at the 1998 Washington Conference on Holocaust-Era Assets,[142] are frequently cited as being soft

---

[136] Erica-Irene Daes, 'The UN Declaration on the Rights of Indigenous Peoples: Background and Appraisal' in Stephen Allen and Alexandra Xanthaki (eds.), *Reflections on the UN Declaration on the Rights of Indigenous Peoples* (Studies in International Law, Oxford: Hart, 2011), p. 38. This can be seen in the context of the 1970 UNESCO Convention.

[137] Kenneth W. Abbott, Robert O. Keohane, Andrew Moravcsik, Anne-Marie Slaughter and Duncan Snidal, 'The Concept of Legalization' (2000) 54 *International Organization* 401, 418.

[138] Chris Brummer, *Soft Law and the Global Financial System: Rule Making in the 21st Century* (Cambridge: Cambridge University Press, 2012), p. 100.

[139] See Lixinski's commentary on this practice: Lixinski, *International Heritage Law for Communities*, p. 7.

[140] E.g. the Burra Charter promulgated by ICOMOS Australia.   [141] In property law terms.

[142] Washington Conference Principles on Nazi-Confiscated Art: www.state.gov/washington-conference-principles-on-nazi-confiscated-art/ (last accessed 20 December 2022).

law,[143] even though these principles were not formally voted on but were instead adopted by consensus.[144] They are clearly stated to be non-binding.[145] Nevertheless, they directly guide the work of restitution committees across Europe, as well as contribute to the overall project of researching the provenance for objects lost during the Nazi era in the 40-plus nations that took part in that conference. In this way, they have an impact on important issues of title to property, where committees recommend the legal transfer of cultural heritage objects from museums to claimants. The effect of this is to circumvent the legal position that has been created by the application of statutes of limitation and consequently the recommendations of the committees arguably represent *quasi*-legal principles.[146]

3.7.2 National Legislation and Case Law

The next category of nested practices of care is national legal norms found in legislation; some of these may have been enacted in response to the international norms set out in treaty commitments.[147] Others originate from debates in Parliament on specific issues such as designated heritage assets[148] and the secondary legislation made in pursuance of these policies. Furthermore, case law necessarily interprets, applies and develops these statutory provisions, particularly in areas such as planning law in developments affecting heritage assets as well as specific consent for work affecting listed buildings and scheduled monuments.

The various legal instruments and associated case law may affect those who directly care for cultural heritage (for example, owners of heritage places) or impose obligations or duties more generally on the public to ensure that specific cultural heritage is not harmed and thus is cared for more appropriately.[149] The cultural heritage frameworks may have a wider reach,

---

[143] Evelien Campfens, 'Restitution of Looted Art: What About Access to Justice?' (2018) 4 *Santander Art and Culture Law Review* 185, 198.

[144] See Stuart E. Eizenstat, *Imperfect Justice: Looted Assets, Slave Labor and the Unfinished Business of World War* (New York: Public Affairs, 2003).

[145] Washington Conference Principles, Preamble.

[146] See Charlotte Woodhead, 'Creative Equity in Practice: Responding to Extra-Legal Claims for the Return of Nazi Looted Art from UK Museums' (2022) 73 *Northern Ireland Legal Quarterly* 650, 664.

[147] Such as the Cultural Property (Armed Conflicts) Act 2017. Lixinski has pointed out the difficulties in translating notions from international law to domestic law in the field of cultural heritage: Lixinski, *International Heritage Law for Communities*, p. 55.

[148] See Section 4.1.

[149] This includes specific criminal offences applicable to cultural heritage (e.g. under the P(LBCA) A 1990, s. 9, Planning (Listed Buildings and Conservation Areas) (Scotland) Act 1997, s. 8, Planning Act (Northern Ireland) 2011, s. 85(1) and the Treasure Act 1996, s. 8(3) and the Dealing in Cultural Objects (Offences) Act 2003. Another way that care is effectuated is through the sentencing guidelines, which treat harm to heritage assets as an aggravating factor dealing with physical harm to cultural heritage when determining appropriate criminal sentences for general offences such as criminal damage, arson or theft: the Sentencing Act

restricting the ability of owners of nearby land to develop their land if this has the potential to adversely affect the specific heritage asset, the setting of that asset, or more generally the area which may be designated as of importance either locally, nationally or internationally.[150]

National legislation, together with the associated statutory instruments and cases, may impose direct obligations on the private owners of cultural heritage to care for cultural heritage, or they may provide for public intervention where the cultural heritage is at risk of physical harm due to neglect or a failure to undertake necessary remedial work. Such intervention may be undertaken by institutional communities of care, whether governmental or non-governmental,[151] assuming responsibility for its immediate care by undertaking remedial work or for its long-term care through concepts such as guardianship of monuments.[152] Statutory provisions may provide for acquisition by community groups.[153] Ultimately provision may be made for the public acquisition of cultural heritage.[154] Individual owners of cultural heritage objects may be subjected, through legal mechanisms, to restrictions on their powers to export these abroad.[155]

Legislation is also used to establish organisations[156] and prescribe their roles in the direct and indirect care of cultural heritage,[157] including providing care for particular places[158] or collections, including setting out frameworks within

---

2002, s. 59(1)(a) requires courts to follow any sentencing guidelines relevant to the offender's case with 'damage caused to heritage and/cultural assets' being general aggravating factors for these offences: www.sentencingcouncil.org.uk/crown-court/ (last accessed 20 December 2022). See generally Chapter 7.

[150] The obligations to consider historic assets when deciding whether or not to grant permission for sustainable development derive not only from statutes and secondary legislation, but also from the related planning policies.

[151] For example, by the local authority, a council (in Northern Ireland), the Secretary of State, the Welsh Ministers, Historic England, Historic Environment Scotland, Cadw (Wales) and Department for Communities (Northern Ireland). See Section 5.2.7.

[152] See Section 7.5.4.2.   [153] E.g. the situation in Scotland. See Section 7.5.4.3.

[154] See ibid. This would be coupled with appropriate financial compensation for the private owner who would otherwise be deprived of the cultural heritage *qua* private property in contravention of the human right to peaceful enjoyment of one's possessions under Article 1 of the First Protocol of the European Convention on Human Rights, enshrined into UK law through the Human Rights Act 1998.

[155] E.g. through the Export Control Act 2002 (as well as by the associated secondary legislation made pursuant to the Act and the relevant guidance under this): see Chapter 8.

[156] E.g. Historic England (formally the Historic Buildings and Monuments Commission for England), established under the National Heritage Act (NHA) 1983, s. 32(1), the National Memorial Fund, established by the NHA 1980, s. 1(1) and the National Trust (which was originally incorporated in 1894 as an Association under the Companies Act 1862 to 1890 limited by guarantee and was established as the National Trust for Places of Historic Interest or Natural Beauty under the National Trust Act 1907, s. 2).

[157] E.g. Historic England is the statutory advisor to the DCMS. As to these expert communities of care, see Section 5.2.10.

[158] English Heritage, Cadw, Historic Scotland, National Trust for Scotland and the National Trust.

which they care for these.[159] The various legal instruments[160] may also place obligations on existing government agencies or NGOs who are responsible for aspects of the care of cultural heritage,[161] or some of these organisations might undertake statutory functions on behalf of the Secretary of State.[162] Legislation and associated case law can also be used to construct collections in legal terms, thus providing the framework within which to care for cultural heritage, preventing its future dispersal or seeking to avert irreparable harm.[163]

The practices of care through statute law, associated statutory instruments and case law are nested together to provide a legal framework, but in some instances are also supplemented by statutory or non-statutory guidance which may inform practice and assist the court in the determination of a matter. The enforceability and status of these instruments deserve specific untangling below.[164]

3.7.3 Appropriated and Evolving Cultural Heritage Law Principles

It has been suggested that some laws and policies have been appropriated for the purposes of 'attempt[ing] to build national collections of antiquities'.[165] This has the effect of bringing more objects into the public care of museums. Whilst the initial aim of these laws might have been different from seeking to care for cultural heritage, they have nevertheless come to be used for that purpose and can be understood as falling within the framework of cultural heritage law. Carman described how the common law of treasure trove was appropriated by archaeologists.[166] His book predates the enactment of the Treasure Act 1996, which developed from the common law of treasure trove, but whose enactment was firmly framed within the context of seeking to 'preserve portable antiquities if they are made of gold or silver',[167] rather than as a means of dealing with 'masterless wealth'.[168]

---

[159] E.g. the establishment of national museums such as the British Museum in 1753. Legislation can also be used to solidify bequests that have been made to the nation, for example in the case of the Sir John Soane's Museum Act 1833 (although this has since been substituted by the Charities (Sir John Soane's Museum) Order 1969 SI 1969 No. 468).

[160] In tandem with planning policies and statutory and non-statutory guidance – see Section 3.7.5.

[161] E.g. Historic England.

[162] E.g. Arts Council England (ACE) carries out certain statutory functions on behalf of the DCMS under the Inheritance Tax Act 1984 (Acceptance in Lieu Scheme), the Export of Objects of Cultural Interest (Control) Order 2003 (export licensing) and the NHA 1980 (Government Indemnity Scheme): DCMS, *Tailored Review of Arts Council England* (April 2017), p. 20.

[163] This includes specific provisions within the governing statutes of national museums, but also extends to principles of charity law. Discussed at Section 7.3.2.

[164] At Section 3.7.5.   [165] Carman, *Valuing Ancient Things*, p. 45.   [166] ibid., p. 46.

[167] Earl of Perth, Treasure Bill, HL vol. 552 (9 March 1994), col. 1484.

[168] Which was said to be the reason for the old common law of treasure trove: see Carman, *Valuing Ancient Things*, p. 46, citing George Hill, *Treasure Trove in Law and Practice from the Earliest Time to the Present Day* (Oxford: Clarendon Press, 1936), p. v.

Rather than strictly being an appropriation of the law (as Carman envisaged[169]) it is possible to observe the evolution of laws used instrumentally for the care of cultural heritage in ecclesiastical law. The ecclesiastical law system of the Church of England developed as a separate body of legal principles administered by a distinct system of adjudication.[170] Whilst it has at its heart the mission of the church and its pastoral role, more recently one can observe a changing attitude of the ecclesiastical courts[171] in recognising the wider obligation of the Church to protect and provide access to cultural heritage objects, recognising the concept of national heritage and assuming responsibility for its care.[172] The court has identified its changing role as a guardian of national treasures in recent cases where permission was sought to sell church treasures and the court's response was to prioritise public access to them – either in the church or in a museum.[173] The Church of England, together with other churches across the nations of the UK, has been granted an exemption from the application of the listed building system as administered by the planning system and in turn the secular courts. This ecclesiastical exemption is restricted to certain named religious organisations and allocates the responsibility for the care of churches which are listed buildings to them.[174]

3.7.4 Regional-level Laws

Parliament has given certain authorities and organisations the power to formulate specific local practices of care which have the authority of law and can thus provide appropriate levels of care in a locality. In this way, at the regional level, local authorities[175] have a general power in respect of their area to 'make byelaws for the good rule and government ... and for the suppression of nuisances'.[176] However, more specific powers, relevant to the care of cultural

---

[169] Carman, *Valuing Ancient Things*, p. 112.

[170] See Mark Hill, *Ecclesiastical Law* (Oxford: Oxford University Press, 2007).

[171] Specifically in the context of the Church of England. Here the ecclesiastical courts comprise the consistory court, the Court of Arches, the Chancery Court of York and the Court of Ecclesiastical Causes Reserved. There is a further 'rarely exercised jurisdiction of the Privy Council to hear and determine further appeals from the Court of Arches and Chancery Court of York': Mark Hill, *Ecclesiastical Law* (4th ed., Oxford: Oxford University Press, 2018), p. 45. In the Church of Scotland, the General Trustees, as a corporation, hold property and make decisions about disposal. In the Church in Wales, the Representative Body of the Church in Wales owns the content of churches and must also receive the approval of the Bishop of the Diocese through the church's faculty jurisdiction: The Constitution of the Church in Wales, chapter III, para. 23(1).

[172] *Re St Lawrence, Wootton* [2015] Fam 27 (Arches Court). This is dealt with at Section 5.2.5.

[173] See Section 5.2.8.2.

[174] The Ecclesiastical Exemption (Listed Buildings and Conservation Areas) (England) Order 2010; The Ecclesiastical Exemption (Listed Buildings and Conservation Areas) (Wales) Order 2018; Planning (Listed Buildings and Conservation Areas) (Scotland) Act 1997, s. 54 and Planning (Northern Ireland) Act 2011, s. 85(8).

[175] Specifically, the council of a district or of a London borough.

[176] Local Government Act 1972, s. 235(1). Parish councils also have the power to make byelaws: The Byelaws (Alternative Procedure) (England) Regulations 2016, reg. 11(1); Local

heritage, are included in the enabling provisions relating to open spaces,[177] for this permits byelaws which regulate metal-detecting activities[178] as well as legislation relating to public museums. The latter can aid regulation of the use of museum facilities and the conduct of people using those facilities in England and Wales[179] or 'all or any matters and things whatsoever connected with the control, management, protection and use of any property, articles or things under [the] control' of the museum and art gallery authority in Scotland.[180] Being backed up with criminal sanctions, byelaws provide legal bite to the provision of care for cultural heritage at the local community level.[181]

Organisations such as the National Trust, the National Trust for Scotland and the Board of Trustees of the National Museums and Galleries of Northern Ireland also have the power to make byelaws for specific purposes.[182] These can be used to assist in navigating harm to cultural heritage and are explored in Chapter 7.

Under the new expedited system of making certain byelaws in England[183] (a similar process exists in Wales for those byelaws not requiring confirmation),[184] there is public involvement in the law making process itself. As part of preparing the local authority's statement of assessment[185] about the regulatory burden of the proposed byelaw[186] the authority must consult with 'such persons as it considers are potentially affected by the proposed byelaw',[187]

Government Byelaws (Wales) Act 2012, s. 2(1); Local Government (Scotland) Act 1973, s. 201 and Local Government Act (Northern Ireland) 1972, s. 90.

[177] Open Spaces Act 1906, s. 15(1). In the case of London this also applies to 'any other public park, heath, common, recreation ground, pleasure ground, garden, walk, ornamental enclosure or disused burial ground'.

[178] Guidance to local authorities encourages them to exercise caution when making provision for restrictions on metal detecting activities since restrictions should be limited to areas in need of 'special protection' and byelaws seeking to prohibit metal detectors in all areas 'may be seen as overly restrictive and unreasonable': Ministry of Housing, Communities and Local Government, *Guidance: Model Byelaw Set 2: Guidance Notes* (updated 7 September 2018), para. 41. Furthermore, it entreaties local authorities to ensure that 'adequate local consultation has taken place before adopting such measures': *Model Byelaw Set 2*, para. 7, thus demonstrating a dialogic approach to care.

[179] Public Libraries and Museums Act 1964, s. 19(1) (England and Wales).

[180] For the purposes of the Act: Public Libraries Consolidation (Scotland) Act 1887, s. 22.

[181] These are explored at Section 7.7.

[182] These are set out in National Trust Act 1971, s. 24(1); National Trust Act 1907, s. 33 (relating to buildings); the National Trust for Scotland Order Confirmation Act 1935, ss. 33 and 35 and Museums and Galleries (Northern Ireland) Order 1998.

[183] This does not include byelaws made under the Public Libraries and Museums Act 1964, s. 19(1) which require confirmation from the DCMS, but would include those made under the Local Government Act 1972, s. 235(1) and the Open Spaces Act 1906, s. 15(1)

[184] Local Government Byelaws (Wales) Act 2012, s. 6.

[185] The Byelaws (Alternative Procedure) (England) Regulations 2016, reg. 5(2)(c).

[186] ibid., reg. 5(2)(b).

[187] ibid., reg. 5(3). In Wales the obligation is to consult any person who 'is likely to be interested in, or affected by, the issue': Local Government Byelaws (Wales) Act 2012, s. 6(2)(b).

and publish the statement of assessment.[188] In England, once the Secretary of State has given 'leave to the authority to make the byelaw',[189] the authority must publish the proposal[190] with a consultation period of no fewer than 28 days.[191] Where the authority receives written representations in response[192] then these shall be considered[193] before they decide whether or not the byelaw is made.[194] In Wales there is no requirement to send the proposed byelaw to the Secretary of State, but a second written statement (following the initial consultation with interested parties) is published and 6 weeks before the byelaw is intended to be made notice of intention is published.[195]

The use of byelaws therefore provides a targeted means of caring for cultural heritage which has a sanction for non-compliance and is created, in some instances, within a spirit of public participation. Byelaws, as a practice of care, are nested within the international and national legal systems to provide local, democratic care that can be tailored for cultural heritage.

3.7.5 Policy and Guidance

Supporting national legislation in some areas of practice relating to cultural heritage are policies and national guidance or codes of practice provided by government departments, or other NGOs acting on behalf of the Secretary of State in specific circumstances.[196] These instruments take the form of statutory guidance or codes of practice as prescribed in the legislation.[197] Other guidance can be non-statutory in nature,[198] originating from government or those acting on behalf of the Secretary of State. As part of these nested practices, the decision-

---

[188] See The Byelaws (Alternative Procedure) (England) Regulations 2016, reg. 5(4)(b) and (c) and Local Government Byelaws (Wales) Act 2012, ss. 6(2)(a) and 6(4) which provides for a second published statement after the consultation.

[189] The Byelaws (Alternative Procedure) (England) Regulations 2016, regs. 7(1) and 7(2)(a).

[190] ibid., reg. 8.

[191] Ministry of Housing, Communities and Local Government, *Local Government Legislation: Byelaws – Guidance*, Step 4: www.gov.uk/guidance/local-government-legislation-byelaws (last accessed 20 December 2022).

[192] Which must be for a period not less than 28 days: The Byelaws (Alternative Procedure) (England) Regulations 2016, reg. 8(3)(d).

[193] ibid, reg. 9.   [194] ibid, reg. 10. The byelaw is then made under reg. 11.

[195] Local Government Byelaws (Wales) Act 2012, s. 6(5).

[196] Examples include ACE in the context of export licensing, Historic England in the context of listed buildings and scheduled monuments. These 'announcements by particular administrative bodies of the course which it is proposed to take in the administration of particular statutes' have been described as 'quasi-legislation': Robert E. Megarry, 'Administrative Quasi-Legislation' (1944) 60 *Law Quarterly Review* 125, 126.

[197] E.g. listed buildings (DCMS, *Principles of Selection for Listed Buildings* (London: DCMS, 2018)); export licensing (DCMS, *Export Controls on Objects of Cultural Interest: Statutory Guidance on the Criteria to be Taken into Consideration When Making a Decision about Whether or Not to Grant an Export Licence* (London: DCMS, 2020) under the Export Control Act 2002, s. 9(6)); treasure (DCMS, *Treasure Act 1996 Code of Practice* (3rd Revision, London: DCMS, 2023), under section 11(1) of the Treasure Act 1996).

[198] Historic England, *Conservation Principles, Policies and Guidance* (2008).

makers involved in individual cases may derive advice and support from organisations in the execution of the powers conferred by the overarching statutory regime.

Certain professional bodies and other membership organisations publish guidance, including codes of ethical conduct which set out obligations for their individual and institutional membership to follow; these obligations extend beyond their legal ones and assist them in navigating particular issues in practice.[199]

3.7.5.1 Statutory Guidance, Policies and Non-statutory Guidance Issued by Government Departments and Related Bodies

Legislation prescribing that the Secretary of State promulgates codes of practice or guidance may require them to set out relevant principles and practice to apply when making determinations under the statute.[200] Furthermore, legislation may require the publication of guidance for the public or for institutions in matters relevant to their activities under the Act.[201] As part of this legislative process the Secretary of State can be required to consult 'such persons appearing to him to be interested as he thinks appropriate' before preparing or revising a code[202] and to lay the guidance before Parliament.[203]

It is clear from *Laker Airways* v. *Department of Trade*[204] that statutory guidance can explain, amplify or supplement the general objectives of the enabling legislation, but cannot 'reverse or contradict' those objectives.[205] Guidance denotes neither an order nor a command[206] and thus 'has the implication of leading, pointing the way' in contrast to 'direction', which 'echoes its Latin root of regere, to rule'.[207]

Policies represent statements of applicable principles that may be applied at the national or local levels. The National Planning Policy Framework (NPPF) is a national policy applicable to planning law. It includes principles relating to conserving and enhancing the historic environment[208] which represent a material consideration to be taken into account within the overall framework of achieving sustainable development[209] in planning decisions.[210] The NPPF,

---

[199] These include museum and archaeologists and are considered in turn below.

[200] Treasure Act 1996, s. 11(2). See also Export Control Act 2002, ss. 9(3) and (4) and DCMS, *Export Controls on Objects of Cultural Interest*.

[201] E.g. the Treasure Act 1996, s. 11(3), which states that the Secretary of State may include in the Code guidance for '(a) those who search for or find treasure; and (b) museums and others who exercise functions in relation to treasure'. See also Export Control Act 2002, s. 9(2).

[202] E.g. the Treasure Act 1996, s. 11(4).

[203] Treasure Act 1996, s. 11(6) and the Export Control Act 2002, s. 9(6).

[204] [1977] 1 QB 643 (CA).   [205] ibid., 699 (Lord Denning MR).   [206] ibid.

[207] ibid., 725 (Lawton LJ).

[208] Ministry of Housing, Communities and Local Government, *National Planning Policy Framework* (2021), pp. 55–8.

[209] NPPF 2021, p. 5.

[210] Town and Country Planning Act 1990, s. 70(2)(c); *Hopkins Homes Ltd.* v. *Secretary of State for Communities and Local Government and another* [2017] 1 WLR 1865 (SC) at 1876 and 1878 (Lord Carnwath JSC).

which was created by the Secretary of State with powers derived under statute,[211] acts as 'nothing more than "guidance"',[212] which should 'not be interpreted as if it were statute'.[213] Similarly, Written Ministerial Statements are policies considered as material considerations[214] in the planning decision-making process, as are local development documents, created by the local planning authority in the form of development plans.[215]

Policies are treated in the same way as statutory guidance in the sense that they explain and amplify the law,[216] rather than permitting the Secretary of State to effectuate a change to the primary objectives of the legislation by using that policy document to constrain the way in which the organisation specified by the legislation can act. In turn, the role of practice guidance is to 'amplify published policy' which 'supplements and explains policies in the NPPF, and assists in their application'.[217] It therefore should be interpreted objectively in context rather than in isolation and should be considered as neither a statute nor a contract.[218] In the case of *Knox* v. *Causeway Coast and Glens BC*[219] in Northern Ireland the Protocol for the Operation of the Causeway Coast and Glens Borough Council Planning Committee was described as 'the kind of instrument which is not to be equated with statute, whether primary or subordinate. Notwithstanding, it has statutory parentage. Thus it is invested with a certain measure of solemnity and gravity.'[220] In terms of the interpretation of these instruments: '[s]uch Guidelines are not enactments; they are practical guidelines to be read in a common sense way and not in a pedantic or legalistic manner'.[221]

Memoranda may be published by government departments outlining the scope of a legislative framework and providing guidance when administering the provision of a scheme related to cultural heritage. Such an example is found in the HM Revenue and Customs *Capital Taxation and the National Heritage* memorandum, which guides the operation of the capital taxation provisions relating to heritage.[222]

Non-statutory guidance falls into several different categories. The first category covers the actions of formal advisors in administering schemes on behalf of the government. Such guidance may be published by the responsible government department, or by the NGO advisors themselves to set out how

---

[211] *Hopkins Homes*, 1876 (Lord Carnwath JSC).   [212] ibid.   [213] ibid., 1890 (Lord Gill).
[214] NPPF 2021, p. 4.
[215] Town and Country Planning Act 1990, s. 70(2)(a) (Local development plans were introduced by the Planning and Compulsory Purchase Act 2004, s. 17(3)).
[216] See *Laker Airways*, above.
[217] *R. (on the application of Save Britain's Heritage)* v. *Liverpool City Council and Regeneration Liverpool and Neptune in Partnership Ltd.* [2016] EWCA Civ 806, para. 26 (Lindblom LJ).
[218] ibid., para. 26 – applying the approach relating to interpreting planning policy set out by the Supreme Court in *Tesco* v. *Dundee CC* [2012] UKSC 13.
[219] *Knox* v. *Causeway Coast and Glens BC* [2019] NIQB 34, 31 (QB).   [220] ibid., para. 31.
[221] Said in the context of conservation area guidelines: *R. (on the application of Majed)* v. *Camden LBC and Adam Kaye* [2009] EWCA Civ 1029, para. 24 (Sullivan LJ).
[222] HM Revenue & Customs, *Capital Taxation and the National Heritage* (2013, updated 2022).

the powers are exercised.[223] These instruments, whilst not statutory in nature, can assist in determining whether the powers have been carried out appropriately. They have been described as *quasi*-legislation and are found in both secular[224] and canon law, playing a supplementary role, filling 'gaps in formal law'.[225]

The selection guide, used by Historic England when selecting historic battlefields, is such a type of document[226] and has been recognised in court as not being drafted with the precision of statute. It was written and was intended 'as a collection of principles and advice to guide the exercise of judgment in individual cases' and 'to promote decision-making which is sound, consistent and reasonably predictable'.[227] Furthermore, it was to guide Historic England in both its statutory powers[228] and its general functions.[229]

A second type of guidance is instruments aimed at particular communities engaged in specific activities taking place within a formal legal structure. This includes guidance to exporters of cultural heritage objects,[230] owners of historic assets,[231] and agencies responsible for the prevention and enforcement of heritage crime.[232] But guidance is also provided to other communities who care for, search for,[233] or transact with cultural heritage which highlights their legal obligations and supplements these with enhanced ethical obligations in certain circumstances; such an example relates to when museums acquire cultural heritage objects.[234]

[223] E.g. Historic England's Guides for Listing: https://historicengland.org.uk/listing/selection-criteria/listing-selection/ (last accessed 20 December 2022).

[224] Megarry 'Administrative Quasi-Legislation', 125, 126.

[225] Norman Doe, 'Ecclesiastical *Quasi*-Legislation' in Norman Doe, Mark Hill and Robert Ombres (eds.), *English Canon Law: Essays in Honour of Bishop Eric Kemp* (Cardiff: University of Wales Press, 1998), p. 95.

[226] Historic England, Battlefields: Registration Selection Guides HEAG072, English Heritage (2012, reissued by Historic England 2017).

[227] *R. (on the application of Charles Jones)* v. *English Heritage and others* [2014] EWHC 2259 (Admin), para. 55 (Lindblom J).

[228] NHA 1983, s. 33(5)(d).   [229] *R. (on the application of Charles Jones)*, para. 55.

[230] E.g. an ACE Notice provides guidance for exporters of works of art and other cultural goods: Arts Council, *UK Export Licensing of Cultural Goods: Procedures and Guidance for Exporters of Works of Art and Other Cultural Goods* (An Arts Council Notice, 2021, issue 1) since ACE administers the export licensing regime on behalf of the Secretary of State for Digital, Culture, Media and Sport.

[231] E.g. Historic England, *A Guide for Owners of Listed Buildings* (2016) and Historic England, *Scheduled Monuments: A Guide for Owners and Occupiers* (2013).

[232] Historic England, *Heritage Crime Impact Statements* (2023) and Historic England, *Interventions: Prosecutions and Alternative Disposals* (HEAG 189, 2023).

[233] Portable Antiquities Advisory Group, *Code of Practice for Responsible Metal Detecting in England and Wales* (2017 revision): https://finds.org.uk/documents/file/Code-2017.pdf (last accessed 20 December 2022).

[234] DCMS produced due diligence guidance for museums which emphasised the need for provenance research and the importance of the date of 1970: DCMS, *Due Diligence Guidelines for Museums, Libraries and Archives on Collecting and Borrowing Cultural Material* (October

Thirdly, guidance has been created to support how particular types of objects are cared for, such as human remains[235] and objects with gaps in their provenance between 1933–1945.[236] Guidance also assists in the overall approach to how museums deal with repatriation requests,[237] issues concerning acquisition and the difficulties in navigating issues concerning cultural heritage with contentious histories (so-called contested heritage).[238] Other guidance is also provided for those working in the art market, setting out the legal and enhanced obligations expected of them.[239]

A fourth category of guidance is those instruments produced by associations and professional bodies for their own membership and this category deserves specific analysis, to which the discussion now turns.

3.7.5.2 Guidance and Codes of Ethics by Professional and Membership Organisations[240]

In several international instruments state parties have undertaken to encourage institutions to adopt codes of conduct.[241] Most notable is the 1970 UNESCO Convention, which states in its Preamble that 'museums . . . should

2005), p. 4. The date of 1970 has been described as an ethical rather than a legal watershed when the world was put on notice, see Section 7.6.2.1.

[235]   DCMS, *Guidance for the Care of Human Remains in Museums* PP 847 (London: DCMS, 2005) and Museums Galleries Scotland, *Guidelines for the Care of Human Remains in Scottish Museums* (2011).

[236]   Including the UK's National Museum Directors Conference, *Statement of Principles and Proposed Actions* (1998, updated 2016): www.nationalmuseums.org.uk/what-we-do/contrib uting-sector/spoliation/spoliation_statement/ (last accessed 20 December 2022) and the comparable principles published by the then Museums Libraries and Archives Council which apply to non-national museums. The Washington Conference Principles guide the overarching approach of just and fair solutions which has been adopted by European restitution committee, including the UK's Spoliation Advisory Panel.

[237]   ACE, *Restitution and Repatriation: A Practical Guide for Museums in England* (London: ACE, 2022).

[238]   E.g. Historic England, *Contested Heritage*: https://historicengland.org.uk/whats-new/state ments/contested-heritage/ (last accessed 20 December 2022); Church of England, *Contested Heritage in Cathedrals and Churches Guidance* (London: Church Buildings Council and Cathedrals Fabric Commission for England, 2021).

[239]   See for example HMRC, *Anti-money Laundering Supervision: Guidance for High Value Dealers* (2018) which states (in the context of contrasting the use of the word 'must' to denote legal obligations) that: 'The word "should" is a recommendation of good practice, and is the standard that HMRC expects to see. HMRC will expect you to be able to explain the reasons for any departures from that standard', p. 2.

[240]   'Laws restrict activities and define methods or means of compliance. They serve as the minimum standards of social behavior. Ethics defines and describes correct actions for persons working in a specialized profession': Gary Edson, 'Ethics' in Gary Edson (ed.), *Museum Ethics: Theory and Practice* (London: Routledge, 1997), p. 9. Examples of professional codes of ethics include: the ICOM, *Code of Ethics for Museums*; MA, *Code of Ethics*; Chartered Institute of Archaeologist, *Code of Conduct: Professional Ethics in Archaeology* (2014) and National Council for Metal Detecting, *Code of Conduct* (amended by the AGM, June 2012): www .ncmd.co.uk/code-of-conduct/ (last accessed 20 December 2022).

[241]   E.g. Resolution adopted by the United Nations General Assembly on 18 December 2014 – 69/ 196 International Guidelines for Crime Prevention and Criminal Justice Responses with Respect to Trafficking in Cultural Property and Other Related Offences, Guideline 5.

ensure that their collections are built up in accordance with universally recognized moral principles'.[242] It has thus been described as a 'strong pressure instrument' in establishing ethical codes.[243] By treating codes of ethics as 'mini-systems of collective government'[244] formed by 'self-regulatory associations'[245] undoubtedly one lapses into the language of regulation rather than care.[246] Nevertheless, analysing them in this way enables an appreciation of how care is provided for cultural heritage, for the effect of them is to act as a type of 'soft law' (without direct legal sanction),[247] certainly at a local level amongst professional members.[248] However, codes have a much wider function which is evident in the context of museums, archaeology and other aspects of the care of cultural heritage. They can be educative,[249] acting as a marker of best ethical practices,[250] and also demonstrate the general consensus of a particular community.[251] They provide 'a principled pathway to help ... to navigate through contested moral territory'[252] rather than prescribing the appropriate actions to take.[253] Codes have the significant advantage that they

[242] Convention on the Means of Prohibiting and Preventing the Illicit Import, Export and Transfer of Ownership of Cultural Property UNESCO, Paris (adopted 14 November 1970, entered into force 24 April 1972 823) UNTS 231.

[243] Frigo, 'Ethical Rules', 51. As to its pivotal role in developing an 'ethical watershed' of the year 1970, see generally Section 7.6.2.1.

[244] Julia Black, 'Constitutionalising Self-Regulation' (1996) 59 *The Modern Law Review* 24.

[245] ibid.

[246] In practice as well, codes can inform the development of future legal obligations: Intergovernmental Committee on Intellectual Property and Genetic Resources, Traditional Knowledge and Folklore, *Preliminary Systematic Analysis of National Experiences with the Legal Protection of Expressions of Folklore*, WIPO/GRTKF/IC/4/3 (20 October 2002), para. 121 (referring to Australia's *Report of the Contemporary Visual Arts and Craft Inquiry* (Commonwealth of Australia, 2002)).

[247] Robert K. Paterson, 'The Caring and Sharing Alternative: Recent Progress in the International Law Association to Develop Draft Cultural Material Principles' (2005) 12 *International Journal of Cultural Property* 62, 65.

[248] A series of writers have placed them within the scope of soft law: Sophie Vigneron, 'Les codes de déontologie en Angleterre: entre droit souple et droit dur' in Géraldine Goffaux Callebaut (ed.), *Éthique et patrimoine culturel: Regards croisés* (Paris: L'Harmattan, 2016), p. 67; Manlio Frigo, 'Codes of Ethics' in Francesco Francioni and Ana Filipa Vrdoljak (eds.), *The Oxford Handbook of International Cultural Heritage Law* (Oxford: Oxford University Press, 2020), p. 803.

[249] Patrick J. O'Keefe, 'Codes of Ethics: Form and Function in Cultural Heritage Management' (1998) 7 *International Journal of Cultural Property Law* 32, 49.

[250] Judith Chelius Stark, 'The Art of Ethics: Theories and Applications to Museum Practice' in Janet Marstine (ed.), *The Routledge Companion to Museum Ethics* (London: Routledge, 2011), p. 39.

[251] Edson, *Museum Ethics*, p. 112; although Marstine suggests that in this context 'consensus has come to signal an exclusivity and like-mindedness among contributors, as well as a fixity of thought' and she argues for recognising ethic's contingent nature, which emphasises 'the conditional and relational qualities of the discourse': Janet Marstine, 'The Contingent Nature of the New Museum Ethics' in Marstine, *The Routledge Companion to Museum Ethics*, pp. 7, 8.

[252] Tristram Besterman, 'Museum Ethics' in Sharon Macdonald (ed.), *A Companion to Museum Studies* (Oxford: Blackwell, 2006), p. 431.

[253] 'Ethics not only provide a framework to guide actions, but they are also intertwined with the social structure, its powerful institutions, and its understanding of "good" and "bad"': Miriam Clavir, *Preserving What is Valued: Museums, Conservation, and First Nations* (Vancouver: UBC Press, 2002), p. 27.

are much more responsive and adaptable in a relatively short period of time and their drafters can therefore respond to the changing nature of cultural heritage, its importance for particular communities, or the relevance of repatriation requests and the need to do justice in particular circumstances. A disadvantage of codes is the lack of the force of formal sanction and they thus depend more often than not on the goodwill of those who are members of the relevant professional body.[254] As Abbott et al. observe though, '[c]ompliance with rules occurs for many reasons other than their legal status. Concern about reciprocity, reputation, and damage to valuable state institutions, as well as other normative and material considerations, all play a role.'[255] A primary driver of compliance with codes may be the risk of professional embarrassment[256] which comes with failing to adhere to ethical principles, and the removal of funding sources[257] which would flow from losing accreditation under the Arts Council England (ACE) Scheme.[258]

Principles set out in codes of ethics can be given legal force between parties; the Museums Association (MA) Code of Ethics encourages its members to specify that contractors adhere to the principles of the Code and to make these contractual terms.[259] In the case of the Chartered Institute for Archaeologists, voting members are required, by the Institute's byelaws, to 'so order their conduct as to uphold the dignity and reputation of the profession'[260] with a provision setting out the framework for the General Meeting of the Institute to establish (and update) rules for regulating conduct.[261] Some professional bodies have in place disciplinary systems that can ultimately sanction the exclusion of an individual or institutional member in the event of a serious breach of the code.[262] Even where sanctions exist, these may be of relatively

---

[254] O'Keefe suggests that the educative function of codes of ethic should take priority over their enforceability subject to sanction: O'Keefe, 'Codes of Ethics', 32, 49.

[255] Abbott et al., 'The Concept of Legalization', 419.

[256] This is recognised as a potential incentive for compliance in other sectors – e.g. the financial services sector: Brummer, *Soft Law and the Global Financial System*, p. 121.

[257] In the UK a museum may lose its accredited status (which is conferred by the Arts Council) as a result of breaching the MA, *Code of Ethics*, for example by deaccessioning for financially motivated reasons. This would impact on the ability of the museum to access certain funding sources. In the context of the USA it has been pointed out that bad publicity following breaches of ethical codes can lead to museums losing out on private funding (on which they rely heavily): Kate Fitz Gibbon, 'Dangerous Objects: Museums and Antiquities in 2008' (1 March 2009), p. 9: http://doi.org/10.2139/ssrn.1479424 (last accessed 20 December 2022). In the UK, deaccessioning from museum collections in contravention of ethical codes may discourage donors from transferring objects to the collection either by gift or bequest in the future if the risk is that they will be sold by the recipient for short-term financial gain.

[258] Parallels can be drawn here with what Abbott and Snidal describe as the countermeasures available under the WTO legalized regimes which 'legitimizes retaliation and clarifies its intent': Kenneth W. Abbott and Duncan Snidal, 'Hard and Soft Law in International Governance' (2000) 54 *International Organization*, 421, 427.

[259] MA, *Code of Ethics* (2015), p. 21.

[260] Chartered Institute for Archaeologists, *Charter and by-law* (2014), byelaw 9.2.

[261] ibid., byelaw 9.3.

[262] See, for example, the MA, *The Disciplinary Regulations for the Members of the Museums Association* (2001, updated 2015) which includes the powers to cancel membership: para. 10.1.

short duration. Despite all of this, codes of ethics do provide an important framework for those who directly care for cultural heritage (i.e. those in whose care cultural heritage is), demonstrating ethical obligations which exceed the usual legal ones. Although there may be some causes célèbres where codes have been breached, codes nevertheless provide a principled road map for professionals and the governing bodies of museums to follow. The strict legal position requires a certain level of care (in the context of national museums this is usually specified as a duty to care for and preserve the collection in the governing statute[263]), but ethical duties can go further. They can, for example, set out the way in which museums might engage in dialogue with other communities in the care of cultural heritage.[264]

How a code is formulated can also influence the wider perception of it, and the extent to which it is authoritative. This can be enhanced, for example, where the code has been formulated by communities of members themselves[265] as a result of a democratic process.[266] In the case of the MA Code of Ethics, earlier drafts of the 2015 revision were circulated and open for consultation, with the final version being voted upon in the annual general meeting of the association, under statute.[267] Engaging the entire community of members and the public with the activity of the drafting of the code and with sessions run afterwards by the MA to discuss and embed ethical practices in the community strengthens the authority of the code as a nested practice of care. Similarly, the ICOM Code is reviewed and consulted upon.[268]

The fact that these codes are drafted as a result of a democratic process and active participation,[269] representing the consensus of the membership of the professional body, may avoid the risk of 'passive adherence'.[270] This can be a problem with prescriptive codes formulated by others and not through the active participation of its membership.[271] Vigneron highlights the strength of the UK's Museum Association Code of Ethics as soft law through the concept of legalization espoused by Abbot et al., who analyse it in terms of obligation, precision and delegation.[272] She concludes that the level of obligation is an enhanced one in the context of the UK MA Code of Ethics as compared with the ethical codes applicable to UK art dealers.[273]

---

[263] See Section 6.4.1.   [264] E.g. ICOM, *Code of Ethics for Museums*, principle 6.2.

[265] For, as Fiss points out, 'Rules are not rules unless they are authoritative, and that authority can only be conferred by a community'. Owen M. Fiss, 'Objectivity and Interpretation' (1982) 34 *Stanford Law Review* 739, 745.

[266] Cf. the authoritative nature of legal texts: James Boyd White , 'Interview with James Boyd White' (2007) 105 *Michigan Law Review* 1403, 1415.

[267] MA, *Annual Report 2016*, p. 10.

[268] ICOM, *The 2021–2022 Review*: https://icom.museum/en/resources/standards-guidelines/code-of-ethics/ (last accessed 20 December 2022).

[269] See Emma Faulkner, 'The Policy Column: Drafting a New Code of Ethics', *Museums Journal*, 30 June 2015.

[270] Roger Homan, 'Problems with Codes' (2006) 2 *Research Ethics Review* 98, 103.   [271] ibid.

[272] See Abbott et al., 'The Concept of Legalization', 401, 419.

[273] Vigneron, 'Les codes de déontologie', p. 74.

In addition to codes of ethics by professional bodies, codes can be established by membership organisations, such as the National Council for Metal Detecting, to guide the way in which they carry out activities relating to cultural heritage and as a means of caring for it.[274]

3.7.5.3 The Status of Guidance and Codes of Ethics in Law: The Court's Interpretations of Cultural Heritage Guidance

Both secular and ecclesiastical courts have to interpret and apply statutory provisions relating to cultural heritage. They may also need to interpret and apply the policies set out in both statutory and non-statutory guidance to individual cases. Resulting from this, further norms are developed and clarified in case law.

Recent *obiter dictum* of the English court has indicated that relevant ethical codes and other guidance can assist a court when considering the judicial review of a decision to significantly reduce the provision of a local authority museum.[275] In *ex parte Hall,* Blake J. specifically observed that having sight of the various codes and guidance of DCMS, Heritage Lottery Fund, Art Fund and the MA would have been helpful in reaching his decision – although he was still able to deliver judgment without them.[276] However, expectations of adherence to codes and the ability to rely on them clearly depend on being a party to them. In *Kingdom of Spain* v. *Christie Manson and Woods Ltd*[277] the court considered the Dealers Code of Practice (of which Christie's, together with other dealers and several institutions, were signatories) but concluded that the Spanish government, who claimed that an oil painting by Goya had been exported with false export documents, could not rely on the code as it was not a party to it.[278]

Professional codes setting out the expected standards of an organisation can be of relevance to a court when assessing whether a contractual party has acted to the appropriate standard of care expected of the reasonable professional[279] or whether that party has acted negligently.[280] The appropriate standards of due diligence expected of professional members, set out in codes relating to dealers or museums, may assist the court when determining whether there is a defence to a claim for conversion. (Where a current possessor seeks to rely on section 4(2) of the Limitation Act 1980 and bears the burden of proving that they are a good faith purchaser unconnected to a theftuous conversion.[281])

---

[274] National Council for Metal Detecting, *Code of Conduct.*

[275] *R (on the application of Hall)* v. *Leicestershire County Council* [2015] EWHC 2985 (Admin) (Blake J), para. 44.

[276] *ex parte Hall,* para. 44.   [277] [1986] 1 WLR 1120 (Ch).   [278] ibid., 1125.

[279] Under section 13 of the Supply of Goods and Services Act 1982.

[280] The test is the reasonable care and skill of a competent professional. See Michael A. Jones and Anthony Dugdale (eds.), *Clerk & Lindsell on Torts* (23rd ed., London: Sweet and Maxwell, 2020), para. 9.18.

[281] Ruth Redmond-Cooper, 'Limitation of Actions in Art and Antiquity Claims: Part II' (2000) 5 *Art Antiquity & Law* 185, 187. Similarly, the DCMS Due Diligence Guidance might be of assistance in this regard. See also Janet Ulph and Ian Smith, *The Illicit Trade in Art and Antiquities: International Recovery and Criminal and Civil Liability* (Oxford: Hart, 2012), pp. 192–3.

3.7.6 Advice and Recommendations of Advisory Committees

A further nested practice of care exists in the form of the advice and recommendations provided by various advisory bodies to the Secretary of State. These committees and panels exist as advisory non-departmental public bodies (NDPBs) sponsored by the Department for Digital, Culture, Media and Sport[282] and exist as expert communities of care.[283] These include the Export Reviewing Committee and the Treasure Valuation Committee.[284] The Spoliation Advisory Panel, when originally established in 2000, also took the form of an advisory non-departmental public body. However, in 2010, following the budgetary cuts to the DCMS the Spoliation Advisory Panel ceased to be an advisory NDPB.[285] It now exists as a group of expert advisers, convened by the Secretary of State as and when necessary.[286] The advisory NDPBs advise the Secretary of State on aspects of their statutory obligations.[287] In the case of the Export Reviewing Committee, statutory guidance prescribes its powers. Whilst the committee gives advice and recommendations, the Secretary of State is the actual decision-maker, whose discretion when exercising this power 'must be exercised reasonably'.[288]

Other panels and committees of experts are convened by ACE (an executive NDPB) for specific purposes connected to its functions. Amongst these are the Acceptance in Lieu Panel, the Designation Panel and the Accreditation Committee; they draw on expertise relevant to the particular issues at hand.[289] Some professional organisations also convene committees relating to ethics and represent further practices of care.[290] Other advisory committees

---

[282] Non-departmental public bodies (NDPBs) have 'a role in the process of national government but are not part of a government department', which operate at arm's length and may have advisory functions: Cabinet Office, *Public Bodies Handbook Part 1: Classification of Public Bodies: Guidance for Departments* (27 April 2016), p. 13. These non-department public bodies are reviewed on a triennial basis, assessed against three tests relating to whether it is a technical function requiring external expertise, whether it can be 'delivered with absolute political impartiality' and whether it needs to be 'delivered independently of ministers to establish facts and/or figures with integrity': Cabinet Office, *Tailored Reviews: Guidance on Reviews of Public Bodies* (May 2019), p. 15.

[283] See Section 5.2.10.   [284] See ibid.

[285] See DCMS, *DCMS Public Bodies Directory 2010: Information and Statistics* (December 2010), p. 89.

[286] Spoliation Advisory Panel, Terms of Reference, para. 1: www.gov.uk/government/groups/spoliation-advisory-panel#terms-of-reference (last accessed 20 December 2022). It can also be convened by the Secretary of State as the 'Advisory Panel' for the purposes of section 3(1) of the Holocaust (Return of Cultural Objects) Act 2009: SAP ToR, paras. 2 and 4.

[287] Like other NDPBs such as ACE , these advisory NDPBs are subjected to periodic review: The triennial reviews of the Treasure Valuation Committee and the Export Reviewing Committee both took place in 2012. Even though the Spoliation Advisory Panel is differently convened, it too was subjected to an independent review in 2015: Sir Paul Jenkins KCB QC, *Independent Review of the Spoliation Advisory Panel* (March 2015).

[288] Arts Council, *UK Export Licensing of Cultural Goods*, para. 73.

[289] These various expert communities of care are considered at Section 5.2.10.

[290] MA, *Ethics Committee*: www.museumsassociation.org/campaigns/ethics/committee/ (last accessed 20 December 2022).

support the work of organisations such as Historic England[291] and the specific work of caring, for example for World Heritage Sites.[292]

The recommendations of all these bodies provide expert insights into how cultural heritage should be cared for and guide the official decision-makers in exercising their functions. However, the Spoliation Advisory Panel has a supplementary role in making recommendations to the parties to a dispute about important matters of title to cultural heritage objects. For that reason, the panel can be considered as a *quasi*-legal body.[293]

3.7.7 Institutional Level

Institutional legal frameworks providing support for how particular collections are maintained, including in some cases restrictions of or prevention of the dispersal of collections,[294] represent the next nested practice of care. The governing statutes of national museums provide the framework which allocates legal responsibilities, usually to a board of trustees and director, vesting in them the collections, and granting them specific powers for the care of the collections and places for which they have responsibility.[295] As Arms-Length NDPBs, the decisions made by the governing bodies of museums could be subject to judicial review and in theory could be subject to the provisions of the European Convention on Human Rights if they have a sufficiently public nature.[296]

Specific institutional policies provide an additional nested practice of care detailing precisely how a collection is cared for (through maintaining it, displaying it, lending it, as well as how claims for repatriation or return are

---

[291] E.g. the Historic England Advisory Committees which advises Historic England on 'those cases which are novel, contentious, of exceptional sensitivity or technical or academic complexity or which raise broader policy issues . . .': HEAC, *Terms of Reference* (April 2015), para. 1: https://historicengland.org.uk/content/docs/committees-panels/termsofreference-pdf/ (last accessed 20 December 2022).

[292] E.g. the City of Bath World Heritage Site Advisory Board: https://dev .bathworldheritage.org.uk/advisory-board (last accessed 20 December 2022).

[293] See Woodhead, 'Creative Equity'.   [294] See Section 7.3.2.

[295] E.g. British Museum Act (BMA) 1963, ss. 6(1) and 8(3); Imperial War Museum Act 1920, s. 4(2); National Maritime Museum Act 1934, s. 5(1); Museums and Galleries Act 1992, ss. 2(2) (a), 2(3)(a) and 2(4)(a); NHA 1983, ss. 2(1)(a), 10(1)(a), 18(2)(a) and 24(1)(d) and Museums and Galleries (Northern Ireland) Order 1998, SI. 1998 No. 261 (NI 2). ord. 4(1)(a).

[296] The High Court in *Fearn and others* v. *The Board of Trustees of the Tate Gallery* [2019] Ch 369 (Mann J), paras. 123–4 concluded that the board of trustees of the Tate Gallery was not a hybrid authority for the purposes of the Human Rights Act 1998 (this finding was not challenged in the Court of Appeal). Mann J adopted a 'multi-factorial' approach: see generally Alexander Williams, 'Public Authorities and the HRA 1998: Recent Trends' (2020) 25 *Judicial Review* 179. See also See *R (on the application of Hall)* v. *Leicestershire County Council* [2015] EWHC 2985 (Admin). Chamberlain explored the public nature of museums for the purposes of the HRA 1998 in the context of claims for the repatriation of human remains: Kevin Chamberlain, 'We Need to Lay Our Ancestors to Rest: Repatriation of Indigenous Human Remains and the Human Rights Act' (2005) 10 *Art Antiquity and Law* 325, 334.

handled[297]). These instruments may refine or restrict how their legal powers are exercised.[298] Where such institutions are public bodies[299] any policies committing them to acting in a particular way, such as undertakings to carry out consultations, could raise legitimate expectations that such policies will be followed; these decisions could ultimately be judicially reviewable where the policies are not followed.[300]

Particular objects may be subject to individual practices of care because of the terms of individual gifts or bequests by which they entered collections; these may restrict how they are cared for – often ensuring the long-term place of objects within particular collections. Caring then takes place through individual curatorial decisions about how they are maintained and displayed through quotidian care,[301] but also about how information about objects is entered on the collection's database and communicated to the public.[302] Terms may also prescribe how objects are cared for on a short-term basis when museums act as safe havens.[303]

3.7.8 Other Initiatives

The civil society and public participation initiatives considered in this book are those directly relevant to caring for cultural heritage, linking directly (or interweaving) with the legal framework of dealing with cultural heritage.[304] Some of these initiatives derive support from international organisations and act within a framework set by the state parties to international organisations such as UNESCO. These include the Memory of the World initiative comprising both national lists[305] and an international one.[306]

Other public participation initiatives can plug gaps left by the law. In England and Wales, the Portable Antiquities Scheme provides a voluntary reporting scheme for finds of archaeological objects that fall outside the statutory definition of treasure.[307] In Scotland, a public participation initiative which records intangible cultural heritage (in the absence of the UK government ratifying the 2003 Intangible Cultural Heritage Convention) shows Scotland's care of intangible cultural heritage. Although the UK has not ratified

---

[297] E.g. human remains policies, repatriation policies – such policies are considered in Chapter 9.
[298] E.g. British Museum loans policy and also its policy on deaccessioning in response to a recommendation of the Spoliation Advisory Panel: see Section 9.6.3.
[299] Either because the institution is a national museum (and thus a NDPB) or a local authority museum or a university.
[300] Legitimate expectation 'comes into play when there is a promise or a practice to do more than that which is required by statute': *R (on the application of Majed)* v. *Camden LBC and Adam Kaye* [2009] EWCA Civ 1029, para. 14 (Sullivan LJ).
[301] See Section 6.7.1.   [302] See ibid.   [303] See Section 7.5.4.4.
[304] As to which see Section 1.5.3.
[305] See: https://unesco.org.uk/portfolio/memory-of-the-world/ (last accessed 20 December 2022).
[306] See: https://en.unesco.org/programme/mow (last accessed 20 December 2022).
[307] Under the Treasure Act 1996. For a background to the scheme see: Roger Bland, 'The Treasure Act and Portable Antiquities Scheme: A Progress Report' (1999) 4 *Art Antiquity and Law* 191.

the 2003 UNESCO Intangible Cultural Heritage convention, in Scotland an informal list has been created to record the cultural heritage practices in Scotland.[308] This scheme, administered by Museums and Galleries Scotland (MGS), has an inclusive concept of cultural heritage which recognises the multiple communities present in Scotland. It therefore extends beyond Scottish intangible heritage to include all intangible heritage practised in Scotland. For that reason it adopts the terminology of 'ICH in Scotland' rather than 'Scottish ICH'.[309] It includes Mehndi[310] as well as the traditional Scottish practice of tossing the caber, foods such as cullen skink[311] and celebrations including Hogmanay.[312] UNESCO has approved MGS as a non-governmental organisation accredited to provide advisory services to the Intergovernmental Committee for the Safeguarding of Intangible Cultural Heritage.[313] Members of the public can contribute to this inventory by sharing details of the ICH activity.[314]

The most frequent use of public participation initiatives is to actively engage the public with cultural heritage. This can be engagement with the designation process, through applying for a place to be entered on the list of historic buildings,[315] but also extends to contributing to the richness of information about cultural heritage, for example by encouraging members of the public to contribute photographs and information about existing listed buildings.[316] Like the ICH initiative in Scotland, this provides an opportunity for communities beyond any relevant expert communities to contribute to the care of cultural heritage which they care about.

3.7.8.1 Accreditation Schemes and Standards

Schemes which recognise the adherence to appropriate standards of care provide a further level of practices of care. At the institutional level, these include the established scheme of accreditation for museums in the UK,

---

[308] ICH Scotland, *From First Footing to Faeries: An inventory of Scotland's Living Culture*: https://ichscotland.org/ (last accessed 20 December 2022).

[309] Historic Environment Scotland, *Intangible Cultural Heritage Policy Statement* (Edinburgh: Historic Environment Scotland, 2018), p. 5.

[310] https://ichscotland.org/wiki/mehndi-hindi-%E0%A4%AE%E0%A5%87%E0%A4%B9%E0%A4%81%E0%A4%A6%E0%A5%80-urdu-%D9%85%DB%81%D9%86%D8%AF%DB%8C (last accessed 20 December 2022).

[311] http://ichscotland.org/wiki/cullen-skink (last accessed 20 December 2022).

[312] http://ichscotland.org/wiki/hogmanay (last accessed 20 December 2022).

[313] The procedure for accreditation is found in UNESCO, *Operational Directives for the Implementation of the Convention for the Safeguarding of the Intangible Cultural Heritage* (adopted by the General Assembly 16–19 June 2008), para. 97. MGS was accredited in 2012: UNESCO, Intangible Cultural Heritage, *Non-Governmental Organizations Accredited to Provide Advisory Services to the Committee*: https://ich.unesco.org/en/accredited-ngos-00331?pg=00436&lg=en (last accessed 20 December 2022).

[314] https://ichscotland.org/categories (last accessed 20 December 2022).

[315] https://historicengland.org.uk/listing/apply-for-listing/ (last accessed 20 December 2022).

[316] https://historicengland.org.uk/listing/enrich-the-list/ (last accessed 20 December 2022).

administered by ACE[317] in partnership with the Welsh Government,[318] Museums Galleries Scotland[319] and the Northern Ireland Museums Council.[320] Established in 1988, originally as the Registration Scheme, it provides standards for museums to abide by. Outstanding collections recognised as pre-eminent and nationally significant can be designated under the Designation scheme.[321] Schemes of accreditation for recognised standards of professional competency exist, through fellowship programmes[322] or chartered status.[323] Additionally, adopting particular standards of care is encouraged through the British Standards designation (for conservation of cultural heritage)[324] and through the Collections Trust Spectrum standard (relating to museum collections).[325] In the context of archaeology, the Chartered Institute of Archaeologists has three grades of professional accreditation as well as institutional accreditation.[326] All of these schemes contribute to ensuring that the care for cultural heritage is appropriate care and provide a means of revisiting standards through regular review.[327]

3.8 Case Law Applying Non-heritage Principles as Nested Practices of Care

The binding nature of the law, specifically in the form of the application of non-heritage legal principles in case law, can provide challenges for translating the human dimension to cultural heritage and for constructing appropriate care for cultural heritage. Here the law needs to grapple with the nature of cultural heritage, whilst applying specific legal principles that have neither originated as 'cultural heritage law' nor been appropriated as such.

---

[317] ACE, *About Accreditation*: www.artscouncil.org.uk/accreditation-scheme/about-accreditation#section-1 (last accessed 20 December 2022).

[318] Welsh Government, *Museum Accreditation Scheme: Standard*: https://gov.wales/museum-accreditation-scheme-standard (last accessed 20 December 2022).

[319] Museums Galleries Scotland, *Accreditation and Recognition*: www.museumsgalleriesscotland.org.uk/accreditation-recognition/ (last accessed 19 August 2022).

[320] Northern Ireland Museums Council, *Accreditation*: https://nimc.co.uk/accreditation/ (last accessed 20 December 2022).

[321] See ACE, *Pearls and Wisdom: Arts Council England's Vision for the Designation Scheme for Collections of National Significance* (Manchester: ACE, 2014).

[322] E.g. the MA fellowship scheme: www.museumsassociation.org/careers/fellowship/ (last accessed 20 December 2022).

[323] E.g. the Chartered Institute of Archaeologists.

[324] These include: BS4971 – Exhibition and storage aspects of conservation [formerly PD5454]; EN 16893:2018 – Conservation of Cultural Heritage (specifications for location); PAS 197:2009 – Code of Practice for cultural collections management; BS EN 16790:2016 – Conservation of cultural heritage. Integrated pest management (IPM) for protection of cultural heritage.

[325] Collections Trust, *Spectrum 5.0*: https://collectionstrust.org.uk/spectrum/ (last accessed 20 December 2022).

[326] CIfA, *Professional Accreditation*: www.archaeologists.net/regulation/accreditation (last accessed 20 December 2022).

[327] See Section 2.5.6 regarding the need to revisit care periodically to ensure that it is appropriate.

On occasions, although a claim is dealing with cultural heritage its nature as cultural heritage may be more peripheral to the issue under consideration. Here, the outcome of the application of these general legal principles may not negatively impact on the cultural heritage itself and the overall allocation of the responsibility for its care. This might be because the technical point of law only affects how the object, place or practice is translated in legal terms; it may lead to a counterintuitive position of, for example, treating an Old Master painting as 'plant' and therefore a wasting asset.[328] However, that decision affects someone's tax liability and does not negatively affect how the cultural heritage is currently enjoyed. The judgment would not affect the public's access to the cultural heritage or any associative value that it might have to a particular place, to a person, or to other objects (as a collection).[329]

In some legal cases, the outcome of the application of non-heritage law principles may have a negative impact on the cultural heritage itself. In such cases, the importance of the cultural heritage in dispute, specifically its human dimension, may not feature amongst the formal legal principles relevant to determining the matter. Instead, the object's or place's status as property trumps the appropriate care of it *qua* cultural heritage. A range of different cases falling into this category are analysed in depth in the next chapter.

The judge's task is often made more difficult by not having the benefit of a previously drafted definition of cultural heritage (or a synonym) set out in a specialist legal instrument to apply to the case. Instead, the judge will have to construct cultural heritage within the framework of the relevant community and its mores. In this way, because any legal judgment by the court will be made at a particular time, in a particular context, there is arguably more scope for taking into account the dynamism[330] of cultural heritage than there is with statute law or international conventions. All of these varied cases, heard by the courts, demonstrate the clearest way in which cultural heritage is translated into legal terms. They thus not only show how the law plays a central role in caring about (and for) cultural heritage but also present a window on how the UK or the international community recognises its commitments to cultural heritage and cares for it.

At first sight, such case law does not appear to fit easily with the notion of nested practices of care; the legal principles applied by the court do not form part of any existing framework of care for cultural heritage and are most likely developed without earlier reference to cultural heritage (or with very little application to it). Nevertheless, how the court treats the subject matter and

---

[328] *Commissioners of HM Revenue & Customs* v. *Executors of Lord Howard of Henderskelfe* [2014] EWCA Civ 278; [2014] 1 WLR 3902. This related to Joshua Reynold's *Portrait of Omai* (now renamed *Portrait of Mai*).

[329] Although in the *Portrait of Mai* claim the painting was by the time of the 2014 judgment in private ownership, albeit occasionally lent to public collections.

[330] As to which see Lisanne Gibson and John Pendlebury, 'Introduction' in Lisanne Gibson and John Pendlebury (eds.), *Valuing Historic Environments* (Farnham: Ashgate, 2009), pp. 8–9.

translates notions of cultural heritage does provide care (even though the nature and the extent of the care may be minimal). As Tronto observes in the context of Narayan's work on care and colonialism, there may still be care even though it does not amount to what she describes as 'democratic care'.[331] Therefore, how courts translate cultural heritage and the care to be provided are still nested practices of care to be considered in this context. Criticism of the outcomes of these cases[332] may be more warranted than of cases which apply more formal cultural heritage frameworks developed in law and practice. It will become clear, though, that in some cases the strict legal principles relating to property, tax or administrative procedure may constrain any attempt to care for cultural heritage.

3.9 Instrumental Use of Law to Create Nested Practices of Care

The law provides a range of mechanisms that communities can use to assume responsibility for the caring for cultural heritage. These include legal devices providing for the creation and maintenance of charities. In all countries of the UK,[333] to establish a charity the organisation needs to meet one of the charitable purposes, there needs to be a public benefit to the charity[334] and it must be entered on the register of charities, unless it is an exempt charity or satisfies other exceptions.[335] The 'advancement of the arts, culture, heritage or science' is a prescribed charitable purpose, set out in legislation.[336] Relevant guidance[337] and case law support the interpretation of legislation relating to charities; once established as a charity, and subject to the jurisdiction of the Charity Commission, it receives certain tax benefits relating to VAT and gift aid.[338]

---

[331] Bernhard Weicht, '"As Long as Care is Attached to Gender, There is No Justice": An Interview with Joan C. Tronto' (2014) 17 *Tijdschift voor Genderstudies* 259, 263.

[332] Found in Chapter 4.

[333] Under the Charities Act 2011 – for England and Wales, Charities and Trustee Investment (Scotland) Act 2005 and Charities Act (Northern Ireland) 2008.

[334] Under Charities Act 2011, s. 4; Charities and Trustee Investment (Scotland) Act 2005, s. 7(1)(b) and Charities Act (Northern Ireland) 2008, s. 3.

[335] Under Charities Act 2011, s. 30(2). In Scotland charities must be entered on the Scottish Charity Register: Charities and Trustee Investment (Scotland) Act 2005, s. 3(1). In Scotland particular types of charities which may be relevant for different community groups to use: Development trusts (community organisations): www.dtascot.org.uk (last accessed 20 December 2022) and social enterprises: https://socialenterprise.scot/ (last accessed 20 December 2022). In Northern Ireland charities must be registered in the register of charities held by the Charity Commission for Northern Ireland: Charities Act (Northern Ireland) 2008, s. 16(2).

[336] Charities Act 2011, s. 3(1)(f); Charities and Trustee Investment (Scotland) Act 2005, s. 7(2)(g) and Charities Act (Northern Ireland) 2008, s. 2(2)(f).

[337] Charity Commission, *The Review of the Register of Charities: Museums and Art Galleries*, RR10 (August 2002): https://assets.publishing.service.gov.uk/government/uploads/system/uploads/attachment_data/file/358894/rr10text.pdf (last accessed 20 December 2022).

[338] HM Revenue & Customs, *Guidance – Chapter 3: Gift Aid* (updated 21 April 2022): www.gov.uk/government/publications/charities-detailed-guidance-notes/chapter-3-gift-aid (last accessed 20 December 2022).

Collections and museums may be considered as more usual examples of charities, but this legal device can also be used to care for intangible cultural heritage.[339]

Other types of legal bodies that can be created as instruments to care for cultural heritage are companies limited by guarantee,[340] community interest companies, charitable incorporated organisations,[341] Scottish charitable incorporated organisations[342] or community benefit societies in Scotland.[343]

Certain categories of voluntary or community bodies in England and Wales[344] are recognised in a process through which they nominate land to be entered on a local authority's list of local community assets.[345] The effect of entry on the list is that the community bodies are notified when there is a proposal to sell the land, giving them an opportunity to acquire the land for the community and care for it in the longer term. In Scotland, community-controlled bodies and community participation groups are recognised as groups that can participate in decisions[346] and can acquire land where it is at risk.[347] In Northern Ireland, there is no equivalent of the community nomination of public assets. However, there is a system of community asset transfers, which can result in the ownership or management of assets being transferred to community groups.[348]

3.9.1 Multiple Interactions with Law and Guidance

The various legal encounters of Joshua Reynolds' painting *Portrait of Mai*[349] serve to demonstrate the way in which law may translate something as cultural heritage, showing the fluid or dynamic interventions. The law may only have a transitory and temporary effect on the cultural heritage object without any lasting impact. This example shows how one cultural heritage object may intersect with law at different times, triggering a reconsideration of its nature against particular definitions. It is thereby transformed from personal property to a national treasure, to goods or even to a wasting asset.

---

[339] E.g. National Life Stories (part of the British Library) was established as a separate charity – www.bl.uk/projects/national-life-stories?_ga=2.259859917.632109661.1620922026-486435493.1602450562 (last accessed 20 December 2022).

[340] In England, Wales, Scotland and Northern Ireland. E.g. Stonehenge World Heritage Site Ltd, Company number 12591715, incorporated 7 May 2020.

[341] Under the Charities Act 2011, Part 11, chapter 1 relating to England and Wales.

[342] Under the Charities and Trustee Investment (Scotland) Act 2005, chapter 7. See also the Scottish Charitable Incorporated Organisations Regulations 2011 (SSI) 2011/44.

[343] Set out in Localism Act 2011, s. 89(2), as to which see Section 5.2.6.

[344] Defined in the Localism Act 2011, s. 89(1)(b).   [345] Localism Act 2011, ss. 87(1) and 87(2).

[346] Community Empowerment (Scotland) Act 2015, s. 139.   [347] See Section 5.2.6

[348] See Northern Ireland Department for Communities, *Community Asset Transfer: Guidance for Asset Owners* (14 November 2018).

[349] In 2023, the decision was taken by the National Portrait Gallery and the Getty Museum (who jointly acquired the painting) to rename it; its previous title had been *Portrait of Omai*.

Following its creation at the hands of Reynolds as property, the painting's early legal status changed into special property, as the subject matter of a bailment whilst it was on loan for an exhibition at the Royal Academy in 1776.[350] On Reynold's death, *Portrait of Mai* would have been classified as personal property (choses in possession) bequeathed under his will and then as 'goods' for the purposes of the subsequent studio sale at Greenwood's Rooms in Saville Row.[351] It was then owned for many years by Lord Howard of Henderskelfe; however, it was loaned to Castle House Estate Ltd and displayed in Castle Howard. This would have rendered it subject to the law of bailment and any contractual terms. Once more, when consigned to auction in 2001, the painting would have been temporarily defined as goods under the consignment arrangement and for the purposes of the Sale of Goods legislation when title was transferred to the purchaser at the auction.[352] The painting was the subject matter of litigation relating to the amount of tax payable on that sale and a successful argument was put forward that, rather counterintuitively, this painting by one of the Old Masters could be defined as 'plant'[353] and therefore a 'wasting asset' with a deemed predictable life of less than 50 years for the purposes of section 44(1)(c) of the Taxation of Chargeable Gains Act 1992. This recognised that for the preceding years it had legally been 'plant'.

Portrait of Mai's first brush with legal designation as 'heritage' properly so-called was following its sale when its new owner made an application for an export licence, as required under the export controls then in place, but in any event would fall within the current definition of an 'object of cultural interest' and the relevant financial and age thresholds.[354] The Export Reviewing Committee applied the criteria set out by the statutory guidance (the Waverley Criteria) to make its recommendation to the Secretary of State whether it was appropriate to grant or refuse an export licence or to defer the granting of an export licence on the grounds of the object's national importance. The Reviewing Committee found that the painting met all three Waverley Criteria; the Secretary of State accepted the Committee's

---

[350] Martin Postle and Mark Hallet, 'Catalogue' in Martin Postle (ed.), *Joshua Reynolds: The Creation of Celebrity* (London: Tate, 2005), p. 218.

[351] See Martin Postle, *Sir Joshua Reynolds: The Subject Pictures* (Cambridge: Cambridge University Press, 1995), p. 277. Postle commented how the *Portait of Mai* received the joint highest price at that sale of 100 guineas and said that the portrait had 'acquired *quasi*-mythological status) … [and] was certainly perceived more as public property than a private portrait': Postle, *Sir Joshua Reynolds: The Subject Pictures*, p. 278.

[352] Sale of Goods Act 1979, s. 57(2). It could be argued that the painting would remain 'goods' for as long as the purchaser would have had the ability to bring a claim for breach of any conditions or warranties under the sale, which would be six years from any breach of contract: Limitation Act 1980, s. 5.

[353] Since it had been on loan to the Company and fell within the definition of plant set out in *Yarmouth v. France* [1887] 19 QBD 647, 658.

[354] See The Export of Objects of Cultural Interest (Control) Order 2003, SI 2003/2759, art. 2.

recommendation and deferred the grant of an export licence to provide an opportunity for an institutional purchaser to 'save' it for the nation.[355]

Once the Secretary of State accepted the recommendation of the Export Reviewing Panel that *Portrait of Mai* had met the criteria for determining it to be of national importance and deferred the granting of an export licence, it was only at this point cultural heritage in a legal sense, specifically recognised as a national treasure. Whilst an offer to purchase was made by a UK institution, this was refused by the then owner; the application for the export licence was therefore refused at that time. Since that time *Portrait of Mai* has been temporarily exported to Italy for the touring exhibition *Joshua Reynolds: The Creation of Celebrity* in Italy and then returned to the UK to be included in the UK leg of the exhibition at Tate Britain. Whilst it was on loan to the latter its care would have been subject to policies, guidance and the MA Code of Ethics. The owner of the painting may also have benefited from an indemnity from the Secretary of State against loss or damage under the Government Indemnity Scheme.[356] In 2005 a further temporary export licence was granted to enable the owner to lend the work to the National Gallery of Ireland in Dublin for a period of over 6 years.[357] Following *Portrait of Mai*'s return to the UK a further application was made by the owner to temporarily export the painting to Ireland; however, this application was refused by the Secretary of State on the basis that the process for applying for export licences for long-term loans should not be used to circumvent the export licensing process.[358] A subsequent short-term loan to the Rijksmuseum for the *High Society* exhibition in 2018 was permitted following reassurances to ACE that the painting would be returned promptly after the exhibition.[359] It was reported that the fact that the loan was to another EU country with the legal safeguards that, at that time, were in place to ensure its return made it easier and it has been suggested that it would have been more difficult to acquire a licence were the loan to a non-EU country.[360]

For those years when it was not subject to an export licence process, it was arguably an inchoate national treasure, as the painting had been designated on several occasions so far as a national treasure and it is most likely that the Secretary of State would consider that it still met one or more of the Waverley Criteria and is likely to only grant an export licence subject to deferral period in the future. Barring a significant reattribution or some other consideration which fundamentally questioned its importance, it is likely that it would continue to be

---

[355] As to the rhetoric of 'saving for the nation', see Chapter 8.

[356] Under the NHA 1980, s. 16.

[357] Culture, Media and Sport Select Committee Sixth Report (2006–2007), *Caring for Our Collections*, HC 176-1, 25 June 2007, Written Evidence, Annex.

[358] DCMS, *News Story: Refusal of Further Temporary Export Licence for Joshua Reynolds' Omai* (2 July 2012): www.gov.uk/government/news/refusal-of-further-temporary-export-licence-for-joshua-reynolds-omai (last accessed 20 December 2022).

[359] Martin Bailey, 'British Government Gives 11th-Hour Permission for Joshua Reynolds' Omai to Leave UK', *The Art Newspaper*, 25 February 2018.

[360] ibid.

considered to be a national treasure. Indeed, in 2021 a further application was made to export it permanently from the UK. Again the Reviewing Committee found that it met all three Waverley Criteria and the Secretary of State accepted its recommendation to defer the granting of an export licence.[361] Following a series of deferral periods, the National Portrait Gallery and the Getty Museum in the United States announced in 2023 that they will jointly purchase *Portrait of Mai*.[362]

In brief, *Portrait of Mai* has not been labelled consistently as cultural heritage. Instrumental legal labels have been applied as it navigates the world of museums, the art market and its role as an asset. Its label as a national treasure has acted as a processual label (applied as it passes through the export licensing process) and an inchoate one at times. However, its status as a national treasure has impacted the owner's ability to treat it as unencumbered private property.

Given its unquestionable status as important cultural heritage, recognised by communities of care including museums, expert communities of care, and national communities, the legal interventions themselves do not give value to it, but rather shift the focus of who has responsibility for the care of it. However, it is also difficult to see how the law is the means by which *Portrait of Mai* was given value.[363] Instead, it can be acknowledged that a community (here the UK) cares about a cultural heritage object and wishes to care for it and its fluctuating legal status *qua* property or *qua* national treasure does not directly impact this. If anything, though, the lack of recognition more broadly as cultural heritage in legal terms and the absence of any right of pre-emption for cultural heritage objects or a requirement of public access means that its private property law status trumps any public 'interest' (in a non-law sense) and the owner can keep it out of the public view for much of the time.

Having considered the legal life of this object it is possible to see that the fragmented system of law and even the fragmented system of the cultural heritage law principles in the UK mean that this is far from a straightforward notion of designating something as official heritage because of the shifting nature of designation.

3.10 Conclusion

Given the, at times, uncomfortable relationship between law and cultural heritage, it is unsurprising that non-law principles have been used instead to care for cultural heritage. These practices of care, nested one in the other, all

---

[361] Reviewing Committee on the Export of Works of Art and Objects of Cultural Interest, note of case hearing on Wednesday, 9 June: *Portrait of Omai,* Sir Joshua Reynolds (Case 19, 2020–21) and DCMS Press release, *Reynolds' Portrait of Omai at Risk of Leaving UK* (11 March 2022): www.gov.uk/government/news/reynolds-portrait-of-omai-at-risk-of-leaving-uk (last accessed 24 May 2023).

[362] National Portrait Gallery, *The Portrait of Mai:* www.npg.org.uk/support/the-portrait-of-omai (last accessed 20 May 2023).

[363] See the discussion at Section 3.1 regarding the role of law in giving value, espoused by John Carman in *Valuing Ancient Things*.

actively contribute to the care of cultural heritage. The general law also provides tools for communities to assume responsibility for the care of cultural heritage, enabling the creation of civil society initiatives to care for cultural heritage.

Law is therefore central to the endeavour of caring for cultural heritage, but it is not an end in itself, nor should it interfere with the appropriate care of cultural heritage. Law is therefore supported by other instruments which supplement it when it falls short, and by civil society and public participation initiatives which step up to the mark to help communities, all of which contribute to care within the UK. The next two chapters turn to the specifics, by looking at the way in which the importance of cultural heritage is recognised, and how communities of care come together to assume responsibility for its care.

4

Translating How and Why Communities Care about Cultural Heritage

4.1 Introduction

A key way of assessing how far cultural heritage is cared about and how provision is made to care for it is to analyse how it is translated into legal and non-law instruments. This helps to construct a picture of the communities of care within the UK which are analysed in more detail in the next chapter. The terminology used to describe cultural heritage varies in the nested practices of care (both legal and non-law instruments). It includes: designated heritage assets,[1] undesignated heritage assets, World Heritage Sites, listed buildings, locally listed buildings, scheduled monuments, archaeological areas, conservation areas, in Northern Ireland state care monuments, pre-eminent objects, treasure, treasure trove, portable antiquities, cultural heritage, cultural property, cultural objects, objects of cultural interest, national treasures, protected wrecks, registered battlefields, registered parks and gardens, heirlooms, community assets and church treasures. All of these contribute to the varied tapestry of terminology used across the UK to describe cultural heritage.[2]

The various definitions which accompany these terms reflect, to differing degrees, the extent to which each instrument shows how communities care about cultural heritage and care for it. Furthermore, at times, law necessarily labels cultural heritage reactively, when the subject matter of the dispute is cultural heritage, but the court needs to apply non-heritage law principles. Thus, the court's approach to cultural heritage provides a particular window on how cultural heritage is translated.

---

[1] These include World Heritage Sites, listed buildings, scheduled monuments, archaeological areas, registered battlefields, registered parks and gardens and protected wrecks under the Protection of Wrecks Act 1973: Ministry of Housing, Communities and Local Government, NPPF, Glossary, p. 66.

[2] Individual practices or products therefore may have specific designation in legislation. For example, Harris Tweed is defined under section 8(1) of the Harris Tweed Act 1993 and the process and circumstances in which Scotch whisky must be manufactured are defined under the Scotch Whisky Regulations 2009, art. 3(1): discussed below, Section 7.4.3.1.

One of the key difficulties encountered in the field of cultural heritage law has been the issue of definition, both outwith and within the law.[3] Translation between different domains is always imperfect,[4] but the act of translation forces us to respect other languages or other people and, as Boyd White suggests, this serves as a model for all political and ethical thought.[5] This is particularly relevant in the context of contested cultural heritage where the differing viewpoints of members of communities, in particular those who have previously been excluded from the discourse on the appropriate treatment of cultural heritage, are considered and acted upon.

This chapter explores the extent to which communities care about cultural heritage and how language is used in definitions to emphasise the strength of that importance and to recognise the need for care. It starts by analysing the extent to which the strength of the importance of cultural heritage to communities is recognised within the definitions of cultural heritage and its synonyms, as used in various instruments designed to care for cultural heritage (within the cultural heritage frameworks identified in Chapter 3). It then proceeds to consider how the need to care for cultural heritage is addressed in case law, by analysing the courts' treatment of cultural heritage and how far they recognised the reasons why communities care about it. The final part of the chapter considers situations where importance is assumed, without the degree of that importance being defined.

4.2 Recognising the Extent to Which Communities Care about Cultural Heritage and the Strength of that Care

The next section focuses on how cultural heritage is translated in practice and how the reasons for which communities care about it are reflected in instruments. It covers those circumstances where cultural heritage is not at risk of immediate harm. Subsequent chapters will consider in more detail the efforts made to care for cultural heritage, by addressing the way in which quotidian care is provided in the UK, how communities navigate harm or loss and the role played by cultural heritage in the context of justice and memory.

---

[3] See for example, Janet Blake, 'On Defining the Cultural Heritage' (2000) 49 *International and Comparative Law Quarterly* 61, 63; Kathryn Last, 'The Resolution of Cultural Property Disputes: Some Issues of Definition' in *The International Bureau of the Permanent Court of Arbitration, The Resolution of Cultural Property Disputes: Papers Emanating from the Seventh PCA International Law Seminar, 23 May 2003* (Kluwer, 2004), p. 58 and Andrea Biondi, 'The Merchant, the Thief and the Citizen: The Circulation of Works of Art within the EU' (1997) 34 *Common Market Law Review* 1173, 1180.

[4] James Boyd White , 'Interview with James Boyd White' (2007) 105 *Michigan Law Review* 1403, 1414.

[5] James Boyd White , *Justice as Translation: An Essay in Cultural and Legal Criticism* (London: University of Chicago Press, 1990), p. xvii.

4.3 Strength of Importance and Interest

The language found in the individual definitions of designated cultural heritage in the UK (regardless of whether the definitions derive from international or domestic instruments) is primarily focused on the superlative and the monumental. However, at times one can see the statutory definitions expressing the monumental 'tamed' by accompanying practical guidance which takes into account more local, community factors to determine whether to designate something as a designated heritage asset. Furthermore, cultural heritage in non-law instruments may provide scope for recognising its dynamism and the link with communities. These various approaches form the subject matter of this section and the terminology used in these instruments includes value, significance, interest, importance and uniqueness.

4.3.1 Value

Value is a central means of assessing the ways in which communities care about cultural heritage and various types of value which make up the cultural heritage value of a particular object, place or practice have been identified. The sum total of these different types of value is said to represent the cultural heritage object's, place's or practice's significance.[6] Focusing on value, rather than significance, has the advantage of greater particularisation, because, as Mason suggests, the overall term of 'significance' can act as a 'black box' which risks 'collapsing all values to an aggregate statement of significance, the different types of heritage value are mystified or rendered secondary and are thus neglected'.[7] Some legal and non-law instruments use the broader terminology of significance, and these will be considered below; however, the terminology of value, which can focus on the components that comprise overall significance, can overcome the, at times, subjective assessment of significance.[8] Using the concept of value permits an opportunity to focus on the varying elements that make up the subject matter's value to different people and for different reasons.

---

[6] Lisanne Gibson and John Pendlebury (eds.), *Valuing Historic Environments* (Farnham: Ashgate, 2009), p. 7; Erica Avrami, Randall Mason and Marta de la Torre (eds.), *Values and Heritage Conservation: Research Report* (Los Angeles: The Getty Conservation Institute, 2000), p. 7; English Heritage, *Conservation Principles: Policies and Guidance* (2008 – reissued by Historic England), p. 61. These same principles are adopted by Cadw in Wales: https://cadw.gov.wales/advice-support/conservation-principles/conservation-principles (last accessed 20 December 2022).

[7] Randall Mason, 'Assessing Values in Conservation Planning: Methodological Issues and Choices' in Marta de la Torre (ed.), *Assessing the Values of Cultural Heritage: A Research Report* (Los Angeles: The Getty Conservation Institute, 2002), p. 8.

[8] See the various criticisms of significance, discussed at Section 4.3.2.

A traditional approach to preservation of cultural heritage has been to treat it as being imbued with some inherent value,[9] objectively ascertainable by professional experts,[10] which required it to be preserved because of the vital information stored within it.[11] This has now made way for the constructive approach to value[12] and an approach which shifts its focus away from 'observed qualities of fabric' to acknowledge the 'multiple, valid meanings of a particular place'.[13] This change of focus in practice shifts management from 'a bureaucratic typological exercise' to an 'intellectual exercise'[14] and places 'the emphasis on values and cultural significance as opposed to the traditional emphasis on fabric [which] is an important though subtle shift'.[15] If value is treated as wholly intrinsic then the effect would be to treat cultural heritage as static, and it would mean that those who care for it would be unable to respond to the changing importance of the cultural heritage over time to different people.[16]

At the highest, the standard set out in the World Heritage Convention uses the language of 'outstanding universal value'. This represents not only the strength of the value, as outstanding – something beyond the usual and which shines above all others – but also its breadth in that it is universal. This means that even though the cultural heritage place is located in the territory of one state party, its value is recognised beyond those borders, extending to all humanity. The World Heritage Committee's Operational Guidelines[17] give further guidance on the interpretation of outstanding universal value and particularise it as having a significance which 'is so exceptional as to transcend national boundaries and to be of common importance for the present and future generations of all humanity'.[18] Although this definition is not directly translated into UK law, it is nevertheless directly applicable in the UK for it represents the criteria according to which the places that have been entered on the World Heritage List have been assessed. Yet the representative nature of

---

[9]   David Throsby, 'Cultural Capital and Sustainability Concepts in the Economics of Cultural Heritage' in de la Torre, *Assessing the Values of Cultural Heritage*, p. 101.

[10]   Gibson and Pendlebury, *Valuing Historic Environments*, p. 1; Laurajane Smith, 'Deference and Humility: The Social Values of the Country House' in Lisanne Gibson and John Pendlebury (eds.), *Valuing Historic Environments* (Farnham: Ashgate, 2009), p. 35.

[11]   See the manifesto for SPAB: www.spab.org.uk/about-us/spab-manifesto (last accessed 20 December 2022).

[12]   Gibson and Pendlebury, *Valuing Historic Environments*, p. 1.

[13]   Randall Mason, 'Theoretical and Practice Arguments for Values-Centered Preservation' (2006) 3 CRM: *The Journal of Heritage Stewardship* 21, 31.

[14]   Jeffrey H. Altschul, 'Archaeological Heritage Values in Cross-Cultural Context' in George S. Smith, Phyllis Mauch Messenger and Hilary A. Soderland (eds.), *Heritage Values in Contemporary Society* (Walnut Creek: Left Coast Press, 2010), p. 83.

[15]   Mason, 'Theoretical and Practice Arguments', 34.

[16]   Joseph A. Tainter and G. John Lucas, 'Epistemology of the Significance Concept' (1983) 48 *American Antiquity* 707, 714–15.

[17]   World Heritage Committee, *Operational Guidelines for the Implementation of the World Heritage Convention*, UNESCO (10 July 2019), WHC.19/01.

[18]   ibid., para. 49.

the list[19] means that it is not necessarily the case that all places which would match these criteria have been assessed and designated in this manner. It is clearly a dynamic category, meaning that some places may not have met the criteria in the past, but when reassessed would then have been designated as being of outstanding universal value. Furthermore, it is clear that the World Heritage List is a 'select' one 'of the most outstanding of' places that are 'of great interest, importance or value … from an international viewpoint' and therefore there is no assumption that a place of 'national and/or regional importance will automatically be inscribed on the Word Heritage List'.[20] In determining whether a place should be designated as a World Heritage Site, the Committee then assesses a place against one or more criteria using terminology such as 'masterpiece', 'unique or at least exceptional … ', or 'outstanding'.[21]

The outstanding nature of value is relevant to the Secretary of State's exercise of their power to issue an exemption certificate for the sale of certain objects which are made of ivory.[22] The test set out in statute is whether an object is pre-1918 and 'is of outstandingly high artistic, cultural or historical value'.[23] As part of this determination the Secretary of State takes into account the 'rarity of the item', 'the extent to which the item is an important example of its type' and any other relevant matters specified in regulations.[24] In making this decision, the Secretary of State is advised by expert communities of care, in the form of the institutions which can be prescribed in regulations.[25]

Various typologies of value applicable to cultural heritage have been advanced in academia and in practice. In the context of cultural heritage places Historic England makes use of a typology which overlaps with the well-known typology of value set out in the Burra Charter, promulgated by ICOMOS Australia and with Mason's typology of values.[26] Historic England has adopted the terminology of: historical value (expressly said to cover associative values including associations with families, individuals, events or particular movements as well as developments in the arts[27]); aesthetic value; communal value (which includes social value[28] and incorporates the commemorative);[29] symbolic value;[30] and spiritual types of value[31] (set out by Mason and in the Burra Charter). The final category adopted by Historic England is that of

---

[19] As to which see ibid., para. 50. See also the DCMS, *World Heritage for the Nation Identifying, Protecting and Promoting Our World Heritage: A Consultation Paper* (2 December 2008).

[20] *WHC Operational Guidelines*, para. 52.   [21] ibid., para. 77.   [22] Ivory Act 2018, s. 2(2).

[23] ibid.   [24] ibid., s. 2(3).

[25] ibid., s. 2(5) and The Ivory Prohibitions (Exemptions) (Process and Procedure) Regulations 2022, sch.

[26] Mason, 'Assessing Values', p. 9 in which he separates the separates sociocultural values from economic ones; he identifies sociocultural values as including: cultural/symbolic value, historical value, spiritual/religious value, social value and aesthetic value.

[27] Historic England, *Conservation Principles*, p. 29.   [28] ibid., p. 32.   [29] ibid., p. 31.

[30] ibid., p. 32.   [31] ibid.

evidential value, which focuses on what those features can do (that is to say their functions) in terms of providing evidence about the past by saying how it considers 'the potential of a place to yield evidence about past human activity'.[32]

There are still occasional references to cultural heritage having an intrinsic value, sometimes without further explanation; for example, *Values and Vision: The Contribution of Culture*[33] gives 'The intrinsic value of culture' as the first of its 'Values and core principles'. This approach seems at odds with more inclusive conceptions of valuing which take account of wider types of value than purely aesthetic and historical ones.[34] In the DCMS document on Scheduled Monuments, the introduction still takes as its starting point the notion that ancient monuments have an intrinsic value, but says 'in addition' to this they 'can contribute to our perceptions of cultural identity and spirit of place, including the character of our landscapes and seascapes'.[35]

At the other end of the spectrum from the universal value of the WHC is the test of value to the local community used in the process of designating assets of community value under the Localism Act 2011. Under this process the local authority considers the actual current use of the building furthering 'the social wellbeing or social interests of the local community'[36] and whether such continued use is realistic.[37] Within this scheme the local value is translated into the local interest which is central to the definition.

4.3.2 Significance

Significance at the international level can be centred within the narrative of the common heritage, as seen in the International Guidelines for Crime Prevention and Criminal Justice Responses with Respect to Trafficking in Cultural Property and Other Related Offences in which it was recognised that 'the significance of cultural property as part of the common heritage of humankind and as a unique and important testimony of the culture and identity of peoples . . . '[38]

Shifting to the national level, the National Gallery is the only national museum in the UK with a statutory provision specifying that the cultural

---

[32] ibid., p. 28.

[33] Arts Council, NMDC, MLA, The Association of Independent Museums, The Group for Large Local Authority Museums, MA and the University Museums Group: www
.nationalmuseums.org.uk/media/documents/publications/values_and_vision_no_pics.pdf
(last accessed 20 December 2022).

[34] Such as those of Mason, 'Assessing Values', p. 10; David Throsby, 'The Value of Cultural Heritage: What Can Economics Tell Us?' in Kate Clark (ed.) *Capturing the Public Value of Heritage: The Proceedings of the London Conference* (London: English Heritage, 2006), p. 43 and see generally Cornelius Holtorf, 'Heritage Values in Contemporary Popular Culture' in Smith et al., *Heritage Values*, p. 43.

[35] DCMS, *Scheduled Monuments & Nationally Important But Non-scheduled Monuments* (London: DCMS, 2013), para. 2.

[36] Localism Act 2011, s. 88(1)(a).   [37] ibid., s. 88(1)(b).

[38] The Resolution adopted by the General Assembly on 18 December 2014 – 69/196, Preamble.

heritage objects that are acquired by its governing body should have a particular importance. In that instrument it is expressed in terms of 'maintaining a collection of works of art, primarily consisting of pictures, of established merit or significance . . . '[39] Nowhere is significance defined; in practice this would be a curatorial decision. The National Gallery's Acquisitions Policy (2012) does not refer to established merit or significance, but instead talks in terms of 'obtaining masterpieces of outstanding quality . . . developing the canon' and 'building on strength'. Later the criteria for acquisition are identified as considering (1) quality (2) narrative significance (3) association with the Gallery (4) condition (5) price and (6) provenance.[40]

Significance is a central concept in the policies relating to the historic environment in the National Planning Policy Framework (NPPF). Heritage assets should be 'conserved in a manner appropriate to their significance'[41] so that they might be 'enjoyed for their contribution to the quality of life of existing and future generations'[42] and the NPPF clearly considers there to be a scale from those of more 'local historic value' to the internally recognised World Heritage sites as being of 'the highest significance'.[43] Significance is defined in the NPPF's glossary but there is a significant mixing of terminology, for it is initially defined as 'The value of a heritage asset to this and future generations because of its heritage interest'. It then proceeds to explain that the interest 'may be archaeological, architectural, artistic or historic'. But what is clear is that significance can derive not only from the tangible (its 'physical presence') but also from the intangible dimension (its setting).[44]

Once an assessment of value has been undertaken, heritage professionals create a statement of significance detailing the reasons for its significance (based on the identified types of value).[45] Such a statement is required when 'a site on which development is proposed includes, or has the potential to include, heritage assets with archaeological interest . . . '[46] Although the terminology of significance is used by Historic England in its listing process (and has the potential to act as a black box as Mason suggests where the use of the term 'significance' masks the detail of the different types of value which make up significance[47]), the *Conservation Principles* published by Historic England

---

[39] Museums and Galleries Act 1992, s. 2(1).

[40] *The National Gallery's Acquisitions Policy* (November 2012): www.nationalgallery.org.uk/media/16208/acquisitions-policy_2012.pdf (last accessed 20 December 2022).

[41] NPPF (2021), para. 189.   [42] ibid.   [43] ibid.   [44] ibid., Glossary, pp. 71–2.

[45] Historic England, *Managing Significance in Decision-Taking in the Historic Environment: Historic Environment Good Practice Advice in Planning: 2* (27 March 2015), para. 11: https://historicengland.org.uk/images-books/publications/gpa2-managing-significance-in-decision-taking/ (last accessed 20 December 2022). Statements of cultural significance originated in *The Burra Charter: The Australia ICOMOS Charter for Places of Cultural Significance* (Australia ICOMOS 2013), art. 26.2 which in turn influenced the English Heritage (now Historic England) principles: Kate Clark, 'Values in Culture Resource Management' in Smith et al., *Heritage Values*, p. 91.

[46] NPPF 2021, para. 194.   [47] Mason, 'Assessing Values', p. 8. See Section 4.3.1.

set out the different types of value[48] and provide the overall significance of a heritage place as 'high-level principles', enabling significant places to be managed in such a way as to sustain their values.[49] For that reason, the types of value identified earlier may assist in the compilation of such a statement. It has been suggested that significance should be approached 'as a quality that we assign to a cultural resource based on the theoretical framework within which we happen to be thinking',[50] although this can 'vary between individuals and change over time'.[51] There is therefore a risk that significance can be subjective in nature.[52] However, this changing significance, or more specifically the different value components, is relevant as the composition of a cultural group changes over time and also the appreciation of the existing corpus of cultural heritage.

4.3.3 Interest

The exceptional nature of the interest of cultural heritage is evident in the Council of Europe's Granada Convention, which recognises the architectural heritage as 'an irreplaceable expression of the richness and diversity of Europe's cultural heritage' and includes monuments and groups of buildings of 'conspicuous' 'historical, archaeological, artistic, scientific, social or technical interest'.[53]

At the national level, interest forms part of the test for determining whether certain cultural heritage objects or collections or group of objects (when taken as a whole) are pre-eminent for their 'national, scientific, historic or artistic interest'.[54] This definition is used in the context of the conditional exemption scheme,[55] the acceptance in lieu scheme,[56] and the cultural gifts scheme.[57] Whilst this is statutory terminology, its practical application is supported by criteria adopted initially by the Museums Libraries and Archives Council (now used by Arts Council England).[58] This particularises the process by which pre-eminence is determined, but translates these national, scientific, historic or

---

[48] Discussed at Section 4.3.1.   [49] Historic England, *Conservation Principles*, principle 4.
[50] Tainter and Lucas, 'Epistemology of the Significance Concept', 714.   [51] ibid., 714–15.
[52] Frank G. Fechner, 'The Fundamental Aims of Cultural Property Law' (1998) 7 *International Journal of Cultural Property* 376, 380.
[53] Preamble and art. 1(1).
[54] Historic Buildings and Ancient Monuments Act 1953, s. 5(1)(a); Inheritance Tax Act (IHTA) 1984, ss. 31(1)(b) and (c) in respect of land and buildings (note the test of pre-eminence is used for objects).
[55] IHTA 1984, ss. 31(a) and 31(aa).   [56] ibid., ss. 230(4)(a) and (b).
[57] Finance Act 2012, sch. 14, para. 22(1). Under this scheme an individual or a company may make a qualifying gift of pre-eminent property and a proportion of the individual's liability for income tax or capital gains tax and the company's liability for corporation tax may be treated as satisfied: Finance Act 2012, sch. 14, paras. 3(1) and 13(1).
[58] Which is inspired by the Waverley Criteria used to identify national treasures (originating from Report of the Committee on the Export of Works of Art 1952 (chaired by Viscount Waverley)): see Section 8.1.2.

artistic interests into an 'especially close association with our history and national life', 'of especial artistic or art-historical interest' and of 'especial importance for the study of some particular form of art, learning or history'.[59] Thus, interest becomes association and also importance, demonstrating the interchangeable nature of these terms. When it comes to the acceptance of buildings under the conditional exemption scheme, the focus is on them as buildings 'for the preservation of which special steps should in the opinion of the Treasury be taken by reason of its outstanding historic or architectural interest'.[60] Here the importance of the building is recognised as relating directly to the need to preserve it.[61] The work of the National Trust focuses on interest, specifically preserving 'buildings of national interest or architectural historic or artistic interest . . . '[62] When it comes to objects owned by the National Trust, these are judged according to whether they have 'national or historic or artistic merit'.[63] The concept of pre-eminence is also deployed in the context of collections which have been designated by the Arts Council as being 'collections of outstanding resonance, that deepen our understanding of the world and what it means to be human'.[64]

The particular interest of buildings and conservation areas as being of 'special architectural or historic interest' is recognised in planning legislation across the nations of the UK.[65] What comprises elements of both architectural and historic interest is set out in the statutory criteria.[66] Special interest, though, does not provide sufficient nuance for the system of listed buildings. Therefore, the statutory guidance for England provides greater specificity detailing Grade I as relating to buildings of 'exceptional special interest', Grade II* as 'particularly important buildings of more than special interest' and Grade II as those of 'special interest'.[67] In Scotland the categories are buildings of 'special architectural or historical interest', which in the case of Category A is 'outstanding examples of a particular period, style or building type', Category B is 'major examples' and Category C is 'representative examples'.[68] In Northern Ireland Grade A are 'buildings of greatest

---

[59] HM Revenue & Customs, *Capital Taxation and the National Heritage* (2017), p. 122.

[60] IHTA 1984, s. 31(1)(c).   [61] ibid.

[62] The National Trust Act 1937, s. 3(c) and the National Trust for Scotland Order Confirmation Act 1938, ss. 3(a) and (b), which includes the promotion of 'the preservation of buildings of architectural or artist interest and places of historic or national interest' and the 'preservation of articles and objects of any description having artistic or antiquarian interest'.

[63] The National Trust Act 1937, s. 3(b).

[64] Arts Council England, *Designated Collections* (2019), p. 3.

[65] P(LBCA)A 1990, ss. 1(1) and 69(1); Planning (Listed Buildings and Conservation Areas) (Scotland) Act 1997, ss. 1(1) and 61(1) and Planning Act (Northern Ireland) 2011, ss. 80(1) and 104(1).

[66] DCMS, *Principles of Selection for Listed Buildings* (November 2018), para. 16.

[67] ibid., para. 7. These same grades are used in Wales: Welsh Government, *Understanding Listing in Wales* (Cardiff: Cadw, 2018), p. 5.

[68] Historic Environment Scotland, *Categories of Listing*: www.historicenvironment.scot/advice-and-support/listing-scheduling-and-designations/listed-buildings/what-is-listing/#categories-of-listing_tab (last accessed 20 December 2022).

importance to Northern Ireland', Grade B+ are 'high quality buildings ...
clearly above the general standard set by B1 buildings', Grade B1 are 'good
examples of a particular period or style' and Grade B2 are 'special buildings
which meet the test of the legislation'.[69]

'Interest' without the use of a superlative or other qualifier adjective is found
in several definitions in UK domestic law. One such definition includes objects
of 'historical, architectural or archaeological interest'[70] which are classed as
cultural objects protected by the regime of the Dealing in Cultural Objects
(Offences) Act 2003. The Preamble of the Ancient Monuments and
Archaeological Areas Act (AMAAA) 1979 also sets out that the Act relates to
matters of archaeological or historical interest, although the statutory test is one
of monuments that appear to be of 'national importance'.[71] According to the
DCMS's Principles of Selection for Scheduled Monuments, a monument's significance is derived from both its archaeological and historic interest, thus
linking the concepts of importance and interest together.[72]

In the provisions applicable to Wales in the AMAAA 1979, 'interest' is
specifically used to refer to the interests of particular individuals. In section
1AA, which relates to serving notice and inviting written representations from
appropriate persons (when a monument is to be removed from the schedule or
when amendments are made in relation to the monument[73]), an appropriate
person includes someone who has an interest in a particular monument or in
monuments of special historical archaeological interest more generally.[74]

4.3.4 Importance

Another measure of the connection between cultural heritage and its communities is 'importance'. This terminology is used quite extensively at the international level, with the 1954 Hague Convention recognising the 'great
importance' of cultural heritage 'for all peoples of the world'.[75] Article 1 of
the 1970 UNESCO Convention sets out cultural property as having been
specifically designated by Member States and as 'being of importance for
archaeology, pre-history, history, literature, art or science' and which belongs
to certain categories.[76]

---

[69] Department for Communities, *Criteria for the Scheduling of Historic Monuments and the
Listing of Buildings of Special Architectural or Historic Interest with Associated Procedures* (DfC
Historic Environment Division, 2019), pp. 16–17.

[70] Dealing in Cultural Objects (Offences) Act 2003, s. 2(1).   [71] AMAAA 1979, s. 1(3).

[72] DCMS, *Scheduled Monuments*, Annex 1 – Principles of Selection for Scheduled Monuments,
pp. 10–11.

[73] AMAAA 1979, ss. 1AA(1) and (2).   [74] ibid., s. 1AA(3)(d).

[75] 1954 Hague Convention, Preamble and art. 1 (which is adopted wholesale by the Cultural
Property (Armed Conflicts) Act 2017).

[76] Although neither the 2001 Underwater Cultural Heritage Convention nor the 2003 Intangible
Cultural Heritage Convention has been ratified by the UK both refer to the notion of importance
of cultural heritage.

At the national level, the Wedgwood collection of pots and papers was described in case law as 'part of our cultural heritage and of immense importance'.[77] This is dealing with 'importance' in much more abstract terms, referring to 'our cultural heritage', which might be assumed to refer to the national viewpoint, and there is no reference to its importance for what – whether it is culture, history or the nation.

As discussed above, whilst 'national importance' is the statutory test for whether a monument is entered on the schedule of monuments by the Secretary of State, nevertheless the focus shifts to the archaeological and historic interest, which is then translated into considering factors including period, rarity, documentation/find, group value, survival/condition, fragility/vulnerability, diversity and potential.[78] Historical, archaeological or artistic importance, regardless of any connection with the national interest, are relevant matters to take into consideration when protecting vessels in UK waters by means of designating the area of the site around it a restricted area.[79] Importance in the context of the Iraq (UN Sanctions) Order 2003 focuses on the detailed reasons why it is important – specifically Iraqi cultural property 'or any other item of archaeological, historical, cultural, rare scientific or religious importance'.[80] 'Illegally removed Syrian cultural property' has a comparable definition in the Syria (United Nations Sanctions) (Cultural Property) (EU Exit) Regulations 2020.[81]

4.3.5 Recognition of Uniqueness

One way of assessing the importance of cultural heritage is by focusing on its uniqueness, linked to which is the notion that because something is unique its loss would be sorely felt by those who care about it. Uniqueness is a relevant consideration when assessing universal value for the purposes of listing under the World Heritage Convention.[82] This can be seen in one of the very early listings – Stonehenge – which is recognised as unique not only because of its engineering ('featuring huge horizontal stone lintels capping the outer circle and the trilithons, locked together by carefully shaped joints') but also because of its unique use of two types of stone (Pembroke Bluestones and Wiltshire Sarsens).[83] The overall uniqueness of Stonehenge was identified in the early twentieth-century

---

[77] *Re Wedgwood Trust Ltd. (In Administration)* [2012] Pens LR 175 (Ch), para. 56.

[78] DCMS, *Scheduled Monuments*, Annex 1 – Principles of Selection for Scheduled Monuments, pp. 10–11.

[79] Protection of Wrecks Act 1973, s. 1(1).　　[80] Art. 8(4).　　[81] SI 2020 No. 1233, art. 5(1).

[82] Specifically under criterion (iii), which relates to places bearing 'a unique or at least exceptional testimony to a cultural tradition or to a civilization which is living or which has disappeared', but it can also be relevant to (i), which covers places which 'represent a masterpiece of human creative genius', which is the context in which Stonehenge is identified as having unique attributes. The criteria are set out in the *WHC Operational Guidelines*, 43 COM 11A, p. 25.

[83] World Heritage List, *Stonehenge, Avebury and Associated Sites*: https://whc.unesco.org/en/list/373/ (last accessed 20 December 2022).

case of *Attorney General* v. *Antrobus*[84] where Farwell J recognised the 'unique character and great archaeological interest of Stonehenge'.[85] Similarly, in *Re Wedgwood*, the Wedgwood collection was recognised as 'a unique collection of pottery and other artefacts and items of historical importance built up over many decades',[86] reflecting at least elements of its listing on the national UK Memory of the World Register.[87]

Uniqueness is relevant to the question of whether damages would be an inadequate remedy in the context of the instrumental use of the remedy of delivery up (for the tort of conversion), which can provide some incidental care for cultural heritage.[88] It is also recognised by the court as a factor when determining whether to give permission for the sale of heirlooms.[89] Thus in *Re Hope*,[90] even though the Hope diamond was no longer one of a kind in terms of it being the largest blue diamond in the world, at first instance its name, taken from the family who owned it, was recognised around the word and as Byrne J said: 'I cannot from that circumstance say on the evidence that the diamond itself does not stand out as a jewel unique from its size, from its circumstances connected with its history, and from its being a world-wide known diamond.'[91]

Speaking there in 1899 Byrne J drew an analogy with the Warwick vase both in terms of the object's uniqueness and connection with a particular family.[92] Eighty years later that same vase was assessed against the Waverley Criteria and, whilst the Expert Adviser recognised that there 'was no shortage in British collections of Roman marble vases and other decorative items, the Warwick Vase was by common consent the most splendid example'.[93] On that basis, the Reviewing Committee found it to meet both the first and third Waverley Criteria.[94]

The uniqueness of cultural heritage may also justify international intervention. When discussing customary law regarding the Bamiyan Buddha – specifically in a discussion about the scope of intervention – Roger O'Keefe asked how culturally significant something would need to be for States and the UN to intervene. In answering this, he highlighted the use of the words 'unique', 'irreplaceable' 'priceless historic value', 'vital importance' and among the world's great cultural treasures.[95]

---

[84] [1905] Ch 188.   [85] ibid., 199.   [86] *Re Wedgwood*, para. 2.

[87] United Kingdom National Commission for UNESCO, *Memory of the World*: https://unesco .org.uk/portfolio/memory-of-the-world/ (last accessed 20 December 2022).

[88] And the remedy of specific performance in response to a claim for breach of contract.

[89] See Section 5.2.6.3.   [90] [1899] 2 Ch 679.   [91] ibid., 687.   [92] ibid.

[93] Export of Works of Art 1978–79, Twenty-fifth Report of the Reviewing Committee Appointed by the Chancellor of the Exchequer in December, 1952, Cmnd. 8050, Item (xiii) *A Marble Roman Vase, 2nd Century AD*, p. 22.

[94] It was acquired by the Burrell Collection: http://collections.glasgowmuseums.com/mwebcgi/ mweb?request=record;id=40016;type=101 (last accessed 20 December 2022).

[95] Roger O'Keefe, 'World Cultural Heritage: Obligations to the International Community as a Whole?' (2004) 53 *International & Comparative Law Quarterly* 189, 206.

4.3.6 Value, Interest, Importance and Significance Nested within Each Other

In many cases the concept of interest sits nested within that of importance; the two concepts therefore appear to be interwoven, particularly in the domestic scheme relating to the care of cultural heritage. This can be seen in the context of the Agreement relating to RMS *Titanic* when it is described as being of 'exceptional international importance having a unique symbolic value'.[96]

4.3.7 Identity

A notable absence in the various definitions of cultural heritage (or its synonyms) in the UK is any reference to the importance of cultural heritage to the identity of communities. Given the centrality of identity to the recognition of how important cultural heritage is to communities it is noteworthy that this does not feature in any of the particular legal frameworks recognising and caring for cultural heritage.

4.4 Instrumental Nature of Cultural Heritage

The more modest nature of cultural heritage and its importance to current and future generations for a variety of reasons is evident in several international instruments. The first of these is the 1992 Council of Europe Valetta Convention, ratified by the UK, which defines archaeological heritage as 'essential to a knowledge of the history of mankind'[97] and as a 'source of collective memory' and 'an instrument for historical and scientific study'.[98]

The second instrument is the Venice Charter of 1964 produced by ICOMOS, which, as an instrument promulgated by an NGO, is not legally binding, but has had a significant impact on cultural heritage practice.[99] Although not a formal international legal instrument, it talks of historic monuments being '[i]mbued with a message from the past' and a recognition that 'People are becoming more conscious of the unity of human values and regard ancient monuments as a common heritage'.[100]

---

[96] *Agreement Concerning the Shipwrecked Vessel RMS Titanic*, London, 6 November 2003 (agreement entered into force on 18 November 2019) CP 205 (previously published as Miscellaneous Series No. 4 (2003) Cm 5798), art. 2(b). See Section 7.5.3 for an explanation of the nature of this.

[97] European Convention on the Protection of the Archaeological Heritage (Revised), Valetta, 16 January 1992, Preamble.

[98] ibid., art. 1(1).

[99] International Charter for the Conservation and Restoration of Monuments and Sites (the Venice Charter, 1964), which Lixinski observes has been treated by some scholars as being binding in nature: Lucas Lixinski, *International Heritage Law for Communities: Exclusion and Re-Imagination* (Oxford: Oxford University Press, 2019), p. 7.

[100] Venice Charter, Preamble.

4.5 Focusing on the Misfortune of Loss

A measure of the extent to which cultural heritage is cared about by communities is the misfortune that would be occasioned if it were lost. This is the gap that would be left by an object, place or practice were it to be irreparably damaged. It is evident in the context of property for personhood, for 'One may gauge the strength or significance of someone's relationship with an object by the kind of pain that would be occasioned by its loss'.[101] Loss can be felt by people even if they have never before seen or experienced a cultural heritage place, object or practice, as was evident in the international response to the potential loss of cultural heritage with the development of the Aswan Dam (reflected in the response of the Nubian Campaign) and the destruction of the Bamiyan Buddhas. Even though communities may care about cultural heritage, they may only care for it when it is at threat of loss. Often the cultural value of cultural heritage is only articulated by the public or by heritage professionals 'when the existence of places or practices are threatened or celebrated'[102] and 'Nothing arouses affection for a legacy as much as the threat of its loss'.[103]

There is a general theme of the image of the risk of loss of cultural heritage from the UK represented by the looming figure of the American collector. This stems from the time when country houses and their contents had to be sold off to satisfy death duties. Even when Shakespeare's birthplace was offered for sale, it was reported that there was a chance that it could be acquired by PT Barnum, an American circus showman, who planned to relocate it to the United States.[104] The way in which the trope of the American collector has influenced specifically the export licensing process and the rhetoric of 'saving for the nation' is explored further in Chapter 8. In practice though, the statutory criteria used to determine whether an object is a national treasure and whether efforts ought to be made to keep it within the UK include specifically whether 'the object's departure from the UK would be a misfortune'.[105]

In the context of heritage crimes, loss occasioned by damage to, or destruction of, cultural heritage is a relevant consideration within the context of sentencing of offenders. In the case of *R* v. *William Simon Jacques*[106] Moses

---

[101] Margaret Jane Radin, 'Property and Personhood' (1981) 34 *Stanford Law Review* 957, 959.

[102] Tracey Avery, 'Values Not Shared: The Street Art of Melbourne's City Laneways' in Gibson and Pendlebury, *Valuing Historic Environments*, p. 140.

[103] David Lowenthal, 'Patrons, Populists, Apologists: Crises in Museum Stewardship' in Gibson and Pendlebury, *Valuing Historic Environments*, p. 19.

[104] Melanie Hall, 'Plunder or Preservation? Negotiating an Anglo-American Heritage in the Later Nineteenth Century in the Old World and the New: Shakespeare's Birthplace, Niagara Falls, and Carlyle's House' in Astrid Swenson and Peter Mandler (eds.), *From Plunder to Preservation: Britain and the Heritage of Empire, c. 1800–1940* (Oxford: Oxford University Press, 2013), p. 249.

[105] DCMS, *Export Controls on Objects of Cultural Interest: Statutory Guidance on the Criteria to be Taken into Consideration When Making a Decision and Whether or Not to Grant an Export Licence* (March 2015), para. 11.

[106] [2010] EWCA Crim 3233.

LJ recognised that the individual books owned by the Royal Horticultural Society were 'not of the greatest value' but, 'as part of a collection adding to the sum of cultural wealth of the library, their value may on occasion be literally priceless since the library, once it loses those books, may never be able to replace them again'.[107] Heritage crime impact statements can also provide a means of setting out the specific loss that the damage or destruction has caused to communities.[108]

4.6 Measuring Importance with Reference to Financial Value

Several instruments use financial thresholds to set the parameters of whether something should be classified as cultural heritage or one of its synonyms. The UK has adopted financial thresholds for the granting of UK export licences. Rather than setting out financial amounts in statutory provisions, as discussed above, the Secretary of State has granted an Open General Export Licence (OGEL) for lower-value objects.[109] However, in the context of the ethics of making public the financial rather than cultural value of cultural heritage, the Museums Association (MA) Code and accompanying guidance explain that museums should avoid giving objects within their collections a financial value (save for the purposes of insurance valuation).[110]

4.7 Measuring Importance with Reference to Age: Should Cultural Heritage Stand the Test of Time?

As set out in Chapter 1, cultural heritage is not necessarily something from the distant past that needs to be passed on, but can be generated in the present, with it becoming apparent that it is something to be enjoyed, used and passed on to future generations.

There are, though, several established legal and non-law instruments in which age plays a role in determining whether or not something is identified as cultural heritage and therefore whether additional care is to be put in place because of its status as such.[111] The idea of something acquiring 'cultural significance' with the passage of time is evident in the 1964 non-binding ICOMOS Venice Charter, which states that 'not only ... great works of art but also ... more modest works of the past, which have acquired cultural significance with the passing of time'.[112]

---

[107] ibid., para. 1.   [108] See Section 7.7.   [109] See Section 8.1.1.
[110] MA, *Code of Ethics: Additional Guidance*, para. 3(a).
[111] Lixinski suggests in the context of international heritage law that 'the processes through which heritage is recognized and authorized by these instruments seem to create this one-way relationship with time, in which heritage is (re)created by the act of international safeguarding': Lixinski, *International Heritage Law for Communities*, p. 111.
[112] Venice Charter, art. 1.

It is clear when applying the statutory test to list a building that time is of relevance when determining whether it has 'special historic or architectural interest' with a presumption against listing where the building is less than 30 years old.[113] The justification that has been given for this is that 'they have yet to stand the test of time', although it is possible to list more modern buildings if there is a clear justification for departing from this general approach.[114] There is therefore an opportunity for more respectful and empathetic care of cultural heritage by responding to the changing nature over time of cultural heritage which is recognised as worthy of care. Contrastingly, a more fluid concept of time is found in the context of 'ancient monuments' for the purposes of the AMAAA 1979 where no specific age is given.

In the context of export licensing the Export of Objects of Cultural Interest (Control) Order 2003 states that the relevant objects of cultural interest are those 'manufactured or produced more than 50 years before the date of exportation' (except for certain objects of a philatelic nature, certain certificates relating to personal matters, letters written by the exporter or his/her spouse or certain personal property of them – or a widow/er).[115] The justification for a period of 50 years is that this is taken to be two generations.[116]

Age is a relevant factor under the statutory definition of treasure applicable in England, Wales and Northern Ireland, for in most cases an object or coin must be over 300 years old[117] to qualify as treasure (although objects which fall within the old definition of treasure trove also constitute treasure and are not subject to the age requirement).[118] Additional categories of objects have been introduced by statutory instrument. Firstly, objects 'of prehistoric date' are defined as 'dating from the Iron Age or any earlier period'.[119] Secondly, with effect from July 2023, metal objects can be classed as treasure, regardless of age, if they provide 'exceptional insight into an aspect of national or regional history, archaeology or culture' based on three prescribed bases relating to rarity, find location or connection with a particular person or an event.[120] There is no requirement relating to the age of the object in the Scots law principle of treasure trove.[121]

Although the UK has not ratified the 2001 UNESCO Underwater Cultural Heritage Convention, nevertheless its principles guide practice and therefore the date of 100 years set out in the law[122] is directly applicable to the UK, albeit in a non-binding manner.[123]

---

[113] DCMS, *Principles of Selection for Listed Buildings*, para. 19.   [114] ibid.

[115] Export of Objects of Cultural Interest (Control) Order 2003 (SI 2003 No. 2759), sch. 1, para. 1.

[116] *Waverley Report*, p. 35.   [117] Treasure Act 1996, s. 1(1)(a).

[118] See Treasure Act 1996, s. 1(1)(c) and DCMS.

[119] Treasure (Designation) Order 2002, art. 3(1)(a) and (b).

[120] ibid, arts. 3(1)(c) and 3(2), as amended by Treasure (Designation) (Amendment) Order 2023.

[121] See Treasure Trove in Scotland, *A Code of Practice* (July 2014, revised January 2016), p. 13.

[122] 2001 UNESCO UWCH, art. 1(1)(a).

[123] Although it can be incorporated into agreements between parties and thus have a binding nature: see Section 3.7.1.1.

Despite these approaches focusing on older cultural heritage, there are also instances where more recently created works have been recognised as forming part of a community's cultural heritage.[124] One English local planning authority seems to have adopted at least some of the arguments in favour of treating street art as cultural heritage. Cheltenham Borough Council upheld an application for retrospective listed building consent for the alteration of a listed building in the form of an addition of an artwork by Banksy entitled *Spy Booth* on a building which was already designated as a Grade II listed building.[125] However, by granting the consent for the work, this meant that the removal of the work would require listed building consent. Thus, parasitically the artwork had achieved listed building status since it was found to be a fixture[126] and in any event through the retrospective consent became part of the listing. This case demonstrates the evolving nature of the legal imaginings of cultural heritage over time.

Cultural heritage can be created in an impromptu manner, as seen with the development of the UK's National Covid Memorial Wall, evolving on the South Bank of the river Thames, and the desire to care for this for current and future generations.

4.8 Cultural Heritage Conceptualised in Case Law

In some legal cases judges will refer to cultural heritage by its legal label even if that is not directly relevant to the legal matter in dispute. This can be seen in situations where the status of a place as a designated heritage asset may not be directly at issue, but the judges still emphasise the nature of the site in legal terms. Therefore, throughout the judgment in *ex parte Hall*[127] the heritage place was referred to by its legal identity as a scheduled monument treated in practice as what has been referred to as 'official heritage'.[128] However, where the cultural heritage in question is not so designated in law, the judge adopts their own terminology to refer to the cultural heritage, at times emphasising its

---

[124] Holtorf suggests that 'even something as mundane as car wrecks' can now be heritage: Cornelius Holtorf, 'The Changing Contribution of Cultural Heritage to Society' (2011) 63 *Museum International* 8, 14.

[125] In the circumstances it was not the owner who was seeking retrospective listed building consent to regularise the situation. Instead, it was a third party who applied for listed building consent with the motive of protecting it as part of the listing. The owner of the building wanted to undertake remedial work on the building. Apparently, the artwork was destroyed as part of the remedial work which was undertaken: BBC News, *Lost Banksy Spy Booth Mural 'Not Saveable' Says Council* (22 November 2016).

[126] Another Bansky mural – 'Art Buff' – was considered as part of the building; when it was removed by the tenant, there was found to be an implied term that the removed artwork was owned by the landlord: *The Creative Foundation* v. *Dreamland Leisure Ltd. and others* [2016] Ch 253, 266 (Arnold J).

[127] *R (on the application of Hall)* v. *Leicestershire County Council* [2015] EWHC 2985 (Admin).

[128] See Harrison's approach to official and unofficial heritage in Rodney Harrison (ed.), *Understanding the Politics of Heritage* (Manchester: Open University and Manchester University Press, 2010).

nature or difference from everyday property and in some cases acknowledging the extent to which communities care about it.

4.8.1 Imprecise and Interchangeable Labels

There is no consistent approach to the terminology used by judges to describe cultural heritage in case law, although more recently there has been an increased reference to cultural heritage in legal cases applying non-heritage law principles.

At one end of the scale is the approach by judges which fails to engage with the fact that the objects or places at issue are cultural heritage. This can be seen in some early cases in which the judges sanitize cultural heritage within the judgment, focusing on the objects as property, by describing them as property[129] or 'articles in question', rather than treating them *qua* cultural heritage.[130] However, even by the 1980s in the Court of Appeal judgment in the oft-cited cultural heritage law case *Winkworth* v. *Christie Manson and Woods Ltd and another*[131] the judges made no reference at all to the subject matter of the claim. The Japanese netsuke were never described as such, but were referred to as 'certain works of art'[132] and then swiftly transformed into 'goods' when the judgment considered them for the purposes of the law relating to possession in England and specifically the action in detinue and conversion.[133] There was no consideration by the court of whether these were important as a collection or to their owner. They were merely treated as property and the technical rules of the conflicts of laws were applied to them.

In some instances, specific wording contained in a legal instrument such as a bequest which is indicative of the nature of the objects as cultural heritage needs to be interpreted by a court. In *Re Baroness Zouche*,[134] a case relating to a collection of books at Parham House, provision was made in the will for 'articles of virtu', which, as a term, was interpreted by the court as requiring artistic merit.[135] However, Lawrence J said that 'there may be articles which are very rare and which are of great interest to men of taste and education which could not be properly described as "articles of virtu"'.[136]

In some cases the court emphasises the importance of the cultural heritage objects through the terminology used. For example, in 1918, in *The King of Italy and the Italian Government* v. *Marquis Cosimo de Medici Tornaquinci, Marquis Averardo de Medici Tornaquinci, and Christie, Manson, and Woods*[137] manuscripts, letters, books and files from the Medici family were described as

---

[129] *Princess Paley Olga v. Weisz and others* [1929] 1 KB 718, 725 (Scrutton LJ).

[130] ibid., Sankey LJ used the terminology of 'the articles in question . . . originally her property' (at 725–6). Russell LJ talked of 'The articles, which are the subject of the action, are, to quote the statement of claim: "furniture, tapestries, pictures, carpets and other chattels of great value" (at 732).

[131] [1980] 1 Ch 496.   [132] ibid., 498.   [133] ibid., 499.   [134] [1919] 2 Ch 178.

[135] *Re Baroness Zouche* [1919] 2 Ch 178, 185.   [136] ibid.   [137] (1918) 34 TLR 623.

documents 'of historical and archaeological importance' of which 'Italy was very jealous about the exportation'.[138] Here the importance of the objects to the national community of care is recognised by the court.

Even sacred objects of significant importance to communities have been translated by the courts into artistic works. Thus, in *Attorney-General of New Zealand* v. *Ortiz and others*[139] the House of Lords dealt with preliminary issues involving the application of section 12(2) of New Zealand's Historic Articles Act 1962.[140] The subject matter of the case was certain wooden carvings known as the Motunui (or Taranaki) panels carved before 1820 by Te Ātiawa artists and hidden in a swamp.[141] They had been illegally exported and the New Zealand government claimed that the Crown was the owner of the panels due to the effect of forfeiture under the 1962 Act. The language used in the judgments, both at first instance, in the Court of Appeal, and in speeches by the Law Lords, demonstrate that these objects, which were cultural heritage objects of importance to a particular Maori community, were translated by the courts into artistic works.

Of particular note, though, is the focus by the court on these objects being of interest to collectors,[142] rather than focusing on the importance of them from the community from which they originated. To this end, the judges charted the various dealers' involvement with what was termed primitive art or tribal art,[143] at the expense of considering their importance to the community who deeply cared about them.

A contrasting approach was found in the judgment of Lord Denning MR who – as was his particular style – started by setting the scene. He focused on the cultural heritage object itself and its creation by saying: 'Years ago in New Zealand a great chief of the Maoris had a treasure house [he proceeded to describe the door, its composition and the way in which it was carved] ... This great door was lost for centuries in a swamp near Waitara in the province of Taranaki in North Island ...'[144] This approach was in the minority though, for although the value of the panels in cultural or historical terms was recognised,[145] it was primarily taken to be from the viewpoint of the dealer who 'realised at

---

[138] ibid., 623.   [139] [1984] AC 1.

[140] The House of Lords was sitting as the judicial committee of the House of Lords, rather than as the Privy Council hearing an appeal from New Zealand, because the panels were located in England; the court was therefore applying New Zealand law as a foreign law under conflicts of law rules. Counsel for the plaintiff pointed out in argument that technically the preliminary issue about the construction of the 1962 Act was one of fact rather than law; it would have been a question of law had the House of Lords been sitting as the Privy Council, but that it would be artificial to treat it as such: ibid., 35.

[141] Arapata Hakiwai, *The Motunui Panels: Returned to New Zealand* (9 July 2014): www .friendsoftepapa.org.nz/motunui-panels-returned-new-zealand/ (last accessed 20 December 2022).

[142] At first instance Staughton J focused on the notion of collecting abroad: [1982] QB 349, 352. In the Court of Appeal O'Connor LJ started by focusing on the consignment by Ortiz of the panels to the auction house: [1984] AC 1, 34.

[143] ibid., 41 (Lord Brightman) and [1984] AC 1, 13 (Lord Denning).   [144] ibid., 13.

[145] E.g. the focus on artistic value through the reference to cultural heritage in the first instance decision of Staughton J.

once that it was of much value. It was of the highest importance to the study of Maori art and civilisation and Polynesian sculpture.'[146]

Although one of the law lords recognised the panels as being 'a valuable Maori relic . . . ',[147] which might have given some indication of the importance to the original community, nevertheless, it was the loss to New Zealand, rather than to Maori, that was emphasised when he observed that: 'If the statement of claim is correct, New Zealand has been deprived of an article of value to its artistic heritage in consequence of an unlawful act committed by the second respondent.'[148] It is noteworthy that Lord Brightman emphasised the subjectivity of the artistic value and heritage of the panels by saying 'If the statement of claim is correct', suggesting that it was not necessarily a belief that was universally acknowledged.[149]

How the narrative of an object's history is presented can demonstrate how cultural heritage is cared *about* and cared *for*. Thus, a judge opening their judgment by setting out how a finder realised that he had found something financially valuable sets a different tone from a judgment starting by taking the reader back to the object's origin. Several cases demonstrate these different approaches.

In *Bumper*[150] Purchas LJ began his judgment by focusing on the discovery of the Siva Nataraja, specifically pointing to the finder's realisation that he had found something valuable.[151] The judge described the Nataraja in detail, setting out the design and its component parts. In contrast, when Eady J introduced the fragment of an Achaemenid limestone relief in *Iran* v. *Berend*,[152] by explaining that the 'chronology in [the] case begins, unusually in 531B.C.'[153] he thus focused on the object itself and its origins, rather than starting with its discovery as in *Bumper*.[154] This more sensitive treatment of cultural heritage, focusing at the outset on the cultural heritage itself, can also be seen in *Hoos* v. *Weber*,[155] where the judge began by talking about Rembrandt and his self-portraiture and then charted the ownership of the painting through history.[156]

There is no clear and consistent terminology that ensures that the nature of cultural heritage is taken into consideration when an object, place or practice comes before the court but where non-heritage principles are applicable, for judges use interchangeable terminology to refer to cultural heritage, even within the same case when dealing with the same subject matter. The case of

---

[146] *AG of New Zealand* v. *Ortiz*, 13 (Lord Denning MR).   [147] ibid., 41 (Lord Brightman)
[148] ibid.   [149] Cf. the approach in *Iran* v. *Barakat*, discussed overleaf.
[150] *Bumper Development Corp Ltd.* v. *Commissioner of Police of the Metropolis and others (Union of India and others, claimants)* [1991] 4 All ER 638 (CA).
[151] ibid., 640.   [152] *The Islamic Republic of Iran* v. *Denyse Berend* [2007] EWHC 132 (QB).
[153] ibid., para. 1.
[154] Although by the end of the first paragraph Eady J had explained how the relief had 'lay buried from the time the city was sacked by Alexander the Great in 331 B.C. until excavations in the early 1930s': ibid., para. 1.
[155] (1974) 232 EG 1379.   [156] ibid.

Government of the Islamic Republic of Iran v. *The Barakat Galleries Ltd*[157]concerned eighteen chlorite jars, bowls and cups, dating from 3000-2000BC and originating from the Jiroft region of Iran.[158] The case dealt with certain preliminary issues relating to Iran's title to these objects that were alleged by Iran to have been recently illegally excavated. Lord Phillips of Worth Matravers CJ in the Court of Appeal focused on the subject matter in general terms as 'cultural objects'. He then created a subset of cultural objects which he called 'antiquities' and proceeded to recognise the jars as being part of a nation's 'cultural heritage'.[159] By pointing out that the 'unlawful excavation and trafficking of antiquities has become very big business'[160] he recognised the financial value of the cultural heritage in question. Nevertheless, the overall tenor of the judgment was to imagine cultural heritage and the world in which it is placed as something for which states have moral obligations to respect and protect.[161] His Lordship then proceeded to consider the 1970 Convention in which the term 'cultural property' is used.[162] Despite this varied terminology, the court was still able to recognise the importance to Iran of the cultural heritage objects at issue and the concomitant responsibilities on the UK to recognise their moral obligations to uphold the international commitments it had made regarding recognising other states' cultural heritage. This had the overall effect of recognising the UK as being part of the international community[163] and that it had assumed certain responsibilities for the indirect care of the cultural heritage of other nations.

In *R* v. *Farhad Hakimzadeh*[164] a renowned scholar of books including maps and illustrations had stolen books from the British Library and the Bodleian Library.[165] Here the books were treated as a 'cultural and historical resource'.[166] The terminology of 'resource' seems to presuppose its status as property, or arguably as something exploitable, albeit the qualifying words of 'cultural and historical' would distinguish them from commercial resources.[167] Furthermore, Blake J went on to acknowledge that the books contributed to the nation's cultural heritage.[168] The Court of Appeal then shifted its judicial gaze to the books' rarity and specifically how their importance far exceeded the value of easily replaceable shop-bought novels (i.e. fungibles[169]), for Blake J, giving the judgment of the court, said: 'Cultural property cannot be valued in the same way as cash or readily replicable items, and the gravamen is the damage to rare items of historical, intellectual and cultural importance.'[170]

---

[157] [2009] QB 22 (CA).   [158] ibid., 30.   [159] ibid., (Lord Phillips of Worth Matravers CJ), 63.
[160] ibid., 29.   [161] ibid.   [162] ibid.   [163] Discussed further at Section 5.2.2.
[164] [2010] 1 Cr App R (S) 10 (CA).   [165] ibid.   [166] ibid., para. 8.
[167] ibid., para. 8. It has been argued that 'cultural resources' provides 'stronger associations with materiality, ownership and usefulness than the word "heritage" does': Marie Louise Stig Sørensen and John Carman, 'Heritage Studies: An Outline' in Marie Louise Stig Sørensen and John Carman (eds.), *Heritage Studies: Methods and Approaches* (London: Routledge, 2009), p. 12.
[168] *Hakimzadeh* [2010] 1 Cr App R (S) 10 (CA), para. 8.
[169] As to which see Radin, 'Property and Personhood', 960.   [170] *Hakimzadeh*, para. 13.

Although the terminology was interchangeable, the court nevertheless recognised its fundamental importance and recognised this in the sentencing of the defendant by drawing an analogy with cases of breach of trust.[171]

4.9 *De facto* Recognition as Cultural Heritage: Assumed Importance

Objects may be indirectly recognised as cultural heritage by virtue of their status as part of a museum collection, without any label of cultural heritage or a synonym being ascribed to them. Museums have been described as having 'come to serve the important role of transforming commodities into cultural property',[172] not acting as neutral keepers of things, but playing an active role in value creation.[173] The legal structures of museums may have been determined by the way in which the collection came into being and the particular structure may have been more by accident than pre-planned. The museum's legal status may derive from the way in which its objects were transferred, perhaps by way of gift or bequest on terms relating to the public benefit which make it a charitable trust.[174] On other occasions Parliament intervened to prescribe how the collection is held in legal terms and to impose restrictions on the power of the governing body to change the composition of the collection (by way of acquisition, disposal or temporary loans),[175] which is how national museums are governed.[176] The governing statute may also place on trustees the duty to care for objects.[177] Although an express legal act of care took place when the statute was enacted, the curator, by bringing an object into the collection (most usually by formally entering it in the accessions register[178]),

---

[171] As to which, see Section 7.7.

[172] Peter H. Welsh, 'The Power of Possessions: The Case Against Property' (1997) 21 *Museum Anthropology* 12, 15.

[173] Anthony Alan Shelton, 'In the Lair of the Monkey: Notes Towards a Post-modernist Museography' in Susan Pearce (ed.), *Objects of Knowledge* (London: The Athlone Press, 1990), p. 97. Lowenthal suggests that museums 'epitomize what we value' and that curators 'regard accession as an eternal act': Lowenthal, 'Patrons, Populists, Apologists', pp. 19, 25, 26.

[174] See for example *In Re Spence* [1938] Ch 96, which dealt with the collections of arms and antiques given to the corporation of Stockton-on-Tees by Gilbert Ormerod Spence: https://prestonparkmuseum.co.uk/highlights/military/ (last accessed 20 December 2022) and *Re Holburne, Coates v. Mackillop* [1885] 53 LT 212, which forms the basis of the collection at the Holburne Museum, Bath: www.holburne.org/the-collection/history-of-the-collection/ (last accessed 20 December 2022). Although the son of General Pitt Rivers had indicated to his father that on inheritance of the estate he would continue to allow public access to the museum that was in a house adjoining the Rushmore estate (although General Pitt Rivers had never wanted to go as far as giving any rights to the public which would be enforceable against him, (p. 409)), no charitable trust of the museum was created: *In re Pitt Rivers, Scott v. Pitt Rivers* [1902] 1 Ch 403 (CA), 410.

[175] E.g. British Museum Act 1963; Museums and Galleries Act 1992; National Heritage Act 1983 and Imperial War Museum Act 1920.

[176] As to national museums, see Section 7.3.2.

[177] This can include using the language of care and preservation – see Section 6.4.1.

[178] See Collections Trust, *Spectrum: The UK Museum Collections Management Standard, Spectrum 5.0* (London: Collections Trust, 2017), p. 30.

translates that object into a cultural heritage object and performs a practice of care, transforming it into part of a national collection. As part of this transformation most objects (with only very few exceptions) become *de facto* inalienable objects which are to be kept for future generations.[179] Although the statutes use neither the label of cultural heritage nor a synonym and have no specific definitions about required attributes of an object, the object's status as part of that collection impacts on the way in which it is cared for.[180] As mentioned above in the context of 'significance', the National Gallery is the only national museum for which the importance of the objects acquired is mentioned. There is a passive (or indirect) legal designation and translation which happens, although unaccompanied by any formalised process of applying certain criteria.[181] The law is playing a secondary role here – not in designating something as cultural heritage, but in recognising its importance through restricting the circumstances in which it can leave the collection. The restrictions on how objects in collections are cared for are akin to the way in which heritage places (using the terminology of designated heritage assets) are cared for. Therefore, it is appropriate to draw an analogy with designated heritage assets and treat them as being indirectly designated as cultural heritage.

The act of accession into a museum collection can affect both the legal and ethical status of the object. Legal restrictions on powers of transfer are placed on the governing bodies of most national museums by their governing statutes and where non-national collections are charities there are restrictions on the trustees' powers of disposal of charity property.[182] However, in the case of non-national museums, which have a variety of different legal structures, the restrictions on the ability to transfer from their collections may only be ethical in nature. This could be put in place by the status of the collection either as a designated or an accredited collection under the Arts Council schemes or where the museum is an institutional member of the MA. Thus, financially motivated sales are discouraged,[183] yet curatorially motivated sales may be possible[184] without ethical sanction. More recently in *ex parte Hall*, there was judicial recognition of the deleterious effect of transferring objects from museum collections in the judgment of Blake J where he warned that the 'irreversible decision to "de-accession"' objects from a museum collection 'by open market sale . . . may mean that such a public authority forfeits all trust in

---

[179] *Treasures in Trust: A Review of Museum Policy* (Department of National Heritage, 1996).

[180] E.g. as a charity.

[181] Only in a limited number of provisions governing national museums are the types of object which can be added to the collection by the trustees proscribed by the statute. In the case of other national collections there are no such restrictions; consequently, it is for the curators and the trustees as expert to determine what is admitted to the collection: see Museums and Galleries Act 1992, s. 2.

[182] Thus, charity law is used instrumentally to care for cultural heritage: see Section 7.3.2.

[183] See generally, Section 6.6.1.   [184] As to which see Section 7.3.2.2.

the future as a guardian of [cultural] assets',[185] although this did not translate in the case into any activity of direct care which could prevent the loss.

There are two situations where cultural objects are labelled as such, but where the importance to communities is assumed. The first is in the context of the claims process before the Spoliation Advisory Panel. This involves 'cultural objects' whose owners lost possession of them during the Nazi era and where those objects are now in a national collection, or other collection established for the public benefit. The term 'cultural objects' has been defined in neither the Panel's Terms of Reference nor its recommendations. The Panel has dealt with a variety of different objects but has never questioned whether or not an object qualifies as a cultural object. So far these have been uncontentious in that they have been paintings, drawings, tapestries, porcelain and the like, which are unlikely to be disputed as being cultural objects. It is clear, though, that if there were a doubt about this the Panel has the power to 'make such factual or legal inquiries (including the seeking of advice about ... cultural objects and about valuation of such objects) as the Panel consider appropriate to assess the claim as comprehensively as possible'.[186]

Similarly, the term 'cultural object' is used in the title of Part 6 of the Tribunals, Courts and Enforcement Act 2007, although again is not defined, and does not feature in the substantive sections of the Act.[187] The provisions deal with 'protected objects' which are immune from seizure or forfeiture in limited situations[188] whilst on temporary loan for the purposes of public display.

In both sets of circumstances, whilst the terminology is not defined anywhere, and the term 'cultural objects' is applied immediately to those objects, their status as such is uncontentious. There is no need to assess any of their characteristics to determine whether they are cultural objects. Common to both situations is that there has already been indirect designation of the objects as cultural objects by the curators, for they are either already part of the museum collection or are being borrowed by a museum for a public exhibition. Consequently, the label is of secondary importance within the process, being applied to the object simply to show that it comes within the bailiwick of a particular process. When it comes to the Spoliation Advisory Panel, the process is aimed at determining whether the cultural object has a problematic Nazi-era provenance, in which case the Panel may conclude that there is sufficient moral strength to the claim to warrant transfer of the object itself from the public to the private domain or another remedy.[189] In the case of the

---

[185] *The Queen (on the application of Hall)* v. *Leicestershire County Council* [2015] EWHC 2985 (Admin), para. 46 (Blake J).

[186] SAP Terms of Reference, para. 15(a).

[187] Similarly, The Protection of Cultural Objects on Loan (Publication and Provision of Information) Regulations 2008, SI 2008 No. 1159 makes no reference in the substantive provisions to 'cultural object'.

[188] Defined in Tribunals, Courts and Enforcement Act 2007, s. 135.

[189] Such as an *ex gratia* payment or the display of a commemorative label next to the retained object.

process under Part 6 of the Tribunals, Courts and Enforcement Act 2007 an object would be a 'cultural object' and a 'protected object' under the Act because a museum or gallery deems it appropriate to borrow it from an overseas owner which they will then publicly display at the museum or gallery. It then receives protection of immunity from seizure in certain circumstances.[190]

4.10 Conclusion

Whilst fragmented in approach, the labelling of something as cultural heritage or a synonym can represent an activity of care, bringing that object, place or practice within a framework of care. When courts have to deal with cultural heritage as the subject of a dispute, it can be difficult to translate this concept into law in the absence of a particular legal label of cultural heritage (or a synonym) to apply to the facts. Where labels are deployed by the judges, these can be used imprecisely and interchangeably within case law and non-cultural heritage law principles can intervene to trump a desire to provide appropriate care of cultural heritage.

What is clear, though, is that the strength of the importance of why communities care about cultural heritage can be recognised in the definitions of cultural heritage. Many of these descriptors have focused on value, interest and significance, specifically recognising how cultural heritage is important but not linking this directly with a community's identity. Nevertheless, whilst not consistent, definitions which cover cultural heritage from the pre-eminent to the vernacular have the scope to express within them many of the very strong connections between the cultural heritage and the communities for whom it is important. It is to those communities that the analysis now turns.

---

[190] As specified under Tribunals, Courts and Enforcement Act 2007, s. 135(1).

5

Creating Communities of Care
Assuming Responsibilities

5.1 Introduction

Communities are central to caring about and caring for cultural heritage, and having considered the instruments by which care is recognised in the UK, it now falls to consider in more detail the nature of the communities who come together to care for cultural heritage.

According to article 27 of the Universal Declaration on Human Rights 1948, 'Everyone has the right freely to participate in the cultural life of the community ... ' Both participation and communities form central elements of this right, leading to initial questions about who comprises a community and about what form participation in cultural life takes.[1] Communities can be international, national, regional and local. They can be formal or informal – being created by legal instruments or on an *ad hoc* basis.

The terminology of communities has a troubled history. It has been criticised in the context of New Labour's approach to communities,[2] as well as because of its 'colonial load',[3] and can be 'politically charged'.[4] If not used carefully,[5] the term 'community' has the potential to set apart a particular group and treat that group as 'them' rather than 'us'.[6] However, in this book

---

[1] The contribution of communities to the designation of intangible cultural heritage is recognised in the 2003 UNESCO ICH Convention, although the UK has not ratified this. 'Participation refers to a process in which two or more parties influence each other in making certain plans, policies, and decisions. It is restricted to decisions that have future effects on all those making the decisions and on those represented by them': John R. P. French Jr., Joachim Israel and Dagfinn Ås, 'An Experiment on Participation in a Norwegian Factory: Interpersonal Dimensions of Decision-Making' (1960) 13 *Human Relations* 3.

[2] Emma Waterton and Laurajane Smith, 'The Recognition and Misrecognition of Community Heritage' (2010) 16 *International Journal of Heritage Studies* 4, 6.

[3] Lucas Lixinski, *International Heritage Law for Communities: Exclusion and Re-Imagination* (Oxford: Oxford University Press, 2019), p. 23.

[4] Elizabeth Crooke, 'The Politics of Community Heritage: Motivations, Authority and Control' (2010) 16 *International Journal of Heritage Studies* 16.

[5] Specifically, 'critically and cautiously': Rhiannon Mason, 'Museums, Galleries and Heritage: Sites of Meaning-Making and Communication' in Gerard Corsane (ed.), *Heritage, Museums and Galleries: An Introductory Reader* (London: Routledge, 2005), p. 299.

[6] See Laurajane Smith and Emma Waterton, *Heritage, Communities and Archaeology* (London: Bloomsbury, 2009), pp. 23–4.

'communities' refers to groups of people occupying different spaces relating to the care of cultural heritage. Therefore, the term is not restricted to Indigenous communities or to local communities living around or with heritage[7] or to those who 'create and attribute value to heritage by virtue of heritage's importance to their identity'.[8] Instead, the terminology of communities of care arises in a variety of different situations. There are overlaps between the approach taken here and the concept of heritage communities in the Council of Europe's Faro Convention.[9] This treats such communities as 'people who value specific aspects of cultural heritage which they wish, within the framework of public action, to sustain and transmit to future generations'.[10] It is clear that both communities with a geographical link to cultural heritage as well as those with a common interest, such as archaeology, would fall within that definition.[11] Similarly, communities of care have been recognised recently to extend to those 'enthusiast groups' as well as amateurs.[12] However, the approach in this book goes further.[13] It includes the international community, both in terms of the collections of states and as recognised in institutions such as the UN, UNESCO, the Council of Europe and the European Union and through their law making roles. National law makers, including Parliament, the law making bodies of England, Scotland, Wales and Northern Ireland separately, the Ministers exercising powers to create delegated legislation, and the courts, are all also included as communities caring for cultural heritage. Here they are acting in a representative capacity, on behalf of the UK as a whole, or on behalf of one or more of the nations of the UK. In this regard they may be indirectly caring for the cultural heritage, facilitating or regulating the powers of those who provide direct care for it, as well as representing communities who care about cultural heritage. Assisting in this care are communities of experts who provide advice and recommendations for decision-makers.

Individual groups of people come together to form communities of care, because they care about a locality,[14] a particular style of cultural heritage, or a particular cultural heritage place, object or practice. In turn, they may wish to care for them. Such communities may have been established in a precautionary manner because they generally care about a style and want to prevent future potential harm, or in a reactionary manner in response to a perceived threat of harm to the cultural heritage. Here they have

---

[7] This is the approach taken by Lixinski, *International Heritage Law for Communities*, p. 23.

[8] ibid.

[9] Council of Europe Framework Convention on the Value of Cultural Heritage for Society CETS 199, 27 October 2005 (although this has not been ratified by the UK).

[10] ibid., art. 2(b).   [11] ibid.

[12] Anna Woodham, Rhianedd Smith and Alison Hess, 'Introduction' in Anna Woodham, Rhianedd Smith and Alison Hess (eds.), *Exploring Emotion, Care, and Enthusiasm in 'Unloved' Collections* (Leeds: Arc Humanities Press, 2020), p. 11.

[13] C.f. Explanatory Report to the Council of Europe Framework Convention on the Value of Cultural Heritage for Society, p. 6.

[14] Such as civic groups.

self-identified as a community by constructing themselves as a legal entity or simply as an unincorporated association.[15] The community may exist only temporarily, purely for the purposes of instigating proceedings for judicial review to challenge a decision that has been made about the care of cultural heritage. Contrastingly, they may be longstanding communities, some of whom may be formally recognised as consultees within a legal process (e.g. amenity societies) or who may be legally incorporated bodies.[16] However, the way in which courts approach these cases shows how communities are recognised. Boyd White suggests that 'law should take as its most central question what kind of community we should be, with what values, motives and aims'.[17] Where the courts apply non-heritage law principles, it is a prime opportunity to analyse the community that they create and how they care for cultural heritage.

Communities are, by their nature, constructed and it is important to engage with them as 'social relationships in all their messiness'.[18] Identifying a group of people as a community is not seeking to prioritise them over others. The approach taken here does not homogenise the community, for it is important to recognise that even within a community, with members sharing a common interest, views differ and there may be internal dissonance. Furthermore, one should recall that communities, like culture and identity, are dynamic concepts.[19] It will, however, be possible to see how these communities become communities of care through the manifestations created by them, such as legal instruments, instruments of professional practice or guidance for the community's members. This analysis will also reveal how they engage with, use and care for cultural heritage. Communities of care may come about as a result of groups forming, to call upon the public to help fund the purchase of places or objects. A community of interested parties spearheaded the campaign to purchase Shakespeare's Birthplace and a community of interest established a trust with the aim of relocating Temple Bar to the City of London.[20]

Although communities are considered here from the point of view of how cultural heritage is cared for in the UK, the communities for whom cultural heritage is important will not necessarily be located in the UK. Therefore, in addition to recognising the international community and the community of

---

[15] In the case of community interest companies for the purposes of the 'community interest test' under The Community Interest Company Regulations 2005, 'any group of individuals may constitute a section of the community if – (a) they share a readily identifiable characteristic; and (b) other members of the community of which that group forms do not share that characteristic': reg. 5.

[16] Some of which received Royal Charters, e.g. Arts Council England.

[17] James Boyd White , 'Law as Rhetoric, Rhetoric as Law: The Arts and Cultural and Communal Life' (1985) 52 *The University of Chicago Law Review* 684, 698.

[18] Waterton and Smith, 'Recognition and Misrecognition', 5.

[19] Peter Davis, 'Place Exploration: Museums, Identity, Community' in Sheila Watson (ed.), *Museums and their Communities* (London: Routledge, 2007), p. 70.

[20] See Section 7.8.4.

other nations, it is also important to recognise the communities within those other nations and the resultant plurality of communities across the globe. Cultural heritage which is cared about by communities abroad may be in the UK for historical reasons, or because of more recent illegal removal. For that reason, such communities, as communities of care, and the claims that they make for cultural heritage located in the UK, will also be considered.[21]

As recognised in the 2017 Heritage Statement, 'England's heritage sector is broad and multifaceted' ranging from 'large national public bodies and charities to numerous local organisations, charities and voluntary organisations, small- and medium-sized business and many thousands of private owners, volunteers, academics and campaigners. Together they protect and care for, manage and research' cultural heritage.[22] The same sentiment applies in respect of Wales, Scotland and Northern Ireland and it is these plural communities which form the focus of this chapter, not only in respect of cultural places but also objects and practices.

This chapter is structured around communities of care, focusing on the relational nature of care by considering how communities are imagined and how they care about cultural heritage. In some instances these communities also assume responsibility for caring for cultural heritage. As part of this analysis it will be considered to whom these responsibilities are owed and what opportunities exist for engagement in the decision-making about that care.

Whilst in some cases responsibility for the care of cultural heritage may be assigned by the international community or the state to other communities, there can still be gaps in the coverage of the care provided. In such cases communities may actively assume responsibility for care. This leads to questions about the source of the authority of such communities to assume such responsibility and about the efforts taken to review this to determine whether the particular care provided is appropriate in the circumstances.

5.2 Care, Communities and Responsibilities

Communities can self-identify as such without using any formal structure. They may have evolved over time. Other communities may form in an informal manner by gathering together in a particular set of circumstances without the need to satisfy any formalities in their creation. Communities can be formally created and mandated with the care of cultural heritage instrumentally using the law to give them structure, powers and responsibilities. Some individuals can be considered to be part of a common community, even though they have not formed together in a conscious manner, and may indeed

---

[21] In Chapter 9 the terminology of challenges to the *status quo* rather than 'claims' is preferred and justified.

[22] DCMS, *Heritage Statement 2017*, p. 6.

not know the other members of that community. However, they share common characteristics as owners of particular categories of cultural heritage with
shared interests.

5.2.1 Imagining the International Community of All Peoples in International Instruments

The international community, comprising 'all peoples of the world', is recognised
in several UNESCO Conventions.[23] Amongst them is the 1954 Hague Convention,
which, by its nature, is designed to deal with situations involving breakdowns of at
least part of the international community, for most of its provisions apply to states
at war.[24] The Hague Convention nevertheless imagines the entire international
community by recognising that the damage to cultural property which belongs to
any people 'means damage to the cultural heritage of all mankind'.[25] It thus
identifies the interconnectedness of people by saying that 'each people makes its
contribution to the culture of the world'.[26] Similarly, the World Heritage
Convention conceives of 'the international community as a whole'.[27] Whilst it
has been suggested that there is no direct obligation owed by one state to the
international community to respect the cultural heritage located in its territory,
'the international community as a whole, jointly and severally, is permitted by
general international law to subject a State's peacetime treatment of such heritage
to scrutiny, comment and, where appropriate, criticism'.[28]

The Preamble of the International Covenant on Economic, Social and
Cultural Rights creates a strong international community, quite separate
from the state or a collection of states, by referring to the 'human family'.[29]
It is not simply the peoples of the world, but the cultures of the world that
contribute to the international community, as is evident in the Declaration on
Principles of International Cultural Co-operation,[30] which recognises that 'all
cultures form part of the common heritage belonging to all mankind'. The
effect of destruction of cultural heritage on the international community is

---

[23] 1954 Hague Convention, Preamble, which sets cultural heritage preservation as 'of great
importance for all peoples of the world' and 1972 World Heritage Convention, Preamble,
which set out that safeguarding the unique and irreplaceable property is of importance for all
the peoples of the world.

[24] The remaining provisions relate to measures that are put in place in peacetime but are for the
purposes of dealing with times of war – e.g. arts. 3 and 7.

[25] 1954 UNESCO Hague Convention, Preamble.   [26] ibid.

[27] 1972 UNESCO World Heritage Convention, Preamble, arts. 6 and 25 (the latter omitting the
word 'whole').

[28] Roger O'Keefe, 'World Cultural Heritage: Obligations to the International Community as a
Whole?' (2004) 53 *International & Comparative Law Quarterly* 189, 207.

[29] International Covenant on Economic, Social and Cultural Rights, United Nations, OHCHR
General Assembly Resolution 2200A (XXI) 1966 (adopted 16 December 1966, entered into
force 3 January 1976).

[30] Declaration on Principles of International Cultural Co-operation1966 (adopted
4 November 1966), art. 1(3).

clearly emphasised in the UNESCO Declaration concerning the Intentional Destruction of Cultural Heritage[31] and is framed as those who would be affected by the intentional destruction of cultural heritage.

Although references to 'all peoples' and 'all cultures' in the preceding conventions have focused primarily on present generations, an inter-generational international community is clearly imagined by the Declaration on the Responsibilities of the Present Generations Towards Future Generations.[32] This recognises that there is a common heritage of humankind which can be used by present generations but not compromised 'irreversibly'.[33] This notion was reaffirmed in the context of the intentional destruction of cultural heritage[34] and has been reflected in the work of the Special Rapporteur on cultural rights, who talks of 'our collective role as custodians of the past achievements of humanity'.[35]

5.2.1.1 Respect

Respect both to cultural heritage and to other parties to a convention is a key element of creating the international community.[36] In the Hague Convention this is reflected in provisions in which state parties undertake to respect cultural property of other parties to the Convention[37] to safeguard and to preserve cultural property of an occupied country.[38] Additionally, parties to the Hague Convention undertake during peacetime to foster in their armed forces 'a spirit of respect for the culture and cultural property of all peoples'.[39] This notion of a 'spirit of respect' gets to the heart of the notion of caring for cultural heritage since respecting cultural heritage and the people for whom it is important are central components of appropriate care for cultural heritage and for those communities for whom the cultural heritage is so important.[40] It also demonstrates a commitment to care which goes beyond the state level, to incorporate care undertaken by the armed forces who will be in direct contact with the cultural heritage which may be in danger or require appropriate care for the benefit of others. Even though, at times, criticised as a convention focusing on nationalism rather than internationalism,[41] the 1970 UNESCO

---

[31] (adopted 17 October 2003).

[32] (adopted 12 November 1997). As to Roger O'Keefe's observations about the choice of the word 'responsibilities' rather than 'obligations', see a discussion of O'Keefe, 'World Cultural Heritage', 189, 203 at Section 5.2.1.3.

[33] Declaration on the Responsibilities of the Present Generations Towards Future Generations, art. 8. As Lixinski points out, though, the obligation is to future generations rather than past ones: Lixinski, *International Heritage Law for Communities*, p. 110.

[34] UNESCO Declaration concerning the Intentional Destruction of Cultural Heritage, art. I.

[35] Karima Bennoune, *Cultural Rights: Report of the Special Rapporteur in the Field of Cultural Rights: Intentional Destruction of Cultural Heritage* (A/71/317 UN), p. 21.

[36] The notion of respect for each culture is reflected in article 1(1) of the UNESCO Declaration of the Principles of International Cultural Co-operation, UNESCO (adopted 4 November 1966).

[37] 1954 UNESCO Hague Convention, art. 4(1).   [38] ibid., art. 5(1).   [39] ibid., art. 7(1).

[40] See Section 2.5.4.

[41] John Henry Merryman, 'Two Ways of Thinking about Cultural Property' (1986) 80 *American Journal of International Law* 831, 832.

Convention nevertheless creates an international community of care concerned about the negative impact of the illicit trade in cultural heritage objects. For whilst the national projects necessary to fulfil the state parties' obligations under the Convention form the focus of article 5, the Preamble demonstrates the importance of state parties working together at the international level[42] and the moral obligations that each state has 'to respect its own cultural heritage and that of all nations'.[43] This notion of respect across the international communities found in the Convention (which recognises the importance of cultural heritage for other countries) has influenced domestic case law[44] in England and Wales as well as non-law instruments such as the UK's *Due Diligence Guidance for Museums*, which recognises 1970 as an ethical marker.[45]

5.2.1.2 Co-operation, Collaboration and Assistance

Co-operation is a central element to creating international communities,[46] not just in recognising that various states care about cultural heritage, but more pragmatically at the level of actively co-operating together in caring for cultural heritage.[47] Therefore, in the 1970 Convention the provisions of article 7 cement the idea of the international community through the international co-operation necessary to provide the mechanisms for prohibiting the illicit

---

[42] By recognising that the effective protection of cultural heritage can only be achieved 'if organized both nationally and internationally among States working in close co-operation': 1970 UNESCO Convention, Preamble.

[43] ibid., Preamble.   [44] In *Iran* v. *Barakat*, discussed in Section 4.8.1.

[45] DCMS, *Combating Illicit Trade: Due Diligence Guidelines for Museums, Libraries and Archives on Collecting and Borrowing Cultural Material* (October 2005), p. 4. The 1970 Convention has similarly influenced guidelines in other countries. E.g. in the USA, Guidelines on the Acquisition of Archaeological Material and Ancient Art (Association of Art Museum Directors, revised 2013), para. E. It has been suggested that in 1970 'the international community was put on notice that a rule against reckless acquisition was in the course of adoption': Lyndel V. Prott, 'The History and Development of Return of Cultural Objects' in Lyndel V. Prott (ed.), *Witnesses to History: A Compendium of Documents and Writings on the Return of Cultural Objects* (Paris: UNESCO, 2009), p. 10.

[46] See, for example, International Covenant on Economic, Social and Cultural Rights, art. 2(1) which sets out both international assistance and co-operation as being necessary to achieve the 'full realization of the rights recognized in the present Covenant'. See also art. 15(4). For 'a cooperative approach to caring for cultural material' see International Law Association (ILA) – 'Caring and sharing' – middle ground – ILA Conference Report Berlin 2004; RESOLUTION No. 4/2006, Cultural Heritage Law Committee of ILA, (Preamble), demonstrating a relational approach to care.

[47] Nafziger and Paterson recognise cooperation as one of the five interrelated functions of the 'legal regimes within this UNESCO-orientated framework' – the other four being protection, rectification, criminal justice and dispute resolution: James A. R. Nafziger and Robert Kirkwood Paterson, 'Cultural Heritage Law' in James A. R. Nafziger and Robert Kirkwood Paterson (eds.), *Handbook on the Law of Cultural Heritage and International Trade* (Cheltenham: Edward Elgar, 2014), p. 6. Co-operation is evident in the efforts to protect cultural heritage from intentional destruction: UNESCO Declaration concerning the Intentional Destruction of Cultural Heritage, art. VIII.

import of inventoried cultural property stolen from another state party and ensuring its return through diplomatic channels.[48]

Co-operation is elevated to a prescribed duty in the context of the 1972 World Heritage Convention, with the 'international community' being recognised in article 6 as having a duty to co-operate for the purpose of protecting the cultural and natural heritage of outstanding universal value. International protection for World Heritage Sites is therefore seen as synonymous with 'the establishment of a system of international cooperation and assistance'.[49]

Developing an international community is not simply achieved through the grouping together of state parties of specific international organisations. The relationship between international organisations also contributes to a holistic international community. In the context of participatory governance of cultural heritage, it has been highlighted that this can be enhanced by co-operation between international organisations such as the EU, the Council of Europe and UNESCO.[50] This therefore imagines an international community, not only of the state parties to a specific convention, or members of a particular organisation, but also of the members of other organisations. It thus extends coverage beyond the state parties, to a broader concept of the international community through the medium of the organisations themselves, representing those collections of states.

Further contributing to an ethos of a community looking out for its fellow members is the concept of mutual assistance, as recognised in UNESCO's Constitution. It identifies an international community through the fact that the 'wide diffusion of culture' is 'indispensable to the dignity of man and constitute[s] a sacred duty which all nations must fulfil in a spirit of mutual assistance and concern'.[51]

The recognition of assistance is not merely a hortatory sentiment but is recognised in practical terms in several conventions. Assistance from the international community can be called upon by any state party under article 19 of the World Heritage Convention – this is undertaken through an application for emergency assistance,[52] conservation and management assistance[53] or preparatory assistance,[54] which, if successful, is primarily financed by the World Heritage Fund.[55] In practice, therefore, assistance is not simply

---

[48] See Charlotte Woodhead, 'Article 7b(i) – Prohibition of Import of Inventoried Cultural Property' in Ana Vdroljak, Alessandro Chechi and Andrzej Jakubowski (eds.), *Oxford Commentaries on International Cultural Heritage Law: Commentary on the 1970 UNESCO and 1995 UNIDROIT Conventions* (Oxford: Oxford University Press, 2023 forthcoming).

[49] 1972 UNESCO World Heritage Convention, art. 7.

[50] Council conclusions on participatory governance of cultural heritage OJ 2014 No C431, p. 3, para. 26.

[51] UNESCO Constitution (adopted on 16 November 1945, as amended).

[52] Intergovernmental Committee for the Protection of the World Cultural and Natural Heritage, *Operational Guidelines for the Implementation of the World Heritage Convention* (31 July 2021), WHC.21/01, para. 235(a).

[53] ibid., para. 235(b).   [54] ibid., para. 235(c).

[55] Established under 1972 UNESCO World Heritage Convention, art. 15. ibid., para. 234.

provided in response to cultural heritage that is at risk, but also to assist in the general care of cultural heritage. This contrasts with the provision for assistance in article 9 of the 1970 UNESCO Convention, which applies where a state party's 'cultural patrimony is in jeopardy from pillage of archaeological or ethnological materials'. This commitment of the other state parties to the 1970 Convention is then to bring in 'concrete measures' to control the export and import of such materials.[56] This demonstrates how the international community shows empathy towards other members of that community in the care of cultural heritage and recognises the need for one member of that international community to call upon others to come to its assistance. This does not represent the imposition of care, but rather the opportunity to raise the need for assistance with care.

Under the Second Protocol to the 1954 Hague Convention, parties may call upon the Committee for the Protection of Cultural Property in the Event of Armed Conflict[57] for international assistance, not only regarding enhanced protection of cultural property, but also in creating the legal and administrative procedures necessary to ensure the enhanced protection.[58] Furthermore, parties to the conflict, even if not a party to the Second Protocol, may request international assistance.[59] The Hague Convention envisages that during wartime there may be situations in which an occupying power may need to take certain measures to preserve cultural property when the competent national authorities are unable to do so.[60] Provision is also made in the accompanying regulations for other state parties to set up improvised refuges for cultural property and to be able to place those under special protection.[61] When it comes to state parties discovering that cultural property from an occupied territory has been imported into their territory, they undertake to take such cultural property into their custody.[62] This may be at the request of the occupied country, but will not necessarily be – for the undertaking is to automatically take the cultural property into their custody on importation.[63] Such cultural property must then be returned to 'the competent authorities of the territory previously occupied'.[64]

On first sight, legal provisions under which states take it upon themselves to care for the cultural heritage of another country demonstrate care without dialogue and which may not be empathetic. It may necessarily involve

---

[56] 1970 UNESCO Convention, art. 9.

[57] Established under the Second Protocol to the Hague Convention of 1954 for the Protection of Cultural Property in the Event of Armed Conflict, The Hague, 26 March 1999, art. 24(1). Funding is available from the Fund for the Protection of Cultural Property in the Event of Armed Conflict (established under art. 29(1) of the 2nd Protocol).

[58] ibid., art. 32(1).   [59] ibid., art. 32(2).   [60] 1954 Hague Convention, art. 5(2).

[61] Regulations for the Execution of the Convention for the Protection of Cultural Property in the Event of Armed Conflict, art. 11(1).

[62] Protocol to the Convention for the Protection of Cultural Property in the Event of Armed Conflict, The Hague, 14 May 1954, art. 2.

[63] ibid.   [64] ibid., art. 3.

imposing on others care and assuming responsibility for it. It might be considered to be paternalistic in nature. However, in the context of war, where intervention may be a necessity to avert irreparable harm, there is a stronger argument that care, without initial consultation, and with the assumption of responsibility on a temporary basis, may still be empathetic and respectful despite the absence of direct dialogue and informed consent.[65] It is at the end of hostilities when cultural heritage should be returned that particular efforts need to be made to ensure that care is both empathetic and respectful to ensure that cultural heritage is returned appropriately (particularly in situations where borders have shifted).

5.2.1.3 International Responsibilities

In international law, state parties place themselves under obligations and duties in law which, if they violate, lead to state responsibility.[66] This notion of responsibility is different from the broader approach which is taken to responsibility within this book (derived from the ethics of care). In many ways the international discussion between the members of an international organisation such as UNESCO, which may then result in the acceptance and ratification of an international legal instrument, demonstrates that those states, together forming the international community, care about cultural heritage and care for it by making provision for its care within the international legal framework. Prescribing duties and obligations, and by committing to uphold these, would, in the language of care, demonstrate the assumption of responsibility for the care of cultural heritage. However, in international legal terms, responsibility would only be engaged in the event of states breaching their obligations. But responsibility within the ethics of care is broad enough to incorporate both elements. Therefore, international responsibility is taken here to include the way in which states have initially committed themselves to those legal duties and obligations[67] and the direct responsibility for care in the form of making good on any violations of the legal duties or obligations.

The notion of responsibility outside this strict legal meaning is found in international legal instruments. Roger O'Keefe suggests that use of the word 'responsibility' in the Declaration on the Responsibilities of Present Generations Towards Future Generations was 'a subtle but significant avoidance of the formal legal terms "obligation" and "duty", and a semantic ploy common to diplomatic drafting'.[68] Again, the notion of the common responsibility at the international level 'to safeguard' common heritage for future

---

[65] The topic of safe havens and the assumption of the responsibility for the temporary care of cultural heritage in wartime is considered in Section 7.5.4.4.

[66] International Law Commission, Draft articles on Responsibility of States for Internationally Wrongful Acts with commentaries (adopted at the 53rd session of the General Assembly, (2001) 2 *Yearbook of the International Law Commission* 31, 32, art. 1(1)).

[67] Such as in the provisions set out in the preceding section.

[68] O'Keefe, 'World Cultural Heritage', 189, 203.

generations is found in the Venice Charter[69] – the non-law instrument promulgated by ICOMOS.[70]

The international community, with its associated responsibilities, both jointly and severally is a community caring about, and for, cultural heritage. The discussion now turns to the courts, as communities of care, which recognise why the international community cares about cultural heritage and the fact that they do actually care about it.

5.2.2 Imagining International Communities in Case Law in the UK

English common law has translated the notion of comity of nations – 'the body of rules which sovereign states observe towards one another from courtesy and convenience'[71] – by upholding the idea of the community of friendly nations for whom the UK, as a member, should recognise and respect their cultural heritage. This is clear from cases such as *Bumper* where the primary question for the court was whether a temple could be recognised as a juristic entity who could sue for conversion for a Siva Nataraja.[72] Purchas LJ said that he could not 'see that in the circumstances of this case there is any offence to English public policy in allowing a Hindu religious institution to sue in our courts for the recovery of property which it is entitled to recover by the law of its own country. Indeed we think that public policy would be advantaged'.[73] However, he arrived at that conclusion having worked through a hypothetical situation, derived from *Salmond on Jurisprudence*, involving a Roman Catholic cathedral which had been given legal personality under foreign legislation, and from that he was able to draw an analogy with a Hindu religious institution to conclude that standing ought to be granted.[74] An argument had been advanced that the Sivalingam of the temple[75] should also have standing in the case. At first instance Ian Kennedy J held, in the alternative, that 'the "pious" intention of the twelfth-century notable who gave the land and built the Pathur temple remained in being and was personified by the Sivalingam of the temple, which itself had a title superior to that of Bumper'.[76] However, the Court of Appeal, having held that the temple had been recognised as a juristic entity, deemed it unnecessary to determine whether the Sivalingam was also a juristic entity.[77]

---

[69] ICOMOS, International Charter for the Conservation and Restoration of Monuments and Sites (The Venice Charter, 1964).

[70] ibid., Preamble. The obligation to future generations is also evident in the Preamble of the Granada Convention on Architectural heritage, which recalls 'the importance of handing down to future generations a system of cultural references . . . '.

[71] *Re St Mary the Virgin, Hurley* [2001] 1 WLR 831, 834 (Oxford Consistory Court).

[72] *Bumper Corporation* v. *Commissioner of Police of the Metropolis and others* [1991] 4 All ER 639 (CA), 648.

[73] ibid.   [74] ibid.

[75] This is a stone within the temple which was added as a fifth claimant: ibid., 642.

[76] A description of the finding at first instance given by Purchas LJ in the appeal: ibid., 643.

[77] ibid., 648 (Purchas LJ).

The idea of the comity of nations was also evident in the consistory court judgment regarding the application for a faculty to exhume Hipólito José Da Costa, a Brazilian national hero, from an English church, St Mary the Virgin, Hurley.[78] The court, in determining whether there was a 'good and proper reason for exhumation'[79] (which could justify granting a faculty when the general presumption is against exhumation), took into account the comity of nations. It was relevant to finding in favour of granting a faculty that the petitioner was the Brazilian ambassador and that the UK 'undoubtedly enjoys friendly relations with the sovereign state of Brazil'.[80] The appreciation that the court should recognise difference derives from the notion of comity of nations, but there is a clear development of the notion of an international community which translates the importance of the cultural heritage of other nations and in particular the moral obligations regarding that cultural heritage in respecting it into action. This is evident in *Iran v. Barakat* where, under the conflict of laws rules, the court recognised the ownership rules of Iran.[81] The matter at issue was whether something could be recovered by another nation on the basis that the object was part of that nation's cultural heritage. Whilst none of the international conventions relating to cultural heritage were directly applicable to the facts of the case, Lord Phillips of Worth Maltravers CJ observed that these conventions 'illustrate the international acceptance of the desirability of protection of the national heritage'.[82] However, in these cases there were no direct challenges to the cultural heritage of the UK. Had there been a question about whether these were national treasures for the purposes of export licensing then there may have been more resistance to this.[83] Rather than recognising the importance of the cultural heritage and framing it as being important to the UK or to the international community more broadly (in terms of its universal importance) the court instead recognised its importance to the claimant country and the moral obligation incumbent on the UK to help other countries to recover their national heritage.[84] This derived from the international obligations to which the UK had subscribed in the UNESCO 1970 Convention[85] and was expressly referenced.

UK organisations demonstrate their membership of the international community of care in many practical ways. This can be seen in the context of the war in Ukraine, with the Institute of Conservation's *Emergency Guidance for Caring for Cultural Property*, which provides bilingual practical guidance on dealing with fires and handling soot and smoke to historic surfaces during wartime.[86] Safe havens, discussed below, also provide practical help to other countries,

---

[78] *Re St Mary the Virgin, Hurley.* See Charlotte Woodhead, 'Exhumation of a National Hero and the Return to His Homeland: *In re St Mary the Virgin, Hurley*' (2003) 8 *Art Antiquity and Law* 289.

[79] The test that had been established in *Re Christ Church, Alsager* [1999] Fam 142, 151.

[80] *Re St Mary the Virgin, Hurley*, 834.

[81] *Government of the Islamic Republic of Iran* v. *The Barakat Galleries Ltd.* [2009] QB 22 (CA).

[82] ibid., 65.   [83] See Chapter 8.   [84] *Iran v. Barakat*, 29.   [85] ibid.

[86] ICON: www.icon.org.uk/resource/emergency-guidance-for-caring-for-cultural-property.html (last accessed 20 December 2022).

demonstrating assumption of responsibility for the cultural heritage of other countries within the international community.

5.2.3 Imagining the Commonwealth as a Community

In the Charter of the Commonwealth,[87] the community of the Commonwealth of nations is recognised, in particular, in the emphasis on 'the special strength' which 'lies in the combination of our diversity and our shared inheritance in language, culture and the rule of law; and bound together by shared history and tradition'.[88] Talking in the context of the Commonwealth Scheme to Protect Cultural Treasures,[89] Patrick O'Keefe observed that no binding obligations between the members of the Commonwealth are brought about by the scheme; rather, it would be for the members to introduce legislation to bring the principles of the scheme into operation.[90] Nevertheless, as an established community of members, it has been recognised that the cultural heritage of the members of that community requires care and this instrument facilitates that.

5.2.4 Imagining European Communities

At the European level, the European Community is created in various instruments from both the Council of Europe and the European Union. Of direct relevance to the approach in the UK are the Council of Europe Conventions relating to archaeological and architectural heritage, which seek in their preambles to demonstrate a common heritage of Europeans,[91] which, as a community, has a collective memory.[92] In the context of archaeological heritage it is clear that the countries within Europe and Europe as a whole (in terms of the members of the Council of Europe) are jointly and severally responsible, thus 'responsibility for the protection of the archaeological heritage should rest not only with the State directly concerned but with all European countries'.[93]

5.2.5 Imagining National Communities

Even within the international community, individual nations have a significant role to play in caring for cultural heritage and the responsibility to do so is often placed on them in the first instance. This can be seen by the detailed

---

[87] Charter of the Commonwealth (adopted by the Commonwealth Heads of Government, 14 December 2012).

[88] ibid.   [89] Agreed by the Commonwealth Law Ministers, Mauritius, November 1993.

[90] Patrick J. O'Keefe, 'Protection of the Material Cultural Heritage: The Commonwealth Scheme' (1995) 44 *International & Comparative Law Quarterly* 147, 148.

[91] Council of Europe Convention for the Protection of the Architectural Heritage of Europe, Granada, 1985 (adopted 3 October 1985, entered into force 1 December 1987) CETS 121, Preamble.

[92] European Convention on the Protection of the Archaeological Heritage (Revised) Council of Europe, Valetta (adopted 16 January 1992, entered into force 25 May 1995) CETS 14, art. 1(1).

[93] ibid., Preamble.

provisions of the 1970 UNESCO Convention setting out the expected national initiatives relating to cultural property[94] as well as in the 1972 World Heritage Convention.[95] The responsibility[96] rests on state parties to prepare themselves for war and to respond to the need to care for cultural heritage through the provisions of the 1954 Hague Convention and its Protocols. UN Security Council Resolution 2347/2017 stresses that 'Member States have the primary responsibility in protecting their cultural heritage and that efforts to protect cultural heritage in the context of armed conflicts should be in conformity with the Charter, including its purposes and principles, and international law, and should respect the sovereignty of all States'.[97]

Often the nation is the framework within which the concept of heritage is constructed where there is concern that cultural heritage will be 'lost' to the nation. This can happen where there is a proposed sale and potential export abroad.[98] As well as the UK, as a whole, being a national community, the individual nations of the UK (England, Scotland, Wales and Northern Ireland) are also recognised as national communities in legislation relating specifically to them or within broader UK schemes. Thus, in Wales respecting Welsh language by 'promoting and facilitating' its use and placing it on an equal footing with English recognises the national community of Wales, set out within its own legislative scheme.[99] The Bòrd na Gàidhlig has been established in Scotland[100] to promote and facilitate the promotion of the use and under-standing of the Gaelic language as well as Gaelic education and culture.[101] In respect of Northern Ireland the Northern Ireland Act 1998, section 78F[102] requires public authorities 'carrying out functions relating to Northern Ireland' to 'have due regard to the national and cultural identity principles'. These principles take into account the idea that everyone is free to 'choose, affirm, maintain and develop their national and cultural identity' and to express and celebrate this 'in a manner that takes account of the sensitivities of those with different national and cultural identities and respects the rule of law'. Furthermore, provision is made for public authorities to 'encourage and promote reconciliation, tolerance and meaningful dialogue ... with a view to promoting parity of esteem, mutual respect and understanding, and cooper-ation'. Section 78J of the Northern Ireland Act 1998 provides for the official recognition of the Irish language and the 2023 amendments to the Act have

---

[94] 1970 UNESCO Convention, art. 5.   [95] 1972 WHC, arts. 4 and 5.
[96] Used here in the broader sense of the ethics of care, rather than the technical international law sense: discussed at Section 5.2.1.3.
[97] UN Security Council Resolution 2347/2017 (adopted by the Security Council at its 7907th meeting on 24 March 2017), S/RES/2347 (2017), art. 5. This idea is reflected in the Council of Europe Framework Convention with the notion of responsibility set out in article 1(b) that there is both 'individual and collective responsibility towards cultural heritage'. It should be noted that this convention has not been ratified by the UK.
[98] See Section 8.3.   [99] Welsh Language Act 1993, Preamble.
[100] Gaelic Language (Scotland) Act 2005, s. 1(1).   [101] ibid., s. 1(2).
[102] As inserted by the Identity and Language (Northern Ireland) Act 2023, s. 1(1).

introduced the appointment of the Irish Language Commissioner[103] and the Commissioner for the Ulster Scots and the Ulster British tradition.[104]

The 'Scottish interest' in a cultural heritage object has been given a statutory footing in the context of the UK-wide Acceptance in Lieu Scheme. This means that it can be made a condition of the acceptance of a pre-eminent object in satisfaction of tax by the transferor that an object should be displayed in Scotland, or transferred to a Scottish institution.[105] The more recently enacted Finance Act 2012, which sets out the cultural gifts scheme, recognises the interests of each of the nations of the UK and depending on which interest (or combination of nations) there is, the relevant Minister from each country or the Secretary of State (for England)[106] determines the object's pre-eminence and where it might be located, if associated with a particular building.[107]

Consistory courts also focus on the importance of national heritage when preventing objects from churches being sold on the open market, because of the perceived risk that they will be purchased by collectors who might export them abroad. The focus is clearly on the national viewpoint, rather than solely the local one. In several consistory court cases, the object in question had been on long-term loan to a museum and so had already been separated from the local church and the community for some time.[108] In *Re St Lawrence, Wootton* it was said that such separation by itself would not justify allowing disposal.[109] When sales are anticipated, the recognised risk is that the objects may be lost to the public view. Earlier cases indicated that the local community interest, specifically those of the parishioners and the local community, were of paramount concern and that churches were not museums and were not responsible for the national heritage.[110] Specifically, the courts had treated the concept of the national heritage as being the proper concern of the export licensing system, which would prevent an object from leaving the country.[111] *Wootton* was a case concerning the proposed sale of a fifteenth-century Flemish armet that had hung above the marble monument to Sir Thomas Hooke in the Church of St Lawrence, Wootton. Although the beginning of the judgment focused on the physical object, the Dean of Arches proceeded to highlight the importance of maximising access to cultural heritage objects and set out a sequential approach for churches, petitioners and Chancellors to adopt when considering whether to remove an

---

[103] Northern Ireland Act 1998, s.78K (as inserted by the Identity and Language (Northern Ireland) Act 2023, s. 2(1).

[104] Northern Ireland Act 1998, s. 78R (as inserted by the Identity and Language (Northern Ireland) Act 2023, s. 3(1).

[105] IHTA 1984, ss. 230(6) and (7).   [106] Finance Act 2012, sch. 14, para. 23.

[107] ibid., sch. 14, para. 22.

[108] E.g. *Re St Mary's, Warwick* [1981] Fam 170 and *Re St Bartholomew's, Aldbrough* [1990] 3 All ER 440.

[109] [2015] Fam 27, 54 (Arches Court).

[110] *Re St James, Welland* [2015] Fam 27, 44 (Mynors Ch).

[111] *Re St Gregory's, Tredington* [1972] Fam 236, 244 (Arches Court of Canterbury).

object from a church.[112] Firstly, it should be considered whether it is possible to lend an object (thereby safeguarding the object's security but also providing a level of continued public access). Secondly, it is necessary to consider whether to dispose of the object by 'limited sale' – that is to say a sale to a museum, art gallery or to the diocesan treasury as a means of ensuring continued public access.[113] Therefore, churches may be expected to forego the market value of an object to ensure public access to the object (within national borders).[114] The final option (perceived as the last resort) would be a disposal by an outright sale – this would potentially take place at an auction when private purchasers could also acquire the object and so there would likely be a loss of public access to the object.[115] Even in such a case the consistory court has made the faculty (permission) to sell an object subject to conditions in the ultimate contract of transfer between the church and the purchaser or donee that objects are sold to a locally based purchaser[116] or that the objects or collections cannot be resold.[117]

The community imagined by the judgment is one which recognises the national interest in something owned by the church, but at the same time owing a responsibility to the wider public, beyond the parishioners of the church. It thus centres the church and the consistory court at the heart of the national community which cares for cultural heritage, by prioritising its access and availability to that wider community.

When it comes to the work of committees such as the Export Reviewing Committee and the Acceptance in Lieu Panel, the Waverley Criteria act as the basis for the tests to establish whether an object deserves special treatment, either by seeking to prevent its export or to justify it in being accepted for the nation in lieu of tax.[118] Here the care expressed by the work of the committees is firmly focused on the nation as a community.[119] Care is therefore viewed from the perspective of the nation and the desire to keep something rather than either to look after it *per se* or to take responsibility for it. This can be seen in the context of the consideration by the Export Reviewing Committee of the current condition of the object; where the object's physical condition is in some way diminished, this can result in it not being considered a national treasure under the Waverley Criteria.[120]

---

[112] *Re St Lawrence, Wootton* [2015] Fam 27 (Arches Court), 44–5.   [113] ibid., 44.

[114] It appears that a sale at an undervalue may be possible by a museum established as a charity: see the position of the Charity Commission as explained in Janet Ulph, 'The Sale of Items in Museum Collections' in Nicholas Hopkins (ed.), *Modern Studies in Property Law*, vol. 7 (Oxford: Hart, 2013), p. 218.

[115] *Re St Lawrence, Wootton*, 45.

[116] *Re St John the Baptist, Stainton-by-Langworth* 9 Ecc LJ 144 (condition that every effort should be made to sell to a Lincolnshire-based buyer).

[117] *Re St Mary's, Warwick*.

[118] The Waverley Criteria are used by the Export Reviewing Committee whereas the Acceptance in Lieu Panel uses criteria based around the Waverley ones, albeit without reference to the misfortune of loss.

[119] Although this is both the entire nation but also local communities in the context of cultural heritage of importance to a locality: see the next section.

[120] Discussed further at Section 8.1.2.

5.2.5.1 The National Incorporating the Local

Several definitions of cultural heritage used in the UK ostensibly focus on the national interest or importance. However, accompanying guidance (whether statutory or non-statutory) then translates the national interest into something that does not necessarily have to be of direct interest for *all* areas of the UK. This is certainly the case for listed buildings where the criteria for listing focuses on the national interest but then recognises that the list can include 'the most significant or distinctive regional buildings' and representative vernacular buildings which 'represent a nationally significant but localised industry'.[121] The Export Reviewing Committee have adopted the practice of translating the notion of the closeness of the object to national life as recognising the closeness to local life.[122] The more regional approach is evident in the Inheritance Tax Act (IHTA) 1984 in the context of the conditional exemption scheme, as well as the Acceptance in Lieu Scheme, which explains that reference to 'national interest' 'includes interest within any part of the United Kingdom'.[123] This clearly shows a relational view of the need to care and the interconnectedness that comes of something that is of local interest also being of national interest and worthy of designation, justifying enhanced levels of care.

5.2.6 Imagining Local or Regional Communities

Local or regional communities can be created in a variety of different ways. These can form from the general geographical area, or when a particular county or region feels a sense of common identity, through either shared cultures or experiences. At times, the connections between communities and cultural heritage can be translated into requests for objects originating from a particular place to be returned or repatriated to that area. Such strong feelings have been evident in the context of requests made for the Lewis Chessmen to be transferred from the British Museum to the Isle of Lewis[124] and for the Lindisfarne Gospels to be returned from the British Library to Lindisfarne.[125] Similarly, on occasions where finds of treasure have been found in a local area, members of that local community have requested that finds are allocated to their local museums, rather than to a national museum.[126] There is increased recognition, though, that local communities may have strong connections with cultural heritage places, as is evident from the schemes relating to assets of community value in England and Wales found in

---

[121] DCMS, *Principles of Selection for Listed Buildings* (November 2018), para. 22.

[122] See Waverley Committee Report, para. 189, discussed at Section 8.1.2.

[123] IHTA 1984, s. 31(5) (conditional exemptions scheme) and ITA 1984, s. 230(5) (the acceptance in lieu scheme), which also makes specific interest to the Scottish interest.

[124] *Hansard* HC vol. 507, col. 124WH, *Repatriation of Historical Objects* (10 March 2010).

[125] UK Parliament, Early Day Motion: Return of the Lindisfarne Gospels to the North, EDM 576: tabled on 24 February 1997.

[126] See, for example, *Bring the Hoard Home to Herefordshire! – The Hub at St Peters* (23 July 2022): www.visitherefordshire.co.uk/whats-on/bring-hoard-home-herefordshire-hub-st-peters (last accessed 21 May 2023).

the Localism Act 2011. Assets of Community Value can be nominated by community organisations including parish councils, neighbourhood forums,[127] parish councils in England,[128] community councils in Wales[129] or 'a person that is a voluntary or community body with a local connection'.[130] The power to nominate is firmly placed in the hands of the community, for assets cannot be nominated by a local authority.

Language or dialect is another aspect of a local community's identity and cultural heritage. The Council of Europe Charter has recognised not only languages used in the different countries forming the UK – specifically Welsh, Scots, Scottish Gaelic, Irish, Manx Gaelic and Ulster Scots – but also the local community through its designation of Cornish as a minority language.[131]

Further initiatives recognising local communities include the community empowerment provisions in Scotland enabling rural and crofting communities to buy land and for purchases to be made of land which is at risk.[132] Community participation bodies in Scotland[133] (which include community-controlled bodies[134]) 'can make a request to a public service authority to participate in the outcome improvement'.[135] As part of this they must, among other things, set out their reasons for participating in this and also detail their 'knowledge, expertise and experience' as well as an explanation of the improvement that might come about.[136]

The importance of provincial collections of cultural heritage to local communities is recognised in a number of different situations.[137] In the case of *R (on the application of Hall)* v. *Leicestershire City Council*, involving the Snibston Discovery Centre, the judge emphasised the social and cultural importance of provincial museums and sought to avoid a London-centric approach to the issue.[138] The context of the case was the announcement of the proposed reduction in provision at the Snibston Discovery Centre in Leicestershire. A volunteer at the museum judicially reviewed the decision to close the existing museum and demolish the building in which it had been housed, resulting in a reduced provision of the museum elsewhere with a smaller collection.[139] Whilst Blake

---

[127] The Assets of Community Value (England) Regulations 2012, reg. 51. Town and Country Planning Act 1990, s. 61F(3) recognises generally neighbourhood fora, the conditions for recognition of them are set out in s. 61F(5).

[128] Localism Act 2011, s. 89(2)(b)(i).   [129] ibid., s. 89(2)(b)(ii).   [130] ibid., s. 89(2)(b)(iii).

[131] A civil society initiative entitled the Cornish Language Fellowship is established as a charity to promote Cornish language: https://cornish-language.org/ (last accessed 20 December 2022).

[132] Community Empowerment (Scotland) Act 2015, Part 4.   [133] ibid., s. 20.

[134] Defined under ibid., s. 19.   [135] ibid., s. 22(1).   [136] ibid., s. 22(2).

[137] These include the recommendations of the Export Reviewing Committee, which are considered in Chapter 8.

[138] *R (on the application of Hall)* v. *Leicestershire County Council* [2015] EWHC 2985 (Admin), para. 45.

[139] There were four legal issues which the administrative court had to consider: (1) whether the public consultation exercise was fair (2) whether the product of consultation had been fairly considered (3) whether due regard of the impact on vulnerable people such as the claimant had been given and (4) whether there had been lawful consideration of an alternative bid made by

J used the language of the administrative court, he nevertheless set out the context by providing the background information about the museum in the opening paragraphs.[140] In addition to the cultural heritage context, Blake J. presented the social and economic issues, specifically pointing out the council's decision to reduce the service was due to the reduced support grant.[141] After the richness of the contextual information, the judge waited until the sixth paragraph of the judgment to set out the legal point that was raised in the case – specifically the judicial review of the significant change to the museum provision. The judge adopted the language of museums by talking about 'the irreversible decision to "de-accession"', using inverted commas perhaps to emphasise the technical use of the term in a professional context. However, he clearly treated the local authority as the 'guardian' of its cultural assets.[142]

Although the strict legal point at issue was the fairness of the consultation that had been carried out and how far the results of that consultation had been considered in the decision-making process, Blake J went further and made *obiter dictum* giving some insight into the community created in this case. Specifically, it was a community which values museum collections and which recognises the need for access to collections not only in London but also in the regions, emphasising the importance of public access to such regional museums.[143] When setting out his conclusions he clearly situated the museum within that community rather than focusing on its collection for its own sake. The museum, he said, 'has plainly added both value to the local economy and the quality of life of visitors, volunteers and staff, and also houses unique exhibits to which the public will no longer have access'.[144]

The community created by the court was one which recognised the procedural processes that needed to be followed, and acknowledged that these are the ones which facilitate discussion. It also recognised that where there has been appropriate discussion, then the decision, even if it hampers access to collections in the future, should nevertheless be upheld.

Blake J indicated that transfers of cultural assets to a 'viable community trust'[145] would ensure continued access (particularly in the regions) at the same time as avoiding burdening local authorities.[146] For that reason, he suggested that local authorities are under a duty to undertake active searches for viable partnerships before cultural assets are removed from public access 'let alone the irreversible decision to "de-accession" such assets by open market sale which may mean that such a public authority forfeits all trust in the future as a guardian of such assets'.[147]

The judge clearly demonstrated an awareness of the need for multivocality and dialogic care. He expressed the view that he would have liked to have heard the voices of the sector in its various policy guidance. He said: 'Before reaching

a group called the Friends of Snibston to take over the running of the Discovery Centre: ibid., para. 9.

[140] ibid., paras. 1–3.   [141] ibid., para. 11.   [142] ibid., para. 46.   [143] ibid., para. 45.
[144] ibid., para. 42.   [145] ibid., para. 45.   [146] ibid.   [147] ibid. para. 46.

any general conclusions on the requirements of a local authority in such circumstances, I would have welcomed and preferred examination of any available policy from the DCMS, the HLF, the Art Fund and the Museums Association.'[148]

In this case there was a strong judicial recognition of the public trust relating to museums. Blake J. elevated the concept of public guardianship to one of trust – the risk that selling off the objects through an open market sale would mean that the public authority 'forfeits all trust in the future as a guardian of such assets'.[149] This solidified the ethical concept of public trust found in the MA's Code of Ethics[150] into legal terms (albeit as persuasive *obiter dicta*). The judge thus performed an act of translation, translating the museum language of 'public trust', 'deaccessioning' and 'guardianship' into legal language and therefore giving it persuasive legal force for the future.[151]

The local community as one which cares about their provincial collections is translated in the recommendations of the Export Reviewing Committee in the designation of national treasures.[152] The Export Reviewing Committee high-lighted the importance of provincial collections from an early stage of its existence by interpreting the Waverley criteria in a more generous manner if the prospective purchaser was a local, rather than a national, museum.[153]

In the context of the Church of England, it has been recognised how '[t]he Church, particularly in rural areas, depends heavily on the enterprise, enthusiasm, expertise and simple hard work of a small, sometimes a tiny, number of devoted followers',[154] yet '[e]verybody who works within a church community, or who cares for a church building and its contents, is operating under the constraints of a trust, not merely in a religious and moral sense, but also in a manner defined by law'.[155] Thus the way in which the consistory court, the local community and the churchwardens in whom the property is vested all interact depends on trust and respect. However, ultimately the extent of the appropriateness of the care provided by the local community is subject to the court's jurisdiction.

Those governing and working in museums and heritage places are increas-ingly encouraged to engage with communities, in particular local ones. Museums do hold privileged positions and are 'perceived centres of knowledge and authority'.[156] They should ideally incorporate 'a participatory approach

---

[148] ibid., para. 44.   [149] ibid., para. 46.

[150] UK MA, *Code of Ethics for Museums* (2015), principle 3.

[151] The familiarity with the terminology of museums may derive from his role as a former trustee of the National Portrait Gallery: *Judicial Commissioner*: www.ipco.org.uk/who-we-are/judi cial-commissioners/ (last accessed 20 December 2022).

[152] See Chapter 8.   [153] See Section 8.3.1.

[154] *In the Matter of the Bells of the Church of Saint Michael, Michael Church Escley and in the matter of a confirmatory amendment to faculty 2013/136 and in the matter of an application for costs* [2020] ECC Her 1 (Deputy Chancellor Mark Ockelton), para. 2.

[155] ibid., para. 3.

[156] Corinne Perkin, 'Beyond the Rhetoric: Negotiating the Politics and Realising the Potential of Community-Driven Heritage Engagement' (2010) 16 *International Journal of Heritage Studies* 107, 109.

that values the contributions, knowledge and perspectives of local people and integrates these into professional museum practice'.[157]

Local or regional communities, may be in nations many miles away. Yet, the importance of cultural heritage to them may be of relevance to how the UK cares for cultural heritage, where that cultural heritage originates from those communities.

5.2.6.1 Specific Interest Communities

Held suggests that 'In civic associations, members develop enough empathetic feeling for one another to engage in common projects: to save a historical building'.[158] Various groups of interested individuals may establish themselves as communities because they care about cultural heritage. To achieve this, they may use law instrumentally, or may gather together informally as unincorporated associations. They may not take it upon themselves to assume responsibility for the direct care of any particular cultural heritage, but they may nevertheless demonstrate how they care about cultural heritage. This could be through public talks or by providing support for their members engaging in a cultural practice, such as the Embroiders Guild or the National Council for Metal Detecting. This may, though, very quickly amount to providing indirect care for the cultural heritage and its communities.[159] Indirect care may be given by responding to consultations or campaigning where a specific cultural heritage object, place or practice is at risk. Part of the role of these communities may be to encourage the flourishing of certain cultural heritage practices, or bring to the public's attention the risks of irreparable harm to objects, places or practices. These communities can play educative roles, such as the work of the UK Blue Shield.[160] Eventually, these communities may evolve to care for specific cultural heritage for which they assume responsibility.[161]

Throughout the UK there are a significant number of building preservation trusts which exist to provide care where buildings are at risk and to facilitate the sustainable use of these places. Whilst many are established in local communities, others exist across the UK or focus on particular types of buildings.[162] Further support is provided by the Prince's Foundation and

---

[157] ibid., 112.

[158] Virginia Held, *The Ethics of Care: Personal, Political and Global* (Oxford: Oxford University Press, 2006), p. 131.

[159] Lixinski suggests that 'in non-Indigenous contexts, too, communities are often seen as objects. In the English case, local history societies who initially made the push for heritage protection soon found themselves in the position of only being relevant if they were part of the professional, expert archaeologists' narrative of that place. Failing that, communities were more likely to be an obstacle to heritage protection than an agent in those processes': Lixinski, *International Heritage Law for Communities*, p. 99.

[160] Blue Shield UK: https://ukblueshield.org.uk/ (last accessed 1 June 2023).

[161] See Section 5.2.18.

[162] Historic England, *Building Preservation Trusts*: https://historicengland.org.uk/advice/hpg/publicandheritagebodies/bpt/ (last accessed 1 June 2023).

there are multiple preservation trusts to support the care of places of worship, whether still used for active worship, as well as those which are disused.[163]

5.2.6.2 Diaspora Communities

Diaspora communities may care about cultural heritage that is local to them now, but which originates from the communities in which they were born. In the context of the discussions regarding Hinemihi, which is the wharenui (meeting house) from Te Wairoa, Aotearoa, which has been located at the National Trust property Clandon Park in Surrey since 1892,[164] the diaspora community regularly met in Hinemihi and have been involved in the dialogue regarding its long-term care.[165]

5.2.6.3 Familial Communities of Care

It has been suggested that the public are to private people as heritage is to family history.[166] Nevertheless, although families are firmly within the private, rather than the public domain, there are several situations where families form communities of care in respect of cultural heritage.

The law recognised the interests of the landed gentry and wealthy, often well-known families, in the context of the law of heirlooms as a legal scheme incidentally caring for cultural heritage.[167] The direct relationship between certain cultural heritage and the family who has owned it for many years is evident in *dicta* in this field. The decision in *In re Hope*[168] demonstrates how the feeling of the Hope family towards the 'Hope Diamond' was a factor which should not be minimised (as counsel in the case had submitted should be done). Romer LJ observed: 'We sitting here as men of the world must in dealing with questions of this kind take cognizance of the fact that many families do take pride in possessing a jewel so widely known and of such a unique character as this diamond.'[169]

The link between the family and the cultural heritage was based on the many years of ownership which had created such a connection that the object itself had absorbed this within its identity with its name indicating the association with the family. In that case, different members of the family were in dispute about what should happen to the object. Whilst the link with the family was recognised in the 1899 litigation, in a later case other factors were taken into consideration when the sale of the diamond was ultimately approved by the court.[170]

---

163 ibid.
164 See generally Dean Sully and Alan Gallop, 'Introducing Hinemihi' in Dean Sully (ed.), *Decolonizing Conservation: Caring for Maori Meeting Houses Outside New Zealand* (Walnut Creek: Left Coast Press, 2007), p. 127.
165 See generally www.hinemihi.co.uk/page.php?id=24 (last accessed 20 December 2022).
166 John Carman, *Valuing Ancient Things: Archaeology and Law* (Leicester: Leicester University Press, 1996), p. 21.
167 See generally Norma Dawson, '"Heirlooms": The Evolution of a Legal Concept' (2000) 51 *Northern Ireland Legal Quarterly* 1.
168 [1899] 2 Ch 679.   169 ibid., 690 (Romer LJ).
170 The Hope diamond is now in the Smithsonian Institute, Washington: www.si.edu/spotlight/hope-diamond/history (last accessed 15 December 2022).

Familial communities of care for cultural heritage can also be observed when a family makes a claim for a cultural heritage object which was owned by one of their ancestors who lost possession of it.[171] They are simultaneously a community of justice,[172] seeking, and in some cases receiving, justice in respect of cultural heritage. However, familial communities can be the communities *providing* justice through repatriation. Some families discover that their ancestors obtained possession of cultural heritage with a troubled history and consider it to be more appropriately cared for by that community and so return it to them, or at least locate it elsewhere in an attempt to rectify that injustice. The grandson of Captain Walker,[173] who had taken part in the punitive expedition to Benin Kingdom, restituted certain objects which he had inherited from his grandfather. The Haggard family restituted a Jibbah to the Khalifa House Museum in Sudan.[174]

5.2.7 Institutional Communities of Care

Various institutions are themselves communities of care, acting in a representative capacity for the broader community, but acting at the same time as a community on their own behalf.

5.2.7.1 Parliament

Parliament can, as a whole, be identified as a community of care. However, it is sensible to separate out the different sub-communities within Parliament which all contribute to the care of cultural heritage.[175] One may primarily think of Parliament in its law making role, debating issues about cultural heritage when considering bills which may, or may not, eventually become Acts of Parliament. In this role, Parliament can make tangible changes to how cultural heritage is cared for, although the care that is provided by it may be considered indirect, since it does not involve looking after the physical cultural heritage itself. Nevertheless, its actions affect the way in which cultural heritage is cared for. But there are other sub-communities within Parliament caring for cultural heritage. Members of the House of Commons or the House of Lords may make statements in Parliament, highlighting important matters about cultural heritage and concern about its care.[176] In doing so, this dialogic community

---

[171] E.g. Nazi-era claims brought before the Spoliation Advisory Panel. Overall in this book the language of challenging the *status quo*, rather than claims is preferred and is explored in Chapter 9.

[172] Discussed at Section 5.2.8.3.

[173] See Samuel Reilly, 'Private Enterprise – The Individuals Who are Taking Restitution into Their Own Hands', *Apollo Magazine*, 1 August 2020.

[174] Mallinson Architects and Engineers, *Western Sudan Community Museum Project*: www .mallinsonae.com/western-sudan-community-museums (last accessed 1 May 2023).

[175] Described by Waterton as 'a "third" body [after the DCMS and Historic England] that holds sway in the processes of formulating heritage legislation and policy': Emma Waterton, *Politics, Policy and the Discourses of Heritage in Britain* (Basingstoke: Palgrave Macmillan, 2010), p. 81.

[176] See, for example *Hansard* HL vol. 820, col. 1602, *British Museum: Ethiopian Sacred Altar Tablets* (30 March 2022).

contributes to the way in which cultural heritage is cared for, encouraging action which furthers the appropriate care of cultural heritage. Other communities of care within Parliament include select committees which challenge how cultural heritage is cared for, making significant inroads into ensuring that the UK cares for cultural heritage appropriately. In the 7th Report of the 2000/2001 session of the Select Committee for Culture, Media and Sport[177] important statements were made about the need to address the continued retention by museums of cultural objects spoliated during the Nazi era as well as the illicit trade in cultural objects. In the follow-up report of the Committee in 2003/2004, when the issue of spoliation was revisited, the Select Committee held to account the government for the lack of progress that had been made in bringing about a change in the law to enable national museums to deaccession objects spoliated during the Nazi era, as well as the lack of progress in creating databases of illegally removed cultural objects.[178] These, therefore, provide places in which law makers who provide care for cultural heritage are held to account for any perceived shortcomings in that care. Select Committees can also be instrumental in the care of individual cultural heritage; the 1998 Report by the House of Commons Committee for Culture Media and Sport[179] was credited with being instrumental in saving HMS *Cavalier*.[180] In Scotland the remit of the Culture, Tourism, Europe and External Affairs Committee includes the ability to consider and report upon culture and tourism matters.[181] In 2019, the committee reported in *The Glasgow School of Art Mackintosh Building: The Loss of a National Treasure* on its hearings and findings relating to the 2014 and 2018 fires that damaged the Glasgow School of Art. In this report the committee commented not only on the fires themselves and governance issues relating to the school's custodianship and safeguarding of the historic building but also on the broader issue of whether a sub-category of Grade A listed buildings should be introduced which 'are of significant cultural and historical importance to Scotland'.[182]

Another way in which Parliament cares for cultural heritage is through All Parliamentary Groups established to consider particular issues of interest across the political divide; in this regard, a host of parliamentary groups consider different aspects of the care of cultural heritage,[183] contributing to

---

[177] House of Commons, Culture, Media and Sport Committee, Seventh Report, Session 1999–2000, *Cultural Property: Return and Illicit Trade*, HC 371-I, July 2000.

[178] House of Commons, Culture, Media and Sport Committee, First Report, Session 2003–04, HC 59, pp. 22, 27.

[179] House of Commons, Culture, Media and Sport Committee, Third Report, Session 1997–98, HC 561.

[180] House of Commons, Culture, Media and Sport Committee, Fourth Report, Session 2004–05, *Maritime Heritage and Historic Ships*, HC 296.

[181] https://archive2021.parliament.scot/parliamentarybusiness/PreviousCommittees/117355 .aspx (last accessed 20 December 2022).

[182] *The Glasgow School of Art Mackintosh Building: The Loss of a National Treasure*, p. 39.

[183] The register of All-Parliamentary Groups [as at 25 August 2021]: https://publications .parliament.uk/pa/cm/cmallparty/210825/contents.htm (last accessed 20 December 2022) included: Archaeology; Arts and Heritage; British Museum; Historic Vehicles; Holocaust

the dialogue surrounding its care. In Scotland Cross-party Groups of members of the Scottish Parliament include groups on 'Culture and Communities', Gaelic and Scotch whisky.[184] In Wales, relevant Cross Party Groups of the Senedd include 'Arts and Health' and 'Intergenerational Solidarity'[185] and in Northern Ireland this includes the All Party Group on Arts.[186]

5.2.7.2 Government Departments

The care of cultural heritage in the UK is split across several different government departments, further contributing to the patchwork of care provided for cultural heritage. The Department for Digital, Culture, Media and Sport (DCMS) is responsible for 'protect[ing] and promot[ing] our cultural and artistic heritage … ',[187] which includes ultimate responsibility for cultural property, museums, the illicit trade in cultural objects, and World Heritage Sites. However, responsibilities for the care of cultural heritage places are also placed on the Department for Levelling Up, Housing and Communities, specifically when dealing with the planning and development policies, including the National Planning Policy Framework (NPPF), which affects the historic environment. Thus, the recent policies regarding public statues and the presumption in favour of retaining and explaining their relevance emanated from the Secretary of State for what was then called Housing, Communities and Local Government, rather than the Secretary of State for Digital, Culture, Media and Sport, and was solidified in the NPPF.[188] Whilst both the DCMS and the Department for Levelling Up, Housing and Communities are geared towards dealing with cultural heritage because the subject is clearly within their usual remit, other departments may only have a tangential relationship with cultural heritage and its care, only undertaking care in more limited circumstances, with potentially less of an overall holistic approach than the DCMS or the Department for Levelling Up, Housing and Communities have. The scheme for cultural gifts is ultimately the responsibility of HM Revenue and Customs as it falls within the provisions relating to various taxes, even though it relies on the expert advice of the Acceptance in Lieu Panel, which is hosted at Arts Council England (ACE). The Ministry of Justice is responsible for granting licences to exhume human remains when archaeologists anticipate

---

Memorial; Industrial Heritage; Listed Properties; Metal, Stone and Heritage Crime; Museums; and War Heritage.

[184] The Scottish Parliament, *Current and Previous Cross-Party Groups*: www.parliament.scot/get-involved/cross-party-groups (last accessed 1 June 2023).

[185] Welsh Parliament, *Cross Party Groups*: https://business.senedd.wales/mgListOutsideBodiesByCategory.aspx (last accessed 20 December 2022).

[186] Northern Ireland Assembly, *All Party Groups*: http://aims.niassembly.gov.uk/mlas/allpartygroups.aspx#current (last accessed 20 December 2022).

[187] UK Government, *What the Department for Digital, Culture, Media & Sport does*: www.gov.uk/government/organisations/department-for-digital-culture-media-sport (last accessed 20 December 2022).

[188] NPPF 2021, para. 198.

that they may find human remains, or where they have discovered some during excavations.[189] In the case of wrecks not only would the Ministry of Defence have involvement in the discovery of certain wrecks, but also the Receiver of Wreck, which sits within the Maritime and Coastguard Agency.[190]

In Wales Cadw, as part of the Welsh Government's Arts and Sports Department,[191] is responsible for caring for the historic environment.[192] In Scotland, the Arts, Culture and Sports department has responsibility for cultural property, museums and World Heritage Sites. The Department for Communities in Northern Ireland is responsible for the arts, cultural heritage, language and the historic environment.[193] All these government departments across the four nations thus contribute their own varied communities of care, creating and using nested practices of care.

5.2.7.3 Local Authorities

Local authorities have a dual role in the care of cultural heritage. First, in their role as local planning authorities, with responsibility for the administration of planning laws and policies. Part of this responsibility involves considering applications for development that are likely to affect designated heritage assets or their settings. This role is therefore one of ensuring that the care of cultural heritage undertaken by others is appropriate and that it is undertaken according to the relevant legal provisions and associated policy. The second role of local authorities is in providing direct care for cultural heritage of which they are owner or guardian.[194] This includes cultural heritage places that the local authority make use of itself (e.g. civic halls or offices), or monuments, theatres, parks and gardens, but also includes any cultural heritage objects which it owns and which may be part of collections. These may be housed in museums owned and run by the local authorities themselves, or both the collections and the museums in which they are housed may be administered by third parties on behalf of the local authority. In its role of directly caring for cultural heritage, it is clear that the local authority, as the extended museum community, has a responsibility based on public trust. The court in *Snibston* provided strong judicial recognition of the public trust where Blake J elevated the concept of public guardianship to one of trust, highlighting the risk that the

---

[189] As was the case in the context of the licence application to disinter the remains of Richard III, discovered in Leicester: *R (on the application of Plantagenet Alliance Ltd.)* v. *Secretary of State for Justice, the University of Leicester and others* [2014] EWHC 1662 (QB), para. 43.

[190] See Maritime and Coastguard Agency, *Guidance: Wreck and Salvage Law*: www.gov.uk/guidance/wreck-and-salvage-law (last accessed 20 December 2022).

[191] Which is also responsible for museums and the arts.

[192] The language of 'caring for the historic environment' is used, particularising it as conserving and protecting it: Welsh Government, *Introducing Cadw* (Bedwas: Cadw, 2019), p. 4.

[193] Department for Communities, *Topics*: www.communities-ni.gov.uk/topics (last accessed 1 June 2023).

[194] Regarding guardianship, see Section 7.5.4.2.

public authority, in selling off objects on the open market, 'forfeits all trust in the future as a guardian of such assets'.[195]

Within local authorities, Heritage Champions (usually one of the councillors) act as advocates 'to help ensure the proper care of the historic environment is embedded in all activities over which the authority has influence'.[196] Through this scheme, the responsibility for ensuring that cultural heritage places are appropriately cared for is placed on an advocate who can speak up for cultural heritage within a local community, providing dialogic care. In some cases, local authorities may also set up additional bodies to contribute to the care of cultural heritage, such as conservation advisory fora, which may evaluate and advise on applications affecting heritage assets.[197]

5.2.7.4 Domestic Non-governmental Organisations (NGOs)

Various NGOs are tasked, as communities of care, with facilitating the work of government in caring for cultural heritage, either by administering schemes on their behalf, advising them or by performing regulatory functions. In some cases, NGOs also take responsibility for the direct care of cultural heritage places or objects, either by virtue of their existing rights of ownership, by compulsorily purchasing them if they are at risk, or by assuming responsibility (but not taking ownership).[198] In other cases they are tasked with the care of publicly owned collections, such as the English Heritage Trust, a charity, which cares for the National Heritage Collection,[199] and has 'responsibility' as one of four elements of its vision and values.[200]

In some cases, statutory provisions place wide-ranging legal duties on NGOs. This can be seen in the case of the Historic Buildings and Monuments Commission for England (now known as Historic England), which has responsibility, through a prescribed legal duty, for historic places broadly, including those in private ownership. This duty (so far as practicable) is 'to secure the preservation of ancient monuments and historic buildings situated in England'.[201] The meaningfulness of this responsibility (in terms of how it may be effectively carried out) is evident from the powers of prosecution that Historic England has in England.[202] In effect, Historic England is a prescribed guardian, tasked with direct responsibilities for the care of cultural heritage places; it describes its role

---

[195] *ex parte Hall*, para. 46.
[196] Historic England, *Heritage Champions Handbook* (2016) HEAG127, p. 2.
[197] Such fora were suggested in Historic England, *Managing Local Authority Assets: Advice for Local Government* (reissued 2017) HEAC152, p. 9. They have been established in Warwick District Council: www.warwickdc.gov.uk/info/20386/submit_a_planning_application/529/conservation_advisory_forum (last accessed 20 December 2022) and Derbyshire Dales District Council: www.derbyshiredales.gov.uk/planning-a-building-control/conservation/conservation-advisory-forum (last accessed 20 December 2022).
[198] E.g. through the scheme of guardianships of ancient monuments. See Section 7.5.4.2.
[199] See DCMS, *English Heritage New Model: Consultation Response* (October 2014).
[200] English Heritage, *Our Vision & Values*: www.english-heritage.org.uk/about-us/our-values/ (last accessed 20 December 2022).
[201] NHA 1983, s. 33(1)(a).   [202] ibid., s. 33(2A). These are considered at Section 7.7.

as helping people 'care for, enjoy and celebrate England's spectacular historic environment' by, inter alia, 'championing historic places', 'identifying and protecting our heritage' and 'understanding historic places'.[203]

Arts Council England performs various roles in the care of cultural heritage. It does this by administering schemes on behalf of the government[204] and on its own behalf, as well as owning cultural heritage.[205] Creative Scotland, as a public body, supports the arts, heritage and crafts, including by distributing funding.[206] Arts Council Northern Ireland has several functions, which include advising the Department for Education, other government departments, district councils and relevant bodies as well as 'develop[ing] and improv[ing] the knowledge, appreciation and practice of the arts' and 'increase[ing] public access to, and participation in the arts'.[207] Further non-governmental bodies playing a significant role in directly caring for cultural heritage include the National Trust[208] and National Trust for Scotland. The roles and responsibilities of these communities of care are set out in statute.[209]

5.2.7.5 Communities of Reform

Established in 1965, the Law Commission reviews the laws of England and Wales and undertakes projects, consulting widely, which analyse the existing legal structures and evaluate the appropriateness of reforms, at times drafting bills which eventually become law. In the Law Commission's 13th Programme of Law Reform *Museum collections* was identified as a future project.[210] This will focus on 'setting out how objects are held and can be dealt with by museums'.[211] In part its aim is to overcome problems where there is insufficient information about an object in a museum to determine whether it is only on loan rather than whether it entered the collection as a gift.[212] In the context of a broader project, the Scottish Law Commission considered specifically whether separate rules of prescription were needed for cultural objects and considered the case of treasure trove. It ultimately concluded that treasure trove should be excluded from the rule of positive prescription.[213] The Northern Ireland Law Commission, which

---

[203] *Historic England's Role*: https://historicengland.org.uk/about/what-we-do/historic-englands-role/ (last accessed 1 June 2023).

[204] E.g. the export licensing scheme, the Acceptance in Lieu Scheme, the conditional exemption scheme, the Government Indemnity Scheme and the Immunity from Seizure process: see ACE, *Supporting Collections and Cultural Property*: www.artscouncil.org.uk/supporting-arts-museums-and-libraries/supporting-collections-and-cultural-property (last accessed 20 December 2022).

[205] The Southbank Centre manages the collection on behalf of ACE, thus providing the direct care for the collection: Arts Council Collection, *About Us*: www.artscouncilcollection.org.uk/about-us (last accessed 20 December 2022).

[206] www.creativescotland.com/what-we-do (last accessed 21 May 2023).

[207] The Arts Council (Northern Ireland) Order 1995, art. 4(1).

[208] Including National Trust for Northern Ireland.   [209] See Section 3.4.4.

[210] Law Commission, *Museum Collections*: (last accessed 21 May 2023).   [211] ibid.   [212] ibid.

[213] Scottish Law Commission, *Report on Prescription and Title to Moveable Property* (SCOT LAW COM No. 228), pp. 16–17.

was established in 2002, has unfortunately not been operational since 2015.[214] Whilst operational, its two programmes of reform did not deal directly with issues relating to cultural heritage.[215]

These reformative communities of care exist more broadly to care for society in general, rather than specifically to care for cultural heritage. Nevertheless, they have the potential to care for cultural heritage (as seen in Scotland), and through its future law reform programme relating to museum collections, the Law Commission in England and Wales can play a key role in developing how cultural heritage is cared for in the future. It provides an opportunity to revisit the existing provision of care and considers the appropriateness of that care, which is an essential element of challenging the *status quo*. It interrogates the current legal framework and assesses how it might be used to provide appropriate care in the future.

5.2.7.6 Communities of Scrutiny

Various communities which care for cultural heritage are subject to scrutiny. In the context of the discussion of nested practices of care and the nature of non-departmental public bodies (NDPB), it is possible to see how the activities of these bodies are periodically monitored.[216] Select Committees, as discussed above, can challenge more broadly the approaches taken by communities of care towards the care of cultural heritage.

Where communities make instrumental use of available legal structures such as charities to facilitate the care of cultural heritage these activities are subject to scrutiny.[217] Thus, charities may be established for specific purposes, including the installation of particular statues, or may be used instrumentally to effect the recovery of cultural heritage and its reinstallation (e.g. the Temple Bar Trust was only ever viewed as a temporary charity). However, the Charity Commission provides an important regulatory role in ensuring that these small organisations which are established are for the public benefit and are not established for private gain. The role includes investigating the actions of the charity trustees, but also includes making orders to banks to hold the funds of the charity and not to make payments without the approval of the Commission, as well as the power to suspend a trustee, charity trustee, office, agent or employee of a charity.[218] Furthermore, the Charity Commission may play a direct role in determining whether or not objects which are charity property may be transferred out of the charity, for example, in response to repatriation claims.[219]

---

[214] www.nilawcommission.gov.uk/ (last accessed 21 May 2023).

[215] Although in principle the project on coroners – set out in the second programme of reform but which has not yet been undertaken – might extend to the way in which it deals with treasure.

[216] See Section 3.7.6.   [217] As seen in Section 6.4.2.   [218] Charities Act 2011, s. 76(3).

[219] See for example, the need for the Charity Commission's approval for restitution in the case of the Courtauld Institute returning drawings to the heirs of Arthur Feldmann following the recommendation of the Spoliation Advisory Panel: www.artandarchitecture.org.uk/images/gallery/3166e2a5.html (last accessed 1 June 2023).

These are therefore communities of scrutiny, providing an important mechanism for ensuring the appropriateness of care for cultural heritage. In many cases that role is not established for the purpose of caring for cultural heritage, but the scrutiny element of their role is effectively appropriated for the benefit of caring for cultural heritage.

In the case of government buildings in England, the Government Historic Estates Unit produces a biennial report on the condition of the government's historic estate[220] and requires returns from individual departments and agencies updating the status of their compliance with the *Protocol for the Care of the Government Historic Estate.*[221] The government sees this as setting a good example in the care of historic estate.[222] By scrutinising the practices of care on a community-by-community basis, this provides an opportunity to analyse whether care is appropriate and avoids maintaining the *status quo* in an unquestioning manner.

In Northern Ireland, it is recognized that the conduct and quality of the museum service would come under the jurisdiction of the Ombudsman, as the majority of museums are run by public bodies.[223]

5.2.8 Judicial Communities of Care

As outlined in Chapter 3, there has, at times, been a difficult relationship between the courts and the care of cultural heritage. Where secular courts deal with cultural heritage law principles it is clear that they play a central role in the care of cultural heritage by upholding the principles set out in the legislation and, where relevant, guidance. This ensures appropriate levels of scrutiny in decision-making where judicial review challenges are made. This may also include ensuring that appropriate consultation has taken place with expert communities of care, or the public more generally, and that this has been taken into consideration when making decisions about cultural heritage. However, the role of the court does not extend to revisiting the substantive elements of a decision. The court cannot substitute its own approach to caring for the cultural heritage for the one undertaken by the appointed decision-maker. The judicial role is therefore one of taking indirect responsibility for the care of cultural heritage by ensuring that those who have a voice have been heard and that the process is fairly and appropriately carried out. But it does not extend to ensuring that those who have direct responsibility for its care (in terms of the day-to-day or quotidian care) are providing appropriate care. It therefore

---

[220] See https://historicengland.org.uk/services-skills/our-planning-services/advice-for-government-historic-estates/#Section1Text (last accessed 20 December 2022).

[221] Historic England, *Protocol for the Care of the Government Historic Estate* (2017). A similar protocol exists for Northern Ireland: Northern Ireland Environment Agency, *Protocol for the Care of the Government Historic Estate*: Northern Ireland Guidance, February 2012.

[222] Historic England, *Protocol for the Care of the Government Historic Estate*, p. 1.

[223] Northern Ireland Museums Council, *Governance and Management of Museum* (2013), p. 8.

ensures that care is dialogic and to an extent empathetic to those other interests. It does not, though, ensure that the nature of the care, in a more holistic sense, is appropriate (in terms of being empathetic or respectful) because the decision itself is not substitutable.

Additional types of court also deal peripherally with cultural heritage matters. It has already been seen how the consistory court, in addition to dealing with listing matters under the ecclesiastical exemption, also applies principles which have evolved into ones caring for cultural heritage in the context of so-called church treasures.[224] The coroner's court plays a limited role in the care of cultural heritage when it carries out treasure inquests; here it applies existing cultural heritage laws under the Treasure Act 1996 and its power extends to applying those legal principles objectively to assess whether or not the objects in question are treasure. The work of the First-tier Tribunal (Tax) also plays a role in the care of cultural heritage, both in terms of the recognition of art or cultural heritage for tax purposes, and in the variation of undertakings for conditionally exempt objects as well as for rateable values for cultural heritage places.[225]

In situations where non-heritage law principles apply, the care provided tends not consistently to be care that would be considered appropriate. It is thus difficult to conceptualise of the courts in England and Wales assuming a general responsibility for the care of cultural heritage in the absence of any specific legal obligations to do so. The decision in *Iran* v. *Barakat*[226] discussed above does reveal the moral obligation (derived from the UK's international commitments) to recognise that other countries care about their cultural heritage and that this, and their efforts to care for it, should be respected.[227] But it is clear that any moral obligation to care for cultural heritage does not override legal provisions affecting the cultural heritage more directly. In this regard, the case of *AG* v. *Trustees of the British Museum*[228] considered whether the British Museum could respond to the claim of the family of a Jewish man whose drawings were seized by the Gestapo by returning looted drawings to them. Despite strong moral arguments that appropriate care for the cultural heritage and the people for whom it was important would result in a transfer from the collection, nevertheless the legal provisions which restricted the circumstances in which the museum could dispose of objects could not be circumvented by any moral desire to transfer the cultural heritage object elsewhere.[229]

5.2.8.1 The Ethos of the Court

Whilst the case of *AG.* v. *Trustees of the British Museum* was considering the recognition of a possible moral obligation of the museum (in its application of the principle in *Re* Snowden), judges often make it clear in their judgments that

---

[224] See Section 3.7.3.

[225] E.g. *The Roald Dahl Museum and Story Centre* v. *The Commissioners for Her Majesty's Revenue and Customs* [2014] UKFTT 308 (TC).

[226] [2009] QB 22 (CA), see Section 4.8.1.   [227] At Section 5.2.2.   [228] [2005] Ch 397 (Ch).

[229] ibid., 412.

they are dealing with legal questions rather than moral ones. In rhetorical terms, highlighting this demonstrates the court making clear its *ethos*[230] as a place to determine specific points of law rather than as a place to deal in morals.[231] Judges, when recognising that the subject matter of a claim is cultural heritage and that it may be important to particular groups, or when recognising that there are strong arguments in favour of keeping a collection of cultural heritage objects together, have on several occasions set out the ethos of the court, distancing themselves from the applicable legal principles which commit them to dealing with the claim in a particular way. In the case of *Thompson v. Shakespeare* heard in 1860, the Lord Chancellor observed (in the context of the validity of a bequest to honour the birthplace of Shakespeare) that 'We must all feel such an inclination in favour of giving effect to the bequest, that it is necessary to enter into a covenant . . . not to violate the rules which governed the Courts on such subjects'.[232] In the context of applications for judicial review, the court may make it clear early on that its power to review decisions is just that – a review of the process that does not allow it to substitute its own decision. Thus, in *ex parte Rose Theatre Trust*[233] Schiemann J set out the ethos of the court by saying 'the court is not empowered under our law to consider whether it is desirable that the remains of the Rose Theatre should be scheduled. My personal views on that are legally irrelevant and I am obliged by law to lay them to one side.'[234] In a similar fashion, when considering a claim about the authenticity of a painting attributed to Egon Schiele, the judge in *De Balkany v. Christie Manson and Woods*[235] made it clear that 'this is a judicial decision based upon the evidence and is not, and it does not purport to be, a contribution to the academic debate, in which I am not qualified to participate'.[236]

Several cases demonstrate how judges distance themselves from the final outcome of the case, recognising that the subject matter is important cultural heritage, yet highlighting that 'the law' has tied their hands in reaching the final judgment. In *AG New Zealand v. Ortiz* one law lord distanced himself from the result and what the law had directed them towards deciding.[237] This shows how the judicial committee of the House of Lords was not taking responsibility for the care itself, but emphasised how the law lords were restricted in their ability to care appropriately for the cultural heritage in question. In this regard, Lord Brightman ended his speech with: 'I have every sympathy with the appellant's claim. If the statement of claim is correct, New Zealand has been

---

[230] See generally Peter Goodrich, *Reading the Law: A Critical Introduction to Legal Method and Techniques* (Oxford: Basil Blackwell, 1986).

[231] Again, demonstrating the ethos of the court.

[232] *Thomson* v. *Shakespear* [1860] 1 De G F & J 399, 405. Despite stating that 'All must be delighted at anything that can be done to do honor to the memory of such a remarkable man as *Shakespeare*' the bequest was void in the circumstances: at p. 405.

[233] *R* v. *Secretary of State for the Environment (ex parte Rose Theatre Trust Co)* [1990] 1 QB 504.

[234] ibid., 507.   [235] (1995) 16 TR LR 163.   [236] ibid., 2.

[237] [1984] AC 1, 49 (Lord Brightman).

deprived of an article of value to its artistic heritage in consequence of an unlawful act committed by the second respondent.'[238] Whilst empathetic, and showing that the judicial committee cared *about* cultural heritage, nothing could be done to override the statutory provisions which might have enabled the court to provide more appropriate care *for* the wooden panels from Motunui.

A case which demonstrates how traditional property law concepts may prevent a court from being able to take into account cultural heritage as a distinct category requiring specific care, or to recognise the communities for whom it is important, is the case of *Tower Hamlets London Borough Council* v. *Bromley London Borough Council.*[239] Here a dispute arose over the ownership of a Henry Moore sculpture, entitled 'Draped Seated Woman' and fondly known as 'Old Flo'.[240] In 2012 the then mayor of Tower Hamlets proposed to sell the sculpture, which had originally been acquired by London County Council and sited in a council-run housing estate.[241] Old Flo had been on long-term loan to the Yorkshire Sculpture Park since 1996. When news of the proposed sale was made public, the London Borough of Bromley claimed ownership of Old Flo (as the successors to the London Residuary Board in whom all personal property of the abolished London County eventually vested)[242] and committed itself to retaining Old Flo within East London. Tower Hamlets then sought a declaration from the High Court regarding the ownership of the sculpture. The question for the court was whether the sculpture was a fixture (in which case Tower Hamlets was the owner) or personal property (in which case Bromley was the owner). Although the sculpture was found to be personal property, Tower Hamlets was held to have the best title as it had converted the sculpture and the statute of limitation had extinguished both Bromley's claim and legal title.[243] Whilst it would seem that the 'fate' of Old Flo, as public art in East London, was at risk with such a finding, ultimately the mayor of Tower Hamlets resigned and the borough did not sell the sculpture.[244]

---

[238] ibid.

[239] *London Borough of Tower Hamlets* v. *London Borough of Bromley (as successor to the London Residuary Board)* [2015] EWHC 1954 (Ch).

[240] The sculpture was a reflection by Moore on his wartime experiences: ibid., para. 1. See generally Alice Correia, 'Draped Seated Woman 1957–8, cast c.1958–63 by Henry Moore OM, CH', catalogue entry, November 2013, in *Henry Moore: Sculptural Process and Public Identity* (Tate Research Publication, 2015): www.tate.org.uk/art/research-publications/henry-moore/henry-moore-om-ch-draped-seated-woman-r1172099 (last accessed 21 May 2023). For further details of the case itself, see Janet Ulph, 'Frozen in Time: Orphans and Uncollected Objects in Museum Collections' (2017) 24 *International Journal of Cultural Property* 3, 10–17.

[241] Maev Kennedy, 'Henry Moore Sculpture May Be Sold by Tower Hamlets Council', *The Guardian*, 3 October 2012:.

[242] There was strong public opposition to the sale, including a campaign by the Art Fund.

[243] [2015] EWHC 1954 (Ch), para. 49; under Limitation Act 1980, s. 3(2).

[244] Maev Kennedy, 'Henry Moore's Sculpture "Old Flo" Returns to East London', *The Guardian*, 25 October 2017.

In the first paragraph of the judgment Norris J engaged with the historical context of the sculpture and explained the social background to the installation of the sculpture, including policy issues supporting the acquisition of public art.[245] However, by the end of the paragraph he had clearly distilled the issue into one of ownership and articulated the basic premise that an object's owner was free to deal with the object as they wished.[246] There was no mention in the judgment of the contemporary social context of Old Flo, specifically the risk of her being sold and the potential loss to the community. The arguments put forward by Bromley in its application for permission to appeal suggested that the public interest was relevant (presumably because it had set out its commitment to 'retaining' 'Old Flo' for Londoners). However, this was not seen as relevant to the matter at hand. In the hearing of the request for permission to appeal the judge said, in denying permission:

> My judgment considers ownership: it does not contemplate a 'purpose trust', and the case was not so argued. The only question is whether the sculpture should be in the ownership and control of one local authority or the other. They may have differing ideas about how it should be dealt with and what moral limits should be placed on their statutory powers having regard to the history of the sculpture. But that is not a legal question.[247]

In the circumstances, Bromley clearly saw the moral limits on its purported ownership as curtailing any right to sell and ensuring instead that it was kept for the benefit of the public. Although not bound in the circumstances by the MA Code of Ethics (as this was a public sculpture rather than an accessioned object in a museum collection), it nevertheless saw itself under moral obligations akin to those set out in the code. However, Tower Hamlets (specifically its mayor at the time) saw no moral limits on its ability to sell the sculpture. Whether Bromley or Tower Hamlets was the owner of the sculpture, if the sculpture was recognised as a heritage asset, as a local authority, either one of the London boroughs would be expected (although not obligated) to comply with the document *Disposal of Historic Assets*.[248] As part of this, rather than maximising financial return, the local authority would be expected to secure 'the best value for the taxpayer'.[249] This would include taking into account the provision of statutory development, 'government planning policy for the historic environment', the fact that the 'most appropriate long-term use' may not align with the use bringing the greatest financial gain, state of repair and maintenance costs and wider regeneration benefits relating to the environment, culture and the like.[250]

---

[245] [2015] EWHC 1954 (Ch), para. 1.   [246] ibid.   [247] ibid., para. 10.

[248] Although technically only binding on central government, rather than local authorities, nevertheless, it represents best practice for local authorities: Historic England, *The Disposal of Heritage Assets: Guidance Note for Government Departments and Non-departmental Public Bodies* (English Heritage, 2010), para. 1.4: https://historicengland.org.uk/images-books/publi cations/disposal-heritage-assets/ (last accessed 1 June 2023).

[249] ibid., para. 9.1.   [250] ibid.

By highlighting that what the competing parties ultimately wanted to do with the object was a moral question rather than a legal one, the court failed to assume any responsibility towards the care of cultural heritage and left it for others to deal with. In *Tower Hamlets* the sculpture was neither translated into its status *qua* public art nor *qua* cultural heritage. Furthermore, its link with a particular place or community was absent from the discussion. The public's voice was neither acknowledged nor listened to in the circumstances. All in all, in this case the law failed to effectuate the policies or the widely held view that 'Old Flo' should not be sold off to the highest bidder – that is to say, saving it from sale to a potential private seller. Instead, ownership had primacy, thus demonstrating how the English courts (in the absence of specific legislation) may need to prioritise property rights over any public interest in cultural heritage. There was strong public opposition to the proposed sale of the sculpture; indeed, the support for the sale within Tower Hamlets council itself was by no means unanimous – it was the elected mayor who was in favour of the sale. Ultimately, the only reason that 'Old Flo' was 'saved' from the auction sales room was because of the change in mayor, leading to a change in policy which stopped the sculpture being sold.

Care was therefore not a central concern for the court. Instead, the issue came down to ownership, which is objectively determined and does not depend on whether or not they intended to keep it in its original place (or as near to it as possible) and maintain its association with the local people. Having said that, at no point has it been considered whether the public connection with the sculpture was a manufactured one for the purposes of keeping it within East London. Although there was much local public support for the 'Save Old Flo' campaign, many inhabitants of the locality may have had little or no direct experience of the statue given that it had been on loan to the Yorkshire Sculpture Park since the mid-1990s. Yet a strong feeling of the community in the form of East London was evident in the efforts to avoid it being sold. Ultimately it was 'returned', not to its original location, but to a public–private space within a corporate area of the city, for Old Flo now resides in Canary Wharf, London,[251] which is far removed from the context of public social housing in which she was originally located. Nevertheless, she was still considered to have returned to the East End. This idea of a constructed link with the community is an interesting one and has a similarity to the sudden public feeling of a desire to save an object for the nation which is at risk of being sold abroad but which may have been in a private collection for many years.[252]

Moving back now to comparable case law, a similar instance of a judge distancing himself from the law that had led him to the outcome of the case is

---

[251] Press Release, *Henry Moore Sculpture Draped Seated Woman Returns to the East End after 20 Years* (25 October 2017): https://group.canarywharf.com/media/press-releases/henry-moore-sculpture-draped-seated-woman-returns-to-the-east-end-251017/ (last accessed 15 December 2022).

[252] Discussed in Chapter 8.

found in *Re Wedgwood Trust Ltd (In Administration)*.[253] The question before the court was whether the Wedgwood collection of pottery and other objects of historical importance was available as an asset to meet the £134.7 million pension deficit of the Wedgwood company (in which case it was at risk of sale and dispersal)[254] or whether it was held as a charitable trust and therefore out of reach of the creditors.[255] Ultimately the collection was found to be an asset of the company. At the end of the judgment Judge Purle QC again acknowledged the collection's importance, but at the same time distanced himself from this, by saying: 'This is a sad conclusion for those who are concerned to preserve a collection which is, as everyone recognises, part of our cultural heritage and of immense importance . . . '[256] On the one hand he acknowledged that everyone recognises this as part of 'our' cultural heritage and thus created a shared community which valued cultural heritage (although it was unclear whether this was a local, national or international community); on the other hand he seemingly treated *others* as being the ones concerned with preserving the collection. Through this he seemingly tried to absolve the court of any responsibility for the care of cultural heritage. By the very end of the judgment he had clearly separated himself not only from the decision of the court (for the 'sad conclusion' was 'the combined result of the pension protection and insolvency legislation'[257]) but also from the collection itself by observing that 'Quite what will happen to the collection next will be a matter for the administrators and not, at least at this stage, for me'. Through that statement he effectively allocated responsibility to the administrator (whose legal duties to the creditors would not include any positive duty to provide appropriate care for the collection *qua* cultural heritage) without acknowledging any role for the public, or for the court acting on its own behalf.

The judge sought to contextualise the relative harms that were involved in the determination of the case, for he pitted the human tragedy of those with pensions who were affected by the pension deficit against the tragedy to the collection,[258] but without seeking to find any way around this. In practice his hands were tied by the legal principles, since there are no general principles relating to cultural heritage which must be considered in all cases.[259] Ultimately the collection was purchased by the Victoria and Albert Museum and lent on long loan to the Wedgwood museum in Staffordshire.[260]

---

[253] [2012] Pens LR 175 (Ch).

[254] In effect the museum company was the last company standing as part of the Wedgwood group. The collection had a financial value of £11.5–£18 million.

[255] *Re Wedgwood*, para. 3.   [256] ibid., para. 56.   [257] ibid.   [258] ibid., para. 56.

[259] An argument has been made for a general statute requiring cultural heritage principles and norms to be taken into account by decision-makers, including the courts: Charlotte Woodhead, 'A Critical Analysis of the Legal and Quasi-Legal Recognition of the Underlying Principles and Norms of Cultural Heritage' (thesis submitted for the degree of Doctor of Philosophy at the University of Leicester, April 2014).

[260] See V&A Board Meeting Minutes, 3 July 2014.

5.2.8.2 The Courts as Guardians

When it comes to the ecclesiastical courts and the relationship with cultural heritage, it is clear that the Chancellors have envisaged their role as one of guardian. As discussed above, they have started to see themselves as having a role in the care of cultural heritage by assuming responsibility for recognising the national interest, even when traditionally the role of the church had been recognised by its courts as one of church rather than museum.[261] It is clear that the courts treated the faculty jurisdiction as the guardian of both the future and of the past in a need to future-proof its decisions.[262] Therefore, in assuming responsibility for the objects in their care, the courts would take into account the views of parishioners, but even if the majority of them were in favour of the proposal, that was not, by itself, conclusive.[263]

In *Re Wootton* (discussed above in the context of creating national communities) one can observe how the court treated the sale of cultural heritage objects as being a last resort.[264] The judgment creates a community in which an organisation whose mission is entirely different from 'heritage organisations' – and is neither established to care for cultural heritage, nor is primarily concerned with the day-to-day care of cultural heritage – nevertheless recognises the role of the churchwardens as guardians of art treasures.[265] What is clearly important to the court is not only the public visibility – both for objects of local and national distinction – but also the public access to them. Care is translated here into an assumption of responsibility for the national interest by averting the risk of loss abroad or to the private sector. This is not a contested dispute which involves location elsewhere; the rhetoric of 'saving for the nation' is not used here, but that is in effect what it does. Whilst the church (with support from the consistory court) had direct physical care and custody of the cultural heritage, it saw care as a continuing duty, acting here on behalf of the nation. The courts, in recognising these guardians, are themselves acting as guardians.

5.2.8.3 Developing Alternative Communities of Justice: Providing Space to Resolve Dissonance

As discussed above, families may act as communities of justice when seeking justice for past wrongs. However, the committees set up to determine such claims as well as museums responding to repatriation requests all form part of the community of justice. In an ideal world, all members of the community involved in that dialogue (which would be the ideal terminology, rather than dispute) would be considered as the community of justice. The community would

---

[261] At Section 5.2.5 – specifically discussing the case of *Wootton*.

[262] See generally *Re St Stephen's, Walbrook* [1987] Fam 146 (Court of Ecclesiastical Causes Reserved).

[263] ibid., 164. This was in the case of an application for a faculty to install an altarpiece by Henry Moore.

[264] See Section 5.2.5.

[265] It thus treats the approach in *Re St James, Welland* as being too narrow. In that earlier case Mynors Ch had pointed out that churches are not museums and were not formed to be guardians of art treasures for their own sake.

therefore include those making the claim, those responding to the claim and those determining the claim (whether independent committees or the museum itself acting as decision-maker).

Individual people come together to form a community because they care *about* cultural heritage but in the act of coming together to form communities they exercise care *for* the culture heritage itself. In this way, the creation of communities established for the purpose of bringing a claim or for challenging a decision that has been made is in itself, an act of caring. Once established, the active care that these communities provide for the cultural heritage functions as ongoing care.

Communities of justice who challenge the *status quo* are usually intergenerational in nature, for the basis of the challenges relate to the claims of their forefathers, for which they have assumed responsibility for pursuing in an attempt to seek justice. This may be seen as a duty owed to their forefathers. In the context of Nazi-era dispossessions, the family members bringing the claim have standing to bring the claim based on the notion of inheritance – they would have inherited their forefather's property but for their persecution – so therefore take on the claim that their forefather would have had.[266] However, in situations involving claims by other countries, or communities where borders have changed over the years, or where there is uncertainty about the links between the modern-day communities and the original communities which are linked with the cultural heritage, more difficulties arise in determining the nature of the claim and the appropriate response.[267] The language of challenging the *status quo* may, therefore, be more helpful and is explored further in Chapter 9.

In some cases the communities seeking justice had already formed as communities before commencing the claim and remain as communities after claims are resolved. Nevertheless, some communities of justice may only be temporary in nature; they may have been solidified as a community in legal terms (e.g. if they have been established as a company limited by guarantee or using some other legal device) solely for the purposes of bringing a claim and assuming responsibility for the care of cultural heritage by challenging the *status quo*.[268] In the context of claims brought regarding the proposed development of Stonehenge, a community was established as a company limited by guarantee.[269] This community could be described as an instrumental one, with the aim of demonstrating it has have standing for the purposes of pursuing litigation, thus assuming responsibility for cultural heritage, by instrumentally using the law. If its status is not recognised and the claim is not upheld, its assumption of responsibility may be thwarted. Its authority to assume direct responsibility for particular cultural heritage is therefore challenged – in some cases because the connection between the cultural heritage and the community is insufficient. In the *Rose Theatre Trust* case, the group was found by the court not to have standing on a stricter test of *locus standi* for

---

[266] See Section 9.3.5.   [267] See ibid.
[268] As to challenges to the *status quo*, see generally Chapter 9.
[269] Company number 12591715 incorporated on 7 May 2020: https://find-and-update.company-information.service.gov.uk/company/12591715 (last accessed 21 May 2023).

judicial review.[270] Were such a review to be brought now it is likely that a court would find sufficient *locus standi* in the circumstances based on the liberalisation of the test of standing.[271] The difficulty in establishing standing can be seen in the context of a claim made before the European Court of Human Rights in respect of the Parthenon Marbles by a Greek association, established in 1895 to ensure the protection and maintenance of 'monuments and works of art connected with the history of Athens'.[272] None of the Convention articles cited would give a right to an association such as the applicant to have a right to have the marbles returned to Greece, or to require the UK to engage in international mediation for their return.[273]

In a similar vein, in a report following a public consultation about a claim made by Council of British Druid Orders against the Alexander Keiller Museum in Avebury, it was recognised that the members of the group did not have a sufficiently close link with the human remains to claim them and to assume responsibility for their direct care through reburial.[274] Following extensive public consultation, English Heritage and the National Trust concluded in a joint report that the group was deemed to have a relationship which was only as significant as any other member of the Western European population and for that reason its claim was unsuccessful.

Choosing the appropriate legal structure is important. Certainly community interest companies cannot be created by people who wish to form a community of care specifically to promote or oppose changes in the law, or oppose changes to proposed or existing policies promulgated by government or other public bodies.[275] However, if those activities are incidental to other activities which a reasonable person considered to be for the benefit of the community then it will be allowed.[276]

5.2.9 Museums as Communities of Care

The discussion now moves closer to the direct care provided for cultural heritage by focusing on those traditionally considered to be caring for much cultural heritage – museums. At times it is only too easy to think of museums simply as institutions, as a homogeneous whole, but in fact they consist of members forming

---

[270] Although the editors of *De Smith* suggest that it would have been advisable for the applicants to argue that as an 'agglomeration of individuals' they had standing, because some of them had relevant expertise: Harry Woolf, Jeffrey Jowell, Catherine Donnelly and Ivan Hare, *De Smith's Judicial Review* (8th ed., London: Sweet & Maxwell, 2018), para. 2–044.

[271] See *De Smith's Judicial Review*, para. 2–045. See also *R. (on the application of Save Stonehenge World Heritage Site Ltd.* v. *Secretary of State for Transport* [2021] EWHC 2161 (Admin) where a company limited by guarantee was granted standing to judicially review the Secretary of State for Transport's grant of a development consent order.

[272] *Syllogos Ton Athinaion* v. *UK*, Application no. 48259/15, 31 May 2016, p. 1.   [273] ibid., p. 3.

[274] See the final report: https://historicengland.org.uk/advice/technical-advice/archaeological-science/human-remains-advice/avebury-reburial-results/ (last accessed 20 December 2022).

[275] The Community Interest Company Regulations 2005, reg. 3(1).   [276] ibid., reg. 3(2).

a community.[277] This community includes not only the governing body of the institution, those who work in the museum either as staff or volunteers, those who engage with the museum to develop its practices, those who visit museums and those whose cultural heritage may be displayed there. A central element of the work of museums, and of those who work in them, is caring for their collections – something which is enshrined in the UK Museums Association (MA) Code of Ethics.[278] When it comes to national museums, responsibilities for the care of a museum's collections are often set out in the governing statute.[279] In the case of non-national museums established as charities, the responsibility for care is partially a responsibility owed to the public to look after charity property.[280]

The role of museums is often seen as one by which they hold their collections as ethical guardians, on behalf of others – specifically for the benefit of society.[281] This is reflected in the various codes of ethics governing museums. It is clear that in legal terms museum curators can be seen as being in a heightened position of responsibility than members of the public.[282]

5.2.9.1 Paternalistic Communities of Care

One form of community, considered in more detail in Chapter 9, is that of paternalistic communities of care which may be evident in museums. Paternalistic care is where a community of care continues to maintain the position that it is best placed to bear the responsibility for the care of cultural heritage without revisiting that decision. These are formed in situations where responsibility for care is either assumed, without consulting those for whom the cultural heritage is important, or where the current provision of care is maintained without revisiting that decision. Here there is an absence of critical engagement in an empathetic and respectful manner with dialogue to determine whether the continued provision of direct care by that particular community (such as the museum) is appropriate. Arguments may be advanced that another community of care is more suitably placed to assume responsibility for the direct care of the cultural heritage.

5.2.10 Expert Communities of Care

Experts contribute at different stages to the care of cultural heritage and represent, in themselves, communities of care.[283] Criticism has been levelled

---

[277] As Lixinski points out, there are issues in exactly how a museum's 'community is defined': Lixinski, *International Heritage Law for Communities*, p. 86.

[278] UK MA, *Code of Ethics for Museums*, principle 2.   [279] See Section 6.4.1.

[280] See Section 6.4.2.

[281] This is the approach taken in the International Council of Museums (ICOM) Code of Ethics (Principle 2) and they are seen as preserving the 'inheritance of humanity' (Principle 1), ICOM, *Code of Ethics for Museums* (2017).

[282] *R v. Hakimzadeh* [2010] 1 Cr App R (S) 10 (CA). Discussed at Section 7.7.

[283] This fits with the approach taken by Lixinski, who seeks in his book to look at experts as a group, rather than as individuals: Lixinski, *International Heritage Law for Communities*, p. 71.

at the enhanced role that experts have, at the expense of communities for whom the cultural heritage is important.[284] Involvement of experts in the designation and care of cultural heritage has the potential to contribute to the Authorized Heritage Discourse.[285] This is based, in part, on the notion that a governance structure that privileges experts may have the effect of marginalising local voices.[286] Lixinski suggests that experts could be seen as 'stage managers'[287] and that it might be possible to 'downgrade experts to just another interested community'. By doing so the 'parity could potentially open the field more widely to engagement by other non-state actors, whose interests would not need to be filtered by the expert in its stage manager role'.[288]

At the national level, heritage experts can facilitate efforts to proactively care for cultural heritage, by preventing harm from development or sale, and 'saving' a place or object. Although experts advise on the designation of listed buildings, public participation is possible in setting the designation process in motion by nominating places.[289] It has been observed that 'communities of expertise have been placed in a position that regulates and assesses the relative *worth* of other communities of interest, both in terms of their aspirations and their identities'.[290] For this reason, it is said that '"Other" communities, therefore, have endured a less than equal footing from which to make claims about their past, their heritage and their self-image'.[291] One therefore has to be mindful of the need to be alert to the potential power imbalances and the risk of paternalistic care imposed on other communities. For this reason, ensuring that care is empathetic, respectful and dialogic can guard against this.

The recommendations of bodies of advisors who assist decision-makers such as the Secretary of State have already been considered in the context of the nested practices of care of cultural heritage and their status as NDPBs.[292] These bodies represent individual expert communities of care, whose advice in most cases will be followed by those with the actual power to make decisions. Therefore, as part of their process of reaching their recommendations, these expert communities have a responsibility for the care of cultural heritage. Determining the appropriate financial reward for finds of treasure is dealt with by such a committee of experts in the form of the Treasure Valuation Committee. The Export Reviewing Committee recommends to the Secretary

---

[284] ibid., p. 71.   [285] Laurajane Smith, *Uses of Heritage* (London: Routledge, 2008), p. 11.
[286] See generally Lixinski, *International Heritage Law for Communities*, p. 77.   [287] ibid., p. 101.
[288] ibid.
[289] See see Historic England, *How to Get Historic Buildings or Sites Protected Through Listing* https://historicengland.org.uk/listing/apply-for-listing/ (last accessed 3 June 2023); Department for Communities, *Nominating a Building for Listing in Northern Ireland* https://www.communities-ni.gov.uk/articles/nominating-building-listing-northern-ireland (last accessed 3 June 2023); Welsh Government, *Understanding Listing in Wales*, Cadw 2018, p. 19; and Historic Environment Scotland, *Propose a building for listing* https://www.historicenvironment.scot/advice-and-support/listing-scheduling-and-designations/listed-buildings/propose-a-building-for-listing/ (last accessed 3 June 2023).
[290] Waterton and Smith, 'Recognition and Misrecognition', 4.   [291] ibid. 13.
[292] See Section 3.7.6.

of State which objects are national treasures and for a large part the Secretary of State is dependent on the expertise of that group.[293] The Spoliation Advisory Panel has a dual role, advising both the Secretary of State and the parties to a claim (the governing body of the respondent museum and the claimants).[294]

In some cases the role of experts, as advisors, has a statutory footing.[295] When deciding where an object that has been accepted in lieu of tax because of its significant association with a place should be located, the Secretary of State 'shall obtain such expert advice as appears to him to be appropriate'.[296] Historic Environment Scotland, as an expert community of care, has the power to give advice in respect of matters relating to Historic Maritime Protection Areas. This includes advice relating to matters which might damage or otherwise affect the historic asset as well as how they might further the preservation objectives and identify any possible hindrance to these.[297] Designated institutions advise the Secretary of State of any exemption certificates under the Ivory Act 2018.[298] These include experts at museums such as the Victoria and Albert Museum.

Communities of experts are also consulted in a formal manner on certain aspects of the care of cultural heritage. Experts participate in the way in which a decision is reached about what to do with a particular heritage place, specifically organisations such as Historic England, the Church Buildings Council as well as amenity societies who are interested in the preservation of historic buildings and in some cases buildings of a particular historical period.[299] It was observed in *Re St Mary, Sherborne*[300] by the Court of Arches (in the context of the rights of Historic England and the national amenity societies to participate in faculty proceedings) that: 'True it is that that public interest recognises the legitimate wishes of those who worship God in places where over the centuries thousands have worshipped before them, but it also recognises that the concerns of conservationists and others must be properly examined and taken into account in the decision-making process.'[301] This passage imagines the integrated communities of care – both caring about and for cultural heritage. In talking about the public interest it very much recognises the wider communities for whom the cultural heritage is important. Similarly, the Planning (Listed Buildings and Conservation Areas) (Heritage Partnership Agreements) Regulations 2014 states that the local

---

[293] The recommendations of the Export Reviewing Committee are analysed in more detail in Chapter 8.

[294] The recommendations of the Spoliation Advisory Panel are analysed in more detail in Chapter 9.

[295] For example, see the role of Historic England: Section 3.7.2.   [296] NHA 1980, s. 9(5).

[297] Marine (Scotland) Act 2010, s. 80A(1).   [298] See Section 4.3.1.

[299] E.g. the Society for the Protection of Ancient Buildings, the Ancient Monuments Society, the Council for British Archaeology, the Georgian Group, the Victorian Society and the Twentieth Century Society are informed where there is a proposal for the demolition of a listed building or works for altering a listed building which involves demolition of part of the building: Arrangements for Handling Heritage Applications – Notification to Historic England and National Amenity Societies and the Secretary of State (England) Direction 2021, para. 4(b).

[300] [1996] Fam 63.   [301] ibid., 70.

planning authority must consult with Historic England during a consultation period of 28 days before making a Heritage Partnership Agreement (HPA)[302] and take into account any representations from the Commission received during the consultation period.[303] Once the HPA is made there is a reporting obligation to Historic England.[304]

In charity law, expert opinions are necessary to determine whether an institution is a museum under charity law[305] and in ecclesiastical law, there are circumstances in which there is mandatory consultation with the Church Buildings Council in the case of faculties relating to various matters concerning heritage objects or places, including the removal of articles of 'special historic, architectural, archaeological or artistic interest'.[306] The role of experts within a process needs to be carefully managed and can be beneficial where there are long-term relationships between experts and communities for whom the cultural heritage is important and where the local communities can influence experts' research questions.[307]

Communities of experts can also form as professional organisations, providing support for each other, working towards common frameworks and providing advice, and in some cases upholding standards. These include the major membership organisations such as the MA, the Collections Trust, the National Museum Directors' Council as well as those with specialist interests, such as the Museum Ethnographers' Group and the Touring Exhibitions Group. In addition to their own principles relating to professional conduct, they often also produce guidance for their members to follow which may include establishing appropriate standards of care. This expertise supports fellow members, encouraging and enhancing the appropriate care of cultural heritage. These communities also, by responding to consultations, contribute to the wider discussions that take place beyond the sector and which may reform policies in the area if they are called upon.

5.2.11 Artists' Communities: Foundations and Authentication Boards

The estates of artists, or their foundations, can play two distinct roles in the care of cultural heritage. Firstly, they may hold collections of artists' work, and be responsible for their day-to-day and long-term care.[308] Secondly, they may

---

[302] Planning (Listed Buildings and Conservation Areas) (Heritage Partnership Agreements) Regulations 2014, reg. 4(2)(b). HPAs are considered at Section 6.5.

[303] ibid., reg. 4(2)(c).   [304] ibid., reg. 6.

[305] Charity Commission, *The Review of the Register of Charities: Museums and Art Galleries*, Report 2002, p. 3 and see *Re Pinion* [1965] 1 Ch 85, 89.

[306] The Faculty Jurisdiction Rules 2015, as amended, r. 9.6(1). See, for example, *Re Emmanuel Church Leckhampton* [2014] Gloucester Cons Ct, 44. In the Church in Wales the relevant expert is the Committee on Church Art and Architecture.

[307] Lixinski, *International Heritage Law for Communities*, p. 99.

[308] E.g. The David Hockney Foundation: www.thedavidhockneyfoundation.org/ (last accessed 1 June 2023).

care for an artist's legacy in terms of the integrity of the body of work. In this role they may authenticate work, promote the artist and (if they have sufficient funding) finance the care of the artist's works which are owned by others, but which might be at risk of harm.[309] The origin of this responsibility may derive from the terms of a bequest or may have been established during the lifetime of the artist. In some cases artists' foundations, or the trustees of the estate, may ensure that the wishes of the deceased artist, if enshrined in a legal obligation, are met.[310]

5.2.12 Ethical Communities of Care

Ethical care of cultural heritage is central not only to professional practices such as museums and archaeology but more fundamentally to the assessment of cultural heritage value.[311] States are encouraged by international conventions to be alert to their moral obligations[312] reflecting the notion of ethical treatment of cultural heritage as part of the 'common themes' of heritage.[313] The museum sector exemplifies a strong ethical community with its ethical mandate from the international community, set out in the 1970 UNESCO Convention, as follows: 'museums ... should ensure that their collections are built up in accordance with universally recognized moral principles'.[314] The museum profession, both nationally and internationally, has developed codes of ethics (discussed above in the context of nested practices of care) which apply to both its individual and institutional members.[315] Further institutional policies relating to matters such as acquisitions, disposals, collections management, spoliation, human remains and in some cases repatriation more generally will support the work of individual museums. This is supplemented by government guidance which also adds to the ethical nature of the community, in some cases binding

---

[309] For example, in the case of the risks to the long-term care of Paolozzi's *Piscator* at Euston station, the Paolozzi Foundation was willing to fund the restoration: see Section 7.6.1.

[310] E.g. the Turner Bequest: see Section 7.3.2.2.

[311] See Smith et al., citing various authors in support, who suggest that 'Any discussion of values, including heritage values, begins in the realm of ethics and morals': George S. Smith, Phyllis Mauch Messenger and Hilary A. Soderland, 'Introduction' in George S. Smith, Phyllis Mauch Messenger and Hilary A. Soderland (eds.), *Heritage Values in Contemporary Society* (Walnut Creek: Left Coast Press, 2010), p. 16.

[312] Convention on the Means of Prohibiting and Preventing the Illicit Import, Export and Transfer of Ownership of Cultural Property UNESCO, Paris (adopted 14 November 1970, entered into force 24 April 1972 823) UNTS 231, Preamble.

[313] These have been described as being duty, honour, including stewardship, fairness and responsibility as well as social obligations: Smith et al., 'Introduction', p. 16.

[314] 1970 Convention, Preamble. This has been described as a 'strong pressure instrument' – regarding the establishment of ethical codes: Manlio Frigo, 'Ethical Rules and Codes of Honor Related to Museum Activities: A Complementary Support to the Private International Law Approach Concerning the Circulation of Cultural Property' (2009) 16 *International Journal of Cultural Property* 49, 51.

[315] E.g. UK MA, *Code of Ethics for Museums* and ICOM, *Code of Ethics for Museums*.

them to ethical obligations in excess of the legal ones. Professional archaeologists also bind themselves to codes of ethics[316] and other specialised guidance.[317]

5.2.13 Communities of Concern: Proactively Taking on Responsibilities

A 'sense of community' is a 'strong motivator for participation' and an absence of identity can 'militate against participation'.[318] At times groups are established to proactively assume responsibility for the care of cultural heritage, reacting directly to a threat in order to avert direct and irreparable harm to cultural heritage, or to stop the loss of cultural heritage abroad.[319] Here groups of people use the law instrumentally to establish themselves as communities and bring claims to challenge decisions which may affect the integrity of the cultural heritage.[320] They may seek to take ownership of the cultural heritage to prevent the harm or loss, thus assuming responsibility for the long-term care of the cultural heritage in question. These communities, and the way in which they assume the responsibility for the care of cultural heritage, are explored further in Chapter 7.

Where individual members of the public, or community groups, respond to consultations, this demonstrates indirect care for cultural heritage. The act of responding primarily demonstrates that they care about cultural heritage enough to contribute to the discourse about issues (usually) involving the long-term care of the cultural heritage. Some small communities, as organisations, may be established solely with the purpose of caring *for* certain cultural heritage, rather than more distantly caring *about* it. When groups of non-experts come together to form communities, this is clearly about caring for cultural heritage and demonstrates an assumption of responsibility towards cultural heritage and community inter-relationality. This might be through establishing public interest companies, or trusts, or where other organisations use the law instrumentally to further their desire to care for culture heritage.

Participation in the form of impromptu organisations established to care for heritage shows non-experts caring for heritage. Participation in the care of cultural heritage by what may be very small organisations, set up purely for the

---

[316] Chartered Institute for Archaeologists, *Code of Conduct: Professional Ethics in Archaeology* (London: CIfA, 2014) and World Archaeological Congress which has specific codes of ethics for dealing with indigenous peoples, human remains and the display of human remains and sacred objects: https://worldarch.org/code-of-ethics/ (last accessed 1 June 2023).

[317] Discussed at Section 3.7.5.2.

[318] Vivien Lowndes, Lawrence Pratchett and Gerry Stoker, 'Diagnosing and Remedying the Failings of Official Participation Schemes: The CLEAR Framework' (2006) 5 *Social Policy & Society* 281, 287.

[319] This can be not only cultural heritage objects, but also cultural heritage places, which occasionally may be removed, brick-by-brick, and relocated abroad: see Section 7.8.4.

[320] Discussed at Section 5.2.13.

purpose of caring for cultural heritage, is perhaps the strongest form of participation. It demonstrates the centrality of relationships and the willingness to assume responsibility in response to the government or local authority or other institution (for whatever reason) failing to step up to the mark to care appropriately for cultural heritage. The question then becomes whether this care, provided in whole, or in part, by non-experts, is appropriate care in the circumstances.

5.2.14 Communities Providing Safe Havens

It will be seen in Chapter 7 how, in the context of the 1954 Hague Convention, state parties may provide temporary refuges in times of war for illegally imported cultural property.[321] The use of safe havens[322] in the context of cultural heritage raises particular issues in terms of law enforcement and objects crossing borders. Questions also arise about the assumption of responsibility, at times without full dialogue and consent, where decisions may be made urgently without informed consent.[323] In recent times museums in exile have been created and major museums such as the British Museum have played a role in temporarily caring for cultural heritage until it is safe to return it to its country of origin. As part of this caring process these communities of temporary care – the safe havens – may contribute to the overall care of the cultural heritage in terms of its flourishing by undertaking additional research which can supplement the historical record regarding the objects and contribute more broadly to knowledge, providing a greater understanding of the cultural heritage.[324] The necessity of this, and the pressured circumstances, may mean that responsibility may be assumed without full informed consent of the state party from which the cultural heritage originates, but that this care can still be considered empathetic and respectful even in the absence of direct dialogue.[325]

5.2.15 Private Communities of Care

It is recognised that whilst some of the 'best known' historic buildings and sites are 'in the care of major national organisations . . . most of our heritage is cared for by private owners'.[326] Privately owned cultural heritage places designated as listed buildings or scheduled monuments, or located within conservation areas, are cared for through the legislative provisions restricting the way in

---

[321] At Section 7.3.1.
[322] Whilst safe havens are something that countries may establish in advance of war as a means to care for their cultural heritage, here safe havens refers to those situations where other states or organisations take care of cultural heritage from another state on a temporary basis. See Section 7.5.4.4 for a discussion of safe havens.
[323] For a discussion of some of these problems, see Section 7.5.4.4.   [324] ibid.   [325] ibid.
[326] DCMS, *Heritage Statement 2017*, p. 7.

which private owners can use their property with a view to averting irreparable harm to cultural heritage.[327] These owners form an overall community of care which has transcended the public/private divide. They are a collection of individual owners who, by virtue of owning a heritage asset, find that they are responsible for its care. Their private property rights are therefore subordinated (in part) to the public interest in caring about cultural heritage and therefore have to care for cultural heritage.

In contrast to the legal provisions relating to cultural heritage places, there is no similar regime for designating cultural heritage objects and restricting the owner's actions. This led the authors Lawson and Rudden, in their second edition of *The Law of Property*, to observe that providing that a private owner of a painting by Vermeer does not cause a nuisance he could place it on a bonfire.[328] There are some limited situations, though, where specific obligations of care are placed on the owners of personal property which is cultural heritage. This occurs in the context of the conditional exemption of tax where owners of cultural heritage objects considered as pre-eminent[329] undertake both to provide public access to the heritage objects and to preserve them, in return for receiving tax dispensation. Through this scheme they care for the cultural heritage. Again, this is a community of individual owners who may not be aware of other members of that community. Here they are not coming together collectively but they are people with a common interest and as a community are affected by relevant legal decisions.[330]

Nevertheless, they do contribute to the overall care of cultural heritage in the UK in return for a financial benefit to them. They therefore assume that responsibility. It is likely that because these objects are valuable items of personal property the private owners would care for them appropriately (by averting harm to them), either because they are of importance to them *qua* cultural heritage or *qua* financial asset. Nevertheless, they also have a responsibility to care for them because of the public interest in that object occasioned by the public foregoing the payment of tax to the value of that object.

In some cases private communities of care exist, formed of the families who care about and care for cultural heritage by virtue of inheritance. They have become the custodians of cultural heritage places and have assumed a responsibility for their care. Their desire to care and continue to care for, and provide access to these places may stem from their long-term connection with the place, but may in part be grounded in a feeling of responsibility towards the national heritage. These private communities of care at times can form together as organised communities of care, for example in communities such as the Historic Houses Association.

---

[327] See Section 7.4.1.

[328] Frederick Henry Lawson and Bernard Rudden, *The Law of Property* (Clarendon Law Series, 2nd ed., Oxford: Oxford University Press, 1982), p. 116.

[329] See Section 4.3.3.

[330] E.g. *Re an application to vary the undertakings of A; Re an application to vary the undertakings of B* [2005] STC (SCD) 103.

5.2.16 Market-focused Communities of Care

Various actors are involved in the trade of cultural heritage. This includes smaller-scale dealers, auction houses, as well as the internationally known major auction houses. Given London's major role in the international art market, this forms a large community and network of communities. Although the primary objective of these communities may well be a financial one, nevertheless they too form communities of care since, as discussed in Chapter 2, care takes a variety of forms. Care is provided by these communities, even if not always appropriate for cultural heritage (in the sense of being empathetic, respectful or dialogic). At times market-focused communities of care adopt their own codes and agree to abide by these.[331]

The sort of care provided by these communities of care is varied and includes care in researching the provenance of objects and making these visible to the public.[332] This contribution to the historical record can add to the knowledge about the object, whilst at the same time having the instrumental effect of making the object more marketable.

Other forms of care provided by the market include, in the case of the major auction houses, the work of their restitution departments. They work to uncover gaps in provenance and where they have identified potential acts of spoliation, they may act to achieve just and fair solutions.[333]

5.2.17 Facilitative Communities of Care

Some communities of care, acting very much on the periphery, provide the practical means by which other communities of care can provide appropriate care to cultural heritage. These communities provide, among other things, funding to support the activities of other communities of care. This includes foundations such as the Wolfson Foundation, which supports communities by providing financial assistance for the care of 'sites of outstanding historic, architectural and cultural significance',[334] as well as the Heritage Fund.[335] These various organisations, and the frameworks within which they act, are considered in the context of quotidian care in the next chapter.

---

[331] E.g. the British Art Market Federation Principles of Conduct: www.bada.org/bamf-principles-conduct (last accessed 22 December 2022).

[332] It is acknowledged that some commentators may dispute this and have concerns regarding due diligence of auction houses and dealers alike, calling for less autoregulation: see Sections 3.4.4 and 7.6.2.

[333] See generally Section 9.7.2.2.

[334] The Wolfson Foundation, *Funding for Historic Buildings & Landscapes*: www.wolfson.org.uk/funding/funding-for-places/funding-for-historic-buildings-landscapes/ (last accessed 1 June 2023).

[335] They do not define heritage and consequently a very large group of projects relating to cultural heritage could receive funding: Heritage Fund, *What We Fund*: www.heritagefund.org.uk/funding/what-we-fund (last accessed 1 June 2023).

5.2.18 Evolving Communities of Care

Communities of care can evolve over time. They may begin as a group of interested individuals, either drawn from the local community or from a pool of experts, and develop into non-departmental advisory bodies or independent organisations directly sponsored by the government departments. This can be seen in the context of the organisation National Historic Ships UK, which administers the National Register of Historic Vessels. It grew from the National Historic Ships Committee, which began following a seminar in 1991, was succeeded by the Advisory Committee on National Historic Ships (a non-departmental advisory body) in 2006 and more recently was established as an independent organisation in the guise of National Historic Ships UK. It is funded by the government and 'provides objective advice to UK governments and local authorities, funding bodies, and the historic ships sector'.[336] The evolution of communities in such a way may show the formalisation and centralisation of care. It demonstrates clearly how individuals who care about cultural heritage and come together as a community to actively care for cultural heritage can steer, and indeed spearhead, the overall care for cultural heritage in a significant way at the national level. Concerns had been expressed (as reflected in several Select Committee reports[337]) about the appropriateness of the provision of care of historic ships. Therefore, the Select Committee, as a formal community of scrutiny, together with the community of care formed as the National Historic Ships Committee at a seminar, contributed in a concrete manner to the development of the national-level care of historic ships.

5.2.19 Shared Care: Integrated Communities of Care

Most communities of care identified in this chapter have been identified as individual ones, but it is important to remember that practices of care are nested; therefore multiple communities of care may share the direct and indirect care of cultural heritage concurrently. The responsibility may have been prescribed in those instruments forming the practices of care, but in other situations communities may have made use of general legal principles to assume responsibility for care. Taking just one example – here World Heritage Sites – it is possible to see this notion of shared care. The World Heritage Committee has overall responsibility for the nomination of World Heritage Sites (derived from the World Heritage Convention and its Operational Guidelines) and recourse can be had to the Committee when applications for development are made which may affect the universal value of the heritage site. Therefore, the World Heritage Committee has the ultimate sanction of being able to remove a World Heritage

---

[336] National Historic Ships UK, *About Us*: www.nationalhistoricships.org.uk/about (last accessed 22 November 2022).

[337] House of Commons, Culture, Media and Sport Committee, Fourth Report, Session 2004–05, HC 296.

Site from the list. As part of the designation of World Heritage sites, ICOMOS, as an advisory body to the World Heritage Committee, advises on the implementation of the Convention.[338] Within the UK the DCMS has overall responsibility for the scheme. The UK National Commission for UNESCO provides policy advice and supports the UK's agenda regarding UNESCO.[339] In turn, the appropriate NGOs or government departments in each of the nations of the UK assume responsibility through the provision of guidance notes regarding the World Heritage Sites.[340] As part of this the NPFF plays a role in making it clear that harm to WHSs should be 'wholly exceptional'.[341]

World Heritage UK is a community of care, established as a charity and a membership organisation, which developed from the Local Authority World Heritage Forum. Its aim is to draw together the UK World Heritage Sites and to represent and support them, helping communities to get involved with World Heritage Sites by focusing on advocacy, professional development and promotion.[342]

The local planning authority is also tasked with caring for individual World Heritage Sites by taking into account the potential effect that any development would have on the WHS itself and on its setting.[343] Each World Heritage Site has a management plan which supports it and sets out the responsibilities, acting as a framework 'for long-term decision-making on the conservation and enhancement of the WHS and the maintenance of its OUV'.[344] These plans are updated following consultation with the community.[345] Advisory bodies[346] or partnerships[347] may be formed as part of these management plans, thereby also taking responsibility for the care of the WHS. Local landowners who seek to develop their land in a way which may affect the World Heritage Site will also be subject to local planning laws and guidance in place.

[338] WHC, art. 14(2).

[339] The Role of the UK National Commission for UNESCO: https://unesco.org.uk/the-role-of-the -uk-national-commission-for-unesco/ (last accessed 1 June 2023).

[340] Historic England, *The Protection and Management of World Heritage Sites in England: English Heritage Guidance Note to Circular for England on the Protection of World Heritage Sites* (2008); Welsh Government, *Managing Change in World Heritage Sites* (Cadw, 2017).

[341] NPPF 2021, para. 200.

[342] https://worldheritageuk.org/about-world-heritage-uk/what-we-do/ (last accessed 18 August 2022).

[343] This is set out in the NPPF and discussed at Section 7.4.1.1.

[344] i.e. outstanding universal value. E.g. Historic Scotland, *The Heart of Neolithic Orkney World Heritage Site, Management Plan 2014–19*, 14 March 2016, p. 3. See generally www .historicenvironment.scot/advice-and-support/listing-scheduling-and-designations/world-heritage-sites/download-world-heritage-site-information/; https://cadw.gov.wales/advice-support/historic-assets/other-historic-assets/world-heritage-sites and www.daera-ni.gov.uk/ topics/land-and-landscapes/world-heritage-site (last accessed 1 June 2023).

[345] Historic Environment Scotland, *The Community View: Heart of Neolithic Orkney World Heritage Site* (1 April 2020).

[346] E.g. Bath World Heritage Site: https://www.greenwichworldheritage.org/about/administra tion (last accessed 21 May 2023).

[347] E.g. Maritime Greenwich World Heritage Site, *Administration:* https://www .greenwichworldheritage.org/about/administration (last accessed 21 May 2023).

Another way in which it is possible to see the shared care of cultural heritage is in the bringing together of different cultural heritage communities who care about cultural heritage to work collectively together with a common goal of caring for cultural heritage. This can be seen in the work of the UK's Heritage Alliance, which brings together more than 140 independent heritage groups from larger organisations such as English Heritage and the National Trust, to smaller specialist bodies.[348]

5.3 Developing Sustainable Relationships: Encouraging Participation of Communities in Decisions

Writing in 1905, Baldwin Brown suggested that the ultimate authority for monument preservation was public opinion.[349] But who exactly is the public? It can be seen that there was a recognition of this general interest when it came to the early litigation concerning Stonehenge, where the judge expressed the view that there was a public interest in Stonehenge and that: 'It is only fair to the defendant to say that he is not acting capriciously but on expert advice for the preservation of the stones.'[350]

It could be said that the public are given indirect responsibility for the care of listed buildings and scheduled monuments by virtue of the offences that they would be committing if they undertook work on a designated heritage asset without appropriate consent.[351] Certainly, the more general terminology of 'public interest' is used in the context of ancient monuments that are not formally included in the Schedule of Monuments, but which the Secretary of State considers to be of public interest because of their 'historic, architectural, traditional, artistic, or archaeological interest'.[352]

Participation provides the means of demonstrating respect and empathy (essential elements of the care of cultural heritage). It facilities opportunities to listen to, engage with and re-evaluate the care that is provided for cultural heritage and for the communities for whom it is important to contribute to this dialogic activity. Participation needs, though, to be relevant and meaningful, rather than partial or pseudo.[353] Equally, though, excessive participation can stifle the way in which care is provided for cultural heritage.[354]

---

[348] The Heritage Alliance, *The Heritage Manifesto 2019*: www.theheritagealliance.org.uk/wp-content/uploads/2021/02/Manifesto-2019.pdf (last accessed 20 December 2022). A further example is The Association of Charitable Foundations: see www.acf.org.uk/ (last accessed 1 June 2023).

[349] Gerard Baldwin Brown, *The Care of Ancient Monuments* (Cambridge: Cambridge University Press, 1905), p. 31.

[350] *Attorney General* v. *Antrobus* [1905] Ch 188, 209.   [351] See Section 7.4.1.

[352] AMAAA 1979, s. 61(12).

[353] A distinction is made by Pateman between full, partial and pseudo participation: Carole Pateman, *Participation and Democratic Theory* (Cambridge: Cambridge University Press, 1970), pp. 69–71.

[354] See Jim Rossi, 'Participation Run Amok: The Costs of Mass Participation for Deliberative Agency Decisionmaking' (1997–8) 92 *Northwestern University Law Review* 173, 217, who highlights the risk of excessive participation.

There is no common law duty to consult.[355] However, several situations show how participation, particularly public participation, is embedded within how the UK cares for cultural heritage. The first is the provision for consultation about developments that may affect the special character of listed buildings.[356] As part of this process the public in general is consulted on the way in which proposed developments may affect the historic or architectural interest of the building. Similarly, in the context of both changes to churches which are listed buildings and sales of objects from churches, members of the public can contribute, as active participants, to the consultation process.[357] In *Re St Bartholomew's, Aldborough*[358] the Chancellor observed that: 'The helmet has been in the de facto possession of the parish since the fourteenth century and it has at least a considerable moral claim to express a view as to what should happen to it now, subject of course to my ruling under the faculty jurisdiction.'[359] In the context of listed buildings Lord Reed has observed that 'The purpose of this particular statutory duty to consult must, in my opinion, be to ensure public participation in the local authority's decision-making process'.[360]

In the absence of a common law duty to consult the public, a local authority,[361] as a public organisation, may opt to consult on a particular matter. If it does so then that consultation needs to be undertaken fairly. Furthermore, if the public body has made it clear that it is going to take its results into account when making the decision then that public body needs to do so in a fair and reasonable manner.[362] A lawful consultation must 'be at a time when proposals are still at a formative stage . . . the proposer must give sufficient reasons for any proposal to permit intelligent consideration and response . . . [and] the product of consultation must be conscientiously taken into account'.[363] The public's role is cemented by the requirement that the local planning authorities must publish statements of community involvement,[364] which are 'intended to promote a culture of open and participatory decision-making'.[365]

In the case of *ex parte Hall*, involving the Snibston Discovery, the *obiter dictum* there shows that there is a greater need for participation and consideration of proposals from community groups who might have an interest in

---

[355] *Plantagenet Alliance*, para. 98.   [356] Under the P(LBCA)A 1990.

[357] This is part of the faculty jurisdiction.   [358] [1990] 3 All ER 440.   [359] ibid., 456.

[360] *R (on the application of Moseley)* v. *Haringey LBC* [2014] 1 WLR 3947, 3962 (SC).

[361] Here referring to local government.

[362] *R (on the application of Easyjet Airline Company Ltd.)* v. *Civil Aviation Authority* [2009] EWCA Civ 1361 (Dyson LJ), para. 46 and see *Snibston*, para. 31, which emphasises that where a public authority has chosen to consult then this should be in accordance with the *Gunning principles*.

[363] Citing Hodgson J in *R* v. *Brent London Borough Council, ex parte Gunning* (1985) 84 LGR 168, 189, this approach was recently approved by the Supreme Court in *R (on the application of Moseley)*, 3957.

[364] Planning and Compulsory Purchase Act 2004, ss. 18–20.

[365] *R (on the application of Majed)* v. *Camden LBC and Adam Kaye* [2009] EWCA Civ 1029 (Arden LJ), para. 35.

purchasing and running a museum if it would otherwise be closed.[366] The recent Historic England and Historic Environment Scotland AHRC project entitled *Outreach to Ownership* is tasked with exploring innovative approaches to community engagement and is beginning with a pilot scheme, partnering with organisations to (amongst other things) develop and sustain inclusive community outreach, networks and partnerships.[367] This community partnership, which brings together communities of care, has the potential to encourage and support empathetic, respectful and dialogic care.

Direct, public participation at the international level is found in the context of the World Heritage Committee, who 'may at any time invite public or private organizations or individuals to participate in its meetings for consultation or particular problems'[368] and 'may create such consultative bodies as it deems necessary for the performance of its functions'.[369]

5.3.1 Consultation as an Act of Care

The indirect caring of cultural heritage through consultation focuses on developing the relational aspect of caring for cultural heritage by engaging with a broader group of people who may be interested in the way in which cultural heritage is cared for. This process therefore facilitates active engagement with the way in which care is provided, ensuring that it is not solely the ultimate decision makers (who have assumed responsibility or on whom responsibility has been placed) who make the decision about the appropriate care. Instead, appropriateness of care, as Tronto recognises, needs to be revisited[370] and consequently such a programme of consultation permits this. An essential element of care in a caring relationship is that of trust and empathy.[371] Therefore, central to consultation is the need to ensure that the views expressed during the consultation are respected, including being taken into account and directly acted upon. For that reason, requiring that the elicited views obtained in a consultation are taken into account through a legislative requirement facilitates this.

5.4 Conclusion

Adopting a wide approach to the concept of communities has provided the opportunity to view the varied range of people who get involved in the care of cultural heritage in the UK. In some cases, that involvement is at the

---

[366] Discussed at Section 5.2.6.
[367] Historic England and Historic Environment Scotland, *Outreach to Ownership: Grants and Capacity Building Programme Call for Partners* (November 2021): https://historicengland .org.uk/content/docs/research/outreach-ownership-call-for-partners-pdf/ (last accessed 20 December 2022).
[368] 1972 World Heritage Convention, art. 10(2).   [369] ibid., art. 10(3).   [370] See Section 2.5.
[371] See Section 2.5.4.

periphery – in an indirect, but nevertheless important way such as scrutinising the law makers who themselves provide indirect care for cultural heritage. All of these communities contribute to how cultural heritage is imagined in the UK and how it is cared for. Some communities are far removed from the cultural heritage itself, but there are equally ones for whom it is vitally important for their sense of identity and for whom it forms an essential part of their everyday life. The next chapter will explore how the access to, use and enjoyment of cultural heritage are recognised in the nested practices of care. But what the overall picture of communities of care in the UK shows us is again the importance of looking beyond the legal provisions and considering the varied non-law nested practices of care used by the different communities in different ways. Appreciating the roles played by all of these communities helps to map out the cultural heritage landscape of the UK: from the institutions to the individuals and everything in between.

As will be seen in subsequent chapters, the court, as a community of care, may not always provide the most appropriate care. Nevertheless, it seeks to imagine cultural heritage in its many different forms. Even where legal questions are seemingly about something other than the heritage dimension to an object or place – there is still scope for judges to take into account the importance of heritage within the broader community. Although traditionally there has been a clear focus on property rights, and as the *Re Wedgwood* case shows, these take priority, it is also possible to see, in recent cases, a widening concept of the importance of cultural heritage, to not only the nation, but also local communities and international communities. Although only *obiter dictum*, the case of *ex parte Hall* demonstrates how a judge can construct the idea of a community which values cultural heritage. Such a community recognises that it is incumbent on those who control that cultural heritage when exercising their public functions to be cognisant of viable alternatives to closing down or significantly reducing the provision of cultural heritage within an area. These judicial statements, whilst persuasive rather than binding, can nevertheless provide support for the sector and emphasise the need for museums to look into viable options when deaccessioning entire collections.[372] This demonstrates how the community that is created in these cases has a wider importance to heritage within the wider community.

---

[372] MA, *Museums Facing Closure – Legal and Ethical Issues* (2017), para. 20.

6

Quotidian Care

6.1 Introduction

Everyday care can take a variety of forms. At its most basic, the opportunity for communities to use and enjoy cultural heritage is central to ensuring flourishing of cultural heritage and its communities of care. Those who care for cultural heritage on behalf of others have day-to-day responsibilities which can include ensuring that it is cared for appropriately, that appropriate access is provided and that access is balanced with any other risks. This may be facilitated through a system of licensing giving permission to do activities which might otherwise be prohibited for the purpose of averting unnecessary harm to the cultural heritage in question.

Quotidian care also includes navigating how communities engage with each other and with the cultural heritage, and how participation is enabled and encouraged. This includes the everyday management of collections and how cultural heritage is displayed and presented to other communities.

Communities participate in cultural heritage in various ways by making tangible contributions to its ongoing care. This can be reactive, by contributing to public consultations on specific issues to do with cultural heritage, or proactive, by forming where members of the public individually, or collectively, recognise a need, as communities, to care for particular cultural heritage. Given that central elements of care are the relationships between communities, assumptions of responsibilities for care and the need to revisit those allocations of responsibilities, the extent to which meaningful participation is facilitated and how far it is taken into account is central to determining the appropriateness of care.

This chapter begins by setting out the importance of appropriate quotidian care for the flourishing of cultural heritage and for the communities who care about it. The chapter then analyses how communities are allocated responsibility or assume responsibility for the direct quotidian care of cultural heritage. The focus then shifts to the broader notion of encouraging participation in cultural heritage and providing access to those opportunities. The final part considers the standards of care that are expected and contrasts these with general legal standards of care found in other areas of civil law.

6.2 The Importance of Quotidian Care for Flourishing of Cultural Heritage and Communities of Care

Appropriate everyday care is essential for cultural heritage and for the communities for whom it is important. Frequently, focus is placed on the need to care for cultural heritage so that obligations owed to future generations are met, but the living nature of cultural heritage and its importance to current generations is increasingly recognised in international conventions. According to the UN Universal Declaration of Human Rights, 'Everyone has the right freely to participate in the cultural life of the community, to enjoy the arts . . .'[1] This is mirrored in the cultural rights to enjoy cultural heritage and the right to access it and to take part in cultural life. As observed in the more recent UNESCO Declaration on Cultural Diversity, cultural heritage is recognised as 'the wellspring of creativity', for 'creation draws on the roots of cultural tradition, but flourishes in contact with other cultures'.[2] Whilst this is a right enjoyed by all humanity it is also reinforced in the context of the UN Declaration of the Rights of Indigenous Peoples.

Everyday engagement with cultural heritage is recognised as contributing to the flourishing of cultural heritage, and at the international level it has been linked to sustainable development.[3] Specifically, it is recognised as being central to sustainable development and necessary for well-being in the context of Wales. This means that public bodies in Wales, such as local authorities, the Arts Council of Wales, the National Library of Wales and the National Museum of Wales,[4] as part of their duties to carry out sustainable development,[5] must set and publish objectives designed to maximise the achievement of well-being goals and take all reasonable steps to meet those goals.[6] These well-being goals include 'A Wales of vibrant cultural and thriving Welsh language', which is defined as 'A society that promotes and protects culture, heritage and the Welsh language, and which encourages people to participate in the arts, and sports and recreation'.[7] The Public Services Boards for each local authority in Wales[8] must also publish assessments of the cultural well-being of an area[9] and a local well-being plan which sets out objectives and how they propose to meet them.[10] Community councils must also take all reasonable steps to meet the objectives in the local well-being plans.[11] When it comes to UK museums, these are recognised as having 'a duty to care for objects entrusted to them for the benefit of the public'.[12]

---

[1] Art. 27(1).   [2] UNESCO Declaration on Cultural Diversity (2 November 2001), art. 7.

[3] United Nations, *Transforming Our World: The 2030 Agenda for Sustainable Development* (A/RES/70/1), Goal 11.4 – 'Strengthen efforts to protect and safeguard the world's cultural and natural heritage'.

[4] Set out in the Well-being of Future Generations (Wales) Act 2015, ss. 6(1)(b), (i), (k) and (l) respectively.

[5] ibid., s. 3(1). This includes improving the cultural well-being of Wales: s. 2.   [6] ibid., s. 3.

[7] ibid., s. 4, Table 1.   [8] ibid., s. 29(1).   [9] ibid., s. 37.   [10] ibid., s. 39.   [11] ibid., s. 40(1).

[12] *Treasures in Trust: A Review of Museum Policy* (Department of National Heritage, 1996), para. 3.2.

6.3 Quotidian Care: Facilitating Use, Enjoyment of and Access to Cultural Heritage

In this part, we consider both 'care' as an express term in legal and non-law instruments as well as other language used to describe particular elements of care such as preservation of cultural heritage. Some instruments treat 'care' as closely entwined, or synonymous, with custodianship and link it with collections management. 'Care' is often separated from preservation, for example in the DCMS Guidance on the Care of Human Remains.[13] In some ways then 'care' as conceptualised in these instruments is more akin to what is treated here as quotidian care, whereas 'preservation' used in those same instruments is closer to the notion of preventing harm, which forms the subject matter of the next chapter. Regardless of this, it is helpful at this juncture to look at the different ways in which these concepts of care, custody and preservation are represented in the various instruments.

Central to the quotidian care of cultural heritage and the facilitation of use, enjoyment and access is the strong ethical basis to care.[14] Ethics play a vital role in ensuring that the day-to-day care of cultural heritage supplements the legal obligations and responsibilities that have been placed on communities of care, and encourage ethical care and stewardship of collections,[15] as well as recognising its importance to particular communities.[16] These ethical principles will again be treated as nested practices of care and the discussion of the legislative regime, and relevant case law, will be interwoven with consideration of the ethical principles enlarging these legal responsibilities.

6.4 Allocating and Assuming Responsibility for Quotidian Care

Responsibility for the care of cultural heritage can be allocated, but can also be assumed, and this can be done in different ways. These will be considered in turn in this section. First, it is helpful to consider those situations where responsibility is imposed, most usually through statutes, and how concepts of care have been translated into these instruments. Secondly, those situations in which responsibility is assumed for the care of cultural heritage will be considered. These are where a public interest has been generated in the cultural heritage because of a benefit received by the private owner (there is therefore

---

[13] E.g. part 2 of the document is separated into curation, care and use of human remains: p. 7.

[14] The first principle of the MA, *Code of Ethics* emphasises the importance of public engagement and public benefit, which includes active engagement, equal, honest and respectful treatment, access and enjoyment of collections: MA, *Code of Ethics* (2015).

[15] This is the second of the three broad principles of the MA, *Code of Ethics*.

[16] 'The care for collections, and especially so for human remains, is grounded in ethics, which are influenced by worldviews, cultural beliefs and/or politics, and lead to policies and practices whose success are largely dependent on access to resources': Myra Giesen, 'Introduction: Human Remains Curation in the United Kingdom' in Myra Giesen (ed.), *Curating Human Remains: Caring for the Dead in the United Kingdom* (Heritage Matters Series, Woodbridge: Boydell Press, 2013), p. 16.

a *quid pro quo*). In this context the responsibility for care, taking into account the public interest, is assumed by the private owner in return for a tax break, or the management and control of the cultural heritage place has been transferred to a public body.[17] Attention will then turn to situations where a community has voluntarily assumed responsibility for cultural heritage and how that quotidian care is translated into either ethical or legal principles.

6.4.1 Imposition of Responsibility

Care is recognised as a concept in the statutes governing the British Museum, the National History Museum, the Imperial War Museum and the National Maritime Museum. These instruments place responsibility for care on the museum directors rather than on the boards of trustees.[18] This emphasises how care is envisaged as the direct care provided for the collection in curatorial terms, rather than in terms of the broader policies that might be developed at trustee level.

Using the phrasing of 'in the care of', the British Museum Act (BMA) 1963 demonstrates a notion equivalent to stewardship, presenting the idea that the object is within the confines of the care of a particular institution. It can be observed that the use of this phraseology in the 1963 Act, without further clarification of its meaning, treats it as a static concept which recognises that the director, on behalf of the trustees, has the care of the particular objects. It does not identify, or set out specifically, on whose behalf the care is given or of the need to care for the individuals. In particular, it does not detail the communities or public for whom the cultural heritage is important.

Care is clearly central to the work of the British Museum and is specifically recognised by the establishment in 2019 of the Department of Collection Care, whose team 'conserves, preserves and investigates the collection for the benefit of present and future generations'.[19]

There is no specific statutory provision placing the trustees under a duty to preserve the collection; instead, their duty is expressed as a duty to keep the objects in the collections in the particular authorised repositories.[20] Preservation is referenced in the context of making objects available for inspection by members of the public with the trustees being given a power to impose certain conditions on the access for the purposes of ensuring their safety.[21]

---

[17] The terminology of *assuming* responsibility rather than the *imposition* of responsibility is used because these are undertakings which are assumed in the context of what amounts to a contractual arrangement.

[18] BMA 1963, ss. 6(1) and 8(3); Imperial War Museum Act 1920, s. 4(2) and National Maritime Museum Act 1934, s. 5(1).

[19] British Museum, *Department of Collection Care*: www.britishmuseum.org/our-work/depart ments/collection-care (last accessed 21 December 2022).

[20] BMA 1963, s. 3(1).   [21] ibid., s. 3(3).

Whilst the statutes governing the British Museum, the Natural History Museum, the Imperial War Museum and the National Maritime Museum represent an older style of approach to museums, as they were enacted between 1920 and 1963, more recently enacted statutes governing national museums have placed the obligations to care for their collections on the governing bodies of institutions themselves. These statutes have also distinguished 'care' from 'preservation' and this might therefore indicate that 'care' equates to the more quotidian nature of caring for cultural heritage identified in this chapter. Thus, in the context of the National Gallery,[22] National Portrait Gallery,[23] Tate Gallery,[24] the Wallace Collection,[25] Victoria and Albert Museum,[26] Science Museum,[27] the Royal Armouries,[28] National Museums and Galleries of Northern Ireland[29] and the National Museums of Scotland,[30] the governing bodies are required to 'care for' and 'preserve' the objects in their collections.[31]

There is no indication in either the statutes or in case law of how to interpret 'care' for the purposes of any of these statutes, nor is there any express statement of what the expected standard of care is. It is likely that if a court were faced with the need to determine the appropriate standard of care it would apply the standard expected of a reasonable national museum director in the relevant circumstances. This is in line with the common law approach to standards of care found both in the law of tort and in contract law.[32]

In some instances, the language of preservation, rather than that of care, is used in both legal and non-law instruments. Preservation seems to focus on ensuring the future of the cultural heritage in question, whereas care encompasses more activities and is not necessarily geared towards securing the future of the heritage, but rather focuses on looking after it on an ongoing basis. This can be seen in the context of the National Trust, whose purposes include 'the preservation of buildings of national interest or architectural historic or artistic interest ... and the protection and augmentation of the amenities of such buildings'[33] as well as 'the preservation of furniture pictures and chattels of any description having national or historic or artistic merit'.[34] The slightly differently worded provisions applying to the National Trust for Scotland are '[t]he preservation of buildings of architectural or artistic interest and places of

---

[22] Museums and Galleries Act 1992, s. 2(1)(a). In the National Gallery Act 1856 the terminology used was pictures and other works of art that 'have been placed under the Care and Ordering' of both the trustees and the director: s. 1.

[23] Museums and Galleries Act 1992, s. 2(3)(a).   [24] ibid., s. 2(2)(a).   [25] ibid., s. 2(4)(a).

[26] NHA 1983, s. 2(1)(a).   [27] ibid., s. 10(1)(a).   [28] ibid., s. 18(2)(a).

[29] Museums and Galleries (Northern Ireland) Order 1998, SI 1998 No. 261 (NI 2). ord. 4(1)(a).

[30] National Heritage (Scotland) Act 1985, s. 2(1)(a).

[31] In the case of the Royal Botanic Gardens, Kew, the duty is to care for the collections: NHA 1983, s. 18(1)(a). The trustees of the National Museum of Wales 'have custody of, retain, collect, preserve, maintain, record and lend or provide access to objects, things or information': Royal Charter and Statutes (December 2013), para. 5(i).

[32] See Section 6.11.1.   [33] The National Trust Act 1937, s. 3(a).   [34] ibid., s. 3(b).

historic or national interest' and '[t]he preservation of articles and objects of any description having artistic or antiquarian interest'.[35]

The Historic Monuments Commission for England has a duty, 'so far as practicable . . . to secure the preservation of ancient monuments and historic buildings situated in England' as well as to promote 'the preservation and enhancement of the character and appearance of conservation areas' in England.[36] Here, the focus on enhancement of conservation areas extends beyond the need to navigate actual or potential harm, and also includes the enhancement of the character and appearance of these areas (which includes not only the physical appearance but also the character which might incorporate more intangible elements of cultural heritage). As part of the nested practices of care British Standards provides guidance to those involved in cultural heritage conservation.[37]

6.4.2 Assumed Responsibility as *quid pro quo*

Non-national museums which have been established as charities owe obligations toward the public in terms of how the trustees exercise their powers and functions. By establishing themselves as charities these communities have assumed the responsibility and committed themselves to caring for cultural heritage.[38] They have thus used the law instrumentally. This legal status imposes certain elements of responsibility in return for which the charity receives certain tax breaks and is bound to satisfy the public benefit test and therefore need to show that it is providing sufficient access. The need to provide access to museums is central to the idea of the public benefit test in charity law[39] and there is an expectation that even small museums would need to be open to the public for at least half of the year.[40] Yet it is recognised that the public benefit is also linked to the need to preserve objects, and therefore access can be restricted if necessary for physical preservation of the collections.[41] Respectful care is central to the access

---

[35] National Trust for Scotland Order Confirmation Act 1935, ss. 3(a) and 3(b).

[36] NHA 1983, s. 33(1).

[37] British Standards; it is clear that these are 'statements of good practice' rather than mandated expectations: British Standards Institute, *What is a Standard – Benefits*: www.bsigroup.com/en-GB/about-bsi/uk-national-standards-body/about-standards/what-is-a-standard-benefits/ (last accessed 21 December 2022). They cover a range of issues relating to cultural heritage conservation, from the characterisation of mortars used in cultural heritage (BS EN 17187:2020) and guidelines relating to load-bearing timber structures (BS EN 17121:2019) to more general guidance such as *Conservation of Cultural Heritage. Main General Terms and Definitions* (BS EN 15898:2019).

[38] One of the charitable purposes is 'the advancement of the arts, culture, heritage or science': Charities Act 2011, s. 3(1)(f).

[39] Charity Commission, *Museums and Galleries*, RR10 (Version 08/02), para. A19.

[40] ibid., para. A21.

[41] ibid., para. A22. This mirrors Merryman's hierarchy of preservation-truth-access: John Henry Merryman, 'The Public Interest in Cultural Property' (1989) 77 *California Law Review* 339, 355. However, museums will need to find other means of providing non-physical access such as internet, lectures and media coverage: RR10, para. A28.

requirements mandated by the Charity Commission because it is clear that there needs to be transparency in that museums should publicise visitor numbers.[42] This reflects the public nature of charities, in that, in return for tax advantages, the museum should be accessible. In addition to their legal responsibilities, the charity regulators in all nations of the UK have Codes of Good Governance, which charities are expected to uphold, with principles covering matters including organisational purpose, leadership, integrity, risk and control, openness and accountability, and effectiveness.[43]

The supervision or surveillance of charities by the Charity Commission, the Office of the Scottish Charity Regulator (OSCR) and the Charity Commission for Northern Ireland ensures that objects are cared for appropriately by the trustees in the long term.[44]

When it comes to cultural heritage objects, private owners are free to care for cultural heritage in any way that they deem appropriate until the public benefit is recognised through the tax system when the private owner receives a tax break. Where a cultural heritage object is conditionally exempt from capital gains tax or inheritance tax (on the basis of its pre-eminence[45]) the public has an interest in its long-term care. The owners then enter into undertakings regarding levels of preservation and public access to the object and an agreement not to remove it from the UK.[46] In this way, the private owner assumes additional responsibilities towards the object and ultimately towards the public in its treatment of their otherwise private property.

Where the Secretary of State or Historic England has been constituted as the guardian of a monument, they are under a duty to maintain the monument,[47] and also have the full control and management of the monument.[48] Maintenance is interpreted as including repairs and doing 'any other act or thing which may be required for the purpose of repairing the monument or protecting it from decay or injury'.[49] In return for handing over responsibility

---

[42] RR10, para. A30.

[43] See Charity Commission, *Charity Governance Code for Smaller Charities* (2020): www .charitygovernancecode.org/en/pdf (last accessed 21 December 2022); Scotland's Third Sector Governance Forum, *The Scottish Governance Code for the Third Sector* (2018): http://good governance.scot/wp-content/uploads/2019/10/Scottish-Governance-Code-Final-PDF.pdf (last accessed 21 December 2022) and Charity Commission for Northern Ireland, *The Code of Good Governance* (3rd ed., 2021): www.nicva.org/sites/default/files/d7content/attachments-resources/code_of_good_governance_0.pdf (last accessed 21 December 2022).

[44] Two of the Charity Commission's objectives are the 'public benefit objective' and the 'compliance objective': Charities Act 2011, s. 14. The same objectives are found in the Charity Commission of Northern Ireland: Charities Act (Northern Ireland) 2008, s. 7(2). The various charity regulators in England, Wales, Scotland and Northern Ireland can instigate inquiries into the activities of a charity: Charities Act 2011, s. 46 (England and Wales); Charities Act (Northern Ireland) 2008, s. 22 and Charities and Trustee Investment (Scotland) Act 2005, s. 28. Ultimately charities can be removed from the register: Charities Act 2011, s. 34(1)(a) (England and Wales); Charities Act (Northern Ireland) 2008, s. 16(5) and Charities and Trustee Investment (Scotland) Act 2005, s. 30.

[45] See Section 4.3.3.   [46] IHTA 1984, s. 31(2).   [47] AMAA 1979, s. 13(1).   [48] ibid., s. 13(2).

[49] ibid., s. 13(7).

for the management and control of the cultural heritage place to a public body, the private owners then have encumbered land with an undertaking (prescribed in statute) to provide access and preservation.[50]

6.4.3 Voluntary Assumption of Responsibility

People may come together as informal communities to care for cultural heritage, taking the form of unincorporated associations. As seen in the previous chapter, in some cases these evolve on an *ad hoc* basis. Over time the members of that community might choose to use other legal structures to solidify its legal status. These choices might be with the view to making it easier for them to apply for funding in the future to support their work, or to benefit from tax advantages which come from converting the organisation into a charity. In some instances, communities may use the legal structure of a company limited by guarantee to assume responsibility for the care of cultural heritage. A clear advantage of having a recognised legal structure is that this may help a community who wishes to challenge the *status quo,* or to challenge a decision about the care of cultural heritage. The community interest and public nature of these communities, focusing on the people who care about and for cultural heritage, can be demonstrated by the public benefit test in charities,[51] and the community test in the context of community interest companies.[52] In this context, assessing whether something is being carried on for the benefit of the community depends on applying the community interest test, which involves considering whether a reasonable person would consider the activities were being carried out for the benefit of the community.[53]

The law provides a level of assurance that those communities who have established themselves to care for cultural heritage keep that cultural heritage together and there are restrictions on this by virtue of the different legal structures used. For that reason, charity trustees need the permission of the Charity Commission before disposing of certain charity property[54] and the use of the 'asset lock' in the context of community interest companies[55] also provides a means of ensuring the continued care of cultural heritage by restricting the way in which central assets, such as museum collections, might be disposed of.

When groups of people have come together to establish themselves as small communities they are not closed communities, but instead have a public-facing element to them. Charities are answerable to the Charity Commission and must satisfy the public benefit test. When it comes to community interest companies there is a requirement that they describe in their annual reports 'the steps, if any,

[50] AMAAA 1979, s. 19(1).   [51] Charities Act 2011, s. 4.
[52] The Community Interest Company Regulations 2005, reg. 3(1).   [53] ibid.
[54] Charities Act 2011, s. 105.   [55] The Community Interest Company Regulations 2005, sch. 1.

which the company has taken ... to consult persons affected by the company's activities'.[56] This therefore provides the relational element to care. Whilst not mandating consultation, it nevertheless demonstrates an expectation that they might do so when writing their report. This would be something that they would need to think about, and even if they had not consulted that year, it might encourage them to do so in the future. It would – one would hope – encourage respectful, empathetic and dialogic care of cultural heritage. When community interest companies and charities apply for funding from organisations such as the National Lottery Heritage Fund there is a clear expectation of public involvement and specifically it is a mandatory outcome of funding that 'a wider range of people will be involved in heritage'.[57]

In Scotland, social enterprises have been used for activities such as *Inclusive Images*, which used funding from the Heritage Fund to undertake a project entitled *Picturing Our Past* which supported people with disabilities and those from socially deprived areas to participate more fully in engaging with their local and national heritage.[58] Here, funding facilitates active participation in cultural heritage for not only those who might usually participate but specifically supporting those who may not have had the opportunity to do so before. This enables them to have access to, and to engage with, cultural heritage.

Carole Pateman distinguishes between partial participation and full participation.[59] The former refers to situations in which, although the public participates in discussions, ultimately the decision rests with the other party to the discussions. Contrastingly where a community group is formed to care for cultural heritage, participation can be full. This is perhaps a truly democratic example of participation because the self-selecting group, based on membership of a community, has assumed responsibility for the care of cultural heritage and makes the decisions about the most appropriate care in the circumstances.

Through professional guidance and a commitment to particular schemes of accreditation, including the Accreditation Scheme, and the Museums Association (MA) Code of Ethics, the notion of care is extended to encompass the consideration of other factors when making decisions about the long-term care of cultural heritage objects within national museums. Further support for a concept of care is also provided in the institutional guidance dealing with acquisition, disposal and lending of objects within the collection.

[56] ibid., reg. 26(1)(b).

[57] Heritage Fund, *Outcomes for Heritage Projects* (updated 27 January 2022): www .heritagefund.org.uk/funding/outcomes (last accessed 21 December 2022).

[58] Heritage Fund, *Picturing the Past: Access to Heritage for Excluded Groups in Scotland*: www .heritagefund.org.uk/projects/picturing-past-access-heritage-excluded-groups-scotland (last accessed 21 December 2022).

[59] Carole Pateman, *Participation and Democratic Theory* (Cambridge: Cambridge University Press, 1970), pp. 70–1.

6.4.4 Practical Measures to Support Care, Preservation and Maintenance

Funding for the care and maintenance of cultural heritage may be provided by different communities of care in various ways. These include communities established for the purpose of philanthropy.[60] Other communities who play an active role in the care of cultural heritage also have powers enabling them to provide funding to support other communities in the care of cultural heritage. These include the power for the Historic Monuments Commission for England (Historic England) to defray or contribute to certain costs relating to protected wrecks,[61] which includes costs of preservation and maintenance.[62] However, other organisations may provide funding for the ongoing care of cultural heritage. The War Memorials (Local Authorities' Powers) Act 1923 gives local authorities the power 'to incur reasonable expenditure in the maintenance, repair and protection of any war memorial within their district whether vested in them or not'.[63] Again, there is clear statutory support for very practical provision of expenditure to preserve or enhance the character or appearance of any conservation area in England and grants or loans can be made to cover the whole or part of the costs.[64]

6.5 Caring about Cultural Heritage and Facilitating Quotidian Care

In drawing together communities of care in a dialogue about quotidian care, heritage partnership agreements (HPAs)[65] demonstrate the relational nature of care in the context of certain designated heritage assets.[66] HPAs are agreements which provide consent for the owners of designated heritage assets, such as listed buildings or scheduled monuments, to carry out routine work without having to obtain formal consent each time (providing that this does not affect the special characteristics of the historic asset).[67] They are described in the Welsh context as being voluntary agreements 'for the long-term management of listed buildings' of designated heritage assets.[68]

Before HPAs are agreed, there is a requirement for the local planning authority to consult with both Historic England[69] and the public,[70] and to

---

[60] E.g. www.wolfson.org.uk/funding/funding-for-places/funding-for-historic-buildings-landscapes/ (last accessed 22 November 2022).

[61] Under the Protection of Wrecks Act 1973, s. 1.   [62] NHA 1983, s. 33C(1).

[63] War Memorials (Local Authorities' Powers) Act 1923, s. 1. In Wales there is the document: Welsh Government, *Caring for War Memorials in Wales* (Cadw, 2014).

[64] P(LBCA)A 1990, s. 77.   [65] ibid., s. 26A for England and s. 26L for Wales.

[66] See also The Scheduled Monuments (Heritage Partnerships Agreements) (Wales) Regulations 2021 and The Listed Buildings (Heritage Partnership Agreements) (Wales) Regulations 2021.

[67] Historic England, *Setting Up a Listed Building Heritage Partnership Agreement*, Historic England Advice Note 5, HEAG008 (2015), p. 1.

[68] Cadw, *Heritage Partnership Agreements in Wales*, WG43299 (Welsh Government, 2021), p.6.

[69] During a consultation period of 28 days before making a HPA (see Planning (Listed Buildings and Conservation Areas) (Heritage Partnership Agreements) Regulations 2014, reg. 4(2)(b)). Once the HPA is made there is a reporting obligation to Historic England: reg. 6.

[70] During a consultation period of 28 days (as required by the Planning (Listed Buildings and Conservation Areas) (Heritage Partnership Agreements) Regulations 2014, reg. 5(1)(a))

take into account any representations made during the consultation period.[71] Not only can the person who has 'an interest in the listed building'[72] and any occupier of it[73] be a party to the agreement, but also 'any other person who appears to the relevant local planning authority appropriate as having special knowledge of, or interest in, the listed building, or in buildings of architectural or historic interest more generally'.[74] Consequently, this provides opportunities for communities of care including local community groups, interest groups or amenity societies to participate directly in decisions about the long-term care of specific cultural heritage places. Participation, as a partner in this manner, by these communities of care is arguably more meaningful than when they contribute as consultees to applications for planning permission or listed building consent. Furthermore, as part of the HPA, provision can be made for a variety of things, including provision of 'public access' and 'the provision to the public of associated facilities, information or services'.[75] Equally, provision can be made for the restriction of 'access to, or use of, the listed building'.[76] Here, at least in theory, responsibility for care can be negotiated and assigned by the parties to the HPA.

6.5.1 Collections Management

As observed in a 2006 Select Committee Report, 'If we care about our collections, we must also take proper care of them'.[77] As part of the Accreditation Scheme of museums, administered by Arts Council England, accredited museums are expected to follow certain standards when caring for their collections, including undertaking care and conservation of their collections.[78] This includes following the Spectrum system of collections management published by the Collections Trust. Museums are also expected to have their own collections development policies setting out details of the types of objects that form their collection and which they may acquire and dispose of in the future.[79] These documents also set clear policies about their approach to care and conservation, detailing the activities undertaken to safeguard their collections, including 'organisational policies, security, storage, cleaning, maintenance, handling, scientific investigation, environmental monitoring and control, exhibitions and loans, conservation, provision of surrogates and emergency planning'.[80] On the whole, the way in which monitoring and review of the appropriateness of care takes place is through

---

information should be physically available near the listed building, Council building, etc. and online: reg. 5(1)(b).

[71] Including from Historic England and the public: ibid., regs. 4(2)(c) and 5(3).

[72] P(LBCA)A 1990, s. 26A(2)(d).   [73] ibid., s. 26A(2)(e).   [74] ibid., s. 26A(2)(g).

[75] ibid., s. 26A(6)(d).   [76] ibid., ss. 26A(6)(e) (England) and 26L (Wales).

[77] Culture, Media and Sport Select Committee Sixth Report (2006–2007), *Caring for Our Collections*, HC 176-1, 25 June 2007, para. 158.

[78] Arts Council England, *Accreditation Standard* (November 2018), para. 6.2.

[79] ibid., para. 6.1.   [80] *Caring for Our Collections*, p. 4.

the individual institutional collections' policies, which state the way in which collections are reviewed over time and how questions relating to the everyday care of the cultural heritage are undertaken.

6.5.1.1 Hindering Care

At times questions of ownership can hinder the appropriate care of cultural heritage. In the next chapter, it will be seen that when there is a risk of damage or deterioration to cultural heritage doubts about its ownership can stymie appropriate care; the uncertainty about who owns particular cultural heritage means that it is unclear on whom the responsibility falls. However, in some situations, museums may have come into possession of objects many years earlier but may lack the documentation specifying on what basis the object is within their collection – either owned by them or on a long-term loan.[81] This makes it difficult to carry out certain activities with those cultural heritage objects, for example, museums may be unable to lend the objects to other museums or dispose of the objects if they are no longer relevant to their collecting policies.[82]

6.6 Access to Cultural Heritage

Access is recognised as a central element of the use and enjoyment of cultural heritage. It is recognised as a cultural right, taking the form of physical access, economic access (i.e. affordable to all), access to information (across borders) and access to decision-making processes.[83] Facilitating access to cultural heritage can take a variety of forms. First, instruments recognising access and facilitating use of cultural heritage where it was previously unavailable will be discussed. Second, the shifting of cultural heritage from private to public ownership will be explored as will be the notion of bringing cultural heritage into the public domain without a transfer of ownership. The third element of access to be considered is where parties negotiate levels of access, or restriction of access, through collaboration. Next, the way in which participatory initiatives outside formal schemes are used to provide access will be considered. Fifth, the practical matter of the role of funding will be considered in terms of initiatives including free entry to museums as well as provision of funding for other activities. Attention will then turn to the balance between providing access, and the risk that that might bring.

---

[81] Janet Ulph, 'Frozen in Time: Orphans and Uncollected Objects in Museum Collections' (2017) 24 *International Journal of Cultural Property* 3, 8.

[82] It is for this reason that the Law Commission has recognised this area as a topic for review: see Section 5.2.7.5.

[83] Set out in Report of the independent expert in the field of cultural rights, Farida Shaheed, UN General Assembly Human Rights Council, 17th session, A/HRC/17/38, p. 16.

6.6.1 Provision of Cultural Heritage

Caring for cultural heritage includes providing opportunities for communities to engage with it. This can include institutions that care for cultural heritage, such as museums, specifically the provision of them, including by local authorities. It also includes how access is provided to them. Certain institutional communities may act on behalf of the wider community in amassing local or national collections for the benefit of the present communities, as well as those of future generations. Access to cultural heritage, often expressed in the form of facilitating admission to museums, has a long history. The MA was instrumental in encouraging the enactment of the Education Act 1918, which allowed schools to pay for museum trips. The facilitation of access to cultural heritage has judicial recognition, for case law from the European Court of Human Rights shows that a state can legitimately interfere with the private property rights of an owner of cultural heritage (a recognised human right) where those measures are 'designed to facilitate in the most effective way wide public access to them, in the general interest of universal culture'.[84] Local authorities in Scotland have specific powers to erect or maintain a statue or monument in a public place.[85]

The law can be used to solidify the responsibilities to provide access to museums. National museums[86] are required to secure that their collections are exhibited to the public[87] and available for research and study,[88] and these museums are generally required to promote the public's enjoyment and understanding of their particular collections.[89] The availability of public access to museums is central to those with charitable status satisfying the public benefit test.[90] Entry to the main collections of national museums is free of charge.[91]

---

[84] *Beyeler v. Italy* (2001) 33 EHRR 52, para. 113.

[85] Civic Government (Scotland) Act 1982, s. 96.

[86] Which are Arms Length Public Bodies, governed by statute and sponsored by the DCMS (DCMS, *Strategic Review of DCMS-Sponsored Museums* (2017), p. 6).

[87] See Museums and Galleries Act 1992, s. 2(1)(b) (National Gallery); s. 2(2)(b) (Tate Gallery); s. 2(3)(b) (National Portrait Gallery); s. 2(4)(b) (Wallace Collection) and NHA 1983, s. 2(1)(b) (V&A); s. 10(1)(b) (Science Museum); s. 18(2)(b) (Armouries). The BMA 1963, uses the terminology of a duty on the Trustees to secure 'so far as appears...practicable' that the collection is 'when required for inspection by members of the public, made available...': s. 3(3).

[88] See Museums and Galleries Act 1992, s. 2(1)(c) (National Gallery); s. 2(2)(c) (Tate Gallery); s. 2(3)(c) (National Portrait Gallery); s. 2(4)(c) (Wallace Collection) and NHA 1983, s. 2(1)(c) (V&A); s. 10(1)(c) (Science Museum); s. 18(2)(c) (Armouries).

[89] See Museums and Galleries Act 1992, s. 2(1)(d) (National Gallery); s. 2(2)(d) (Tate Gallery); s. 2(3) (d) (National Portrait Gallery); s. 2(4)(d) (Wallace Collection) and NHA 1983, s. 2(1)(d) (V&A); s. 10(1)(d) (Science Museum); s. 18(2)(e) (Armouries). The Museum of London Act 1965 relates to 'understanding and appreciation of historic and contemporary London and its society and culture': s. 3(1)(c).

[90] See Section 6.4.2.

[91] This was introduced in 2001, and was enabled by additional funding by the DCMS and the ability of free museums (as well as fee-charging ones) to reclaim VAT: see Alex Brocklehurst, *House of Lords Library Note: Debate on 7 February Museums* (1 February 2008), para. 2. See Maev Kennedy, 'Museums to Scrap Entry Charge: Vote Makes Free Admission to All National Collections Inevitable', *The Guardian*, 24 May 2001.

In the context of one of the older museum governing statutes (relating to the British Museum), researchers are referred to as 'students' and the impact on them is considered in the context of deciding whether or not to lend out certain objects from the collections.[92]

Again, making use of legal instruments, one of the central purposes of the National Trust is to promote 'The access to and enjoyment of such buildings places and chattels' that is to say those that are of 'national interest or architectural historic or artistic interest . . . ').[93]

Public access to cultural heritage is central to the justification for seeking to acquire national treasures under the UK's export licensing scheme and is reflected in the so-called Ridley Rules, which permit the acceptance of offers from private purchasers, providing that there is an appropriate level of public access.[94]

As will become clear in the context of navigating harm,[95] when disposing of cultural heritage objects it is recognised as important to make every effort to maximise the public access to them. This can be done through the system of prioritising disposals to other museums in the first instance, thus ensuring maximised public access. Furthermore, even though charities or local authorities would usually not sell property below the market value, the sale of cultural heritage objects at an undervalue may be permitted in order to ensure public access.[96] The importance of maintaining public access in such a context is found not only in the context of museum collections, under their ethical principles,[97] but also when government assets are sold (where usually the best value for money should be obtained)[98] and when the consistory court considers applications for faculties, it focuses on the sequential approach set out in *Re St Lawrence, Wootton*.[99] Here the financial value of the object is secondary to the social and cultural value of the object, and to the desire to keep it in the public domain to ensure continued access to it. The system thus demonstrates empathic care of cultural heritage.

---

[92] BMA 1963, s. 4.

[93] The National Trust Act 1937, s. 3(c) and National Trust for Scotland Order Confirmation Act 1935, s. 3(3).

[94] See Section 8.2.1.   [95] In Chapter 7.

[96] See Janet Ulph, 'The Sale of Items in Museum Collections' in Nicholas Hopkins (ed.), *Modern Studies in Property Law*, vol. 7 (Oxford: Hart, 2013), p. 218.

[97] MA, *Off the Shelf: A Toolkit for Ethical Transfer, Reuse and Disposal* (2023), p. 5., para. 2.33. (2014).

[98] *The Disposal of Heritage Assets: Guidance Note for Government Departments and Non-departmental Public Bodies* produced by English Heritage, the Office of Government Commerce (OGC) and the DCMS (it was confirmed and reissued by Historic England), 2010: https://historicengland.org.uk /images-books/publications/disposal-heritage-assets/guidance-disposals-final-jun-10/ (last accessed 29 August 2022). Whilst this is applicable to central government and the bodies for which it is responsible, it also provides elements of best practice more broadly to public bodies: para. 1.4.

[99] [2015] Fam 27 (Arches Court). See Section 7.8.1.4.

6.6.2 Navigating the Public/Private Divide

It has been suggested that 'two-thirds of the nation's built heritage is privately owned and maintained'.[100] Even the most important places, such as those recognised as World Heritage Sites, can include both private and public owners. For example, whilst Blenheim Palace has a single owner, the City of Bath has thousands of different owners and occupiers.[101] In their introduction to *Circles of Care*, Able and Nelson emphasise the public/private divide in the context of care. When it comes to cultural heritage clear questions arise as to whether care is more effectively provided by public rather than private institutions. However, it should be emphasised that provision of care within the public sector is not synonymous with public ownership. It may be that simply providing care for the cultural heritage on behalf of the public ensures that it is appropriately cared for without necessitating a transfer of ownership to a public institution. This can have certain advantages, for example, the cost of providing care will be significantly less than the cost of acquiring an object or place, and so available funds can be targeted on ensuring the continued physical integrity of the object or place.

Private owners of cultural heritage places or objects are under no common law obligation to facilitate access to them.[102] In contrast, in circumstances where a monument has been taken into guardianship (where ownership remains in private hands, but responsibility for direct care, in terms of its management, has been transferred to a guardian such as the Secretary of State, English Heritage or a local authority), then the public shall have access.[103] The same applies to monuments in public ownership.[104]

Conservation covenants provide an opportunity to prescribe access to cultural heritage places as ancillary purposes to the conservation purposes of the agreement.[105] These covenants (promises made under deed) created between landowners and responsible bodies (which include heritage organisations) are discussed more fully in the context of how they can be used to care directly for cultural heritage and its setting in the next chapter. However, the provision for access is not independent and must be undertaken in the context of a conservation purpose.[106] The effect of these covenants is not only to bind the current landowners but also any successors in title.

---

[100] House of Commons, Culture, Media and Sport Committee, Third Report, Session 2005–06, *Protecting and Preserving Our Heritage*, HC 912-I, para. 119.

[101] Historic England, *The Protection & Management of World Heritage Sites in England*, p. 4.

[102] This was seen in *Attorney-General* v. *Antrobus* [1905] 2 Ch 188 (Ch).

[103] AMAAA 1979, s. 19(1).   [104] ibid.   [105] See Section 7.4.1.5.

[106] The Law Commission considered the arguments relating to the importance of public access to satisfying the public benefit and the strong arguments put forward by the National Trust, but also recognised the potential harm of public access in some situations, for example in protection of birds relating to the natural heritage: Law Commission Report, *Conservation Covenants*, Law Com. No. 349, HC 322, 2014, paras. 3.35 and 3.36. Conservation purposes are discussed at Section 7.4.1.5.

Where a private individual has received a tax exemption on a cultural heritage object or place, then reasonable public access is required as an undertaking provided by the owner of a cultural heritage.[107] The requirement that 'reasonable access' should not be restricted to access requiring a prior appointment has a statutory foundation[108] – providing the public with so-called 'open access'[109] to the cultural heritage which, whilst privately owned, has a recognised public interest attached to it be dint of the fact that the owner has received a tax benefit funded by the public purse.

6.6.3 Negotiating Access

Part of the care of cultural heritage has been focused on providing access to it, not only for the community for whom the cultural heritage is important but also for the wider communities, since access to cultural heritage is both a cultural right and important for well-being. Some communities of care may need to negotiate with museums or research institutions to provide access to specific objects to enable them to perform particular cultural or religious practices. The trustees of national museums have the duty to make collections available for inspection (so far as practicable).[110] However, it is likely that where the community from which the object originated wishes to obtain access to undertake particular practices, this would fall beyond any right to have access for inspection and it would be necessary to negotiate directly with the museum for very specific access for undertaking particular practices. It should be emphasised, though, that access does not always mean providing the fullest access possible. In some cases it may be important to restrict access and communities may need to negotiate with the current possessor to remove the cultural heritage from public display and to restrict access by researchers or the broader public because of very specific cultural or religious reasons. This can be seen in the case of the Ethiopian Tabots held by the British Museum.[111] On the basis of agreements with the Ethiopian Orthodox Church the British Museum does not place the Tabots on public display and these are not viewable by the museum's curators but instead are only accessible by a limited number of people from the church. This is despite the objects being part of the British Museum's collection, vested in the trustees under

---

[107] See Section 5.2.15.   [108] IHTA 1984, s. 31(4FA).

[109] HM Revenue & Customs, *Capital Taxation and the National Heritage* (2017), p. 134. In *Re an application to vary the undertakings of A; Re an application to, vary the undertakings of B* [2005] STC (SCD) 103, para. 177 the Special Commissioners balanced the public access requirements with the individual situation of the owners, including risks of theft and damage to the owner's belongings.

[110] E.g. BMA 1963, s. 3(3) (referring to the public) and Museums and Galleries Act 1992, s. 2 (referring to exhibiting to the public and making them available to those wishing to inspect them for research and study).

[111] These are considered to be the Ark of the Covenant by the church.

the 1963 Act[112] and which the trustees have a duty to make available to the public in so far as is practicable.

6.6.4 Participatory Initiatives Outside Formal Schemes

Intangible practices may be recognised through public participation initiatives rather than through any formal legal designation. The chalking of the White Horse at Uffington, Oxfordshire, provides such an example. This is a 3,000-year-old tradition called 'scouring', which involves weeding and cleaning.[113] At its heart is the act of caring for cultural heritage which is carried out by communities of care who care about the White Horse. It demonstrates an intermingling of the practice of cultural heritage with the practice of care. Whilst the National Trust may co-ordinate the activity, it is the individual members of the public who volunteer and carry out the direct practice of care. They actively participate in the practice, as communities of care, in directly caring for cultural heritage. Any member of the public can join in the chalking, thereby providing an opportunity for the interlinking of local, national and international communities in the pro-active caring of cultural heritage. Community archaeology activities also represent public participation activities which involve communities directly in the care of cultural heritage.[114]

6.6.5 Practical Matters: Funding

6.6.5.1 Charging as Hindering Access

Payment for entry to museums may hamper access. As discussed earlier, national museums are accessible by the public free of charge.[115] Although it is possible for a local authority in England and Wales to charge for admission to a museum or gallery established under the 1964 Act,[116] when exercising that power 'a local authority shall take into account the need to secure that the museum or gallery plays its full part in the promotion of education in the area, and shall have particular regard to the interests of children and students'.[117] In Scotland, museums and galleries established under the equivalent Act 'shall be open to the public free of charge'.[118] Where museums are charities, the Charity Commission assesses the reasonableness of the charges to ensure that they are 'appropriate to the overall purposes of the organisation and set at a rate which balances the current and future activities of the organisation and are not set at

---

[112] British Museum, *Maqdala Collection*: www.britishmuseum.org/about-us/british-museum-story/contested-objects-collection/maqdala-collection (last accessed 21 December 2022).

[113] Philip Schwyzer, 'The Scouring of the White Horse: Archaeology, Identity and "Heritage"' (1999) 65 *Representations* 42.

[114] See generally Suzie Thomas, 'Community Archaeology' in Gabriel Moshenska (ed.), *Key Concepts in Public Archaeology* (London: UCL Press, 2017), p. 14.

[115] See Section 6.6.1.   [116] Public Libraries and Museums Act 1964, s. 13(1).

[117] ibid., s. 13(2).   [118] Public Libraries Consolidation (Scotland) Act 1887, s. 32.

a level which excludes a substantial proportion of the public'.[119] In assessing the appropriateness of levels of access to museums, the Charity Commission considers not only physical access (including loans) but also online, radio and television coverage of the collections.[120]

6.6.5.2 Funding to Promote Access

The provision of funding can promote access to cultural heritage and this is reflected in a number of statutory provisions enabling the funding of cultural heritage to support communities of care. The National Heritage Memorial Fund was established as a memorial to those who lost their lives for the UK.[121] The fund can be used to provide financial assistance for things relating to historic archaeological, aesthetic or artistic interest, specifically for the purposes of securing the preservation or enhancement of them, encouraging the study, understanding or dissemination of information about them, securing or improving access to them or the display or enjoyment of them, as well as encouraging the maintenance and development of the skills necessary for the preservation enjoyment of them.[122] Therefore, as part of this, the projects can assist in acquiring property, or providing education or training.[123] The trustees also administer the National Lottery Heritage Fund, providing the means of enhancing the provision of cultural heritage with 'a wider range of people will be involved in heritage' as a mandatory outcome of funding.[124]

6.6.6 Balancing Risk of Access

As discussed above, the physical safety of the objects is clearly important and the responsibility for this is placed on the governing bodies of national museums. Specifically, the duty of the trustees to secure that the objects are available for inspection by members of the public is subject to the proviso that such access can be made under conditions necessary for the preservation of the safety of the collection.[125] Therefore the risk of harm is mitigated against through the provisions of the Act. Whilst facilitating the access to cultural heritage objects from within the collections through a legal power to lend objects for public exhibition including specifically abroad, nevertheless an element of consideration is not only the gap that is left behind during the loan (that is to say the interests of students and those persons visiting the museum) but also the physical aspect of harm. In particular, the physical condition and any risks to which it is likely to be exposed are further factors that are relevant when considering any outward loan.[126] The risk involved in lending works of art abroad has also been recognised in the context of the export licensing system, where the Export Reviewing

---

[119] Charity Commission, *The Review of the Register of Charities: Museums and Art Galleries* (2002), para. A26.
[120] ibid., para. A28.   [121] NHA 1980, s. 1(1).   [122] ibid., ss. 3(1) and 3(2).   [123] ibid., s. 3(3).
[124] Heritage Fund, *Outcomes for Heritage Projects*.
[125] BMA 1963, s. 3(3). See also Museums and Galleries Act 1992, s. 2.   [126] BMA 1963, s. 4.

Committee recommended that the Secretary of State did not grant a temporary export licence for Michelangelo's marble relief known as 'Taddei Tondo' by the Royal Academy in the late 1970s to the Metropolitan Museum of Art in New York for a temporary exhibition.[127] The concern was the potential harm to its fragile state and the risk of damage to it.[128]

6.7 Understanding Cultural Heritage and Its Communities

Understanding cultural heritage is an essential element of caring for it, and for the communities who care about it. Cultural heritage is not simply comprised of objects, places or practices, but instead its relationship with communities – essentially the human dimension to cultural heritage is key. A very basic element of this understanding is appreciating the nature of the cultural heritage objects that a museum has in its possession. This can, in some extreme situations, simply involve needing to understand what the object actually is, but more often it is about understanding the role played by the cultural heritage objects and their significance to communities for which they are important. This can include the responsibility to maintain records relating to collections.[129] Objects collected during colonial times may have been taken with little awareness of what the object was. In other situations there may be no contextual information available. Absence of, or inadequacies with the provision of information can mislead the public, or hinder their understanding of the particular cultural heritage concerned. However, the act of misattributing an object and displaying it in that way could be extremely distressing for the descendants of the communities from which it originated.[130] In order to provide appropriate care, particularly in terms of it being respectful and empathetic, it may be necessary for museums to engage in dialogue with the communities from whom the objects were taken. This can enable them to better understand the cultural heritage itself, its role with practices and its past and present importance to the communities, and ultimately to provide appropriate care.

When acquiring objects, whether through purchase, receipt of a gift or by a bequest, museums need to ensure that these are not stolen or 'illegally removed Iraqi cultural property', 'illegally removed Syrian Cultural Property' or cultural objects illegally removed from a designated heritage assets. Acquiring such objects would open them up to potential legal challenge.[131]

---

[127] *Export of Works of Art 1978–79 – 25th Report of the Reviewing Committee*, Cmd 8050, case (iii) *A Marble Relief of the Madonna and Child with the infant St John by Michelangelo, c. 1504–5*, March 1980.

[128] ibid.

[129] In the case of the Royal Armouries, the board of trustees 'maintain a record (which may include books, pictures and other articles) relating to their collection, to arms, and armour generally and to the Tower': NHA 1983, s. 18(2)(d).

[130] See generally Elazar Barkan & Ronald Bush (eds.) *Claiming the Stones Naming the Bones* (Los Angeles: Getty Research Institute, 2002).

[131] See Section 4.3.4.

The act of researching the provenance of objects in museums has shifted from being essentially an art historical exercise, seeking to understand the cultural heritage object from the point of view of its authorship and authenticity, to enquiring much more closely into an object's ownership history. To this end, museums need to ensure that there are no gaps in provenance. From an ethical point of view, the museum should be clear that it is acquiring a valid title to an object, rather than simply a strict legal title. The latter might only have been acquired due to the passage of time and the statute of limitation, in circumstances where, in the past, the original owner may have been dispossessed of it.[132]

Other non-law instruments require museums to consider the provenance of a cultural heritage object at different stages of the cultural heritage object's interactions with the museum. Therefore, when acquiring objects, or considering them for inward loans, there is an obligation to research the object's provenance. Similar principles require provenance checks to determine whether there are any gaps in the information available about an object for the years 1933–1945. There also seems to be an ongoing responsibility on the part of the museum to revisit any gaps in provenance information and to ensure that the collection has been appropriately researched and that the provenance is clear with has no problematic gaps.[133]

The importance of recording and displaying information about cultural heritage and its use extends beyond a responsibility to current generations to future generations. This is also about maintaining the historical record, and can help facilitate direct engagement with the cultural heritage objects. Even as far back as 1857 it was recognised how the public ought to have access to information about the objects of art, historical interest or science in various public collections and a return was made from those institutions about the measures that they had in place to provide such information 'sparing [the visitor] the Expense of a Catalogue'.[134]

6.7.1 Display: Transparency

The public places a great deal of trust in museums and it is recognised that, as part of their responsibility towards the public, museums should act ethically by being transparent about their actions. The MA Code of Ethics places a responsibility on museums, and on the people who work in them, to be honest and open with the public about what is on display. Therefore, museums need to make it clear whether something is a replica rather than the original.[135]

---

[132] ICOM, *Code of Ethics*, principle 2.2.

[133] Report of the Spoliation Advisory Panel in respect of an oil painting by John Constable, 'Beaching a Boat, Brighton', now in the possession of the Tate Gallery (26 March 2014) (2014 HC 1016).

[134] National Collections, *Further Return to an Address of the Honourable House of Commons, dated 19 February 1857*.

[135] MA, *Code of Ethics: Additional Guidance* (2015), para. 2(b).

An argument has been made in the context of objects taken during the Nazi era that museums are responsible to the public to ensure that they do not implicate the public in the past wrongdoing that took place (even though in most cases the museum will not have been directly responsible for that wrongdoing), for it has been suggested that the public may be complicit where an object that was improperly taken from its original owners (and has not been returned) is on public display and its troubled history is known.[136] This applies equally to objects that were taken in other circumstances. Overall, then, it is important for museums to appropriately represent the objects within their collections, based on the responsibility to the communities for whom the cultural heritage is important and the responsibility to the wider public is not misleading them in any way.

6.8 Lending: Facilitating the Use of Cultural Heritage as a Good Ambassador

Art and cultural heritage have been recognised as having the potential to act as good ambassadors,[137] representing a form of soft power.[138] During periods of international political tensions, major loans of cultural heritage to overseas institutions can fulfil an ambassadorial role. The UK's national cultural institutions (which include national museums) have been described, in view of their 'public service nature', as 'effective, but unofficial, ambassadors for the UK while their public appeal makes them a valuable bridge between diplomacy, international relations and public opinion'.[139] It has been suggested that because the UK's institutions are custodians of global resources they have both the legal and moral obligation 'to look after what they hold on behalf of source communities and of future generations, but they also have an obligation to make their collections as widely available as possible'.[140] It is incontrovertible that the lending of artworks to other institutions, whether within the UK or overseas, widens access to that cultural heritage. However, it should be acknowledged, that this notion of the good ambassador has also been used as a defence by major Western museums to justify maintaining the *status quo* and holding on to cultural heritage objects which originate from other national or local communities overseas.[141] For that reason, this idea must be navigated carefully to ensure that it does not encompass paternalistic care.[142] Several initiatives in the UK encourage the lending of cultural heritage objects. These include the Government Indemnity Scheme, which enables the Secretary of

---

[136] Baroness Deech, *Hansard* HL vol. 712, cols. 907–908 (10 July 2009).

[137] Paul M. Bator, *International Trade in Art* (London: University of Chicago Press, 1983), p. 30.

[138] Leanne Hoogwaerts, 'Museums, Exchanges, and Their Contribution to Joseph Nye's Concept of "Soft Power"' (2016) 14 *Museums and Society* 313.

[139] Kirsten Bound, Rachel Briggs, John Holden and Samuel Jones, *Cultural Diplomacy* (London: DEMOS, 2007), p. 40.

[140] ibid., p. 43.   [141] See the discussion of the universal museum in Section 9.5.2.3.

[142] As to which see Section 9.5.1.

State to give lenders of objects to UK institutions[143] an indemnity in respect of any loss or damage to the object whilst on loan.[144] This facilitates intra-UK loans as well as loans to the UK from overseas. It does not apply to loans of objects from UK collections abroad. The reassurance that the government can give to lenders means that this encourages loans and provides wider access to cultural heritage within the UK. A similar provision of reassurance to lenders (specifically those from overseas) is found in the immunity from seizure legislation, which gives protected status to cultural objects during the currency of a loan.[145]

Recent principles relating to lending, published by the National Museums Directors' Council, identified the nature of lending as a partnership between institutions, suggesting that lending is seen as a dialogic way of caring for cultural heritage.[146] The importance of widening access to nationally important collections through the means of lending and reaching diverse audiences, as well as new research and interpretations, is recognised in this document,[147] which seeks to facilitate such loans, with a presumption in favour of lending, for the principles expect lenders to 'lend unless there is a compelling reason not to'.[148]

The Arts Council's Collection is entirely a lending collection, designed to 'reach different audiences and enhance people's everyday environment and their enjoyment of the visual arts'.[149] The raison d'être of this collection is thus a democratic one, seeking to reach out to people to experience art, as a form of cultural heritage.

Donors or legatees may place legal restrictions on the use of collections or on particular gifts or bequests to museums. These can prohibit particular activities, or restrict how the cultural objects can be used. This may impact on the lending of these to other institutions. It will be discussed in Chapter 7 how, until relatively recently, the terms of the Wallace Collection bequest were considered to preclude the lending of objects to other institutions. However, the reinterpretation of the terms, which now favours lending, has been approved by the Charity Commission (even though no such express power is set out in the Museums and Galleries Act 1992, unlike the comparable powers enjoyed by the other museum trustees under the Act).[150] In the case of the Tate Gallery, National Gallery and National Portrait Gallery, if an object is subject to terms or conditions restricting the governing body's power to lend objects, if 50 years have elapsed since the

---

[143] These include museums, libraries and the National Trust and National Trust for Scotland.
[144] NHA 1980, s. 16.
[145] Tribunals, Courts and Enforcement Act 2007, s. 134. With thanks to Alex Herman for highlighting this link.
[146] National Museum Directors' Council and the Touring Exhibitions Group, *Principles for Lending and Borrowing* (June 2021).
[147] ibid., p. 3.   [148] ibid., p. 4.
[149] *Arts Council Collection Loans Policy & Procedure*: https://artscouncilcollection.org.uk/sites/default/files/1_Loans_0.pdf (last accessed 24 May 2023).
[150] Museums and Galleries Act 1992, s. 5.

object vested in the trustees, or if the original donor or their personal representatives have consented, the trustees can lend in contravention of these conditions.[151] This is clearly designed to facilitate access to cultural heritage. In the case of the Burrell Collection in Glasgow, it was necessary under Scots law to use statute to circumvent the terms of the bequest and to give Glasgow City Council the power (with written agreement from the Burrell Trustees) to lend and to borrow objects both within the UK and abroad.[152]

6.9 Licensing Activities

In the next chapter, it will be seen how the legal and non-law instruments seek to navigate rather than completely avert harm, and that it is recognised that one cannot keep cultural heritage in aspic. As part of this, certain activities involving cultural heritage are prohibited in the absence of a licence or consent. These permissions then facilitate the use and enjoyment of cultural heritage. This can be seen in the context of the listed building regime, where developments are permitted to listed buildings or scheduled monuments when consent has been obtained beforehand. In the context of activities around wreck sites, the Marine Management Organisation has powers to grant licences for certain activities, which include the situation when a vessel is used to remove any object from the seabed.[153] Furthermore, it is possible for individuals to dive around a protected site, providing that they obtain permission to do so,[154] and licences can be obtained for carrying out 'salvage operations in a manner appropriate to the historical, archaeological or artistic importance of any wreck'.[155]

6.10 Memory and Information

People and places are memorialised in a variety of different ways. Statute law can recognise them, for example, the National Heritage Memorial Fund was established in memory of all of those who have died for the UK.[156] Places themselves may act as memorials, such as the University of Leicester, which was originally established as Leicester, Leicestershire and Rutland University College in 1921 as a living memorial to 'the local people who made sacrifices' during the First World War.[157] The *Titanic* was recognised as being both a memorial to those who perished and a historical wreck of 'exceptional international importance having a unique symbolic value'.[158]

---

[151] ibid., s. 5(3).   [152] Burrell Collection (Lending and Borrowing) (Scotland) Act 2014, s. 1(1).
[153] Marine and Coastal Access Act 2009, s. 66(1)(8).
[154] Protection of Wrecks Act 1973, s. 1(3)(b).   [155] ibid., s. 1(5).   [156] NHA 1980, s. 1(1).
[157] University of Leicester, *History and Campus*: https://le.ac.uk/about/history/campus-history (last accessed 22 May 2023).
[158] *Agreement Concerning the Shipwrecked Vessel RMS Titanic*, London, 6 November 2003 (agreement entered into force on 18 November 2019) CP 205 (previously published as Miscellaneous Series No. 4 (2003) Cm 5798), art. 2(b).

The blue plaque scheme which is run by English Heritage in London provides a mechanism for maintaining the association between particular people and the places where they were born, lived, worked or died.[159] This does not have any particular legal structure, but where buildings are listed, appropriate consent will be needed before a blue plaque is installed. Similar schemes exist across the UK, run locally and by different groups, with English Heritage providing relevant support and guidance where necessary.

The Department for Constitutional Affairs has published guidance on war memorials, using the language of custodians to recognise the fact that those who maintain war memorials may be quite separate from those who own them, and also frequently using the term 'care'.[160] Such language emphasises the importance of the care that is required to maintain the memory of those who lost their lives and the information forms an essential part of cultural heritage.

6.10.1 Place Names

Place names are a central element of identity and may be important in raising awareness of the value of place names. This can be seen in the context of Welsh historic place names as a form of intangible cultural heritage where there is a statutory requirement for the Welsh Ministers to 'compile and maintain a list of historic place names in Wales'.[161] Wales clearly benefited from a recent consideration of its cultural heritage provision with the 2016 Act,[162] which provides the basis for recording historic place names. Contrastingly, where the laws have not undergone such a recent review in other nations of the UK, civil society initiatives have been used to instigate the recording of similar information in both Northern Ireland and Scotland.[163] In Northern Ireland, a civil society initiative entitled Northern Ireland Place-Name Project has, with support from Queen's University Belfast, Land & Property Services, the AHRC and Foras na Gaeilge, put together a database of place names.[164] In Scotland ScotlandsPlaces is a database of place names which draws from

---

[159] English Heritage, *The History of Blue Plaques*: www.english-heritage.org.uk/visit/blue-plaques/about-blue-plaques/history-of-blue-plaques/ (last accessed 22 May 2023).

[160] Department for Constitutional Affairs, *War Memorials in England and Wales: Guidance for Custodians* (2007): https://assets.publishing.service.gov.uk/government/uploads/system/uploads/attachment_data/file/326678/war-memorial-guidance.pdf (last accessed 22 May 2023).

[161] Historic Environment (Wales) Act 2016, s. 34. This is available at *List of Historic Place Names*: https://historicplacenames.rcahmw.gov.uk/ (last accessed 24 May 2023).

[162] But it is recognised that the 2016 Act resulted in heavily amended legislation which is difficult to navigate and the Welsh Government plans to work on a consolidation bill: https://gov.wales/welsh-government-programme-to-make-law-more-accessible (last accessed 24 May 2023).

[163] These are less public participation initiatives and more civil society in nature, albeit that certainly in the case of Scotland they are closely linked with government and may not represent the truest form of civil society initiative: see Section 1.5.3.

[164] www.placenamesni.org/ (last accessed 24 May 2023).

Historic Environment Scotland, National Records of Scotland and the National Library of Scotland.[165] All of these initiatives contribute to maintaining the historical record relating to information about places.

6.11 Standards of Care Expected: Translating Care Into and Out of Law

In the analysis so far in this book the emphasis has been placed on assuming responsibility, but what if the appropriate person fails to assume responsibility or takes on the responsibility but provides inappropriate care? How does someone who cares about cultural heritage require others who have either been assigned responsibility or who have assumed responsibility to actually provide the appropriate care? How is it enforceable and does it translate into a duty?

In law the standards of care relating to quotidian care of cultural heritage are those found in the tort of negligence[166] or in contract.[167] These translate into an obligation of a person exercising the reasonable care and skill that would be expected of the relevant professional. A similar test is also found in the context of the duties of directors under the Companies Act 2006. In the context of bailment, where someone is undertaking work on a chattel[168] (such as conservation or restoration), the bailee has a duty not only to exercise reasonable care and skill but also to take care of it.[169] Supplementing these legal rules, though, are guidance and ethical codes, augmenting the strict legal standards of the professionals who care for cultural heritage by placing on them additional ethical obligations relating to care.

The reasonable man test is frequently found in the common law and has been equated to the 'Man on the Clapham omnibus'.[170] When it comes to the legal test of standards of reasonable care and skill of professionals it is not expected that the standards reflect those of the passenger on the Clapham omnibus but instead are context-specific; the courts assess the standard expected of the reasonable practitioner in the context, judging an individual's actions against those recognised standards objectively. In these legal terms, therefore, the standard of 'reasonable' seems to equate with competent care that was identified by some academics as the expectation in the context of the ethics of care.[171] The expected standard of care depends on the particular attributes of the individual – the specialist auction house

---

[165] https://scotlandsplaces.gov.uk/about (last accessed 29 August 2022).
[166] Which is the test of reasonable care and skill: *Hall* v. *Brooklands Auto Racing Club* [1933] 1 KB 205, 217 (CA). Negligence is described as 'the omission to do something which a reasonable man, guided upon those considerations which ordinarily regulate the conduct of human affairs, would do, or doing something which a prudent and reasonable man would not do': *Blyth* v. *The Company of Proprietors of the Birmingham Waterworks* (1856) 11 Ex 780, 784.
[167] Supply of Goods and Services Act 1982, s. 13.   [168] i.e. personal property.
[169] This is clear from case law applicable both in England and Wales (*Leck* v. *Maestaer* (1807) 1 Camp 138 and *Clarke* v. *Earnshaw* [1818] Gow 28, 30) as well as in Scotland (*Sinclair* v. *Juner* [1952] SC 35, 45 (Lord Russell)).
[170] *Hall* v. *Brooklands Auto Racing Club*, 205, 224.
[171] See discussion of Tronto at Section 2.5.3.

will have a higher standard expected of it than the provincial dealer in antiques[172] and presumably the standards expected of the curator of a national museum would differ from those expected of a volunteer-run local museum. Nevertheless, when addressing such expectations the standards set out in any professional guidance or codes of practice may assist the court in determining whether the appropriate level of care and skill was exercised in the circumstances.

6.11.1 Requirements of Due Diligence

Although not ratified in the UK, the 1995 Unidroit Convention provides a useful starting point when considering standards of due diligence in the context of cultural heritage. The Convention requires states to have regard to 'all the circumstances of the acquisition'. This includes price, character of the parties, whether reasonably accessible registers and agencies were accessed as well as 'any other relevant information and documentation which it could reasonably have obtained'; finally, due diligence requires consideration of whether they 'took any other step that a reasonable person would have taken in the circumstances'.[173] This test places a duty on purchasers which is akin to the duty in the context of determining whether a purchase has been made in good faith for the purposes of the Limitation Act 1980.[174]

The MA Code of Ethics treats due diligence as 'ensuring that all reasonable measures are taken to establish the facts of a case before deciding a course of action, particularly in identifying the source and history of an item offered for acquisition or use before acquiring it, or in understanding the full background of a sponsor, lender or funder'.[175]

6.11.2 To Whom Is the Duty Owed?

Where there is a legal duty of care, this duty is owed to the owner of the cultural heritage in question, either in the law of tort, contract or bailment. However, the question arises as to how far third parties might complain, where the person who has assumed (or who has been assigned) the responsibility for the care of cultural heritage fails to provide appropriate care. In some circumstances it may be possible for an individual or a particular community with sufficient standing to make an application to the administrative court to judicially review a decision of a public body where it was illegal, irrational or *Wednesbury* unreasonable.[176]

A local community could apply to assume responsibility for the care of cultural heritage in circumstances where the current provision of care was

---

[172] *Luxmoore-May* v. *Messenger May Baverstock* [1990] 1 WLR 1009, 1020 (CA).
[173] Unidroit Convention, art. 4(4).   [174] Limitation Act 1980, s. 4(4).
[175] MA, *Code of Ethics*, p. 23.
[176] Under the principle in *Wednesbury Corp* v. *Ministry of Housing and Local Government (No 2)* [1966] 2 QB 275 (CA).

considered by them as inappropriate.[177] This provides an opportunity for proactive care of cultural heritage which is appropriate in the context.

6.11.3 Enhanced Duties of Care for Curators

Trust is central to the care of cultural heritage and is reflected in the enhanced duty placed on curators. Where anyone who accesses a collection harms it by causing physical damage to any object within it, this is treated as a breach of trust.[178] Nevertheless, a more stringent duty is placed on those who have had the responsibility for the care of cultural heritage placed on them (specifically curators). Thus, in *R v. Farhad Hakimzadeh*[179] Blake J indicated, *obiter dictum*, that had the harm to the books been caused by those who were tasked with caring for the collection then this would have justified the severest level of sentencing on the basis of breach of trust.[180] This clearly demonstrates the caring responsibility placed on those who care for cultural heritage and the expectation of the public trust.[181] The relationship of trust between carers of cultural heritage and the public demonstrates the relational nature of the caring relationship.

6.11.4 Standards of Care for Temporary Custodians

6.11.4.1 The Care Expected of a Borrower: Bailment
Where cultural objects are loaned, legal duties of care are placed on borrowers. Here, the duty can arise under any contractual arrangement in place dealing with the loan of the object of cultural heritage. Where a borrower owed a duty of care in negligence and acted negligently, then this could lead to liability in tort. However, there is a basic, common law duty of reasonable care which arises under the law of bailment. It is a simple case of being required to care for something that is not one's own, but has been borrowed, or where someone has simply come into possession of it, and not to expose it to unnecessary risks.

We often focus on taking care of others rather than ourselves, and the responsibilities that are owed to others. Therefore, it is not surprising that there are duties of care owed in respect of taking care of the personal property of others – in this situation cultural heritage objects.

The elements of appropriate care set out in Chapter 2 exceed the standard of care required under the common law of bailment.[182] This basic standard which

---

[177] See Section 7.5.4.2.

[178] This is considered in the next chapter in the context of harm to cultural heritage acting as an aggravating factor in sentencing.

[179] [2010] 1 Cr App R (S) 10 (CA).   [180] ibid., para. 14.

[181] BritainThinks, *Public Perceptions of – and Attitudes to – the Purposes of the Museums in Society* (A report prepared by BritainThinks for MA, March 2013 which set out the strong public trust in museums).

[182] Which is a duty to take reasonable care: *Yearworth* v. *North Bristol NHS Trust* [2010] 1 QB 1, 22.

is expected of anyone who takes chattels into their possession provides a first level of care in averting physical harm, but does not include the other elements of appropriate care recognised in Chapter 2, in particular the dialogic and empathetic elements. However, in the context of averting harm, the common law duty which arises in bailment covers the basics and seeks to discourage physical harm by placing a legal burden on the bailee. Therefore, in situations where a borrower (the bailee) has borrowed an object a duty is owed relating to preventing physical harm, but not in terms of how it is displayed – therefore the care required by the law is not necessarily empathetic, respectful or dialogic, but practical in terms of ensuring physical integrity.

6.11.5 Setting Examples and Revisiting the Appropriateness of Care

One situation in which example-setting has been identified as good practice is the policy to appropriately care for cultural heritage that underlies the Protocol for the Care of the Government Historic Estate.[183] Here the sentiment of the document is clearly framed within an idea of setting the tone for others to follow suit, and the idea that one cannot expect others to care for cultural heritage if one does not do so oneself. The government therefore regularly questions how its departments care for cultural heritage. It involves a series of questions which departments who care for cultural heritage should ask themselves periodically and upon which they report centrally for a biennial report; this sets out the extent to which these principles are adhered to.

6.12 Conclusion

The concept of care within the various national museum statutes clearly recognises obligations relating to physical preservation, provision of access and the care of the objects as part of a collection. The basic notion is about looking after cultural heritage, with the vast majority of national museum trustees having a further duty to preserve their collections as well. Very few of the activities require consideration of other viewpoints when making these decisions. This demonstrates overall a very traditional notion of curation and care as a dependent relationship, with this specific responsibility lying on the trustees and the director.

Whilst the UK approach to cultural heritage permits people to freely participate in the cultural life of the community and to enjoy the arts, thus upholding the principles set out in article 27 of the Universal Declaration on Human Rights 1948,[184] it does go further than what is envisaged by that provision. It is clear that participation is about more than passively enjoying

---

[183] Historic England, Protocol for the Care of the Government Historic Estate, 8 November 2017.

[184] And which is also reflected in article 15(1) of the Economic, Social and Cultural Covenant, which states that 'The States Parties to the present Covenant recognize the right of everyone: (a) To take part in cultural life'.

or consuming pre-existing opportunities to experience culture, but extends to actively participating in ways of ensuring continued access to cultural heritage. By providing opportunities for making instrumental use of civil society initiatives to assume responsibility for the care of cultural heritage this upholds the notion that '[e]very people has the right and the duty to develop its culture'.[185] The emphasis on preserving and caring for national museum collections goes some way to upholding the principle that '[e]ach culture has a dignity and value which must be respected and preserved'.[186]

---

[185] Declaration of principles of International Cultural Co-operation, art. 1(2).
[186] ibid., art. 1(1).

7

Navigating Harm to Cultural Heritage

7.1 Introduction

Physical harm, in the form of intentional destruction of cultural heritage, is seen as a significant threat to human dignity and human rights.[1] It has been described as 'a plague accompanying humanity throughout all phases of its history and involving many different human communities either as perpetrators or victims'.[2] But intentional destruction and harm to cultural heritage cannot always entirely be averted. At times it is necessary to sanction harm to cultural heritage for the purposes of development, yet at the same time try to mitigate the effects of that harm. It is therefore necessary to care for cultural heritage by navigating harm in a respectful, empathetic and dialogic manner. For these reasons, the approach taken here is to use the language of navigating, rather than averting harm.

The harm to cultural heritage that requires navigation takes a variety of different forms which were explored in Chapter 1. Traditionally the focus of concern has been on the risk of irreparable physical harm to a place, object or practice, but the risk of irreparable harm to the setting, the context or to the special character of cultural heritage is of equally grave concern.[3] Both physical and intangible harm are recognised internationally and nationally. Harm occurs because of genocide, war, development, looting of archaeological sites, natural disasters or through deterioration and decay caused by inaction. Where cultural heritage objects have been collected together, the sum of those objects may be greater than the individual elements, and if some objects are irreparably damaged or lost, this can affect the entire collection.[4] Collections may be associated with a particular person and where this association is

---

[1] UNESCO Declaration Concerning the Intentional Destruction of Cultural Heritage (adopted at the General Conference of the 32nd session of UNESCO, 2003).

[2] Federico Lenzerini, 'Intentional Destruction of Cultural Heritage' in Francesco Francioni and Ana Filipa Vrdoljak (eds.), *The Oxford Handbook of International Cultural Heritage Law* (Oxford: Oxford University Press, 2020), p. 75.

[3] Caring for the past should not just involve 'pickling it', as Caitlin DeSilvey highlights (Caitlin DeSilvey, *Curated Decay: Heritage Beyond Saving* (London: University of Minnesota Press, 2017), p. 188), and in some cases palliative care may be appropriate (p. 161). Therefore, the focus later is this chapter is also on how harm is navigated and mitigated.

[4] *R v. Simon Jacques* [2010] EWCA Crim 323, para. 1.

removed there may be a risk of harm, as can the association between an object and a person or between a place and a person. At times there can be a risk of loss abroad and efforts may be made to keep them within the UK – this particular notion is dealt with in Chapter 8 in the context of the rhetoric of saving for the nation.

Harm may also be directly caused to the community for whom the cultural heritage is important – for example, if cultural heritage is displayed inappropriately, is in the possession of an institution against the wishes of the community, is misused or has been culturally appropriated. Significant harm can be caused to communities and their individual members by the continued display or commemoration of a public figure because of their association with slavery or other harmful activities.

Navigation of harm involves preparation for possible harm, by responding to an actual or perceived threat of harm through provision of appropriate care. Such care needs to be tailored to the dynamic nature of cultural heritage. Furthermore, the use and enjoyment of cultural heritage have to be balanced with a desire to pass it on to future generations.

This chapter begins by setting out the various caring activities that seek to navigate harm – specifically precautionary care, preventative care and reactive care. The second part of the chapter analyses how the UK deals with loss. This includes the use of criminal offences and example-setting, as well as the efforts to mitigate the negative effects of harm and loss.

7.2 Caring Activities to Navigate Harm

Caring activities to navigate harm are carried out by different communities of care. International or national communities may provide precautionary, preventative or reactive care, but so too may institutional communities, who take a variety of different forms. However, smaller communities of care may be more directly involved in the practical care of cultural heritage. Writing in 1971, Ashworth observed that 'Much of the will to conserve has been expressed through individuals, either members of voluntary bodies or semi-official advisory boards or councils'.[5] For that reason, once again the multiple communities of care using varied legal and non-law instruments forming the nested practices of care will be considered.

7.3 Precautionary Care

Precautionary care has at its heart the notion of communities anticipating future risks to cultural heritage that they care about. Even though it may be uncertain whether harm will actually befall cultural heritage in wartime – because it is

---

[5] Graham Ashworth, 'Contemporary Developments in British Preservation Law and Practice' (1971) 36 *Law and Contemporary Problems* 348, 356.

unclear whether there will be a conflict in the future and what form it might take – it is, nevertheless, prudent to take action in peacetime as a precautionary measure.[6] States thereby prepare for these possible eventualities, even if they are relatively unlikely.[7] Where cultural heritage has been brought together, and there is a risk of it being separated or sold off in the future and removed from the public domain, it may be prudent to guard against that possibility. This is important even if there is no present suggestion that there is a risk of this happening. This section considers how frameworks are created to provide precautionary care, as well as certain legal devices which can be used instrumentally by communities of care to put in place precautionary care for cultural heritage that they care about.

7.3.1 Establishing Frameworks of Care as a Precautionary Measure

The 1954 UNESCO Hague Convention includes provisions that apply *in the event* of armed conflict[8] and are thus there "just in case". Some provisions of the Convention and the Protocols (which is brought into effect wholesale by the Cultural Property (Armed Conflicts) Act 2017) are specifically precautionary efforts to take during peacetime.[9] Central to the regime set out in the 1954 Convention, its Protocols and Regulation are the notions of respect and safeguarding of cultural property.[10] Respect, as part of appropriate care, is a key element of the Convention's coverage. Safeguarding is seen as the preparedness undertaken during peacetime 'against the foreseeable effects of an armed conflict'.[11]

---

[6] Although not ratified by the UK, pre-emptive action can be seen in the context of the Convention for the Safeguarding of the Intangible Cultural Heritage, which has 'an element of actual or perceived threat to cultural heritage inherent in the concept, hence requiring preservation': Katya S. Ziegler, 'Cultural Heritage and Human Rights' in Giuffrè Milano (ed.), *Alberico Gentili: La Salvaguardia Dei Beni Culturali Nel Diritto Internazionale*, Working Paper No. 26/2007 (Oxford Legal Studies Research Paper Series, Faculty of Law, University of Oxford, 2007): http://ssrn.com/abstract=1002620 (last accessed 22 May 2023).

[7] For the precautionary principle in international environmental law see: Consolidated Version of the Treaty on the Functioning of the European Union [2010] OJ C83/61, art. 191(2) and the *Bergen Statement,* Ministerial Meeting of the OSPAR Commission, Bergen, 23–24 September 2010, para. 25. Principle 15 of the Rio Declaration on Environment and Development, United Nations Conference on Environment and Development (1992) states that a 'lack of full scientific certainty shall not be used as a reason for postponing cost-effective measures to prevent environmental degradation'. This approach has also been applied to cultural heritage using the language of 'preventive conservation' in ICOMOS Principles for the Preservation and Conversation/Restoration of Wall Paintings (2003), art. 4 and 'preventive maintenance' in ICOMOS Charter-Principles for the Analysis, Conservation and Structural Restoration of Architectural Heritage (2003), para. 3.2.

[8] Convention for the Protection of Cultural Property in the Event of Armed Conflict UNESCO, The Hague (adopted 14 May 1954, entered into force 7 August 1956) 249 UNTS 240.

[9] Second Protocol to the Hague Convention of 1954 for the Protection of Cultural Property in the Event of Armed Conflict, The Hague, 26 March 1999, regarding safeguarding, art. 5.

[10] 1954 Hague Convention, art. 2.   [11] ibid., art. 3.

Mechanisms which allocate responsibility for the direct care of cultural heritage in the event of armed conflict are prescribed for by the convention. As soon as a state party is engaged in war or armed conflict (and in the case of whole or partial occupation of a state),[12] it assumes responsibility for the care of its own cultural property by appointing a representative for cultural property and if it is in occupation of another territory that state would appoint a special representative situated in that territory.[13] Further provision for identifying a particular individual who assumes responsibility for the care of cultural heritage is made in the requirement to appoint a Commissioner-General for Cultural Property by agreement between the Party and the Protecting Power acting on behalf of the opposing sides.[14] Certain cultural property can be placed under special protection and an international register of such property should be made.[15] It is possible to provide improvised refuges for cultural property under special protection,[16] taking direct and temporary care to avert potential harm. The Second Protocol also introduced the enhanced protection scheme, which places cultural property 'of the greatest importance for humanity'[17] (once designated as such by the state party) under 'immunity from attack or from any use of the property or its immediate surroundings in support of military action'.[18] Further direct care is found in the First Protocol under which the parties undertake 'to take into its custody cultural property imported into its territory either directly or indirectly from any occupied territory'[19] and to return at the end of hostility.[20] The Convention and its associated legal instruments assign responsibility for the care of cultural heritage to avert unnecessary harm to cultural heritage. Such responsibility is not simply assigned to a state in general terms. Instead, the Convention ensures that practical measures are in place for personnel on the ground in war zones to assume direct responsibility for the care of cultural heritage. Although the desire to avert physical harm is clearly expressed, it is not absolute and the obligation to respect cultural property may be waived in the event of military necessity.[21] Therefore, this framework assists in navigating and mitigating against harm, rather than entirely averting harm to cultural heritage.[22]

---

[12] As set out in ibid., art. 18.

[13] Regulations for the Execution of the Convention for the Protection of Cultural Property in the Event of Armed Conflict, art. 2.

[14] ibid., art. 4.   [15] ibid., art. 12.   [16] ibid., art. 11.

[17] Second Protocol to the 1954 Hague Convention, art. 10.   [18] ibid., art. 12.

[19] Protocol to the Convention for the Protection of Cultural Property in the Event of Armed Conflict, The Hague, 14 May 1954, art. 1(2).

[20] ibid., art. 1(3).

[21] 1954 Hague Convention, art. 4(1). The use of such a waiver may only be invoked in very limited circumstances and for a limited period of time, detailed in Second Protocol to the 1954 Hague Convention, art. 6.

[22] The concept of mitigating harm, particularly in the context of development, is explored at Section 7.8.

Directed at the potential illicit trade in objects taken from places of conflict, the Cultural Property (Armed Conflicts) Act 2017 (implementing the requirements of the Convention and its protocols) brought in an offence of dealing in unlawfully exported cultural property[23] from a territory which at the time it was occupied was a state that was a party to the First or Second Protocol or where cultural property was exported from the territory of an occupied state that was party to either Protocol.[24] 'Dealing' is acquiring or disposing of the cultural property or importing or exporting it as well as agreeing to do those activities.[25] Here the *mens rea* is whether they knew, or had reason to suspect, that it was unlawfully exported.[26]

7.3.1.1 Recognising Cultural Heritage as *res extra commercium* or Making It Inalienable

Harm can be caused to cultural heritage and to those communities of care for whom it is important when its care shifts from a publicly accountable community of care (which can provide or is mandated to provide access to the cultural heritage) to the private domain. This is because the care that is provided might be determined wholly or partly by the private owner, without any concern for broader interests of other communities. One way of pre-empting this possibility is to provide a protective legal cloak around certain categories of cultural heritage, which treats them as being beyond the reach of commerce. The effect of this can be to prevent their sale in any circumstances, to make it illegal to sell without appropriate consent, or to require a process to be followed before a sale takes place, thus making any sale subject to scrutiny. These notions are found in the contexts of *res extra commercium* and inalienability of property.[27] As a general principle, the notion of treating cultural heritage as being outside commerce is found at the international level in UNESCO's Universal Declaration on Cultural Diversity, 2 November 2001, which states that cultural goods and services 'must not be treated as mere commodities or consumer goods' because they are 'vectors of identity, values and meaning'.[28] This idea thus distinguishes between cultural heritage as a financial asset and as

---

[23] Which contraventions either the laws of the territory from which it was exported, or international law: s. 16(3).

[24] Cultural Property (Armed Conflicts) Act 2017, s. 16(1).   [25] ibid., s. 17(3).

[26] ibid., s. 17(1).

[27] These concepts are found in various countries: see Kurt Siehr, 'The Protection of Cultural Heritage and International Commerce' (1997) 6 *International Journal of Cultural Property* 304, 318. The concept of inalienable state museum collections is found in France, although more recently there have been some instances of laws being passed to transfer specific objects from collections in response to claims for repatriation or restitution: see loi no 2020–1673 du 24 décembre 2020 relative à la restitution de biens culturels à la République de Bénin et à la République du Sénégal. In the context of Nazi-era claims, see Corinne Hershkovitch, 'Restitution of Nazi-Looted Art: The French Law of 2022' (2022) 27 *Art Antiquity and Law* 13.

[28] UNESCO Universal Declaration on Cultural Diversity (2 November 2001), art. 8.

something of importance to communities.[29] In the UK there is no general principle which recognises cultural heritage as being *res extra commercium*. However, the law acts to create what are in effect such categories in some limited situations.

The first is in the context of the consistory court, which treats 'church goods' as being 'not in the ordinary way in commerce or available for sale and purchase'.[30] These objects can only be sold or given away by the churchwardens where the appropriate consent is given and where a faculty is granted by the court.[31] Whilst this is not strictly speaking the doctrine of *res extra commercium* prohibiting sales entirely, its effect is to subject to scrutiny any decision about the long-term care of the cultural heritage and the possible harm that might occur if it is sold.[32] The legal brakes are applied to any potential sale, or other disposal by the churchwardens. This provides an opportunity for the court (with relevant expert advice and contributions from other communities of care) to fully evaluate the appropriateness of the current provision of care, to consider whether that should continue, or whether transfer elsewhere would be more appropriate in the circumstances. As part of this process the court may take into account the financial reasons for the sale. These reasons can include churches requiring money to finance urgent repairs and where the sale prices would be used to cover these repairs. Nevertheless, there is a strong presumption against the disposal of such objects.[33] Where a petition relates to a proposed disposal of an object of 'special historic, architectural, archaeological or artistic interest' the Chancellor must seek the advice of the Church Buildings Council,[34] thus relying on an expert community of care to advise them about the appropriateness of the potential sale. In addition, as with every petition for a faculty, there is a requirement to display a public notice which permits representations to be made and considered.[35] Where church treasures are involved (as distinct from any other personal property owned by the churchwardens) a faculty should

---

[29] This is also reflected in the MA, *Code of Ethics* (2015), principle 2, which states that collections should be treated 'as cultural, scientific or historic assets, not financial assets'.

[30] Adopting passages to that effect from Blackstone and Phillimore: *Re St Gregory's, Tredington* [1972] Fam 236, 240.

[31] A valid sale or gift appears to act as a process of metamorphosis, for it is said that they then 'become ordinary things in commerce and are wholly divested of any sacred character' (*Legal Opinions Concerning the Church of England* (2020), Part 5 'Churchwardens', para. 9). Although there is a *de minimis* principle which permits mouldy old hassocks to be thrown away without the need for a faculty from the consistory court: see *Re Emmanuel Church Leckhampton* [2014] Gloucester Cons Ct., p. 9.

[32] Although the concept of *res extra commercium* has been interpreted more widely to mean 'restricting the free alienability of certain forms of property': Oliver Metzger, 'Making the Doctrine of Res Extra Commercium Visible in United States Law' (1995–6) 74 *Texas Law Review* 615, 621.

[33] *Leckhampton*, p. 54.   [34] Faculty Jurisdiction Rules 2015 (as amended), r. 9.6(1) and (2).

[35] ibid., r. 5.7.

'seldom if ever be granted without a hearing in open court',[36] thus providing an opportunity for communities of care to contribute to discussions relating to the long-term care of cultural heritage. The sequential approach to dealing with applications for faculties involving church treasures, by treating a sale on the open market as the last resort,[37] further demonstrates how harm is averted where at all possible.

The second category of property treated with more stringent limits on transfers is certain property owned by the National Trust and the National Trust for Scotland which is deemed to be inalienable.[38] This includes those properties listed in the first schedules of the National Trust Act 1907 and the National Trust for Scotland Order Confirmation Act 1935, any that may be designated as such by a resolution of the National Trust[39] or the National Trust for Scotland,[40] or a mansion house or amenity lands assured to the National Trust under the National Trust Act 1939.[41] This notion of inalienability is clearly set in the context of when property becomes vested in the National Trust 'for preservation for the benefit of the nation'.[42] Therefore, the focus here is on the idea of retaining it within the public domain for the benefit of the wider national community, and preventing its transfer to the private domain.[43] Where there is a proposed compulsory purchase of inalienable land for the purposes of development, the National Trust can object to this. Where it makes an objection, compulsory purchase can only take place if the special parliamentary procedure is followed and the purchase approved.[44] This procedure subjects the decision about the long-term care of these important cultural heritage places to scrutiny at the highest level, demonstrating particularly heightened levels of care applied to avoid depriving the national community of the enjoyment of this cultural heritage. Further enhanced levels of care are provided by prohibiting the use of

---

[36] *Re St Gregory's, Tredington*, 236, 246 (Arches Court of Canterbury) (GH Newsom QC).

[37] Discussed at Section 7.8.1.4.

[38] National Trust Act 1907, s. 21(1) and National Trust for Scotland Order Confirmation Act 1935, s. 22(1). See also National Trust Act 1939, s. 8 regarding mansion houses or amenity land.

[39] National Trust Act 1907, s. 21(2).

[40] National Trust for Scotland Order Confirmation Act 1935, s. 22(2).

[41] National Trust Act 1939, s. 8.

[42] National Trust Act 1907, s. 4(1) and National Trust for Scotland Order Confirmation Act 1935, s. 4(1).

[43] The context in which the National Trust acquired many mansion houses was to avoid the houses being sold to private purchasers, thus saving them for the nation. These powers were often exercised in conjunction with the granting of leases to the original owners, allowing them to continue living there: see the Preambles to the National Trust Act 1937 and the National Trust for Scotland Order Confirmation Act 1935.

[44] Acquisition of Land Act 1981, s. 5(1). In the case of inalienable National Trust land to be compulsorily purchased for the purposes of the proposed A303 road improvement scheme, the National Trust withdrew its objection to the compulsory purchase: Hilary McGrady, Director General of the National Trust, *Our Position on the Compulsory Purchase of Our Land* (26 September 2019): www.nationaltrust.org.uk/stonehenge-landscape/features/our-position-on-the-compulsory-acquisition-of-our-land (last accessed 22 May 2023).

inalienable property as security for loans.[45] Although the National Trust may grant leases over inalienable land, for such leases to be valid, they must be sanctioned by the Charity Commission.[46] The power of the Board of Trustees to resolve that certain property is inalienable applies only to lands or tenements and not to personal property.[47] Therefore collections of cultural heritage objects, or cultural heritage objects associated with a particular cultural heritage place could well be sold but would be subject to the disposals policy of the National Trust or the National Trust for Scotland.[48]

7.3.2 Using the Law Instrumentally: The Creation of Collections

One area of contestation, considered in Chapter 1, was the often-expressed concern about the effects of disposal of an entire collection, or elements of it. These effects include the risk to a collection's encyclopaedic nature, the loss of association between the objects themselves, or between the object and a place or the objects and a person, as well as the loss of current and future public access to the collection. There is also a concern that disposing of objects from museums which were gifts or bequests might dissuade future donors and risk a loss of the public's trust. Instances of misguided past disposals (deaccessions) are cited to support arguments aimed at curtailing the disposal of objects from museum collections, in particular prohibiting disposals based solely on financial motivations.[49] In response to this, various communities place legal restrictions on the ability of museums to dispose of the whole or part of any collection. It is clear that museums are under a recognised moral obligation not to dispose of their collections for purely financial motives, articulated not only in the MA Code of Ethics,[50] but also by the Select Committee on Culture, Media and Sport. The latter made these observations in the context of local museums by saying that they believed that 'there is a moral duty on councils to hold cultural collections in trust for the wider community'.[51] This notion is further recognised by the Arts Council in their Accreditation Scheme, and more widely by the museum sector.[52]

[45] National Trust Act 1907, s. 21(1) and National Trust for Scotland Order Confirmation Act 1935, s. 22(1).
[46] National Trust Charity Scheme Confirmation Act 1919, sch., para. 1.
[47] National Trust Act 1907, s. 21(2). For the most part the properties listed as inalienable in the schedule to the 1907 Act are land in a traditional sense of being open land or buildings, although certain monuments are also listed: Specifically, the Monuments to Viscount Falkland, Vice-Admiral Sir Thomas Hardy and John Ruskin: National Trust Act 1907, sch. 1, Parts I and II.
[48] National Trust for Scotland, *Developing Collections: A Policy to Reflect and Enrich Lives* (2019).
[49] See Iain Robertson, 'Infamous De-accessions' in Anne Fahy (ed.), *Collections Management* (London: Routledge, 1995), p. 168.
[50] MA, *Code of Ethics*, principle 2.9.
[51] House of Commons, Culture, Media and Sport Committee, Sixth Report, Session 2006–07, *Caring for Our Collections*, HC 176–1, para. 142.
[52] As to which, see the 2015 *Joint Statement – Unethical Sale from Museum Collections*, signed by ACE, Museums and Galleries Scotland, Northern Ireland Museums Council, Federation of Museums and Art Galleries of Wales, AIM, MA, AIM, Art Fund, National Archives, NMDC

Carefully crafted legal structures, used in circumstances where there is no immediate threat of harm to collections, can be used to ensure both appropriate quotidian care[53] and appropriate care if direct threats materialise in the future. This enables communities concerned to navigate more appropriately any threat to the collection and to respond with appropriate care. Creating a collection in legal terms can serve to ensure its integrity as a whole, or at a minimum to subject any proposal to dispose of the whole or part of it to legal scrutiny.[54] Thus, the law can be used instrumentally to create a collection which may serve, in a precautionary manner, to avert any future harm that might be caused if either the entire collection or individual objects from within it were sold.

The onus is on those who care for collections to take positive action to make use of the available legal structures. A failure to clothe the collection with such a legal structure means that little can be done to prevent its dispersal, since the recognition in legal terms of a collection cannot be imposed after the fact by a court. This shortcoming in the law is analysed below in the context of reactive care.[55] Differing degrees of restrictions on powers of disposal can be created through legal means.

7.3.2.1 The Extent of Precautionary Care Provided to Collections

At one end of the legal spectrum are those collections governed by legal provisions entirely prohibiting acquisitions or disposals, thus keeping the collection entirely static. The Wallace Collection, comprising paintings and works of decorative art from France and Europe – bequeathed by Lady Wallace to the nation in 1897 on condition that it should be kept together intact, 'unmixed with other works of art'[56] – provides one such example. Despite this prohibition, the trustees have interpreted their power as permitting acquisitions, only in exceptional circumstances, 'to complete a work of art or set or ensemble within the Bequest'.[57] Additionally, the trustees have acquired objects for the Hertford House Historic Collection and Archive, which is treated as separate from the Wallace Collection.[58]

Until relatively recently the terms of the Wallace Collection bequest had been interpreted so strictly as to prevent the Board of Trustees from lending objects (and no such power was present in its governing statute).[59] However,

---

and Heritage Lottery Fund: https://www.nationalmuseums.org.uk/news/nmdc-joins-sector-bodies-joint-statement-against-unethical-sale-collections/ (last accessed 30 May 2023).

[53] See Chapter 6.   [54] E.g. through consideration by the Charity Commission.

[55] Discussed at Section 7.5.

[56] As set out in the original bequest: Wallace Collection, *Collections Management Policy* (July 2016), p. 7. This sentiment is reflected in the Museums and Galleries Act 1992, s. 4(6), which states that the Board 'shall neither add any object to their collection nor dispose of any object'.

[57] ibid., p. 7.   [58] ibid.

[59] Museums and Galleries Act 1992, s. 5 only refers to the governing bodies of the National Gallery, the National Portrait Gallery and the Tate having such a power.

following a reinterpretation of the terms of the bequest, at the request of the trustees, the Charity Commission made an Order permitting the Board of Trustees to lend objects, including for public exhibition. These are on terms in line with the comparable powers given to the other governing bodies of national museums subject to the 1992 Act.[60]

Moving along the legal spectrum one finds collections where acquisitions and disposals are permitted, but either only in very limited circumstances, or subject to onerous legal hoops which must be gone through before any disposal is permitted. Most of the national museums governed by statutes have prohibitions along these lines; their provisions are analysed in more detail below.[61]

The next category involves legal structures requiring certain pre-requisites to be met before disposals can take place, albeit less onerous ones. These include charities, which are considered in more detail below.[62]

Finally, for some museums the particular legal structures used to administer the collections do not give any accompanying formal legal designation to the objects themselves as a collection. In these situations there are no legal prohibitions or restrictions on disposal. Many local authority museums fall into this category.[63] The absence of restrictions on disposal makes the collection susceptible to financially motivated disposals, particularly in circumstances where the local authority is under other budgetary pressures. There may, though, be ethical restrictions placed on them due to their professionally agreed ethical obligations, or due to accreditation requirements. Once more, these are discussed below.[64]

7.3.2.2 Communities of Care and Their Methods of Providing Care by Constructing Collections in Legal Terms

Museum collections can come into existence because of the actions of benefactors, either donating or bequeathing large collections which form entire museum collections (as seen with the Wallace Collection), or an element of it. The legal structure of a museum or part of its collection can, therefore, be determined by the actions of these benefactors who may make the transfer of a collection or of individual objects to a museum subject to certain conditions.

The nature of the restrictions may extend beyond prohibition of disposal to include other requirements about how cultural heritage is cared for. These may include a prohibition on lending objects, which may be aimed at averting

---

[60] ibid., s. 5. The relevant parts of the Charity Commission Order are extracted in: Wallace Collection, *The Wallace Collection Loans Out Policy* (2022): www.wallacecollection.org/documents/622/The_Wallace_Collection_Loans_Out_Policy_2022.pdf (last accessed 30 May 2023).

[61] At Section 7.3.2.2.   [62] ibid.

[63] Although in some cases local authorities have established museums as charitable trusts, the collections themselves remain owned by the museums and are lent to the trust: Janet Ulph, 'Dealing with UK Museum Collections: Law, Ethics and the Public/Private Divide' (2015) 22 *International Journal of Cultural Property* 177, 186.

[64] At Section 7.8.1.4.

physical harm,[65] or maintaining associations between a place and a person (such as requirements that the donation is linked to the name of the benefactor), or prescribing how objects are displayed.[66]

A mere expression by a benefactor of a particular wish to keep a collection together, or to preserve it for future generations, may have a moral standing but has no legal significance.[67] Any such desire would need to be supported by a legal device to make it binding on the recipient museum. One way of doing this would be to establish a charitable trust,[68] or to make a conditional gift.[69] Acts of Parliament have been used to solidify in legal terms bequests of certain collections where they have been given to the nation with restrictive conditions attached.[70]

An institutional community of care, in the form of Parliament, has created national museums through statute law, and has constructed them in such a way that their governing bodies[71] tend to have a qualified power to dispose of objects; however, this is in a manner which prevents the widespread or indiscriminate deaccessioning of objects. These restrictions prevent disposals except where an object is a duplicate,[72] where the object consists of printed material printed not earlier than 1850 and where a copy can be made,[73] where the object is unfit to be retained, provided that it can be disposed of without detriment to the interests of students[74] (and to the public[75]) or where the object is considered useless because of its damaged state, physical deterioration or infestation.[76] The National Portrait Gallery Board can also dispose of an

---

[65] This was seen in the context of the Burrell collection in Glasgow where a prohibition on lending overseas was based on a concern about the fragility of objects during transit. It was eased through private legislation (a device existing in Scots Law) on the recommendation of a Parliamentary Commission but by introducing suitable safeguards: see Ian McCulloch and Jessica Koravos, 'The Burrell Showcase' (1998) 3 *Art Antiquity and Law* 193, 199.

[66] JMW Turner bequeathed two paintings to the National Gallery with a stipulation that they were to be displayed between paintings by Claude Lorrain: see Lyndel V. Prott and Patrick J. O'Keefe, *Law and the Cultural Heritage, Volume 3: Movement* (London: Butterworths, 1989), p. 306. Henry Vaughan bequeathed some watercolours by Turner to National Galleries Scotland and one stipulation was that they were all to be exhibited to the public for free each January: www .nationalgalleries.org/art-and-artists/features/scottish-tradition-jmw-turner-and-vaughan-bequest (last accessed 30 May 2023).

[67] *Butler* v. *Butler* [2016] 4 WLR 133, para. 92. See Section 7.6.1.1.

[68] See generally Jeremy Warren (ed.), *The Legal Status of Museum Collections in the United Kingdom* (London: Museums and Galleries Commission, 1996).

[69] See Janet Ulph, *The Legal and Ethical Status of Museum Collections: Curatorially Motivated Disposals* (2016), p. 25: www.museumsassociation.org/app/uploads/2020/06/30082016-disposal-document-2.pdf (last accessed 30 May 2023).

[70] E.g. the Wallace Collection, discussed above, and the Sir John Soane's Museum.

[71] With the exception of the Wallace Collection and the National Gallery.

[72] BMA 1963, s. 5(1)(a); NHA 1983, ss. 6(3)(a) (V&A), 14(3)(a) (Science Museum) and 20(3)(a) (Armouries) and Museums and Galleries Act 1992, s. 4(5)(b) (National Portrait Gallery).

[73] E.g. the BMA 1963, s. 5(1)(b). [74] ibid., s. 5(1)(c).

[75] NHA 1983, ss. 6(3)(b) (V&A), 14(3)(b) (Science Museum) and 20(3)(b) (Armouries) and Museums and Galleries Act 1992, s. 4(4)(b) (Tate Gallery).

[76] BMA 1963, s. 5(2); NHA 1983, ss. 6(3)(d) (V&A), 14(3)(d) (Science Museum) and 20(3)(d) (Armouries) and Museums and Galleries Act 1992, ss. 4(4)(c) (Tate Gallery) and 4(5)(d) (National Portrait Gallery).

object where the formally accepted identification of a portrait is discredited.[77] Many national museums can transfer objects to institutions listed in schedule 5 to the Museums and Galleries Act 1992[78] and this provision creates, in effect, a composite national collection which permits inter-museum transfers, yet at the same time keeps the national collection as a whole. The only institution with an absolute prohibition on disposal is the Wallace Collection, already discussed.[79] Whilst the National Gallery is prevented from disposing of objects from its collections,[80] it may transfer objects from within its collections to other institutions listed in schedule 5. Of particular interest is the fact that not all the institutions listed in schedule 5 are other national museums – instead transfers can be made to National Trust properties as well as English Heritage. These transfers are not financially motivated but are the result of collections management decisions. However, the provision can be used to facilitate a transfer to a more appropriate place in which an object can be cared for or enjoyed; at the same time, the object remains in the public domain and is available for continued public access. This happened when the V&A returned the interior of Sizergh Castle (which it had purchased in 1891) to be reinstalled there because it was owned by the National Trust.[81] The result of such a composite national collection is that decisions about the appropriate care of cultural heritage can be made in a holistic manner, enabling a review of the current provision of care and consideration of whether it is more appropriate for the cultural heritage to be placed in a location with which it has particular associations. It can also place objects together with other similar ones, to provide a stronger narrative and emphasise the associations between objects.

Given the highly restrictive manner in which the powers of transfer outside the limited schedule 5 scheme have been interpreted in recent years, the collections are to a certain extent otherwise *de facto* inalienable. In the DCMS's Strategic Review, it was observed that these provisions have been interpreted by the museums more strictly than necessary.[82] Yet, in *AG v. Trustees of the British Museum*[83] it was held that even where the previous owners of certain drawings in the museum's collection had been deprived of them when they were seized by the Gestapo, this did not render them 'unfit to be retained' by the board of trustees.[84] Consequently, the trustees had no power to transfer the drawings to the heirs of the original owner despite the museum considering themselves under a moral obligation to do so.[85]

---

[77] Museums and Galleries Act 1992, s. 4(5)(c).
[78] ibid., s. 6 and sch. 5, which lists those which can act as transferors and transferees and those only as transferees.
[79] At Section 7.3.2.1.   [80] Museums and Galleries Act 1992, s. 4(3).
[81] Maev Kennedy, 'V&A Returns Tudor Bedroom to Original Sizergh Castle Setting', *The Guardian*, 2 January 2017.
[82] DCMS, *Strategic Review of DCMS-Sponsored Museums* (2017), p. 43.
[83] [2005] Ch 397 (Ch).   [84] ibid., 411.
[85] Although the position is now different for claims relating to cultural objects of which the original owners lost possession during the Nazi era following the enactment of the Holocaust

When it comes to non-national museums, no legal provisions automatically prescribe the circumstances in which a collection should be retained. Instead, it will depend on individual communities of care to translate their collections into legally recognised collections, where appropriate. The relevant communities of care who establish the museum (whether a local authority exercising its powers under the Public Libraries and Museums Act 1964,[86] local communities or benefactors) will prescribe the initial legal structure. Once established, the museum's governing body – as a community of care – may, during the course of the museum's legal lifetime, respond to changes in circumstances by altering that structure as they re-evaluate the current provision of care effected through the particular chosen legal structure.

Where a community wishes to care for a collection by using charity law, the institution would need to pass the public benefit test.[87] In some cases, permission from the Charity Commission is needed before disposing of certain objects from their collections.[88]

Depending on their legal nature, some collections are more fluid than others because they are subject to less restrictive powers of disposal. Thus, museum collections of local authorities may be owned by the local authority and decisions about disposals or the long-term care of them fall to councillors to make. Where separate charities are formed these have several advantages for the museums, including benefiting from the fiscal advantages of being charities.[89] Universities may hold collections of objects which they use for teaching and research purposes, or as museum collections; whether these are separate or part of the university will depend on the legal structure.

7.3.2.3 The Bright and the Dark Sides of Legally Constructed Collections

These various legal devices, imposing restrictions on the circumstances in which objects from a collection can be transferred, act in a precautionary manner. They avoid future potential loss and ward against reduced access occasioned by moving cultural heritage from the public to the private domain. Nevertheless, the legal protection given to collections has a potential dark side as well as a bright side.[90]

(Return of Cultural Objects) Act 2009, the position remains unchanged for other cultural heritage objects. Although, see discussion at Section 9.5.1 relating to the Ethiopian Tabots held by the British Museum.

[86] S. 12(1).   [87] Discussed at Section 6.4.2.

[88] See, for example, the Charity Commission Order relating to the restitution of objects to the Feldmann heirs from the Courtauld Institute: www.artandarchitecture.org.uk/images/gallery/3166e2a5.html (last accessed 30 May 2023).

[89] Adrian Babbage, Rosemary Ewles and Julian Smith, *Moving to Museum Trust: Learning from Experience – Advice to Museums in England and Wales Part 1: Strategic Overview* (London: Museums, Libraries and Archives Council, and Renaissance, 2006), para. 6.

[90] Cf. Lixinski, who talks about bright sides and dark sides to heritage protection in the context of the UNESCO conventions on heritage and the effect on communities: see Lucas Lixinski, *International Heritage Law for Communities: Exclusion and Re-Imagination* (Oxford: Oxford University Press, 2019), p. 131.

The bright side of the process, in terms of solidifying and making more difficult disposals to subject them to scrutiny, has been highlighted. However, on the other side of the coin one must consider the benefits, on occasions, to disposals from collections. There may be sound curatorial reasons for disposing of objects from a collection. Where collections are so heavily protected by legal restrictions that disposal is either impossible or so heavily qualified that it is difficult to fit such a disposal within the scope of the powers of the governing body, this then has the effect of either preserving the entire collection in aspic, or at least rendering it relatively static and something far removed from the needs of the communities that it serves.

Of more concern is the fact that restricting the power of disposal entirely has the potential to impede appropriate care of cultural heritage within the collection, as there is no scope for dialogue or empathetic and respectful consideration of how the collection and objects within it are currently cared for. Furthermore, there is no opportunity for reviewing the appropriateness of care in terms of considering whether the museums are those most appropriately placed to have responsibility for the care of the cultural heritage in question. This can be seen to a stark extent in the context of the Wallace Collection and Sir John Soane's Museum. These restrictive provisions, solidified by Acts of Parliament, prevent dialogic care and risk turning into paternalistic care in the event that others who care about the cultural heritage within these collections seek to challenge the museum's continued retention of an object.[91]

Contrastingly, whilst there is a risk that museums without legal restrictions on disposals may dispose of cultural heritage objects for financially motivated reasons, those same institutions have the freedom to exercise dialogic care and to accede to repatriation requests in circumstances where that is considered most appropriate. These powers are considered below in Chapter 9.

7.4 Preventative Care

Where there is an identified actual, or potential risk to cultural heritage of harm or loss, preventative care may be appropriate. Appropriate care seeks to navigate this anticipated harm by putting in place measures in a respectful, empathetic and dialogic manner. The notion of preventative conservation is evident in several international and national instruments, particularly when concerned with the practical efforts to avert harm to the physical object or place.[92]

---

[91] See Section 9.5.1. The idea of 'paternalistic care' derives from Uma Narayan, 'Colonialism and Its Others: Considerations on Rights and Care Discourses' (1995) 10 *Hypatia* 133, 135.

[92] E.g. ICOMOS, Principles for the Preservation and Conservation/Restoration of Wall Paintings (October 2003), art. 4 deals with preventative conservation and. It is described as 'cover[ing] the measures necessary to slow down or minimise deterioration of museum objects and specimens and structures' and National Museums Northern Ireland, *Collections Care and Conservation Policy* (2015), p. 5.

The broader concept of 'care', which covers all activities relating to cultural heritage,[93] is used here in the context of preventative measures.

7.4.1 Establishing Frameworks through Law or Other Designation

Private owners may provide direct preventative care for cultural heritage places that they own, with a view to avoiding any physical harm to them. They may well have in mind a desire to avert harm which could affect the special interests of it as a cultural heritage place. Yet there may be a tension between an owner's use of a building, as a home or for their business, and its status as a cultural heritage place. Parliament, as a community of care, has therefore for many years[94] made provision for ensuring that certain designated cultural heritage places, even though privately owned, are nevertheless cared for.

Baldwin Brown observed in 1905 that one should 'gladly recognise that both individuals and public bodies are often as jealous for the safe keeping and proper treatment of their artistic possessions as any outsiders could possibly be'.[95] Nevertheless, he recognised that despite monuments often having an important aesthetic or historical value, occasionally some owners may cause them harm through neglect, injury or sometimes outright destruction.[96] Here Baldwin Brown recognised that property interests were at the forefront of discussions about the proper care of ancient monuments. Concern with spoliation or interference with property rights at times prevented action to care for heritage places. Even though, at the time of his writing, the Ancient Monuments Protection Act 1882 had been in force for a number of years, nevertheless he saw Britain's approach as being one of laissez-faire in relation to the state of monuments.[97] He acknowledged that it represented interference with private rights which were necessary for the purposes of development. Nevertheless, he said that it seemed that there was less compulsion on grounds that 'many regard as sentimental'.[98]

To provide such care, statute law places the responsibility to avoid engaging in direct physical harm to designated heritage assets not only on the owners of the specific places, but on everybody in the UK by criminalising activities which may cause harm.[99] In the context of listed buildings, this is effected through the use of criminal offences relating to activities which would affect their character as buildings of 'special architectural or historic interest' undertaken without consent[100] and the connected sanctions.[101] It is also an offence

---

[93] As set out at Section 2.3.
[94] The first statute was the Ancient Monuments Protection Act 1882.
[95] G. Baldwin Brown, *The Care of Ancient Monuments* (Cambridge: Cambridge University Press, 1905), pp. 4–5.
[96] ibid., pp. 4-5.   [97] ibid., pp. 4–5.   [98] ibid., p. 9.
[99] Such as listed buildings, scheduled monuments and protected wrecks.
[100] P(LBCA)A 1990, s. 7(1); Planning (Listed Buildings and Conservation Areas) (Scotland) Act 1997, ss. 6 and 7 and Planning Act (Northern Ireland) 2011, s. 85(1).
[101] P(LBCA)A 1990, s. 9(4); Planning (Listed Buildings and Conservation Areas) (Scotland) Act 1997, s. 8(1) and Planning Act (Northern Ireland) 2011, s. 85(6).

to intend to cause damage to a listed building or to permit any act which causes or is likely to cause damage.[102] Relevant care is extended to something which is fixed to a listed building in such a way as to have become a fixture and thus part of the building.[103] Any damage or destruction of a protected monument without a lawful reasonable excuse is treated as an offence.[104] Here, protected monuments include scheduled monuments (which are officially designated heritage assets) and those monuments owned by, or under the guardianship of, the Secretary of State.[105]

Preventative care is also provided through statutory provisions permitting local authorities to make grants or loans for the repair or maintenance of listed buildings or a building which is not listed, but which 'appears ... to be of architectural or historic interest'.[106] The authority can make it conditional on the owner agreeing to public access.[107] Similar provisions permit the support of 'the preservation or enhancement of the character or appearance of any conservation area'.[108]

Once historic wrecks are discovered in UK waters,[109] they can be designated as having protected status due to the 'historical, archaeological or artistic importance of the vessel, or of any objects contained or formerly contained within it',[110] or as scheduled monuments[111] or, in Scotland, as Historic Marine Protected Areas.[112] Certain activities relating to those wrecks require licences[113] and specific offences which may cause harm to these importantly historic places are provided in the legislation.[114] These instruments therefore

---

[102] P(LBCA)A 1990, s. 59(1); Planning (Listed Buildings and Conservation Areas) (Scotland) Act 1997, s. 53 and Planning Act (Northern Ireland) 2011, s. 103(1).

[103] P(LBCA)A 1990, ss. 1(5)(a) and 7 which includes alterations of buildings and similarly Planning (Listed Buildings and Conservation Areas) (Scotland) Act 1997, s. 1(4)(a) and Planning Act (Northern Ireland) 2011, s. 80(7)(a).

[104] AMAAA 1979, s. 28(1).   [105] ibid., s. 28(3).

[106] P(LBCA)A 1990, s. 57(1) and Planning (Listed Buildings and Conservation Areas) (Scotland) Act 1997, s. 51(1). In Northern Ireland the Department has the power to make grants or loans: Planning (Northern Ireland) Act 2011, s. 199(1).

[107] P(LBCA)A 1990, s. 57. Under the Planning (Listed Buildings and Conservation Areas) (Scotland) Act 1997, ss. 51(4) and (5A) grants and loans can be made subject to conditions. In Northern Ireland the department may make grants or loans which are subject to conditions which secure public access: Planning (Northern Ireland) Act 2011, s.199(4).

[108] P(LBCA)A 1990, s. 77(1) (England); Planning (Listed Buildings and Conservation Areas) (Scotland) Act 1997, s. 69 and Planning (Northern Ireland) Act 2011, s. 106(1).

[109] Defined in Protection of Wrecks Act 1973, s. 3(1).   [110] ibid., s. 1(1).

[111] AMAAA 1979, s.61(7)(c) 'monument' includes any vessel.

[112] Marine (Scotland) Act 2010, s. 73.

[113] Such as tampering with, damaging or removing parts of a wrecked vessel, carrying out diving or salvage operations or depositing anything that might fall or on the wreck site: Protection of Wrecks Act 1973, s. 1(3). However, such actions are excused in the context of emergencies and necessity 'due to stress of weather or navigational hazards'. In Scotland this includes using a vehicle, vessel, etc. to remove any object from the seabed, to carry out dredging or to 'scuttle any vessel or floating container' in a Scottish Marine Area: Marine (Scotland) Act 2010, s. 21(1) which sets out the full list of licensable marine activities.

[114] In Scotland prohibited activities include removing, altering or damaging a marine historic asset or carrying out activities which do or are likely to damage or interfere with such an asset,

provide a framework of care which can mitigate against potential harm. Even in the case of undesignated wrecks, a licence is needed for someone to remove an object from the seabed, which includes removing something from a wreck.[115]

Removal of cultural heritage objects from a designated heritage asset can also cause harm,[116] as can subsequent dealings with them (either by sale, export or import). The Dealing in Cultural Objects (Offences) Act 2003 makes it an offence for someone to dishonestly deal in such an object knowing it to be a tainted cultural object.[117] The Act was introduced as a means of criminalising dealing in objects that have been unlawfully removed from designated heritage assets.[118]

Enacting such legislative frameworks with criminal sanctions gives them appropriate legal 'bite' and shows how the UK, as a community, has acknowledged and assumed responsibility to care for cultural heritage places which are recognised as forming part of the UK's cultural heritage.

7.4.1.1 Indirect Harm: Harm to Setting

Legislation and planning policies across the nations of the UK provide for the care of cultural heritage. This care relates not only to acts which directly affect the physical heritage and the actions of anyone in respect of that, but also the actions of private owners of neighbouring land where they seek to develop in such a way as to potentially impact the surrounding heritage.[119] This is recognised, through legislation, in the broader general duty of local planning authorities to consider, when granting planning permission, the effect not only on any listed building but also on its setting.[120] Setting is widely interpreted and can extend beyond 'visual and physical considerations' to include

---

or 'have a significant impact on the protected area': Marine (Scotland) Act 2010, s. 96(2). Such an act would be carried out intentionally or recklessly and 'the act has significantly hindered, or may significantly hinder, the achievement of the stated preservation objectives for the protected area': Marine (Scotland) Act 2010, s. 96(1).

[115] Marine and Coastal Access Act 2009, ss. 65(1) and 66(1)(8). The appropriate licensing authorities for the nations of the UK are listed in s. 113.

[116] This would include removal of a fixture from a listed building as well as something illicitly excavated from a scheduled monument or archaeological area, or something removed from a protected wreck: under the Dealing in Cultural Objects (Offences) Act 2003, s. 2(2).

[117] ibid., s. 1(1), which applies to England, Wales and Northern Ireland.　　[118] ibid., s. 1(1).

[119] By treating the effect on designated heritage assets as a material consideration in applications for the development of land: see P(LBCA)A 1990, s. 66(1) which refers to the 'special regard to the desirability of preserving the building or its setting or any features of special architectural or historic interest'. This phrasing is mirrored by the Planning (Listed Buildings and Conservation Areas) (Scotland) Act 1997, s. 59(1) and the Planning (Northern Ireland) Act 2011, s. 91(2).

[120] P(LBCA)A 1990, s. 66 and R (on the application Williams) v. Powys County Council [2017] EWCA Civ 427; [2018] 1 WLR 439. The NPPF defines 'setting' in the context of England and the Conservation principles for the sustainable management of the historic environment in Wales, Cadw March 2011 defines setting of historic assets in a similar way to the NPPF definition in England.

'economic, social and historical' ones, including 'the historic relationship between place'.[121]

Similarly, in the context of works that might affect conservation areas, their 'character and appearance' is a relevant factor to take into account in planning decisions.[122] This incorporates 'matters such as historic uses and the contributions which they make to the character of the area by influencing the understanding of that area and reflecting experiences that are not simply visual'.[123] Care extends beyond and around World Heritage Sites. When considering planning applications, not only is the impact on the site's setting a material consideration, but also the impact on buffer zones around World Heritage Sites.[124]

7.4.1.2 Participation

Advice derived from various communities of experts informs decision-makers. In some cases, these communities of experts are required to be consulted, such as Historic England[125] and the amenity societies.[126] These communities therefore have a voice in the process and can express objections to proposals that would affect cultural heritage places from particular eras.[127] However, other interested parties who care about cultural heritage may also submit representations for consideration as part of that process. These participants in the decision-making process provide multivocality and proactively provide care for the cultural heritage, forming a network of communities of care. They might already have formed communities of care, such as local or architectural interest groups, who decide to respond to public consultations. However, the public are also able to respond to calls for the expression of views about any works that might be undertaken to a listed building. Therefore, in some cases individual members of the public who are likely to be directly or indirectly

---

[121] These comments were made in the context of a development that had the potential to affect Kedleston Hall in Derby: *Catesby Estates* v. *Steer* [2018] EWCA Civ 1697; [2018] JPL 1375, para. 26.

[122] P(LBCA)A 1990, s. 72(1).

[123] *R (on the application of Historic Buildings and Monuments Commission for England (known as Historic England))* v. *Milton Keynes Council and St Modwen Developments Ltd.* [2018] EWHC 2007 (Admin) (Dover J), para. 63.

[124] Historic England, *The Protection and Management of World Heritage Sites in England: English Heritage Guidance Note to Circular for England on the Protection of World Heritage Sites* (2008), para. 7.2.

[125] See Section 5.2.10.

[126] These are the Society for the Protection of Ancient Buildings, the Ancient Monuments Society, the Council for British Archaeology, the Georgian Group, the Victorian Society and the Twentieth Century Society. They are informed where there is a proposal for the demolition of a listed building or works for altering a listed building which involves demolition of part of the building: Arrangements for Handling Heritage Applications – Notification to Historic England and National Amenity Societies and the Secretary of State (England) Direction 2021, para. 4(b). In the case of the Church of England's faculty jurisdiction: Faculty Jurisdiction Rules 2015 (as amended), r. 4.5(2).

[127] The role of the Joint Committee of that National Amenity Societies: http://heritagehelp.org.uk /about (last accessed 30 May 2023).

affected by the proposed development may participate in the dialogue by responding to the consultation call.[128] Provision is also made in the context of World Heritage Sites for consideration of the effect on the world heritage status of the place.[129]

The former refers to situations in which, although the public participates in discussions, the traditional form of consultation about listed buildings and the granting of faculties allows communities of care to participate in discussions, but ultimately the decision rests with another community of care. This therefore accords more with Pateman's notion of partial, rather than full participation.[130] The entire system, therefore, draws on consultation and participation in the decision-making process. It thus engages with communities who care about cultural heritage and enables participation in longer-term decisions about cultural heritage. It therefore provides the space for dialogic care.[131] This demonstrates how the UK is a community which simultaneously cares about, and for, cultural heritage places by seeking to avoid physical harm or alterations to designated heritage assets as well as prohibiting or restricting development activities on other property which has the potential to negatively affect the designated cultural heritage. However, ultimately, because the decision of whether or not to grant permission rests with the Secretary of State any position reached following dialogue can be overturned. Having said that, any decision can be challenged through judicial review and so cannot be arbitrary, unreasonable or illegal.[132]

7.4.1.3 Restricting Specific Activities Relating to Cultural Heritage

It has already been seen how one element of the framework of preventative care for cultural heritage places is the use of criminal offences seeking to avert harm. Other criminal offences which aim to discourage certain activities that have the potential to cause harm to cultural heritage also provide preventative care. They exist in addition to the general crimes which might be committed when harming cultural heritage, such as theft, handling stolen goods, criminal damage or arson.

The activity of metal-detecting is sometimes seen as posing a risk to previously unexcavated cultural heritage objects. For that reason, it is one recognised as in need of some degree of regulation so that any cultural heritage discovered as a result of the activity is appropriately cared for. The use of metal detectors without appropriate permission is illegal on protected places in

---

[128] See the Planning (Listed Buildings and Conservation Areas) (Amendment) (England) Regulations 2010 (SI 2010 No. 568).

[129] NPPF 2021, para. 200.

[130] Carole Pateman, *Participation and Democratic Theory* (Cambridge: Cambridge University Press, 1970), pp. 70–1.

[131] Whether in practice dialogue is meaningful and participation is fully engaging is outside the scope of this book.

[132] See Section 3.7.7.

England, Wales and Scotland.[133] In Northern Ireland the offence is much stricter in that it is an offence simply to be in possession of a detecting device in a protected place.[134] Further care is provided for archaeological objects more generally in Northern Ireland where a licence is required from the Department of Communities to excavate 'for the purpose of searching generally for archaeological objects or of searching for, exposing or examining any particular structure or thing of archaeological interest'.[135] This applies to searching on any type of land.

Local authorities have the power to make metal detecting illegal in other open spaces through byelaws. It is recognised, though, that restricting the activity of metal detecting in local spaces may prove controversial. Therefore, in the government advice to local authorities regarding the model byelaws it is recognised, that whilst it may be appropriate to introduce byelaws restricting metal detecting in areas requiring special protection (including cultivated flowerbeds and the like as well as 'sites of archaeological interest'[136]), wider restrictions have the potential to be seen as 'overly restrictive and unreasonable'.[137] Therefore, before adopting byelaws which would restrict metal detecting in pleasure grounds and open spaces there should be adequate local consultation.[138]

Guidance exists to support the use of metal detectors. This includes the Code of Practice for Responsible Metal Detecting in England and Wales,[139] led by the Portable Antiquities Scheme and endorsed by various organisations, including the National Museum of Wales, the British Museum, Historic England and the Royal Commission on the Historical & Ancient Monuments of Wales.[140] The members of the National Council for Metal Detecting agree to abide by the terms of their Code of Conduct.[141] Central to this code is the emphasis on following the law, in particular by not trespassing, familiarising themselves with PAS as a voluntary scheme and only 'working on ground that has already been disturbed (such as ploughed land or that which has formerly been ploughed').[142]

---

[133] AMAAA 1979, s. 42(1). Protected places are scheduled monuments, monuments in the ownership or guardianship of the Secretary of State, Historic Scotland, Historic England or a local authority or areas of archaeological importance: AMMAA 1979, s. 42(2).

[134] 1995 Northern Ireland Order, art. 29(1). Protected places are scheduled monuments or those under the ownership or guardianship of the Department for the Environment: art. 29(2).

[135] Historic Monuments and Archaeological Objects (Northern Ireland) Order 1995, art. 41(1).

[136] Ministry of Housing, Communities and Local Government, *Model Byelaw Set 2: Guidance Notes* (2018), para. 41.

[137] ibid., para. 7.   [138] ibid.

[139] Portable Antiquities Scheme, *Code of Practice for Responsible Metal Detecting in England and Wales* (2017): https://finds.org.uk/getinvolved/guides/codeofpractice (last accessed 20 December 2022).

[140] ibid.

[141] NCMD, *Code of Conduct* (amended June 2012): www.ncmd.co.uk/code-of-conduct/ (last accessed 22 May 2023).

[142] Code of Practice for Responsible Metal Detecting.

By virtue of their statutory powers, the National Trust and the National Trust for Scotland can make certain byelaws,[143] enabling them to care for cultural heritage by deterring harm. Byelaws can include provisions relating to 'prohibiting or regulating an act or thing tending to injure or disfigure such lands or property'[144] and 'for permitting the public or any specified persons or person to view and to make copies or reproductions of or extracts from any chattel vested in the National Trust on such terms in all respects as may be from time to time prescribed by the Board of Trustees'.[145] Very practical levels of direct care are provided through these byelaws, including provisions affecting the care of cultural heritage. These specifically relate to malicious damage through defacing any building, structure or fixed or movable equipment,[146] prohibiting photographs in a Trust building without permission of the National Trust,[147] and prohibiting the touching of furniture or sitting 'upon any chair or other article of furniture' without permission.[148] The use of teasels or thistles to deter visitors from sitting on chairs in National Trust and National Trust for Scotland properties arguably serves as a material manifestation of this law by in effect indicating that permission has not been given to sit down.

Similar powers to make byelaws relating to admission, conduct of persons on the premises, for preservation of property and for 'otherwise securing the efficient administration of any premises … '[149] are enjoyed by the Board of Trustees of the National Museums and Galleries of Northern Ireland.[150]

Criminal sanctions for contravening byelaws are discussed below.[151] These provide targeted means of deterring future conduct which risks harm to cultural heritage and thereby provide preventative care.

7.4.1.4 Designation of Railway Heritage

In some cases cultural heritage objects may be recognised as being sufficiently important to communities that there is a general consensus that they should not be lost to future generations. Yet there is no general framework to designate these as cultural heritage in law, or to proactively provide care for them by avoiding harm where they reach the end of their utilitarian life. Therefore, there is a risk that they could be sold to private owners, or disposed of, including through destruction. In such cases, the focus is on

---

[143] These are set out in National Trust Act 1971, s. 24(1); National Trust Act 1907, s. 33 (relating to buildings) and the National Trust for Scotland Order Confirmation Act 1935, ss. 33 and 35.

[144] National Trust Act 1971, s. 24(1)(n) and National Trust for Scotland Order Confirmation Act 1935, s. 33(o).

[145] National Trust Act 1971, s. 24(1)(q).

[146] Byelaws enacted by the National Trust include: The National Trust for Places of Historic Interest or Natural Beauty: Byelaws 1965 and The National Trust for Places of Historic Interest or Natural Beauty: Byelaws 1968 (Northern Ireland), para. 6.

[147] ibid., para. 23(c).   [148] ibid., para. 23(d).

[149] Museums and Galleries (Northern Ireland) Order 1998, ss. 7(1)(a)–(d).

[150] ibid., s. 7(1). The board is established by s. 3(1) of the Act.   [151] See Section 7.7.

ensuring that an institutional community of care in the public domain assumes responsibility for the future care, not only so that the object's physical future is ensured, but also to ensure that contextual information is retained. Nevertheless, provision is made to care for railway heritage through a system of designation by the board of trustees of the Science Museum[152] of records or artefacts owned by bodies (which are broadly successor companies to the previously publicly owned railway).[153] Where one of those companies proposes to dispose of an artefact or object that has been designated by the board they have to give notice to the board of trustees.[154] Here disposal means not only outright disposal through transfer but also includes any loans of the object for more than 12 months,[155] as well as the use of the object as security for a loan.[156] These provisions therefore prevent the object from crossing into the private domain, ensure that information about the object is retained (by avoiding it being decontextualised), thereby providing appropriate care.

7.4.1.5 Controlling the Use of Land: Individual Initiatives through Covenants

In 1966 Lord Denning eloquently expressed how the owner of land, caring about the beauty of a place – here natural heritage rather than cultural heritage – wished to ensure it remained so for future generations.[157] Describing a 'lovely inlet of the sea called the Helford River',[158] he explained how the owner had granted the National Trust a covenant 'to see that the beauty and character of her land should not be impaired.'[159] This demonstrates how owners of cultural heritage places have at their disposal the means of providing direct covenants (promises under deed) to the National Trust or National Trust for Scotland,[160] undertaking to provide enhanced levels of care for their land by restricting its use and 'planning development use' and by binding future owners of the estate in land to do likewise. These restrictive covenants, unlike those found in Equity,[161] do not require the National Trust to own a dominant tenement (i.e. a specific estate in neighbouring land which benefits from the covenant). Instead, the National Trust and National Trust for Scotland have the power to enforce these covenants against successors in title to the covenantor, 'in the like manner and to the like extent as if the National Trust were possessed of or entitled to or

---

[152] Through the Railway Heritage Designation Advisory Board: www .sciencemuseumgroup.org.uk/about-us/railway-heritage-designation-advisory-board/ (last accessed 30 May 2023).

[153] Set out in Railway Heritage Act 1996, s. 1(1).   [154] ibid., s. 4(1).   [155] ibid., s. 7(1)(a).

[156] ibid., s. 7(1)(b).

[157] *Gee* v. *The National Trust for Places of Historic Interest or Natural Beauty* [1966] 1 WLR 170 (CA), 172.

[158] ibid., 172.   [159] ibid., 172.

[160] National Trust Act 1937, s. 8 and National Trust for Scotland Order Confirmation Act 1935, s. 7.

[161] Established in *Tulk* v. *Moxhay* (1845) 47 ER 1345.

interested in adjacent land and as if the covenant had been expressed to be entered into for the benefit of the adjacent land'.[162]

With these provisions, Parliament (being itself a community of care) created two clear communities of care with responsibilities for the care of cultural heritage. The first is the owners of the land – the original covenantor – who seeks to bind their successors in caring for cultural heritage, but also the subsequent owners. The second is the National Trust or National Trust for Scotland, with each one being a community of care, and having responsibility for enforcing that against successors in title to question whether that development is appropriate. Here the restrictive covenants provide an extra layer to the planning law enforced by the local planning authority – a more specific care focused on potential harm to the cultural heritage. In *Gee* v. *the National Trust* Lord Denning said that the National Trust are, 'under the statute, the custodians of the natural beauty of our land, the cliffs and downs, fields and woods, rivers and shores; and at the stately home's historic buildings cottages and barns. In respect of any injury to their interest as custodians of our natural beauty, I think they would be qualified to insist on these covenants'.[163] It is clear from this case though that 'the last word' is not with the National Trust and that the enforceability of these covenants must relate to their particular interest and injury which would damage 'the amenities or beauty of the district'.[164] If it does not, then the Lands Tribunal can choose to discharge or modify the covenant if it is appropriate to do so under section 84 of the Law of Property Act 1925.[165]

When it comes to restrictive covenants used to restrict the use of neighbouring land to inalienable property owned by the National Trust, the Lands Tribunal cannot discharge or modify these under section 84 of the Law of Property Act 1925[166] if the covenants have been imposed to preserve, protect or augment the amenities or to secure access to and enjoyment of the public to any inalienable property of the Trust.[167] The long-term effect of this is to prevent neighbouring land from changing with the times, particularly as it applies both to the discharge and to the modification of these. However, it ensures that the long-term care is provided to the National Trust places, but without any mandated dialogue.

The mechanism for creating covenants with the National Trust, and the more general statutory covenants that landowners can enter with local planning authorities, provide a means of restricting the use of land.[168] Nevertheless, the Law Commission recognised that there was scope for a wider power to make covenants.[169] This led to the introduction of conservation covenants, a new

---

[162] National Trust Act 1937, s. 8; National Trust Act (Northern Ireland) 1946, s. 16(1) and National Trust for Scotland Order Confirmation Act 1935, s. 7. *Gee* v. *The National Trust*, 174.

[163] *Gee* v. *The National Trust*, 174–5.   [164] ibid., 175.   [165] ibid.

[166] National Trust Act 1971, s. 27. Property of the National Trust which is inalienable is discussed at Section 7.3.1.1.

[167] ibid., ss. 27(a)–(c).   [168] Town and Country Planning Act 1990, s. 106(1).

[169] Law Commission Report, *Conservation Covenants*, Law Com. No. 349, HC 322, 2014.

form of binding agreement in England and Wales entered into between land-owners and certain responsible bodies (prescribed by the Secretary of State).[170] Conservation covenants bind successors in title to the land, meaning that responsible bodies can enforce them against subsequent landowners.[171] Covenants must have a 'conservation purpose' which includes 'conserv[ing] land as a place of archaeological, architectural, artistic, cultural or historic interest' or 'conserv[ing] the setting of land ... which is a place of archaeological, architectural, artistic, cultural or historic interest'[172] and must be intended to be made for the 'public good'.[173] Under such covenants the owner of a legal estate[174] could agree 'to do, or not to do, something on land in England'.[175] Therefore, unlike covenants agreed with the National Trust, discussed above, the new conservation covenants can be positive in nature. The introduction of these covenants enhances the nuanced measures of care that can be provided by National Trust covenants, which relate only to restrictions on the use of and development of the land, rather than actively requiring the owner to preserve the land. A further difference is that the responsible body can also promise the landowner to do something on that land.[176] This means that expert communities of care, such as a preservation society, can contribute to the care of the cultural heritage place, without needing to own the estate or, in the context of monuments, without there needing to be a guardianship arrangement.[177] The terminology of 'conserving' is explained in the statutory provision as including 'a reference to protecting, restoring or enhancing it'.[178] The Law Commission envisaged that conservation covenants could be used by heritage organisations that had undertaken work to preserve a cultural heritage place and who then wanted to sell it, but at the same time ensure that it would be preserved by future owners.[179] The use of these covenants to care for war memorials relating to more recent conflicts, and therefore there is no need for a specific 'historic' interest, was also recognised by the Law Commission.[180]

The Scottish scheme of conservation burdens[181] permits landowners to create real burdens in favour of certain designated conservation bodies[182] for

---

[170] The Environment Act 2021 (Commencement No. 2 and Saving Provision) Regulations 2022, reg. 5(a) set the date of 30 September 2022 for Part 7 relating to conservation covenants to come into force. See Colin T. Reid, 'Conservation covenants' (2013) Conv. 176.

[171] Environment Act 2021, s. 122(2) and is registered as a local land charge: Environment Act 2021, s. 120(1).

[172] ibid., ss. 117(3)(b) and (c).

[173] ibid., s. 117(1)(a)(iii) and Law Commission Report, para. 2.93.

[174] A fee simple (freehold) or a leasehold estate for more than 7 years: Environment Act 2021, s. 117(4).

[175] ibid., ss. 117(2)(a)(i) and (ii). Covenants, by default, last for the length of the qualifying estate unless the parties agree to a different length of time: s. 121(2).

[176] ibid., s. 117(2)(b).   [177] See Section 7.5.4.2.

[178] Environment Act 2021, s. 117(4); this terminology was expressly consulted on by the Law Commission: Law Commission Report, para. 3.10.

[179] Law Commission Report, para. 2.17. Specifically in three circumstances set out by English Heritage (now Historic England): para. 2.18.

[180] ibid., para. 3.34.   [181] Title Conditions (Scotland) Act 2003, s. 38(1).

[182] Prescribed by the Scottish Minsters under Title Conditions (Scotland) Act 2003, s. 38(4).

the purpose of 'preserving, or protecting, for the benefit of the public – (a) the architectural or historical characteristics of any land; or (b) any other special characteristics of any land'.[183] These therefore provide further opportunities for direct assumption of responsibility for care, and for passing these responsibilities on down the generations.

7.4.2 Alerting the Public to Cultural Heritage at Risk

Expert communities of care may identify certain cultural heritage as being at risk of imminent harm, necessitating preventative care. They may identify deterioration to the physical integrity of a place which requires immediate reactive care.[184] Some communities of care keep watch to identify potential harm or the existence of harm which needs to be addressed. Several schemes provide opportunities to put communities of care on notice of the need to navigate particular identified harm. As part of the framework established by UNESCO's World Heritage Convention, the list of World Heritage in Danger[185] lists those cultural properties for which there is either ascertained[186] or potential danger.[187] Entry of a site on this list can cause embarrassment to state parties, in particular if the danger has come about because of the state party neglecting the site, or permitting development which negatively impacts the setting of the World Heritage Site.[188] Yet, the actual or imminent danger to the site can be caused by a natural disaster or fire, rather than due to any fault by the state party.[189] Where a site is designated as being in danger (or is at risk of being so-designated), there may be censure at the international level from the World Heritage Committee. In practical terms, designation of a World Heritage Site as being at risk acts as a precursor to removal from the World Heritage list itself.

At the national level, Historic England publishes a Heritage at Risk Register, updated every year. Historic England applies criteria to assess whether a heritage place is at risk and warrants entry on the register.[190] Similarly, a Buildings at Risk Register is published in Wales[191] with a similar list

---

[183] ibid., s. 38(1).   [184] As to which see Section 7.5.
[185] World Heritage Convention1972, art. 11(4) and World Heritage Committee, *Operational Guidelines for the Implementation of the World Heritage Convention*, 10 July 2019, WHC.19/ 01, para.177.
[186] *WHC Operational Guidelines*, para. 179(a).   [187] ibid., para. 179(b).
[188] For the full list, see ibid., paras. 179(a) and (b). See the recent 'delisting' of Liverpool because of threats from development: UNESCO World Heritage Committee, *Liverpool – Maritime Mercantile City (United Kingdom of Great Britain and Northern Ireland)* (C1150) Decision 44 COM 7A.34.
[189] E.g. Notre Dame Cathedral in France.
[190] Historic England, *Selection Criteria*: https://historicengland.org.uk/advice/heritage-at-risk /search-register/selection-criteria/ (last accessed 30 May 2023).
[191] Cadw, *Listed Buildings at Risk*: https://cadw.gov.wales/advice-support/historic-assets/listed-buildings-listed-buildings-risk#section-managing-listed-buildings-at-risk (last accessed 30 May 2023).

published by Historic Environment Scotland.[192] The latter has also identified castles and tower houses that 'could be successfully restored and reused' and compiled the Castle Conservation Register.[193] As part of the assessment, the cultural significance of the tower or castle is considered. Part of the care here is to assess the potential new uses to which the cultural heritage place could be put and to find an alternative community of care to provide that care in the future. In Northern Ireland, the Heritage at Risk register includes not only designated heritage assets, such as listed buildings and scheduled monuments but also unlisted historic buildings of local interest.[194] Where cultural heritage places are entered on these registers, the Historic Environment Division of the Department for Communities 'works with owners, developers, heritage groups, building preservation trusts, local communities and other stakeholders to find solutions for the issues faced by these assets and to help realise their latent potential'.[195]

Whilst the registers discussed so far are officially recorded by organisations with responsibility for the designation schemes themselves, certain civil society initiatives also recognise heritage that is at risk. These include not only cultural heritage places, but also intangible cultural heritage. In the absence of any legal regime directly caring for these aspects of intangible heritage, such civil society initiatives provide a means of alerting people to the risk faced by these practices of potential loss to current and future generations. Civil society initiatives include the International Council on Monuments and Sites (ICOMOS), which produces periodic Heritage at Risk – World Reports,[196] and some National Amenity Societies[197] have lists of heritage in danger.[198] The Heritage Crafts Association[199] and the Pilgrim Trust in the UK produce a Red List of

---

[192] Historic Environment Scotland, *Buildings at Risk Register*: www.historicenvironment.scot/advice-and-support/planning-and-guidance/buildings-at-risk-register/ (last accessed 30 May 2023).

[193] Historic Environment Scotland, *Castle Conservation Register*: http://data.historic-scotland.gov.uk/pls/htmldb/f?p=2920:10:0 (last accessed 30 May 2023).

[194] Department for Communities, *Historic Environment: Heritage at Risk*: www.communities-ni.gov.uk/articles/heritage-risk (last accessed 30 May 2023). This is a partnership with Ulster Architectural Heritage. Members of the public can send in information about buildings or structures about which they are concerned: www.ulsterarchitecturalheritage.org.uk/built-heritage-risk/ (last accessed 30 May 2023).

[195] Department for Communities, *Historic Environment: Heritage at Risk*.

[196] ICOMOS, *Release of the New Heritage at Risk Report* (3 February 2021): www.icomos.org/en/what-we-do/401-english-categories/what-we-do/heritage-at-risk (last accessed 30 May 2023).

[197] As to which see Section 5.2.10.

[198] These include the Twentieth Century Society, which publishes a biennial list of Buildings at Risk: Twentieth Century Society, *Buildings at Risk*: https://c20society.org.uk/buildings-at-risk (last accessed 30 May 2023), and the Victorian Society, which holds an annual campaign to identify the top ten Victorian buildings which are most endangered: Victorian Society, *Victorian Society's Top 10 Most Endangered Buildings List 2021*: https://www.victoriansociety.org.uk/news/the-victorian-societys-2021-top-10-endangered-buildings (last accessed 30 May 2023).

[199] Designated in 2016 as a non-governmental organisation accredited to provide advisory services to the Intergovernmental Committee for the Safeguarding of Intangible Cultural

Endangered Crafts which ranks crafts in the UK according to the likelihood of them surviving to the next generation.[200] These warning bells provide a means of alerting those who care about the cultural heritage in question to act, by assuming responsibility for caring for it, in an attempt to prevent its loss to current and future generations.

7.4.3 Duties to Report Finds

The mechanisms for assessing discovered cultural heritage objects against the criteria of treasure[201] and treasure trove[202] provide a means within the UK of providing preventative care. Requiring finders to inform the authorities of the objects and by bringing such objects into public ownership, both the object and information that can be gleaned from research about the archaeological objects are not lost. The system of treasure in place in England, Wales and Northern Ireland has been insufficiently far-reaching to provide appropriate care for all cultural heritage objects of archaeological importance. Nevertheless, recent calls for reform to this area of law have resulted in an expanded definition of treasure.[203] Whilst in England and Wales a person is only required to report a find of treasure (as defined under the Treasure Act 1996), the more extensive reporting requirement in Northern Ireland requires any person who finds an 'archaeological object' to report this to the relevant authority,[204] although only those objects falling within the definition of treasure would vest in the Crown. The system in Scotland differs, and portable antiquities represent a subset of *bona vacantia*, which belong to the Crown.[205] Portable antiquities in Scotland are defined as portable property manufactured or modified, normally at least 100 years before their discovery, and which are not integral to a site or monument.[206] Although there is a common law of treasure trove under which the Crown has rights to objects wholly or partly composed of precious metal, in practice the wide scope of the rules relating to *bona vacantia* mean that this does not need to be used.[207] The wider nature of the scheme in

---

Heritage: https://ich.unesco.org/en/accredited-ngos-00331?pg=00436&lg=en (last accessed 30 May 2023).

[200] In 2021 there were 56 critically endangered crafts, 74 endangered crafts and 110 currently viable crafts. Four crafts had been identified as extinct: The Heritage Crafts Association, *Red List of Endangered Crafts* (2021): https://heritagecrafts.org.uk/wp-content/uploads/2021/05/HCA-Red-List-2021-leaflet-optimised.pdf (last accessed 22 May 2023).

[201] England, Wales and Northern Ireland: see Section 4.7.   [202] Scotland: ibid.

[203] This has included a revision of the definition of treasure based on its archaeological and historic importance rather than its age or precious metal content: DCMS, *Consultation Outcome: Revising the Definition of Treasure in the Treasure Act 1998 and Revising the Related Codes of Practice – Government Response to Public Consultation* (December 2020), para. 3.5. This has been brought into effect through the Treasure (Designation) (Amendment) Order 2023.

[204] Historic Monuments and Archaeological Objects (Northern Ireland) Order 1995, art. 42(1).

[205] Scottish Code of Practice, para. 2.5.   [206] ibid., p. 12.   [207] ibid., p. 13.

Scotland achieves a higher degree of care as it 'safeguards portable antiquities of archaeological, historical, and cultural significance found in Scotland'.[208]

Although discoveries of treasure and portable antiquities arise in circumstances not necessarily giving rise to direct, immediate threats of harm to the cultural heritage, if a find is not reported, there is possible harm. This harm could take the form of loss of access where objects enter private collections, or where hoards are dispersed, or where there is a loss of information relating to the archaeological context when excavations are illicit. There may also be potential harm to a particular site where the object was found (either because further objects might be discovered, or archaeologists may need access to the site for further study). The discovery sets in motion the provisions of the Treasure Act 1996 requiring a finder to notify the coroner where they know, or suspect, that the discovered object is treasure.[209] It is then for the coroner to determine whether in fact the object meets the statutory criteria, in which case ownership vests in the Crown or one of its franchisees[210] under section 4(1). Criminalising a failure to report a find of treasure[211] encourages the reporting of finds, and avoids losing important information about the findspot, which could cause unnecessary harm to the historic record. It should be recalled that this works in tandem with the provision of a reward of the market value of the treasure in the event that it is properly recorded.[212] Under the treasure regime, responsibility for the care of cultural heritage objects is assumed by the state in the first instance (through a legally mandated reporting requirement) once the legal label is applied. Direct, long-term care is then assumed by the museum which offers to pay the reward[213] which has been recommended by the Treasure Valuation Committee. In Scotland, museums are expected to meet the *ex gratia* payment, although financial assistance can be provided by the National Fund for Acquisitions.[214]

Where an object does not fall within the definition of treasure, it is returned to the finder or landowner, because legal title to the object is determined by the common law of finding.[215] In such a context, the Portable Antiquities Scheme (PAS), as a public participation initiative, provides a mechanism of preventative care to record information about the object and its archaeological context.

---

[208] ibid., para. 2.2.   [209] Treasure Act 1996, s. 8.

[210] These were those people granted the right to treasure – e.g. the Duchy of Lancaster.

[211] Under the Treasure Act 1996, s. 8(3).

[212] See DCMS, *Treasure Act 1996 Code of Practice* (2nd Revision, London: DCMS, 2008), para. 71.

[213] Such a reward is usually shared between the finder and landowner: ibid., para. 72.

[214] Treasure Trove in Scotland, *A Code of Practice* (July 2014, revised January 2016), para. 9.12. In Scotland there is also the concept of museums of last resort, who are approached where no other museums have shown an interest in acquiring the find: Scottish Treasure Trove Code of Practice, para. 10.

[215] See generally, Robin Hickey, *Property and the Law of Finders* (Oxford: Hart, 2010). According to the authorities of *Parker* v. *British Airways Board* [1982] QB 1004 (CA) and *Waverley Borough Council* v. *Fletcher* [1996] QB 334 (CA) it is likely that the landowner would have the better title than the finder where an object is found in the ground, although the owner may have entered into an alternative agreement with the finder.

Consequently, it avoids harm that could be caused by a loss of that information.[216] It therefore goes some way to addressing the shortfall in the legal coverage of direct care through the definition of treasure. Future reforms of the statutory definition would seek to extend the care that is provided by museums, and the consequent public access to a wider category of objects.

There is one situation in which the usual voluntary reporting of objects to the PAS is given a legal footing. Where a person who searches along the Thames foreshore with a permit from the Port of London Authority finds an object of archaeological interest (which is not treasure), the terms of that licence require them to report the find to the Portable Antiquities Scheme Finds Liaison Officer at the Museum of London.[217]

In a similar vein to the requirement to report treasure, where wreck is discovered, there is a legal requirement to report it to the Receiver of Wreck.[218] This requirement applies not only to historic wrecks, but to all types of wreck, including both a vessel and its cargo.[219] Where someone takes possession of cargo or 'other articles belonging to or separated from the vessel' they must be delivered to the Receiver of Wreck, otherwise an offence is committed.[220] Whilst these provisions are not aimed directly at caring for cultural heritage, they incidentally have that effect, for as part of the process the Secretary of State will be informed of the historic wreck and can then designate it as a protected wreck or scheduled monument.[221]

7.4.3.1 Caring for Intangible Cultural Heritage through Individual Initiatives

Several individual initiatives, using either law or policy, provide preventative care for cultural heritage. These are geared primarily towards intangible cultural heritage. These smaller-scale initiatives demonstrate how the UK, as a community, and a network of communities, cares for cultural heritage in response to identified risks of harm. One way in which a broad category of intangible cultural heritage is cared for is through the scheme of geographical indications. This protects the geographical names of certain foods which are connected with a place or the traditional methods.[222] Thus, the way in which the UK cares for its culinary heritage is provided through a scheme of ensuring the integrity of the output and the continued practice of making it. Even as far back as 1934 the quality of blue-veined Stilton made in England and Wales was mandated by legal regulations.[223] Provision can be made by specific legislation

---

[216] Portable Antiquities Scheme: https://finds.org.uk/ (last accessed 30 May 2023).

[217] Port of London Authority, *Thames Foreshore Permits*: www.pla.co.uk/Environment/Thames-foreshore-permits (last accessed 30 May 2023).

[218] Merchant Shipping Act 1995, s. 236(1)(b).   [219] ibid., s. 237(1).   [220] ibid., s. 237(2).

[221] As discussed at Section 5.2.7.2.

[222] Department for Environment, Food and Rural Affairs, *Guidance: Protected Geographical Food and Drink Names: UK GI Schemes*: www.gov.uk/guidance/protected-geographical-food-and-drink-names-uk-gi-schemes (last accessed 30 May 2023).

[223] The Agricultural Produce (Grading and Marking) (Stilton Cheese) Regulations 1934 (SI 1934 No. 1354).

to prescribe the ingredients, process of production and the place of production for particular foods or drinks.[224] Particular products of craftsmanship may also be cared for through trademark law, but further legislation may be required. The Harris Tweed Act 1993 is one such example.[225] The Act makes provision for ensuring the integrity of the tradition of Harris Tweed, both in terms of the process and the materials used.[226] It was expressly stated in the Preamble to the Act that the reason for introducing a statutory framework, including the establishment of the Harris Tweed Authority,[227] was because the use of a private company was 'no longer a satisfactory body fully to safeguard the Harris Tweed industry and to secure for the future its goodwill and enterprise'[228] and could therefore not provide the appropriate care for the practice.

A further individual initiative which cares for cultural heritage is the consistory court's willingness to protect the timbre of bells through its jurisdiction to grant faculties for work to churches and their contents. The case of *Re St Michael, Michael Church Escley*[229] involved the question of whether to tune bells that had been installed in 1732 and were a complete ring of five casts by the same founder. There the Deputy Chancellor recognised that sounds, such as those particular bells, which had been preserved since before the advent of sound recordings were 'a valuable part of our heritage' and something which it was right to be proud of.[230] He did not completely rule out the possibility of retuning old bells, in circumstances where the sound was 'so bad that the mission of the Church was affected' or that they 'let the church down in some way'.[231] Neither of those factors applied in that case and since the tuning of the bells was irreversible, and no good case had been made for returning them there was, according to the Deputy Chancellor, 'no reason to destroy the heritage'.[232] There is something quite evocative of the thought of a sound that has been heard, and experienced, by a community's forefathers still ringing out to that community today and a court, as a community of care, recognising its importance to these communities.

At times other legal devices may be used instrumentally to care for cultural heritage and to avert harm. The National Trust for Scotland had been concerned about companies using the names of some of their National Trust for Scotland places in commercial activities, suggesting an association with those places or with the Trust which had not been authorised. With the risk that those place names might be registered as trade marks, rather reluctantly the National Trust for Scotland felt it necessary to use trademark law as a defensive measure[233]

---

[224] For example, the Scotch Whisky Regulations 2009 (SI 2009 No. 2890).
[225] The trademark of the orb and Maltese Cross was registered in 1909.
[226] See Harris Tweed Act 1993, s. 7.   [227] ibid., s. 3(1).   [228] ibid., Preamble.
[229] 30 May 2014 (unreported).   [230] *Re St Michael, Michael Church Escley*, para. 1.
[231] ibid., para. 3.   [232] ibid., para. 6.
[233] National Trust for Scotland, *Trust and Trademarks* (7 August 2017): www.nts.org.uk/stories/trust-and-trademarks (last accessed 30 May 2023).

to protect the association with a particular place and reputation with some of the places for which it cares – specifically Glencoe and St Kilda.

7.5 Reactive Care

Where cultural heritage is in the process of being harmed, or harm has already taken place, it may be appropriate for one or more communities of care to respond to this. Most likely, the owner of the cultural heritage object or place would respond to this actual or potential harm and care appropriately, by seeking to navigate the harm in such a manner as to minimise the effect of any harm. Often the individual importance of cultural heritage to them, possibly also including the reduced financial value of the cultural heritage caused by that physical harm, might incentivise their action. The potential harm may extend to the communities for whom the cultural heritage is important. How this is minimised depends on the individual circumstances of the case. It may be that other communities of care will need to contribute to the care of the cultural heritage.

Care provided in response to potential harm needs to be tailored towards a particular community of care. The importance of dialogue, and 'timely and open discussion', was highlighted in a statement by a group of institutional communities of care in support of organisations whose long-term future or their collections had been put at risk because of the COVID-19 pandemic.[234] Here a clear statement committed them to working together to provide advice, and to discuss appropriate responses; it thus represented an important first step in addressing, and responding to harm to cultural heritage.[235]

7.5.1 Financial Assistance

Care may be provided by other communities of care through the provision of grants or funding which can support the owners who are directly responsible for the cultural heritage.

A practical means of institutional communities of care providing care for cultural heritage places or objects (regardless of whether privately or publicly owned) is through the powers of Historic England and the Scottish Minister to make grants or loans for the preservation of not only historic buildings[236] but

---

[234] Northern Ireland Museums Council, English Heritage, Federation of Museums and Art Galleries of Wales, MA, National Archives, Museum Development UK, National Trust, Army Museums Ogilby Trust, University Museums Group, National Directors Council, ACE, Historic England, Association of Independent Museums, Museums Galleries Scotland, Heritage Fund, Art Fund and the Collections Trust, *Statement on Heritage, Museums and Collections and Risk* (July 2022): www.artscouncil.org.uk/sites/default/files/download-file/Statement%20on%20heritage% 20museums%20and%20collections%20at%20risk_1.pdf (last accessed 30 May 2023).

[235] ibid.

[236] Here buildings of 'outstanding historic or architectural interest': Historic Buildings and Ancient Monuments Act 1953, ss. 3A(1) and 4(1).

also the objects 'ordinarily kept' in those buildings.[237] In return for this financial care, a condition can be imposed requiring public access to the whole or part of the property concerned.[238] The National Heritage Memorial Fund[239] has a broader remit. This includes providing financial assistance 'in the case of things of any kind which are of scenic, historic, archaeological, aesthetic, architectural, engineering, artistic or scientific interest, including animals and plants which are of zoological or botanical interest'.[240] This can be for reasons not only of securing their preservation or enhancement, but also for encouraging the study and understanding of them, securing or improving access to them, encouraging enjoyment of them, or for encouraging the maintenance and development of preservation and enhancement skills relating to them.[241]

As discussed in the context of preventative care, at the local level a local authority can make a grant or loan towards the repair or maintenance of a listed building.[242] It also has such a power in respect of an unlisted building which 'appears . . . to be of architectural or historic interest'.[243] The authority can make the grant or loan conditional on the owner agreeing to terms[244] which could include providing public access. These grants, or loans, can be used for preservation as well as maintenance. They can therefore be made in response to harm in situations where the current provider of care (usually the owner) is otherwise able and willing to provide appropriate care but for the need for financial assistance.

Clearly framed within the context of the UK as part of the international community, and the need to recognise the importance of other national communities' cultural heritage, the UK established in 2016 the International Cultural Heritage Protection fund.[245] This is a joint initiative between the DCMS and the British Council.

7.5.2 Bringing Places or Objects into Existing Frameworks of Care

Since designated heritage assets benefit from enhanced levels of care to prevent harm which would affect their special characteristics, where non-designated heritage assets are at risk of harm, efforts may be made to bring these within existing frameworks of care by seeking to designate them. Therefore, where a building is at risk of danger of demolition or alteration and, although not listed, is nevertheless recognised as being of special architectural or historic

---

[237] ibid.   [238] ibid., ss. 3A(4) and 4(3).   [239] Established by the NHA 1980, s. 1(1).
[240] ibid., s. 3(1).   [241] ibid., s. 3(2).
[242] P(LBCA)A 1990, s. 57(1); Planning (Listed Buildings and Conservation Areas) (Scotland) Act 1997, s. 51(1) and Planning Act (Northern Ireland) 2011, s. 199(1).
[243] ibid.
[244] P(LBCA)A 1990, s. 57; Planning (Listed Buildings and Conservation Areas) (Scotland) Act 1997, s. 51(4) and Planning Act (Northern Ireland) 2011, s. 199(2).
[245] British Council, *Cultural Protection Fund*: www.britishcouncil.org/arts/culture-development /cultural-protection-fund (last accessed 30 May 2023).

interest, the local planning authority (LPA) can serve a building preservation notice on the owner or occupier to halt the demolition or other work to the building.[246] This notice would explain that the LPA has requested the Secretary of State to consider listing the building.[247]

Urgency can justify muting dialogue about the appropriate care of cultural heritage. In particularly urgent cases the LPA can simply fix a notice to the building to prevent any work being carried out which would harm it.[248] There is no similar power for emergency or temporary listing in the case of conservation areas, and it is clear that the desire to prevent the demolition of a building cannot be *the* impetus for designating somewhere as a conservation area, but can be *an* impetus.[249] The court, therefore, has the power to strike down the decision if the true reason is to prevent demolition of a building.[250]

Where it is necessary to urgently designate a wreck as a protected one, the need for consultation with appropriate persons may be dispensed with.[251] In Scotland urgent designation of a historic marine protection area can be made and the order remains in place for two years where 'the Scottish Ministers consider there is an urgent need to protect the area . . . or (as the case may be) to protect a marine historic asset within the area . . .'[252]

In these various situations, the risk of irreparable harm can justify intervention with rapid reactive care. This means that the responsibility for care may be assumed without full dialogue, because of the pressures of time. However, following any intervention (whether through emergency designation or halting the immediate physical harm) there is a need for reflection on this decision. This would take place in the absence of any pressure caused by the threat of harm and with dialogue, empathy and respect to ensure that this type of care is appropriate in the longer-term.

7.5.3 Bespoke Frameworks of Care

It may be necessary to construct frameworks of care once a threat of harm to specific cultural heritage has been identified. When the wreck of RMS *Titanic* was discovered in 1985, there was significant concern that artefacts might be

---

[246] P(LBCA)A 1990, ss. 3(1) (England) and 3A(1) (Wales); Planning (Listed Buildings and Conservation Areas) (Scotland) Act 1997, s. 3(2) and Planning Act (Northern Ireland) 2011, s. 81(1).

[247] P(LBCA)A 1990, s. 3(1); Planning (Listed Buildings and Conservation Areas) (Scotland) Act 1997, s. 3(2) and Planning Act (Northern Ireland) 2011, s. 81(2).

[248] P(LBCA)A 1990, s. 4(1); Planning (Listed Buildings and Conservation Areas) (Scotland) Act 1997, s. 4(1) and Planning Act (Northern Ireland) 2011, s. 82(1).

[249] *R (on the application of Arndale Properties Ltd.)* v. *Worcester City Council* [2008] EWHC 678 (Sullivan J), para. 26.

[250] *R (on the application of Silus Investments S.A)* v. *London Borough of Hounslow* [2015] EWHC 358 (Admin) (Lang J), para. 36 citing *Metro Construction* v. *Barnet* [2009] EWHC 2956 (Admin) (which in turn had cited Sullivan J in *ex parte Arndale Properties*).

[251] Protection of Wrecks Act 1973, s. 1(4).   [252] Marine (Scotland) Act 2010, s. 77(1).

removed from the wreck. It was recognised that there was a need for international efforts to ensure the in situ preservation of the site as far as possible. This led to co-operation between the United States of America, the UK, Canada and France in the form of the *Agreement concerning the Shipwrecked Vessel RMS Titanic.*[253] In furtherance of its commitments under this agreement, the UK enacted domestic legislation criminalising certain activities in the absence of a licence from the Secretary of State[254] and giving effect to the rules concerning activities agreed between the state parties.[255] As part of the general principles adopted by the state parties, a preferred policy of in situ preservation was set out, as was a statement that activities 'shall avoid disturbance of human remains', non-intrusive, non-destructive sampling should be preferred, with activities having 'the minimum adverse impact on RMS Titanic and its artifacts'.[256] A further principle was to ensure 'proper recording and dissemination to the public of historical, cultural and archaeological information'.[257] As part of this framework of care, provision was made for the appropriate design and funding of proposed projects. Design of projects included the need to demonstrate, *inter alia*, appropriate conservation and planning, arrangements for collaboration with museums (if appropriate) and anticipating the deposit of archives and a programme of publication where appropriate.[258] It was clear that funding for projects should not derive from the sale of artefacts recovered from the wreck, given the real risk of artefacts and documentation being 'irretrievably dispersed' if sold.[259] Appropriate expertise of those involved was identified as being essential; as part of this the Secretary of State must approve the identity, qualifications, experience and responsibilities of team members for any project relating to RMS *Titanic.*[260] Central to the agreement, and to the principles laid down in the schedule to the 2003 Order, was the need for a conservation plan to be put in place if objects had to be removed from the wreck, and the notion that the project collection (including artefacts and relevant documentation) 'shall be kept together intact in a manner that provides for public access, curation and its availability for educational, scientific, cultural and other public purposes'.[261]

This individualised programme of care reacted to the identified harm that had already begun to take place. It not only covered the immediate physical care of the site, but also sought to navigate the harm that would be occasioned by any further dispersal of the objects and sought to provide appropriate care by seeking to create a collection that would be maintained intact.

---

[253] London, 6 November 2003 (agreement entered into force on 18 November 2019) CP 205 (previously published as Miscellaneous Series No 4 (2003) Cm 5798).

[254] The Protection of Wrecks (RMS Titanic) Order 2003, SI 2003 No. 2496 (as amended by SI 2021 No. 470) made under the power in the Merchant Shipping and Maritime Security Act 1997, s. 24, which is concerned with implementing international agreements relating to the protection of wrecks.

[255] As set out in the schedule to SI 2003 No. 2496.   [256] ibid., sch., paras. 1–4.

[257] ibid., sch., para. 5.   [258] ibid., sch., para. 6.   [259] ibid., sch., para. 12.

[260] ibid., sch., paras. 17–18.   [261] ibid., sch., paras. 23 and 28.

7.5.4 Interventions: Assuming Responsibilities

In response to harm to cultural heritage or the immediate threat of it, certain communities of care may intervene and assume responsibility for its care, displacing the current communities of care from their existing responsibilities. These interventions can be made, not only by institutional communities, such as the Secretary of State, local planning authorities or Historic England, but also by local communities. The different ways in which these interventions can take place are explored in this section.

7.5.4.1 Emergency Interventions

Discussed above in the context of developing international communities of care, provisions of various international conventions[262] enable a state party to call upon other states to assist it where its cultural heritage is threatened. The first of these is article 19 of the World Heritage Convention, which sets out various assistance that can be given by the World Heritage Committee, including emergency assistance[263] and conservation assistance,[264] financed primarily by the World Heritage Fund.[265] The second provision is found in article 9 of the 1970 UNESCO Convention, where a state party whose 'cultural patrimony is in jeopardy from pillage of archaeological or ethnological materials' may call upon other state parties who are affected (for example if heritage is likely to be imported into their territory) to participate in 'concrete measures' to control the export and import of such objects.[266] Finally, in the context of armed conflict the High Contracting Parties of the 1954 Hague Convention in addition to being able to call upon UNESCO for assistance, whether technical or otherwise,[267] specific provision is made for High Contracting Parties to request international assistance from the Committee.[268] These demonstrate requests for assistance *with* care rather than substituting one provider of care with another. Such substitutions are found in UK domestic law and will be considered later in this section.

The first situation is where work has been carried out to a designated asset without consent, and 'has affected its character as a building of special architectural or historic interest'.[269] Such unauthorised work can be required to be undone. In the case of listed buildings, where work has been carried out which affects the special historical architectural interest of the building, the local planning authority may issue building enforcement notices requiring the building to be restored to its former state, or to comply with any terms and conditions of the listed building consent, where that had been granted but

---

[262] Both of which are ratified by the UK.

[263] *WHC Operational Guidelines*, para. 235(a) [Decision 30 COM 14A and Decision 36 COM 13.I].

[264] ibid., para. 235(b) [Decision 30 COM 14A and Decision 36 COM 13.I].

[265] Established under 1972 UNESCO World Heritage Convention, art. 15. ibid., para. 234.

[266] 1970 UNESCO Convention, art. 9.   [267] 1954 Hague Convention, art. 23.

[268] Second Protocol to the 1954 Hague Convention, art. 32.   [269] P(LBCA)A 1990, s. 7(1).

where the works had been undertaken in contravention of that.[270] Similar enforcement notices can be made where work is undertaken to scheduled monuments in contravention of the Ancient Monuments and Archaeological Areas Act (AMAAA) 1979.[271] Provision is made to restrain unauthorised works to scheduled monuments in Scotland (where there is either 'an actual or apprehended breach of the controls'); this takes the form of having an application for interdict.[272]

Secondly, in situations where a designated asset has fallen into a state of disrepair, emergency interventions can be made. There is no general legal responsibility placed on owners of cultural heritage to avoid harm caused by deterioration to cultural heritage places or objects. Even where cultural heritage places are designated historic assets, there is no direct responsibility placed on owners to care for the places.[273] However, mechanisms exist which permit intervention by another community of care where it becomes apparent that repair work is necessary.

Specifically, the local planning authority, or the Secretary of State, can take action by assuming responsibility for the care in such urgent cases. First, it is necessary to serve a notice on the owner requiring the emergency work to be carried out.[274] In situations where emergency work is not completed by the owner following the service of a notice,[275] local authorities or the Secretary of State can assume responsibility for the direct care of designated assets by causing the repair work to be undertaken.[276] The circumstances in which such intervention would take place are restricted to emergency works, interpreted as situations such as ensuring that the building is wind-and watertight or safe from collapse.[277] Limitations are placed on this power where a listed building is occupied.[278] The Secretary of State can also carry out urgent work

---

[270] ibid., s. 38(2); Planning (Listed Buildings and Conservation Areas) (Scotland) Act 1997, s. 34(1); Planning Act (Northern Ireland) 2011, Pt. 5.

[271] In respect of Wales, see AMAAA 1979, s. 9ZC and in respect of Scotland see s. 9A.

[272] ibid., s. 9O(1).

[273] DCMS, *The Upkeep and Repair of Historic Building: The Use of Sections 47, 54, 55 and 76 of the P(LBCA)A 1990 as Amended* (March 2022), para. 1.

[274] Planning (Listed Buildings and Conservation Areas) (Scotland) Act 1997, s. 49(5).

[275] The Secretary of State or Historic Environment Scotland may serve notice on the owner indicating an intention to execute certain emergency works for the preservation of a scheduled monument: AMAAA 1979, s. 5. In turn, in England the Secretary of State may authorise Historic England to undertake this work on their behalf: AMAAA 1979, s. 5(3).

[276] In the case of listed buildings in England and Wales, P(LBCA)A 1990, s. 54 and in Scotland the Planning (Listed Buildings and Conservation Areas) (Scotland) Act 1997, s. 49(1). Provision is made for 7 days' written notice of an intention to carry out such works under section 54(5) and in Scotland and Planning (Listed Buildings and Conservation Areas) (Scotland) Act 1997, s. 49(5). Any expenses incurred in carrying out these emergency works can be recovered from the owner of the listed building under s. 55 of the P(LBCA)A 1990 and Planning (Listed Buildings and Conservation Areas) (Scotland) Act 1997, s. 50.

[277] DCMS, *The Upkeep and Repair of Historic Buildings*, para. 4.

[278] In England and Scotland work can only be carried out on those parts that are not occupied: P(LBCA)A 1990, s. 54(4) and Planning (Listed Buildings and Conservation Areas) (Scotland) Act 1997, s. 49(4), whereas in Wales if the building is for residential use, it is only possible to

on unoccupied buildings in conservation areas in England, Wales and Scotland, to maintain the appearance and character of the area.[279]

These are short-term mechanisms providing reactive care for cultural heritage places by a publicly recognised community of care that assumes direct responsibility for care. In reacting to the immediate harm, the Secretary of State may consider whether it is appropriate to take on responsibility for the long-term care of monuments through guardianship[280] or may consider using their compulsory purchase powers (in respect of certain designated heritage assets[281]) in the event that the long-term care by the private owners is of concern. These mechanisms will now be considered in turn.

7.5.4.2 Taking on the Management and Care of Cultural Heritage Places

The scheme of guardianship of ancient monuments[282] provides a mechanism to substitute more appropriate care for the current care provided by a private owner. It achieves this not by transferring the monument into public ownership, but instead by the Secretary of State, Historic England or the local authority assuming responsibility for its quotidian care.[283] The care given by this publicly accountable community of care to assist the private owner through managing and general caring for the cultural heritage place is only given in return for public access to that place.

Guardianship can be framed within the ethics of care, demonstrating how appropriate care can be provided to navigate harm. However, it can also be seen as a state-regulated activity. Where a scheduled monument is subject to guardianship, this operates as a local land charge in England and Wales[284] and must be entered on the Register of Sasines in Scotland,[285] thereby binding successors in title to the legal estate forming the particular cultural heritage place. Furthermore, guardianship impacts directly on the owner's use and enjoyment of their private property by requiring public access, and by taking the responsibility for the management of the place out of the hands of the owner. During the debates for the original Ancient Monuments Act 1882, it was described as a 'measure of spoliation' by Cavendish Bentinck.[286]

Shifting focus now away from places to the broader activities of care of cultural heritage, one can see how communities of care may assume responsibility for care which at present might not be considered to be appropriately undertaken. Where services, including cultural-based activities such as

---

carry out works where this would 'not interfere unreasonably with that use' (P(LBCA)A 1990, s. 54(5A)) and where the occupier as well as the owner has been given 7 days' notice: s. 54(5A).

[279] P(LBCA)A 1990, s. 76(1) and Planning (Listed Buildings and Conservation Areas) (Scotland) Act 1997, s. 68.

[280] See Section 7.5.4.2.   [281] See Section 7.5.4.3.

[282] Under the AMAAA 1979, s. 12 (this relates to England, Wales and Scotland) under which the owner of the monument constitutes the Secretary of State, or Historic England or the local authority as a guardian.

[283] Regarding quotidian care, see Chapter 6.   [284] AMAAA 1979, s. 12(7).   [285] ibid., s. 12(8).

[286] Brown, *The Care of Ancient Monuments*, p. 152.

museums, are provided by a local authority and local communities are concerned about the current provision of them, certain communities can intervene. These communities, identified in legislation,[287] can challenge the current provision of services by a local authority[288] and can express an interest in providing those services themselves. They may wish to ensure that there is a continued provision in a local community, but by transferring responsibility for its care to a different community of care can enable the cultural heritage to be more appropriately cared for. This can help to address any lapses in the existing care of cultural heritage by the local authority. On the one hand guardianship involves an institutional community of care, supported by advisers who are expert communities of care. In contrast, through the Localism Act 2011, non-expert local communities of care can assume responsibility for care where they see shortfalls in it, or where there is a risk of removal of a particular activity of care relating to cultural heritage.

7.5.4.3 Taking on Ownership

In some cases, the risk of harm to cultural heritage is so acute – and the various means to encourage or require the owners of heritage places to provide appropriate care to avoid the harm have failed – that more dramatic intervention is required. In such cases, the national, or international, communities of care may assume direct responsibility for the care of cultural heritage through ownership of the cultural heritage. This is facilitated in the case of designated heritage assets through the scheme of compulsory purchase of listed buildings or scheduled monuments that are in need of repair.[289] Prior to this, the Secretary of State must have served on the owner a 'repairs notice' and have consulted with Historic England,[290] as an expert community of care. Clearly, this interferes with private property rights but would be compatible with

---

[287] Which include a voluntary or community body, 'a body of persons or a trust which is established for charitable purposes', a parish council, two or more employees of the relevant local authority or such other persons specified by the Secretary of State by regulations made under the Localism Act 2011, s. 81(6). In *ex parte Hall* Blake J observed that the Act did not prescribe formal requirements of how the bodies should be constituted and that 'it is perfectly feasible for an expression of interest to be submitted that contains a timetable to progress the bid from an existing status of an organisation to move to charitable or other status . . . in order to provide the service': para. 80.

[288] Defined as 'relevant authority' under the Localism Act 2011 and which means county councils, district councils, London borough councils and such other person or body carrying out a public function which the Secretary of State designates by regulations under the Act: s. 81(2).

[289] P(LBCA)A 1990, s. 47; Planning (Listed Buildings and Conservation Areas) (Scotland) Act 1997, s. 42 and Planning (Northern Ireland) Act 2011, s. 161(1). In England and Wales the Secretary of State will need to consult Historic England (P(LBCA)A 1990, s. 47(3)). There is a procedure for any person with an interest in the building applying to the court for an order to stay the proceedings (1990 Act, s. 47(4) and 1997 Act, s. 42(4)). Similar provisions exist in respect of scheduled monuments under AMAAA 1979, s. 10 and Historic Monuments and Archaeological Objects (Northern Ireland) Order 1995, art. 7(1).

[290] P(LBCA)A 1990, s. 48 and Planning (Listed Buildings and Conservation Areas) (Scotland) Act 1997, s. 43.

Article 1 of the First Protocol of the European Convention on Human Rights[291] on the basis that it is pursuing a legitimate interest of society in preserving cultural heritage. These principles are clear from the European Court of Human Rights cases of *Beyleur* v. *Italy*[292] *and Kozacioğlu* v. *Turkey*[293] where statements were made about the importance of caring for cultural heritage and the value placed on these important places or objects to people. Transfer of ownership to the Secretary of State, or to the local authority, would be compatible with human rights since the transfer is on payment of compensation.[294] This transfer of a place from the private to the public domain also means that the public can now access the cultural heritage.

General powers exist to purchase cultural heritage, regardless of whether it is at risk of harm. These have the effect of passing, with ownership, the responsibility for the care of the cultural heritage to the public domain. These are found in the context of the general power of councils, county boroughs, districts, London boroughs or joint planning board for Greater London to purchase buildings, whether listed or not, if they have 'special architectural or historic interest', as well as nearby land which may be necessary to preserve, provide access or for appropriate management and control of that building.[295]

Whilst provision is made for the assumption of ownership of designated heritage assets that are in a significant state of disrepair, there are no comparable statutory provisions relating to cultural heritage objects. However, there are other opportunities for public purchase of cultural heritage. Although not a provision directly aimed at caring for heritage at risk of harm, the Historic Buildings and Monuments Commission for England has a power to purchase, or to accept by way of gift, any building of 'outstanding historic or architectural interest' or any building in a conservation area.[296] Historic England can also purchase 'any objects which it would be ... historically appropriate[297] to keep in' a building which the Commission has an interest in, or has management, custody or guardianship of any building, or any National Trust building.[298] Additional support exists for purchasing objects (reactively rather than proactively) through funding schemes such as the Art

---

[291] Protocol to the Convention for the Protection of Human Rights and Fundamental Freedoms, Paris, 20 March 1952 (entered into force 18 May 1954), art. 1.

[292] *Beyeler* v. *Italy*, Application no. 33202/96 (ECHR, 5 January 2000); (2001) 33 EHRR 52, paras. 111–13.

[293] *Kozacioğlu* v. *Turkey*, Application no. 2334/03 (ECHR, 19 February 2009) (Grand Chamber), para. 53.

[294] P(LBCA)A 1990, s. 49. Where a building has been deliberately left derelict, provision is made for minimum compensation: s. 50 and Planning (Listed Buildings and Conservation Areas) (Scotland) Act 1997, s. 44, again provision is made for minimum compensation: s. 45.

[295] P(LBCA)A 1990, s. 52(1) and Planning (Listed Buildings and Conservation Areas) (Scotland) Act 1997, s. 47.

[296] Historic Buildings and Ancient Monuments Act 1953, s. 5A(1). Regarding Scotland, these powers are set out in s. 5.

[297] Defined in ibid., ss. 5A(2) and (5).   [298] ibid., ss. 5A(1) and (2).

Fund.[299] Grants for local authorities or the National Trusts in England and Scotland to purchase historic buildings can also be made by Historic England.[300]

One way for these places or objects to continue in their current use, or to maintain the association with, or as, a collection of cultural heritage is by being 'saved for the nation' through acquisition by the National Trust. This brings them into the public domain by ensuring their long-term care, where places are made inalienable, whilst at the same time allowing in some cases the owners to continue to live there.[301] The National Trust's Acquisitions Policy makes it clear that for it to consider acquiring a property it 'should normally be under threat'.[302]

These provisions play an instrumental role in responding to emergencies relating to the physical integrity of cultural heritage places as well as where financial reasons necessitate some development or sale.

When companies go into liquidation their, often vast, business archives may be at risk of dispersal through sales by liquidators. Obviously, liquidators are under a duty to the creditors to achieve the best value.[303] However, various civil society initiatives have been used to respond to this harm and to provide reactive care for the archives. The Business Archives Council can spearhead efforts to find a home for the business archives of companies in liquidation through their Crisis Management Team.[304] When the Thomas Cook archive was at risk they were able (with the Association for Business Historians) to coordinate efforts to save it.[305] The archive is now available at the Record Office for Leicestershire, Leicester and Rutland following a decision in 2019 of a panel comprised of the Business Archives Council, the Official Receiver, representatives from the archive profession and academics.[306] They all considered where it would be most appropriate to care for the archive.[307] Constructing this panel and hearing from representatives allowed dialogic care to take place. As part of this process it was possible to consider who was best placed to assume responsibility for the archive's care as well as what appropriate care entailed in the circumstances.

Often an assumption is made that public ownership provides the best opportunity for the most appropriate care of cultural heritage. Therefore, frequently,

---

[299] This is an independent charity not in receipt of government funding: www.artfund.org/about-us (last accessed 30 May 2023).
[300] Historic Buildings and Ancient Monuments Act 1953, ss. 5 and 6.   [301] See Section 7.3.1.1.
[302] National Trust, *Annual Report 2020/21*, p. 73.   [303] Insolvency Act 1986, s. 143(1).
[304] https://businessarchivescouncil.org.uk/ (last accessed 30 May 2023) and Business Archives Council of Scotland.
[305] See Stephanie Decker, 'Why Historians are Fighting to Save Thomas Cook's Enormous Archive', *The Conversation*, 30 September 2019 and Caroline Parry, 'Staying Alive' [2019] 12 *Museums Journal* 20.
[306] The Record Office, *Thomas Cook Comes Home* (13 January 2020): www.recordoffice.org.uk/news/thomas-cook-comes-home/ (last accessed 30 May 2023).
[307] ibid.

efforts are made to bring cultural heritage into the public domain through public acquisition. However, in some situations, particularly in times of austerity, there is a strong argument for a shift outside the public domain – but not entirely to private ownership. Community asset transfer schemes allow previously publicly owned property to be brought into seemingly private ownership, although in reality this is community ownership. Thus, the public–private divide is blurred in some respects because of the intervention of communities in the ownership of these cultural heritage assets under which they assume responsibility for their care and displace the state.[308] This mechanism of community asset transfers permits an immediate response to risks of long-term loss of cultural heritage caused by threats of demolition of a building or through the removal of provision of a museum because of funding cuts. A major stumbling block to successful community asset transfers though is the need for these endeavours to be commercially viable. How these communities are set up depends on the circumstances. They can take the form of charities, public interest entities, or companies limited by guarantee. A way in which to ensure that they continue to care for cultural heritage and do so for the benefit of a community, rather than for personal benefit, is the insistence on the use of an asset lock. This means that the assets must either be retained by the community interest company, or transferred subject to certain requirements including that it is transferred for its market value to another asset-locked body, with the consent of the Regulator, and that it is 'for the benefit of the community'.[309]

The community assets scheme clearly enables a local community to assume responsibility for the long-term care of cultural heritage. Using this instrument provides them with an opportunity to acquire an asset, thus providing reactive care in what may be pressured circumstances which risk harm to cultural heritage. In *ex parte Hall* the judge clearly articulated the importance of exploring all opportunities for the transfer of assets to 'a viable community trust' before a local authority should make the difficult decision of reducing the provision of a local museum.[310] In Scotland, community-controlled bodies and community participation bodies have the right to buy abandoned, neglected or detrimental land.[311] There is also a requirement for local authorities in Scotland to maintain common good registers[312] which detail property

---

[308] This process is different from the one provided for in chapter 3 of the Localism Act 2011 where land has been nominated as an asset of community value and where voluntary or community groups are given an opportunity to bid for it in the event that it is sold. The scheme under chapter 3 of the Localism Act 2011 also represents a means of reacting to potential harm and, arguably, if used proactively could be a means of preventative care.

[309] Department for Business, Energy & Industrial Strategy, *Office of the Regulator of Community Interest Companies: Information and Guidance Notes, Chapter 6: The Asset Lock* (May 2016), para. 6.1.1.

[310] *Ex parte Hall*, para. 45.

[311] Part 3A Land Reform (Scotland) Act 2003 [brought in by the Community Empowerment (Scotland) Act 2015].

[312] Community Empowerment (Scotland) Act 2015, s. 102.

'owned by the local authority which has been passed down, through local government reorganisation, from former burghs'. This 'includes land and buildings, and moveable items such as furniture and art'.[313] It must publish the details of any proposed disposal of common good property or any change of use[314] and must take into account representations from certain bodies made before disposing of the property.[315] These provide local communities who care about cultural heritage with the opportunity to assume responsibility for its direct care. These processes involve dialogue, not only with relevant local authorities but also with 'any community body that is known by the authority to have an interest in the property'.[316]

7.5.4.4 Taking Cultural Heritage into Temporary Custody: Safe Havens

Cultural heritage – displaced from elsewhere – may be in need of temporary refuge until it is safe to be returned to its community of origin. Safe havens provide such a place for temporary safekeeping. The International Law Association (ILA) defines safe havens as 'facilities created in order to care for cultural material that has been endangered by armed conflict, natural disasters, illegal excavation, or other insecurity and has therefore been removed for safekeeping and preservation from the territory of the source state'.[317] In its guidelines (which are not legally binding in the UK) it indicates that state authorities should supervise such safe havens.[318] Specifically, museums – as expert communities of care, with suitable storage facilities to provide appropriate care – are frequently the best placed to act as such safe havens or repositories of last resort.[319]

Through means of a civil society initiative, the British Museum provides direct physical care of cultural heritage objects that have been illicitly removed from conflict zones and for which short-term refuge is needed.[320] This temporary care is given following direct consultation with the country of origin, and in some cases with the institution from which the object was illicitly removed; it consequently appears to be dialogic in nature.

---

[313] Scottish Government, *Community Empowerment and Common Good Property: Guidance for Local Authorities* (July 2018), para. 2.

[314] Community Empowerment (Scotland) Act 2015, s. 104. See also *East Lothian District Council v. National Coal Board* [1982] SLT 460 and *Stirling District Council (Re Application for Authority to Dispose of Common Good Land* [2000] ScotCS 128.

[315] Community Empowerment (Scotland) Act 2015, s. 104(6).   [316] ibid., s. 104(5).

[317] Guidelines for the Establishment and Conduct of Safe Havens as Adopted by the ILA at its 73rd Conference held in Rio De Janeiro, Brazil, 17–21 August 2008.

[318] ibid., para. 3.

[319] The ICOM, *Code of Ethics* states that nothing in the code 'should prevent a museum from acting as an authorised repository for unprovenanced, illicitly collected or recovered specimens or objects from the territory over which it has lawful responsibility': principle 2.11.

[320] St John Simpson, *Art in Crisis: Identifying and Returning Looted Objects* (November 2019): https://blog.britishmuseum.org/art-in-crisis-identifying-and-returning-looted-objects/ (last accessed 30 May 2023).

Part of the care given to the cultural heritage objects whilst in the care of the British Museum has been their cataloguing, together with research into them. The question then becomes – who is entitled to the outputs of this research? Here, the focus of compiling such catalogues is clearly on the historical record and sharing this information with scholars and countries by making it publicly available. On occasions, museums which act as safe havens to cultural heritage also display it in temporary exhibits, thereby providing public access to it.[321] This arguably also benefits the host museum that has acted as a safe haven. Furthermore, academic works or exhibition catalogues are produced, adding to cultural exchange.

Permission to exhibit the objects, to use them for research, and to produce outputs requires dialogue with, and informed consent by, the community of origin. The circumstances in which the community finds itself must also be taken into account to ensure that any agreement is freely made and that the ultimate use by the communities providing the safe haven amounts to respectful, empathetic and dialogic care. The ILA Safe Haven Guidelines envisage the public exhibition of objects, but make it clear that any proceeds from exhibitions 'may be used only for safekeeping and preserving safe haven material'.[322]

More controversial though are situations where objects come to light on the art market and are purchased with a view to being taken into temporary care until they can be returned to their place of origin (or more specifically the institution where they are officially housed). In such circumstances there is a clear ethical question about whether the purchase of such objects fosters the illicit trade in the cultural objects. However, this risk of encouraging the illicit trade is balanced against the potential loss of the object if it is left on the open market and disappears into a private collection, out of the public view and specifically lost to the institution or country of origin.

7.5.4.5 Safe Havens: Duty of Care

The language of safekeeping is used in the context of situations where the UK is acting as a depository for protected cultural property[323] under the Cultural Property (Armed Conflicts) Act 2017 as well as in the ILA Guidelines.[324] During this time the cultural property in question would be immune from

---

[321] The Minister of Culture in Baghdad consented to a display of a Sumerian temple wall plaque in the British Museum following its arrival at the museum as part of the Metropolitan Police's investigations. The Prime Minister of Iraq subsequently proposed an extension of that display 'so that more . . . visitors could see it after the second lockdown [during the COVID-19 pandemic]': St John Simpson, *Combatting Illicit Trade: Identifying and Returning a 4,000-Year -Old Relief to Iraq,* 14 December 2020: https://blog.britishmuseum.org/combatting-illicit-trade-identifying-and-returning-a-4000-year-old-relief-to-iraq/ (last accessed 30 May 2023). See also Martin Bailey, 'Seized Antiquities Sent from Ukraine to Go on Show at British Museum', *The Art Newspaper,* 31 May 2022.

[322] ILA Guidelines, paras. 4(e) and (g).

[323] Cultural Property (Armed Conflicts) Act 2017, s. 28(6).   [324] ILA Guidelines, para. 4(a).

seizure or forfeiture under any legislation or rule of law.[325] In the case of cultural heritage under special protection during armed conflict, the depository 'shall extend to it as great a measure of care as that which it bestows upon on its own cultural property of comparable importance'.[326]

Specific information about the obligations of those acting as safe haven, outside the scope of the 2017 Act, are set out in the ILA Guidelines on Safe Havens.[327] This includes taking 'all reasonable measures to avoid deterioration or endangerment of cultural material by applying the highest standards of care'.[328] This document is not enforceable in the UK, but those people who are in possession of cultural heritage which is owned by someone else are under a legal duty of care in bailment.[329]

7.5.5 Seizure

The power of officials to seize cultural heritage objects provides a practical and effective means of caring for cultural heritage by removing it from harm. Where recently illicitly excavated or stolen cultural heritage objects are illegally imported into the country, customs officials have the power to seize them, taking them into temporary custody pending a criminal investigation. Ultimately these are returned to their legal owners. Cultural heritage objects may even be seized when exported by their owners if they have not obtained the appropriate export licence.[330] The ability to seize cultural heritage objects is an important means of direct care which permits intervention to stem the flow of circulation of illicitly excavated or illegally exported cultural heritage objects.

Under the Cultural Property (Armed Conflicts) Act 2017 there is a power to seize cultural property[331] and ultimately to forfeit it[332] where a person has committed the offence of dealing in unlawfully exported cultural property.[333] The general criminal law also provides opportunities to seize property, thus further assisting in caring for cultural heritage that has been stolen or illicitly excavated by preventing its loss and continued circulation on the market. Specifically, a constable may seize anything for which they have reasonable

---

[325] Cultural Property (Armed Conflicts) Act 2017, s. 28(1).

[326] ibid., sch 2, para. 18(a) (as set out in the Regulations for the Execution of the Convention). See Andrzej Jakubowski, 'International Protection of Cultural Heritage in Armed Conflict: Revising the Role of Safe Havens' (2019) 16 *Indonesian Journal of International Law* 169.

[327] ILA Guidelines.   [328] ibid., art. 4(a).   [329] As to which see Section 6.11.4.1.

[330] Under the Export of Objects of Cultural Interest (Control) Order 2002, the Commissioners have a duty to take such action as considered appropriate to enforce the export requirements, which includes the application of the Customs and Excise Management Act 1979 (which includes the power to seize goods): ACE, *UK Export Licensing for Cultural Goods: Procedures and Guidance for Exporters of Works of Art and Other Cultural Goods* (ACE Notice, 2021), para. 34.

[331] Following the issuing of a warrant by the court: Cultural Property (Armed Conflicts) Act 2017, s. 23(1), (2).

[332] ibid., s. 18(1).   [333] Defined in s. 16(1), see Section 7.3.1.

grounds for believing may they have 'been obtained in consequence of the commission of an offence'.[334] Such an object can then be retained for 'so long as is necessary in all the circumstances',[335] which includes time to establish its lawful owner ('when there are reasonable grounds for believing it has been stolen or obtained by the commission of an offence'[336]). The money laundering regime within the UK provides an additional means by which to seize the proceeds of crime, including cultural heritage objects which may have been illicitly acquired.[337] All of these mechanisms provide reactive care, responding to the direct risk occasioned by the illicit trade in cultural heritage objects.

Efforts are also made to avoid cultural heritage being used to fund or support terrorism. The Anti-terrorism, Crime and Security Act 2001 furnishes an authorised officer[338] with the power to seize any item of property if they have reasonable grounds for suspecting it as a listed asset (which includes precious metals, whether or not manufactured, precious stones, watches and artistic works falling within the definition of the Copyright Designs and Patents Act 1988).[339] This power of seizure exists in respect of property intended to be used for the purposes of terrorism, or which is part of the resources of an organisation, or the property is earmarked as terrorist property.[340]

7.5.5.1 Standards of Custody of Seized Property

Care is legally mandated for all property temporarily in the possession of someone else. Therefore, where someone has assumed responsibility for the temporary care of cultural heritage, by seizing it, they owe obligations in the common law of bailment.[341] In the event that the police are in possession of cultural heritage temporarily for the purposes of law enforcement they owe similar duties in respect of it.[342]

Where listed assets have been seized under the Anti-terrorism, Crime and Security Act 2001, under its framework of 'safekeeping of property' the authorised officer is under a duty to arrange for the property to be safely stored throughout the period of seizure, putting a direct obligation onto the police or other officers to care for seized property.[343]

---

[334] Police and Criminal Evidence Act 1984, s. 19(2). This power is available in circumstances where the constable is lawfully on any premises: s. 19(1).

[335] ibid., s. 22(1).

[336] Police and Criminal Evidence Act (PACE) Code B, revised *Code of Practice for Searches of Premises by Police Officers and the Seizure of Property found by Police Officers on Persons or Premises*, para. 7.14(iv).

[337] See Janet Ulph and Ian Smith, *The Illicit Trade in Art and Antiquities: International Recovery and Criminal and Civil Liability* (Oxford: Hart, 2012), pp. 101–16.

[338] Defined in Anti-terrorism, Crime and Security Act 2001, sch 1, para. 19(1).

[339] ibid., sch. 1, para. 10A(1).   [340] ibid., sch. 1, para. 10B.

[341] Norman Palmer and Janet Ulph, 'Bailment, Crime and the Proceeds of Crime' in Norman Palmer (ed.), *Palmer on Bailment* (3rd ed., London: Sweet & Maxwell, 2009), section 35-054.

[342] ibid.   [343] Anti-terrorism, Crime and Security Act 2001, sch. 1, para. 10E(2).

Officials may transfer the direct physical care of cultural heritage to an expert community of care such as a museum. This means that the seized cultural heritage object can benefit from specialised care which takes account of its nature and can therefore be appropriate in the circumstances. Museums such as the British Museum may be tasked with caring for seized cultural heritage objects, since the museum has specialist, secure facilities and the relevant curatorial experience to provide appropriate quotidian care for the objects whilst awaiting the outcome of a dispute.[344]

7.5.5.2 Return or Reunification: Attempts to Overcome Loss of Association

Where cultural heritage objects have been separated from their place of origin, or where statues have been dismembered and one part is found elsewhere, the process of return has been conceptualised in terms of reunification.[345]

The notion of the integrity of cultural heritage and the reunification of an element of heritage with its place of origin (such as an element of a church or a part of a statue) can be seen in the context of the Export Reviewing Committee's decision to recommend that the Secretary of State grant an export licence for certain choir stalls which originated from a church in Germany.[346] Although they may have met the Waverley criteria and thus be considered a UK national treasure, nevertheless the importance of both the European and international cultural heritage and the integrity of the heritage as a whole, specifically the aesthetic and cultural significance, were factors considered by the committee in reaching its recommendation.[347]

A recent example of reunification was seen in the case of a statue of Eros, whose dismembered head, which had originally formed part of a sarcophagus which was located in Turkey, was part of the collection of the V&A. The head of Eros was reunited with the rest of the sarcophagus as part of a 'renewable cultural partnership' with Turkey. In legal terms, though, this was a long-term loan;[348] the head was attached in a non-permanent manner, presumably reflecting this fact. It was within this context that the current director of the museum suggested that it might be appropriate to revisit the governing statutes, which prohibit the transfer of ownership to reunite the head of the statue with the rest of it on a permanent basis.[349]

---

[344] E.g. in the case of a Libyan funerary statue which had been seized by HM Revenue and Customs : Joseph Lee, *British Museum Turned into Temporary Court* (31 March 2015): www .museumsassociation.org/museums-journal/news/2015/03/31032015-bm-turned-into-court/ (last accessed 30 May 2023).

[345] See for example Kalliopi Fouseki, 'Claiming the Parthenon Marbles back. Whose claim and on behalf of whom?' in Louise Tythacott and Kostas Arvanitis (eds.), *Museums and Restitution: New Practices, New Approaches* (Farnham: Ashgate, 2014), p. 173.

[346] See Section 8.3.2.   [347] ibid.

[348] Martin Bailey, 'Victoria and Albert Museum Returns – and Reattaches – a Third-Century Marble Head of Greek God Taken from Turkey', *The Art Newspaper*, 1 July 2022.

[349] Gareth Harris, 'Victoria & Albert Museum Director Says it is Time to Change UK Law that Stops Museum from "Disposing" of Works', *The Art Newspaper*, 4 July 2022. Since then potential reform of the NHA 1983, which governs the V&A, has been debated in Parliament:

7.6 Challenges to Providing Reactive Care

Despite well-meaning communities wanting to assume responsibility for care as a response to harm, at times practical or legal challenges can hinder them from doing so, thereby precluding appropriate care.

7.6.1 The Challenges of Ownership

Uncertainties about who actually owns specific cultural heritage objects or places – and therefore on whom the responsibility to care for them and respond to harm falls – can present challenges to the effectiveness of implementing appropriate care, particularly when at risk of immediate harm.

Above, it was discussed how the Secretary of State or the local planning authority can assume responsibility for the care of certain monuments by taking them into guardianship, or in the case of listed buildings and ancient monuments, by taking ownership of them.[350] Lapses in the care of cultural heritage places in Scotland can be plugged by the public assuming responsibility by purchasing those places which are in danger; this statutory regime is not restricted to historic places, but can facilitate a shift in ownership which can provide more appropriate care.[351] However, there are no comparable powers to assume guardianship, or to compulsorily purchase undesignated public art works that have fallen into a state of disrepair, for the purpose of avoiding further harm.

In some limited situations involving publicly sited artworks, the close relationship between ownership and responsibility has hindered the appropriate care of cultural heritage where there were uncertainties about who owned it. It is to this situation that the discussion now turns.

In establishing who is the owner of an artwork in a public space, it is not a simple question of identifying the landowner, because artworks such as sculptures are not necessarily fixtures (and therefore part of the land). Instead, they may remain as chattels. This was made particularly clear in the case of *Tower Hamlets* v. *Bromley* involving the Henry Moore sculpture *Draped Seated Woman* where the court had to grapple with the issue of whether it was real or personal property.[352]

Even in the absence of being able to categorically determine ownership, one community of care may decide to assume responsibility for the necessary care – although this may follow years of uncertainty. This can be seen in the references in Baldwin Brown's early work on legislation affecting ancient monuments, when he discussed the uncertainties surrounding the ownership of the Eleanor Cross, located in Northampton, where it was unclear which local authority was

---

Lord Vaizey, *Hansard* HL vol. 824, col. 168GC (13 October 2022). However, the UK government's position is that there are no plans to reform this Act: Lord Kamal, *Hansard* HL vol. 824, col. 184GC (13 October 2022).

[350] P(LBCA)A 1990, s. 47(1) and the Ancient Monument and Archaeological Areas Act 1979, s. 10(1). See Sections 7.5.4.2 and 7.5.4.3, respectively.

[351] See Section 7.5.4.3.   [352] [2015] EWHC 1954 (Ch). See Section 5.2.8.1.

responsible for its care.[353] According to Baldwin Brown, responsibility was eventually assumed by the County Council, who held it under the 1900 Act. However, a 2017 BBC News report suggested that the County and Borough Councils still did not know which one of them owned it. A subsequent news report indicated that the Borough Council had said that it would make sure that the Cross was maintained, thereby at a minimum assuming responsibility for its care[354] and enabling repair and conservation work to be carried out, which was ultimately part-funded by Historic England.

External communities of care may wish to intervene in situations where they care about cultural heritage but may be reluctant to do so if they need to access a site and would need the permission of the owner of land. In 2016 Eduardo Paolozzi's sculpture *Piscator*, located at Euston Station, was in need of repair. The question arose as to where ownership lay following the privatisation of British Rail. According to information now available via the Arts Council England (ACE), it had been commissioned by the British Railways Board (Great Britain) Ltd, Sir Robert McAlpine & Sons Ltd, Norwich Union Insurance Group and Pensions Fund Securities Ltd, and installed outside offices in Euston Square.[355] However, even though in 2016 the artist's foundation was willing to assume responsibility for the care of the statue in terms of funding the necessary repair work, it still needed to establish who owned the sculpture in order to obtain permission to both undertake the work and access the site.[356] Ultimately it was reported that ownership had been transferred by British Rail to ACE.[357] Therefore, ACE, as a recognised community of care for cultural heritage, assumed responsibility through a transfer of ownership.

In situations where no one acknowledged ownership of a sculpture, it would arguably be possible for someone to intervene and assume responsibility for its care, and to avert physical deterioration on an emergency basis, under the doctrine of agency of necessity.[358] This has been suggested as a concept that could be deployed by museums to conserve an object in the event that they were unclear who had loaned a cultural heritage object to them.[359]

---

[353] Brown, *The Care of Ancient Monuments*, pp. 162–3.

[354] BBC News Online, *Northampton's Eleanor Cross Memorial Has Summer Repair Plan* 8 May 2018. Ultimately the work was undertaken and financed by Historic England and Northampton Borough Council: BBC News Online, *Eleanor Cross: Conservation of Northampton Monument Complete* 15 November 2019.

[355] Art UK, *Piscator*: https://artuk.org/discover/artworks/piscator-309797 (last accessed 22 May 2023).

[356] Dalya Alberge, 'Major Paolozzi Sculpture Facing Decay Because No One Wants to Own it', *The Guardian*, 28 November 2016.

[357] Dalya Alberge, 'Arts Body Criticised for Leaving Paolozzi Sculpture on Euston Building Site', *The Guardian*, 11 November 2019.

[358] This was considered by Janet Ulph in the context of disposal of an object where it was unclear who had loaned it to them: Janet Ulph, 'Frozen in Time: Orphans and Uncollected Objects in Museum Collections' (2017) 24 *International Journal of Cultural Property* 3, 8.

[359] Norman Palmer, *Art Loans* (London: Kluwer Law International and International Bar Association, 1997), p. 179.

One unequivocal act of care provided by the UK national community (in the form of the general public) without concern about whether something was privately or publicly owned was seen in the crowdfunding campaign to facilitate the repair of Peter Laszlo Peri's *The Sunbathers*. This had been commissioned and displayed at the Festival of Britain in 1951 but by 2016 its location was unknown. Historic England instigated a public project to locate various public artworks that had disappeared over the years;[360] in response to this *The Sunbathers* was located in the garden of a hotel. The public participated in an effective crowdsourced funding operation which raised a sum in excess of the initial funding target. During this whole process, no questions appear to have been raised online about the ownership of the sculpture and whether it remained in private hands or had been transferred into public ownership. The focus was firmly on 'saving' the work. When the initial funding target was met so quickly, it was announced that further funds would be used to support the long-term curation of the sculpture. In this case, the imperative was to ensure its physical safety and its restoration ahead of the South Bank Summer exhibition, irrespective of whether the owner of the sculpture might receive a windfall from a fully repaired sculpture. Following its return to Waterloo Station in 2020 (albeit to a different wall) it was made clear that the sculpture was on loan for a five-year period and the generosity of the lenders, the O'Donnell family and the Clarendon Hotel in Blackheath, was acknowledged.[361]

7.6.1.1 Difficulties Where No Collection Is Established

It has already been seen how law facilitates the legal construction of a collection.[362] This can provide greater control over how the collection is administered, and a certain level of care is provided, in terms of averting the physical and intangible harm which might be occasioned by separating it. However, the legal question in some cases is whether there was any legal structure in place which created such a collection. Two cases show how the property status of the objects is prioritised over the recognition of the cultural heritage nature of a collection. The first case in which this arose was that of *Re Wedgwood Trust Ltd (In Administration)*,[363] discussed above. In this case, the question was whether the Wedgwood collection of pottery and other artefacts was available as an asset to meet the pension deficit of the Wedgwood company.

The first paragraph of the judgment focused on the legal issue, specifically whether the collection was available to meet the liabilities of the Wedgwood

---

[360] Historic England, *Help Find Our Missing Art* (December 2015): https://historicengland.org.uk/campaigns/post-war-public-art/missing-public-art/ (last accessed 22 May 2023).

[361] Historic England, *1950s Sculpture 'The Sunbathers' at London Waterloo Station*: https://historicengland.org.uk/campaigns/post-war-public-art/sunbathers-at-london-waterloo/ (last accessed 22 May 2023); Historic England, *News: Festival of Britain Sculpture Returns to London Waterloo* (24 August 2020): https://historicengland.org.uk/whats-new/news/sunbathers-returns-waterloo/ (last accessed 22 May 2023).

[362] Section 7.3.2.   [363] [2012] Pens LR 175 (Ch).

company (which, as the last company in the group still standing, was responsible for the liabilities of the entire group regarding pensions).[364] Even though in the second paragraph the collection was introduced as 'a unique collection of pottery and other artefacts and items of historical importance built up over many decades ... ', this statement does not fully reflect its status as part of the UK UNESCO's Memory of the World where it is expressed in the following terms as:

> one of the most complete ceramic manufacturing archives in existence ... Unparalleled in its diversity and breadth the 80,000 plus documents embrace every imaginable subject from pot to people, transport to trade, society and social conditions.[365]

In this case, the museum had failed to create a suitable trust vehicle to separate the collection from the rest of company and thus take it outside the property that could be called upon to fulfil the pension deficit of the Museum Company. Despite the collection being recognised as internationally important, there was no legal requirement for it to be maintained as a whole or which prevented it from being treated as an asset of the pension scheme. Treating the collection as an asset excluded from the dialogue about care the various communities of care who cared about it (the international, national and local communities as well as the museum community). The voices of their members were not considered as part of the decision-making process. As discussed above, the judge – in setting out the ethos of the court – separated himself from the outcome of the case, showing how it was the combination of the pension and insolvency rules that had led to the conclusion[366] and left the collection's fate in the hands of the administrators.[367] In the absence of appropriate care from the courts, it was for others to intervene to assume responsibility for the cultural heritage.[368] It was only because of a public appeal for funding that the collection was saved from dispersal. To ensure that the collection was kept together, the Art Fund asked the Victoria and Albert Museum to take ownership of it and then make a long-term loan to the Wedgwood museum in Barlaston.[369] In this way it would benefit from more restrictive provisions relating to disposal.[370]

The second case of particular relevance in demonstrating how the common law has treated efforts to maintain the integrity of collections involves the collection of Chinese vases amassed by Sir Michael Butler, which he displayed in a museum at his house.[371] Over several years Sir Michael and his wife transferred the vases to the Butler Family Collection trust. A dispute arose between Sir Michael's four children after his death. Two of the disputing siblings wanted to retain the collection as a museum, whilst the other two wanted to take vases out of the collection to keep for themselves. The court therefore had to

---

[364] ibid., para. 12.   [365] UK UNESCO Memory of World Register, 2011.
[366] [2012] Pens LR 175 (Ch), para. 56.   [367] ibid.
[368] As was the case with the Rose Theatre, see Section 5.2.8.1.
[369] See V&A Board Meeting, 3 July 2014, para. 5.1.   [370] Under the NHA 1983, s. 6(3).
[371] *Butler* v. *Butler*.

consider a technical legal point about the division of co-owned chattels (personal property) under section 188 of the Law of Property Act 1925.

The judge's language mirrored that of the judge in *Re Wedgwood* in talking about the collection, noting its uniqueness and 'outstanding importance'[372] to the study and appreciation of Chinese art and culture in the 17th century'.[373] This language is reminiscent of how heritage places are categorised for the purposes of the World Heritage Convention, focusing on the more traditional approach to cultural heritage as being monumental and of universal value.

The court concluded, though, that Sir Michael and Lady Butler's prime concern, as donors, had been to make a gift of the contents of the collection to their children in such a way as to take advantage of tax benefits; this trumped any intention of making a gift or transfer of the Chinese porcelain 'pots'[374] *qua* 'The Butler Family Collection'.[375] The judge made it clear that it had been open to the donors to have effected the transfer in that way had they so wished.[376] The deed of gift clearly stated that the objects were to be transferred to the donees, to be held as beneficial tenants in common. Consequently, any of the tenants in common could take their share. In circumstances such as the facts of *Butler*, where two co-owners apply to the court to divide the chattels,[377] a court can order that each of the co-owners takes turns to select an object until none remain.[378]

In *Butler* v. *Butler*,[379] the court treated the cultural heritage nature of the collection and its importance as irrelevant. Counsel for the claimants (the siblings who wanted to remove 'pots' from the collection) had argued that the uniqueness of a collection and its recognised importance might lead to a desire to keep it together and ensure its integrity as a collection but were 'insufficient to trump the rights and wishes of an owner'.[380] In support of this they cited *Re Wedgwood Trust Ltd (In Administration)*.[381] The judge did not fully address this argument and specifically the analogy that the claimants drew with that case, instead dismissing it on the basis that *Re Wedgwood* had 'not been directly concerned with that point'.[382] But *Re Wedgwood* was clearly a case where the private property dimension to the cultural heritage took priority over any argument that the collection's integrity would be lost by a negative court decision. It therefore appears to be a clear case of ownership trumping the subject matter's status *qua* cultural heritage.[383] These two cases therefore

---

[372] 'Immense importance' in *Re Wedgwood*.   [373] *Butler* v. *Butler*, para. 77.
[374] The terminology that had been used by the family and the court adopted at times: ibid., para. 1.
[375] ibid., paras. 40 and 74.   [376] ibid., para. 41.
[377] Under section 188 of the Law of Property Act 1925.
[378] *Butler* v. *Butler* (Ch). In the circumstances of the *Butler* litigation neither of the opposing pairs of siblings favoured the outright sale of the collection and sharing the proceeds of sale (para. 68).
[379] ibid.   [380] ibid., para. 93.   [381] [2012] Pens LR 175 (Ch).   [382] *Butler* v. *Butler*, para. 93.
[383] In the *Tower Hamlets* case discussed at Section 5.2.8, ownership was engaged in an attempt to prevent the sale of public art. Therefore, in that case, the answer of *who* was the owner had the potential to 'save' it from sale. Ultimately though, even though the legal arguments were unsuccessful a change in the mayor of the council meant that the sale was thwarted: see Section 5.2.8.1.

illustrate how important it is to establish collections in legal terms, as a preventative measure to avoid problems where circumstances arise which risk the integrity of the collection.

7.6.2 Gaps in Coverage

7.6.2.1 The Illicit Trade in Cultural Heritage

A significant gap in the care of cultural heritage relates to illicit trade in cultural heritage objects. It was identified earlier how this area of law represents a space where there is insufficient law to deal with the problem of the illicit trade in cultural heritage. The 1970 UNESCO Convention represented a watershed moment in the international approach to illicit trade in cultural objects. It established what has been described as an ethical marker, putting everyone on notice that they need to act ethically when acquiring cultural heritage.[384] This has been translated into guidance for museums which places them under an ethical obligation not to acquire objects which have a questionable provenance after 1970. The DCMS Due Diligence Guidance states that museums 'should reject an item if there is any suspicion about it, or about circumstances surrounding it, after undertaking due diligence ... Museums should acquire or borrow items only if they are certain they have not been illegally excavated or illegally exported since 1970.'[385] There is a worldwide problem with the illicit trade in cultural heritage objects, although exact figures are difficult to determine.[386] Recent work has identified the importance of focusing on the demand for cultural heritage objects, rather than on the supply, emphasising the need to put in place strong legal provisions which disincentivise the purchase of illicitly excavated, illicitly exported and imported cultural heritage objects.[387] Part of this also includes the need for strategies to encourage good behaviour.[388]

Various practical measures are in place to tackle the illicit trade, such as codes of ethics for museums and dealers, specific offences relating to cultural heritage, and general criminal offences. Nevertheless, there is a problem of enforceability of these instruments across the world and difficulties with

---

[384] The 1970 date is an ethical rather than legal watershed: Neil Brodie, 'Provenance and Price: Autoregulation of the Antiquities Market?' (2014) 20 *European Journal on Criminal Policy and Research* 427, 440. It was the point in time when 'the international community was put on notice that a rule against reckless acquisition was in the course of adoption': Lyndel V. Prott, 'The History and Development of Return of Cultural Objects' in Lyndel V. Prott (ed.), *Witnesses to History: A Compendium of Documents and Writings on the Return of Cultural Objects* (Paris: UNESCO, 2009), p. 10.

[385] DCMS, *Due Diligence Guidelines for Museums, Libraries and Archives on Collecting and Borrowing Cultural Material* (October 2005), p. 4.

[386] European Commission, *Illicit Trade in Cultural Goods in Europe: Characteristics, Criminal Justice Responses and an Analysis of the Applicability of Technologies in the Combat Against the Trade* (2019), p. 78.

[387] Neil Brodie, Morag M. Kersel, Simon Mackenzie et al., 'Why There is Still an Illicit Trade in Cultural Objects and What We Can Do About It' (2021) 46 *Journal of Field Archaeology* 1.

[388] ibid., 123.

available provenance information. Often it is unclear exactly when an object was imported into a country, which can present a problem for establishing the elements of a criminal offence, specifically in terms of ensuring that the illicit removal happened after the Act came into force.[389] Provenance documentation can be forged, causing problems for unsuspecting purchasers and making it difficult to prove the elements necessary to make a claim. In some cases, provenance documentation is unavailable, or statements about provenance are vague and unsubstantiated, and have been taken at face value by purchasers. Even where purchasers have suspicions, they may be willing to take a risk and purchase the object even if it turns out to have been illicitly excavated. All of these factors make curbing the illicit trade in cultural heritage difficult, and can fuel demand for more illicitly excavated objects, encouraging looters to acquire more objects.[390] For that reason there is a gap in coverage of care.

7.7 Responding with Criminal Sanctions

Where harm has already taken place which was a criminal offence, the fact that the community cares about cultural heritage is evident through the prosecution of those crimes, and the sentence that is passed. This has the effect of recognising publicly the severity of the harm done to cultural heritage, punishing the perpetrators and acting as a deterrent to others. At the international level this was seen when Ahmad Al Faqi Al Mahdi was convicted by the International Criminal Court of war crimes relating to the intentional destruction of cultural heritage in Timbuktu.[391]

Criminalising certain activities, and providing legal 'bite' through the use of sanctions, demonstrates how care is provided by seeking to discourage harm. Historic England has powers of prosecution for offences relating to harm to designated heritage assets.[392] This community of care, which is well-placed to appreciate the harm to the significance of heritage assets, can spearhead action which demonstrates the national community's care for cultural heritage and can act as a deterrent for future harm to cultural heritage places.

At the local level, communities of care provide criminal sanctions against those contravening a byelaw since that person commits an offence; the byelaws can prescribe that a defendant is liable, on summary conviction, to pay a fine,[393] or can provide for the forfeiture or seizure and retention of certain property.[394] Alternatively, in the case of specific byelaws made by the Secretary of State, the byelaw may prescribe that an authorised officer may issue a fixed penalty

---

[389] The Dealing in Cultural Objects (Offences) Act 2003 is not retroactive in nature. However, the Iraq (United Nations Sanctions) Order 2003, art. 8 applies to all Iraqi cultural property illegally removed since 6 August 1990.

[390] See generally Brodie et al., 'Why There is Still an Illicit Trade in Cultural Objects'.

[391] *The Prosecutor* v. *Ahmad Al Faqi Al Mahdi*, ICC-01/12-01/15.   [392] NHA 1983, s. 33(2A).

[393] Under Local Government Act 1972, s. 237 (read in conjunction with the Criminal Justice Act 1982, s. 46), and Local Government Act (Northern Ireland) 1972, s. 92.

[394] Local Government Act 1972, s. 237ZA (England).

notice;[395] in the case of local authority museums and galleries anyone contravening the byelaws may be excluded or removed from the premises.[396]

Whilst the criminalisation of certain activities demonstrates care, the development of sentencing practices specifically dealing with cultural heritage, and the ability to increase sentences where there is harm to cultural heritage, demonstrates the importance of the impact of loss or harm to cultural heritage. It thus seeks not only to punish offenders but also to act as a deterrent, thus providing both current reactive care and future preventative care.

Several cases show the court treating harm to cultural heritage, in the absence of sentencing guidelines at the time, as a breach of trust.

In *R v. Jonathan Aidan Tokeley-Parry*,[397] which involved the deliberate export of cultural heritage and direct contribution to the illicit trade in cultural heritage objects, Beldam LJ specifically highlighted the need to deter others, and justified the use of a deterrent sentence by saying that 'It is important that the courts of this country should prevent those who seek to profit from the theft and removal of antiquities from other countries from doing so.'[398]

Two further Court of Appeal cases, *R v. Hakimzadeh*[399] and *R v. William Simon Jacques*,[400] recognised that harm to cultural heritage, and to collections, had a sufficient gravity to represent an aggravating factor, warranting longer sentences than other situations involving theft or damage to property.

The Court of Appeal on both occasions made visible the UK as a community in which cultural heritage collections (in both cases, of books) are valued, and where harm to them should be punished in a manner reflecting a breach of trust.[401] The cases demonstrate how the courts, as judicial communities of care, recognise the importance of cultural heritage collections and the harm that is caused where individual elements of the collection are destroyed or stolen, thereby irrevocably harming the integrity of the whole.

More recently the sentencing guidelines have been altered to reflect the severity of the commission of offences that harm cultural heritage. When assessing the category of harm that an offence falls into,[402] 'damage to heritage assets' is cited as one example of 'significant additional harm'.[403] Heritage Crime Impact Statements also provide a means by which to present to the police, and to the court, information about the impact that a particular crime has had on the cultural heritage and members of the community for whom it is

---

[395] ibid., s. 237A. In Wales such a power exists under Local Government Byelaws (Wales) Act 2012, s. 12.

[396] Public Libraries and Museums Act 1964, s. 19(2).   [397] 8 December 1998 (CA) (unreported).

[398] ibid., p. 10   [399] [2010] 1 Cr App R (S) 10 (CA).   [400] [2011] 2 Cr App R (S) 39 (CA).

[401] *R v. Farhad Hakimzadeh.*

[402] Under s. 143(1) of the Criminal Justice Act 2003, 'the court must consider the offender's culpability in committing the offence and any harm which the offence caused, was intended to cause or might foreseeably have caused'.

[403] Sentencing Council, *Theft Offences: Definitive Guideline* (2015).

important.[404] This can be of use where there is an out-of-court disposal (such as a reprimand) and also for the prosecution in court at the sentencing stage.[405]

Criminal damage cases relating to memorials can be heard by the Crown Court (and therefore have longer sentences) based on recently amended legislation. Memorials are buildings, structures, 'or any other thing erected or installed on land'[406] as well as gardens[407] and things planted which have 'a commemorative purpose'. This extends to any moveable things left at the site as well, such as flowers.[408]

7.8 Responding to Loss: General Mitigation of Harm and Loss

It is not always possible to entirely avoid harm to, or loss of, cultural heritage. In some circumstances it is recognised that some harm to cultural heritage is necessary to pursue other goals, such as development. Here, the concern of communities of care is to determine how to appropriately navigate this harm through mitigation.

7.8.1 Sanctioned Harm: Mitigating Harm and Loss

7.8.1.1 Sustainable Development

Where an application for development is made which will affect a heritage asset, the applicant is required to provide the local planning authority with a statement about the asset's significance, as well as details of the contribution of its setting.[409] The effect on the significance of the heritage asset or on its setting is a material consideration for the local planning authority.[410] In determining what are appropriate levels of harm in particular circumstances, where harm to cultural heritage is inevitable, issues of proportionality are taken into account. In the context of planning and sustainable development,[411] the terminology used reflects the importance of the cultural heritage affected. Thus, where a proposal is likely to affect scheduled monuments, protected wrecks, registered battlefields and Grade I or II* listed buildings parks or gardens, or where a World Heritage Site is involved, substantial harm or loss should only be 'wholly exceptional'

---

[404] Historic England, *Heritage Crime Impact Statements* (2023).   [405] ibid., p. 15.

[406] Magistrates Courts Act 1980, s. 22(11A)(a), inserted by the Police, Crime, Sentencing and Courts Act 2022, s. 50.

[407] Magistrates Courts Act 1980, s. 22(11A)(b).   [408] ibid., s. 22(11B).

[409] NPPF 2021, para. 194.

[410] ibid., para. 195. In Wales these are described as Heritage Impact Statements: Planning (Listed Buildings and Conservation Areas) (Wales) Regulations 2012 (as amended), reg. 6(1).

[411] This has been defined as 'development that meets the needs of the present without compromising the ability of future generations to meet their own needs': Gro Harlem Brundtland, *Our Common Future: Report of the World Commission on Environment and Development* (1987), p. 41: https://sustainabledevelopment.un.org/content/documents/5987our-common-future.pdf (last accessed 22 May 2023).

circumstances.[412] Furthermore, where the local planning authority has approved an application for 'a World Heritage Site development' – which is a development which 'would have an adverse impact on the outstanding universal value, integrity, authenticity and significance of a World Heritage Site or its setting, including any buffer zone or its equivalent'[413] and where Historic England objects to this, the Secretary of State shall be consulted.[414] The Secretary of State can then make a direction for the application to be referred to them for determination.[415] Very specific requirements for developments within a World Heritage Site or a conservation area are given which mitigates the harm that the particular development might cause.[416] The general approach of Historic England to conservation is to ensure that 'if some negative impact or loss of fabric is unavoidable, mitigation should be considered to minimise harm'.[417]

For Grade II listed buildings, or Grade II parks or gardens, substantial harm or loss should be 'exceptional.[418] Finally, in the case of non-designated heritage assets balanced judgements will be required, having regard to the scale of any harm or loss and the significance of the heritage asset.'[419] By adopting such an approach, enhanced levels of care are provided where communities care more about certain cultural heritage because of its importance.

In Scotland, Historic Environment Scotland, which is responsible for the listed buildings and scheduled monuments scheme, when exercising this regulatory function, 'must contribute to achieving sustainable economic growth, except to the extent that it would be inconsistent with the exercise of those functions to do so'.[420]

Statutory provisions or memoranda entered into between those developing infrastructure can particularise the extent to which cultural heritage will be affected, and can mitigate against harm. As part of the Crossrail works in London a significant number of listed buildings were either altered or demolished as prescribed in the Act.[421] Harm that might be caused by major infrastructure, such as roads and rail networks, are mitigated through standards[422] which guide behaviour[423] or heritage memoranda. In the case of the construction of the High Speed (HS2) railway, a Heritage Memorandum

---

[412] NPPF 2021, para. 200(a).
[413] The Town and Country Planning (Consultation) Direction 2021, para. 6.
[414] ibid., para. 10.   [415] Under Town and Country Planning Act 1990, s. 77.
[416] The Planning (General Permitted Development) Order 2015, sch. 1. The Planning (General Permitted Development) Order (Northern Ireland) 2015.
[417] Historic England, *Conservation Principles: Policies and Guidance* (2008), p. 47.
[418] NPPF 2021, para. 200(b).   [419] ibid., para. 203.
[420] Regulatory Reform (Scotland) Act 2014. See also Andrea Ross and Agne Zasinaite, 'The Use of Presumptions and Duties in Sustainable Development Equations: Promoting Micro-Renewables and Preserving Historic Buildings' (2017) 19 *Environmental Law Review* 93.
[421] Cross Rail Act 2008, sch. 9.
[422] Standards for Highways: https://www.standardsforhighways.co.uk/ (last accessed 30 May 2023).
[423] See Section 3.7.8.1.

was entered into between the Department for Transport and High Speed Two (HS2) Ltd.[424] The High Speed Rail (West Midlands – Crewe) Act 2021 disapplies section 59 of the Planning (Listed Buildings and Conservation Areas) Act 1990 (P(LPCA) A 1990) with respect to committing any offence where harm is caused to a listed building. In a table it sets out the details of removal of listed structures and their reinstallation when work is completed.[425]

7.8.1.2 Rescue Archaeology and Archaeological Archives

Cultural heritage objects of archaeological interest, or the remains of cultural heritage places, may be discovered during building development work. It is recognised that these sites need to be cared for through investigation by trained archaeologists; consequently, an opportunity is provided for them to do so before the development progresses. This is clear from the National Planning Policy Framework (NPPF), which requires developers 'to record and advance understanding of the significance of any heritage assets to be lost (wholly or in part) in a manner proportionate to their importance and the impact, and to make this evidence (and any archive generated) publicly accessible'.[426] It is clear though that 'the ability to record evidence of our past should not be a factor in deciding whether such loss should be permitted'.[427] The archives can lead to an abundance of cultural heritage and there are very practical difficulties, at times, in maintaining the large archives of material generated from these reactive excavations.[428] Historic England and ACE are working with other partners to initiate the Future Archaeological Archives Programme to tackle this problem.[429]

In some cases, as part of the design of new developments, archaeological remains are incorporated within the framework of modern buildings and may be opened up to the public.[430] Where human remains are discovered during archaeological excavations, the approach taken in recent years has been that, even if the excavation site was not previously used as a burial ground, a licence for exhumation is required from the Ministry of Justice under the Burial Act 1857.[431] The grant of a licence is usually made subject to a condition that any human remains discovered should be reburied within a particular timeframe and at

---

[424] High Speed Rail (London-West Midlands), *Environmental Minimum Requirements Annex 3: Heritage Memorandum* (February 2017).

[425] The High Speed Rail (West Midlands – Crewe) Act 2021, sch. 15, table 1.

[426] Ministry of Housing, Communities and Local Government, *NPPF* (2021), para. 205.

[427] ibid. 'Copies of evidence should be deposited with the relevant historic environment record, and any archives with a local museum or other public depository': NPPF 2021, para. 205.

[428] See for example, Planning for Archives: Opportunities and Omissions: Historic England Project Code: 7756 *End of Project Report* (2019): https://historicengland.org.uk/images-books/publications/planning-for-archives/planning-for-archives/ (last accessed 22 May 2023).

[429] Historic England, *Future for Archaeological Archives Programme (FAAP)* https://historicengland.org.uk/research/support-and-collaboration/future-for-archaeological-archives-programme/ (last accessed 24 May 2023).

[430] E.g. the archaeological remains of the Rose Theatre in London and the London Mithraeum under the Bloomberg Building.

[431] Under section 25.

a particular location. It was for this reason that the remains of Richard III were reinterred in Leicester, at the cathedral, which was in keeping with the terms of the licence originally granted by the Ministry of Justice.[432]

7.8.1.3 Maintaining Associations

Provision is made to ensure that particular associations (between cultural heritage objects, places or people) are retained which might otherwise be lost when something is being designated as cultural heritage or one of its synonyms. When a pre-eminent cultural object is accepted in lieu of tax, it is taken out of the private domain and enters the public domain.[433] One implication of this shift across the public/private divide is that an object may lose its context, or its association with a particular place, thus risking harm to the cultural heritage. For that reason, when allocating an object that has been accepted in lieu of tax under the UK-wide scheme, the Secretary of State can take into account any significant association with the place and if it is appropriate for the object, collection or group to be kept in that place then the Secretary of State can allocate it accordingly, thus maintaining that association.[434] To assist them in making the decision, the Secretary of State can obtain expert advice.[435] Ultimately, it may remain at the object's original location, with its previous owner, to ensure that the association with the place remains, providing that sufficient public access is provided.[436]

Although not developed as a scheme with the aim of caring for cultural heritage, the concept of heirlooms provides a means of retaining associations between places or families.[437] Heirlooms, properly so-called, are chattels that, through legal drafting, were effectively annexed to the land and therefore passed with the land on death; they could only be sold with permission of the court.[438] The law relating to heirlooms developed in such a way that it was possible for the court to order the sale of heirlooms by the tenant for life (who had mere enjoyment of them).[439] Nevertheless, the courts were sympathetic to

---

[432] R (on the application of Plantagenet Alliance Ltd.) v. Secretary of State for Justice, the University of Leicester and others [2014] EWHC 1662 (QB) 23 May 2014.

[433] At Section 5.2.15.

[434] IHTA 1984, s. 230(5). Although when it comes to objects with a Scottish interest, the Scottish Ministers exercise separate functions under IHTA 1984, s. 230(7). See Section 5.2.5.

[435] NHA 1980, s. 9(5).

[436] The Secretary of State will obtain appropriate expert advice relating to the 'significant association with a particular place': ibid., s. 9(5). The requirement for the owner of the associated building (usually the previous owner of the object which has been given in satisfaction of tax) would undertake to care, maintain and preserve the object in addition to providing sufficient public access: HM Revenue & Customs, Capital Taxation and the National Heritage (2017), para. 11.33.

[437] The uniqueness of the Hope Diamond, which was an heirloom, and its link with a family was discussed at Section 5.2.6.3.

[438] Under the Settled Land Act 1925, s. 67. See 'The Sale of Heirlooms' (1932) 73 The Law Journal 185. They can no longer be created as settlements: Trusts of Land and Appointment of Trustees Act 1995, s. 4(1).

[439] Norma Dawson, '"Heirlooms": The Evolution of a Legal Concept' (2000) 51 Northern Ireland Legal Quarterly 1.

associations between objects and particular places and the links with particular families.[440] Therefore, the associative value of the object to the land could be recognised where delivery up was considered in respect of heirlooms.[441]

7.8.1.4 Where There Is Disposal of an Object from a Collection

The sequential approach adopted by the consistory court to determine how a church treasure might be disposed of from a Church of England church was considered in the context of how that creates a national community of care.[442] This seeks to mitigate harm when an object in a church is to be disposed of, by prioritising public access and maintaining it in the public domain, with sales to a private purchaser seen as a last resort.[443] A similar sequential approach to disposal is found in the context of those museums who have a power to transfer an object out of their collection.[444] In the the MA's toolkit, *Off the Shelf*[445] priority is given to retaining objects within the public domain with a gift or gratuitous transfer to another accredited museum or a gift or gratuitous transfer to another public domain organisation which might not be an accredited museum but which would provide regular public access.[446] In the case of the potential disposal of cultural heritage objects that have been donated to a museum, return of an object to the donor is only appropriate after offering it first to a public domain organisation.[447] The next consideration is whether to sell the object within the public domain or to transfer it to a museum outside the UK.[448] Only after considering all of these options would it be appropriate to consider a transfer, or a sale, outside the public domain.[449] In limited situations it might be necessary to recycle or destroy an item.[450] The clear thread weaving through these passages of *Off the Shelf* is the importance of museums acting altruistically in the first instance (by transferring or gifting an object) and the importance of keeping things in the public domain, thereby ensuring more widespread access to cultural heritage objects. Whilst the principles set out in the *Off the Shelf* are not mandatory, they are nevertheless recognised as central to implementing the presumption against disposal set out in the Code of Ethics of the Museums

---

[440] *In re Hope* [1899] 2 Ch 679, 690 (Romer LJ).   [441] *Pusey* v. *Pusey* (1684) 1 Vern 273 (Ch).

[442] Section 5.2.5. Specifically the approach set out in *Re St Lawrence, Wootton* [2015] Fam 27, 54 (Arches Court).

[443] See Section 5.2.5. The Church in Wales adopts a similar sequential approach and its policy makes clear that '[o]pportunities for the loan of a treasure to an appropriate institution, such as a national museum, should also be considered to avoid outright disposal': The Church in Wales, *Contents of Churches: Policy and Guidance*, para. 6, 23 August 2019.

[444] This would be non-national museums, which are not governed by the statutes that prevent transfer.

[445] Which was produced by the Museums Association *Off the Shelf: A Toolkit for Ethical Transfer, Reuse and Disposal* (2023). Specific disposals guidance is also provided by ICOM: *Guidelines on Deaccessioning of the International Council of Museums* (2019).

[446] *Off the Shelf*, p. 22.   [447] ibid., p. 24.   [448] ibid., pp. 24 & 26.   [449] ibid., p. 26.

[450] ibid., pp. 27 & 29.

Association (MA), which both their institutional and individual members have undertaken to uphold.[451]

The care provided here seeks to maximise the chance of continued public access to the cultural heritage. It thus ensures that there is no breach of the public's trust by making a short-term financial gain at the expense of longer-term public access. Any loss of access is therefore very much a last resort.

On occasions the government may need to dispose of cultural heritage. Traditionally sales of government assets should maximise receipts. The *Disposal of Heritage Assets: Guidance note for government departments and non-departmental public bodies*[452] applies to central government, government departments and non-departmental public bodies for which they are responsible as well as some executive agencies. Although not binding on the wider public sector as a whole, it represents best practice for them and would therefore apply to local authorities and public corporations.[453] It recognises in the case of sales of heritage assets that the aim should not be one of maximising receipts, but of achieving the best value for money for the taxpayer and that this can take into account the wider recognition of the cultural benefit,[454] the recognition that the most appropriate long-term use of the heritage asset is not necessarily the one that generates the most money[455] and government policy on the historic environment.[456] However, it is clear that special disposal procedures may be applied in exceptional cases 'to secure appropriate ownership, repair or use of the asset'.[457] The methods of sale discussed here are by means of a competitive tender process, rather than a sale by auction. In exceptional cases a sale by private treaty may be allowed. It is clear that if a heritage asset is to be transferred to the private sector, a statement of significance needs to be provided as well as an explanation about the restrictions that are going to be placed on its use. Bidders would need to show how they were going to make use of the heritage assets in both heritage and service terms.[458] The emphasis here is on keeping heritage assets in good repair and in use, in preference to being mothballed.[459] It is clear as well that the guidance is alive to the concern of separating the ownership of heritage sites if this has the potential to damage the integrity of the sites.[460]

---

[451] As to the risk of making financially motivated sales on the sanctions for non-compliance with the Code of Ethics, see Section 3.7.5.2.

[452] Produced by English Heritage, the Office of Government Commerce (OGC) and the DCMS (it was confirmed or reissued by Historic England), 2010: https://historicengland.org.uk/images-books/publications/disposal-heritage-assets/guidance-disposals-final-jun-10/ (last accessed 30 May 2023).

[453] *Disposal of Heritage Assets*, p. 1.   [454] ibid., pp. 8 and 20.   [455] ibid., p. 20.

[456] ibid., p. 20.   [457] ibid., p. 17.   [458] ibid., p. 9.   [459] ibid., p. 9.   [460] ibid., p. 18.

7.8.2 Restoration and Repair

A key difficulty in caring for cultural heritage places is in identifying the appropriate way in which to respond to physical harm and how to repair this.[461] Historic England's approach to repair is a conservative one which has the aim of retaining as much of this 'significant historic fabric' as possible, keeping changes to a minimum.[462] It recognises that the 'unnecessary replacement of historic fabric, no matter how carefully the work is carried out, will in most situations have an adverse effect on character and significance'.[463]

It has already been shown how the listed buildings and scheduled monuments regimes ensure that no work is carried out on an historic asset without consent having been obtained.[464] This has the effect of ensuring that restoration of designated heritage assets is subject to control and review, carried out in accordance with appropriate principles relating to repair, such as the Historic England document. In determining the specifics of the appropriate care, the advice of communities of experts will be drawn on, and the wider public community also have opportunities to contribute their views on the planned work.[465]

There is no direct legal regulation of restoration, repair and conservation work more generally in the UK; however, the British Standards associated with certain aspects of heritage work provide further nested practices of care which encourage appropriate care of cultural heritage.[466] Furthermore, there is an accreditation scheme for conservators,[467] and professional codes of ethics which the members of the Institute of Conservation (ICON), agree to abide by which support this community of care in the care of cultural heritage.[468] In the case of the Church of England, there is direct control over any restoration and repair work that might be undertaken. Whether the proposed work is on a listed or an unlisted building, or on cultural heritage objects such as bells, permission must be sought from the consistory court and work can only be carried out once the court has granted a faculty giving such permission.[469] Much of the day-to-day care of cultural heritage would be undertaken by the local community, that is to say the parish, in the form of willing volunteers of that community. Nevertheless, mechanisms are in place to ensure that any care provided is appropriate in the circumstances. This system of checks and balances – the consistory court – is an important one, for it ensures that where communities assume responsibility for care it can be ensured that the care is appropriate and does not cause damage to the cultural heritage in question.

---

[461] In some cases it may be necessary for 'nature to take its course' and 'we perhaps need to develop modes of care that help us negotiate the transition between presence and absence': Caitlin DeSilvey, *Curated Decay*, p.179.

[462] Historic England, *Principles of Repair for Historic Buildings* (updated 17 September 2018): https://historicengland.org.uk/advice/technical-advice/buildings/principles-of-repair-for-historic-buildings/ (last accessed 22 May 2023).

[463] ibid.   [464] See Section 7.4.1.   [465] See Section 7.4.1.2.   [466] See Section 3.7.8.1.

[467] ICON, *Accreditation* www.icon.org.uk/accreditation.html (last accessed 24 May 2023).

[468] The Institute of Conservation, *Ethical Guidance* (2020).

[469] Canons of the Church of England, canon F13.

The judicial community of care therefore ensures that the cultural heritage is available to enjoy by current generations, as well as to pass on to future generations.

7.8.3 The Ethics of Rebuilding

In the previous section, the discussion of restoration and repair was set in the context of situations where objects or elements of places are repaired, often as a response to deterioration that has taken place over time. In some situations, catastrophic events such as fires may have caused such irreparable harm that repairing the existing fabric is impossible since entire elements of the cultural heritage have been destroyed. This raises difficult questions about how far these places or objects should be rebuilt or reconstructed.[470] These include the potential risk to the cultural heritage's authenticity and integrity, as well as concerns about any rebuilding creating a pastiche of the original. The cultural heritage place itself, and its use, may be so fundamentally important that it will be necessary to contemplate rebuilding the entire place rather than simply rebuilding lost elements of the building. This then leads to questions about how this should be rebuilt, whether it is to the style of the place immediately before the harm, or whether it is to the specifications of the building in a particular era. Principles found in guidance documents such as the ICOMOS Dresden Declaration[471] and *Historic England's Approach to the Reconstruction of Heritage Assets*[472] inform decisions about rebuilding. This latter document emphasises that reconstruction will not always be appropriate, for example, if a lack of information inhibits credible reconstruction, 'when any elements of the significance of the asset may be unnecessarily damaged or lost', 'when the fact of loss or damage is of high significance' and 'when (a) key stakeholder(s) do not support reconstruction'.[473] Central to a decision about the appropriateness of reconstruction is consideration of the aspects of the significance of what has been lost, what might be gained from reconstruction, and the particular views of communities who object to the reconstruction. The terminology of stakeholders[474] is used and it is of particular

---

[470] See Gareth Harris, 'The Glasgow School of Art Dilemma: Rebuild, Leave in Ruins or Design a Whole New School?', *The Art Newspaper*, 10 July 2018.

[471] The Declaration of Dresden on the Reconstruction of Monuments Destroyed by War (ICOMOS, 1982): www.icomos.org/en/charters-and-texts/179-articles-en-francais/ressources/charters-and-standards/184-the-declaration-of-dresden (last accessed 22 May 2023).

[472] https://historicengland.org.uk/advice/planning/the-reconstruction-of-heritage-assets/historic-englands-approach/ (last accessed 22 May 2023).

[473] ibid.

[474] Legget's working definition of stakeholders was 'Museum stakeholders are individuals or organisations who have an interest in, or influence on, a museum's ability to achieve its objectives': Jane Legget, 'Shared Heritage, Shared Authority, Shared Accountability? Co-generating Museum Performance Criteria as a Means of Embedding "Shared Authority"' (2018) 24 *International Journal of Heritage Studies* 723, 724. This terminology is also found in MA documents.

note that even if one of those stakeholders is unsupportive, this may lead to a decision that reconstruction is inappropriate.[475] Following the fire at Windsor Castle in 1992 a Restoration Committee, chaired by the Duke of Edinburgh, considered the different possibilities regarding restoration. Whilst some rooms were restored to their '14th century appearance, but with a 20th-century reinterpretation' (St George's Hall), in other cases rooms that had been destroyed in the fire were replaced with entirely new rooms, for example, the Lantern Lobby took the place of the private chapel.[476] There are arguments in favour of leaving a place as a modern ruin, rather than rebuilding it, as is the case with the decision in 2022 taken by the National Trust to leave Clandon Park as a modern ruin following the fire that took hold in 2015 to give visitors 'a unique "X-ray view" of how country houses were made'.[477]

In some cases fires may occur during restoration works.[478] Difficult questions then arise about the appropriateness of the care that was provided and whether there were failings in how the risk of harm from fire was dealt with. The Culture, Tourism, Europe and External Affairs Committee of the Scottish Parliament investigated the two fires at the Glasgow School of Art and raised questions about governance. Particular problems occur where buildings have multiple purposes. This issue was identified in the case of Glasgow School of Art because the buildings were used for the purposes of a practising educational establishment in which students necessarily made use of various materials, some of which were highly flammable. The buildings also formed a museum and a cultural heritage place which communities hoped to be able to pass on to future generations. This particular case serves to demonstrate the tensions that arise when determining the appropriate care for a cultural heritage place. To ensure the continued use of the place, this requires a balancing exercise to be undertaken with the place's long-term survival, ensuring that future communities of care who will also care about it will have access to it.

7.8.4 Physical Relocation

Often the in situ preservation of cultural heritage is seen as the paramount concern.[479] In many situations this will ensure that particular cultural heritage places such as archaeological sites (whether underwater or underground)

---

[475] *Historic England's Approach to the Reconstruction of Heritage Assets.*

[476] Royal Collection Trust, *The Fire at Windsor Castle*: www.rct.uk/visit/windsor-castle/the-fire-at-windsor-castle#/ (last accessed 22 May 2023).

[477] National Trust, *Clandon Park* www.nationaltrust.org.uk/visit/surrey/clandon-park/index (last accessed 24 May 2023).

[478] For example the Glasgow School of Art and Cutty Sark: www.rmg.co.uk/cutty-sark/history/fire (last accessed 22 May 2023) and Uppark in 1989: www.nationaltrust.org.uk/uppark-house-and-garden/features/the-fire-at-uppark (last accessed 22 May 2023).

[479] For example, the *Agreement Concerning the Shipwrecked Vessel RMS Titanic* (2003), which recognised that '*in situ* preservation is the most effective way of ensuring such protection, unless otherwise justified by education, scientific or cultural interests', Preamble.

continue to benefit from their context and that important elements of them are not harmed. In the case of cultural heritage objects, keeping them in place may ensure that there is no loss of association between those objects and other objects within a collection or the association between an object and the place. However, in some situations it may not be possible to maintain this association because of development.

One way in which it may be possible to avert irreparable physical harm to buildings is by relocating them elsewhere. Some might be moved to a location relatively close by, but others may be relocated across borders. This happened during the Nubian Campaign, where the temple complex of Abu Simbel was dismantled and moved further up the hill, whereas the Temple of Dendur was removed from Abu Simbel and reconstructed in the Metropolitan Museum, New York.[480] In some cases entire buildings are relocated to outdoor museums whose primary purpose is to care for dislocated cultural heritage buildings. In Wales this includes St Fagan's Museum and in England the Black Country Museum in the West Midlands and the Weald and Downland Museum. Other museums such as the Crich Tramway Museum in Derbyshire house heritage trams, but also relocated buildings and street furniture. Whilst these efforts ensure the physical preservation of the fabric of the building, they do not succeed in maintaining the intangible association or connection with its original place of location. However, this association can be brought to the public's attention through labels setting out the narrative about a building's past use and location displayed with it in its new location. It may take many years for the reconstruction of some buildings or interiors in their original settings (or at least somewhere near to the original location). Temple Bar was removed from the Strand in 1878 and only returned to London in 2004 when it was installed in Paternoster Square. This followed a campaign spanning many years by the Temple Bar Trust (which was created as a community of care solely for the purpose of returning and relocating Temple Bar to the City of London).[481] Entire interiors of rooms from country houses were sometimes kept intact, but moved and reconstructed elsewhere, including in museums.[482]

Where the Secretary of State or Historic England are guardians of monuments under the AMAAA 1979 they have the express power 'to remove the whole or part of a monument to another place for the purpose of preserving it'.[483] This could be interpreted as giving the power to relocate it on a permanent basis if that is clearly necessary for the purpose of preserving it.

---

[480] See Cyril Aldred, *Temple of Dendur* (Metropolitan Museum of Art Bulletin, Summer 1978).

[481] 'The return of Temple Bar to the City of London': www.thetemplebar.info/history.html (last accessed 30 May 2023).

[482] See generally, John Harris, *Moving Rooms: The Trade in Architectural Salvages* (Paul Mellon Centre for Studies in British Art, London: Yale University Press, 2007). In some cases, these were ultimately returned to their original location, for example Sizergh Castle's interior which was transferred by the V&A, see Section 7.3.2.2.

[483] AMAAA 1979, s. 13(4)(c).

7.8.5 Digital Record

Where harm has been sanctioned, either in the form of the destruction of a particular place or the sale of an object on the open market, where there is a risk of loss of public access, it may be possible to mitigate the loss of information by making a digital record of the cultural heritage concerned. This could be in the form of photographs of the object or place in situ, or through the recording of information about the cultural heritage and its provenance. However, Historic England has cautioned that the potential to reconstruct a heritage asset or to create comprehensive digital records does not, by itself, provide valid justifications for demolition or for permitting a cultural heritage place to fall into a state of disrepair.[484]

In several consistory court cases the chancellor has made the granting of a faculty subject to a condition that a digital record is created, or in some cases that a replica is made. Maintaining a record, 'in writing and by photography', of a cup and cruet was clearly seen as a means of diminishing the loss that would happen if they were sold, which was identified as 'the loss of a piece of history' and 'the loss of connexion with a particular family' as well as the 'lost opportunity to demonstrate by reference to the physical object the variation in the practice of holy communion at a particular time in the history of the church in this area'.[485] In the case of *Re St Bartholomew's, Aldbrough*[486] it was said that '[b]y severing the ownership of the helmet from the ownership of the tomb there is, of course, a further step in the separation, but this I think can be mitigated by appropriate records being made of the provenance of both items and their historical connection'.[487]

Replicas can also assist in mitigating harm. In *Re Oldland St Ann*,[488] where a faculty confirming the loan of a painting to Bristol Museum and Art Gallery was approved, the Chancellor also stated that: '[a] high quality copy of the painting is to be provided in a suitable frame by the Museum. There is to be a plaque placed by the painting setting out a brief history of the painting.'[489] By requiring the display of both a replica and the narrative about the cultural heritage object, this sought to mitigate the harm that might be caused by disposal.

The Export Reviewing Committee can recommend that an export licence is granted, but that a digital or photographic copy of it is made available to the British Library for the purposes of scholarship. Provision is made for such a copy to be made, but access to it is embargoed for a period of seven years after the licence has been granted.[490] The seven-year requirement is aimed at ensuring that the owner of the cultural heritage object can commercially exploit it. The information that was contained in the object is then made available to scholars after a period of seven years. However, in certain

---

[484] *Historic England's Approach to the Reconstruction of Heritage Assets.*
[485] *St John the Baptist, Stainton-by-Langworth*, 9 Ecc LJ 144, 13 April 2006 (unreported), para. 22.
[486] [1990] 3 All ER 440.   [487] ibid., 454.   [488] [2017] ECC Bri 2.   [489] ibid., para. 26.
[490] ACE Notice, para. 14.

exceptional circumstances the Reviewing Committee has recommended that a copy should be made available immediately, rather than having to wait the full seven years. This can be seen in the case of a Cartulary of St Peter's Benedictine Abbey Chertsey when it was exported to the National Library of Australia.[491]

7.8.6 Harm to the Owners

At times, communities of care may require designated heritage assets to be cared for in a particular way that is at odds with the interests of private owners. Here the public interest in the care of cultural heritage intersects with the private interest of cultural heritage *qua* property. In the context of listed buildings the relational nature of care is evident in the recognition that the needs of owners or occupiers of the building must be balanced with the needs of the wider community. For that reason, provision is made for the purchase of listed buildings where the refusal of listed building consent or the granting of consent on conditional grounds means that the building and land 'have become incapable of reasonably beneficial use in their existing state'.[492] Therefore, rather than an owner being burdened by unusable property, this can be purchased from them.

7.9 Conclusion

Harm has been understood in this chapter to include physical harm to physical things, but also harm to the intangible elements of cultural heritage and to intangible cultural heritage, as well as harm to the communities for whom it is important. In some cases, precautionary efforts are made to establish frameworks of care which will provide appropriate care in the event of certain eventualities such as war. Having the foresight to instrumentally use law to create collections also ensures that it is more difficult to separate objects from the collections of which they form part, ensuring that they are kept together. This can thereby maintain their association, as a collection, or with a particular place. Preventative care frameworks, which set out the responsibilities of the public and the responsibilities of those who own cultural heritage places, backed up with the force of criminal law, provide a means of discouraging both physical harm and harm to the setting of heritage places. It is a highly intrusive framework, because firstly it affects the private owners of neighbouring properties where developments may affect the heritage assets concerned,

---

[491] *Report of the Reviewing Committee on the Export of Works of Art* 1974–75, 21st Report, Cmd 6624, Case (v) 'A Cartulary of St Peter's Benedictine Abbey Chertsey'. This was accompanied by a condition that the National Library of Australia also make the Cartulary available to the British Library when it was required by them for research and exhibition purposes: para. 151.

[492] P(LBCA)A 1990, s. 32(2)(a); Planning (Listed Buildings and Conservation Areas) (Scotland) Act 1997, s. 25(1); Planning Act (Northern Ireland) 2011, s. 181 and AMAAA 1979, s. 7.

and secondly has the strength of criminal sanctions. Other preventative care frameworks are used to encourage reporting of finds of archaeological objects and shipwrecks with associated cultural heritage. But it is clear that individual initiatives can provide very targeted and appropriate care for cultural heritage. Whilst the legal recognition in the UK of intangible cultural heritage is rather limited, it is nevertheless possible to see the recognition of certain practices as intangible cultural heritage and the provision of care for them through the use of individual statutes relating to things as diverse as cheese, whisky and tweed. Yet public participation initiatives also contribute to the overall care of cultural heritage. Furthermore, alerting communities of care to the risk of potential harm to particular cultural heritage can also facilitate responsive care.

Despite all these efforts, made in advance, to care for cultural heritage and to prevent harm, sometimes care needs to be provided to cultural heritage reactively rather than proactively. This can be done by making use of existing frameworks, such as seeking to list a building when it is at risk of demolition, with the aim of preventing it from being destroyed. However, whilst there is hope in individualised schemes to care for cultural heritage, there are significant gaps in coverage, such as consistent mechanisms to deal with the illicit trade in cultural heritage.

Communities have an important role to play in navigating harm; they are consulted in the case of any development to cultural heritage places themselves or to nearby places where that development may risk its setting. Legal challenges can be mounted in the event that the relevant communities are not consulted, or if the fruits of that consultation are not taken into consideration appropriately when a decision is made. The very practical issue to do with the effectiveness of these consultations is a matter for other research to ensure that consultation is meaningful and that participation is not merely tokenistic. However, structurally mechanisms are in place for various communities to be listened to through mechanisms of dialogic, respectful and empathetic care. These communities include local communities, expert communities of care and wider communities for whom the cultural heritage is important and for whom taking an active part in the care of cultural heritage is important.

8

The Rhetoric of Saving for the Nation

8.1 Introduction

The rhetoric of 'saving for the nation', frequently used to refer to attempts to prevent cultural objects from being sold to overseas collectors, is reflected in the UK's export licensing system through which objects are designated as 'national treasures'. The system encourages the UK's national community to care about particularly important cultural heritage, even though they may not have previously been aware of it and are now entreated to care for it, by saving it from 'loss' to the UK public. The potential loss is not necessarily a loss to the wider international public, for the proposal may be for the object to enter a public collection overseas.

The export system demonstrates how the UK (through a developed policy since 1952[1] and initially as part of the export controls during and after the Second World War[2]) cares *about* the potential loss of cultural heritage to the UK public. Yet, it does not necessarily demonstrate the most appropriate care *for* cultural heritage as it fails to take account of whether cultural heritage might be more appropriately cared for by a community abroad. To untangle the extent to which the export licensing system, aimed at 'saving objects for the nation', cares for cultural heritage this chapter analyses how national treasures are identified and designated, and the nature of care provided. After setting out the background to, and outlining the overall process of, designating national treasures within the UK export licensing system, it proceeds to analyse the rhetoric of 'saving'. To this end it focuses on what the rhetoric of saving refers to, and from whom the cultural object is being saved. The next part analyses the relational nature of the care provided as well as the communities who are recognised within the system. This is followed by analysis of how the public and other parties participate in the process, and of the assumption of responsibility for care, particularly the moral dimension to this. Overall, this chapter analyses the extent to which the relational nature of the care for cultural

---

[1] Originating from the Report of the Committee on the Export of Works of Art 1952 (chaired by Viscount Waverley).

[2] See Vivian F. Wang, 'Whose Responsibility? The Waverley System, Past and Present' (2008) 15 *International Journal of Cultural Property* 227.

heritage is recognised, and the extent to which care that enhances the flourishing of cultural heritage is manifested in the export licensing system.

8.1.1 The Origin of 'National Treasures'

As part of the UK's system of export licensing, cultural objects are reviewed with the aim of 'saving objects for the nation' by restricting the export of those identified as 'national treasures'. As far back as 1883 the term 'national treasures' was used in the context of objects in private collections (specifically manuscripts) about which there was a public interest – for they 'may indeed be justly regarded in the light of a national treasure'.[3] The Curzon Report in 1915 set out the problem of private collections being sold off abroad and the 'cry of lamentation' at 'each diminution in the national treasure'.[4] Here, the cries clearly demonstrated the feeling of attendant loss, even in situations where the public may never before have engaged directly with the objects. Despite the absence of any previous relationship between the national community and the object, an expert community of care, acting on behalf of the national community, has a general concern about the future loss of access within national borders. Often the possibility of loss excites a realisation of how important something is and of the need to take action to avert its loss.

The first formal control of the export of artworks was one element of the wider export restrictions introduced during the Second World War, aimed at preventing the depletion of resources through export.[5] However, the application of export restrictions to artworks also came 'at the end of a long period of anxiety' caused by the depletion of private collections and the export of them abroad[6] rather than being introduced to 'safeguard our national treasures'.[7] The early twentieth century saw a raft of sales by the landed gentry of the land forming their estates as well as their contents, often to meet large death duties. However, the export regime introduced during the Second World War, and refined following the report of the Waverley Committee in 1952, was responsive to the potential loss of artworks, rather than proactive[8] in the sense of providing disincentives for sale of pre-identified objects to private individuals and export.[9] As expressed in the

---

[3] HMSO, Historical Manuscripts Commission, Calendar of the Manuscripts of the Most Hon the Marquis of Salisbury, preserved at Hatfield House, Hertfordshire, 1883 C-3777, p. iii.

[4] Report of the Committee of Trustees of the National Gallery appointed by the Trustees to Enquire into the retention of Important Pictures in this Country and other matters connected with the national art collections, 1915, p. 4.

[5] For a history to the export licensing scheme see Wang, 'Whose Responsibility?'.

[6] Waverley Report, p. 2.

[7] Appendix A of history of export controls: *Export of Works of Art 2008–2009*, 55th Report, p. 58.

[8] The possibility of establishing a list of privately owned cultural heritage objects which might be acquired over the years has been rejected on the basis of the potential interference with the private property rights of owners (usually with the attendant financial impact on the value of the objects) and the art market for those objects: Her Majesty's Treasury, *Report of the Committee on The Export of Works of Art Etc.* (London: HMSO, 1952) (Waverley Committee Report), p. 22.

[9] As a counterbalance to this is more proactive means of accepting pre-eminent objects in satisfaction of tax. See Section 5.2.15.

Cottesloe Report of 1964, the system of export deferrals of national treasures gives a chance for them to be saved for the nation and 'is a matter of seizing fleeting opportunities that will not recur'.[10] There is therefore an urgency to the process; simply because an object is designated as a national treasure does not mean that it will be saved for the nation, since rather than being a system of 'a mandatory right of pre-emption',[11] it instead defers the granting of an export licence to give an opportunity for a purchaser to be found who will provide sufficient public access. The opportunity to purchase the object may come out of the blue, and require rapid fundraising to secure significant funds to purchase the object. Therefore, the system is a 'trigger mechanism', providing 'one final period of time for the acquisition of items which are judged to be national treasures and whose export would be a misfortune'.[12] It is seen as a 'safety net'[13] or 'tripwire'[14] and very much as a system of 'last resort'.[15] Until more recently the ecclesiastical (consistory) court relied on the export licensing system as a backstop when it was considering whether to grant faculties to sell church treasures.[16] The consistory court had previously not seen its role as being to protect national heritage, but instead relied on the secular system of reviewing cultural heritage objects against the Waverley Criteria to prevent the ultimate loss abroad.[17] The court was therefore trusting this system to successfully avert loss, yet, as discussed above, the system of designating objects as national treasures is centred on museums or other potential purchasers having to seize opportunities to purchase objects, possibly at times when funding might not be readily available. However, as was apparent in earlier chapters, in several recent cases, rather than relying on the export system to prevent the loss of national treasure, the consistory court has been more proactive in recognising its responsibilities to the national community. It has therefore focused on averting private sales from the outset as there is a risk that this might otherwise take an object out of the public domain and might potentially be lost to the nation if exported.[18]

8.1.2 The Process

When exporting objects of cultural interest from the UK, a valid export licence is required.[19] The Secretary of State has granted an open general export licence applicable to certain categories of cultural objects[20] which can be exported without

---

[10] *Report of the Committee of Enquiry into the Sale of Works of Art by Public Bodies* (London: HMSO, 1964), p. 17.

[11] *Export of Works of Art 2008–2009*, 55th Report, p. 15.   [12] ibid.

[13] *Export of Works of Art 2000–2001*, 47th Report, Cm 5311, para. 5 and *Export of Objects of Cultural Interest 2016–17*, 63rd Report, Foreword by Secretary of State, p. 5.

[14] *Export of Objects of Cultural Interest 2007–08*, 54th Report, Appendix A.

[15] *Export of Objects of Cultural Interest 2009–10*, 56th Report, p. 11.   [16] See Section 5.2.5.

[17] ibid.

[18] See, for example, *Re St Lawrence, Wootton* [2015] Fam 27 (Arches Court). Discussed at ibid.

[19] Export of Objects of Cultural Interest (Control) Order 2003, SI 2003/2759, art. 2. Exports from Northern Ireland to non-EU countries also require an EU licence.

[20] Open General Export Licence (Objects of Cultural Interest) dated 1 January 2021 granted by the Secretary of State: https://www.artscouncil.org.uk/media/16340/download?attachment (last accessed 26 May 2023).

the need for an individual licence. Additionally, certain individuals or institutions have open individual export licences which allow them to export objects under this without having to apply to Arts Council England (ACE) for each object.[21] For cultural objects not falling within these categories, applications for export licences must be sought from ACE,[22] whether the export is temporary or permanent.[23] Where an object has been in the UK for a period of 50 years or more[24] and meets certain prescribed financial thresholds[25] it may be referred to an Expert Adviser[26] who applies the Waverley Criteria[27] to assess whether the object might be considered as a national treasure.[28] These criteria, which were established by the Waverley Committee of 1952, and later amended,[29] comprise three separate questions: '(1) Is [the object] so closely connected with our history and national life that its departure would be a misfortune? (2) Is it of outstanding aesthetic importance? (3) Is it of outstanding significance for the study of some particular branch of art, learning or history?'[30] Where the Expert Adviser concludes that an object satisfies one or more of the Criteria and objects to the granting of an export licence, they refer the matter to the Export Reviewing Committee (a group of independent experts established as a non-statutory body[31]) for consideration.[32] Where the Committee concludes that the object meets one or more of the three Criteria it can then recommend a period of deferral to the Secretary of State, who may follow this recommendation[33] and defer the grant of an export licence to allow time for a UK-based purchaser to come forward to offer to purchase it at the fair market price determined by the Committee. If the owner receives an offer to

---

[21] See ACE Notice, para. 7.

[22] ACE administers the export licensing system, and in particular it exercises the functions prescribed by articles 2 and 3 of the Export of Objects of Cultural Interest (Control) Order 2003 on behalf of Secretary of State. This happens by virtue of the Contracting Out (Functions in Relation to Cultural Objects) Order 2005, SI 2005/1103, arts. 2(c) and 3.

[23] Many national museums will have Open Individual Export licences allowing them to export objects for up to three years to lend objects to museums abroad: ACE Notice, para. 7.

[24] The Export of Objects of Cultural Interest (Control) Order 2003, art. 2, sch. 1.

[25] Set out in Table 2 of the Open General Export Licence: www.artscouncil.org.uk/sites/default/files/download-file/UK%20OGEL%20Value%20limits.pdf (last accessed 26 May 2023).

[26] This is 'usually a director, senior keeper or curator in a national museum or gallery': ACE Notice, para. 10.

[27] These were named after Viscount Waverley, who chaired the 1952 Committee appointed by the Treasury. See generally Wang, 'Whose Responsibility?'.

[28] DCMS, *Export Controls on Objects of Cultural Interest: Statutory Guidance on the Criteria to be Taken into Consideration When Making a Decision about Whether or Not to Grant an Export Licence* (London: DCMS, 2020), para, 16.

[29] By the Quinquennial Review of the Reviewing Committee on the Export of Works of Art, DCMS. This is now set out in ibid., para. 12.

[30] These now form part of the statutory guidance provided under the Export Control Act 2002, s. 9(3).

[31] ACE, *UK Export Licensing for Cultural Goods: Procedures and Guidance for Exporters of Works of Art and Other Cultural Goods* (ACE Notice, 2021), para. 36.

[32] ibid., para. 40.

[33] The Secretary of State clearly has discretion when deciding whether or not to grant or defer the granting of an export licence although they must exercise this discretion reasonably: ibid., para. 76; specific provision is made to take into account the Committee's advice: DCMS, *Statutory Guidance*, para. 19.

purchase the object from either a public institution or a private individual (who gives an undertaking to provide appropriate levels of public access to the object[34]) and the owner refuses that offer, the Secretary of State can then refuse to grant an export licence.[35] More recently, a system of legally binding options following the first deferral period has been introduced.[36] Where there is a serious expression of interest in purchasing the object at the end of the first period, the owner can choose to enter into an option with the prospective purchaser (which would bind them to selling this).[37] If they do not enter into an option at this stage then normally the licence would be refused.[38] Where an option is granted, this would require the seller to sell to the purchaser in the event that, during the second deferral period, the purchaser successfully raises the purchase price.[39]

The success of the export licensing system depends on finding a willing purchaser with sufficient available funds, and a seller willing to accept the offer. The system arguably 'diverts [the] attention' of museums and galleries away from what they may need to acquire and creates a sense of urgency to purchase an object simply 'because it has been in this country and is now about to leave it'.[40] It does not provide any opportunity to consider the relative importance of the deferred object as compared with other objects, but instead offers a one-off opportunity to purchase an important object before it is otherwise exported abroad and 'lost' to the nation.

8.2 The Rhetoric of Saving for the Nation

The role of the Reviewing Committee and the Secretary of State's discretion to defer the granting of an export licence to allow time to purchase designated national treasures is set within the rhetoric of 'saving for the nation'. This can

---

[34] Where the export licence for a national treasure is deferred and the owner refuses an offer from a private collector who would have provided such access; in such a situation the Secretary of State will then normally refuse to grant the export licence: DCMS, *Statutory Guidance*, para. 22.

[35] DCMS, *Statutory Guidance*, para. 13. An owner could make a further application for export, which will be considered in the usual way: DCMS, *Statutory Guidance*, para. 33. If an owner were to make an application within '10 years or so of a licence having been refused' they would need to include a written statement setting out details of any change in circumstances, or other arguments in support: DCMS, *Statutory Guidance*, para. 34.

[36] There had been several examples of owners refusing to sell objects even after a matching offer had been made by a museum; in such circumstances the export licence would then be refused, but time had been wasted in fundraising efforts. The DCMS consulted on the appropriateness of introducing a requirement for owners to enter into a legally binding undertaking to sell where a matching offer has been made: DCMS, Strengthening the Process for Retaining National Treasures: Public Consultation (2018), p. 6. This was then implemented.

[37] This would be entered into following the purchaser commissioning a condition report on the object: ibid., para. 26.

[38] ibid., para. 22.   [39] ibid., para. 24.

[40] The Viscount Radcliffe, 'Spoliation by Purse' in The Viscount Radcliffe, *Not in Feather Beds: Some Collected Papers* (London: The Quality Book Club, 1968), p. 117 (originally published in *The Telegraph*).

be seen in the reports of the Reviewing Committee[41] and how press releases from the Secretary of State announce the deferral of the granting of an export licence.[42] This rhetoric is then repeated in the associated press reports[43] but is also employed by museums leading the efforts to raise the necessary funds to ultimately 'save' the object by offering to pay the purchase price.[44]

The language of 'saving' implies an element of preventing, or averting harm, and specifically the notion of removing something from actual harm or danger.[45] Therefore, the ultimate act of caring for cultural heritage in keeping it away from physical harm and safe because of its importance to the nation might come to mind. This would align with one of the elements of caring for cultural heritage identified in Chapter 1. However, it is much more difficult to position the export licensing system comfortably within the framework of care, for the focus is on saving the objects from loss of specific national access. In practice, the export of the cultural object could well result in more extensive public access abroad if it is to be displayed in a major collection, potentially free of charge. The UK system therefore appears to focus on caring about the UK's interest and prioritising it over the interests of other countries rather than on caring *for* cultural heritage in the most appropriate manner by doing so in a dialogic, empathetic and respectful manner.

What is unusual about the loss in many cases is that it is a new, potential loss of future access to an object which may never have previously been on public display. Frequently the objects that come before the Reviewing Committee have been in private collections and until then may have been unknown to the public. On some rare occasions the objects have been completely unknown to experts as well.[46] Therefore, there is often no extant access that will come to an end if the object is exported. Instead, the loss, in reality, is the loss of a chance of public access at the national level. In effect it is about fostering the future availability of specific cultural heritage and developing the connection with the

---

[41] E.g. *Export of Objects of Cultural Interest 2015–16*, 62nd Report, p. 15 in the sense of a heading 'National treasures that were not saved' and the Secretary of State thanking the Reviewing Committee for playing 'a major role in helping to save national treasures from being lost overseas': 62nd Report, p. 5.

[42] DCMS Press Release, *£10 Million Cézanne Painting at Risk of Leaving UK* (1 April 2022): www .gov.uk/government/news/10-million-cezanne-painting-at-risk-of-leaving-uk (last accessed 26 May 2023).

[43] E.g. Staff and Agencies, 'Turner Watercolour Saved for the Nation', *The Guardian*, 1 March 2007.

[44] E.g. National Gallery Press Release, *Bellotto's 'The Fortress of Königstein from the North' Acquired by the National Gallery* (22 August 2017): www.nationalgallery.org.uk/about-us/ press-and-media/press-releases/saved-for-the-nation-bellotto (last accessed 25 May 2023) and National Gallery Press Release, *Saved for the Nation: Baroque Masterpiece Goes on Display at the National Gallery* (May 2010): www.nationalgallery.org.uk/about-us/press-and-media/ press-releases/saved-for-the-nation-baroque-masterpiece-goes-on-display-at-the-national- gallery (last accessed 26 May 2023).

[45] According to the definition of 'to save': Oxford English Dictionary, save, v. 'To Rescue, Preserve, or Protect; to Make Safe': www.oed.com/view/Entry/171456? rskey=MTBrik&result=1#eid (last accessed 25 May 2023).

[46] *Export of Objects of Cultural Interest 2017–18*, 64th Report, Case 1 *The Schmadribach Waterfall near Lauterbrunnen, Switzerland by Joseph Anton Koch*, p. 18.

nation (or with the local community where the object is of importance to a particular local community within the UK[47]). The act of trying to save the object therefore focuses on bringing something which might otherwise be lost to public eyes into the public domain. At the same time it should be acknowledged that the potential loss which the act of saving is seeking to avoid is the loss of a newly created national or local connection with an object. This importance has been recognised and created by the Reviewing Committee, as an expert community of care, in its recommendation that the object satisfies the Waverley Criteria. The public may have only been aware of the object for a relatively short period of time. Indeed, the importance of the object may only have been made public once the Secretary of State accepted the Reviewing Committee's recommendation and deferred the grant of an export licence. It is only at this stage that the public may be encouraged to care *about* the cultural heritage and subsequently care *for* it, by investing both emotionally and financially in 'saving' the cultural heritage object. This might be through efforts to raise money and through direct financial contributions to public fundraising campaigns in order to purchase the object for a museum.

8.2.1 Saving What?

The category of national treasures deemed worthy of 'saving for the nation' is a superlative one with a special legal status and the language of 'treasures' suggests something beyond the ordinary cultural objects. However, there have been criticisms about how far the concept extends. The system's reach extends beyond the nationally important (in terms of the object's connection with the nation and its history or a particular national historical figure[48]). It also takes account of the object's contribution to aesthetics, learning and scholarship. These contributions, and the connections formed with the UK may apply equally between the object and other nations.[49] This led Lord Radcliffe to observe in 1959 that the notion of 'national importance' in the Waverley Report was the least convincing element.[50] He said: 'It seems simpler to say outright that we want to keep within the country the very best of whatever happens to have been brought into it in the past, and that in this context "national" denotes only its physical location.'[51]

A further factor which appears to shift the focus of 'saving for the nation' away from the ethics of care is the fact that as part of the UK's process of designating national treasures, the Reviewing Committee also considers the physical condition of the objects,[52] and seemingly is concerned about keeping *good* examples of

---

[47] As to which see Section 8.3.1.   [48] Under Waverley Criteria 1.

[49] Waverley Criteria 2 and 3. It thus focuses on maintaining a culturally rich nation, rather than a nation rich in its own culture: Charlotte Woodhead, 'Cultural Heritage Principles and Interference with Property Rights' (2011) 42 *Cambrian Law Review* 52, 65.

[50] Radcliffe, 'Spoliation by Purse', p. 117.   [51] ibid.

[52] In applying the Waverley Criteria, the Expert Adviser may take into account the condition of the object: DCMS, *Statutory Guidance*, para. 13.

national treasures, rather than *important* ones. This much is clear from situations where the Reviewing Committee recognises that an object would meet one or more of the Waverley Criteria were it not for the fact that the overall physical condition of the object was poor. Thus the Committee admitted that, despite the historical uniqueness of Titian's *Port of Giulio Romano*, its condition was insufficiently good to be designated as a national treasure.[53] Contrastingly, in the application to export *The Christening* by Hogarth, the Reviewing Committee recognised that the painting was 'not in good overall condition' but that it could still be designated as a national treasure since it satisfied Waverley Criteria 3. The grant of an export licence was accordingly deferred.[54] Applicants (who ironically may have only recently purchased the object, or who are trying to sell the object to an overseas purchaser) occasionally argue that certain repairs or infilling and repainting have spoiled paintings to such an extent that they should not be considered as national treasures.[55] In both cases, the Reviewing Committee concluded that the object satisfied the Waverley Criteria. The focus is therefore not on saving an object from harm for the purposes of passing it on to future generations, but instead on keeping hold of superlative examples.[56] Rather than the poor condition of cultural heritage encouraging action to conserve it, the nation instead occasionally abstains from treating it as a national treasure, which is seemingly the antithesis of care. The minimal intervention here with preventing physical harm reflects the broader approach to cultural heritage objects in the UK where the state interferes far less with objects than it does with places.[57]

It should not be thought that the Reviewing Committee completely ignores the physical harm to objects. It seeks to avert harm in two ways. The first is by actually refusing export licences on the basis of potential harm to the object. Only one example exists and this is in respect of a temporary export licence sought by the Royal Academy when it wanted to export the *Taddei Tondo* to the Metropolitan Museum in New York. This was refused on the grounds that there was too significant a risk of harm to this important marble relief by Michelangelo.[58] The second way in which attempts are made to avert physical harm to objects is by agreeing to curtail the public access for which a potential purchaser would be required to make an undertaking under the Ridley Rules.[59]

---

[53] *Export of Works of Art 1977–78*, 24th Report, Cm 7635, Case 19, para. 139.

[54] DCMS, *Export of Objects of Cultural Interest 2016–17*, 63rd Report, Case 9, p. 35.

[55] *Export of Works of Art 1992–93*, 39th Report, Cm 2355, Case 1 *A Painting, 'Landscape with Ruth and Boaz'*, p. 13 and *Export of Works of Art1997–98*, 44th Report, Cm 4056, Case 15 Ribera, *Girl with Tambourine*, p. 38.

[56] Having said that, there are some cases where some damage was evident but was insufficient to discount it from consideration as a national treasure: E.g. *Export of Works of Art 1992–93*, 39th Report, Cm 2355, Case 1, p. 13 and *Export of Objects of Cultural Interest 2018–19 and 2019–20*, 65th Report, Case 12 *A Tear-Shaped Bidri Tray*, p. 44.

[57] See Section 5.2.15.

[58] It is the only marble sculpture by Michelangelo in a UK collection: Royal Academy, *How to Read It: Michelangelo's Taddei Tondo By RA Collections Team* (2 April 2017).

[59] In *Export of Works of Art 1989–90*, 36th Report, Cm 1225, para. 21 the Committee noted the deterioration of Heveningham Hall since it was sold to a private purchaser and *Export of Objects*

There is also a further demonstration by the Reviewing Committee of a desire to avert physical harm, but in the specific context of the development of the Ridley Rules. These rules permit the refusal of an export licence where the owner refuses to accept an offer from a private purchaser willing to give sufficient public access. As part of the Reviewing Committee's considerations it was deemed appropriate to require such a purchaser to properly preserve the object which had been acquired as a result of the export licence deferral process.[60] The Committee differentiated between a private owner who may have purchased or inherited an object, and a purchaser who had benefited from the export licensing process and who had acquired an object which then 'come[s] within the public domain'.[61]

Nevertheless, many national museums will have Open Individual Export Licences which permit them to export objects for temporary exhibition without being subjected to the scrutiny of the Reviewing Committee. Consequently, the decision about the safety of objects depends on the national galleries being able to make an objective judgement about the potential physical harm to a cultural heritage object in circumstances where there is a financial benefit to them in lending the object abroad.[62] Thus, when the Parthenon Marble sculpture of *Ilissos* was lent to the Hermitage in 2014, the matter did not come before the Reviewing Committee.

8.2.1.1 Importance of Collections

The UK's definition of national treasures does not, by itself, facilitate saving important collections *qua* collections, since the Waverley Criteria do not require consideration of collections as a whole. However, it is clear that the Reviewing Committee cares about collections and seeks to maintain their integrity where possible. Several causes célèbres have become the focus of the Reviewing Committee's discussions on collections and to which the committee has referred back to over the years. These have included the sale of collections from Chatsworth House[63] and the George Brown Ethnography Collection sold by the University of Newcastle, where calls were made for these to remain together rather than be sold abroad.[64] The Reviewing Committee has therefore been keen

---

of *Cultural Interest 2009-10*, 56th Report, Case 11, p. 29 given the risk to the painting by Domenichino it was agreed that instead of the usual requirement under the Ridley Rules of 100 days in every year, that this requirement would be reduced to 18 months in every 5-year period.

[60] *Export of Works of Art 1989-90*, 36th Report, Cm 1225, para. 23.   [61] ibid., para. 23.

[62] The governing bodies of these institutions are under a statutory duty to consider the potential effect on the physical condition of the objects if loaned: e.g. BMA 1963, s. 4 and Museums and Galleries Act 1992, s. 5(2)(b). Furthermore, these institutions have published loans policies to which they adhere.

[63] 71 objects were sold, export licences were sought in respect of 21; whilst 13 met the standard of the Waverley Criteria, only 1 was retained: *Export of Works of Art 1984-85*, 31st Report, Cm 9818, para. 2.

[64] *Export of Works of Art 1985-86*, 32nd Report. See also Lyndel V. Prott and Patrick J. O'Keefe, *Law and the Cultural Heritage, Volume 3: Movement* (London: Butterworths, 1989), para. 933, who talk of the scale of the collection being 3,000 objects and yet only 19 met the Waverley

to encourage the development of legislation to prevent the dispersal of publicly owned collections and encouraged the Minister to pursue this.[65]

The effect of the rules is that, at times, a collection, as a whole, may not fall to be considered by the Reviewing Committee because only individual objects within the collection will satisfy the relevant financial threshold. Potentially some objects may not have been in the UK for the requisite 50 years. Consequently, some individual objects which formed part of a collection may already have left the country and the Reviewing Committee may then consider only a small remaining part of the collection against the Waverley Criteria. By this time, the integrity of the collection as a whole has been compromised and 'lost' to the nation. The current process therefore provides a gap in the necessary care of cultural heritage and hampers efforts to retain collections together. To address this, the Reviewing Committee has called for the establishment of a fourth Waverley criterion to cover collections, although it admitted that this would be difficult to define; however they gave examples of Holkham Hall and the Three Graces.[66]

Despite the lack of any specific provision relating to collections, the Reviewing Committee has taken a pragmatic approach, and sought to care for the integrity of groupings of objects and collections, where possible, within the framework of the existing process. To this end, the Reviewing Committee has in the past 'strongly urged' the purchase of objects which are connected through forming part of the same collection.[67] It has also facilitated the retention of a collection where possible. The Committee commented in its Thirty Ninth Report that it might not have deferred the granting of a licence of a particular Turner had it not been for the fact that it was part of the collection from Royal Holloway and the fact that Thomas Holloway's 'concept was so striking and the collection so exceptional that it was extremely important that the Turner should be retained in situ'.[68] In a recent case where part of the Archigram architectural archive fell for consideration by the Reviewing Committee, and part did not (because it had not been in the UK for more than 50 years), the Reviewing Panel concluded that the part considered by it satisfied the Waverley Criteria. However, the Secretary of State used their discretion to allow the export of the archive 'on the basis that the issue of overriding importance was that the archive should remain intact'.[69]

Criteria, of which 11 were purchased. This led the authors to conclude that 'the export regulations . . . ensure the disposal of the collection'. Further examples include the armoury at Littlecote House and John Evelyn's library: see *Export of Works of Art 1984–85*, 31st Report, Cm 9818, para. 14.

[65] *Export of Works of Art 1989–90*, 36th Report, Cm 1225, para. 36.

[66] *Export of Works of Art 1993–4*, 40th Report, Cm 2710, paras. 18–19.

[67] *Export of Works of Art 2000–2001*, 47th Report, Cm 5311, Case 7 *A Parcel-Gilt Reliquary Figure of Saint Sebastian, Dated 1497* and Case 8 *A Parcel-Gilt Reliquary Figure of Saint Christopher, Dated 1493*, which were purchased respectively by the V&A and National Museums Scotland, pp. 38 and 40.

[68] *Export of Works of Art 1992–93*, 39th Report, Cm 2355, para. 8.

[69] *Export of Works of Cultural Interest 2018–2019 and 2019–2020*, 65th Report, Case 11 *The Archigram Archive*, p. 40.

8.2.2 Saving from What and from Whom?

At the end of the nineteenth and the beginning of the twentieth centuries, the collections of private owners were seen as falling prey to American and German collectors.[70] Certainly 'international collectors', as a generic category, were considered to have 'coffers . . . filled with gold bars' compared with the more meagre funds available in the UK to purchase the private collections that were being sold off.[71] Specifically, the theme of the American collector has been a strong one. After setting out the context of the export restrictions of cultural objects as 'the threat from America', Wang observes, 'Although new market patterns are emerging (Middle Eastern buyers, for example, are increasingly bidding for British objects) the ambivalence toward the American art-buying millionaire is a recurring theme in the British quest to save its treasures'.[72] The specific focus has also been on the perceived threat of purchase by a 'Los Angeles museum'.[73]

The trope of the American collector may have developed, in part, because of other situations where cultural heritage, important to the UK, was at risk of being sold and where the USA was the likely destination. When Shakespeare's Birthplace in Stratford was offered for sale in 1847 there was a concern that George Jones and PT Barnum were showing interest in purchasing it, with the English press suggesting that the house would be dismantled and shipped to America.[74] Other cultural heritage places were relocated to the USA, including the bomb-damaged church of St Mary the Virgin, Aldermanbury, London, to Westminster College, Fulton, Missouri, as a memorial to, and later a museum in honour of, Sir Winston Churchill.[75] A significant number of architectural furnishings from stately homes also entered US and Canadian museum collections.[76] This preoccupation with American collectors encourages a retentionist approach to cultural heritage policy and whilst, as a system, it can be said to show the extent to which the UK cares about cultural heritage objects, it does not necessarily demonstrate that the UK cares for cultural heritage objects in the most appropriate manner.

8.2.3 Saving for What Purpose?

The policy of the export licensing system is firmly one of retaining cultural objects 'considered to be of outstanding national importance' within national borders.[77] Retention has therefore been seen as being at the heart of the scheme. However, an essential element of this is not simply retention *per se*, but that the

---

[70] *Export of Objects of Cultural Interest 2007–08*, 54th Report, Appendix A, p. 58.

[71] *Export of Works of Art 1988–89*, 35th Report, para. 12.

[72] Wang, 'Whose Responsibility?', p. 229.

[73] See *Re St Mary of Charity, Faverhsam* [1986] Fam 143, 159 (Judge Newey QC Com Gen).

[74] See Section 4.5.

[75] National Churchill Museum: www.nationalchurchillmuseum.org/about-the-winston-churchill -museum.html (last accessed 21 December 2022).

[76] See generally, John Harris, *Moving Rooms: The Trade in Architectural Salvages* (New Haven: Yale University Press, 2007).

[77] ACE Notice, para. 2.

public should be able to have access to these national treasures. Saving for the nation and maximising public access is clearly a priority for those involved in the export licensing system. In the Guidance for Exporters, ACE expresses the Secretary of State's hope that owners will accept offers made by institutional purchasers (or private purchasers who undertake to provide appropriate levels of public access) that will give the greatest possible public benefit.[78] The fact that public access is an objective of the scheme is clear from the discussion by the Reviewing Committee of the then-proposed Ridley Rules. In this they indicated that access and appropriate conservation of the cultural objects 'are the objectives, not the accidental consequences, of public acquisition. Private ownership without enforceable undertakings ensures none of these objectives.'[79] The Ridley Rules were therefore implemented on the basis that the refusal of an export licence by an owner will only be justified where an offer is made either by a public institution (which would necessarily provide public access)[80] or a private individual, provided that this was accompanied by provision of sufficient public access to the object. This equates to a minimum of 100 days per year.[81] However, it appears that deferred access may be sufficient and a focus on enhanced access by future generations is prioritised over the certainty of consistent short-term access. This can be seen in the context of an agreement concerning *da Rimini Scenes from the Lives of the Virgin and other saints*, which was purchased by the National Gallery with the assistance of Ronald Lauder, following the deferral of a grant of an export licence.[82] As part of this agreement, the National Gallery would loan the work to Ronald Lauder for his lifetime and, following its display in London during 2017, it would then be displayed in London once every three years.[83] On his death it would return to London.[84] On the basis of this agreement he was granted an export licence.

---

[78] ibid., para. 74. See also para. 59. *Export of Objects of Cultural Interest 2015–16*, 62nd Report, p. 4.

[79] *Export of Works of Art 1989–90*, 36th Report, Cm 1225, para. 12.

[80] National museums are obliged to provide public access through their management agreement with the DCMS. Furthermore, they are also required to provide free access to the permanent exhibitions: see Section 6.6.1. Museums established as charities also need to provide sufficient public access in order to satisfy the public benefit test of charities and to maintain their privileged status: see Section 6.4.2.

[81] ACE Notice, para. 61.   [82] *Export of Works of Art 2014–15*, 61st Report, p. 23.   [83] ibid.

[84] ibid. This agreement was approved by the DCMS: National Gallery Press Release, *Saved for the Nation: Rare Medieval Panel Purchased by the National Gallery Thanks to Ronald S Lauder* (July 2015): www.nationalgallery.org.uk/about-us/press-and-media/press-releases/saved-for-the-nation-da-rimini (last accessed 21 December 2022). According to an article in the *Burlington*, Lauder was the original purchaser of the painting from the Northumberland Collection and he then agreed to donate it to the National Gallery: Jeremy Warren, 'Editorial: Exports and Acquisitions: Tears or Cheers?' (2017) 159 *The Burlington Magazine 271*. Cf. the acquisition by the National Gallery of two paintings by Vernet which had been designated as national treasures: *Export of Works of Art 2003–04*, 50th Report, Cm 5404, Case 6 A Pair of Paintings by Claude-Joseph Vernet, *Calme: A Landscape at Sunset with Fishermen Returning their Catch* and *Tempête: A Shipwreck in Stormy Seas*. The grant of a licence had been deferred and were acquired thanks to a grant by the American Friends of the National Gallery by an individual and which would be loaned and ultimately returned to the National Gallery. The

In 2000 Sir Denis Mahon applied to export four Italian Baroque paintings that had formed part of his collection. He intended to loan three of the paintings during his lifetime to the Pinacoteca Nazionale di Bologna, Italy, and another one to the National Gallery of Ireland, Dublin, and then to bequeath them to these institutions on his death. The Reviewing Committee concluded that while the paintings met the second Waverley Criterion it was appropriate to sacrifice those potential national treasures and recommended their export (which was approved by the Secretary of State). This was on the basis that a larger number of other objects, likely also to satisfy the test of national treasures, were to be donated by Sir Denis to the nation and the two overseas institutions would be making financial donations to the National Art Collections Fund.[85] Sir Denis had loaned 58 paintings to the National Art Collections Fund to be displayed in public institutions in the UK with a view to the ownership of these being transferred on his death, thus 'saving' them for the nation.[86] Here, rather than caring for individual objects and considering the strength of the link between the objects and the UK, a broader view was taken about the enrichment culturally of the nation by the other objects that were being donated. This was despite the specific loss of certain important cultural objects which, but for Sir Denis' other donation, efforts would otherwise have been made to keep in the UK.

Arguably, where the UK's cultural heritage is exported abroad, and there is widespread public access to it, this facilitates a wider benefit to humanity and appreciation of aspects of UK history, allowing cultural heritage to act as a good ambassador.[87] However, the focus of the system is clearly on the direct benefit to the UK public through access, rather than the wider international public. The Reviewing Committee has considered it irrelevant that the export of particular UK objects and their display abroad would deepen the interest in that particular genre and inform the public overseas. It rejected arguments to this effect by the Museum of Fine Arts, Boston, in the case involving the Mediaeval Stone Statues from St Mary's Abbey, York.[88] This recommendation, having been made in 1954, was in an age where knowledge transfer would have been far less easily facilitated than it would be now with the internet and

Reviewing Committee reported that 'After the term of the loan the paintings will be returned to the National Gallery permanently' (p. 32). According to two newspaper reports the loan was to the individual until his death when they will be returned to the National Gallery:
Nigel Reynolds, 'Gallery Buys Painting but Must Wait for Tycoon to Die', *The Telegraph*, 10 December 2004; Mark Brown, 'Rare Painting Secured for UK in Unique Deal with Cosmetics Heir', *The Guardian*, 28 July 2015.

[85]   *Export of Works of Art 1999–2000*, 46th Report of the Reviewing Committee appointed by the Chancellor of the Exchequer in December 1952, Cm 5019, December 2000, Cases 10, 11, 12 and 13 *Four Italian Baroque Paintings from the Collection of Sir Denis Mahon*, p. 44.

[86]   ibid.

[87]   Paul M. Bator, *International Trade in Art* (London: University of Chicago Press, 1983), p. 30.

[88]   *Export of Works of Art 1955–56*, 2nd Report, Cm 9595, para. 50. Although not specifically mentioned in the report, the potential reunification of a series of figures from St Mary's Abbey with their original location may also have been a relevant factor.

increased international travel; in those circumstances export and public display abroad could well have provided an opportunity for the art to act as a good ambassador and for the appropriate care of the cultural heritage.

Despite the argument about the UK cultural heritage objects being ambassadors for the UK's cultural heritage not being upheld by the Export Reviewing Committee, frequently such arguments are made to justify objects such as the Parthenon Sculptures remaining in London and enhancing knowledge of Greek culture abroad.[89] It seems, therefore, that such arguments about the cultural benefits and contribution to knowledge of cultural heritage abroad are reserved for situations where there is a desire to retain the *status quo* of the location of cultural heritage that may have been acquired in the past during times of unequal power relations, rather than to encourage movement of works out of a country in modern times.

8.3 Constructing Communities: Within and Beyond the Nation?

8.3.1 The National and Local Communities

The link with the nation is primarily based on time, specifically on how long an object has been within the nation's borders. An object will fall to be considered as a national treasure only if it has been in the UK for a period of 50 years (which broadly equates to two generations[90]). An object might satisfy one or more of the Waverley Criteria and have previously been located in the UK, but might have briefly resided abroad in the past 50 years, before returning to the UK. This temporary absence would interrupt the 50-year requirement for the purposes of the Waverley process and it would be exempt from consideration as a national treasure. This means that in practice some otherwise nationally important objects are 'lost' to the nation because of a relatively short sojourn abroad. Nevertheless, the Secretary of State has a discretion to depart from the requirement that the object has been in the UK for the last 50 years which can be exercised in wholly exceptional circumstances. They have exercised this discretion in only one instance to date when the casket of Thomas Becket was at risk of being exported abroad.[91] The matter was never formally heard by the Reviewing Committee, for the Secretary of State exercised his discretion in advance of their meeting. Nevertheless, in commenting on this, the Reviewing Committee acknowledged that the controversy surrounding this decision may have been caused in part because the public had not appreciated that the Secretary of State had discretion to depart from the 50-year rule.[92] The Reviewing Committee concluded that,

---

[89] Declaration on the Importance and Value of Universal Museums [2004] *ICOM News* 4. See generally Tiffany Jenkins, *Keeping Their Marbles: How the Treasures of the Past Ended Up in Museums and Why They Should Stay There* (Oxford: Oxford University Press, 2016).

[90] Waverley Report, p. 35.

[91] *Export of Works of Art 1996–97*, 43rd Report of the Reviewing Committee appointed by the Chancellor of the Exchequer in December 1952, Cm 3768, October 1997, p. 10.

[92] ibid.

providing that the use of the discretion was reserved for exceptional circumstances, this would be sufficient to allay the concerns of the London art market.[93]

Although the rhetoric used in the context of export licensing is that of 'saving for the *nation*', it is clear from as early as the 1952 Waverley Committee Report that importance to local communities was interpreted as equating to national importance. This has been translated into practice in two ways. The first is that even though the Waverley Criteria look at the viewpoint of the loss to a nation, this can be interpreted as a loss to a local community. Consequently, if an object has a particular connection with a person of local interest who might not be known to the wider national public, this object could, nevertheless, be recognised as a national treasure under the Waverley Criteria.[94] The second way in which the local community is recognised is when an object is of interest to a local museum outside London, and the Reviewing Committee may apply a slightly lower standard than usual to determine whether it satisfies the Waverley Criteria.[95] It is not, though, by itself sufficient to warrant a finding that the granting of a licence should be deferred,[96] as it does not represent a fourth criterion. Instead, it is a factor for the Reviewing Committee to consider as part of its consideration of the first criterion relating to national life. Specifically, it 'allows [the Reviewing Committee] to give weight as appropriate to particular regional interests within the national context'.[97]

Here, the policy of encouraging the development of local museum collections is effectuated through facilitation of purchasing objects for their collections. It is therefore apparent from the export licensing regime that the concept of the 'nation' is widely construed and is translated into practice in terms of recognising a network of communities. Where an object is important for one local community, this translates into its importance to the wider national community. This shows how, at the national level, cultural heritage which is important to smaller communities is cared for by enabling those communities to acquire objects which, if lost to them, would represent a misfortune.[98]

In the context of designating national treasures, the 'nation' is imagined as a network of communities. Some of these communities will experience the connection with the object directly; however, other wider communities, such as the national community as a whole, may also feel a connection with the

---

[93] ibid.   [94] DCMS, *Statutory Guidance*, para. 16.

[95] This was envisaged by the Waverley Committee itself: para. 189.

[96] See, for example, *Export of Works of Art 1983–84*, 30th Report of the Reviewing Committee appointed by the Chancellor of the Exchequer in December 1952, Cm 9553, June 1985, Case 33 *A Water-Colour by J. M. W. Turner: 'Cader Idris, North Wales' 1983–84*, p. 40.

[97] 30th Report, p. 3.

[98] This shift from a national viewpoint (or sometimes what is considered as a more London-centric approach which prioritises the major London collections at the expense of the local ones) mirrors the approach taken in *obiter* comments by Blake J. in *R. (on the application of Hall)* v. *Leicestershire City Council* [2015] EWHC 2985 (Admin), para. 11 in the context of the proposed reduction in provision of the Snibston Discovery Centre in Leicester. See Section 5.2.6 for a full discussion of the local community imagined by the court.

object. For this reason, the scheme takes a broader approach to imagining the national interest than might be evident when first looking at the criteria used. In effect the interests of a local community are either scaled up or substituted for the national interest and thus locally important objects are saved for the nation even though they may have little or no relevance to other communities within the UK. This both provides a relational approach to caring for cultural heritage between the local and national communities for whom the cultural heritage is important, and also shows respect for local interests by translating this into a national importance by recognising them.

8.3.2 International Community

On the whole, the relational element of care is narrowly construed in the context of the export licensing as it focuses on the relationship between the object and the nation.[99] This was something specifically envisaged in the Waverley Committee Report, when it stated that in situations where another country 'might justly regard an item as a national treasure, the UK's interest should take precedence'.[100] Rarely is consideration given to the greater importance that an object might have to another nation. Yet, if a system truly focuses on the care of cultural heritage (with the markers of empathy, respect and dialogue) then one would expect to find consideration of the human dimension to cultural heritage and its relative importance for other communities in the Reviewing Committee's recommendations to the Secretary of State. Although the default position appears to be that the Reviewing Committee takes its lead from the Waverley Committee and does not give precedence to the overseas national interest, there are limited situations in which there has been scope to take account of factors beyond the national interest. It should be noted, though, that these pre-date the Statutory Guidance which states that the Reviewing Committee may take into account 'local interest, and the condition of the object, including the extent of any damage or restoration'[101] and 'will advise Ministers about whether or not an object satisfies one or more of the Waverley criteria'.[102] Several categories of objects with potential interest to other countries exist. On occasions this factor is either not considered at all by either the Committee or the Secretary of State, or is specifically addressed but is treated as irrelevant for the purposes of designating the object as a UK national treasure. The Reviewing Committee does not abstain from finding an object to be a UK national treasure simply because an object was created by an overseas national[103] or is inextricably

---

[99] Albeit local communities as well (see the preceding section).

[100] *Export of Works of Art 1981–82*, 28th Report, Cm 8814, para. 82 – based on the approach taken in the Waverley Report.

[101] DCMS, *Statutory Guidance*, para. 10.   [102] ibid., para, 17.

[103] See, for example, *Export of Works of Art 1978–79*, 25th Report of the Reviewing Committee appointed by the Chancellor of the Exchequer in December 1952, Cm 8050, Case 33 *A Silver Plaque by Paul van Vianen*, p. 38.

linked with the history of another country.[104] The Reviewing Committee recommended that a tiara originating from the French Crown Jewels[105] was a UK national treasure[106] worthy of deferring the granting of an export licence for two months. The Reviewing Committee 'noted that the tiara had originally been part of the French Crown Jewels and that the application was intended to return it to the Louvre in Paris'.[107] The Reviewing Committee specifically mentioned that it 'agreed that the Minister of State for the Arts should be made aware of the circumstances of the licence application'. Reading between the lines here, the fact that the Reviewing Committee highlighted the importance of the tiara to France in this way and recommended a relatively short deferral period of two months might indicate that efforts were being made to facilitate (or at least not hinder) the return of the tiara to France.

The issue of recognising the European community and the relative import-ance of an object to another Member State arose in a case involving an application to export a Silver Plaque by Paul Van Vianen. Arguments were made that it was part of the Dutch national heritage and consequently a national treasure for them.[108] The purchaser argued that when considering applications to export cultural objects to other EU Member States and assess-ing whether they were national treasures, the effect of Article 36 of the Treaty of Rome was that only Waverley Criteria 1 was relevant since Waverley 2 and 3 focused on aesthetic importance and the object's importance to scholarship rather than national importance.[109] The Reviewing Committee declined to comment on the application of Article 36, but instead reported on the govern-ment's response in the following report where it stated that the process of assessing objects under all three Waverley Criteria was consistent with Article 36.[110] The Reviewing Committee concluded that the plaque satisfied Waverley Criteria 2 and 3 (not upholding arguments made by the Expert Adviser that the plaque's similarity to a smaller one that had been owned by Charles I, but which had subsequently gone missing, amounted to a sufficient importance to the UK's national history).[111] A deferral period of six months was granted and the Royal Scottish Museum made an offer to purchase the plaque.[112] However, this offer was declined by the Rijksmuseum[113] and a subsequent application for export was made ten years later where further research was presented which emphasised the plaque's direct connection with another plaque in the Rijksmuseum.[114] The Reviewing Committee nevertheless concluded that the plaque satisfied the second Waverley Criteria and the Secretary of State once

---

[104] *Export of Objects of Cultural Interest 2001–02*, 48th Report, Case 28 *An Emerald and Diamond Tiara by Bapst of Paris*, 1819–20.
[105] ibid.   [106] Based on Waverley 2 and 3.
[107] *Export of Objects of Cultural Interest 2001–02*, 48th Report, Case 29, p. 65.
[108] *Export of Works of Art 1978–79*, 25th Report, Case 33, p. 39.   [109] ibid., p. 39.
[110] *Export of Works of Art 1979–80*, 26th Report, para. 12.
[111] *Export of Works of Art 1978–79*, 25th Report, Case 33, p. 39.   [112] ibid., p. 40.
[113] Reported in *Export of Works of Art 1979–80*, 26th Report, para. 13.
[114] *Export of Works of Art 1987–88*, 34th Report, Case 13, p. 20.

again deferred the granting of a licence, but because no matching offers were made, the plaque was exported.[115]

There are situations where for art historical or historical, reasons an artwork might be more appropriately displayed in another country because of the special connection between the artwork's subject matter and that country. This factor appears not to have been brought before, or considered by, either the Reviewing Committee or the Secretary of State in the context of the application to export certain drawings by Stubbs which had a close connection with Australia.[116] However, after the announcement of a deferral period, it was suggested that 'Stubbs's image of the kangaroo, in particular, became the archetypical image of the kangaroo for over fifty years ... The kangaroo on the Australian coat of arms was based on this image.'[117] However, these arguments were not accepted, and ultimately the paintings were acquired by the National Maritime Museum, London.[118] In the case of the application to export Poussin's painting *The Destruction of the Temple of Jerusalem*[119] to Israel it was argued by the applicant's representative that the subject matter was of importance to Israel.[120] However, this argument was not relevant to the Reviewing Committee's decision on designating it as a national treasure and it recommended to the Secretary of State that it met Waverley Criteria 3 and that the granting of a licence should be deferred. Ultimately no purchaser came forward and so the painting was exported.[121]

There are a limited number of cases over the years in which either the Reviewing Committee or the Secretary of State has sub-ordinated the UK national interests for a broader purpose when deciding whether or not to designate something as a national treasure. The first of these is the situation where the granting of an export licence for an object which might otherwise meet the Waverley Criteria has been justified (or at least facilitated) on the basis that exporting the object would allow it to be reunified with the place from which it originated. Reunification and return of objects to their original setting has been recognised by the Reviewing Committee as best practice in conservation in the context of aiming to keep furniture from Spencer House in UK collections in the hope that one day they might be reassembled there.[122] However, the Reviewing Committee took this notion one step further in the case of the application to

---

[115] ibid.

[116] Reviewing Committee on the Export of Works of Art and Objects of Cultural Interest: *Note of outcome: Two paintings by George Stubbs, The Kongouro from New Holland (The Kangaroo) and Portrait of a Large Dog (The Dingo)* (Case 13, 2012–13).

[117] A quote by Dr Ron Radford AM, Director, National Gallery of Australia Media Release, *National Gallery of Australia Announces bid to Acquire Iconic Eighteenth Century Paintings from the UK* (2 April 2013). See also Jack Ashby, 'It's Australia v England, in the Battle over Stubbs Masterpieces', *The Conversation*, 7 November 2013.

[118] Note of outcome, Case 13, 2012–13.

[119] *Export of Works of Art 1998–99*, 45th Report, Cm 4466, November 1999, Case 7 *A Painting, The Destruction of the Temple of Jerusalem, by Nicolas Poussin, 1625–26*, p. 28.

[120] ibid., p. 28.   [121] ibid.   [122] *Export of Works of Art 1981–82*, 28th Report, Case 6, p. 15.

export several seventeenth-century Baroque Choir Stalls Incorporating Carved Wood Figures of Apostles[123] to Germany. Here the purpose of export was to reinstall them in their original location and the licence was granted without any deferral period, even though the choir stalls met the Waverley Criteria and would otherwise be considered as national treasures. The applicant had made an undertaking that the choir stalls would be reinstalled. Here, the Reviewing Committee focused on the public access as part of the care expected of the cultural heritage object in question.[124] The Reviewing Committee was concerned 'on iconographic, aesthetic and art historical grounds, for the re-integration of a major artistic complex with its other surviving elements in its original architectural setting'.[125] In fully acknowledging the position that generally the interests of the UK take priority when making their recommendations, the Reviewing Committee pointed to 'the very special circumstances of this case' which meant that it was 'right to consider the interests of the European, and indeed, the international cultural heritage generally'.[126] In a later case where the Choir Stalls were considered by analogy, the Reviewing Committee described that decision in the context 'of the overwhelming case that had been made that they should be returned and re-installed in their original home in the interests of international cultural co-operation'.[127] The case relating to the Choir Stalls is an important example of the Reviewing Committee taking into account factors other than the Waverley Criteria when advising the Secretary of State and specifically guiding them in a more unusual situation where they considered it justifiable to depart from the usual objective Waverley Criteria by recommending an extraordinary course of action rather than leaving them to exercise discretion based on their own interpretation of the situation. This departure from the usual approach to the sanctity of the Waverley Criteria is despite other strong statements by the Reviewing Committee which indicated their commitments to base their recommendations solely on the Waverley Criteria and not on extraneous factors.[128] Both the Reviewing Committee and ultimately the Secretary of State clearly recognised

---

[123] *Export of Works of Art 1980–81*, 27th Report of the Reviewing Committee appointed by the Chancellor of the Exchequer in December 1952, Cm 8515, March 1982, Case 8 *Baroque Choir Stalls Incorporating Carved Wood Figures of Apostles – 17th Century*.

[124] ibid., p. 16.   [125] ibid., pp. 15 and 17.   [126] ibid., p. 17.

[127] *Export of Works of Art 1995–96*, 42nd Report of the Reviewing Committee appointed by the Chancellor of the Exchequer in December 1952, Cm 3428, October 1996, Case 4 *A Painted Panel, 'The Crucifixion', attributed to Gentile da Fabriano, c. 1385–1427*, p. 20. Discussed at Section 8.3.2.3.

[128] The Reviewing Committee emphasised the fact that the Expert Adviser can only take into account the Waverley Criteria and should not take into account other factors such as whether an interested institution was unable to raise the relevant money: *Export of Works of Art 1987–88*, 34th Report, Cm 526, para. 22. The Committee has made clear that it can only consider the Waverley Criteria when making its recommendations to the Secretary of State: Reviewing Committee on the Export of Works of Art and Objects of Cultural Interest: *Note of case hearing on 4 June 2008: Papers of James Bruce, 8th Earl of Elgin, as Governor of British North America* (Case 2, 2008–2009) and the *Export of Objects of Cultural Interest 2016–17*, 63rd Report, Case 19 *Meissen Figure of 'Pulcinell'*.

the international community and the importance to it of cultural heritage which could be reunified.

8.3.2.1 Recognising the Commonwealth Community

It is clear from the Waverley Report that the approach to designation of objects as national treasures was to apply the Waverley Criteria primarily in the interests of the UK and that 'the proposed destination of an object [was] a secondary consideration. At the same time, while we have thought it our duty to set out all the arguments, we have no doubt that in practice ties of history and sentiment will play an appropriate part in determining the destination of objects which leave the country.'[129] The Waverley Committee indicated 'a good deal of sympathy' with various arguments made in favour of exporting to foreign public institutions in preference to private collectors, and when it came to the question of the appropriateness of giving preference to Commonwealth countries, the Committee concluded that it was inappropriate to adopt a formal set of rules.[130] As in the case of the local importance of objects, there are in practice two aspects to this approach. The first involves subordinating the UK interests where an object is relatively speaking of greater importance to the Commonwealth country than to the UK and the second is facilitating opportunities to encourage the development of Commonwealth museum collections.[131]

An example of the first of these can be seen when an application was made to export the papers of the 8th Earl of Elgin; the Reviewing Committee concluded that they satisfied the third Waverley Criteria because they were of 'outstanding importance for the study of British Imperial history, and of the history of British North America in particular'.[132] Although it was possible to make copies of these documents, the Reviewing Committee concluded that the national interest would not be satisfied by the provision of copies to the National Archives of Scotland.[133] The applicant argued that the papers were more historically significant to Canada than to the UK, on the basis that they were mainly concerned with his time as a diplomat and governor of Canada. This was a case where the proposed overseas purchaser, the Libraries and Archives of Canada (LAC), was a public institution and it was made clear that it would 'ensure the papers were cared for in the best possible way'.[134] Nevertheless, the Reviewing Committee emphasised that the final destination of the papers was not a consideration for it to make within its terms of reference and that it was tasked solely with making 'a recommendation to

---

[129] Waverley Report, p. 31.　　[130] ibid., p. 30.

[131] This may have been an argument with greater force many years ago, but may be of less relevance nowadays in terms of populating museums with works by Western artists.

[132] Reviewing Committee on the Export of Works of Art and Objects of Cultural Interest: *Note of case hearing on 4 June 2008: Papers of James Bruce, 8th Earl of Elgin, as Governor of British North America* (Case 2, 2008–2009), para. 10.

[133] ibid.　　[134] ibid., para. 7.

the Secretary of State as to whether the papers were of national importance to the UK under the Waverley Criteria'.[135] However, in the circumstances, the Secretary of State exercised their discretion and granted the export licence on the basis that the national interest would be met by the terms of the agreement with LAC.[136] In this case, the ability to provide copies mitigated the harm to the national interest.

The Elgin example demonstrates how the Secretary of State can exercise their discretion to depart from the strict application of the Waverley Criteria. However, in limited situations the acts of the Reviewing Committee have also demonstrated a willingness to depart from these.[137] This can be seen in the context of helping Commonwealth nations to build their museum collections by subordinating the UK national interest and not designating an object as a national treasure despite it satisfying one or more of the Criteria. In the application to export Claude Lorraine's painting of *Carlo and Ubaldo Embarking in Pursuit of Rinaldo*, the Committee 'concluded that the painting was of great importance and extreme beauty, one of the finest works by Claude in the country, but that having regard to the desirability of building up collections in Commonwealth countries we should not be justified in seeking to prevent the gift to the Toronto Gallery'.[138] This approach could be interpreted as being based on the notion of comity of nations, which is particularly strong in the context of Commonwealth nations between which there are stronger bonds given the close connection between these countries.[139] However, the way in which the Reviewing Committee's approach was reported conveys a paternalistic tone, to the extent of almost being patronising to the Commonwealth collections.

In 1980, one of only four copies of the Inspexius of Magna Carta by Edward I came for consideration before the Reviewing Committee for the first time.[140] The Reviewing Committee concluded that it met the first Waverley Criteria, but that its proposed export to New Zealand[141] meant that 'its loss to this country would be so mitigated by the proposed destination that the granting of an export licence would be justified, provided certain conditions were fulfilled'.[142] The first condition was that the British Library should be allowed immediate access for the purposes of scientific research[143] and that if the New

---

[135] ibid., para. 9.   [136] ibid., para. 15.

[137] Like the choir stall case (*Export of Works of Art 1980–81*, 27th Report, Case 8), these cases precede the publication of the Statutory Criteria made under the Export Control Act 2002, which mentions specifically the application of the Waverley Criteria, and appear to have been interpreted by the Committee as restricting their ability to apply considerations other than the Waverley Criteria. See, for example, *Export of Objects of Cultural Interest 2016–17*, 63rd Report, Case 19.

[138] HMSO, *Export of Works of Art 1962–63*, Case (b), p. 10.

[139] As to the relevance of the comity of nations in case law, see Section 5.2.2.

[140] *Export of Works of Art 1979–80*, 26th Report, Case 16 *Inspexius of Magna Carta by Edward I – 12 October 1297*. As to the subsequent appearance before the Committee, see Section 8.3.2.3

[141] The New Zealand government had an option to purchase the Inspexius and an application to export was sought before launching an appeal to raise money to purchase it: para. 116.

[142] *Export of Works of Art 1979–80*, 26th Report, Case 16, para. 117.   [143] ibid., para. 117(a).

Zealand government did not exercise the option to purchase it would be returned to the current owner in the UK.[144] The Reviewing Committee was at pains to emphasise that this was 'in no sense to be taken as constituting or endorsing a precedent' and was 'related to the particular conditions of this particular case at this particular time'.[145] It is therefore by no means automatically the case that exports to other Commonwealth countries will be sympathetically treated and export licences granted.[146]

8.3.2.2 The Channel Islands and Republic of Ireland

The Reviewing Committee has been willing in certain circumstances to permit the export of cultural objects to Ireland and the Channel Islands on the basis that they are enjoyed there by their owners during their lifetime and then undertakings are given regarding return to the UK.[147] In the case of two paintings by Richard Wilson, such a licence was granted 'subject to the provision by [the applicant] of a suitable undertaking on their future, which would take into account the interest of the Tate Gallery'.[148] Here it was recognised by the Committee that the 'degree of national importance' meant that it was 'desirable that they should be retained in the United Kingdom in the long-term'.[149] This deferral of enjoyment and access to cultural heritage objects until after a current owner has enjoyed the lifetime benefits of possessing them is similar to the situation involving Ronald Lauder discussed above.[150] However, here the ability for the current owner to enjoy their possessions was clearly a stronger factor, as well as the export being specifically to Ireland.

---

[144] ibid., para. 117(b).   [145] ibid., para. 117.

[146] This can be seen in the context of an application to export a watercolour of Niagara Falls. The applicant argued that the subject matter would be of more interest to North American than to the UK. However, the Reviewing Committee recommended the deferral of a licence and ultimately it was purchased by the National Army Museum: *Export of Objects of Cultural Interest 2015–16*, 62nd Report, Case 3 *An East View of the Great Cataract of Niagara, by Captain Thomas Davies*, p. 22.

[147] *Export of Works of Art 1967–68*, 15th Report, Cm 3849, Cases (s) and (t) 'Venice – The Grand Canal above the Rialto by Guardi, para. 118; *Export of Works of Art 1964–65*, 12th Report, Cm 2809, Case (d) 'Madonna and Child and St. Anne' – by Fra Bartolommeo and Case (e) 'Head of Christ' – by Antonella de Messina, paras. 47 and 78, where the export of two paintings from the Cook collection was permitted to the owner's home in the Channel Island where the owner agreed that they would only export them to the UK and the Reviewing Committee abstained from questioning the national importance of the paintings.

[148] *Export of Works of Art 1971–72*, 19th Report of the Reviewing Committee appointed by the Chancellor of the Exchequer in December 1952, January 1973, Case (e) *Two Paintings by Richard Wilson: 'Rome from the Gardens of the Villa Madama' and 'St Peter's and the Vatican Seen from the Janiculum'*, para. 59. Ultimately the Tate Gallery purchased *St Peter's and the Vatican*: www.tate.org.uk/art/artworks/wilson-rome-st-peters-and-the-vatican-from-the-janiculum-t01873 (last accessed 21 December 2022), whilst *Rome from the Villa Madama* is now in the Yale Center for British Art, Paul Mellon Collection: https://collections .britishart.yale.edu/vufind/Record/1669245 (last accessed 21 December 2022).

[149] *Export of Works of Art 1971–72*, 19th Report, para. 59.   [150] At Section 8.2.3.

8.3.2.3 Indirectly Recognising These Communities

One indirect way in which the Reviewing Committee (and, in turn, the Secretary of State) may recognise the importance of particular objects to European or international communities or of reunifying collections of objects or objects with particular places is through the use of shorter-than-usual deferral periods. This has the practical effect of only giving a small window of opportunity for a UK institution to raise funding to make a matching offer before the deferral period expires and the Secretary of State grants a licence to export the object. By applying the Waverley Criteria strictly, and deferring the grant of a licence, this has the effect of retaining the integrity of the export licensing system and outwardly maintaining its focus on prioritising the national interest. However, the short timeframe means that in practical terms the object is likely to be exported as funding will be more difficult to secure quickly. We have already seen examples of the use of short deferral periods. This can also be seen in the case of an application to export two ivory statuettes which were originally part of a set of four. The other two were already in Germany and the licence was to export them to be reunited with the rest of the set. Here the Secretary of State took into account representations made by the museum in Braunschweig, and by the cultural office of Lower Saxony, and set a deferral period of one month, rather than the three months which might otherwise have been expected.[151] In a further example, the Reviewing Committee was quite open about making use of a 'token' deferral period but was clearly mindful of avoiding setting a 'dangerous precedent'.[152] Here, the Committee was faced with a licence application to export a painted panel by Gentilo de Fabriano which may have been part of an altarpiece of a convent which was suppressed in 1810.[153] If the object were exported then it would be reunited with panels that were 'related stylistically but in a museum rather than in their original setting'.[154] Here, unusually, the Expert Adviser advised the Committee to recommend the grant of a licence despite the panel satisfying the Waverley Criteria, on the basis that 'the acquisition by the Brera Museum would mean a return to its probable original context'.[155] The Reviewing Committee carefully compared this case with that of the German choir stalls,[156] and concluded that the inability to reunite the panels in the original setting in this case distinguished it from the earlier case involving choir stalls which could be reinstated in their original setting, (and which, therefore, had justified departing from prioritising the national interest). The Committee, nevertheless, concluded that 'export to Italy was the desired outcome of the case'.[157] It was for this reason that the Reviewing Committee recommended that a token deferral period of one month (with

---

[151] *Export of Objects of Cultural Interest 2016–17*, 63rd Report, Case 3, *Two ivory statuettes, 'Autumn' and 'Winter', by Balthasar Permoser*, p. 24.

[152] *Export of Works of Art 1995–96*, 42nd Report, Case 4, p. 19.   [153] ibid.   [154] ibid.

[155] ibid., p. 20.   [156] At Section 8.3.2.

[157] *Export of Works of Art 1995–96*, 42nd Report, Case 4, p. 20.

a further one-month deferral in the event of a serious intention to purchase being made) should be made. This was accepted by the Secretary of State. This approach was taken since it was 'important to maintain the principle that works of art that met the Waverley criteria should be made available for acquisition in the UK'.[158]

The cultural relevance of how an object was to be displayed in the future was facilitated by the Reviewing Committee and Secretary by using a shorter-than-usual deferral period in the case of the Inspeximus of Magna Carta by Edward I, which had come before the Reviewing Committee in 1980[159] but which again formed the subject matter of an export application a couple of years later.[160] On this occasion the proposal was for it to be exported to the National Archives in Washington DC and be displayed next to the Declaration of Independence.[161] The Reviewing Committee recommended an initial deferral period of six months but exceptionally recommended to the Secretary of State that if it became clear after two months that no UK purchaser was intending to make an offer an export licence should be granted, which is what happened.[162]

By either directly permitting export without any deferral, or indirectly facilitating export by setting a comparatively short deferral period, the Reviewing Committee, or more usually the Secretary of State exercising their discretion, are in effect recognising the comity of nations. Specifically, they are facilitating an outcome which is beneficial to another country (here at what might be seen as the cultural expense of the UK) on the basis that this is an element of being friendly nations.[163] In this way, although only a very limited number of examples exist, these cases demonstrate the relational nature of care and with that the ultimate form of care that includes self-sacrifice. This is focused on the relativity of the position of the UK potentially losing a national treasure and that of the connection with the proposed destination set out in the licence application; it is clear, therefore, that the Reviewing Committee does not pre-emptively seek to reunite objects with other elements of a set or reunite them with their original location. This can be seen in the case involving the arrangement between the National Gallery and Ronald Lauder discussed above, for there one half of the diptych by da Rimini was the subject matter of the application and yet the other panel was in Rome. Nothing was mentioned in the report about making any efforts to return the panel to Rome

---

[158] ibid., p. 20. The Minister for the Arts was prepared to grant a shorter deferral period than the one recommended by the Reviewing Committee in the case of a sketch by Peter Paul Rubens based on the representations made by the Spanish Minster for Education, Culture and Sport 'that the painting should be allowed to join the many other works from the Torre de la Prada, commissioned by King Philip IV of Spain, on public display in the Prado Gallery, Madrid': *Export of Works of Art 2000–01*, 47th Report of the Reviewing Committee appointed by the Chancellor of the Exchequer in December 1952, Cm 5311, February 2002, Case 5 *An Oil Sketch, 'Diana and Her Nymphs Hunting', by Peter Paul Rubens, c. 1636–37*, p. 33.
[159] Discussed at Section 8.3.2.1.   [160] *Export of Works of Art 1982–83*, 29th Report, Cm 9206.
[161] ibid., para. 77.   [162] ibid., paras. 77 and 79.   [163] See Section 5.2.2.

when the application was made to export it to the USA. Thus, there was no relevance of 'saving' it as a European national treasure so that it might be reunited in Rome.[164] This reflects the very nature of the export licensing system which is reactive to potential loss from the UK, rather than acting proactively to care for cultural heritage in the overall most appropriate way.

8.4 Participation in the Designation Process

8.4.1 Reliance on Experts

One concern to bear in mind when adopting a framework of the ethics of care is the need to avoid paternalism, and to ensure that any care-giver does not exercise inappropriate levels of power and control or fail to revisit the question of what the appropriate level of care is and the appropriate nature and extent of the care provided.

The Expert Advisers and the Reviewing Committee are, as expert communities of care, putting forward recommendations about whether, in their opinions, an object satisfies the Waverley Criteria and constitutes a national treasure. The Reviewing Committee interprets its role as one of delegated authority from the nation, for it has made it clear that the decision on the Waverley Criteria is one made by the nation and that this decision-making power is entrusted to the Committee,[165] which it exercises on the nation's behalf. Rather than treating either the Expert Adviser or the Reviewing Committee as care-givers, it is far more appropriate to take an holistic and relational approach to care which focuses on the interrelationships of the Expert Adviser, Reviewing Committee, Secretary of State and the wider national community to treat the care towards cultural heritage as a process. There is a strong inter-dependence between the national community and the experts who both inform and form the committee to determine whether it is appropriate to attempt to save an object for the nation. However, whilst the Expert Adviser, Reviewing Committee and Secretary of State may formally designate an object as a national treasure, and defer the granting of an export licence, this is only part of the care for the object. It effectively facilitates a more direct form of caring which is providing an opportunity for a museum (or private individual undertaking to give it appropriate levels of public access) to acquire it with the aim of retaining it within the national borders. Throughout this entire process, ACE, as the organisation which administers the export licensing system on behalf of the Secretary of State, facilitates the provision of care for the cultural heritage and is instrumental in the caring process.

The Secretary of State can override the approaches of the experts who appear, on the whole, to be confined to assessing the objects against the Waverley Criteria and can exercise their discretion providing that this is

---

[164] *Export of Works of Art 2014–15*, 61st Report, p. 23.
[165] *Export of Works of Art 1955–56*, 3rd Report, Cm 9882, para. 30.

exercised reasonably.[166] The Secretary of State can therefore take account of the wider public interest in the decision-making process, as well as practising cross-border cultural co-operation by recognising the broader international community and the notion of the comity of nations.[167]

8.4.2 National and Local Communities as the Final Arbiter of Care

The Expert Advisers, the Reviewing Committee and the Secretary of State play the central roles in designation of national treasures. However, the UK public as a national community also play an, at times, indirect role. Although the public (in the form of national and local communities) is not directly involved in the initial designation of the object, the public is indirectly involved in caring for it by raising money to purchase it[168] and thus the public's action (or inaction) often ultimately affects the outcome of whether or not the object is 'saved' from export.

Once an export licence is deferred (because an object has been designated as a national treasure), the nation, or rather the public forming that nation, may only then for the first time become aware of the object's existence. The announcement of the deferral period, and the opportunity to acquire the object to 'save' it, might engender public reaction and support for it, but this will not always be the case. Where there is a strong public campaign to raise money to purchase the object, arguably there is a stronger perception of the object as being a national treasure properly so-called. In such circumstances, there is a real public 'buy-in' to acquiring the cultural heritage for the nation. In situations where there is no tangible public support and the public has not been involved with fundraising, it is arguably a clear example of the Authorized Heritage Discourse (AHD)[169] in action, in the sense that experts (here the Reviewing Committee) are ascribing a value, or a set of values to an object which are then rubber-stamped by the Secretary of State, thus converting the object into what Harrison would describe as part of the official heritage.[170] However, in the many cases where there is a public campaign to raise money to purchase the object, the public are active participants in determining its importance to the nation. If the public are unwilling to provide the final funding, then ultimately the power of the experts and the AHD has not triumphed, but instead the care appropriate to the view of the public is given to the object and it will be exported and 'lost' to the nation. In many cases though, the failure to raise sufficient funds

---

[166] ACE Notice, para. 76.   [167] See the discussion at Section 5.2.2.

[168] Similarly, in a situation where a local group has been established to raise funds to purchase an object or place, it is the public and their willingness to raise money which is the decider as to whether something which has been identified as something to care about is actually cared for.

[169] Laurajane Smith, *Uses of Heritage* (London: Routledge, 2008), p. 11.

[170] Rodney Harrison, 'What is Heritage?' in Rodney Harrison (ed.), *Understanding the Politics of Heritage* (Manchester: Open University and Manchester University Press, 2010), p. 8.

could well be more to do with austerity than a lack of appreciation of the object by the public.

8.4.3 The Role of the Champion

The Secretary of State and the Reviewing Committee can recommend that a champion is appointed to co-ordinate the efforts to raise the money to purchase the object.[171] Here the champion acts, in effect, as an advocate for the object itself with a view to keeping it within the nation's borders because of its importance to the nation, to aesthetics or to learning. The champion might be thought of as an ambassador for the object. Alternatively, in perhaps a more idealistic tone, one could interpret the role of champion as a temporary care-giver who co-ordinates efforts to provide the most appropriate environment in which the cultural heritage can flourish.

In certain, exceptional situations, a champion assumes for themselves the responsibility to the national interest and indicates that they may be prepared to purchase the object to save it for the nation. In the case of Pontormo's *Portrait of a Young Man in a Red Cap*, the National Gallery, which had acted as the champion for the painting, with the support of the government, which had offered a grant of more the £19m towards the purchase, indicated that it was prepared to purchase the painting because it 'had an obligation to the national interest'.[172] Ultimately the matching offer was refused. A champion's preparedness to purchase an object is effectively the ultimate acceptance of responsibility for the care of cultural heritage. In this case, having not initially been interested in acquiring the object but recognising its national importance and having 'exhausted every other possibility of purchase by another public body', the National Gallery recognised its own overarching responsibility to the nation and the government by providing the necessary funding. However, the system does depend on the willingness of the seller to accept the offer, and in the Pontormo case the applicant had already purchased the painting and so could not benefit from a net of tax acquisition.[173] It was also reported that the currency fluctuations which occurred between the purchase (which took place in US dollars) and the time of the application to export the painting meant that the matching offer would have left the owner out of pocket.[174] The cases where the champion may step in demonstrate a recognition of situations where the misfortune is deemed by an expert

---

[171] The introduction of this system was announced in the *Export of Works of Art 1996–97*, 43rd Report, para. 9.

[172] *Export of Objects of Cultural Interest 2015–16*, 62nd Report, Case 10 '*Portrait of a Young Man in a Red Cap*' by Pontormo, p. 39.

[173] ibid., p. 39.

[174] Dalya Alberge, 'US Billionaire Defends Refusal to Sell £30m Pontormo Painting', *The Guardian*, 2 March 2017.

to be so great, and that they care about the cultural heritage object to such an extent, that they need to intervene on behalf of the nation.

8.5 Assuming Responsibility for Care as an Ethical Activity

8.5.1 Care and Tainted Cultural Heritage Objects

The ownership history (provenance) of cultural objects that come before the Export Licensing Unit at ACE is something that is requested as part of the application process. Specific guidance is also provided to exporters about the legal requirements to export objects that may have originated from Iraq or Syria.[175] Both ACE and the Reviewing Committee are clearly alive to the problems of unprovenanced objects.[176] Specifically, the Reviewing Committee has expressed the concern that it was being used 'to give a false legitimacy to the trade in objects which may have been illegally exported from another country'[177] where objects were coming before the Committee to show that they had been in the UK for 50 years and to increase the objects' financial value.[178]

However, frequently the need for provenance information is set within the context of determining whether or not an object has been in the UK for the last 50 years and whether it might meet one of the Waverley Criteria.[179] Provenance is also mentioned in the context of the Reviewing Committee's reports to determine the object's authenticity and its connection with the UK.[180]

How far the Reviewing Committee and the Secretary of State take into account ethical issues surrounding the object in question when designating something as a national treasure is central to determining the nature of appropriate, empathetic and respectful care. Elsewhere it has been argued that the risk of bringing ethically tainted cultural heritage objects within the scope of national treasures has the potential to tarnish the entire category.[181]

There has been little engagement by the Reviewing Committee with the ethical issues of whether objects that are designated as national treasures might have been acquired during colonial times as part of the unequal power relations in play at the time or as parts of punitive raids, and whether these factors

---

[175] ACE, *Cultural Objects from Iraq* (3 January 2012); ACE, *Cultural Objects from Syria* (10 August 2015).

[176] *Export of Works of Art 1993–94*, 40th Report, Cm 2710, para. 23.

[177] *Export of Works of Art 1989–90*, 36th Report, Cm 1225, pp. 9–10.

[178] ibid., Case 7 *An Etruscan Helmet: 5th Century BC*, p. 21.

[179] Although there was some questioning of provenance by the Reviewing Committee where UK archaeological heritage that has been found: *Export of Works of Art 2001–02*, 48th Report, Case 25 *Two Late Bronze Age Gold Hair Rings, c. 1100–750 BC*, p. 54.

[180] *Export of Works of Art 1988–89*, 35th Report, Case 17 *A Pair of Empire Giltwood Chairs in the Gothic Style, Stamped Jacob D R Meslee*, p. 31.

[181] Charlotte Woodhead, 'Tarnished Treasures: Provenance and the UK's Waverley Criteria' (2019) 5 *Santander Art and Culture Law Review* 109. This was in the context of an application for the export of an object that had formed part of the collection of Emma Budge. Her heirs had brought successful claims before the Spoliation Advisory Panel in 2014 regarding several objects sold at the same auction, which was considered by the panel to be a forced sale.

might affect whether or not to designate the object as such. There are several instances where the Reviewing Committee has overtly referred to objects as being 'loot', for example, a pair of Sèvres busts that had come 'to Britain as part of the loot from Seringapatam' and which had originally formed part of the collection of Tipu Sultan, who was the ruler of Mysore.[182] The fact that these objects were looted has not been relevant to assessing whether they were recognised as national treasures. In 2021 the finial from Tipu Sultan's throne was reconsidered by the Reviewing Committee. Although on this occasion it was not described as loot,[183] once again it was considered to be a national treasure and the granting of an export licence was deferred to permit a purchaser to come forward.[184]

On two occasions Benin Bronzes have been considered by the Reviewing Committee; in neither case did the committee engage with any ethical questions about the appropriate care of the objects, specifically because they originated from a punitive expedition.[185] In the end, the bronzes were in both cases found not to satisfy any of the Waverley Criteria, in part because it was relevant to the Reviewing Committee that there were already examples in the Pitt Rivers Museum. Consequently, licences were granted without any deferral periods and the bronzes were not designated as national treasures.[186]

8.6 Conclusion

The approach to care within the framework of export licensing control in the UK and the way in which objects are designated as national treasures and ultimately 'saved for the nation' prioritise the interests of the nation and local communities over the interests of other nations and the international community. Convenient national access is prioritised over the needs of other countries or the connection that they have with the cultural heritage object in question or wider international public access. The fact that an object is nationally important to another country is seldom a factor justifying exempting an object from being considered as a UK national treasure by UK decision-makers. Only in limited circumstances, where there is an opportunity to reunite an object with its original location, has the Secretary of State or the Reviewing Committee

---

[182] *Export of Works of Art 1983–84*, 30th Report, Cm 9553, Case 26 *A Pair of Sèvres Biscuit Porcelain Busts of Louis XVI and Marie Antoinette*, p. 33.

[183] Although the Statement of the Expert Adviser observed that the 'extent of the looting and plunder of the palace [after Tipu's defeat] was unprecedented': p. 3.

[184] Reviewing Committee on the Export of Works of Art and Objects of Cultural Interest, *Note of case hearing on 12 May 2021: A Tipu Sultan Throne Finial* (Case 11, 2020–21); ultimately no purchaser came forward and an export licence was granted: Reviewing Committee on the Export of Works of Art and Objects of Cultural Interest: *Note of outcome: A Tipu Sultan Throne Finial* (Case 11, 2020–21).

[185] *Export of works of Art 1963–64*, 11th Report, October 1964, Cm 2502, Case (h) *Benin Bronze Head* and *Export of Works of Art 1965–67*, 13th Report, October 1966, Cm 3130, Case (d) *Benin Bronze Female Head*.

[186] ibid.

foregone designating an object as a national treasure. In these exceptional circumstances shorter deferral periods which make it less likely to be 'saved for the nation' are used.

However, there is a democratic element to caring for the nationally important cultural heritage, which is that in many instances whether or not an object is ultimately 'saved for the nation' will depend on the practical intervention of the public in the fundraising process. Unless the institution has been able to raise the necessary funds from its own resources, or from a funder such as the Art Fund, it will rely on public fundraising. Ultimately the support of the public determines whether or not the object is saved for the nation and effectively whether the designation of the object as a national treasure will bear fruit by keeping it within the national borders and providing appropriate levels of public access.

Save for the limited exceptions where a more international approach is taken to determining national treasures, the way in which the Waverley Criteria are applied in the UK demonstrates a focus on caring about the UK's national interests (originating from both the local and national level) rather than caring for cultural heritage from an international perspective and truly recognising wider responsibilities than simply the national ones.

9

Challenging the *Status quo*
Cultural Heritage, Care and Justice

9.1 Introduction

Communities may challenge the *status quo* of those who currently care for and possess cultural heritage. This chapter focuses on how the notion of *caring for* transcends generations and deals with claims made by the descendants of past owners, communities of origin or states. It addresses the multivocality in decision-making about how best to respond to these challenges. Frequently the question has been asked: who owns cultural heritage? But it is more helpful to consider whether there is a reason to challenge the *status quo*, to analyse the ways in which decisions are made about the appropriate course of action, and to respond to these. Often the return of cultural heritage objects by museums is not legally mandated, but is instead based on the willingness of a museum to make a purely *ex gratia* transfer to a claimant (whether an individual, group, community or nation) or on the exercise of a specific power given to their governing bodies. Many UK national museums have provisions in their governing statutes preventing their trustees from acceding to repatriation requests (although these have been eased in the context of Nazi-era spoliation and for certain human remains). Some non-national museums, with experience of repatriation requests for human remains or other cultural heritage objects, have developed their own policies and processes in response to one or more challenges. More recently, there are instances of museums proactively drafting such non-legal instruments to inform any future decision-making. In the context of Nazi-era spoliated cultural objects, a growing body of recommendations has been published by the Spoliation Advisory Panel, an independent committee of experts, who can hear claims and assess the moral strength of claims, recommending just and fair solutions.

The first part of this chapter focuses on the benefits of framing disputes about cultural heritage as challenges to the current allocation of care (that is to say, challenges to the *status quo*). This approach avoids using a framework of claims which pits one party against another. The second part of this chapter considers the situations which justify communities challenging the *status quo* regarding how cultural heritage is cared for, and who has responsibility for its direct care. The third part analyses the different types of responses made to challenges to the *status quo*. This includes the responses by those currently responsible for direct care who seek to perpetuate the *status quo*, or who have refused to engage in meaningful dialogue about its appropriateness, representing paternalistic care.[1] Legal restrictions can be used as justification for inaction and certain myths about the possible effects of law reform can hinder rule changes which have the potential to otherwise facilitate appropriate care. This part then explores the greater willingness to engage with claims for cultural heritage, and the efforts made to facilitate such engagement, entreated by national and international calls to respond to injustice in the context of claims for objects taken during the Nazi era and for human remains. It also focuses on individual responses to claims by museums, in some cases responding in a dialogic manner to recognised injustice through the ethics of care. The final part considers responses to injustice through memorialisation and acts of removal of cultural heritage; in the UK, this has recently included the rhetoric of 'explain and retain' in preference to removal.

9.2 Challenges in Preference to Claims

Care as a disposition (in the sense of the feeling of caring about something), as well as care as a process (in terms of caring for the cultural heritage and the communities for whom it is important) interact significantly in the context of seeking justice relating to cultural heritage.[2] Communities who care about cultural heritage may seek to assume responsibility for the care of objects or places which are currently cared for by others. Often these challenges are framed as claims about ownership – in particular, seeking to determine if pre-existing ownership rights enjoyed by the claimants continue to exist, or whether, even if they have been lost, there is a continuing moral entitlement as the 'rightful owners' of the cultural heritage.[3] However, focusing on ownership, at the expense of care, can cause tensions and perpetuate dissonance between the various communities of care involved. Instead, a more dialogic approach (which is advocated for here) is to consider the reasons why communities are justified in challenging the continued care by the current possessor, whether that provision of care ought to be reviewed, and whether the claimants have a role to play in the continued care of the cultural heritage, either as participants in decision-making or in assuming responsibility for the direct care of cultural heritage. This is explored further below in the context of dialogic responses to challenges to the *status quo*.

In putting forward this suggested shift in terminology it is important to emphasise that no naïve assumption is being made that this will solve all of the

---

[1] This notion of paternalistic care is drawn from Uma Narayan, 'Colonialism and Its Others: Considerations on Rights and Care Discourses' (1995) 10 *Hypatia* 133, 135.

[2] In Chapter 2 the nature of care both as a disposition and as a process was set out, Section 2.2.

[3] The difficulties with this term are explored at Section 9.5.2.5.

problems associated with dealing with claims for cultural heritage.[4] Nevertheless, in seeking to reframe these as challenges to the *status quo*, and encouraging dialogic responses which seek to navigate the way through the dissonance, this could result in more appropriate care of cultural heritage.

A true dialogue needs to take place to determine the appropriateness of the current provision of care and whether an alternative community might be better placed to assume responsibility for that care.[5] This might be the community challenging the *status quo*, but will not necessarily be so. Rather than focusing on assessing conflicting positions of ownership, or entitlement to something, it is better to focus primarily on considering how cultural heritage is cared for. This includes considering whether the person who currently provides direct care for it should continue to do so. When considering how to respond to any challenge, it would be relevant to assess whether a transfer of the responsibility for care, together with the transfer of the physical object, is more appropriate.

As part of any dialogue it may become apparent that the community from which the object originated is more appropriately placed to provide appropriate care than the current holder. For that reason, the transfer to it of the object may be appropriate, although that is not to say that transfer of the physical cultural heritage object is always the most appropriate form of care. Instead, dialogue about care, having an active role in the care of cultural heritage or some other cultural collaboration may reflect a more appropriate means of navigating dissonance and overall achieve appropriate care, as recognised by all the communities of care concerned.

9.2.1 Challenging the Language of Claims and the Rules of Engagement

As discussed in Chapter 2, the existence of nested practices of care does not presuppose that care is appropriately provided at any one particular time. For this reason it is important that care is re-visited and re-evaluated at various points in time, and that different viewpoints are taken into account as part of this process. It is central to the arguments for and against removal of the Parthenon Marbles from the British Museum and their placement in Athens that the nature of the care given, and the appropriateness of the care, by the British Museum should be re-evaluated. This does not automatically mean that

---

[4] That is to say, taking heed Scarre's and Coningham's warnings of making naïve assumptions that a 'modicum of mutual understanding and good-will' might lead to resolution of disputes about cultural heritage: in Geoffrey Scarre and Robin Coningham, 'Introduction' in Geoffrey Scarre and Robin Coningham (eds.), *Appropriating the Past: Philosophical Perspectives on the Practice of Archaeology* (Cambridge: Cambridge University Press, 2013), p. 8. Discussed in Section 1.3.5.1.

[5] Sarr-Savoy identified the need to openly speak about restitution because this is to speak of justice and that restitution is 'a way to open a pathway toward establishing new cultural relations based on a newly reflected upon ethical relation': Felwine Sarr and Bénédict Savoy, *The Restitution of African Cultural Heritage: Towards a New Relational Ethics* (Report, November 2018).

the marbles should be returned, but rather that previous decisions and viewpoints should be reconsidered in light, not only the views of the trustees of the British Museum but also the views more widely held by other communities. It is only too clear in the context of objects taken during colonial times that viewpoints are shifting, therefore these nested practices of care require re-evaluation from the point of view of considering the continued appropriateness of care by museums where claimants are vocal in seeking dialogue and restitution.[6]

There is a clear need for museums to respond in an open, dialogic manner emphasising cooperation and collaboration. As part of this, responses need to be in good faith and facilitate negotiation.[7] These ethical precepts are found at both the international and national levels and are vitally important to how museums interact with the public since they are firmly grounded in the notion of upholding the public trust, acting in an ethical manner, and engaging with communities both locally and further afield.[8]

Museums may draft policies dealing with requests for the repatriation of objects within their collections, or include statements about their approach to repatriation in their collections' development plans. Either separately, or as part of these policies, they may adopt procedures for dealing with how they respond to challenges to the *status quo*. This can include setting out requirements for the format of claims or the status of claimants who may approach them. Terms relating specifically to the standing of claimants, establishing their relationship with the object, and in some cases requiring claimants to satisfy certain preconditions before agreeing to hear the substantive elements of the claim, can be included. In some instances, museums also indicate that claims should be supported by government authorities, or require an explanation as to 'why such support is inapplicable in the particular case'.[9] The promulgation of these apparent 'rules of engagement' for presenting, hearing and responding to claims represent a significant amount of power in the hands of the museums, whereas independent claims processes such as the Spoliation Advisory Panel provide terms of reference and rules of procedure which are not dictated by

---

[6] 'The terms "restitution" and "repatriation" do not have any strict legal definition as far as museum practice is concerned. They are frequently used interchangeably, but have traditionally described the process of returning cultural material to its original owners (restitution) or its place of origin (repatriation)': ACE Repatriation and Restitution Guide 2022.

[7] The ILA Resolution 4/2006 from the Cultural Heritage Committee (adopted at the 72nd Conference of the ILA, Toronto, 4–8 June 2006) emphasises the need for good faith when responding to claim and negotiating (principle 2) and sets this in the context of 'emphasizing the need for a cooperative approach to caring for cultural material' (the Preamble).

[8] International Council of Museums, *ICOM Code of Ethics for Museums* (revised 2004), principle 2 and MA, *Code of Ethics for Museums* (2015), principle 3.

[9] University of Cambridge Museum of Archaeology and Anthropology and Cambridge University Museums and Botanic Gardens, *Our Approach to the Return of Artefacts*: https://maa.cam.ac.uk/files/media/maa_-_returns_-_full_guidance.pdf (last accessed 1 June 2023).

museums.[10] The recent Museums Association (MA) Guidance on decolonisation in museums emphasises that museums are not neutral spaces and that it is important to acknowledge power and privilege.[11]

Many of the instruments setting out museums' repatriation policies adopt the language of claims, as does the Terms of Reference of the Spoliation Advisory Panel. However, given the dialogic nature of care, and the focus on responsibilities rather than rights, the central elements to repatriation or restitution claims are the reconsideration of the *status quo* and the start of dialogue. This may be with a view to a reallocation of responsibility for the direct care of the cultural heritage in question, together with the physical control of it, but may be about the power to make decisions about its location and long-term care.

Given the approach adopted in this book, which shifts away from talking about claims for repatriation, what is being challenged is either the current allocation of responsibility for the care of cultural heritage, the way in which the care is being undertaken, or the extent of the care (that is to say its appropriateness). Therefore, whilst some individual communities may express a wish to assume responsibility for the direct care of that cultural heritage, in other situations they may advocate for adaptations to the existing provision of care, for example regarding the manner of display. A process to challenge the current allocation, based on the ethics of care, needs clear criteria on which the current allocation of care is justifiably challenged. This starts with a dialogue which is structured, and based on respectful and empathetic tenets.

As the current community with responsibility for the care of cultural heritage, and for determining how that is appropriately carried out, the museum has the responsibility for navigating harm, often focusing on preservation and avoiding physical harm. It will have cared for it in accordance with the standards expected of the Accreditation Scheme (where it is an Accredited Museum). Transferring cultural heritage to a community operating outside similar systems of recognised standards of care may be challenging for some museums to engage with. However, there are clearly some circumstances which justify communities in challenging the *status quo* and which may ultimately result in such a transfer. These varied categories are considered now.

9.3 Justifications for Revisiting the Current Provision of Care

Simply because an object is in a museum does not necessarily mean that its continued presence needs to be questioned. Instead, it is argued here that communities would only be justified in challenging the current provision of care where there has been some act relating to the object amounting to

---

[10] This idea of power is considered by Isabella Atencio in the context of NAGPRA and the contrast with the approach taken by the UK's Spoliation Advisory Panel.

[11] MA, *Supporting Decolonisation in Museums* (2021), p. 7.

a potential injustice or where the nature of the object itself renders the object's continued presence as a potential injustice. Central to this would be the question of whether the museum's continued caring responsibility is the most appropriate means of caring for it. Communities can establish an entitlement to have care reconsidered in broadly four sets of circumstances, which will each be considered in turn. The first is where there is a particular strength of feeling towards cultural heritage, or where the inherent nature of the cultural heritage in question justifies reconsideration of the current allocation of responsibility for care. The second is where there has been a prior displacement of caring responsibilities that were previously enjoyed by the claimant, or by their predecessors. Third, it is appropriate to reconsider care where someone has circumvented the requirements of a nested practice of care. Fourth, care may be reconsidered where the respondent or their predecessors assumed those caring responsibilities with actual or constructive knowledge of the earlier displacement of care.[12] While these different circumstances justify challenge and starting a dialogue, they do not automatically lead to transfer of ownership.

9.3.1 The Nature of the Cultural Heritage and the Strength of Feeling

There are only a few categories of objects which it is argued, by their very nature, justify communities in questioning whether continued care by the current provider of direct care (usually a museum) is most appropriate.

Communities could demonstrate this by establishing that a particular cultural heritage object has a contemporary importance for their cultural practices or is an object with which they feel a strong connection. For example, it may be possible to show that the cultural heritage in question is of such a nature that it forms an integral part of a community's culture or religion.[13] For that reason, challenges may be justified on the basis that the cultural heritage is either *res extra commercium* or has such an importance, perhaps because of its sacred nature, that its presence in a museum setting rather than with the community of origin is inappropriate. Here the *status quo* is justifiably challengeable. Challenges relating to the human remains of former members of a community may immediately engage a need to respond, in most cases by returning the remains to the community for them to provide appropriate care. Similarly, sacred objects which are essential to a community's practices are categories of object which in themselves justify revisiting the current provision

---

[12] Cf. Vrdoljak's approach, which sets out three rationales for restitution: (1) 'sacred property – the principle of territoriality and the link between people, land and cultural objects'; (2) 'righting international wrongs'; and (3) 'self-determination and reconciliation'a
Filipa Vrdoljak, *International Law, Museums and the Return of Cultural Objects* (Cambridge: Cambridge University Press, 2008), p. 2.

[13] This can be seen in the context of grouphood : John Moustakas, 'Group Rights in Cultural Property: Justifying Strict Inalienability' (1989) 74 *Cornell Law Review* 1179.

of care and may justify being returned because of their importance to the communities of origin. Such a determination might be made in the absence of any wrongdoing by the original acquirers of the object or by a museum when it acquired the object. It is the objects themselves, and their importance to modern-day communities, which justify questioning the museum's current assumption of responsibility for care, regardless of the circumstances in which they were originally acquired or how they arrived at the museum. Here the concern is not with the parties' conduct but with the nature of the object. It is this nature which affects the long-term care of all these objects and which may justify an expedited transfer of responsibility of care from the museum to the claimant community. This is based on the greater importance of the cultural heritage to the originating community than to the local, national or museum communities.

9.3.2 Prior Displacement of Caring Responsibilities: Original Loss

A second way in which communities may establish that they should either have an opportunity to contribute to the dialogue about the continued care of cultural heritage or should have responsibility for care transferred to them is where they are descendants of the community who originally had responsibility for the cultural heritage's care. Where that responsibility was displaced and others have assumed responsibility without the informed consent of the original communities of care the current allocation of care can be challenged. The original responsibility for care might have derived from an individual's ownership of an object, or from the community's use of certain cultural heritage for religious or cultural reasons (in a way that does not necessarily reflect ownership in a private property sense). Here, one can draw on recent work relating to repatriation to assess the circumstances of taking.[14] Although these approaches to taking have focused on the colonial context, it is important to bear in mind that cultural heritage was acquired in a wide variety of circumstances which extended beyond colonialism and included wartime genocide and other instances as well as opportunistic theft, looting of archaeological sites, other heritage crimes, forced sales and gifts made in circumstances involving unequal power relations. In such varied situations, the modern-day communities may have in moral terms standing to challenge the *status quo* (for in legal terms title is likely extinguished under the relevant statutes of limitation).[15] This would include entering into a dialogue to determine whether the current regime of care is appropriate for the cultural heritage in question with a view potentially to transferring entirely the responsibility for the care of cultural heritage (which would also transfer the ownership). However, ownership is a secondary issue

---

[14] See Dan Hicks, *The Brutish Museums: The Benin Bronzes, Colonial Violence and Cultural Restitution* (London: Pluto Press, 2020); Sarr and Savoy, *The Restitution of African Cultural Heritage.*

[15] See Section 9.5.2.5.

here, with the primary concern being about having the direct responsibility for the care and for the control of what happens to the cultural heritage, how it is cared for, where it is cared for and by whom.

Using the terminology of communities who have 'lost the responsibility for care without permission' risks masking the violent takings that may have occurred. Consequently, it is important to emphasise the circumstances in which the original possession and responsibility for care of the cultural heritage was lost. These different circumstances give rise to opportunities to challenge the continued assumption of responsibility for the day-to-day and longer-term care. These original takings represent wrongs which need to be challenged and dialogue may result in resolution in a correction of those wrongs.

Taking up Sarr and Savoy's call to develop typologies based on takings rather than on 'imagined types of object or culture', Hicks identifies seven types of taking within colonial contexts.[16] He separates out looting with violence, physical anthropology collecting of human remains, missionary and other confiscations of religious objects, archaeological collections and tomb raiding, 'scientific' collections of natural history specimens, 'ethnographic' collecting and finally instances of barter, purchase and commissioning.[17] Sarr and Savoy themselves identify the following as objects which justify restitution 'in a swift and thorough manner without any supplementary research regarding provenance or origins ... any objects taken by force or presumed to be acquired through inequitable conditions'.[18] These include objects taken 'through military aggression', by 'military personnel or active administrators on the continent during the colonial period ... or by their descendants', 'through scientific expeditions prior to 1960' and initial loans that were never returned to African museums.[19] Van Beurden's earlier work draws out the different circumstances of acquisition as being: '1. Acquisition by normal purchase or barter, at equal level; 2. Acquisition in accordance with colonial legislation, but at unequal level; and 3. Acquisition in violation of this legislation and at unequal level'.[20] He then sets out five categories of 'colonial cultural objects' as '1. Gifts to colonial administrators and institutions; 2. Objects acquired during private expeditions; 3. Objects acquired during military expeditions; 4. Missionary collecting; 5. Archives'.[21]

The Hunterian Museum's recent repatriation policy lists situations demonstrating unethical acquisition by collectors or donors or vendors which represent a non-exhaustive list of justifiable claims where objects were '(a) acquired as the spoils of war; (b) acquired through the desecration of graves or sacred sites; (c) acquired by theft or under duress; (d) acquired without necessary

---

[16] Hicks, *The Brutish Museums*, pp. 238–9.   [17] ibid., p. 239.
[18] Sarr and Savoy, *The Restitution of African Cultural Heritage*, p. 61.   [19] ibid.
[20] Jos van Beurden, *Treasures in Trusted Hands: Negotiating the Future of Colonial Cultural Objects* (Leiden: Sidestone Press, 2017), p. 41.
[21] ibid.

permits and authority which were in place at the time collecting; (e) which have been subject to spoliation in Europe between 1933 and 1945'.[22]

Whilst Hicks and van Beurden restrict their analysis to takings in the colonial context, and Sarr and Savoy to those involving French colonial takings in Africa, as reflected in the Hunterian's policy there are further categories of takings which affect objects in such a way that the object's continued presence in a museum or the nature and extent of care warrants consideration. These include forced sales resulting from persecution, as well as sales taking place in relative safety after fleeing persecution.[23] A typology of categories is now set out.

9.3.2.1 Removal with Force (Directed at People)

Where cultural heritage objects were removed from the original communities who provided care (whether communities of origin or private owners) with the threat of physical force to people, the continued care of these objects by the current possessors needs reconsideration. This would include, as Hicks suggests, the context of colonialism but also includes physical force used during wartime, as acts of genocide, through persecution towards particular communities as well as during civil unrest.

9.3.2.2 Looting

This category overlaps with the previous one in that it also involves the direct taking of cultural heritage from its original place or from its owner. There is, though, no accompanying physical force or threat of it to the people involved. Such looting can take a variety of different forms, including the looting of historical sites, which may involve the removal of elements of a statue or parts of a temple, a tomb or other important historical buildings. It also includes illicit excavation of archaeological sites where the objects themselves, which have been in the ground for many years, may have been unknown to anyone. Yet the owner of the place or the state in which they are located may have a prior legal entitlement to them. Nevertheless, it may be appropriate to consider carefully whether they are the most appropriately placed to care for the cultural heritage. Communities who could mount challenges to the *status quo* include the national community (in the form of the state) which would have been entitled to the objects through patrimonial laws, or the local community from the place where the object was taken.

Looting can also take the form of plundering existing collections, in particular during times of war. The Baghdad Museum was pillaged during the Second Gulf War, as was the Afghan Museum in Kabul. Looting of museum collections was undertaken by the Einsatzstab Reichsleiter Rosenberg, the Gestapo and others working for the Nazi regime during the Nazi era. Here

---

[22] University of Glasgow, *The Hunterian Repatriation Policy* (June 2021), para. 11.3: www .gla.ac.uk/media/Media_815581_smxx.pdf (last accessed 1 June 2023).

[23] Known as flight goods.

the seizure of objects was not always accompanied by violence towards people. Instead, objects may have been removed directly from their owners or from collections, through direct taking, but where places were at that time unoccupied. However, there are clear injustices that need addressing.

9.3.2.3 Forced Sales

A category of objects of particular relevance in the context of Nazi-era claims is those which were the subject of forced sales by their original owners. These sales took place because of the persecution suffered by their owners and the sales would unlikely have occurred but for the persecution. These are varied in nature but include sales to meet extortionate tax demands made of persecuted groups, to fund exit visas, to fund escape from persecution and to fund setting up a new life in neutral countries after the war.[24] Forced sales were identified during the war as problematic and the Allies put the world on notice of the invalidity of these transactions.[25] For that reason, restitution committees across Europe have treated these as forced sales which justify unravelling and being responded to through extra-legal remedies.

9.3.2.4 Collecting

Where museums themselves were complicit in the wrongdoing, there is a stronger argument in favour of acting now to remedy the wrongdoing. The types of collecting which may give rise to questions of injustice can be separated into two types. The first, primary collecting, is where the museum or its agents collected the objects themselves directly from communities or from archaeological and historical sites in circumstances which may have been illegal or unethical. This may have been through archaeological missions or where individual collectors were sent by museums to acquire objects. Institutional collecting took place on a large scale by universities and museums and at times by private institutes for the purposes of compiling scientific collections. Some collecting – particularly of cranial fragments of human remains – might be described as being pseudo-scientific, relating to now debunked theories of evolution aimed at suggesting Western superiority. Collecting was also undertaken for the purposes of adding to ethnographic collections, at times with little or no idea of the cultural purpose of objects, but where objects were treated as curios or as aesthetically interesting. Similarly, objects may have been collected from historical sites, more for their aesthetic beauty than for their archaeological importance.

Secondary collecting involves acquisitions either from those who initially acquired the objects from their original place, from their original community, or

---

[24] See generally Ruth Redmond-Cooper (ed.), *Museums and the Holocaust* (Builth Wells: Institute of Art and Law, 2021).

[25] In the Inter-Allied Declaration against acts of Dispossession Committed in Territories Under Enemy Occupation or Control, London, 5 January 1943.

from an intermediary.[26] It is the circumstances of the original acquisition, and the knowledge that the museum had about the circumstances of the original collecting, which may trigger questions regarding the appropriateness of the continued care by the museums of these objects within the collection.[27] Collecting was undertaken in a variety of different circumstances, by a variety of different actors. A central consideration is about the circumstances in which collecting was carried out – specifically, whether or not this was undertaken with appropriate permission. Even where permission for removal was given by communities or authorities this has to be understood in its context. If it was during times of unequal power relations, or permission was given by the relevant occupying authority at the time rather than directly from the communities from which the objects originated, then this justifies revisiting the current provision of care.

Private collectors amassed cultural heritage objects during their travels, including the Grand Tour, or during overseas postings in the diplomatic service. Objects may have been acquired from communities (whether or not for financial gain) by someone in a position of authority and because of the unequal positions of power in play at the time do not represent freely informed exchange supported by appropriate consideration.

Gifts may have been made directly to royalty or to the state, or to representatives of the colonial power.[28] Again, the circumstances of those gifts would need to be unravelled before considering whether these circumstances warranted a museum or other institution revisiting the current provision of care and its appropriateness. This would also include a consideration of whether an object might be more appropriately cared for by others, such as the successor community of the community from whom it was originally acquired or taken.

9.3.3 Circumventing the Requirements of a Nested Practice of Care

Where objects have entered the UK following their illegal export from their countries of origin and are in museum collections, there is an argument that this justifies a challenge to the *status quo* even in a situation where these entered many years ago and the museum is recognised in law as having title to them.[29] It is clear that according to current UK government guidance, museums should only acquire or borrow items in situations where they are convinced both of their legal and ethical entitlement to them. In this regard, the DCMS has used the 1970 threshold as a 'clear, pragmatic impracticable watershed that is already widely understood and supported'[30] and states that

---

[26] Which is considered in the next section.   [27] See the next section.

[28] For example, Robert Clive: see www.english-heritage.org.uk/visit/london-statues-and-monuments/robert-clive/ (last accessed 1 June 2023); in his typology of colonial cultural objects Van Beurden includes gifts to colonial administrators and institutions, Van Beurden, *Treasures in Trusted Hands*, p. 41.

[29] By virtue of the operation of the Limitation Act 1939 or the Limitation Act 1980.

[30] DCMS, *Combating Illicit Trade: Due Diligence Guidelines for Museums, Libraries and Archives on Collecting and Borrowing Cultural Material* (London: DCMS, 2006), p. 4.

'Museums should acquire or borrow items only if they are certain they have not been illegally excavated or illegally exported since 1970'.[31]

Museums may, in times gone by, have knowingly (or at least recklessly as to the exact situation) acquired objects which were illicitly excavated contrary to laws in place to protect them. In such situations there would be a clear lack of information about the context of the find spot (the provenience). Again, contemporary guidance warns museums about acquiring such objects. In circumstances where a museum acquired such objects years earlier, even where the passage of time has clothed the museum with a legal title, nevertheless, there is an argument for opportunities to challenge the *status quo*.

9.3.4 Assuming Caring Responsibilities with Knowledge: Circumstances of Acquisition

Communities may also establish an entitlement for care to be reconsidered, and for a dialogue to be entered into, where the communities currently with responsibility for the direct care of cultural heritage assumed that responsibility without the consent of the original communities who cared for it. This would be either knowing, or suspecting, that the original removal from the original communities of care was without consent, or knowing about the illegality of the original loss, or acquisition, of the objects. Here the museums, as the current communities of care with knowledge of the wrongdoing, are culpable and this may ultimately justify an alternative community in assuming responsibility in place of the museum. However, as a minimum, this set of circumstances would justify a dialogue regarding the current provision of care. Strong arguments can be made that museums, as defenders and upholders of the public trust, should not benefit from cultural heritage which they know, or ought to have known, was wrongfully acquired from the original communities of care.

The actual knowledge or constructive knowledge of the museum at the time of acquisition thereby taints the object. It thus opens up a need to assess the appropriateness of the current provision of care, and the allocation of responsibility for that care. Where museums, when acquiring an object, were fully cognisant of the force used and the absence of consent of the original community of care, even if it was generally accepted behaviour at the time, there is still justification for revisiting the current allocation of care as well as the nature and extent of the care. This is arguably even the case where the actions were not legally prohibited at the time.

The knowledge of museums when acquiring cultural heritage objects was a factor which, when first established, the Spoliation Advisory Panel had to take into account when making its recommendations. Its Terms of Reference

---

[31] ibid.

stated that, as part of its 'paramount purpose' of seeking to achieve a fair and just solution for the parties, the Panel would:

> consider whether any moral obligation rests on the institution taking into account in particular the circumstances of its acquisition of the object, and its knowledge at that juncture of the object's provenance.[32]

This approach therefore treats knowledge at the time of acquisition as central to a museum's moral obligation, which can give rise to return, compensation, an *ex gratia* payment or the display of an account of the object's history. In all cases to date, the Panel has considered whether the museum was under a moral obligation, but it has only been central to the outcome of a claim in one case. That involved the claim for the Beneventan Missal in the British Library.[33] When a Captain Nash approached the British Museum[34] with the manuscript in question, the presence of Beneventan script clearly identified it as originating from Benevento and raised the flag that it had possibly been looted.[35] It was on this basis that the deputy keeper of manuscripts refused to purchase the manuscript directly from Captain Nash. The British Museum only purchased the manuscript following its appearance at a public auction.[36] The public nature of the sale, by a seller who was willing to be identified, satisfied the British Museum that it could proceed with the purchase although in reality nothing had changed other than the mode of sale.[37] The Panel therefore considered that the provenance checks did not meet even those standards expected at the time, and the museum had sufficient knowledge about the object's questionable provenance. Consequently, the museum was under a moral obligation to the claimant.

In a more recent claim the Panel criticised the Tate Gallery about its failure to enquire about the provenance of Constable's *Beaching a Boat, Brighton*, which it acquired in the 1980s. The criticism was on the basis that at that time 'Holocaust-related provenance were not ignored in the 1980s to the extent that they had been in the 1950s or 1960s' and on the specialist knowledge of the Tate on works by Constable.[38] This together with the gap in the provenance

---

[32] SAP ToR, para. 7(g) as originally drafted: *Hansard* HC vol. 348, col. 256W (13 April 2000).

[33] *British Library/Benevento* claim (Report of the Spoliation Advisory Panel in respect of a twelfth-century manuscript now in the possession of the British Library (23 March 2005) (2005 HC 406)).

[34] Who was the predecessor in title to the British Library.

[35] Evidenced in a letter from the deputy keeper to Captain Nash: *British Library/Benevento* claim, para. 18.

[36] ibid., paras. 69.1–2.

[37] The Panel concluded that 'We do not think that the terms of the Sotheby's catalogue, and in particular the identification of Captain Ash as the vendor, were sufficient justifiably to allay the previously harboured suspicion as to the missal's provenance, judged by the standard of a reasonable Head of Department': ibid., para. 69.1.

[38] Report of the Spoliation Advisory Panel in respect of an oil painting by John Constable, 'Beaching a Boat, Brighton', now in the possession of the Tate Gallery (26 March 2014) (2014 HC 1016) (*Tate Gallery/Constable*), para. 47.

(particularly during the Nazi era), its sale on the continent in 1908, the general knowledge of the 1944 invasion of Hungary, spoliation, the Inter-Allied Declaration and the ICOM Code of Ethics were all known to museums and their directors. All this led the Panel to conclude that the Tate was under a moral obligation in addition to the sufficiently strong moral strength to the claim that had been established based on the circumstances of loss.[39] Therefore, the success of the claim did not turn on the issue of the museum's moral obligation, but had been considered as part of the process established by the Terms of Reference.

In 2016, in response to recommendations in the *Jenkins Review*,[40] a new paragraph 16 was inserted into the Panel's Terms of Reference stating that:

> The Panel will only consider whether any particular moral obligation rests on the institution if it finds it necessary to do so to enable it to arrive at a fair and just recommendation. For that purpose, the Panel shall take into account any relevant consideration (including the circumstances of its acquisition of the object and its knowledge at that time of the object's provenance).[41]

Only one claim, the *Fitzwilliam/Bing* claim,[42] heard in 2023 has been considered since the standard Terms of Reference were revised; however, the Terms of Reference used by the Panel on this occasion were those existing before 2016 and consequently the Panel was required to consider whether a moral obligation rested on the respondent museum.[43] Therefore, in the report of this claim, the Panel considered whether the museum was under a moral obligation, as part of the general analysis of the circumstances, without justifying any exceptionality which would justify the actions of the museum being considered (as was the approach in the 2016 revisions to the Terms of Reference).[44]

The moral obligation of museums, certainly, in the context of claims for cultural heritage objects taken during punitive expeditions and colonial times would be relevant. The museum would likely have been aware of the source of the objects when it acquired them, and this fact would justify a reconsideration of the current provision of care.

9.3.5 Challenges to the *status quo* (Searching Out the Challengers – aka the 'Claimants')

Having considered the circumstances that may justify challenges to the *status quo*, it is important to fully engage with the question of who can challenge the *status quo* regarding cultural heritage and on what grounds? Simply caring

---

[39] ibid., para. 49. The Panel went further and placed a continuing obligation on the Tate to enquire about provenance after acquisition: paras. 50–2.
[40] Sir Paul Jenkins KCB QC, *Independent Review of the Spoliation Advisory Panel* (March 2015).
[41] SAP ToR Revised 2016, para. 16.
[42] Report of the Spoliation Advisory Panel in respect of the painting 'La Ronde Enfantine' by Gustave Courbet in the possession of the Fitzwilliam Museum, Cambridge (28 March 2023) (2023 HC 1210).
[43] SAP ToR appended to the *Fitzwilliam/Bing claim*.   [44] ibid., para. 22.

about cultural heritage does not by itself give someone sufficient standing to justify a challenge – more is needed. As discussed above, the presence of a small number of cultural heritage objects in museums in itself represents an injustice. For this reason they may be more appropriately cared for by the particular community that justifiably cares about the cultural heritage because of its importance to it as a community due to a pre-existing connection such as being the community of origin. That community is therefore the appropriate one to challenge the *status quo*. In circumstances where there was a past wrong or injustice through which a community lost responsibility for the care of the cultural heritage, it may be more difficult to identify the most appropriate community to challenge the *status quo* and often such challenges revolve around a desire to have the object returned (and will take the form of a claim). An identifiable community, or its heirs, or the modern-day community with the closest connection will be best placed to challenge the *status quo*. This could be justified on the basis of a continuing moral entitlement which comes about by the circumstances in which the previous generations of their community lost the responsibility for care. They could then engage the process through which they question the current provision of care, and look to establish who might be best placed to assume responsibility for the care in the most appropriate manner. Thus, the requirement of sufficient standing is satisfied where there is a link between the current community and the cultural heritage. This can be shown by establishing that they are the successors of the initial community of care (which was displaced at some point in the past due to an injustice), or if they can establish a link with the particular place from which the object originated.

Individuals or communities whose previous generations were wronged may seek to challenge the continued care of objects of which they were dispossessed which are currently located in museums, other similar institutions or private collections. In many situations these wrongs will have crossed generations, resulting in inter-generational obligations.[45] States may also bring claims in a representative capacity, acting on behalf of local communities. In such circumstances caution needs to be exercised to ensure that the representation does not amount to paternalistic care.[46] At times there may be more than one community who could bring a claim in respect of an object. The varied nature of these communities is recognised in the recent Arts Council England (ACE) Guidelines on restitution and repatriation.[47]

In some situations, direct descendants of the original owner seek the return of a particular cultural heritage object – this is more so in situations involving

---

[45] See Janna Thompson, *Taking Responsibility for the Past: Reparation and Historical Justice* (Cambridge: Polity, 2002); Jeremy Waldron, 'Superseding Historic Injustice' (1992) 103 *Ethics* 4.

[46] See Section 9.5.1.

[47] ACE, *Restitution and Repatriation: A Practical Guide for Museums in England* (London: ACE, 2022), p. 10.

Nazi-era dispossessions. The focus is primarily on the property itself, which can be a symbol of the tragedy that befell the original owner, or a symbol of a family member's struggle to locate it and have it returned.[48] In such cases, the importance of the object is intertwined with its loss and with the quest for its recovery. Sometimes works of art are vitally important culturally to a particular owner – but in other situations the objects were part of the overall wealth of an individual family or were the commercial stock of a gallery owned by a member of a persecuted group. Nevertheless, there is still a recognised need to provide justice.[49]

These claims have a much firmer grounding in property concepts – for it can often be established that the original owners had legal title to the object before the loss and usually, but for the Nazi-era persecution, they would not have given up possession of the objects at that time.[50] The line of inheritance down which the object would otherwise have passed and a current heir who was deprived of the chance of receiving that inheritance can be identified. These claims are constructed within a framework of treating the original owner as the 'rightful owner'[51] and the idea that the museums (and ultimately the public) are now wrongfully benefiting from those objects. There is strong public support for facilitating the return of these objects.

Sacred or culturally important objects of significant importance to communities such as Australian Aboriginal, Maori, Native American, Sami or First Nations would have held significance to these communities from the outset. Following misappropriation these dispossessed objects would continue to hold a high degree of significance to communities who would clearly care about them. Their importance lay (and continues to lie) in their use within practices and as part of the manifestation of a particular culture. Entwined with this, though, is the fact that the taking of these objects (in a parallel with the Nazi-era dispossessions) was part of a background of deculturalisation of a group. An example is found in the context of the repatriation of the G'psgolox totem pole from the Haisla Nation, which was related to the banning of the potlach ceremony and also other attempts to remove the indigenous cultures from society through cultural assimilation and the like.[52] The recovery of these objects is important not only for the reconnection with those objects but also with the need to seek to repair the injustices and as a future means of revitalising or reconnecting with the culture and to regenerate communities – therefore in the context of indigenous cultural heritage there are a multitude of benefits to repatriation. The physical return *qua* cultural heritage object is but

---

[48] See, for example, Simon Goodman, *The Orpheus Clock* (Melbourne: Scribe, 2015).

[49] The Spoliation Advisory Panel has not distinguished between these two types of claim. See generally Norman Palmer, 'Spoliation and Holocaust-Related Cultural Objects: Legal and Ethical Models for the Resolution of Claims' (2007) 12 *Art Antiquity and Law* 1, 11.

[50] See Section 9.6.2.

[51] A discussion of 'rightful owners' as a rhetorical device is found at Section 9.5.2.5.

[52] See Stacey R. Jessiman, 'The Repatriation of the G'psgolox Totem Pole: A Study of its Context, Process, and Outcome' (2011) 18 *International Journal of Cultural Property* 365, 368.

one element, but arguably more important for those communities who used the particular object and with which there is a continued connection through use within practices.

Establishing entitlement to challenges can be more difficult where they are made by communities who are not direct descendants of the original dispossessed owners, but are communities who now live at the place from which an object was taken, or are the national community. There are two reasons for identifying the continuity of culture – or the patriae from which they originate.[53] The first is to justify why the cultural heritage in question is of importance to a community (that is to say why they care about it) and secondly for the purposes of determining whether that is sufficient to justify revisiting the question of who provides the care and whether that community is better placed to provide appropriate care (which may ultimately justify a transfer of the object or place to them). This can change over time, for some places are now inhabited by communities or nations which are different from those who were originally there. However, even where the communities may be quite different over time, objects can be important for the identity of a community, as can be seen by the arguments made from those in Greece about the importance of the Parthenon and its sculptures for their identity.[54] Nevertheless, the physical remnants of the Parthenon are in the modern-day country of Greece and there are missing elements of the whole which are found in foreign museums.

9.3.5.1 Involvement of the State in Challenges

The national community (in the form of the state) may have entitlement under patrimony laws and be best placed to challenge the *status quo*. Some national governments have spearheaded efforts to repatriate cultural heritage to communities within their nation, such as the Australian government, which has sought the return of human remains through its diplomatic offices.[55] Other examples include the Ethiopian Embassy in London, which deals with claims relating to cultural heritage objects taken during the Maqdala campaign. In practice, the appropriateness of responding to representatives, particularly at the national rather than local level, needs to be considered carefully, since ultimately returning cultural heritage objects to the state rather than the community from which they were originally taken may not represent appropriate care for the community itself.

The case of *Attorney General of New Zealand* v. *Ortiz* shows an early twist to the issue of representative claims; in effect the argument was that the Crown

---

[53] See generally Jeanette Greenfield, *The Return of Cultural Treasures* (3rd ed., Cambridge: Cambridge University Press, 2007).

[54] This argument is found in academic works as well as Parliamentary debates, e.g. Andrew Dismore MP, *Hansard* HC vol. 412, col. 406 (29 October 2003).

[55] See Australian Government, *Indigenous Repatriation*: www.arts.gov.au/what-we-do/cultural-heritage/indigenous-repatriation (last accessed 1 June 2023).

was the owner of the Maori panels because of the rules of forfeiture. This was despite the panels themselves originating from and being of importance to Maori peoples rather than to the New Zealand state and in the context of colonialism.[56] When the return of the panels was negotiated by the New Zealand government and the Ortiz family, the Panels, on their return to New Zealand, were initially cared for by Te Papa Museum. However, they were eventually returned to Taranaki as part of the Treaty settlement process.[57]

The transfer of cultural heritage, as an act of repatriation, can provide justice to wronged communities. It can also be used as reparations where the government, which was not responsible for the taking itself, nevertheless sought to return it because of its importance to a particular community and as a means of trying to provide justice for other indirect wrongs. Cultural heritage is often the subject matter of a claim and represents the need to respond to an injustice in a particular set of circumstances, requiring a response to correct past injustices.

On some occasions states, rather than the original communities of care, seek to challenge the *status quo* where cultural heritage is held by museums in circumstances in which the original communities of care lost possession during colonial times, as a result of looting, or because of unequal collecting practices in place at the time. The central question becomes: is the state, as a community of care, the one to whom responsibility should be transferred for the direct care of cultural heritage? Alternatively, the state may act as a facilitator such that the transfer is made directly to the community from whom it was originally taken. At least one museum, in its repatriation policy, requires state involvement when considering repatriation requests and in the absence of such support asks for the claimants to justify why they are not involving the state.[58]

9.3.6 Framing Challenges: Translations and the Importance of Analogy

Articulating the strength of feeling that a community has about cultural heritage can be a difficult task. This is particularly so where there is a lack of appreciation for other viewpoints about cultural heritage, and where there is a concern that those in possession of cultural heritage do not fully appreciate the importance of the cultural heritage to a particular community. One way of approaching this has been to translate the feeling of loss that would be occasioned if something were sold or physically harmed or its setting were harmed into something relatable to the person or institution being challenged.

---

[56] [1984] AC 1.

[57] Arapata Hakiwai, *The Motunui Panels: Returned to New Zealand* (9 July 2014): www
.friendsoftepapa.org.nz/motunui-panels-returned-new-zealand/ (last accessed
22 December 2022).

[58] University of Cambridge Museum of Archaeology and Anthropology and Cambridge
University Museums and Botanic Gardens, *Our Approach to the Return of Artefacts.*

This may aid communities in expressing the extent to which they care about cultural heritage and the strength of those feelings and links the disposition of care with the process of caring for cultural heritage. Thus, in the context of claims for restitution analogies have been used by claimants in attempts to situate their own claim within the cultural framework of the respondent. The use of analogies serves an important function in showing the strength of feeling; their use enables the respondents to appreciate that strength of feeling of claimants when considering claims that are made. Whether this perpetuates colonial oppression is a question for another day.

In *Bumper*, in the context of determining whether a Hindu temple might have legal standing, the judge drew an analogy with a foreign Roman Catholic cathedral and concluded that this could apply to a Hindu temple – thus establishing standing.[59] It may be that this decision, now over 30 years ago, is dated and the court would not need to make such an analogy to achieve that same conclusion. Nevertheless, it is possible to see the use of analogies elsewhere, in particular used to emphasise the importance of something to a particular community. Often an analogy is drawn with the Crown Jewels – this can be seen in both media reports and Parliamentary debates. In the 1983 debate about a potential amendment to the British Museum Act (BMA) 1963, it was said in the House of Lords that:

> It is not enough to say that the whole world can come to Britain and see its heritage cared for here, nor even to plead that, but for our ancestors, these precious objects might not now exist, though that may be true. If our Crown Jewels were located in a Greek or Sri Lankan museum gratitude would not be the first emotion to surge into British breasts.[60]

The use of analogies can also play an important role in the repatriation process itself. In the G'psgolox case,[61] which sought the return of an object from the Museum of Ethnography in Stockholm, the originating community compared the importance of the G'psgolox to them with the cultural and historical importance of the Vasa in Sweden (the historic warship from the 1600s which was discovered in the 1950s and is on display in the eponymous museum in Stockholm).[62] They translated the strength of feeling about the extent to which they care about cultural heritage, which therefore necessitated a response or a change to the current way in which the cultural heritage was being cared for. When addressing the 1997 centenary commemoration of the sacking of Benin City, the Oba of Benin compared this case with the return of the Stone of Scone to Scotland and the return of gold to Jewish persons from

---

[59] *Bumper Development Corp Ltd.* v. *Commissioner of Police of the Metropolis and others (Union of India and others, claimants)* [1991] 1 WLR 1362 (CA), 1372.

[60] *Hansard* HL (27 October 1983).

[61] Described by Jessiman, 'The Repatriation of the G'psgolox Totem Pole', 372.

[62] Vasa Museet, *Vasa History*: www.vasamuseet.se/en/explore/vasa-history (last accessed 15 December 2022).

Swiss banks which had been plundered by the Nazis.[63] These analogies were thus drawn not only with the strength of feeling, but also with the need, and way in which, to address an injustice. Such analogies serve to emphasise inconsistent practice, which draws perpetuated injustice into sharp focus.

How other claims have been addressed can assist those challenging the current allocation of responsibility for care. In the report of the Working Group on Human Remains in 2003, in the evidence presented to its chairman by the Tasmanian Aboriginal Centre (TAC), the differential approach taken by the Culture, Media and Sport Select Committee in its 2000 report towards Nazi-era claims as compared with claims for the return of human remains was highlighted. In particular, it was emphasised how claims relating to losses during the Nazi era had benefited from the establishment of an independent panel to hear claims and from the widespread provenance research undertaken by museums.[64] TAC highlighted the difference in pace of legislation, the encouragement to remove statutory bars on transfer in the case of Nazi-era claims, the recognition of the need to subordinate educative value to the vindication of property rights (including subordination of public access to rightful claims) and the expressed commitment to deal with material in private hands as well as that in public hands.[65] Here, the injustice identified was the differing treatment of two very important categories of cultural heritage whose importance to communities could be understood as being different, yet comparable in several respects.

The inconsistencies between how UK museums could respond to comparable claims for the return of objects during the Nazi era were one of the driving forces behind the legislative changes in 2009. Both the successful Feldmann[66] and Rothberger[67] claims, heard by the Spoliation Advisory Panel, had resulted in a recommendation of return of the cultural heritage object where the respondent was a non-national museum. However, in the comparable claims against national museums, those same claimants were given *ex gratia* payments because the governing statute of the British Museum (the national museum in both claims) did not permit the transfer to the claimants of the objects. This was despite the strong moral arguments for so doing.[68] In the debates relating to the

---

[63] Select Committee 7th Report 2000, Vol. II, Minutes of Evidence, Memorandum submitted by Glasgow City Council, para. 2.5.2.

[64] DCMS, *Report of the Working Group on Human Remains* (November 2003), p. 149.

[65] ibid., p. 150.

[66] Report of the Spoliation Advisory Panel in respect of three drawings now in the possession of the Courtauld Institute of Art (24 January 2007) (2007 HC 200) and Report of the Spoliation Advisory Panel in respect of four drawings now in the possession of the British Museum (27 April 2006) (2006 HC 1052).

[67] Report of the Spoliation Advisory Panel in respect of three pieces of porcelain now in the possession of the British Museum London and the Fitzwilliam Museum, Cambridge (11 June 2008) (2008 HC 602).

[68] The Vice-Chancellor in the case of *AG* v. *Trustees of the British Museum* [2005] Ch 397 (Ch), 411 found that the despite a strong moral argument in favour of the trustees transferring an object from its collection, the prohibitive governing statute prevented any transfer.

2009 Holocaust (Return of Cultural Objects) bill those cases were described as resulting in 'downright ludicrous outcomes' where return was permitted from one institution but not from another, despite the claim being made by the same claimant in equally meritorious circumstances.[69]

Analogies can provide a dialogic way of addressing difference, by seeking to understand the importance of cultural heritage from another's viewpoint and appreciating how, and why, someone cares about the cultural heritage involved by recognising the strength of feeling towards it. Being presented with an analogy may encourage those currently in possession to question both that continued presence and the appropriateness of the care that they are providing by determining whether the provision of direct care by another may be more appropriate.

The use of analogies does not negate the fact that claims often raise particular questions requiring individual responses. However, framing claims with the aid of analogies may serve to express the strength of feeling towards the cultural heritage and the importance of questioning the current allocation of responsibility for care, but can also make visible inconsistences which would otherwise perpetuate, or lead to further, injustice.

9.4 Responses

Responses to challenges to the *status quo* can take a variety of forms. Broadly it can be said that at one end of the spectrum of responses sit defensive responses, demonstrating paternalistic care, and at the other end dialogic responses framed within the ethics of care. Approaches by museums (either to specific challenges or challenges through institutional policies) are situated at different points along this spectrum. Indeed, their approaches can change over time, in part when legislative changes facilitate return, but also when institutional policies are revised. The next section considers the range of defensive positions adopted by museums and instances of broader reticence towards attempts to reform the law in order to better respond to challenges to the *status quo*. The discussion then turns to the facilitation of responses to justice (representing first steps) which are found in the context of claims for objects taken during the Nazi era and claims for human remains. The final section considers dialogic responses to claims.

9.5 Defensive Stances

Museums may take defensive stances when faced with what are clearly framed as claims for the transfer of cultural heritage. These can take the form of outright denials of claims in terms of an unwillingness to consider any claim for the transfer of a cultural heritage object or even to entertain any dialogue,

---

[69] Andrew Dismore MP, *Hansard* HC vol. 49, col. 1045 (26 June 2009).

hiding behind legislative provisions. Other museums may defend their current responsibility for care, enshrined by law, but engage, to a limited extent, in dialogue relating to how that museum continues to care for the cultural heritage at issue, or consider the loan of objects. Even where return is permitted by law, museums may still robustly defend claims, whilst others may defend the claim by testing the evidence, on the basis that any return is seen as a limited exception to the norm of maintaining the collections intact and that in maintaining the public interest there must be clear justifications for transfers. Each of these will be considered in turn.

9.5.1 Paternalistic Care (with or without Limited Dialogue)

Paternalistic care, as a concept, was identified by Narayan in the context of colonialism, where the power relations were concealed through a concept of care.[70] Paternalistic care, in situations where there is an unequal balance of power, can therefore 'be wielded as a form of control and domination by the powerful and the privileged'.[71] It is therefore important to have in mind the potential negative effect of such power and control, in particular in responses which are unwavering in their unwillingness to address calls for change.

Tronto identifies the risk of paternalism or maternalism in the sense that '[o]ften care-givers have more competence and expertise in meeting the needs of those receiving care. The result is that care-givers may well come to see themselves as more capable of assessing the needs of care-receivers than are the care-receivers themselves.'[72] 'Such a proprietary sense of being in charge is even more likely to occur among those who have assumed responsibility for some problem, who are taking care of a caring need.'[73] However, Nuala Morse suggests that 'caring is not always simply paternalistic, where care-givers assume that they know better than care-receivers what they need'.[74] It is argued in this chapter that paternalistic care occurs where a community of care has taken it upon itself to assume responsibility for the care of cultural heritage (or has had that responsibility imposed) and consistently maintains the position that it is the most appropriately placed to undertake that care, without revisiting that assumption based on changing views over time. This includes those unwilling to engage in dialogue when a community questions that continued assumption of responsibility for care. There are differing degrees of paternalistic care, ranging from a complete disengagement with any dialogue, to a willingness to engage with some dialogic which may explore mechanisms for collaboration, but premised on the basis of the continued direct care by the

---

[70] Narayan, 'Colonialism and Its Others', 135.   [71] ibid.

[72] Joan C. Tronto, *Moral Boundaries: A Political Argument for an Ethic of Care* (London: Routledge, 1993), p. 170.

[73] ibid., p. 170.

[74] Nuala Morse, *The Museum as a Space of Social Care* (London: Routledge, 2020), p. 190.

museum. This might be with a clear emphasis on the prohibitive nature of the strict legal provision preventing return.

In some situations in the UK, the current legal structures serve to perpetuate more traditional forms of care and marginalise, or at worst ignore, or legitimise attempts to unwaveringly defend the *status quo*. Examples of this include claims for the transfer of objects currently held in the collections of national museums. The disregard for other viewpoints and a determination to maintain the *status quo* through caring for objects in collections may even go as far as what has been described as 'cultural Schutzhaft', where objects acquired during colonialism have been taken into protective custody.[75]

A major stumbling block to attempts to challenge the *status quo* is the way in which care is translated into the English laws governing national museum collections. 'Care' is set out in statute as being the direct activity of the directors[76] or trustees[77] (with the day-to-day care, in practice, delegated to the curators of the museum). Those museums with more recently enacted governing statutes use the terminology of care to denote the relationship between the governing body and the objects forming its collection which are vested in them.[78] The idea is premised on having the objects in their care and the accompanying responsibility to preserve them and to maintain the collection intact for future generations (which is evident in the statutory restrictions on transfers). These restrictions mean that transfer out of their collections can only be justified in limited circumstances.[79] It is quite clear that the general provisions relating to transfer in the Imperial War Museum Act 1920, the National Maritime Museum Act 1934, the BMA 1963, the National Heritage 1983 and the Museums and Galleries Act 1992 all prevent acceding to repatriation requests, even on the basis of a moral compunction to do so. This was made clear in *AG* v. *Trustees of the British Museum*.[80] These statutory provisions thus provide a legal justification for maintaining the *status quo*. They

---

[75] Hicks, *The Brutish Museums*, p. 165.

[76] BMA 1963, ss. 6(1) and 8(3); Imperial War Museum Act 1920, s. 4(2) and National Maritime Museum Act 1934, s. 5(1). See Section 6.4.1.

[77] Museums and Galleries Act 1992, s. 2. See Section 6.4.1.   [78] See Section 6.4.1.

[79] Discussed at Section 7.3.2.2.

[80] [2005] Ch 397 (Ch), 412. Although recently an interesting argument has been advanced relating to the Ethiopian Tabots in the British Museum where it has been suggested that these might be susceptible to transfer on the basis that they are unfit to be retained and can be disposed of without detriment to the interests of students (for the purpose of the BMA 1963, s. 5(1)(c)) because they are not on display and the British Museum has agreed that they shall not be viewed by their curators because of their religious significance (representing as they do in the eyes of the Ethiopian Orthodox Church the Ark of the Covenant): see Alexander Herman, 'British Museum Must Recognise its Owns Powers in Matters of Restitution', *The Art Newspaper*, 29 May 2019. See also British Museum, *Maqdala Collection*: www.britishmuseum.org/about-us/british-museum-story/contested-objects-collection/maqdala-collection#:~:text=What%20are%20they%3F,a%20fortress%2C%20library%20and%20treasury (last accessed 1 June 2023). See also the debate in the House of Lords, British Museum: Ethiopian Sacred Altar Tablets, vol. 820, col. 1602 (30 March 2022).

demonstrate paternalistic care which may involve a museum relying on statutory prohibitions on transfers to resist claims and refusing to take up the opportunity for dialogue.

When faced with repatriation claims, in some cases the trustees of the national museums have emphasised how they are most appropriately placed to care for the cultural heritage concerned, and that there is therefore no need to question their continued responsibility for its care. Therefore, faced with calls for repatriation, as well as direct requests, the British Museum has adopted a published position in respect of the Parthenon Marbles acquired by Lord Elgin.[81] In its response to UNESCO's invitation to engage in mediation with Greece, the trustees stated that they 'have a legal and moral responsibility to preserve and maintain all the collections in their care, to treat them as inalienable and to make them accessible to world audiences'.[82] This has a paternalistic dimension, specifically in making the assumption that the museum is better placed than the community challenging that care who seeks to care for the cultural heritage in question. This is reflective of what has been termed the authorized heritage discourse as the directors and trustees (with the advice of their curators) act as the experts with authority to determine how cultural heritage is cared for.[83]

In the context of other 'contested objects', as described by the museum, the British Museum has set out details of various dialogues that it has entered into with communities seeking the return of specific objects currently in its collections. This includes position statements regarding the Maqdala collection,[84] the Benin Bronzes,[85] human remains[86] and Moai from Rapa Nui.[87]

There tends to be no express statement in the national museums' policies providing for the public to participate in the decision-making process itself. Although, as institutional members of the MA, there is an expectation that they deal 'sensitively and promptly with requests for repatriation'[88] and '[e]nsure

---

[81] British Museum, *The Parthenon Sculptures: The Trustee's Statement*: www.britishmuseum.org/about-us/british-museum-story/contested-objects-collection/parthenon-sculptures/parthenon (last accessed 1 June 2023). It should be noted that recent media reports suggest that representatives of the museum may be in talks with Greece regarding this matter: Helena Smith, 'Greece in "Preliminary" Talks with British Museum about Parthenon Marbles', *The Observer*, 3 December 2022. However, the UK government indicated that it had no plans to reform the NHA 1983 (and one could assume that the same applies to the BMA 1963).

[82] British Museum letter to Alfredo Pérez de Armiñán, Assistant Director-General for Culture, UNESCO, *The Parthenon Sculptures in the British Museum: UNESCO Mediation Proposal* (26 March 2015).

[83] Laurajane Smith, *Uses of Heritage* (London: Routledge, 2008), p. 11.

[84] British Museum, *Maqdala Collection*.

[85] British Museum, *Benin Bronzes*: www.britishmuseum.org/about-us/british-museum-story/contested-objects-collection/benin-bronzes (last accessed 1 June 2023).

[86] British Museum, *Human Remains*: www.britishmuseum.org/our-work/departments/human-remains (last accessed 1 June 2023).

[87] British Museum, *Maoi*: www.britishmuseum.org/about-us/british-museum-story/contested-objects-collection/moai (last accessed 1 June 2023).

[88] MA, *Code of Ethics*, principle 2.7.

that everyone has an opportunity for meaningful participation in the work of the museum'.[89] The recent ACE Restitution and Repatriation Guide aims to guide and empower museums to 'take proactive action in a spirit of transparency, collaboration and fairness'.[90] More recently, though, an increased level of participation has been observed in the context of certain cultural heritage objects of which communities challenge the museum's continued care. Even though there is engagement in some dialogue, arguably the refusal by a museum to actively lobby for a power to transfer presupposes that that museum is the most appropriately placed to provide the direct care.[91]

In some instances, museums (even if legally able to repatriate) may act defensively towards claims made against them. Whilst the museum has a power to transfer objects in appropriate circumstances, nevertheless the museum adopts a defensive position, wanting to retain possession of the object. It therefore takes a more combative or litigious approach to responding to the challenge to the *status quo*.[92]

9.5.2 Hindering Efforts to Respond

Where care is paternalistic and laws specifically prevent the achievement of justice, reform of the law could overcome this. However, previous attempts to amend the law – whether to facilitate wider categories of transfers from national museums with a view to enabling them to respond to claims based on past injustice, or to achieve more targeted reform – have met with several stumbling blocks.

Even if attempts are made to overcome the legal barriers, arguments may be advanced which hinder the development of the law. These include the pre-eminence of the Parthenon sculptures in debates, with an overall shadow of the marbles falling over arguments about repatriation and restitution. Further arguments also suggest that repatriation and restitution can risk the integrity of certain so-called universal museums[93] and that a favourable response to even just one claim would open the floodgates. The risk of political interference has been raised as an issue. Furthermore, the rhetoric of the 'rightful owners' and arguments about the 'culture wars' can hinder responses which might otherwise provide dialogic care. Each of these will now be considered in turn.

9.5.2.1 The Myth of the Marbles
The Parthenon Marbles that formed part of Lord Elgin's collections, purchased by the British Museum in 1816, have frequently been the focus of requests for their transfer to Greece. However, the preoccupation with these marbles has all

---

[89] ibid., principle 1.7.   [90] ACE, *Restitution and Repatriation Guide*, p. 2.

[91] Note the recent increased openness to consider the governing statutes by those in museums. Smith, 'Greece in "Preliminary" Talks with British Museum about Parthenon Marbles'.

[92] This can be seen in claims heard by the Spoliation Advisory Panel, as discussed at Section 9.6.3.

[93] An argument advanced in response to efforts to amend the BMA 1963 in 1983: Lord Trend, *Hansard* HL vol. 444, col. 405 (27 October 1983).

too often shifted the focus in repatriation debates away from the important matter at hand and towards the perceived 'risk' to the marbles. This occurs both in the context of calls for the repatriation of individual cultural heritage objects as well as in the context of broader debates about more generally facilitating repatriation of cultural heritage.

Audi has described the Parthenon Sculptures dispute as the 'myth of the marbles'.[94] He then considered the Elgin Marbles (as he described them) 'as national treasures'; 'as private property'; 'as archaeological treasure'; 'as aesthetic treasure'; 'as humanity's patrimony', additionally considering the 'innocent owner'; and 'national continuity'.[95] This leads to Audi's suggestion that 'The Elgin Marbles issue' has all the elements for a 'template for cultural property disputes' with the marbles themselves being 'active participants in these debates'.[96] It reflects Merryman's approach that the marbles 'symbolize the entire body of unrepatriated cultural property in the world's museums and private collections'.[97] Merryman recognised them, in a perhaps now dated phrase, as being 'a familiar and glamorous example of a class of objects called with increasing frequency cultural property',[98] repeating the notion of glamour as 'a convenient and glamorous context for reasoned discussion'.[99] The marbles thus act as a metaphor for the entire repatriation debate.[100]

Such is the strong link between Elgin's removal of the Parthenon sculptures and the wider concept of removal of elements of a monument that the French have adopted the phrase 'elginisme' to refer to the specific act of vandalism relating to architectural works from which objects are taken and which are then treated as works of art in themselves.[101] This definition thus focuses on the transformation occasioned by the removal from something that was part of a monument to a work of art forming part of a collection.

Not only does the Parthenon cast 'the longest and most influential shadow',[102] but specifically 'the Elgin Marbles narrative casts a dominant, stifling shadow over cultural property argument'.[103] In part this is because of

---

[94] Alan Audi, 'A Semiotics of Cultural Property Argument' (2007) 14 *International Journal of Cultural Property* 131, 142. Specifically, he adopts Barthes' understanding of myth as a second-order cultural meaning and separates out the first level as the marbles in the British Museum and then, on the second level, the story of the Parthenon, Elgin's acquisition, the fact that they are kept by the British Museum and the claims by Greece.

[95] ibid., 144–5.   [96] ibid., 143.

[97] John Henry Merryman, 'Thinking about the Elgin Marbles' (1984–1985) 83 *Michigan Law Review* 1881, 1895.

[98] ibid., 1888.   [99] ibid., 1895.

[100] To adopt David Gurnham's metaphor to describe a metaphor – it is ' . . . a boat, a ferry, a bridge, carrying a freight of meaning between one conceptual shore and another': David Gurnham, 'Introduction to Special Issue on *Law's Metaphors*' (2016) 43 *Journal of Law and Society* 1.

[101] See Larousse online. It has now entered the Encyclopedia Britannica in its anglicised form 'elginism'.

[102] Peter Green, *The Shadow of the Parthenon* (Oakland: University of California Press, 1972), p. 12.

[103] Audi, 'A Semiotics of Cultural Property Argument', 141.

the media focus primarily on the marbles and the use of them as a metaphor for the repatriation debates; as Simpson observes, 'The issue of repatriation is highly complex and political. All too often media attention focuses upon the case of the Parthenon Marbles.'[104] However, it is clear that the marbles can also permeate much of the policies and discussion of the universal museum; the marbles have become central to the discourse on universal museums.[105]

9.5.2.2 Using the Law as a Protective Barrier

Particularly in the context of the Parthenon Marbles, section 5 of the BMA 1963 has been seen as providing a protective barrier around the keepers of the marbles, and in turn, around the marbles themselves. It prevents them from being considered for repatriation or reunification with the Parthenon.[106] The metaphor of the barrier, or walls, is clear in the 1983 Hansard debates about the proposed amendment to section 5. Lord Jenkins, the originator of the attempted legislative amendment, speaking of the then director Dr Wilson, suggested that he 'might perhaps be described as an old lag who clings to his legislative prisonwalls and dreads the fresh air of freedom'. The then chairman of the British Museum Trustees Lord Trend, who spoke against the bill, suggested that the legal provision 'preserved [the trustees] from the random caprice of aesthetic taste, of fashion, moralistic judgments and – even more important – the fluctuations of political pressure, unpredictable, random and varying from day to day'.[107] Yet judgements are made on moral grounds when the British Museum trustees decide whether or not to transfer an object based on the recommendation of the Spoliation Advisory Panel (and approved by the Secretary of State). Similar judgements have been made in respect of human remains. In neither case have issues been raised about the risk of random or unpredictable responses, nor about fluctuations in political pressure.

The myth of the marbles has clearly cast a shadow over parliamentary debates about law reform, even when the bill was not directly targeted at the marbles. Therefore, during debates in past attempts to amend the BMA 1963, success of the bill may have been hindered by the fact that the parliamentary debates refer specifically to the Parthenon Marbles, and to the risk of them being returned. In 1983 the BMA 1963 (Amendment) Bill was introduced and originally titled the British Museum Trustees Liberation Bill, but Lord Jenkins

---

[104] Select Committee 7th Report 2000, Vol. III, Appendices to the Minutes of Evidence, Appendix 42, Memorandum submitted by Moira Simpson.

[105] See Section 9.5.2.3.

[106] Here it is helpful to adopt Kalliopi Fouseki's language of reunification with the rest of the Parthenon (or at least return to the locale) rather than repatriation, which can open up debates about the relevant or appropriate patriae – or the difficulties with the patriae: Kalliopi Fouseki, 'Claiming the Parthenon Marbles Back: Whose Claim and on Behalf of Whom?' in Louise Tythacott and Kostas Arvanitis (eds.), *Museums and Restitution: New Practices, New Approaches* (Farnham: Ashgate, 2014), p. 173.

[107] Lord Trend, *Hansard* HL vol. 444, col. 406 (27 October 1983).

was advised to choose 'a less dramatic title'.[108] The bill's originator expressly stated that the bill was not one to return the Elgin Marbles, but was instead an opportunity 'to abandon the role of international Scrooge'.[109] The bill provided a general power to the trustees to be able to return objects to their countries of origin 'in fulfilment of international obligations'.[110] Nevertheless, very quickly discussion in the debates shifted to the 'Elgin Marbles' and the potential opening of the floodgates to many other claims which could thereby risk the integrity of the collection. In a debate which included several then current and former trustees of the British Museum section 5 of the Act was seen as a welcome protection from political pressure. The amendment would thus be seen by the trustees 'as nothing less than a betrayal of their trust to create a precedent for the piecemeal dismemberment of their collection . . .'[111]

In 2002 a wider bill was placed before Parliament by Edward O'Hara MP.[112] This would have applied to all national museums that were then unable to deaccession objects. Its coverage was clearly aimed at objects beyond the Parthenon Marbles. This bill was introduced at a time when the newly established Spoliation Advisory Panel had already recommended in the *Tate Gallery/ Griffier* claim that return would have been the first option available to the Panel, had the museum been legally permitted to transfer the object.[113] It was also a time when the publication of the report of the Working Group on Human Remains was imminent.[114] Therefore, both human remains and objects which the Spoliation Advisory Panel had recommended to be returned were expressly included in the bill, as were the exchange of cultural objects, return for the purposes of international cultural co-operation and return of objects to their originating communities.[115] This was a comprehensive bill which would have taken a holistic approach to repatriation and restitution from national museums. It included not only a power for the trustees of these institutions to transfer objects, but also a provision enabling the Secretary of State to require the trustees to return objects in certain circumstances. However, this bill did not reach the second reading stage. The theme of protecting the museum from being denuded was emphasised through the use of a metaphorical device by Tim Loughton MP, who said that the 'British Museum should not be treated as some Aladdin's cave to buy power and influence at random'.[116]

---

[108] Lord Jenkins of Putney, *Hansard* HL vol. 444, col. 400 (27 October 1983).   [109] ibid.

[110] Which was a term criticised by several Lords as being too vague including the then Minister for the Arts the Earl of Gowrie, *Hansard* HL vol. 444, col. 416 (27 October 1983).

[111] Lord Trend, *Hansard* HL vol. 444, col. 407 (27 October 1983).

[112] Edward O'Hara MP, *Hansard* HC vol. 379, col. 774 (5 February 2002).

[113] *Tate Gallery/Griffier* claim (Report of the Spoliation Advisory Panel in respect of a painting now in the possession of the Tate Gallery (18 January 2001) (2005 HC 111), para. 51. Ultimately in that claim an *ex gratia* payment and the display of an account of the object's history were made.

[114] DCMS, *Report of the Working Group on Human Remains*.

[115] Edward O'Hara MP, *Hansard* HC vol. 379, col. 774 (5 February 2002).

[116] Tim Loughton MP, *Hansard* HC vol. 379, col. 778 (5 February 2002).

The 2009 attempt to provide a power to transfer the Parthenon Marbles[117] was framed within the wider power of the trustees of the British Museum (or a requirement by the Secretary of State) to transfer objects to another collection where the objects would be 'more widely accessible' or 'more appropriately displayed by reason of historic links' or where the objects 'came to form part of the collections of the Museum in circumstances which make its retention in the collection undesirable or inappropriate'.[118] The marbles were not specifically mentioned in the bill or the explanatory notes but the bill's introducer, Andrew Dismore MP, clearly framed the bill within the context of the Parthenon Marbles and indicated that whilst it was a general power there was really 'only one set of objects to which [the bill] could realistically relate'.[119] This therefore ignored the Benin Bronzes, the Ethiopian Tabots and Hoa Hakanaai'a and Maoi Hava from Rapa Nui, which are now much more strongly in the public mind.

More recently, in 2016, the Parthenon Sculptures (Return to Greece) Bill was presented by Mark Williams;[120] it did not reach the second reading stage. This bill provided for the transfer of ownership of the Parthenon sculptures to Greece following a consultation between the Secretary of State and the trustees of the British Museum, representatives of the government of the Hellenic Republic, and 'any other person, body or institution that the Secretary of State believes to be appropriate'.[121] The transfer of ownership would have been conditional on an agreement relating to transportation, associated costs, arrangements of the conditions and maintenance and display of the collection as well as access to the collection by experts, students and members of the public.[122] Here provision was therefore made for continued care by the UK in terms of involvement in the terms under which the marbles would be cared for in the future, including the provision of access. Again, the exceptionality of the marbles was emphasised, therefore it was expressly stated in the bill that nothing in the Act would apply to any other artefacts in any of the national museums or galleries.[123]

It seems that in parliamentary debates, where a bill specifically referred to the Parthenon sculptures, it did not survive for a second reading. This applied where bills related only to the British Museum as well as those bills dealing more generally with cultural objects in museums, but where it was perceived that it would include the Parthenon Marbles. By contrast, the passage of the Holocaust Return of Cultural Objects Bill 2009 received a friendly response, and arguably succeeded at least in part because it had no application beyond the narrow category of objects within museum collections that had been lost

---

[117] Interestingly the language of the debates shifted from Elgin Marbles in the 1983 bill debates to the Parthenon Marbles by 2003.

[118] Andrew Dismore MP, *Hansard* HC vol. 492, col. 1174 (15 May 2009).   [119] ibid.

[120] Bill 49 House of Commons, 11 July 2016.

[121] Parthenon Sculptures (Return to Greece) Bill, cls. 1(2) and 1(3).   [122] ibid., cl. 1(4).

[123] Cl. 3 of the Bill.

during the Nazi era.[124] It was introduced at the same time as the 2009 attempt to reform the BMA 1963 (discussed above). Andrew Dismore MP, who introduced the Holocaust Bill, emphasised though that 'It is not a Trojan horse for any other art works or cultural items'.[125] This therefore allayed any fears of losing their marbles.

The myth of the marbles has prevented any careful consideration of the appropriateness of changing the statutory provisions preventing deaccessioning by Parliament as a community of care. This myth, together with the rhetoric of the universal museum, has stifled any serious development of the law in this area.

9.5.2.3 Risk to the Universal Museum
In the context of debates about the proposed bill that would permit the trustees of the British Museum to transfer objects from their collection, Lord Trend treated it as a universal museum. He identified the universal museum as one which 'aims to present an integrated picture of the stages in the development of various civilisations of the world their indebtedness one to another' and continued: 'there is a sense in which the British Museum is a microcosm of the whole world ... It is for that reason that the trustees would regard it as nothing less than a betrayal of their trust to create a precedent for the piecemeal dismemberment of their collection.'[126]

This was a very early reference to the notion of the universal museum, a concept which gained traction in 2002 when the Bizot group of museum directors signed the *Declaration on the Importance and Value of the Universal museum*;[127] Greek sculpture was used as the prime example of a collection available to the international public which has led to a 'universal admiration for ancient civilizations'[128] with the marbles effectively becoming a metaphor for the universal museum.[129] Tied up with the notion of ensuring that encyclopedic or universal museums are kept intact is an argument espoused that: 'preservation of antiquities through acquisition and the building of encyclopedic museums' as 'a matter of public trust'.[130] However, in the context of the Declaration, Abungu suggests that by narrowing 'the focus of museums whose collections are diverse and multifaceted' this 'would ... be a disservice to all visitors'. The Declaration is, he says, the self-defining act of creating

---

[124] Albeit that it is not entirely clear that either the House of Lords or the House of Commons had anticipated its wider application than direct or indirect Nazi takings to thus include any loss of a cultural object during the years 1933–45.

[125] Official Report, Commons 26 June 2009, col. 1043 (Andrew Dismore MP).

[126] Debate on the BMA 1963 (Amendment) Bill, *Hansard* (27 October 1983).

[127] Declaration on the Importance and Value of Universal Museums [2004] *ICOM News* 4.

[128] ibid.

[129] See generally Neil Curtis, 'Universal Museums, Museum Objects and Repatriation: The Tangled Stories of Things' (2006) 21 *Museum Management and Curatorship* 117.

[130] James Cuno, 'Introduction' in James Cuno (ed.), *Whose Culture? The Promise of Museums and the Debate over Antiquities* (Oxford: Princeton University Press, 2009), p. 17.

a category of universal museums as a means by which to refuse to engage in a dialogue about repatriation.[131] Besterman[132] sees a refusal to engage with considerations about the *status quo* as a breach of ethical values and states that: 'Placing the need to keep the museum's collections intact above all other considerations is not a defence of integrity but its betrayal. Behaviour that might seek justification within the retentive dogma of universalism is exposed as an unedifying derogation of ethical leadership.'[133] Nevertheless, the trope of the importance of the universal collection continues and was evident in recent debates about the future of the National Heritage Act (NHA) 1983.[134]

9.5.2.4 Opening the Floodgates

Further concern about museums responding to challenges to the *status quo* by transferring objects has been expressed in terms of the risk of opening the floodgates to further claims. Even where calls are made to respond to individual claims, the floodgates argument has been raised in an attempt to quell any calls for transfer of a specific cultural heritage object. Responding to specific repatriation requests (even where specific legislation is needed for that) is seen as a potential precedent for future claims. When restitution and repatriation was facilitated for Nazi-era claims and human remains, these were viewed as *sui generis*, self-contained categories justifying specific responses which did not necessarily set a precedent for other claims because of their unique circumstances. However, in the context of claims for other cultural heritage objects there is sometimes perceived to be a risk that the floodgates would be opened to other claims. This is on the basis that, having responded to one category of cultural heritage, there would be little or no justifications for failing to respond to another given the parallels that might be drawn between them (e.g. forcible removal during colonial times or conquest). For this reason, there may have been reticence in responding to any one claim for fear of opening up challenges in respect of other, not too dissimilar, objects. The discussion above regarding the myth of the Parthenon Marbles as the epitome of cultural heritage claims means that if that is responded to it has the potential to make responding to other claims justifiable, and indeed a failure to do so may be considered to be unjustifiable in the circumstances. Whilst there may be further claims, whether this would lead to a flood of them is unclear – similar arguments were advanced when debates were being heard in respect of seeking to facilitate repatriation of human remains in the early 2000s (before the law was amended). Nearly twenty years after the legislative power was first given to the trustees of the named national museums, there has been no resultant emptying of the collections of human remains held by the national museums;

---

[131] George Abungu, 'The Declaration: A Contested Issue' [2004] *ICOM News* 5.

[132] Tristram Besterman, 'Cultural Equity in the Sustainable Museum' in Janet Marstine (ed.), *The Routledge Companion to Museum Ethics* (London: Routledge, 2011), p. 239.

[133] ibid., p. 243.

[134] Lord Parkinson of Whitley Bay, *Hansard* HL vol. 824, col. 173GC (13 October 2022).

instead, repatriation has been sought, and claims acceded to, on a measured scale.

The argument of potentially opening the floodgates to claims is not a new one. It was made in the House of Lords in 1974 in response to a question about the Ashanti Regalia; Lord Goronwy-Roberts said that if the House were to enact specific legislation regarding the Ashanti Regalia 'a great variety of other cases would immediately arise for consideration'.[135] In the context of the efforts to reform the BMA 1963 in 1983, again those speaking against the bill raised the risk of floodgates.[136] However, refusing one meritorious claim on the basis that other meritorious claims could be made in the future represents neither empathetic nor respectful care.

9.5.2.5 The Difficulty of Terminology: The Rhetoric of Rightful Owners

'Rightful owner' is often used in the context of claims for Nazi-era dispossession, and slightly less frequently in the context of claims for the return of objects taken or exchanged during colonial times. This term has gained currency not only in the way in which the media reports litigation claims, but also in official discussions of the appropriate response to claims based on norms other than legal ones.[137]

The rhetoric of rightful owners is frequently used not to denote ownership, in a legal sense, but as a means of identifying the people who are acknowledged as having a moral entitlement to an object of cultural heritage. They are, in effect, the 'true' owners. It is thus premised on the idea that there are sufficiently strong arguments justifying someone's status as the morally most worthy owner.

In many situations, particularly when talking about cultural *property* rather than cultural heritage, the focus has been on the question of ownership[138] – specifically legal ownership. As discussed earlier, this can be unhelpful when trying to determine how to provide appropriate care for cultural heritage. Specifically, the use of the terminology of 'owners' is problematic for it can demonstrate the disciplinary imperialism of law,[139] focusing on property ownership, and specifically the notion that there is one person who can be an owner in the circumstances. It necessarily pits one person against another in an often seemingly irreconcilable way.

Mixing the terminology, by talking about rightful owners when referring to moral, rather than legal entitlement, has the potential to hinder attempts to

---

[135] *Hansard* HL vol. 355, cc. 534-5 (10 December 1974).

[136] Lord Nugent, *Hansard* HL vol. 444, col. 405 (27 October 1983).

[137] The terminology of 'rightful owner' has been used by the Culture, Media and Sport Select Committee (Select Committee 7th Report 2000, Vol. I, para. 173), Government Press Releases ('UK Government renews its commitment to return Nazi-looted art to rightful owners' 21 July 2017, quote by John Glen) and by the Scottish Legislature (Scottish Legislative Consent Memorandum for the Holocaust (Return of Cultural Objects) Bill, Session 3, 2009 LCM (S3) 21).

[138] See Section 1.1.2.   [139] See Section 3.4.2.

navigate the dissonance which exists where communities are challenging the *status quo* in terms of who is the current holder of the particular cultural heritage. Instead, the primary concern may be one of control, or authority to speak. On occasions, a primary concern has been a lack of understanding regarding the symbolism of the object or the appropriate way in which it is handled (or not).[140] The idea of 'rightful' suggests that it is a clear-cut case which treats one person as having a better (or even the best) entitlement to an object than the other. Here the sense is that one of them is more worthy than the other. However, determining with certainty that one person or community has an unequivocally morally stronger entitlement than the current possessor is often difficult. Claims frequently arise from circumstances that are by no means clear cut. In the context of Nazi-era claims, often losses took place in circumstances other than a direct seizure by the Nazis and therefore one needs to carefully unravel what happened many years ago. For that reason, it is counterproductive to treat the claimant as a rightful owner before a claim is heard, and importantly before assessing the nuances of the claim. This is particularly the case when independent government-appointed panels of experts conclude that the moral strength of the claim is insufficient to justify return but, instead, that some other remedy is approved, such as the display of an account of the object's history. However, the Panel would have considered carefully the available evidence to establish, as far as it can, whether or not the sale had been forced by persecution, or whether it was undertaken because of the financial constraints of the time, such as a result of the 1930s depression.

Focusing on rightful owners reflects to some extent the approach taken at the international level that a person's legal ownership or title might not necessarily coincide with their 'valid title'.[141] This is seen in the ICOM Code of Ethics, which states that museums should be satisfied that they acquire valid title and that '[e]vidence of lawful ownership in a country is not necessarily valid title'.[142] Even if a museum could be sure of acquiring a valid legal title (which it may have by dint of the law extinguishing any better title through the effect of the Limitation Acts 1939 or 1980), this is seen as insufficient.[143] This translates as meaning that the museum should not ethically seek to rely on this legal title, but should instead endeavour to acquire something in ethical circumstances, and in so doing it will also acquire valid title. This presupposes

---

[140] The tethering of the G'psgolox totem pole in the museum with a yoke caused distress for members of the community from which it originated: Jessiman, 'The Repatriation of the G'psgolox Totem Pole', 373.

[141] ICOM, *Code of Ethics*, principle 2.2.

[142] ibid. The code's glossary defines valid title as 'Indisputable right to ownership of property, supported by full provenance of the item since discovery or production'.

[143] Palmer distinguishes between what he considered to be the effect of the Limitation Act 1939, s. 3(2), which is merely to extinguish the original owner's title, compared with the Limitation Act 1980, ss. 3(2) and 4, which he suggested could be interpreted as conferring title on a good-faith purchaser: Norman Palmer, 'Responding to Conscience: The Holocaust (Return of Cultural Objects) Act 2009' (2010) 15 *Art Antiquity and Law* 87, 91.

that there is somebody else who has a valid title to the object and this is where the notion of rightful owners usually sits, for the rightful owner can be said to have a moral claim to the object. In more limited cases the terminology of rightful owner is engaged to refer to the museum's position – this is the case where the museum is adopting a defensive position to a potential or actual claim. In response to the US Court of Appeal's Second Circuit judgment in its favour regarding a claim for Matisse's *Portrait of Greta Moll* by the heirs of Greta Moll the National Gallery stated that: '[t]he Gallery purchased the work from a commercial gallery in London in good faith and is its rightful owner'.[144]

In their efforts to move towards a concept of relational ethics, Sarr and Savoy observe that the idea of 'rightful property owner' has the effect of substituting 'one form of physical and semantic imprisonment by another'.[145] It is argued here that the terminology unnecessarily shifts the focus away from responsive care and towards the dichotomy of ownership, which could, as Sarr and Savoy suggest, represent semantic imprisonment.

At times the phrase 'rightful owner' has become itself a synonym for claimants and, in turn, the phrasing of 'looted' cultural objects has been used to conflate all of the different circumstances in which the original owners lost possession during the Nazi era. However, whilst these circumstances included direct seizure by the Gestapo – clearly synonymous with looting or spoliation or stolen – they also involved other situations. These included forced sales, some of which would have been to fund exit visas, extortionate taxes or flight taxes. These sales may also have been necessitated by financial hardship during escape or where victims of the Nazi regime reached safety in a third country.[146] The financial crash of the 1930s meant that in some cases members of perse- cuted groups sold objects because of, at least in part, financial necessity, thereby raising difficult questions of causation relating to the sale and whether there is sufficient moral strength to the claimant's claim against museums. For these different reasons it is not always straightforward to conclude that a claimant has a strict moral entitlement to that object. Museums may have had no notice of the former owner's interest and could not have done anything more to find out about the circumstances of the loss since there would be nothing on record to show that the original owner had been forced by persecution to sell the object. In such circumstances the moral gravity of the situation may be more nuanced and would not necessarily justify a clear determination that a third party is the rightful owner.

---

[144] *National Gallery and the British Public are rightful owners of Portrait of Greta Moll,* National Gallery Press Release, 11 September 2018: www.nationalgallery.org.uk/about-us/press-and-media/press-releases/national-gallery-and-the-british-public-are-rightful-owners-of-portrait-of-greta-moll (last accessed 1 June 2023).

[145] Sarr and Savoy, *The Restitution of African Cultural Heritage*, p. 39.

[146] E.g. *British Museum/Koch* claim (Report of the Spoliation Advisory Panel in respect of fourteen clocks and watches now in the possession of the British Museum (7 March 2012) (2012 HC 1839)).

Focusing on the notion of the rightful owner introduces a dichotomy between, on the one hand, the current possessor, who is most likely the legal owner, at least in technical terms,[147] and on the other hand, someone who is perceived as having a strong moral claim to the object. A thorny issue in the context of repatriation claims (rather than claims for specific objects removed from an identifiable former owner, such as in the Nazi-era claims) is establishing who might be considered the rightful owner. Whilst it might be obvious in some situations that a particular community could constitute the rightful owner (or at least have a moral claim to the object), in others there may be a lack of cultural continuity between the original owners or the people who lived in the place where the cultural heritage originates from are no longer the same group of people who live in that same place and who now claim an entitlement to the cultural heritage in question. This can happen in the context of shifts in states. Similarly, there are instances where national borders have changed in the years between an object leaving a country and a claim in respect of it being made.

Thus, with rightful owner having become a synonym for claimants, this unnecessarily shifts the focus to the *conclusion* and away from the existence of a claim. It presupposes the outcome of a judgement albeit one of a *quasi*-legal nature whereas an important element of the caring process – dialogue – is at risk of being overlooked. For that reason, it is not helpful to label either of the communities involved as rightful owners, but rather to present them as communities who challenge the *status quo*, and the institutions who currently care for cultural heritage directly and who respond to that. Both communities care about the cultural heritage and may care for it in different ways, now and in the future, and may assume responsibility for its direct care.

9.6 First Steps: Shifts Towards More Dialogue

So far the discussion has focused on the reticence with which claims for the repatriation of cultural heritage objects have often been met. Current possessors have frequently relied on their strict legal rights to defend themselves against challenges to the *status quo*. Efforts to reform the law more broadly, both to avoid paternalistic care and to provide a power to respond to claims, have been stifled by fears of losing their marbles or opening the floodgates. These age-old fears can cloud the judgement of those currently responsible for caring for cultural heritage when considering how to most appropriately care for cultural heritage objects more broadly. The terminology of rightful owners can also set up an unhelpful dichotomy between the parties to a dispute – focusing on the claimant and the respondent and their respective rights rather than focusing on the responsibilities to provide appropriate care and working

---

[147] As they would derive title from the extinction of the original owner's legal title pursuant to the statutes of limitation.

out how to achieve such care. There has been a shift to a more dialogic approach to the treatment of the care of entire categories (Nazi-era objects and human remains) which has received both national and international support and has been backed up by legislation. In other instances, individual museums have responded to claims for more general categories of cultural heritage objects. After exploring these first international and national steps, taken with regard to Nazi-era objects and human remains, the specific examples of museums dealing with challenges with care will be considered.

9.6.1 International and National Consensus for Responding to Nazi-era Claims

The international recognition of the need to respond to Nazi-era claims provided clear justification for the UK putting in place a mechanism for resolving claims. In 2000, the establishment of the UK's Spoliation Advisory Panel was clearly framed as fulfilling its perceived obligations under the 1998 Washington Conference Principles. These principles were non-binding in nature and adopted by consensus at the 1998 Holocaust Era Asset Conference hosted by US State Department. This general consensus to act was also reflected in the National Museum Directors' Conference's development of principles and proposed actions which supported museums in their efforts to identify cultural objects in museums which had gaps in their provenance for the years 1933–1945.[148]

9.6.2 Framing Claims as Ones about Property

Earlier chapters highlighted the tension that can be caused between cultural heritage and property. However, in the context of claims for the return of cultural objects of which their owners were dispossessed during the Nazi era they are *prima facie* identifiable property which was lost in what has been internationally recognised as morally reprehensible circumstances. Treating them as essentially property claims which – because of the circumstances of loss – justify recognition of a persisting moral entitlement, and thus property, has arguably been beneficial to the acceptance of these claims.[149] In particular, this has assisted in justifying an exception to the general approach that national museum collections are, in effect, inalienable in nature. Claims for cultural objects whose owners were dispossessed of them during the Nazi era tend to deal with the broader concept of cultural objects (rather than framing them as cultural heritage). Many of the objects are likely to be cultural heritage because

---

[148] Jacques Schumacher, 'British Museums and Holocaust-era Provenance Research' in Redmond-Cooper, *Museums and the Holocaust*, p. 39.

[149] Elsewhere I have argued that framing these claims within Equity can be helpful: Charlotte Woodhead, 'Creative Equity in Practice: Responding to Extra-Legal Claims for the Return of Nazi Looted Art from UK Museums' (2022) 73 *Northern Ireland Legal Quarterly* 650.

they are important objects which are in a museum, often as a central part of a major collection. It is their presence in a museum which arguably renders them cultural heritage.

The transitional justice efforts relating to the Nazi era and the reparations and restitution made to the victims (and their heirs) of National Socialism in relation to cultural objects have involved objects that are readily identifiable. Therefore, for these claims the objects' status as cultural heritage is to an extent secondary. It is not directly relevant to the requirement of something being a cultural object; therefore, so far the question of whether or not something is a cultural object has not been considered by the Panel. The objects are necessarily cultural heritage objects because they are in the possession of museums, but the relevant issue of concern is that they are objects which have been wrongfully taken, and to which the claimants are identified as having a potential continuing moral entitlement. In many situations the importance of the object to individual family members is cited during the claims. However, the Panel has emphasised that the emotional connection between the object and the claimant is irrelevant to assessing the moral strength of the claim.[150]

In many ways, the ability to follow a line of inheritance through the generations down which an object would have passed has facilitated the resolution of these cases in aligning them more closely with property law. It has, in turn, justified the interference with the circumvention of statutes of limitation in the name of fulfilling justice, returning cultural objects to their rightful owner, and correcting past wrongs.

9.6.3 Still a Place for Paternalistic Care?

The reports of the Spoliation Advisory Panel reveal different approaches by museums when faced with claims. Some respondent museums have already accepted a claimant's position and come before the Panel to facilitate the agreed resolution.[151] In other claims, where there is less certainty about the circumstances of loss of the object and about the moral strength of a claimant's claim, the museum has responded by *testing* the position of the claimant, but with empathy. Finally, there are situations where a respondent museum has *robustly defended* and challenged the claimant's position. This may be where there is real doubt that the claimants lost possession because of persecution, or where there is a suggestion that the claimants have already been compensated for any loss of possession.[152]

---

[150] See Charlotte Woodhead, 'United Kingdom' in Redmond-Cooper, *Museums and the Holocaust*, p. 68.

[151] For example the Panel can then activate the trustee's ability to transfer an object to a successful claimant under the Holocaust (Return of Cultural Objects) Act 2009.

[152] This is discussed in the context of the different defensive stances that may be taken by museums, Section 9.5.

Even in circumstances where the British Museum trustees' limited power to transfer a specific object on the recommendation of the Spoliation Advisory Panel is engaged under section 2 of the Holocaust (Return of Cultural Objects) Act 2009, there are additional hurdles to surmount before return can take place. Through its policy, the British Museum trustees have restricted the circumstances in which they would be prepared to use that limited power.[153] The claimant's claim is effectively reconsidered by the trustees within more restricted parameters than the Spoliation Advisory Panel. To this end, the trustees reassess the strength of the claimant's case and consider whether the claimants represent all of the heirs who might come forward. However, the trustees consider factors to which the Spoliation Advisory Panel has refused to attach significance. First, the trustees would only entertain the possibility of transfer of an object from their collection in circumstances where the loss occurred because of the actions of the Nazis, whereas the Spoliation Advisory Panel has a broader jurisdiction. The Panel has therefore considered a claim relating to loss of a cultural object that occurred during the years 1933–1945 unconnected to Nazi persecution.[154] Second, the trustees will consider the importance of the object to their collection, in the context of whether this is the best solution. They will also consider the circumstances in which it was acquired by the museum.[155] The importance of the object is not a factor that the Panel is prepared to take into account when reaching its decision about whether to recommend the return of an object.[156] The approach of the Panel reflected the views of the Culture, Media and Sport Select Committee in its Seventh Report of 1999–2000, which identified the importance of having an object on public display as being secondary in nature to the importance of returning the object to the 'rightful owner'.[157] By constructing additional policy-based barriers, the British Museum thus perpetuates the paternalistic care.

9.6.4 Caring for Human Remains as a Special Category

Even as far back as the 1990s there were instances of UK museums repatriating human remains from their collections to Australian Aboriginal communities.[158] Whilst the governing bodies of non-national museums would have the power to

---

[153] British Museum Policy, *De-accession of Objects from the Collection*, para. 3.8: www .britishmuseum.org/sites/default/files/2019-10/De-accession_Policy_Nov2018.pdf (last accessed 1 June 2023).

[154] E.g. the *British Library/Benevento* claim.

[155] British Museum Policy, *De-accession of Objects from the Collection*, para. 3.8.4.

[156] *Tate Gallery/Constable* claim, para. 46 and Report of the Spoliation Advisory Panel in respect of a painted wooden tablet, the Biccherna Panel, now in the possession of the British Library (12 June 2014) (2014 HC 209), para. 20.

[157] Select Committee 7th Report 2000, Vol. I, para. 193.

[158] See Moira Simpson, 'The Plundered Past: Britain's Challenge for the Future' in Cressida Fforde, Jane Hubert and Paul Turnbell (eds.), *The Dead and Their Possessions: Repatriation in Principle, Policy and Practice* (London: Routledge, 2002), p. 206.

transfer objects, as well as human remains, from their collections in response to claims, it was not until 2004 that the trustees of national museums had similar powers permitting them to transfer human remains.[159] This legislative change followed the recommendations of the Report of the Working Group on Human Remains,[160] which, in turn, had been prompted, partly, by the Joint Statement made by the British and Australian prime ministers in 2000.[161] Human remains were recognised as a special category for which the *status quo* might be challenged based on their status as former people.

Nevertheless, calls for repatriation brought with them complicating factors. For the current holders the remains also represented potential scientific information which could be lost if the remains were reburied when repatriated.[162] In some cases, the potential future scientific interest could be identified, but in other situations it was merely a potential for being of future interest, with scientific researchers arguing that there were, as yet undiscovered, techniques which might make the human remains of even greater scientific interest. In addition, the encyclopaedic nature of some collections of bones and the contribution made by human remains from communities across the globe were cited as essential from the scientific point of view.[163] This included research into human evolution as well as diseases and other medical conditions which might not be possible with significant gaps within the collections of human remains left by repatriation.[164]

Nonetheless, the importance of the human remains to communities and a modern-day community's link with the remains through historical continuity was recognised in the Report of the Working Group on Human Remains and reflected in the subsequent DCMS Guidance.[165] Curtis observed that there is a greater willingness of museums to repatriate human remains which might be, in part, because of the changing attitudes towards death, and the greater recognition of the need for informed consent.[166] In this regard he identified three significant issues with treating human remains as a distinct category. First, he recognised the tendency to see human remains as having a universal value as distinguished from other objects. Second, he identified that frequently an assumption is made that all indigenous peoples have similar relationships with human remains, when in fact these may differ between groups. Third, he

---

[159] Following the enactment of section 47 of the Human Tissue Act 2004.
[160] DCMS, *Report of the Working Group on Human Remains*, p. 161.
[161] Australian Government, PM Transcripts, *Joint Statement with Tony Blair on Aboriginal Remains* (4 July 2000): https://pmtranscripts.pmc.gov.au/release/transcript-11611 (last accessed 1 June 2023).
[162] DCMS, *Report of the Working Group on Human Remains*, p. 22.   [163] ibid., pp. 26–8.
[164] ibid.
[165] ibid., p. 372 and DCMS, *Guidance for the Care of Human Remains in Museums*, PP 847 (October 2005), p. 26.
[166] Neil Curtis, 'Repatriation from Scottish Museums: Learning from NAGPRA' (2010) 33 *Museum Anthropology* 234, 236.

pointed to the general increased concern about the special treatment of human remains in the West, in particular because of controversies about the retention by some hospitals of the organs of children without informed consent, and also the plastinated human bodies in the Body Worlds exhibition.[167]

For these reasons human remains are now seen as a category of objects which justifies special treatment, but with an eye kept on maintaining responsibility. Even where powers do now exist to transfer human remains from national museum collections, the importance of maintaining collections is very much emphasised, situating that power as an exception to the general position. Therefore, in its Human Remains Policy, the British Museum has articulated its 'primary legal duty' as being 'to safeguard the Collection for the benefit of present and future generations throughout the world'.[168] With this in mind, 'the Trustee's overarching presumption is that the Collection should remain intact'.[169] Specific public benefits to retaining human remains were identified in the policy and details were set out about the only circumstances in which the trustees would normally consider a request.[170] The policy sets out that if a consultation is to take place, the information about who will be consulted and on what matters will be communicated to the claimants. It is made clear that 'an open and ongoing dialogue will take place with the applicants with regard to the request and criteria against which it will be assessed'.[171]

9.7 Dialogic Responses

At the other end of the spectrum of responses from defensive stances, one finds dialogic responses, which likewise can take a variety of forms.

Museums may have identified cultural heritage objects in their collections for which their current responsibility for care, or the appropriateness of that care, needs re-evaluating. Where they proactively alert other communities[172] of this, one sees respectful, empathetic and dialogic care in practice. Rather than responses to challenges, these are proactively dialogic responses to having revisited the current provision of care. They do not need to be brought within a framework of claims because the museums have proactively searched out these communities. The outcome of these dialogic interactions could well result in unconditional return, representing in some situations a truly caring response which is both respectful and empathetic.

Even in the absence of any proactive approach museums can still respond to challenges in a caring manner. Thus, museums may adopt a welcoming and

---

[167] ibid., 237.

[168] British Museum Policy, *Human Remains in the Collection*, para. 5.1: www.britishmuseum.org/sites/default/files/2019-10/Human_Remains_policy_061218.pdf (last accessed 1 June 2023).

[169] ibid.   [170] This included requirements relating to those bringing a claim.

[171] 'Procedure for making a request for the transfer of human remains under Section 47 Human Tissue Act 2004', British Museum Policy, *Human Remains in the Collection*, p. 7.

[172] Some of whom might otherwise be described as claimants.

caring stance, showing an immediate willingness to engage in dialogue with the claimant communities; this may be followed by the museum wholly acceding to the request, and returning the cultural heritage object on an unconditional basis.

Central to a caring approach to repatriation or other transfer is ensuring that different voices from relevant communities are heard, listened to and the views taken into account in decision-making such that there is an active and legitimate dialogue, with genuine collaboration. It is only where such respectful and empathetic dialogue takes place that a truly collaborative resolution to dissonance can take place. A central part of this is identifying the nature of the care that is needed, and who should have responsibility for the care of the cultural heritage involved. It is important, as part of this process, that there is no preconception about what the outcome of any challenge should be, or any conditions subject to which the cultural heritage is transferred.

9.7.1 Developing Caring Practices: Holistic Rather Than Reliant on Legal Rights

As discussed earlier, framing claims for cultural heritage objects of which the owners were dispossessed during the Nazi era within the context of the vindication for previously extinguished property rights may have aided with the recognition of those claims on moral grounds. Nevertheless, the often difficult task of attributing prior ownership of property to some communities who challenge the current allocation of care to cultural heritage objects means that it can be unhelpful.

As Jones observes, there is an ethical issue to rectifying certain wrongs whilst ignoring others[173] that is embedded in the nature of museums which serve the public interest; when they 'see where something is wrong [they] take steps to set it right'.[174] Part of the attempts to set things right is to do so in an empathetic, respectful and dialogic way, demonstrating appropriate care. It is possible to see this in some recent approaches by individual museums when other communities have challenged the *status quo*.

An approach to repatriation focusing on the ethics of care is seen in the context of Aberdeen University. It sets out in its policy that it holds its collection on trust for past and future generations and identifies its 'ongoing responsibilities', together with a 'duty of care to the collections' and 'to encourage access and understanding ... '[175] Further, it recognises that certain cultural heritage objects can be important to other communities and it is on that basis that repatriation may be made. Curtis observed two particularly important aspects to Aberdeen University's decision in 2003 to repatriate a split-horn headdress.

---

[173] Mark Jones, 'Restitution' in Constantine Sandis (ed.), *Cultural Heritage Ethics: Between Theory and Practice* (Cambridge: Open Book Publishers, 2014), p. 167.

[174] ibid.

[175] Aberdeen University, *Repatriation and Deaccessioning from the University Collections*: https://www.abdn.ac.uk/collections/documents/Repatriation-Procedure.pdf (last accessed 1 June 2023).

First, that in contrast to the approach taken by Glasgow City Council when returning the Lakota Ghost Dance Shirt, '[d]iscussions about legal title, association with human remains, or the circumstances of collection did not feature significantly in [Aberdeen] university's decision'. The importance to the Kanai was the primary driver for repatriation 'and thus, [the headdress would] no longer be treated as a museum object'.[176] As part of this recognition of the necessary care towards the cultural heritage, and towards those communities for whom it was important, the university decided that it should 'have no continuing rights after repatriation, such as demands that it be kept on display, available for loan, or conserved'.[177] This act, therefore, transferred responsibility for the care of the headdress entirely to the Kainai, without placing any continuing responsibilities or obligations on them to meet conditions to the satisfaction of the museum. Further empathetic, respectful and dialogic care was demonstrated in the discussions about the appropriateness of making a replica and taking photographs. Since both making a replica and the publication of photographs, were considered by the Kainai to be inappropriate, none were made; however, the museum was able to take photographs and use these for archival, exhibition and lecture purposes.[178]

Working together to ensure respect for the agency of the challenger-community in being able to decide on the form of future care represents appropriate care. This was then cemented by a further act of appropriate care, in the form of return. It therefore avoided presupposing that the appropriate method of care was the approach that the museum itself would take. A true act of respectful, empathetic and dialogic care may, in some circumstances, be to refrain from seeking to impose any further obligations and instead to hand over care entirely and unconditionally. This means that the museum does not assume responsibility for ongoing care by seeking to interfere with that, specifically by prescribing the manner of the care that is adopted in the future. Unconditional transfer can therefore avoid paternalistic care. However, at times, guidance is permeated by assumptions that care equates to the care that a Western museum would give to objects. This can be seen in ACE's Restitution and Repatriation Guide, which suggests that 'an individual without the means to properly care for the object/s may not be viewed as an appropriate claimant',[179] but instead a 'collecting institution (e.g. museum) with a track record in storing and caring for this type of material may be viewed as an appropriate claimant'.[180]

More recently, when the director of the Manchester Museum announced the return of sacred and secret objects from its collections to four Aboriginal communities, she set this act firmly within the context of the ethics of care, noting how '[c]are underpins the work of all museums'.[181] She emphasised

---

[176] Curtis, 'Repatriation from Scottish Museums', 238.   [177] ibid.   [178] ibid.
[179] ACE, Restitution and Repatriation Guide, p. 16.   [180] ibid.
[181] Manchester Museum, Open Letter: The Tide of Change, Esme Ward, Director of Manchester Museum https://blogs.manchester.ac.uk/viewpoint/2019/11/29/the-tide-of-change/ (last accessed 1 June 2023).

how Manchester Museum's approach to the ethics of care was to extend it 'beyond collections to people, ideas, beliefs and relationships'.[182] Repatriation in this context requires 'care, sensitivity, emotional intelligence and patience',[183] which reflect the elements of appropriate care set out in this book.

Taking such an approach has been said to result in 'equitable relationships'.[184] Dialogue undertaken directly with the communities who have authority to speak about the importance of cultural heritage to them is vital in ensuring that care is not assumed by intermediary communities without informed consent. Such a dialogic approach to repatriation is also apparent in how the Hunterian Museum works with claimants in 'a respectful, open, transparent, fair, and timely manner' in accordance with the museum's policy.[185] Its policy makes it clear that questions about what is suitable for repatriation are questions, not to be answered by overseas institutions, but rather by the indigenous communities themselves since they are 'best placed to understand what material is significant and will support their continuing cultural practices or is important to have returned to their communities'.[186] The museum appears to recognise that partnering with, and listening to, communities is essential, seeing them as playing a central role in repatriation. In contrast to some other museums[187] the Hunterian recognises that where claims are made by government agencies, these will only be considered 'if they are being made on behalf of the indigenous communities/peoples (where the community of origin is known) and with the free, prior, and informed consent of the indigenous community/peoples'.[188] This approach focuses on placing control of the care of cultural heritage in the hands of communities for whom it is important, and giving agency to them. The Hunterian's policy also focuses on the living nature of much cultural heritage, in particular the relevance of cultural heritage to living communities.

Prompt, sensitive and confidential responses to repatriation requests are central to the policy of the Royal Albert Memorial Museum and Art Gallery in Exeter. As part of the process of investigating any potential competing claims it undertakes a multifaceted review of factors which include (but are not limited to) the following: the scientific and cultural importance of the artefacts, the strength of the claimants' relationship to the items and the consequences of either retention or repatriation.[189] This approach reflects the approach taken by Glasgow City Council which was set out in the 1990s and was recognised as

---

[182] ibid.   [183] ibid.

[184] Viscount Colville of Culross, *Hansard* HL vol. 824, col. 177GC (13 October 2022).

[185] University of Glasgow, *The Hunterian Repatriation Policy*, para. 11.3.   [186] ibid., para. 3.

[187] Namely the British Museum and the Museum of Archaeology and Anthropology at Cambridge: see Section 9.3.5.1.

[188] University of Glasgow, *The Hunterian Repatriation Policy*, para. 10.4.

[189] Guidelines on the procedure for dealing with repatriation and restitution of objects and human remains from the collection of the Royal Albert Memorial Museum & Art Gallery (RAMM) Exeter, May 2020: https://committees.exeter.gov.uk/documents/s74040/Appendix%20C%20-%20Restitution%20guidelines%202020%20v.5-5-20.pdf (last accessed 1 June 2023).

representing good practice by the House of Commons Select Committee for Culture, Media and Sport in July 2000.[190]

These various examples, extending to varied cultural heritage objects in museum collections, demonstrate how communities may challenge the *status quo*, and how in turn museums undertake to respond in an appropriately caring manner.

9.7.2 Outcomes Infused with an Ethic of Care

Responses to claims can take a variety of forms and the appropriate response is not always the transfer of the object to a claimant, although this will often be the preferred solution sought by the community challenging the *status quo*. Return and restitution have been described recently by the MA as capable of being 'a powerful cultural, spiritual and symbolic act which recognises past wrongs and restores items to their original community'.[191]

The appropriate care of cultural heritage might be putting in place collaborative activities between the parties to the claim in response to that claim. This can include telling different narratives about the cultural heritage concerned, through intercultural exchanges or other fusion of traditions. For example, Curtis talked of the keeper of the Kainai split-horn headdress acquiring a kilt jacket in Scotland to wear when dancing in the headdress, thereby referencing the headdress's time in Scotland, which has become part of its history.[192]

9.7.2.1 The Role of Narrative

Some circumstances might justify a response in which the narrative surrounding the object is set out. This includes explanations about how the object was used in cultural practices, rather than vague statements about the object's possible use, unsupported by direct knowledge of its use, or the object's display as purely an aesthetic object rather than as one important to a community. The necessary response might be about making visible the injustice to the communities whose responsibility for the object's care was displaced.

At times the presentation of a narrative displaying an account of an object's history has been recommended as a remedy to resolve claims relating to objects of which their owners lost possession during the Nazi era. The suitability of these as a standalone remedy instead of return has been doubted[193] and has not received much academic attention.[194] However, narratives play an important role in explaining and making visible troubled pasts and the role of cultural

---

[190] Select Committee 7th Report 2000, Vol. I, para. 199(x).
[191] MA, *Supporting Decolonisation*, p. 26.
[192] Curtis, 'Repatriation from Scottish Museums', 244.
[193] Select Committee 7th Report 2000, Vol. II, Minutes of Evidence, Memorandum submitted by the Commission for Looted Art in Europe, para. 47.
[194] Although has been presented by the author at conferences on the subjects of restitution, provenance and law and humanities.

heritage within those pasts. The use of narrative within the framework of the resolution of disputes concerning Nazi-era dispossessions may be said to have an immediate attraction given that 'Narrative has a unique ability to embody the concrete experience of individuals and communities, to make other voices heard ... '[195] In this way, the otherwise silent stories surrounding the loss by the original owners and the journey taken by the cultural object to the museum's walls might remain untold. The 'poignant ownership history' of objects with a Nazi-era story may even serve, for some viewers, 'to magnify their beauty'.[196]

An 'object on display had relationships not only with other items and with its collectors and curators, but also with its audiences'.[197] Therefore any explanatory text can provide further information that can strengthen the link between the viewer and the object. For a history to be effective, it needs to publicly acknowledge the injury itself.[198] Whilst Maier suggests that 'Remembering and commemoration are perhaps the easiest tasks to accomplish',[199] the question arises as to what is actually remembered and commemorated through the narrative that accompanies these objects. As artworks, with no interpretative explanation, the objects cannot by themselves tell their story or the connection that they have with the Holocaust, and this is the same with memorial camps used by the Nazis;[200] instead, the 'significance derives from the knowledge we bring to them and from their explanatory inscriptions'[201] and these inscriptions 'complete them'.[202]

The UK's Spoliation Advisory Panel introduced the remedy of the display of an account of an object's history, originally in conjunction with one of the monetary remedies available. In 2007, the Panel's Terms of Reference were amended to permit the recommendation of the display of an account of the object's history independently of any other remedy.[203] The first occasion on which the Panel recommended this remedy on its own was in the Curt Glaser case, where the Panel took the view (in contrast to other restitution committees across Europe) that rather than return, a commemorative remedy should be made instead. This remedy was recommended to reflect the fact that there were

---

[195] Peter Brooks, 'The Law as Narrative and Rhetoric' in Peter Brooks and Paul Gewirtz (eds.), *Law's Stories: Narrative and Rhetoric in the Law* (New Haven: Yale University Press, 1996), p. 16.

[196] Geri J. Yanover, 'National Perspective: The "Last Prisoners of the War": Unrestituted Nazi-Looted Art' (2004) 6 *Journal of Law and Social Challenges* 81–98, 88.

[197] Samuel J. M. M. Alberti, 'Objects and the Museum' (2005) 96 *Isis* 559, 569.

[198] Charles S. Maier, 'Overcoming the Past? Narrative and Negotiation, Remembering, and Reparation: Issues at the Interface of History and the Law' in John Torpey (ed.), *Politics and the Past: On Repairing Historical Injustices* (World Social Change Series, Oxford: Rowman & Littlefield, 2003), pp. 296, 299.

[199] ibid., 296.

[200] James E. Young, *Writing and Rewriting the Holocaust: Narrative and the Consequences of Interpretation* (Bloomington: Indiana University Press, 1990), p. 175.

[201] ibid.   [202] ibid.

[203] Report of the Spoliation Advisory Panel in respect of three Rubens paintings now in the possession of the Courtauld Institute of Art, London HC 63 (2007) (revised Terms of Reference appended to the report).

mixed motives for Dr Glaser's sale of the particular artworks in question, that the sums received at auction were 'reasonable market prices'[204] received and that his heirs had previously received a modest sum of compensation.[205]

There is still much work to be done to fully understand the nature of narratives as remedies.[206] However, it is clear that the recommendation for the display of an account of an object's history, rather than return, will not always be welcomed as a remedy, and may be considered to be a second best remedy in the circumstances.[207] For that reason, where a narrative is recommended, this would need to represent the most appropriate care in the circumstances. In particular, there is a strong argument to be made for dialogue in the construction of any narrative so that it reflects the full scope of any agreement. An agreement achieved through consensus was made in relation to Egon Schiele's *Portrait of Wally*; the exact wording of the text that would accompany the display of the painting was made a stipulation of the legal agreement.[208] Furthermore, it was agreed that nothing should be said which contains 'any language that is inconsistent with the contents of the Permanent Signage Statement'.[209]

9.7.2.2 Care through Private Acts to Right Wrongs

So far, the focus of discussion has been on museums and the appropriateness of their care, when faced with challenges to the *status quo*. More difficult questions arise, though, in the context of privately owned cultural heritage when it becomes apparent that another community may have a justifiable moral challenge to the private owner's enjoyment of that cultural heritage.

Often the realisation about potential challenges only becomes apparent where the transfer of ownership is being contemplated. This may happen when a cultural heritage object is consigned to auction, thereby rendering the object visible to the public gaze and raising the possibility of challenge by another community based on a past injustice. In such situations, the private property interests of the current owner will often be indisputable. They would not be under any professional ethical obligations to the communities to enter into a dialogue with anyone who challenges their current responsibility for an object. Similarly, unlike the case of museums, there is no potential breach of public trust or provision of public funding which may justify ethical responses and foregoing of a strict legal entitlement.[210] Therefore, any dialogic response by them is a true act of care.

---

[204] Report of the Spoliation Advisory Panel in respect of Eight drawings now in the possession of the Samuel Courtauld Trust (24 June 2009) (2009 HC 757), para. 41.

[205] ibid., para. 43.   [206] And this is a matter for other research.

[207] See Martin Bailey, 'Glaser Heirs Reject UK Spoliation Ruling', *The Art Newspaper*, 26 August 2009.

[208] *USA* v. *Portrait of Wally, A Painting by Egon Schiele (in rem)* 99 Civ. 9940 (LAP) Stipulation and Order of Settlement and Discontinuance (20 July 2010), para. 7.

[209] ibid.

[210] As Mark Jones observed, museums serving the public interest should take appropriate 'steps to set it right': 'Restitution', p. 167.

In the case of sacred or religious objects, it may be recognised that it is inappropriate to commercialise the sacred. Public pressure can play a role in influencing an owner to decide to withdraw a lot from sale. This can be seen, for example, in the case of the proposed sale of a Maori mat that was consigned to auction at Burstow & Hewett in 2019, but later withdrawn after social media pressure.[211] In some cases this public pressure might lead to a direct dialogue between the owner and the community. However, where there is no such dialogue, or where the dialogue does not manage to resolve the dissonance, there are instances of cultural heritage objects being purchased by those willing to donate them to the communities of care who have demonstrated their connection with them.[212]

Cultural heritage objects about which there is a potential injustice may come to light following provenance research. This may identify an object as having links with particular events, or being the subject of an injustice. Auction houses and art recovery organisations may, as communities of care, intervene to facilitate private acts of care to correct past wrongs. Settlements could involve transfers of the object, whether or not for a part payment to reflect the financial loss that would result from any transfer of the object.

Current owners who, upon inheriting an object, discover its troubled history may feel a strong compunction to respond to challenges or may actively seek out the appropriate communities of care and proactively engage with them with a view to facilitating the restitution of an object. Bronzes taken during the 1897 punitive expedition in the Kingdom of Benin by one of the officers present were inherited by his grandson, Mark Walker. He returned them to Benin and handed them over in 2014.[213] This private act of care, in the form of him forgoing his strict legal entitlement, brought great joy to the affected community of care; this act of return was celebrated by the Oba of Benin and was described by Peju Layiwola as 'one of the most honourable acts of restitution to date'.[214]

9.7.2.3 Facilitating Rather Than Hampering Restitution Efforts?

A potential way in which repatriation can be hampered is by the UK's export licensing system relating to objects of cultural interest. Where objects from UK museum collections or private collections are repatriated abroad, an export

---

[211] Roland Arkell, 'Social Media Storm Stops Maori Cloak Auction', *Antiques Trade Gazette*, 14 September 2019, issue 2408.

[212] Examples include objects from the Summer Palace in China. The notion of purchasing objects with tainted provenance to prevent them from further circulating on the open market is by no means clear-cut ethically since a purchase – even if not legally prohibited – fuels the market and encourages looting and therefore such objects should not be purchased to save them and cared for, even temporarily by museums. A group of art dealers bought objects from Benin in 2020 and returned them: Samuel Reilly, 'Private Enterprise: The Individuals Who are Taking Restitution into Their Own Hands', *Apollo Magazine*, July/August 2020.

[213] Ellen Otzen, 'The Man Who Returned His Grandfather's Loot', *BBC News Online*, 26 February 2015. He subsequently returned some ceremonial paddles: Lanre Bakare, 'Soldier's Grandson to Return Items He Looted from Benin City', *The Guardian*, 17 December 2019.

[214] Quoted in Reilly, 'Private Enterprise'.

licence may be needed, with a chance of them being found to be 'national treasures'. If so, then the grant of an export licence would be deferred to allow time for a UK purchaser to come forward who would provide public access to 'save' the object for the nation'; if they achieved this then this would have the effect of hampering the repatriation process.

The Export Reviewing Committee now only applies the Waverley Criteria without taking other factors into consideration. These objectively determine the importance of the object rather than whether there are strong ethical grounds justifying the object's immunity from consideration. Whilst the Secretary of State may depart from the Committee's recommendation and instead use their discretion to grant the export licences to facilitate repatriation it is unclear whether the Secretary of State would exercise it in such a situation. In the 2021/2022 Report of the Reviewing Committee on Export of Objects of Cultural Interest it was stated that where objects have been slated for repatriation by a museum, they would be treated in the usual way for the purposes of the export licensing process. Therefore, whether or not an object should be repatriated is not a consideration for the Expert Adviser or for the Reviewing Committee but is a consideration for the Secretary of State to make.[215]

This problem could be remedied by adding an additional category of object to the Open General Export licence (OGEL), 'objects which are being repatriated from UK museums to their countries of origin'. This approach has already been taken for objects that were looted during the Nazi era and which have been restituted to claimants following a recommendation of the Spoliation Advisory Panel.[216] In that situation, the export of such an object must be accompanied by a copy of the Panel's report and written confirmation from the claimant that they consent to the export.[217] If this new category were added to the OGEL, with similar requirements, then the exporter of a cultural object would not need to apply for a specific export licence. The object would not be at risk of being designated as a national treasure and instead the export and the repatriation of the object could occur without further delay. Whilst, in the case of Nazi-era claims the Spoliation Advisory Panel (as well as the Secretary of State in the case of national museums) in approving the recommendation acts as a community of scrutiny for the decisions to repatriate or restitute, in most cases involving repatriation of other cultural objects from museums the decision of the museum's governing body would have been subjected to the scrutiny of the Charity Commission, which has to approve transfers from museums. Furthermore, in the cases of repatriation to communities abroad, the cultural heritage object is being returned to the community for whom it is most important. In contrast, in the cases of restituted cultural objects approved

---

[215] DCMS, *Reviewing Committee on the Export of Works of Art and Cultural Interest 2021–22* (London: ACE, 2022), p. 8.
[216] Open General Export Licence (Objects of Cultural Interest) granted by the Secretary of State on 1 January 2021, para. 1(o).
[217] ibid., para. 4.

by the Spoliation Advisory Panel and facilitated under the OGEL, the export might not be made by the claimant themselves, but by a purchaser of the object (providing that the claimant has consented to the export). This is therefore facilitating the sales of the claimant and the ability of new owners to export the object rather than facilitating export for the community who cares about the object most strongly (which is the case for other repatriation acts).

9.8 Memoralising Troubled Histories and Contested Heritage

Where objects or places are associated with a person with a problematic character, perhaps one who has engaged in nefarious activities,[218] or difficult historical events,[219] a balance needs to be struck between recognising that association as part of history and memory, and not celebrating or glorifying the person, event or regime. As part of significant regime changes the removal from display of statues of dictators can take place on a wide scale during the process of state succession.[220]

Such statues may be interpreted as celebrating and memorialising these people and the continued presence may cause harm. Paintings which depict scenes based on historic approaches to race or slavery can cause offence to modern-day communities.[221] Adding contextual statements can explain the historical background to the person or event and may challenge the correctness of their involvement in historical events or their points of view. Such statements or labels may also clarify the position from the point of view of indicating that its continued presence should not be interpreted as supporting the views or themes expressed in the picture. Nevertheless, the continued – now contextualised – display will not necessarily overcome the hurt that can be felt by members of the public encountering the subject matter or the person who is depicted. This hurt has the potential to be heightened in circumstances where the location or prominence of the display might imply commemoration or, worse still, glorification of the events, subject matter or the person.

Recognising differences and memorialising past events can prove difficult where different communities with historic but enduring disputes live in close proximity. An example of how such issues might be addressed can be seen in how the Community Relations Council in Northern Ireland and the Heritage

---

[218] See, for example, Rachel Cooke, 'Eric Gill: Can We Separate the Artist from Abuser?', *The Guardian*, 9 April 2017.

[219] See generally Sharon Macdonald, *Difficult Heritage: Negotiating the Nazi Past in Nuremberg and Beyond* (London: Routledge, 2009).

[220] See generally Harrison, regarding the removal and defacement of statues during the overthrow of political regimes: Rodney Harrison, *Heritage: Critical Approaches* (London: Routledge, 2013), pp. 173–4.

[221] One example is the mural depicting colonialism and slavery by Rex Whistler situated in a restaurant at Tate Britain: Tate Press Release, *Tate Announces Next Steps for Rex Whistler Mural* (16 February 2022): www.tate.org.uk/press/press-releases/tate-announces-next-steps-rex-whistler-mural (last accessed 1 June 2023).

Lottery Fund worked together to develop resources to navigate the Decade of Centenaries.[222] Museums or other heritage places may have to acknowledge the role that the nation, or indeed the institution itself, played in the process, which in the case of cultural heritage objects may include knowledge of the object's provenance at the time of acquisition.

9.8.1 General Approaches

Different responses to contested cultural heritage fall along a spectrum.[223] At one end is the destruction of the statue or other memorial, purging it from memory. Moving along the spectrum one finds destruction of cultural heritage, but where some digital or other archival record of it is made. The next possibility is the removal of cultural heritage and storage, or removal and relocation of it to another place. At the far end is the retention of the memorial in situ. All of these options could be accompanied by the display of narrative text, explaining or setting out the difficulties or assisting viewing communities with the contextualization of the statue or memorial. Such narratives could be equally beneficial where there is complete removal or destruction of the memorial, to explain what led to its removal from display as well as some of the social issues involved with that decision. As with the discussion of narratives as remedies, any version of events that is presented to the public will need to be the result of dialogue and collaboration to ensure that it does not represent a one-sided approach to care, or at worst represent paternalistic care.

9.8.2 Individual Responses

Navigating the question of how to display cultural heritage with a troubled history which has associations with difficult people from the past is one faced by those who have cultural heritage within their care but also those communities of care who are affected by the history in question.

Starting a dialogue regarding contested cultural heritage and beginning to investigate how difficulties may be navigated is a first step, as is determining what form appropriate care should take and how to care for affected communities. Here communities are not faced with short- or long-term risks of physical harm to the cultural heritage but instead the cultural heritage itself, and its continued presence in a particular place, is causing harm to communities.

---

[222] Taking place between 2012 and 2022. This included developing a toolkit as well as *Decade Principles for Remembering in Public Space*: www.community-relations.org.uk/decade-centenaries (last accessed 1 June 2023).

[223] See generally Richard Harwood KC, Catherine Dobson and David Sawtell, *Contested Heritage: Removing Art from Land and Historic Buildings* (London: Law Brief Publishing, 2022).

A short-term way of responding to the difficulties is to acknowledge the existence of these difficulties and leave it for communities visiting it, or coming across it, to navigate this themselves based on information provided.

9.8.3 Wider-scale Approaches

On the macro level, the problem of dealing with contested cultural heritage can be tackled by developing instruments and toolkits to assist communities in navigating the difficulties caused by the continued presence of certain cultural heritage. This links with other cultural heritage in museums which has become contested because of colonisation; specifically, the MA's decolonisation toolkit can assist, but other communities of care have developed instruments to facilitate how harm is navigated. A further example is found in the Church of England's contested heritage document. This encourages churches to undertake research into the significance of contested objects and then 'to ask … whether there is a need for change'.[224] In particular the question is asked whether 'the prominence of the object and its message make worship difficult' and also '[w]ould a change to the object change the nature of that relationship positively enough for the building to be used more widely?'[225]

Across Scotland, Wales and Northern Ireland, heritage places have tackled difficult histories in the displays of information, often engaging head-on with these difficult pasts and to acknowledge what was done.[226] This has included the role of those involved in the slave trade and the wealth derived from it invested in places and collections.[227]

In 2021 the amendments to the National Planning Policy Framework brought all statues, plaques, memorials and monuments within the care of local planning authorities[228] and presupposed the appropriateness of retaining them *in situ* and 'where appropriate, of explaining their historic and social context rather than removal'.[229] At this first level of consideration by the local

---

[224] The Church Buildings Council and the Cathedrals Fabric Commission for England, *Contested Heritage in Cathedrals and Churches* (London: Church Care, 2021), p. 20.

[225] ibid. See *Re The Rustat Memorial, Jesus College, Cambridge* [2022] ECC Ely 2.

[226] E.g. National Trust for Scotland, *Glencoe National Nature Reserve*: www.nts.org.uk/visit/ places/glencoe/the-glencoe-massacre (last accessed 1 June 2023); Amgueddfa Cymru, *Cup, Commemorative*: https://museum.wales/collections/online/object/11c2e413-c279-3ecb-af8c-870c0c93a3be/Cup-commemorative/?field0=with_images&value0=on&field1=string&va lue1=tryweryn (last accessed 1 June 2023); see generally, Elizabeth Crooke and Thomas Maguire (eds.), *Heritage after Conflict: Northern Ireland* (London: Routledge, 2018).

[227] E.g. National Trust, *Penrhyn Castle and the Transatlantic Slave Trade*: www .nationaltrust.org.uk/penrhyn-castle/features/penrhyn-castle-and-the-transatlantic-slave-trade (last accessed 1 June 2023).

[228] By specifically removing them from the permitted development exceptions: see The Town and Country Planning (General Permitted Development) (England) Order 2015, SI 2015 No. 596, sch. 2, Part 11, Class B.1(e) (as inserted by The Town and Country Planning (General Permitted Development etc.) (England) (Amendment) Order 2021, SI 2021 No. 428, ord. 11(2)(b).

[229] NPPF 2021, para. 198.

planning authority, the public would be consulted in the usual way in which they are in planning decisions. Furthermore, as part of the decision, in fulfilling their public sector equality duty, the effect that the granting or refusal of permission would have on those protected communities under the Equality Act 2010 would need to be considered.[230] However, a further level of paternalistic care is provided by the Secretary of State with the power to call in 'commemorative object development' where there is a proposed 'full or partial demolition of a statue, monument or plaque' which has been there for at least 10 years. This call-in power applies other than in the case of such a statue, monument, memorial or plaque which is a listed building, scheduled monument, 'within a cemetery, on consecrated land, or within the curtilage of a place of public worship, within the grounds of a museum or art gallery' or within the 'curtilage of a dwellinghouse'.[231] If a local authority is going to allow the application for removal then they are required to consult the Secretary of State.[232] The Secretary of State can then make a direction for the application to be referred to the Secretary of State for determination.[233]

The continued display of contested cultural heritage, including potentially the commemoration of individuals, has the potential to perpetuate injustices, and to provide inappropriate care to the affected communities. Whilst there is scope for consideration by the local planning authorities of responses to any consultation, where the LPA concludes that removal is appropriate, the Secretary of State then has a discretion to call this in and to overturn that decision without the need for any further consultation. The rhetoric of a presumption that the default position is to 'retain and explain', coupled with the power to call in the application and consider it demonstrates paternalistic care; it does not place the communities who might be affected by the continued display of a memorialisation of individuals on an equal footing.

9.9 Conclusion

Not all cultural heritage objects acquired in the past and cared for by museums represent injustices; however, those cultural heritage objects which by their very nature mean that certain communities have immense feelings about due to the close connection with their practices justify an opening up of dialogue and may ultimately justify return of the objects.

Where there was a clear act of displacement of the caring responsibilities either by force, looting or collecting in times of unequal power relations, these situations represent injustices that trigger the need to revisit the current allocation of the responsibility for care. In these cases there is justification

---

[230] Equality Act 2010, s. 149. See Harwood et al., *Contested Heritage*, pp. 106–107. In Wales, part of the consideration might include the wellbeing goals, as set out in the Well-being of Future Generations (Wales) Act 2015, s. 4.

[231] The Town and Country Planning (Consultation) Direction 2021, para. 9.

[232] ibid., para. 10.   [233] Under the Town and Country Planning Act 1990, s. 77.

for challenging the *status quo* by others who may assume the direct care of the cultural heritage concerned. Furthermore, where the current community with responsibility for the care of cultural heritage acquired that cultural heritage with knowledge of the prior injustice, there may be strong reasons for again revisiting the current provision of care.

In some cases, representatives of governments make calls for repatriation, often on behalf of other claimant communities. Indeed, in some cases, museums will only engage with communities where they receive the support of the national governments. However, such an approach seems to retain the sense of paternalistic care. Whilst challenges may be brought by communities other than those with the closest connection to the cultural heritage, neverthe-less, such communities should only act in a representative capacity where they have direct and informed authority of the community with the closest connec-tion. Failing to do this risks paternalistic care, with communities for whom the cultural heritage is important being excluded from the dialogue altogether, or having their views marginalised, thereby perpetuating injustice. The recent ACE guide on restitution and repatriation sets out how museums should be clear that they are talking to the right people when responding to repatriation claims; specifically, where a claim is made by the state, as representatives of others, the museum should ask whether those communities can be directly involved in the discussions.[234]

Paternalistic care, manifesting itself in an unstinting determination to retain the *status quo*, or with a reluctance to enter into dialogue, perpetuates the injustices that have been occasioned in the past and which remain as continu-ing injustices.[235] Where efforts have been made to reform the law, the myth of the marbles has hindered these efforts, particularly in situations where trustees see the law as a protective barrier against random caprice. Further, a concern is raised about the real risk that would be occasioned to the universal museum if objects were transferred from collections in response to claims.

Whilst there may be a larger number of claims for objects other than human remains or Nazi-era looted art, whether this is a true opening of the floodgates with an uncontrollable deluge is far from clear. But what is clear is that those first steps to responding to injustices may have found some success in part because of the ability to frame the claims within property law. In the case of Nazi-era claims it is much easier to follow a line of inheritance and to recognise the claimants as the heirs of the original owners. The idea of the 'rightful owner' within the context of Nazi-era claims may be problematic because it presupposes that there is somebody who is morally in a better position than the other. Nevertheless, the property nature of claims and a recognition that

---

[234] ACE, *Restitution and Repatriation Guide*, p. 11.
[235] See Vrdoljak, who suggests that restitution is the cessation of the wrong, rather than a remedy: Ana Vrdoljak, 'Genocide and Restitution: Ensuring Each Group's Contribution to Humanity' (2012) 22 *European Journal of International Law* 17, 18.

a wrong displaced the original owner and that morally it is appropriate to return it have helped to resolve claims.

Whilst nationally there may be some vocal views against the use of repatriation to respond to colonial injustices, nevertheless there are increasing numbers of museums who (where legally able to do so) are responding to challenges to the *status quo* in a dialogic manner. Even where they adopt the language of claims they are developing caring practices, drawing on the ethics of care, often without naming it in these terms. Such an approach has a central role to play in trying to correct past injustices, and in the future it is hoped that the ethics of care may provide a way of challenging previous approaches to care which have taken an arrogant stance and relied on a version of care inherently paternalistic in nature.

10

Conclusion

This book started by saying that it was not simply about the monumental or superlative examples of cultural heritage, but about all types of cultural heritage located in the UK. It will end by saying that it is also about the extraordinarily wide range of communities who both care about and care for cultural heritage. These communities use law and non-law as well as civil society and public participation initiatives to care for cultural heritage, to strive to provide appropriate care, and, where possible, to pass it on to future generations.

At times law facilitates that care through detailed statutory provisions applying across the four nations of the UK. On occasions statutes place different emphases in the different nations. In some instances, additional responsibilities are placed on particular communities of care, such as more involvement of the ministers in Wales. There is a recognition of the Scottish interest in allocating cultural heritage objects accepted in lieu of tax. In some nations there are also strong elements of identity such as language and place names recognised through legal instruments. The UK legal landscape is indeed a patchwork which has developed piecemeal, often in response to particular challenges or with the strong backing of supporters for particular subject matter.[1] Therefore, there is no entirely developed system akin to a heritage code. Instead, cultural heritage places are cared for indirectly by the state through law and guidance, whether or not privately owned. In contrast, cultural heritage objects are only cared for by the law where they have entered the public domain. Practices often receive little legal attention at all. But this should not be thought to be an entirely dismal picture of the care of cultural heritage. Various non-law instruments, albeit without the full force of law, nevertheless provide the ethical means by which to provide care for cultural heritage nested within those legal provisions, supporting them, supplementing them and, at times, extending the responsibilities far beyond the legal provisions. They provide care – appropriate care – for the cultural heritage and for the communities for whom it is important.

---

[1] Such as the protection of Ancient Monuments, which had Lubbock as a strong supporter of reform: see Simon Thurley, *Men from the Ministry: How Britain Saved Its Heritage* (New Haven: Yale University Press, 2013).

Legal principles have been appropriated to care for cultural heritage, as Carman observed back in the 1990s.[2] Furthermore, it is possible to see incidental categories labelling objects which recognise the central elements of what makes something cultural heritage and gives these added protection through recognition in legal terms. If you look for it, you find care within the UK system for cultural heritage. The care, on the whole, is appropriate, providing opportunities for dialogue, taking account of feelings towards cultural heritage places. Both expert communities, interested in the care of particular styles of buildings, and the public more widely are consulted; there is clear opportunity and space for that dialogue. Where opportunities are not provided for consultation, or the fruits of those consultations are not adequately taken into account, provision is made to challenge that through the mechanism of judicial review. Some commentators may challenge the efficacy of that participation, and recognise that there remain significant power dynamics at play, which may negate recognising this participation as fully appropriate care as (recognised for current purposes as empathetic, respectful and dialogic). Nevertheless, structurally, mechanisms are in place to provide for the dialogic nature of the care, whether that care functionally is the most appropriate in the circumstances may present research opportunities for the future.[3] This book should not be interpreted as providing a utopian, rose-tinted view of the law and non-law initiatives as nested practices of care in the UK providing entirely appropriate care, but it provides a hopeful view.

Hopeful, because communities of care develop in all sorts of places and can effect change and provide appropriate care. Some are established or mandated by law, others are supported by law in what they do, as well as by official guidance. In the UK, the law facilitates communities who want to come together because they care about cultural heritage, and provides them with the tools to care for cultural heritage. That care might take the form of challenging a decision that has been made by those who have direct care for the cultural heritage. This is possible in situations where the decision-maker is subject to judicial review and challenge through the courts. However, in other situations the law facilitates the establishment of civil society initiatives to care for cultural heritage; care is therefore not the purview of the state. It was vitally important not to take a top-down view of the care for cultural heritage in the UK because it is not about regulation, but instead it is about facilitating care through communities of care. Some people may disagree with the approach taken here, which treats communities as being so broad as to include courts, government departments, the Law Commission as well as the museums and the small groups who have formed together because they care about a specific place or an object. Nevertheless, all of

---

[2] John Carman, *Valuing Ancient Things: Archaeology and Law* (Leicester: Leicester University Press, 1996), p. 45. See Section 3.7.3.
[3] See for example Leila Jancovich and David Stevenson (eds.), *Failures in Cultural Participation* (London: Palgrave Macmillan, 2022).

these people – all of these communities – contribute to the care of cultural heritage in the UK (some better than others) and they should not be overlooked.

This book is the start of a conversation about caring for cultural heritage, and hopefully contributes to a broader discussion about how law can actively provide care. Law and the ethics of care are often seen to be in tension with each other, but this book has sought to show that the law has the potential to provide care. It is acknowledged that it might not always provide the most appropriate care, particularly when issues such as property law or tax rules prevent an outcome which might provide more appropriate care for the cultural heritage and its communities. Nevertheless, the potential to care exists, and law provides care through judgments, whether applying cultural heritage law principles or general legal ones. Pockets of hope are seen in the context of case law with the recognition, for example, of the need to consider codes of ethics and other guidance,[4] the recognition of the UK's moral obligation to recognise the cultural heritage of other countries derived from the 1970 UNESCO Convention[5] and the recognition of the comity of nations[6] when dealing with cultural heritage. All of these demonstrate a contribution to the care of cultural heritage. However, it really is the small communities who use the law instrumentally to form together into legal communities, communities of justice, which can challenge how cultural heritage that they care about is cared for. At times, the way to care for cultural heritage is often a very pragmatic one – raise sufficient funds to acquire the cultural heritage. One only has to look at the overwhelming response to the quest for funding to restore the *Sunbathers*[7] to appreciate the strength of feeling that some communities have towards cultural heritage that they have never before seen. This strength of feeling drives them to provide the funds to restore it, for the purposes of 'saving it' and to temporarily return it close to its original location. The law facilitates many of these activities relating to the care of cultural heritage – it certainly does not prevent them. Whilst the UK law *is* fragmented in the state provision of care and the obligations that it places on private owners of cultural heritage, nevertheless it provides an environment in which others may care for cultural heritage, may assume responsibility for it and in turn may provide appropriate respectful, empathetic and dialogic care.

Power dynamics are clearly at play in respect of cultural heritage. It is acknowledged that, at times, the imbalance between those who are prepared to contribute through communities of care to the dialogue about cultural heritage and those who may be marginalised within society and who feel unable to contribute to that dialogue is significant.

The role of law is not an entirely innocent activity in this space, and it can be used instrumentally to perpetuate paternalistic care of cultural heritage, impeding dialogue in any meaningful way and risking the respectful and empathetic care of cultural heritage, certainly in respect of the communities

---

[4] Section 3.7.5.3.   [5] Sections 4.8.1 and 5.2.2.   [6] Section 5.2.2.   [7] Discussed at Section 7.6.1.

for whom the cultural heritage is important. On paper the cultural heritage in question is receiving quotidian care in terms of being looked after physically. However, the care is not respectful, empathetic or dialogic in circumstances where those who have direct responsibility for the current care by virtue of possession fail to respond to the communities who question a museum's continued possession where it is legally prohibited from transferring it to them.

It is only too easy to anthropomorphise the law and to blame it for this impedance of appropriate care, but we should not do so. Law is not a constant. Laws are the will of the community – a nation – and are enacted by their representatives on their behalf. For that reason, the *status quo* should be challenged in circumstances where the law, as it currently stands, actively hinders the appropriate care of cultural heritage. Law should not be celebrated as protective prison walls which prevent dialogue and the ability to respond empathetically and respectfully to challenges. Changes to the law would not necessarily seek to mandate return in particular circumstances, but would instead facilitate return where that represents appropriate care for cultural heritage and for the communities for whom it is important based on an objective, measured consideration of the issues. Often one considers disputes solely as involving a claimant pitted against a respondent museum. The claimant communities are central to this, but there are other relevant communities who have a voice, such as the visiting public, researchers, or the local community for whom the object is a central part of the museum and those communities for whom its continued presence may be uncomfortable and challenging. For that reason, appropriate care involves a full dialogue with those communities from whom the object originated, communities who the object has been part of more recently and also those who have cared for it in physical terms for many years. A dialogue is just that – a conversation and interaction between these varied parties. It is not simply a back and forth between two of them when there are others to consider as well. It is about listening, responding respectfully, showing empathy to those others involved in that discussion, and it is about trying to find objectively what constitutes the appropriate care for the cultural heritage in a particular context. It is not about coming in with predetermined views about the fate of the cultural heritage in question. It is about discussing the next step in the journey of that cultural heritage object, place or practice and to consider who might be the appropriate companion on that journey to assume responsibility for its direct care, but recognising that there are others who care about it. By acting, by listening, by responding, and perhaps even by giving it away, they are caring appropriately for the cultural heritage and for its many, and diverse, communities.

Index

Printed in the USA
CPSIA information can be obtained
at www.ICGtesting.com
LVHW071540121223
766171LV00006B/198

Friends
~in~
Time

GRACE CHETWIN

Friends ~in~ Time

Bradbury Press

New York

Maxwell Macmillan Canada   Toronto
Maxwell Macmillan International
New York   Oxford   Singapore   Sydney

Bradbury Press
Macmillan Publishing Company
866 Third Avenue
New York, NY 10022

Maxwell Macmillan Canada, Inc.
1200 Eglinton Avenue East
Suite 200
Don Mills, Ontario M3C 3N1

Macmillan Publishing Company is part of the Maxwell Communication
Group of Companies.

First edition
Printed and bound in the United States of America
10 9 8 7 6 5 4 3 2 1
The text of this book is set in Sabon.
Typography by Julie Quan.

Library of Congress Cataloging-in-Publication Data
Chetwin, Grace.
Friends in time / by Grace Chetwin. — 1st ed.
p.   cm.
Summary: Unhappy about her family's upcoming move, twelve-year-old
Emma wishes for a friend and is suddenly confronted with a spoiled,
lonely girl transported from the 1850s by a mysterious doll.
ISBN 0-02-718318-1
[1. Time travel—Fiction. 2. Magic—Fiction. 3. Moving,
Household—Fiction.] I. Title.
PZ7.C42555Fr 1992
[Fic]—dc20   91-33178

For my friend Maureen Hayes
with love and thanks
at least

Friends
~in~
Time

~*1*~

*E*mma paced the living room, her eye on the phone. If they were going to catch the movie, Kim was sure cutting it close. She passed the mirror on the far wall, caught the flash of her red down jacket—and the scowl on her face. "Hey!" She backed, eyeing herself severely. "Lighten up. You look like a snapping turtle." She tried for a smile, without much success.

Emma had a bad feeling about that afternoon, and her stomach ached from the stress of it. Kim wasn't coming, even though they'd made their special, last-Saturday plans in class only the day before, at the final bell. Just after, as Emma rode her bike through the school gates, she'd seen Kim talking with Jessie Fisher by the bus lines. Could have been about anything—but it wasn't, Emma knew.

Please let me be wrong, she prayed, glancing at the clock. Ten to three: Kim was never late. A minute more and Emma would call, even though she'd vowed to hold out.

The phone rang. Kim, at last! "For heavens' sakes!" Emma yelled. "We'll miss the movie!"

"I know," Kim said. "Emma—I'm not coming."

"Not coming? You *promised*."

"Yes, well, it's just that—"

Emma cut her off. "That what?" Silence. "It's Jessie Fisher, isn't it? You're going with her."

"Sorry, Emma."

Sorry? "Oh, you'll be sorry all right."

"Just what do you mean?" Kim's voice went unusually low.

"Whatever you want." Emma knew she was losing it, but too bad. "Look, if you don't come for me right now, I'll—I'll . . ."

"You'll what?"

Emma bit her lip. "I won't be your friend."

A small silence. "Okay," Kim said, and hung up. Emma stared into the receiver, feeling hollow.

Her mother stood in the doorway. "What's up, hon? Kim not coming?"

"No."

"Oh, Em." Nancy Gibson advanced into the room. "What happened?"

Emma shrugged, not trusting herself to speak. *She dumped me, that's what,* she thought. *Because we're leaving.*

"You've had a fight?" Her mother caught Emma in a hug and squeezed. "Oh, Em. And she's your best friend."

My only friend, Emma added silently. "She's gone with Jessie Fisher. Couldn't wait until I left."

"Oh boy," her mother said, patting Emma's back. "It happens. Though I'm surprised at Kim, unless—" Nancy Gibson held Emma at arm's length, scanning her face. "Emma, hon, you haven't . . ."

"Haven't what?" Emma stiffened, bracing for a lecture.

Her mother sighed. "Now don't take this wrong, Em, but lately I've noticed you getting just a bit . . . grabby with her."

Emma pulled away and stood off. "*Grabby?*"

"I know she's the first real friend you've had— which is not your fault, with all the moves we've made, Em. If I were you, I'd be just as upset at the idea of losing her. And I might get possessive, too."

3

Possessive now. Emma was hurt. "You always say I'm too standoffish."

Her mother nodded. "The two can go together. Remember how shy you were in the beginning? How Kim called the shots? Now you're leaving, you're crowding her, and she feels smothered. Hon, loosen up," Nancy Gibson went on. "Moving away is rough, but it's not the end of the world. You and Kim can stay pals. You can write each other, and Kim can visit us in Texas."

"She won't want to."

"Oh, yes she will, given the chance. Look, don't take all this too much to heart. Let matters cool today. Tomorrow, call and patch things up—but don't push, okay?"

Emma stared at her mother. Whose side was she on? "I'm going to start packing," she said stiffly, and went upstairs.

But in her room, she ignored the waiting cartons and huddled on her bed, pulling her old striped afghan up around herself. Beside the bed was a framed snapshot of her and Kim riding their bikes along Main. Reaching over, Emma laid the picture face-down, then, sighing, she sat up again, gazing around.

Emma's mother always said her room was too "cluttered." But Emma didn't agree. To Emma's mind, clutter meant junk. And if her room was rather full, it was with treasures, precious souvenirs of all the places they'd lived.

On the dresser by the window was the crinolined lady from Richmond, Virginia (a trinket pot, really). Beside it was a large pink butterfly hair clip, souvenir of the ponytail she'd had cut off in Bakersfield, California, last year. Nearby a miniature china owl from Birmingham, Michigan, sat reading *Through the Looking Glass*. Beside that lay a purple brush and mirror still intact from her third-grade stint in Chagrin Falls, Ohio—a three-year survival feat.

She glanced to the daffodil-yellow writing set on her desk, complete with matching blotter: a New York birthday gift from Kim.

Emma turned away to her crowded shelves: to frayed picture books long outgrown but which she'd never throw out, nature books and almanacs, and classics from Mom and Dad. In among all these were dog-eared paperbacks, adventures and fantasies that Emma purchased herself to read in bed.

The room looked so cozy and secure, but it was about to change.

Emma shrank into her afghan. Four days from now, the whole shebang would be taken down and shipped off like a traveling sideshow. Or the circus she'd been to once, a magical night of marvels under

5

the big top. The whole vast affair had seemed so settled that Emma was sure it was there to stay. But the next morning, when she went to see, the great tent was gone, leaving an empty, trampled field.

Oh, why, Emma lamented, why did Dad move around so much? "Can't you make him stay put?" she'd pleaded with Mom last month, after Dad announced his work was nearly over, and that they were moving on to Dallas.

"Sorry, Em," her mother had replied. "We can't help it if your dad's a planner. Moving goes with the job."

"It doesn't have to. He could stop planning towns and malls and be a regular architect right here."

Mom shook her head. "Middletown is too small. There's no work."

"But I don't want to go. You don't like moving, either." Mom always grumbled over unpacking and settling in. And she left friends behind, too.

"It's a lot of trouble, and I admit I grouch. However, it goes with the territory. I accepted that when I married your father, hon."

Good for you, Emma thought, resentfully. Mom had made her choice. But what about Emma? Didn't they know how tough it was, starting over each time? New school, new teachers, new work—or the same boring stuff. And the kids! Emma glanced to the downturned snapshot. Making friends was hard for her. "Be more outgoing," Mom and Dad advised. "Lighten up, don't expect miracles overnight." But did they realize? Overnight was all the time she ever had. They'd never understand, she thought glumly. How could they? They weren't shy; being new wouldn't seem like much to them. They'd never walked into a cafeteria at lunchtime and sat down, all alone at one end of the table, with kids crowding the other shouting "No room! No room!" with their eyes. Mom and Dad had never gone on eating, anyway, feeling like a pimple on a wart. Last year, in Bakersfield, Emma had felt so conspicuous that she'd ducked the cafeteria altogether. Instead, she'd hidden in the school yard, eating before the other kids swarmed out to play.

Here, though, it had been different. Kim had taken to her right off, and they had quickly become friends. Ever since, life had been great—until Dad dropped the Texas bombshell.

Paul looked in. "Hi, kiddo."

Emma scowled at her eighth-grade brother's cheery face. "I thought you had a soccer match."

"I did. We won, in case you want to know."

That was no news. The school team was county champion. And, normally, Emma would cheer his victory. But today, Paul's evident good spirits were salt in her wounds. "Rah, rah," she said bitterly.

"Hey—" Paul stepped inside, eyeing her face. "What's up?"

"Nothing." Emma turned away. I just lost Kim, she told him silently. And all because we're leaving, of course.

Paul sat beside her, quite concerned now. "Hang on, Em. Only four more days to go."

"You don't get it, do you?" Emma burst out. "But you wouldn't—Mr. Popular."

"Hey." Paul sounded hurt. "Some kids don't like me."

"Such as who?"

"The guys who get bumped off teams for me. They pick fights sometimes."

"You poor thing."

Paul stood up. "Boy, you sure are feeling bad," he said slowly.

Emma watched her brother out in tight-lipped silence, but the moment her door closed, she was sorry. How could she act so mean with Paul! Was it his fault that he was so good at games, that he'd never known a lonely day in his life? Feeling guiltier by the minute, Emma resolved to make amends. Help him load the dishwasher, maybe. It was his turn to clear the dinner plates.

She surveyed her room, unwilling to start taking

it apart. Then, with sudden purpose, she threw off her afghan, strode to her shelves, and began yanking books, stacking them methodically into the nearest carton.

Method didn't last long.

Growing more and more angry, Emma seized up bigger and bigger armloads until one pile buckled halfway to the box. Books fell all over. As she bent to gather them up again, a dusty, unfamiliar cover caught her eye.

Emma retrieved the book, blew off the dust, then buffed the covers with her sleeve. The thin volume was bound in fake leather, shiny mud brown, and its title was stamped in gold leaf. Frowning, she read the lettering. *Middletown, New York: 1689 to the Present Day.* Ah! Now she remembered. It was a local publication, put out by the Middletown Historical Society—the people who had hired Dad. The family had moved here so he could salvage Middle County's old, abandoned buildings and assemble them onto one site called Colonial Village. Set at the edge of town, it was a mini-Williamsburg; meant to preserve local history and bring in tourist dollars. Dad said the job made a nice break from planning new towns and shopping centers.

Jack Gibson had given Emma the book when they arrived. Still smarting from their latest move, she had spurned the peace offering, slipping it behind a shelf to lie, unread, while her father worked on, assembling the county's ruined houses on their new location.

Now, a year later, his job was done, except for the old, abandoned Bentley mansion next door. But on Monday, it, too, would be trucked across town to its new home. And the Gibsons would move on to Texas, where her dad was to help build a brand-new development in a booming Dallas suburb.

Emma flipped through pages of text and fuzzy prints. She paused at a picture of a farmhouse surrounded by pasture—downtown Main Street now. She was just about to close the book when some painted portraits caught her eye. *Gallery of Bentleys from the Nineteenth Century,* the caption said. A dozen faces stared up from the page: somber men, mutton chops and walrus mustaches turtling out from high, wing collars; ladies in bonnets and lacy caps and shawls. And all posed woodenly against formal drapes and large-leaved plants in pots, never a casual, everyday background. Emma stared back, trying to picture them for real: smiling, frowning, talking, yelling and telling silly jokes. She pictured her own family album filled with snapshots taken at the beach, on the porch, in the yard; on bikes, throwing balls and having a tumble of fun all around. Kids looking at *those* in a hundred years' time will know we were real, she thought.

On the opposite page, there were rows of Bentley kids in the same fake set-ups, looking just as stiff and vacant as their elders. Maybe it's the painters, she thought, scanning the rows of faces. Or maybe that was how you were supposed to look in those days. Wouldn't get me to sit for hours like that, Emma told herself. A picture in the third row snagged her attention. A girl, about her own age: oval face, large eyes, dark ringlets caught back in a headband. Emma ran her hand absently through her own short bangs and curls. They must have paid the painter well, she thought. No one could be that good-looking. Abigail Porterhouse Bentley (q.v.), the legend read. The *q.v.* told Emma to check the index at the back of the book if she wanted to know more about the girl. She found the index, found B for Bentley, and started to look for Abigail's name. All at once, the quarrel with Kim, her mother's lecture, her outburst at Paul, not to mention the sight of her room like this, was too much. Emma snapped the book shut and scrambled to her feet. She felt stifled. If she didn't get out that minute, she'd choke. She grabbed her jacket and ran downstairs. Mom was in the kitchen, wrapping china. "Need a break," Emma called hurriedly.

"Okay, hon," Mom called back. "Don't go far. Dinner's early tonight—I'll ring my bell if you're not back." Mom's beloved brass handbell, a Mother's Day gift from Emma and Paul so she could call them in for meals without screaming.

Emma made for her bike, thinking to pedal off her turmoil. Then, remembering her mother's warning about early dinner, she turned and strode toward the estate next door—or what was left of it.

Once through the tilting gateposts, Emma jammed her hands into her jeans pockets and gazed around, her breath steaming in the chill spring air. The place was deserted. Dad was across town with the work crews, checking the mansion's new foundations. She advanced gingerly over churned-up mud tracks to the cluster of flatbed trucks in the middle. Emma wandered around the semis, gazing up at their plastic-shrouded cargo: sections of house, whole rooms slit open to the sky like a giant dollhouse. Abigail Porterhouse Bentley had lived in that mansion. She had walked the floors, climbed those fancy stairs. In her shiny ringlets and long fancy dresses, Abigail had sat in that very parlor, which at this moment reared above Emma on the nearest rig. What would it have been like?

Grasping the edge of the rig, Emma pulled herself on tiptoe, peering through the plastic. The parlor

12

within looked dark and shabby, like the worn carpets and faded drapes that the workcrews had packed away in crates. Of course, in Abigail's time those furnishings would have been rich and new, and the shabby woodwork, waxed and shiny. Lucky Abigail, Emma thought wistfully. Living in those days might not have been much fun, but at least she'd grown up in the one place, instead of moving every year, making do in rental houses or apartments. Abigail had *belonged*, with lifelong friends and childhood memories solid as that huge old house on its foundations. She had grown up among the family heirlooms, never having to part with good stuff just because it wouldn't fit the final carton.

Emma sighed.

That house was wrenched-up now, though; torn apart by twentieth-century machines. Only the main chimney stack remained in place, rising out of the earth: a tall, stark pillar stripped of tile, its stones neatly numbered. When the rigs were gone, the stack would be dismantled, then rebuilt stone by stone onto the house after it was reassembled on its new foundation. Emma gazed around, at the loaded rigs, and the chimney rearing from the mud. It all looked so sad. Desolate, like a folded circus.

Still. Abigail never knew.

Emma glanced at her wristwatch. By now, she

and Kim would have been coming out of the movie and heading for a milk shake. Instead, Kim was in the mall with her old crowd, Emma Gibson quite forgotten, no doubt.

Emma sighed. This time next week she'd be helping her mother check out a new neighborhood, the stores and post office—not for *her,* though. She wouldn't be getting any mail. Two days after that, she'd head through into a new classroom, watched by curious eyes. *And alone, without Kim at her side.* Emma turned her face skyward. "If I could have just one real friend," she called, to no one in particular.

All at once, Emma shivered. The air had certainly gone colder. Turning up her collar, she made to leave, but as she stepped away, a large black bird started up from the chimney top, making her jump. Emma watched it fly off, her heart thudding. A blackbird? No—too big. More likely a crow. Something had disturbed it. Not her, surely. For weeks, the crews had been tearing up the place with big, loud machines. Emma eyed the chimney thoughtfully. Could there be a nest inside? If so, Dad had better warn the crews to leave it be.

Emma strode to the chimney base, and braced her head against the stone. Leaning in, she looked upward, the reek of ancient soot catching her nose.

Way above, a patch of gray sky showed; nothing blocked the view.

Reassured, she was about to move away, when a tremor passed through the chimney stones, under her palm. As she started back, light flashed. Startled, Emma squeezed up her eyes, then reopened them.

She caught her breath. Instead of stone, a shiny, green-tiled hearth, and in the hearth—a fire. Before she could blink, it was gone, and there she stood once more under the cold spring sky.

Another flash.

The hearth reappeared, and this time the parlor all around it, bright and fully furnished—the very parlor that was up on the rig behind Emma; a dark and shabby shell, faded relic of this former glory.

For an instant, the parlor was all around her, and firelight struck warm on her face. Then it vanished and Emma stood once more under gray sky. She clutched her head and shut her eyes. When she looked again, she was back in the firelit parlor—but not alone this time. By the hearth was a girl about Emma's own age and size. Her hair, a mass of dark ringlets, was caught back in a headband. Her blue satin dress was long, with puff sleeves, and shiny black pumps poked out from under her skirts. Oblivious of Emma, she was standing in front of the fire, holding something to the flames.

15

"Good grief!" Emma exclaimed, recognizing who she was.

The girl leapt back, the object falling from her hands. As it hit the tiles, the fire, the parlor vanished.

But the girl remained, staring with horror into Emma's face.

~2~

Emma held her breath. Abigail Porterhouse Bentley—right out of the Middletown history book! Wind riffled past the stone chimney, stirring the girl's thin skirts. She was real! Emma opened her mouth to speak, the girl opened hers. Emma shut her mouth again, and the girl looked away, down to her black patent slippers in the mud, then up at Emma, fearfully. "Are—are you the dollmaker?"

"Dollmaker?" What a strange thing to say. "No, I'm not."

Abigail frowned, giving Emma the once-over: a

narrow, keen appraisal that Emma knew all too well. Emma scuffed her toe, remembering the dab of bike grease on her sleeve, the tear in her jeans, and her ratty old sneakers. "Are you a farm boy, then?" the girl demanded, sounding surer now.

Farm boy! Emma pulled herself up indignantly. "I'm not a farm boy, or any other kind of boy. Are *you* a ghost?"

"A *ghost?* How dare you!"

"You called me a boy," Emma retorted.

"Your hair is like a boy's, and your breeches," Abigail said. "You *look* like one—but you must be Wabeno," she added, stepping back now. "Why else are you here?"

"Hey," Emma protested.

"Don't deny it. One minute it's nighttime and I am in Grandpapa's parlor, and the next, it is daylight and, and—" Abigail faltered, then finished in a rush. "I'm in this awful place. Only powerful magic like yours could do that."

Magic! Emma stood dumbfounded. If there was any magic here, it came from Abigail.

"Hey," she began excitedly. "Who's talking. Here I am, just minding my own business, when—" The girl looked about to run. Emma took a deep breath, calmed herself, and started over. "What just happened—I had nothing to do with it. I'm just a reg-

18

ular kid. My name's Emma, Emma Gibson, and I live over there." She pointed to the hedge. "As for this 'awful place'—" Emma gestured around. "Don't you recognize it?"

Abigail turned and saw the plastic cocoons perched on the rigs. *"Oh!"* She clapped her hands to her mouth. "What have you done to the house!"

Emma moved to calm her down, but the girl backed off so fast she nearly toppled. "Back, Wabeno! This is your revenge because I tried to burn that, you can't deny it!" Abigail pointed to the object lying on the ground between them. The thing she'd been holding to the fire when the flashes started. A figurine? A doll? "Well, take it," she cried. "It's quite undamaged, as you can—oh." Abigail's hand moved to her chest. "Where is *Grandpapa?* And Mama, and Uncle Ralph? What have you done with them?" Crouching, she snatched up the fallen figure and thrust it at Emma urgently. "Here, I don't want it. Take it back and put things right again."

Emma glanced down. Yes, a doll, and the strangest, ugliest one she'd ever seen. Its crude shape was fashioned from, what? Wood? Hide? Clay? Emma couldn't tell. The body was encased in rough cloth, like burlap. The cloth was hung with metal tags of different shapes daubed with dull pigment: red, and

19

blue, and earthen yellow. Were they charms? One, a blood-red heart shape dangling from the doll's chest, was split down the middle and loosely lashed with wire. Feeling strangely uncomfortable at the sight of it, Emma directed her gaze to the head. The skull was flanked by wide, wing-like ears pierced by dull silver rings, and capped with tufted hair, animal pelt of some kind. And the face! Two round hollow eyes, a sharp beak nose, and the mouth? A small round hole rimmed with lips like a tiny tire. The whole looked grotesque, cartoon-like. But Emma didn't find it comic. She thought of her savings bank, the surveillance camera high in the wall. Every time she went in there, Emma could feel the eye on her, the tiny lens recording every move she made. She looked to the doll uneasily, feeling that way now; as if from within those deep, dark holes someone watched her.

Emma clasped her hands behind her back. "It's not mine," she said. "I don't want it."

Abigail's temper flared. "You lie, dollmaker! Don't think I can't see through your disguise! This is your very own power wand, Grandpapa said so, and just because I tried to burn it the house is wrecked, I'm here, and everyone has disappeared." She straightened up and offered the doll again. "Please, *please!* Uncle Ralph meant no harm, he's just a rip, a darling. Take it and put things back the way they were, I beg of you."

Power wand? Uncle Ralph? "I tell you, I haven't a clue what you're talking about," Emma protested.

And then she thought of her wish. *If I could have just one real friend.*

Now here was Abigail.

Emma took a breath to tell about her wish to the sky, then let it out again. If she told that she knew why Abigail was here, Abigail would be *convinced* she was this Wabby-something. "I've already told you: I'm Emma Gibson from next door. Now you say who you are."

The girl tossed her ringlets defiantly. "You know I'm Abigail Bentley. You know I'm why Uncle Ralph took your wretched doll."

As more wind gusted through, Emma took off her jacket and laid it around Abigail's shoulders. "It's okay," she said quickly, as Abigail shied. "I'm not this dollmaker guy, honest. I don't know how or why you're here. But maybe if you tell your side, we can figure it out together."

Abigail Porterhouse Bentley felt the down-soft nylon jacket curiously, then eyed Emma from over the collar. "If you are Wabeno, then you know already. If you're not, then you might just help me as you say, so what have I to lose?" She sighed.

21

"All right. Today was my birthday—"

"Happy birthday," Emma said, but Abigail went right on.

"Uncle Ralph wrote to say he was bringing me home a special surprise. He has been gone months and months, sailing around South America."

"Neat," Emma said. "Is he an explorer?"

"In a way." Abigail nodded slowly. "The Bentleys are merchants, don't you know? We own the biggest clipper fleet on the East Coast."

"Go on," Emma said, huddling closer, shrinking from the icy wind.

"I was so excited. His letter said that he'd found a doll for me in Brazil. I was sure it would be of real porcelain with golden hair and eyes that open and close. I even picked a name for her: Cassie. This afternoon, when he finally arrived, he gave me *this*." Abigail dropped the doll into the mud. "You can't imagine how awful it was. And Uncle Ralph was so proud.

" 'Abigail, it's unique,' he told me. 'Just think: no other little girl in the world will ever have one like it.' "

"Oh, Abigail," said Emma, sympathizing. "What did you do?"

"What could I do?" Abigail said. "They were all watching me: Mama, Grandpapa, and Uncle Ralph.

I had to say thank you, and hug it to me, just as if it were Cassie—*Cassie*, ugh. I went to my room as soon as I could and—oh, you'll never guess the terrible thing that happened next."

Just then, a bell jangled.

"What was that?" Abigail started back in alarm.

"Only my mom," Emma reassured her hurriedly. "I have to go."

"But—you can't," Abigail protested. "Don't leave me here—*please!*"

Emma threw an agonized glance toward the hedge. "Half an hour, okay? I'll be back, promise." She raised her voice to be heard over the bell. "Look, keep my coat—and stay put!"

~3~

Emma's mother was at the door. Would Emma please hurry? Dinner was getting cold. Emma washed hastily, then took her place at table, glancing at her wristwatch. Eight minutes gone already!

She ate fast and with great concentration while Paul gave their mom and dad a blow-by-blow account of the soccer victory.

Abigail Porterhouse Bentley—not a stone's throw from the house. Of all the fantastic luck. A real, live kid, the answer to Emma's skywish. A friend from another age, whisked magically across to Emma's space and time. Emma pictured Abigail sitting at the table, then running upstairs to visit, even sleeping in her room. She resolved to bring Abigail home, any way she could.

At last the meal was over. Her mom and dad went to catch the news in the living room. Emma ducked out, fast, leaving Paul to clear up alone. Well, it was his turn, she reasoned guiltily, remembering her earlier resolution. She pulled on an old jacket, and slipped away.

It was dark now. Emma pulled the jacket up to her chin, feeling the night wind. Abigail would be freezing—if she was still there.

"I thought you'd never come." Abigail stepped from the chimney wall, scrubbing at her eyes. Had she been crying? Emma could not be sure.

She took Abigail's hands. "Wow, you're icy." Maybe this was the way to get Abigail over to the house. "Tell you what: I'll sneak you up to my room for a while. It's really nice and warm there."

"But I—" Abigail began.

Emma drew her firmly toward the gateposts. "Trust me," she said.

They slipped in through the side door. Paul was still stacking dishes, and Mom and Dad were watching the weather forecast, by the sound of it. Emma led Abigail past the kitchen door to the back stairs, and pointed. Without a word, Abigail gathered up her skirts and climbed.

Emma got them through her bedroom door without a hitch. But when she flipped on the light, Abigail squealed.

"Shush!" Emma squeezed her arm.

Abigail wriggled free, looking at the lighted lamps in alarm. "If that isn't magic, then what is it?"

Oh, boy, Emma thought. She doesn't know electricity. Only candles and oil lamps. "It's . . ." How to explain, when she herself didn't know how it worked, exactly? "It's . . . modern science. See?" Emma pointed to the switch. "There's power—I mean, a sort of current in the wall. . . ." She was making it worse. "Look." Emma seized Abigail's finger and pressed it to the switch, off, and on again. "See? No magic, no spells. Just electricity."

Abigail snatched her hand back, eyeing Emma uncertainly.

Emma moved along. "Excuse the mess. Here." She helped Abigail off with the jacket. "Take a seat."

Abigail picked her way around assorted cardboard boxes and perched warily on the edge of the bed.

"Not like that," Emma said in a reassuring voice. "Lift up your feet."

As Abigail swung her legs up and tucked them under her, Emma set the afghan around her shoulders. Abigail *had* been crying. Emma could see the tear streaks now, but dared not mention them. "Comfortable?"

Abigail nodded, gazing at the ransacked shelves and half-filled cartons. "Where are we? What is this place?" she demanded, but she didn't sound so nervous now. Only curious.

"You first," Emma prompted. "When you got to your room, what then?"

"I was so upset about the doll, as I said." Abigail adjusted the afghan. "I ran to my dresser." She turned to Emma. "There's a big, square mirror over it—you seem not to have one. Don't you like to see yourself?"

"Good grief, no," Emma said quickly. Her thought jumped to the girls in school taking their combs out of their back pockets for the Washroom Parade. Even Kim fussed with her hair at breaktime. But not Emma. She didn't care for that stuff—or so she said. But who was she kidding? She was just too shy to fix herself up in front of others, and that was the plain, honest truth. "Well, maybe some," she admitted. "My mirror's behind the closet door. So then what happened, Abigail?"

Abigail's eyes sparked in remembrance. "I was so

angry, my face looked *fierce* in the mirror. I raised that doll-thing high above my head, and brought it *smack* down on the dresser top. The next thing I knew there was a flash, and then I saw—"

"What, *what*, Abigail?" Emma clasped her hands tightly together.

"A face, floating beside my own reflection, staring out at me."

"Oh no! Who was it!"

"An old, old man. And, oh, you should have seen his eyes!"

"Wabeno?"

Abigail shrank into the afghan. "I thought I'd die. *I see you,* they said. *I see right through you. And there shall be a reckoning.*"

"Oh, Abigail. Then what?"

Abigail slid off the bed to pace, the afghan trailing the floor. "For a moment, I stood, fixed on the man's eyes. Then he faded like candle smoke, and I was staring at myself. I left the doll on the dresser and ran downstairs. But when I reached the parlor, there was such a row going on."

Emma listened, watching Abigail in growing admiration. She's just like a ballerina, she thought. The way she holds her head high and her back so straight. Or even a princess, with my afghan for a royal train.

Under Emma's admiring gaze, Abigail sat down again, crossing her ankles and settling the afghan around her. So *elegant,* thought Emma. She straightened up, crossing her left foot over her right.

"I had never seen Grandpapa so angry," Abigail continued. "He banged his fist on the mantel and said, 'You young puppy! Three generations, and the Bentleys have never stolen so much as a cinnamon stick.'

"Uncle Ralph swore he hadn't stolen anything. Wabeno had simply been driving a hard bargain, he said. The old man had already asked twice the going rate on everything, the way he always did."

"Your uncle knows Wabeno, then?"

"Oh, yes. He's sailed down there with Grandpapa lots of times. But Grandpapa has always done the bargaining. Until this year, when Uncle went alone, on account of Grandpapa's ailment.

"Anyway, Uncle Ralph saw the doll hanging in a back corner of Wabeno's workshop and bid on it. The man said it was not for sale. But only, Uncle Ralph said, to drive up the price. Wabeno even offered him other dolls, but Uncle Ralph stuck to this one. He said it was one of a kind. He bid higher, but Wabeno still refused. Finally, Uncle Ralph left."

"Without the doll?" Emma tried to break in, but Abigail raised her hand imperiously, cutting her off.

"By now Uncle Ralph was really set to get that doll for me, so when all was quiet, he sneaked back, took the doll, and left what he considered a fair sum in its place. Much more than he needed to, he said, for such a crude thing made by a mere jungle native. But after all, it was his favorite niece's birthday doll.

" '*Doll?*' Grandpapa's voice was like a whip. 'You fool—did I teach you nothing? You know those things are more than that.'

"Mama asked what he meant, and I could tell that she was frightened.

" 'I'll not beat about the bush, Elizabeth,' Grandpapa said. 'Those things aren't simply native art. And Wabeno is no *mere jungle native*. He's a healer, a magic man. And those dolls are fetishes—totems, *power wands*.' "

"Wands?" cried Emma, puzzled. "I thought they were sticks, like in fairy tales."

"Me, too," Abigail agreed impatiently, then went on. "Grandpapa said that once Wabeno finished making the dolls, or power wands, he set magic into each, to serve folk in different ways.

" 'Like a lucky charm?' Mama said. 'But that is just superstition.'

" 'Maybe,' Grandpapa said. 'Yet people claim they work: to help a woman get with child, or make a man strong. To cure illness—or bring it on.'

30

" 'You mean those things can do *evil?*' Mama said, and sat down.

" 'If you but knew the half of it,' Grandpapa said, in a really grim voice. Mama asked why Grandpapa bought dolls from Wabeno, if he knew they could be bad. 'But I don't, Elizabeth,' Grandpapa said, and then he grew really furious. 'I know better than to meddle in such things. I buy only Wabeno's regular carvings: dishes, vases, and other domestic items. Wabeno and I have traded goods for thirty years, and never a shadow of trouble until now.' Uncle Ralph said things might not be so bad. Wabeno was way down in Brazil and we were up here in New York.

" 'You fool!' Grandpapa told him. 'You brought Wabeno with you!' "

"Oh, Abigail!" Emma said. "The doll?"

Abigail nodded. "Grandpapa said that it was likely Wabeno's very own personal power wand. He said the old man would have put much magic into it over the years. Goodness only knew what it could do—or what the old man might make it do when he found it gone.

"Mama jumped up and cried out, 'That broken heart—what evil might it work on Abigail!' Then she fell into a faint and they rushed to carry her upstairs. I raced ahead, sure that the curse had already begun. I had to do something, so while they laid Mama on her bed, I picked up the doll—"

"Abigail! Weren't you afraid to touch it?"

Abigail nodded. "I ran it down to the parlor, but the moment I put it to the flames—"

"Lightning flashed, and here you are!" Emma cried.

"But where? Where is that?"

Emma thought for a minute. "Abigail, what year is this?"

"Year?" Abigail frowned. "Eighteen forty-six, everyone knows that."

Emma shook her head. "When the lightning flashed, our times criss-crossed and now you're here—in nineteen ninety-five!"

ou mean that I am in the future? How terrible!"

"I think it's exciting," Emma said. "You don't know how lucky you are. I wish I could take a trip ahead."

"You do?" Abigail leapt angrily off the bed, throwing off the afghan. "And if you didn't know how to get home again, what then?" She stumbled over boxes, heading for the door.

Emma blocked her way. "Wait, where are you going? It's *freezing* out there." Taking Abigail's arm, she tried to draw her back into the room.

33

"Hey," she went on, as Abigail resisted. "Aren't we supposed to be figuring things together?"

"I've changed my mind," Abigail said, though she did stop struggling. "Magic brought me here, only magic can take me back. You haven't any."

Oh, no? thought Emma, remembering her sky-wish. She was tempted to mention it, but thought better of it. "Let's think. Did this Wabeno guy send you here . . . or—"

"Of course he did," Abigail cut in scornfully. "Who else?"

"The doll itself, maybe."

"The doll?" Abigail frowned. "How?"

Good question. Emma rummaged through her books for her illustrated almanac of facts. She opened it at D, found "doll," and slid her finger down the column.

"What does it say?" Abigail asked impatiently.

"A lot," Emma said.

The text was small, and packed tight with bits of information—nothing they needed, so far. She scanned the first column, then the second a way, then paused, her finger on "dolls; kachina."

"Listen, Abigail," Emma went on. "It says here that the kachinas are spirit people sacred to the Hopi Indians. A kachina can be anything: a river, a hill, a star, or even an invisible force. It says 'The Hopis carve small images of these spirits out of cotton-wood. These images or dolls are called kachinas also but'—oh." Emma glanced up, then read on. " 'They are *not* invested with sacred power, but serve merely to teach the children about the real spirits that they represent.' "

"You mean kachina dolls have no magic?"

"I guess."

"Then that doesn't tell us anything," Abigail cried dismissively.

"Yes, it does. It tells us to keep looking." Emma moved happily on down the column. She loved playing detective in her almanac. "Ah, this is more like it, Abigail: 'doll; charm (q.v.)'."

Emma turned to C, then leafed through cats, cat-amarans, catapults, and cataracts, slid her finger down past charisma and charlatan, and there was what she sought: charm; fetish (q.v.); power wand (q.v.); totem (q.v.). Under the heading, a small, doll-like figure dangled in the column.

Abigail drew in her breath. "Heavens, that's it. The mouth, the nose, the ears—almost exactly. What do the words say?"

Emma, puzzled, pointed to the text. "Can't you read?"

"Certainly," Abigail said haughtily. "But not so well, just yet," she added. "I started Miss Bessemer's

Academy for Young Ladies only last year."

"Well, it says pretty much what your granddad said. 'The dolls are totems, charms, fetishes, or power wands.' " Emma turned to "wand" and read down the column, until she found what she sought. "A power wand is a stick or doll for storing magic. When it's a doll, the magic is in the doll's body or the ornaments on its dress—those metal tags," she explained. "It says—hey!"

"What is it?" Abigail leaned over Emma's shoulder.

"There's stuff here about dolls as art. It says in recent times, many kinds of carved dolls, sacred and non-sacred, African, Polynesian, Indian, are fetching huge sums of money from collectors." She whistled. "It says here a kachina doll—that's what we read about just now—was auctioned off in 1991 for over five thousand dollars!" She looked up excitedly. "Wabeno's doll could be worth a *lot* in time." Emma closed the book and set it down.

"Worth a lot?" cried Abigail. "What about right now?"

"Right now it's plain dangerous," Emma conceded. "It could be loaded with spells. Abigail, say it can defend itself."

"What do you mean?"

"Look: when you banged down the doll, the face appeared to warn you off. But that didn't work. So when you tried to *burn* the doll, well, it jumped you to a time when there was no fire to harm it. I guess it could have timeshifted back to before the house was built. But instead, it came forward to when the house was taken up and loaded on those rigs—to now, in fact."

"So how do I get home?"

"I don't know, unless the doll can take you."

"But then I have to hold it. Oh, heavens." Abigail clapped her hands to her head. "I left it by the chimney."

Now they both made for the door. There, Emma stopped. "Wait. You can't go out like that." She got together jeans, a blue sweatshirt, sneakers and socks, and handed them to Abigail. "Here."

"You want me to put those things on?" Abigail eyed the clothes in plain distaste. She took the sweatshirt gingerly and held it to her face, then looked to Emma in surprise. "So soft—and these breeches." She fingered the jeans delicately. "They look quite rough, yet they are woolsey fine. Where may I change?"

Emma looked around, considering. "There's my closet. It's real roomy, and there's a light." Emma opened the door with a flourish, revealing her full-

37

length mirror, of which she was secretly proud. She flipped on the ceiling light. "Will it do?"

"Oh, Emma, how fine. You can see yourself all the way from head to toe." Abigail held the jeans to her blue satin skirt and stared into the mirror. Letting the jeans dangle, Abigail raised her skirts behind them, revealing a frilly petticoat. She hitched this up also, displaying now a pair of long johns trimmed with lace, and eyed herself once more. "How bizarre. Do all the girls in your day dress like farm boys?"

Farm boys again! But no point arguing. "I guess. Look, you can't cram all that underwear into those jeans. Put these on instead," Emma said, adding undershirt and panties from her bureau. "But before you go—" She showed Abigail how to step into the jeans and zipper them up.

Abigail went into the closet and shut the door. Emma heard the rustle as Abigail pulled off her dress. Then her voice came muffled through the door: "Bother these hooks on my underbodice!"

"Need any help?" Emma called.

"Thank you, no," Abigail answered primly. "I'll manage."

Emma moved away, packing up a book or two, while Abigail exclaimed softly inside the closet. Then there came a quick, bright laugh. "These shoes," Abigail called. "They're so big and clumsy."

Clumsy, indeed, thought Emma. The hottest sneakers on the market!

At last Abigail emerged, looking like a TV ad for designer clothes.

Abigail posed before the closet mirror, turning this way and that, fascinated with her new appearance. "I look . . . odd," she said, then smiled. "But I feel fine. Although my hair is quite destroyed."

"No problem." Emma gathered the tangled ringlets into a bushy ponytail, and caught it with her bright pink butterfly clip. "There. That looks great. Okay, let's go."

While Abigail put on the red coat, Emma rolled up the discarded clothes and stowed them back of her closet. If Kim could see me now, thought Emma, pulling on her old jacket. And Jessie Fisher's crowd, though they'd never believe who Abigail was, or how she'd gotten here, for now the girl looked just like one of Mrs. Ferguson's Sixth-Grade Finest. "Come on." Emma drew Abigail from the mirror. "If they see you downstairs, I talk, okay?"

She was just opening the door, when her mother called up to her.

"Em? Paul and I are off to the mall, coming?"

Emma looked at Abigail and rolled her eyes. "Thanks, but I'm busy packing," she shouted.

39

"Oh. Oh, well, enjoy. Dad's in the den, won't be late. Bye."

Emma stood in the hall with Abigail, listening to the front door open and close, waiting while her mother gunned the engine.

"Heavens!" Abigail started. "What's that?"

"Mom's car, don't worry. She says revving's good for the motor."

"Car? Motor?"

"Oh, boy. 'Car' as in *car*riage; 'motor' as in . . . horse." The sound of the car headed down the drive-way toward Main Street and faded. "Okay, Abigail. Let's go." Emma took up a flashlight and tested it. The batteries seemed okay.

"What's that?" Abigail took the flashlight, turning it over. "How does it work?" Emma showed her. Fascinated, Abigail flipped it on and off, staring into the bulb. "But what makes the light, Emma?"

"Same stuff that's in the walls. Electricity."

"But—" Abigail looked to the walls, then closed her hand about the slender flashlight. "How, in here?"

Emma took the flashlight, opened it, and showed Abigail the four batteries neatly stacked inside. "The electricity is in those," she said. "They're a sort of— power store. The trouble is, the more you use, the faster it's used up. Now let's go find the doll, okay?"

40

Emma led the way downstairs. She paused by the den door. Dad was scanning building plans on his video screen and humming tunelessly: no problem there. Emma whisked Abigail out the side door and they fled down the path, heading for the Bentley house.

~5~

Abigail held the flashlight while Emma cast about for the doll, groping in the mud with her bare hands. The search was not easy. Delighted with her new toy, Abigail kept switching the flashlight on and off, casting the beam in all directions. Emma puffed out in irritation. What was Abigail thinking of, playing around, using up the batteries, leaving her, Emma, to do the dirty work? Had she forgotten they were on an urgent errand? Emma was just about to protest, when her fingers encountered any icy lump.

"Abigail—shine the light down here."

It was the doll, all right, plastered in mud. Emma withdrew her hand, leery now of touching it.

"Here, let me." Abigail pushed Emma aside and seized up the doll.

"No need to shove," Emma protested.

"Then move aside," Abigail said haughtily. "The doll's mine, I'm the one to hold it."

"It's *Wabeno's*."

"And what if it had moved in your hands instead of mine?"

Emma stared through the darkness. Abigail had a point there—though that didn't give her the right to act so sharp and domineering, she thought, her resentment rising.

"What next?" she asked shortly. If Princess Abigail was taking over now that the dirty work was done, she could just come up with answers, too.

"That's easy." Abigail raised the doll and banged it smartly against the chimney.

"Hey, don't do that!" Emma warned, recalling what had happened the last time Abigail risked harming it.

"I'll do as I like!" Abigail snapped. "Anyone can see I'm trying to make it shift through time again."

"And what if it goes the wrong way? What

if it takes you even farther forward?"

"I didn't think of that," said Abigail, sounding less haughty now. "Oh, Emma, what am I to *do?*"

Emma didn't know.

"Perhaps . . ." Abigail's voice trailed off. "I know. Perhaps I can *coax* it to shift back home. But how do I show what I want? I know, I'll stand by the chimney just as I did when this whole mess started." She bent, a small, shadowy figure reaching out to non-existent flames.

Nothing happened.

"Not to worry. I'll wait a minute, then try again," Abigail said, sounding a note of confidence. "And I'll just keep going until the doll gets my meaning and puts us back the way we were. It has to, in the end."

Emma listened doubtfully. It seemed to her a hopeless scheme, like trying to get an egg back in its shell.

Abigail repeated her performance, with no success. "Oh, why won't the doll work now?" she cried.

"Maybe its power's used up," Emma suggested, and bit her tongue.

"Are you saying there's no more magic?" cried Abigail. "That I'm stuck here for keeps?"

"Not necessarily," Emma said hastily. "Maybe

the magic's like—like the power in these batteries."
She tapped the flashlight's stem.

"What do you mean?"

"The batteries are rechargeable. They can be refilled with power. Maybe the doll's rechargeable, too."

"How?" Abigail sounded skeptical.

Good question, thought Emma. You plug the batteries into a wall outlet and leave them overnight. But that didn't help with the doll. "Well, you rest batteries," she hedged. "So let's try resting the doll, okay? Oh, boy," she went on quickly. "I'm sick of the dark and it's freezing out here. Let's go back to the house. Are you hungry?"

Abigail thought about it. "A little. What have you to eat?"

"Oh, all sorts of good stuff. Come on."

Still Abigail held back. "We come straight out again after?"

"Trust me," Emma said.

In the kitchen, Emma gathered crackers and potato chips from various pantry shelves. Abigail watched from a kitchen stool, holding the doll out in front of her.

The moment Emma opened the refrigerator door, Abigail was there, elbowing Emma aside. She stuck in her hand and moved it about. "How is this box so cold? I see no ice. And what makes that humming noise?"

"Same stuff that works the lights. Excuse me." Emma fished around the refrigerator shelves, picking out cans of soda, a tube of processed cheese spread, and a jumbo jar of peanut butter. Her arms full, Emma kicked the door shut behind her.

"But this box makes cold and your lights make warmth. This box makes noise, and your lights don't. How's that?" Abigail trailed Emma to the kitchen bench.

"I don't know," Emma said, getting out paper napkins and glasses. She loaded everything onto a tray and hustled her guest back upstairs.

"You don't know very much," Abigail remarked, on the way.

They settled themselves on the bed, the tray between them. "Dig in." Emma pointed to the chips. "Go on," she urged, as Abigail made no move. "What are you waiting for? Knives and forks?"

Abigail wedged the doll between her knees, then picked up a single chip and held it up between her thumb and forefinger. "Salty," she said, after a cautious nibble.

"So try a cracker instead." Emma opened up the

peanut-butter jar, then unscrewed the cap off the cheese-spread tube.

"What is *that?*" Abigail pointed to the tube.

"Cheddar cheese. It's real good," said Emma. "Want to try it?" She squeezed a pile of orange paste onto a cracker and offered it to Abigail.

Abigail made no move to take it. "The color's . . . strange. And I've never seen cheese that comes out like a worm."

"Okay, okay." Emma set a fresh cracker in front of Abigail. "Here. Try the peanut butter. Look, just scoop it out of the jar like this." Emma gouged out a generous portion with her own cracker and took a hearty bite.

Abigail let that cracker lie, too.

While Emma ate on, Abigail took up the doll, turning it about. "Are these really charms? If so, I wonder what each one is for." She fingered the painted tags fastened to the burlap. "Especially this one: it gave Mama a fainting fit . . ." Abigail lifted a jagged half of broken heart.

"Don't touch it!" Emma cried. She dropped her unfinished cracker, her own heart beginning to race. "Here, hide that thing." She found a woolen muffler and threw it across.

Abigail wrapped the muffler around the doll until only the hair tuft showed, poking out from the end of the roll. Then she set the bundle on her lap. "At risk if I hold it; at risk if I don't," she murmured. "Agh, why should I worry? It's dead as a horseshoe nail now."

"But for how long?" Emma said sharply. "That's the way evil works. It waits until you look the other way, then—*pow!*"

"But what if the evil is already accomplished?" Abigail looked up. "What if the aim is to banish me here?"

"I don't think so," Emma said, shaking her head. "Look, the doll is Wabeno's, right? And it's loaded with magic. He's got to want it back."

"Oh, I hope so, Emma."

"So do I," Emma said, but even as she said it, she realized she hated the thought of Abigail's leaving. "So don't give up hope, okay? Meantime, let's treat this like a sort of . . . time out together."

"Time out?"

"A short break. I know: let's make it a slumber party, Abigail."

"Slumber party?"

"It's when you have kids to sleep over," Emma explained. "You talk all night, eat breakfast, then everyone goes home again."

Abigail looked puzzled. "Then why call them

slumber parties if you don't sleep? Actually, in my time, we have something of the sort. We call them house parties but they are for grownups," she said. "I don't like them at all, except for Grandpapa's. I always love to come and visit him," she added, looking happier at the mention of her grandfather.

"Oh, so you don't actually live next door, then?" Emma said, wishing she'd read the county history book, especially the part about her new friend.

Abigail shook her head. "Mama and I live in Boston. But we come to stay here all the time. This house party is especially nice, and private, just for my birthday. There's only me, and Mama, and Grandpapa, and Uncle Ralph."

"What about your father?"

"He died soon after I was born."

"I'm so sorry," Emma said, biting her tongue again.

"Oh, don't be. I have his portrait. And Uncle Ralph and Grandpapa are like fathers to me, anyhow."

But Emma was not convinced. There was something in Abigail's voice, a certain sadness Emma well recognized. Loneliness was bad enough, but to grow up without a father . . . Emma thought thankfully of her own downstairs in his den that very minute. "Any brothers? Sisters?"

Abigail shook her head. "I'm an only child. And you?"

"I have a brother, Paul. He's in eighth grade."

"Eighth grade?"

"He's two classes ahead of me."

"What's he like?"

"Not bad—for a brother. He's real good at sports, so everybody loves him. He has friends wherever we go."

"And you? Do you have friends, also?"

Emma glanced to the turned-down snapshot beside the bed. "I have one—or, at least, I did."

"Oh? What happened, Emma?"

"Well, our family's moving, as you can see. So I've been dumped. Since we move a lot, I get dumped a lot."

"Does Paul get dumped also?"

"No." Emma felt her face grow warm. "Making friends is easy when you get picked for teams. Besides," she went on, honesty winning out again, "he's great company, too. Boy, can he make people laugh." Emma jumped off the bed, seizing her empty soda glass. "He's not shy like me. He's a hit at parties, he does comic stunts, like this." Tilting back her head, Emma balanced the glass on her brow, and got down slowly onto her knees. Then, using her arms for balance, she slid in and out among the boxes, honking in passable imitation of Paul's performing seal—until she bumped blindly into a carton and lost the glass. "And that, ladies and gentlemen, is how the tumbler got its name," she improvised, to save face.

Abigail laughed. "Bravo! Bravo, Emma! You're a good clown, too!"

Gratified, Emma climbed back onto the bed and dug out a handful of chips. Abigail did the same, and they sat, munching side by side. After a bit, Abigail tucked the rolled-up doll under her arm and moved curiously around the room. Stopping by the dresser, she looked at each of Emma's things, picking them up and putting them down in turn. Lifting the crinolined lady, she laughed to find the trinket bowl lying underneath. "What a cunning hiding place for treasures," she said, smiling. "I love secrets—well, nice ones, anyway. Oh." She held up a string of glistening beads. "Are these crystal?"

"Gee, no," said Emma, pleased even so. "Only glass." But they did look pretty, dangling from Abigail's fingers.

Abigail put them to the light. "Emma! Your walls!"

Rainbow specks swirled and darted all around the room. "Like dragonflies!" Abigail cried. She jiggled the necklace, making the "dragonflies" dance.

"Just the way they do on Grandpapa's lily pond."

"They're beautiful." Emma gazed around the walls, thinking how clever Abigail was to turn glass beads into rainbow specks, and think of dragonflies. She'd had those beads for ages, and never once made them dance. And if she had, she'd never have thought of dragonflies.

Abigail dropped the necklace back into the bowl, and carefully replaced the crinolined figure. "Such a pretty lady," she said. "So refined, like Mama." She grabbed the purple mirror and held it up. "But look at me! I'm a filthy wretch!" She scrubbed at a mud patch on her cheek—until the owl caught her eye. "Oh, how exquisite. I've never seen the like." She set down the mirror and took up the owl, turning it over. "It's reading. What's the book, Emma? What does the title say?" She pointed to the tiny gilded letters on the cover.

" 'Alice Through the Looking Glass,' " said Emma, glad to know something at last. "Lewis Carroll—you know?"

Abigail shook her head. "I've never heard of it, or him. And Miss Bessemer keeps all the latest novels in her library."

"Well, maybe the book hasn't been written yet," Emma replied. "Actually, the proper title's 'Through the Looking Glass.' Whoever painted the owl didn't know books too well. But I still like it, don't you?"

Abigail did, a lot, Emma could tell, the way she set it down and stroked the owl's head. "What's the story about, Emma?"

"Oh," Emma said, casting around for words. "There's this olden-day kid called Alice who steps through a mirror into . . ." Emma faltered. "Into a strange world where nothing goes the way . . . it . . . should."

"Oh, Emma."

They stared at each other.

"Does Alice get back home?"

Emma nodded. "In the end—and so will you."

"I certainly hope so," Abigail said, turning sadly away.

Emma moved to cheer her up again. "Would you like the owl, Abigail? Take it home as a souvenir?"

"Oh, could I?" Abigail's eyes lit up, then she looked doubtful. "*If* I get home." She slipped the figure into her coat pocket, nevertheless. "Thank you, Emma. I'm sorry I can give you nothing in return."

"Don't worry," Emma said. "I'm only too glad for you to have it." But she wasn't. She already regretted giving it away. The Michigan owl was one of her favorite things. Oh, well, she told herself. No use dwelling on it now. Besides, think of that title sitting on Abigail's dresser before Carroll even writes it! "I have the actual book somewhere," she said. "Let's see if I can find it."

As Emma searched, Abigail crouched among the cartons also, picking up books, putting them down. "So many," she said. "More than even Grandpapa has on his shelves. And they are so brightly colored. Grandpapa's are all in dull leather: oxblood and olive; and black and brown—like this one, only fatter." She took up a shiny brown one with gold lettering and opened it idly.

Oh no! Emma sat up. The Middletown history! The idea of Abigail finding herself lined up with a bunch of people dead and gone gave Emma the creeps. And the dates! Big numbers, plain as can be, telling their births—and deaths!

"Not that one!" Emma cried and snatched the book away.

t's nothing," Emma went on hurriedly. "Just history and stuff. Hey, look at that mud on your face—you want to clean up?"

Abigail's hand went to her cheek. "Well, yes, please."

Dropping the book, Emma steered Abigail across the hall and into the bathroom. "Watch for the hot water," Emma warned, going to the sink. "When you turn it on, the water rushes out and it's *scalding*."

"Hot water?" Abigail halted inside the door, the doll tucked under her arm. She gazed around at the blue-tiled walls, then at the monstrous bathtub perched on bulldog legs. "Mom says that's a gem," Emma remarked, as Abigail went to take a closer look. "They don't make tubs like that anymore, you see. Today, they're small and all boxed in. And the water barely covers you."

Abigail turned to inspect the rest of the place. "A whole room—just to *bathe* in? Emma, in Grand-papa's house, I have a wash bowl on my dresser that Hester the cook fills with cold water each morn-ing, except on really *freezing* days, when she brings up a hot kettle, too. What's that?"

"The toilet," Emma said, and turned the lever to demonstrate.

Water rushed, and Abigail cried out, backing into the tub.

"It's okay," Emma said.

Water gurgled as the tank filled up again.

When all was quiet, Abigail came forward, peer-ing into the bowl. "Let me try," she said. She pushed the lever gingerly, watched the water flush, en-tranced now. "Where does it come from?"

Emma removed the tank lid. "In here," she said.

Abigail worked the lever again, watching the tank empty and refill, laughing with delight as the float sank down and bobbed up again with the movement of the water. At the fourth go, Emma exclaimed,

"That's enough! Cut it out or you'll have Dad up here to see what's going on! Here, let's get you some soap." A tiny cake of scented soap kept especially for visitors.

"How pretty," Abigail said as Emma handed it over. "Mmmm, lavender," she added, putting it to her nose. "Mama's soap smells of roses."

Not one for half-measures, Emma handed Abigail a visitor's towel, too.

"Now, I'll fill the sink so you don't scald yourself, and all you have to do is wash up then pull the plug when you're through, okay?"

"And the lever, one more time," Abigail said, getting in the last word.

Emma went back into her room. Now was her chance to hide the brown book. But first . . . She paused, weighing the volume in her hands. Abigail was listed in there. When she was born. When she died. Emma glanced toward the door. Dare she check these things out with the real, live girl only steps away? Why not—if she was quick? Emma turned to the index and slid her finger down the margins, looking for the number of Abigail's page. Just as she found it, headlights flashed against her shades and tires crunched up the drive. Her mother, home from the mall! Emma snapped the book shut, slid it beneath her mattress, and went to the bathroom door. "Abigail? Are you nearly done? Mom and Paul are home."

Water rushed in the toilet, gurgled down the washbasin drain.

The door opened and Abigail emerged, her face shiny pink and smelling of soap. "Emma, what shall I do? What shall I say?"

"Nothing. I'll do the talking," Emma said, hustling Abigail back into her room and onto the bed. "I know: you're a friend staying over."

"But your mother doesn't know me."

"That's okay. Let's see. I'll call you Abbie. Abbie, um, Cranston. All I have to do to make it work is say your folks know you're here."

"What about your brother?"

"Paul won't come within a million miles when he hears about you."

"But there's only the one small bed, Emma."

"No problem. We'll put bedrolls on the floor. Hush, Mom's coming."

Emma's mother halted in the doorway. "Hello," she said, looking from Emma to Abigail and back again.

"Oh, hi, Mom," Emma said. "This is Abbie Cranston from school. She's staying over, her mom says it's okay. She's helping me pack."

"She is?" Nancy Gibson surveyed the chaos.

"Do I need to call your mom, Abbie?"

"She's out till after midnight," Emma said quickly. "That's why Abbie came over—the babysitter couldn't make it," she added, for good measure, throwing a smile at Abigail, whose face was now deep red.

"Well," Nancy Gibson said. "Paul's getting a snack, would you like to bring Abbie down?"

"We have stuff, thanks," said Emma. The tray was still on the bed.

"So I see." Her mother smiled. "Well, lucky the sleeping bags are still in the hall closet. I'll leave you to get them out. Night, hon. Night, Abbie," she said, and left.

Abigail let her breath out noisily. "How could you stay so calm? I was scared out of my wits."

"That's just what I wondered about you when I left you by the chimney," said Emma. "Where's the doll?"

"I'm *sitting* on it." Abigail drew the charm from under her and bared the head. "Look at the eyes, Emma. You can almost feel their power."

Emma looked. In the lamplight, the twin holes seemed to go in to a depth far greater than the doll's size allowed. "Cover it up again," she said uneasily.

Abigail did, and set the bundle on her lap. "What am I going to do, Emma? What am I going to *do?*"

"What are *we* going to do, you mean. We'll wait until everybody's in bed, then go back to the chimney the way we planned," Emma said.

"You still think it is the best thing?"

"It's where the magic happened before. Let me get the sleeping bags." Emma went to the huge old family storage closet on the landing and ran her eyes over the jumbled shelves. The bags were up top, of course, at the back of everything. Emma pulled out fishing tackle, two old tennis rackets, scuba gear, and two odd ski poles to reach them. What a mess. No wonder Mom hadn't tackled the closet yet. Emma stuffed everything back and toted the bags to her room. They shook them out and laid them side by side in the middle of the floor. The sleeping bags looked like a refuge in among the mess of packing boxes; cozy, secure.

They turned off all the lights except the nightlight by the door. Now the refuge was a magic island. "A great place for ghost stories," Emma said, sitting herself down cross-legged. Then maybe not, she thought, thinking of Abigail in the brown book. "Come on." Emma patted the sleeping bag beside her. "Tell me about this academy. You say you started it last year?"

"Yes." Abigail lowered herself, tucking her legs in gracefully. "When Miss Bessemer's father died, she started a school for young ladies because she needed the money, Mama said. I am so fortunate. Most girls never have the chance to study reading and writing," she added in a stilty voice, as though quoting someone else.

"And do you like it, Abigail? Reading and writing, I mean."

"Oh, yes. Very much, and I am quite good at it, Miss Bessemer says." With a slight toss of her head, Abigail went on, "But even if I did not, I'd have to do my lessons. Mama says I must learn to stand on my own feet. After Papa died, Mama said that if she were not the daughter-in-law of Josiah Bentley, she would be making bonnets now. 'And rich as your grandfather may be, you never know what winds may strike his sails. I want my girl to be ready for anything,' she said."

"So what else do you learn, besides reading and writing?"

"Algebra and arithmetic—multiplication tables and money sums, you know," Abigail said. "Sewing and manners are extra."

Boring, thought Emma. In her classroom there was Herb the hamster, and an ant farm. There was the computer corner, and the video library. And a camcorder for filming weekly book reviews. And last month, during Whole Earth Week, they turned the entire room into an underwater cave. A real fun place, compared with Abigail's stuffy academy. "What about the other kids?"

As Abigail listed the girls, Emma watched her, comparing her with Kim. Kim with the loud voice that could waste a kid when she so chose. From the first, Emma had envied Kim's loud style and poise, her easy slouch and the way she spread herself as though she owned the place. Beside Abigail, Kim seemed gross. Emma sat up straighter, tucking in her legs. So what if Kim had dumped her? Here was a much better friend—or would be, but for that thing.

Emma's eyes slid resentfully to the doll.

Sooner or later, it was bound to shift with Abigail to their proper time. And she'd be all alone once more. Not fair! She was getting to know Abigail so well, and she hadn't been the least bit shy with her, not once. In fact, they'd both been having so much fun. Emma wished they could stay together longer. What a time she'd have, showing Abigail the modern world. She smiled, recalling how Abigail had jumped when she switched on the lights and when she flushed the toilet.

What would Abigail say to riding a bike, taking a spin in a car? Emma pictured them at the movies, in the mall; sipping soda, shopping for clothes. Oh, if only Abigail did not have to go yet—or at all. . . .

Emma eyed the doll, lost in speculation. If its magic was spent, *and* if it couldn't recharge like a battery, Abigail would be stranded in Emma's time for keeps. Mom and Dad will have to take her in—sworn to secrecy, of course. Abigail will be upset at first, Emma thought uneasily. But then she'll come around, when she starts enjoying herself. Emma pictured the two of them laughing it up in the back seat of Mom's car—Paul could drive with Dad—all the way to Texas. Friends—forever!

In her dreams. The magic was still there, low, perhaps, and recharging. That doll could vanish at any moment, Abigail with it.

Unless . . .

Say Abigail dozed off, let go of the doll, and it rolled out of reach. Then if it shifted, it would leave Abigail behind. . . .

And if Abigail didn't let go?

Emma moved her legs uncomfortably. She might have to help things along. Slip the doll from Abigail's grasp and—and hide it away. And then? Emma flushed at the enormity of the thought, but she finished it, all the same.

Then, no matter what the doll did, Abigail was there to stay.

~7~

Abigail gazed around curiously. "You have no toys. Not even a hoop."

Hoop? "Paul has one. It's over the garage door."

Abigail frowned. "However does he roll it, then?"

"*Roll* it?" Emma echoed, then she remembered the Mother Goose pictures she'd seen of olden-day children with sticks rolling hoops down a cobbled street. "It's not that sort of hoop. This one hangs in the air." She held her hand up horizontally. "And it has a net. The idea is to shoot—I mean, throw a ball over the hoop so it falls through the net. That's a goal, and you try to score the most you—"

"Oh, I love to throw my ball. I wish I could try your brother's hoop. But isn't it a nuisance, climbing for the ball each time it lands in the net?"

"Oh, no. The net has no bottom, you see, so the ball falls right through, and—"

"No bottom? So why have a net at all?"

Emma grinned. "I don't know."

"I see. So if you don't care for your brother's hoop, what else do you do, besides read these books?"

"I ride my bike all over. Saturdays—like today—Kim and I go to the mall, or rather, we did until now, like I said."

"What is a mall?"

"A giant closed-in place that's all stores. Clothes, mostly. Shoes, jewelry. And a big department store—that's lots of small stores all in one."

"What do you buy there?"

"Stuff from all over the world," Emma said, warming to Abigail's interest. "Hong Kong, Taiwan, India, Germany, Japan, England, and so on."

Abigail's eyes opened wide. "There must be so many merchant fleets sailing abroad these days."

"Well, yes," Emma hedged. No time now for steamships and airplanes.

"And this department store is inside the bigger closed-in place, you say?" Abigail clasped her hands around her knees. "It sounds truly magical, a wondrous palace within a vast treasure cave. I wish I could see it."

"So do I," Emma said eagerly. "We could buy you all kinds of things; school clothes and party dresses, clips for your hair. And we could hang out in the ice cream parlor, have ourselves a chocolate cone . . ." And show Kim and Jessie a thing or two, she added silently.

"*Chocolate!* But how costly!" Abigail cried.

Emma shook her head. "No more than any other flavor, not these days, anyhow. After ice cream, if there was nothing else to do, we'd get back on our bikes and ride around until dinnertime."

Abigail sighed wistfully. "Lucky Emma, to go where you please, without a chaperone. To share your pleasure with a friend."

"Yeah—except I have no friend anymore, as I said. But you—you have lots, I'll bet. All those kids in Miss Bessemer's Academy."

Abigail shook her head. "We live so far apart. After school, I'm driven home, and there I stay. I rarely go out, save for walks with Mama."

"So what *do* you do?"

"I sew. And play with Agatha, my old wooden doll. I make clothes for her, but she's not much fun. Her hair is painted on, and her face is almost worn away. That's why I was so looking forward to my new Cassie."

For pete's sake, thought Emma. Abigail is as lonely as I am. "What about your visits here, next door?"

Abigail looked down. "There's not much to do, besides ride my pony. I'm not permitted to go near the farm children, you see, and there's no one else."

"Too bad," Emma murmured, thinking how snobbish and even cruel those grownups were. She'd heard how strict rules were in the old days. To think that Abigail couldn't even play with the kids on the farm! Abigail will be much happier here and now, with me, she told herself. Emma thought again of all the fun she'd have, showing Abigail the present day. Going on bike rides together . . .

Tonight, the bathroom plumbing: tomorrow—
the world!

Emma pictured herself watching TV with Abigail, eating popcorn from the microwave. She could just see Abigail staring in wonder at the screen, Emma beside her, explaining everything. She warmed to the idea. What fun they'd have, if she could only get Abigail away from the doll. . . .

Which I just might do, Emma thought, studying Abigail's face. She didn't look so tired, but she had to be, because it had been already nighttime for Abigail when they met by the chimney.

Emma made a play of yawning and stretching. "Boy, am I tired," she said. "I'm going to get horizontal." She slid down onto her side, propping herself up on one elbow. "You get down, too, Abigail. You might as well. It'll be a while before they're all in bed. Come on," she urged, as Abigail hesitated. "We've got a night ahead of us."

"But what if we fall asleep?"

"Fat chance. We'll watch out for each other, okay?"

"I suppose." Abigail slipped down full length onto her sleeping bag and lay, one hand under her head, the other loosely cupping the rolled-up doll.

Emma stared at the hair tuft uneasily. Was the figure really more than just a carving? A totem, full of magic? Those hollow eyes: could they see her through the muffler? Silly, she told herself. It's just an old made-up dummy; it can't see, it can't think, it can't anything. Still. Something had jumped Abigail to the present, and it wasn't just Emma's sky-wish. Oh, she didn't know what to think. From below, a burst of canned laughter abruptly ceased. "They're through with the TV, Abigail. They'll be coming upstairs now," she said. "Abigail?"

There was no reply.

Abigail was lying on her back, eyes shut. Emma

leaned down. "Abigail?" she repeated, softly. Abigail didn't move. In the glow of the nightlight, she looked more beautiful than ever. Like a doll, a real live doll, Emma thought, admiring the thick, dark lashes, the flush of color on her rounded cheeks. Gentle as a baby. And *trusting*.

Emma's resolution wavered. But, recalling Abigail's sad face, her loneliness, she reached out and, not daring to breathe, took the edge of the rolled-up muffler, and pulled.

To Emma's dismay, the doll would not come free; Abigail was clutching it too tightly. Emma held her breath. Had the move disturbed Abigail? Would she wake up?

To her relief, Abigail stayed put. Come on, you brought her: now let her stay, Emma urged the doll silently, then pulled again.

This time, doll and muffler slid from Abigail's hand, so easily that Emma almost dropped the whole thing. But, bound by her resolve, she stood up cautiously and looked around the room. She must hide the doll, fast!

Heart pounding, Emma thrust the bundle back of the closet with Abigail's clothes. Then she shut the door and leaned against it. Her empty palm crawled as if she'd been carrying a live spider. Emma rubbed her hands together vigorously, to scrub away the feeling. Was that how Abigail had felt, rushing that thing to the parlor fire? She glanced at her new friend. Abigail still slept, arm out, fingers loosely curled.

Emma got back inside her sleeping bag and lay staring toward the closet. Reaction set in with a vengeance. Had she gone crazy? What if Abigail had caught her in the act? What if the doll had shifted time on Emma, alone? She squeezed her eyes, shutting out the fear.

Hey, come on, Emma told herself. Abigail didn't wake up, you didn't timeshift. And you've made your wish come true. . . .

Rolling onto her back, Emma clasped her hands across her chest. Her skywish, answer to her loneliness. She looked again toward the closet. Maybe the doll had gone. She fought the urge to go see. Abigail was here for keeps, no going back now. She pictured Abigail waking up and finding the doll gone. Abigail getting upset.

But only for a while, Emma told herself uneasily.

She curled up, hugging her knees. The totem's eyes were on her, she could feel them. Piercing through clothing, closet door, and dimly lighted space, right into the depths of her wicked heart. Could the doll punish her? Would it?

Emma eyed the closet door nervously.

Her courage was all used up; she was getting the jitters. Maybe she should put things back the way they were.

Emma half rose, then huddled down again, this time pulling the bedroll cover over her head, shutting out the nightlight's glow. Wabeno's power wand had no quarrel with her. Emma tossed in her self-made darkness. She would leave matters as they were. Wasn't it for the best? Because who knew where Abigail might end up with that thing. . . .

"Emma! Oh, please, Emma, wake up!"

Emma felt herself being roughly shaken. Abigail was kneeling beside her, eyes round with horror.

"Emma, the doll has *gone!*"

"Gone? Oh, no." Emma glanced to the door, then to her watch. Half past midnight. The family should be well asleep, even Dad.

" 'Oh, no'," Abigail mimicked, savagely. "That is all you can say?" She leapt up and cast wildly about the room. "What'll I do?" she wailed. "Mama! Grandpapa! Uncle Ralph!"

"*Quiet,*" Emma ordered. "Maybe it's not as bad as you think. Maybe the muffler rolled under your sleeping bag." She made a show of lifting the edge, feeling about beneath.

"It's not there," Abigail said. "I already looked."

71

Emma put on a concerned face. "What will you do now?"

"What *can* I do? You tell me," Abigail snapped.

"Don't yell at me," Emma said. "If I hadn't—"

"Had you not persuaded me to leave the chimney, I'd be gone, too."

"But where?" Emma snapped back, then loosening up, she added, "I only tried to help you."

"Worse luck." Abigail turned her back.

"Boy, are you ungrateful," Emma said. "You could be in a much worse place, you know. At least you're with a friend."

"Friend?" Abigail whipped around again. "Why, you scarcely know me! And I don't know you—nor do I want to. I only want to go home."

"I'm sorry you don't like me," Emma said.

"Don't like? What on earth are you saying? How can you even think of 'like' and 'don't like' at a time like this?"

"It's not so bad. It's not as if you're going to *die*. Count yourself lucky. Kids today get lost all the time, and who knows what happens to them. But you—you're not in any danger. You're here, and now—which is much better than the olden days." Emma reached for Abigail's shoulder. "You can live with me, and go to a real school and learn to read properly, and do all those fun things we talked about. Oh, we'll have great times."

Abigail pulled back, outraged. "I don't want—"

"And Thursday, we move to Texas."

"*Texas!*" Abigail was shocked. "But isn't that dangerous?"

"Not at all," Emma said. "You and I will ride with Mom. She's a safe driver, and the interstate's a breeze."

"But the fighting down there."

"*Fighting?*"

"Have you forgotten the Alamo? Things have gotten so bad, Texas and Mexico are about to go to war."

"You're the one who's forgetting," Emma broke in. "That's history."

"Like me?"

Emma stared. Her big mouth! She'd done it again. "I didn't mean—" She shrugged helplessly, then pressed on. "Texas won, and it's the Lone Star State now. It's huge and rich, and they're building all over, which is why we're going there. My dad's a town planner, you see."

"Good for him, good for you. I am staying here."

"But you can't."

"Who says? I shan't leave Grandpapa's estate."

"What estate? You saw it all torn up. They're running a road through, that's why the house is all cut up. They're moving it Monday—the day after tomorrow—to a sort of museum. And they start the road on Tuesday. So you've got to come with us, you have no choice."

Abigail drew herself up. "Oh no? Listen to yourself. Here am I, lost to my family, to the world I know, and you talk of *fun*. My heart is breaking—and you'd keep me as a pet." Abigail strode to the closet. "I'm going back to the chimney, and in my own clothes."

"No, wait!"

Emma seized Abigail's arm but Abigail shook her off. "Stand back or I'll scream," she threatened. Wrenching open the door, Abigail ducked in to retrieve her clothes.

Move, Emma urged herself. Stop her, quick! But she stood as if under a spell, while Abigail emerged with the clothes and shook them out: pumps fell; chemise, knickers and petticoats fluttered down—then Emma's scarf unrolled.

"*No!*" Emma cried, but the doll slid free and tumbled to the floor.

*A*bigail gazed at the doll. So did Emma, caught up in the awfulness.

"Emma?"

Emma looked up, meeting Abigail's incredulous stare.

"You . . . stole the doll—hid it in my clothes. But why, when you know I'd be stuck without—" Abigail finally saw Emma's plan. "Oh, you low, vile wretch! You meant to keep me here!" Fired up now, she snapped to a crouch and grabbed the doll's feet.

Emma dove also, caught its head, and clung. They

came up slowly, both holding the doll. "Let go," Abigail said, in a flat voice.

"Only if you promise to stay."

"Promise? You—talk of *promise?*" Abigail tugged furiously.

Emma hung on. "I was only trying to help."

Abigail tossed her head vigorously, and Emma's hair clip flew wide. "Let go, *let go, I say.*" She twisted the doll, almost breaking Emma's grasp. But Emma still held on, silent and grim. Abigail lunged, bringing her angry face up close, so close that Emma caught a whiff of lavender. "Here I was, grieving and afraid, and there you were, acting the friend—while all the time planning to fool me. 'Trust me,' you said. Have you no shame? Oh, I wish we'd never met, deceitful creature."

"Don't!" Emma cried, frightened now by Abigail's rage. "Calm down."

"Calm down? I'll calm down all right—once I'm away from here."

"Oh, please." Emma held fast. "Please stay until I've—"

Abigail fixed her eyes fiercely on the doll. "Take me home—*now!*"

At that, light flared, blinding out the room.

"No!" Emma yelled. "Not just yet!"

Another flash came, then another. Emma

squeezed her eyes up tight. Her hands were still locked onto the doll like claws. What was happening out there? She dared not look, dared not let go. Still the flashes came, faster, merging at last into one blinding glare. In that instant, Emma saw her mom and dad asleep; Paul, sprawled, his bedcovers flung wide.

When they wake up, she thought bleakly, they'll find me gone.

Emma stood, dazed, eyes closed. Beside her, Abigail stirred, drawing in a deep, slow breath.

"Oh, my," Abigail said softly.

Emma felt the doll's tug as Abigail tried to turn around.

"Emma Gibson!" Abigail sounded shocked. "You came too?"

"What does it look like?" Emma said, coming out of it. Sharp wind cut across her face. She glanced up into a cold, starlit sky. "Where are we?"

"*I* am home," Abigail said. "Isn't that wonderful?"

"Wonderful?" Emma closed her eyes, feeling sick. Where did that leave her?

"I suppose it's not so wonderful for you," snapped Abigail. "But serve you right: I told you to let go of the doll."

A pungent stink hit Emma's nostrils. Horses? "What is this place?" she asked, letting go of the doll now.

"We're in Grandpapa's stables—where your house will be one day." At the sound of Abigail's voice, there came a whinny and a stomp of hooves. "That's White Star, Grandpapa's hunter," Abigail explained, for the moment sounding almost friendly. "He's good as any watchdog. Come along, I suppose you'd better keep with me. But hurry. Mama will be beside herself." Abigail tugged on Emma's arm.

Stunned, Emma let herself be towed through the darkened stables, close on Abigail's heels, emerging under a starlit, moonless sky. She turned, taking in the long, low spread of the stables. *Where your house will be one day* . . . "I can't get my bearings," Emma said.

"The house is yonder." Abigail pointed left.

Emma peered out into the dark. The darker mass was unfamiliar.

"It's different."

"Different? How do you mean?"

"It's . . ." Emma frowned. "Smaller." She glanced behind. The grounds were different, too. Where were the hedge and wrought-iron entrance gates?

"Things do change, you know, Emma," Abigail

78

said. "Just last year, for instance, Grandpapa laid a new roof and added two gables. Hurry up; Mama will be so relieved to see us."

To see *you*, you mean, Emma thought resentfully, as Abigail hustled Emma on toward the house. Then she remembered how, earlier, she'd babbled on in the same way to Abigail.

As she stumbled along behind Abigail, homesickness welled up inside her.

She had a flash of her mother, packing china in Bakersfield. "You'd think this stuff could pack itself by now," her mom had joked. Emma had not found it funny. But right now she wouldn't care if the Gibsons shipped off to the moon, as long as it was in their time, and they were all together.

Mom would be okay for a while, Emma thought.

On regular Sunday mornings, everybody slept late, then Mom and Dad made brunch. They took forever to eat it, her parents lost in the Sunday papers, she and Paul haggling amicably over the weekend comics. Emma tried to picture how, on this particular day, they'd learn that she was missing. Remembering the visitor, Mom would call upstairs a few times first, then she'd send Paul to fetch her down. Paul would find only two empty sleeping bags, no sign of where she and "Abbie" had gone. Even then, her mom wouldn't panic, not until she got out the phone book to call "Abbie's" mother to see if Emma had gone home with her. But when she found there was no Abbie Cranston in Middletown, that no girl of that name even existed, what then?

A broad flight of wooden steps led to the front door. Emma paused. In her time, there'd been a canopy over the steps, flanked by tall white pillars. Abigail stood waiting at the top for Emma to climb.

"Come on in," Abigail urged, as Emma reached the door.

The entrance hall, lit with lamps and candles, was deserted. Things looked more familiar here, though, Emma found. Smelled familiar, too. Of wood, and wax, and mold, like church.

Abigail called out. "Hello-ho! Mama! Grandpapa! Uncle Ralph!" Her voice echoed around the hall and up the curving staircase. But there was no reply. In fact, there was no sound at all, not even the tick of a clock.

"It's so quiet," Emma remarked, uneasily. And cold. And drafty. Where was the heat?

"It's too quiet," Abigail said. She ran across the hall, past the curving staircase, out of sight. Emma started after, met Abigail coming back. "I don't understand," Abigail said, looking really upset now.

"Hester's gone, too. And Tobias."

Hester was the cook, as Emma recalled. "Who's Tobias?"

"The kitchen boy. Emma, I'm so worried. Hester always stays up until everyone else has gone to bed. She rakes the hearth and turns out all the lamps, you know. Oh, where have they all gone?" She started up the stairs.

"Hey—wait for me."

They ran to the upstairs landing. It was long and narrow, dividing the house from front to back. And it was lined with doors. Abigail made her way forward to the front of the house, looking through each door in turn, Emma at her heels. The last one, in the right wall, was Abigail's own, Emma knew it at once. Not that she could see too well, for the only light came from a single lamp at the top of the stairs. But in the dimness Emma could make out the washstand with the bowl and jug, and the dresser with the mirror, just as Abigail had described them. There wasn't much else: a huge four-poster bed big enough to sleep four, a wooden chest at the foot of the bed, and a child's rocking chair. The polished wooden floor was bare except for one small rug, not much fun to lie on. But then Abigail had no books to read or radio to listen to. Emma shivered, thinking of her own room's cozy clutter.

Abigail crossed to her window, looking out. Then she turned to Emma in appeal. "Where are they? What's happened to them?"

Emma followed, hesitantly. The silence was unnerving. Back home, even in the deep of night, there was always some comforting background noise: the kick of the refrigerator, the click of the radiators, the distant *chunk* of the basement furnace. And during the day, a radio and TV to fill the quiet with human noise. She glanced to the doll. Was this a cruel joke, Wabeno's final punishment? A home, but no one in it?

"You don't think—"

"Shush!" Abigail raised a hand.

Emma listened, caught a creak of wood. "What's that?" she whispered. Abigail looked fixedly at the open doorway.

"*Who* is that, you mean. Emma, someone is on the stair."

A young man burst into the room, a lantern swinging in his hand, his cape thrown back. Wild hair, ruddy face, the lower half covered in straggly whiskers. Kind, blue eyes, creased with worry. Emma liked him at once.

"Uncle Ralph!" Abigail rushed to greet him, her arms outspread. But to Emma's horror, on reaching him, Abigail continued on, passing through him to crash against the wall beyond.

The young man raised the lantern, peering around the room. "Abigail?"

"Here, Uncle Ralph! I'm here!" Abigail pushed

off the wall, and advanced a step or two, but no farther. She turned a stricken face to Emma. "He doesn't see me. He doesn't hear me."

Abigail's uncle stood, seemingly in a quandary. "Oh my word, what a mess." The young man ran his fingers distractedly through his hair. "And all my fault, taking that wretched doll." He spun on his heel and clattered off down the stairs.

"Uncle Ralph! Uncle Ralph!" Abigail dashed after him. "He's gone back outside," she cried as Emma followed. "Oh, Emma, what has happened to us? Are we ghosts?"

"Ghosts? No way." Emma rapped her knuckles on the polished stair rail. "We're solid, this place is solid, too." If anybody's a ghost, she thought, it's Uncle Ralph—but she couldn't bring herself to say that.

Abigail was unpersuaded. "We could still be spirits. Some do throw things, you know."

Emma stayed silent. She knew about those spirits. They were called poltergeists. Abigail's suggestion that they might be ghosts frightened her. But how else to explain their present fix? When Abigail had shifted to the future, she'd stayed quite solid and real, so it couldn't be through timeshifting, unless—

Emma thought back to the moment of shifting.

Abigail, beside herself, had demanded to go home. And Emma had tried to override her.

Take me home—now!

No! Not just yet!

Had those two wishes, tugging against each other, partly canceled each other out? Emma wondered. If so, they were somehow stuck *between*—and it was her fault. No way she was going to mention that.

"Abigail, that's sick."

"Then you explain what just happened. I'm afraid, Emma. What if this place is an illusion? *What if Uncle Ralph's the ghost?*"

Emma shook her head vigorously. "I think—I'm *sure*—this house is real, your uncle, too. And us. So let's stop talking of ghosts and try to figure the situation."

"I know. Wabeno's still punishing me, and you're caught up in it. It isn't over yet, you know," Abigail went on with a shiver. "Now he's made us invisible I daren't think what's next." Abigail raised the doll and pulled down the muffler, looking angrily into the hollow eyes. "How much longer does this go on?"

The totem, its round mouth fixed in silent, secret comment, stared back impassively. Emma had the distinct feeling of being watched from way behind those hollow eyes. She glanced to Abigail nervously. Abigail was growing angry with the doll again.

"You cruel thing," Abigail went on. "To bring me only halfway. Wabeno's punished me enough now. It's time to stop and make me fully real." She shook the doll so hard that the muffler slipped off, exposing the body hung with charms. Freed from the scarf, the metal tags jiggled wildly and the heart halves clinked together.

Emma's hand flew to her chest. "Cover that thing up again, quick," she cried. The fractured heart: a charm, a token, made to what end? She looked from the dull red halves to Abigail's anguished face and back again.

"Abigail, I think the charm is meant for breaking hearts."

"Oh, Emma. Do you think?" Abigail looked about to cry. But setting her mouth firmly, she raised the doll again. "You evil thing, you've broken mine. Now are you satisfied?"

The doll stared back without a sign.

"Don't answer, then," Abigail cried, angrily re-wrapping it. "Come on, Emma. I'm going after Uncle Ralph."

They started for the front door. But just then, a group of people burst in, holding lanterns. In front with Uncle Ralph was a pretty woman wearing a bonnet and shawl, and a silver-haired man in a top hat and coachman's cape.

"Mama!" Abigail ran to the woman, arms open wide. But as with Uncle Ralph, her arms passed through the woman's body. "Mama, it's me, Abigail. Mama—*Mama!*" Abigail's voice cracked. Emma put a hand to her chest, thinking, *How awful.* She watched Abigail's tears and the people's utter weariness in that icy entry hall. Misery rose to Emma's throat, and stuck. She wanted to shout and stamp, to make them aware of Abigail, but she was powerless. And knowing made it worse.

The man turned to a small, birdlike woman at his elbow. "Hester, we'll take hot spice tea in the parlor. Make enough for everyone."

"Yes, Mr. Josiah, sir," the cook said with a show of energy. "Come, Tobias, fill up the kettle." She moved away, driving a young lad before her, off toward the kitchen.

Josiah Bentley turned to the rest. "Good people, go warm yourselves; Hester will provide whatever you wish," he said. "We can't thank you enough for all your support," he called after them gruffly, as the search party tramped after cook and kitchen lad. When they had gone, the old man presented his arm to Abigail's mother. "Come, Elizabeth, let's get you to the fire."

"Josiah, how can you even think of resting at a time like this?" the woman protested, but Old Man Bentley escorted her firmly through an open archway beside the stair.

Abigail stared after them, her face pale. "Come on," she said to Emma, after they had gone. "We must go with them." But in the parlor archway, Abigail stopped short. "This is how it was before," she whispered, pointing. The trio, having shed their capes and hats, were over by the fire. "Mama in her chair, Grandpapa in his wing chair facing her, and Uncle Ralph standing at the hearth."

" . . . But what's the point of going out again right now, Elizabeth?" Josiah Bentley was saying. "We can't see, and she won't answer us."

"Or can't. She may be hurt, Josiah," Elizabeth Bentley urged. "Or worse. Wabeno may have taken her."

"Stop it, Elizabeth," Josiah Bentley commanded.

"Lizzie's right, Papa." Ralph Bentley spoke up now, waving his hands in the air. "Abigail's not anywhere, in or out. Something terrible's happened to her, I know it, and all because of me."

"Ralph, compose yourself. You're distressing Elizabeth even more." Old Man Bentley leaned forward. "We must consider the situation calmly, decide what next to do."

Abigail whispered in Emma's ear. "Oh, dear. Grandpapa looks awful. He's been quite sick, you know. And now he looks worse than ever. Oh, please don't let him have another attack."

Abigail's mother jumped and began to pace about. "Oh, how can you speak of being calm!" she cried vehemently. "Who knows what Abigail's going through at the hands of that dollmaker?"

"It's all my fault," Ralph Bentley repeated. "As I've said a thousand times—I only meant well."

Just then, Hester came through with three hot spiced cups on a tray. "Here you are, Mr. Josiah, sir. Can I get you anything else?" She set the tray down before the hearth, and Emma smelled cloves and cinnamon.

"Thank you, no, Hester. Just make sure the folks out there have all they need. I'll be in presently. Hester—" he called, as she went to the archway. "You did a fine job tonight, helping to call out the search party."

"I were only glad to, sir," Hester said, looking gratified.

"All this talk of being sorry, Ralph," Elizabeth said, as soon as Hester was gone. "It's not one bit of use. We must *do* something. Josiah?"

The old man took his cup. "We must find the power wand and return it."

"Wabeno likely has it back already—along with Abigail, for punishment," Ralph said unhappily.

"I think not," Josiah Bentley said, climbing stiffly to his feet. "I know Wabeno. It's not as simple as that." Sighing, he turned to Abigail's mother. "Elizabeth, go to bed. We can do no more until daylight."

"And then?" The woman stood up.

"We'll see. Go on; you, too, Ralph. I'll send the search party home."

The two obeyed, passing Emma and Abigail by the space of a hair.

Elizabeth Bentley paused in the doorway. "If Abigail doesn't come back, you'll go to Brazil, won't you, Josiah? If so," she went on, as the old man did not answer, "I go with you."

Josiah looked up. "Absolutely not," he said.

"You know," Elizabeth Bentley said quietly, "that I would give my life, my very soul, for my child."

Josiah Bentley looked inclined to argue, but then he bowed his head. "We'll talk in the morning, Elizabeth. Good-night, my dear."

Abigail's mother crossed the room and put an arm around him. "This is a terrible time for us all, Josiah." She kissed his whiskered cheek and hugged him tight. "Good-night," she said, then, turning, made swiftly for the stair.

"Mama—see! Here I am, and the doll! And quite safe—see!" Abigail called after her, waving the doll in the air. But, deaf and blind to Abigail's protestations, Elizabeth began to climb. Abigail ran up behind her, the doll still held aloft.

Emma watched them go. The agonized look on Elizabeth Bentley's face as she turned away: Abigail's, the very same. Emma made no effort to follow them. She had no business here. She was an intruder—worse. A spy.

The moment they disappeared, Uncle Ralph ran back downstairs and into the parlor. After a moment, Emma went after him.

"You don't really mean to journey to Brazil, Papa?" the young man was saying. "Doc Wharton won't even let you go as far as Boston."

"Ha! The man likes his fees, that's all. I'm much better. Now, get upstairs and sleep, my boy. I'll need your help tomorrow."

"If you insist," the young man said, then left.

Josiah Bentley threw himself into his chair and leaned toward the fire. "All those years," he muttered to himself. "I honored Wabeno, gave the man his due. Does that count for nothing?" He shook his head slowly. "I'd have said he was a good man. But whatever his powers, if he's harmed Abigail one whit, I'll have his head."

Emma hovered uncomfortably near the doorway. She was snooping again, eavesdropping on another's pain. But where else to go? Upstairs, to spy on Abigail and her mom?

On a thought, she went to the kitchen.

The search party was sitting around the stove, drinking their tea.

Emma moved forward to stand at the outer edge.

"I'd have bet a week's wage we'd find her in the stables," Hester said. She moved around, refilling cups. "The love she has for that pony."

"Pony!" The man nearest Emma leaned in toward his neighbor. "Pity she ain't got none of it to spare for human beings," he murmured. "You oughta hear the names she calls my Tobias, here. Low, and vile. Common, low creature. *Dirty wretch*. Treats him like scum, just because he helps in the kitchen. So I'm not crying over lost sheep."

"Watch it, Jeb," a nearby woman warned. "She may be more than lost. Don't go saying words you'll rue come morning."

Jeb scowled. "Hey, wishing her a spanking isn't wishing her dead."

"A spanking, is it?" The woman frowned, then moved away.

Jeb sniffed. "Hoity-toity. A man's entitled to his own opinion."

"Miss Abigail ain't so bad," Jeb's neighbor said. "It's them fancy Boston ways. Fine clothes and day schools and learning manners has gone to her head. It's a fact she never plays with no one."

Another woman chimed in. "My Mary ast her over to our place." The woman glanced over to Hester, and went on in a low voice. "That little chit snubbed Mary real bad. Said she wasn't allowed to visit with *farm* kids—but the stable lad overheard Mr. Josiah hisself hasslin' her to go out and make friends. Still, I wouldn't want to wish her any real harm, just a bump and a scratch, and a backside full of teazles, maybe, to bring her down to size."

Emma listened, stunned, remembering how Abigail had said that she was not allowed to play with farm children. She thought back to Josiah in the parlor. He seemed a kind man, considerate of his farm folk. Not one bit the snob Emma had imagined. Abigail had been lying all along.

A silence fell as the kitchen door opened, and Josiah stood in the doorway. "I thank you again for your support," he said. "It's been a rough few hours. If we haven't yet found Miss Abigail, it's not for lack of effort on your part. And I know you're game for more, but I think we've done all we can this night. So sup up, catch some sleep—and I'll see you right for your trouble come morning."

The door swung to on a chorus of good-nights.

"Now there's a gentleman for you," Jeb murmured. "He'll see us right for our trouble, he says, and he will, indeedy."

"Young Ralph, he's okay, too," Jeb's neighbor replied. "Better than the brother, rest his soul. That little miss—she's a chip off her dad's block, and no mistake." He drained his cup and set it down. "I'll say good-night to ye, Hester," he called, and went out the door. That started everyone leaving, and within minutes, the kitchen was empty, save for Hester and Tobias.

Together, they started picking up tea cups and rattling them in the kitchen tub. "Off home with you," Hester said, giving the youth a gentle shove. "I'll finish up. Go on, get after your dad."

The boy needed no urging. He wiped his hands smartly on the towel.

"I'm glad she's lost," he said, pulling on his jacket. "She don't like me. She calls me common and low, but I ain't, my father sez."

Hester put a finger on his lips, glancing to the inner door. "Hush now, Tobias," she said. "Miss Abigail's not half as bad as people think. She's lonely, and scared folk won't like her. And she tries to hide it, you see."

Tobias snorted. "She's right to be scared. Folk

don't like her. And you know why? Because she thinks she's too good to play with us *common* kids, that's what."

"There you go again!" Hester cried. "Here, I'm not about to stand and argue the case with you. Off to bed, and from now on mind your tongue. I've told you before not to speak of Mr. Josiah's flesh and blood that way. Now, go on—home." She shooed Tobias out, then went to the sink.

Emma wandered back into the hall and slumped onto the stair. That talk about Abigail acting proud to hide her loneliness. Just now, Emma had pounced on her for lying. But was she, Emma, any better? Admit it, moving wasn't why she'd lost Kim as a friend.

Abigail came slowly down the stairs, the doll dangling from her hand. "Mama's in bed with the lamp lit, and that's bad. She's huddled up, so I can't see her face, but I know she's crying."

"Oh, Abigail." Emma's heart went out to her. She stood up. "Come on," she said. "Let's get ourselves out of this mess."

~10~

They went up to Abigail's room and shut the door. Abigail set the doll down on her bed and, with a taper from the landing, lit her oil lamps: three, in all. But at their very brightest, the room was dim and yellowish. Like when Mom lit candles during a power loss, Emma thought, gazing around at the shadowy walls. No wonder they told so many ghost tales in olden times. Even today, in movies, the lights went out when spooks got into the act.

"Now what?" Abigail picked up the doll again.

"I'm working on it," Emma said. Abigail was

acting cool. The princess, waiting for her servant to deliver. But she didn't fool Emma this time. Abigail was frightened. And no wonder.

Abigail spoke up. "Wabeno is an evil man, to leave me here like this."

Emma shook her head. "It's not over."

"How do you know that?" Abigail looked scornful.

"You still have the doll. I wouldn't call Wabeno evil, either."

Abigail frowned. "You called him that yourself."

"That was before."

"Before what?"

Emma shrugged. She could hardly say "Before I eavesdropped on your grandpa in the parlor." Josiah had been clearly shocked and much confused. *All those years, I honored Wabeno, gave the man his due. . . . I'd have said he was a good man. . . .* Josiah had been around. He was no fool. Wabeno must have earned that trust. According to Josiah, the man was a healer, not the sort to dump a kid in limbo and abandon her.

Emma went to the great, square mirror. She stood before it, gazing at her reflection. Behind her, Abigail watched intently. Emma pressed her palms into the solid dresser top. This was where Abigail had banged down the doll and seen Wabeno's face: *A face, floating beside my own reflection, staring out at me . . . and, oh, you should have seen his eyes!* Emma leaned in, half expecting Wabeno to appear. But there was only Abigail holding the doll.

Turning, Emma held out her hand. "Here, let me have that thing."

Abigail clutched the doll with both hands. "No."

"You don't need it now," Emma argued. "You're home. In fact, you ought to put it down, in case it shifts again."

"I'm *not* home!" Abigail cried angrily. "Only in the cruelest of ways. It's evil, and useless, so take it, and good luck." She thrust the doll into Emma's hands, and threw herself onto the high four-poster bed.

Emma unwound the scarf, laying bare the figure lying in its folds. She took hold of it gingerly and turned it over. The charm tags shifted with the movement, and the fractured heart disk clinked.

She frowned, staring into the doll's eyes. Somehow, it didn't seem so evil now. And the eyes had lost their menace. In fact—they seemed to be asking her something.

"You don't have any answers, do you?" Abigail sat up again, her eyes fiery bright. "You always act as though you do, but you're all talk."

Emma whirled around. "And so are you, *Miss*

Hoity-toity. That's what they call you downstairs. They hope you get a spanking, or thorns in your butt, because you're such a rotten *snob.*" Even as Emma blurted it out, she knew it wasn't as simple as that. For while Abigail ducked the local farm kids, she also dodged her posh schoolmates in Boston.

"How dare you!" Abigail leapt down off the bed. "I hate you, sly, deceitful . . . *grasping* creature that you are!"

Grasping! "You can talk, *princess.* You haven't thought once of me. Only of yourself. No wonder kids can't stand you. I wouldn't cross the street to be with you."

"Why, you loud, common wretch!" Abigail's voice rose. "I could never be as low as you. I'd *never* steal to keep a friend!"

Abigail didn't look so pretty now. In fact, her face looked almost plain, screwed up in that fierce scowl. Emma glanced to the mirror and saw her own. What a pair they made: Miss Grabby. Miss Snob.

"Don't quarrel, Abigail," Emma said quietly. "I'm only trying to help."

"Oh, please," Abigail retorted. "You've helped enough."

Emma looked at the doll, the broken heart tag

dangling at the chest. A heartbreak charm . . . joined by coils of wire!

She caught her breath. All this time, they'd been looking at the broken halves—and had missed the point entirely!

"Now I *truly* know," she said slowly. "About Wabeno, the doll, and why we're stuck like this."

"That's what you said before. But you're a cheat and a liar," Abigail said. "You don't know anything."

"But I *do*. And I was almost right before. Now I know the rest of it. What the charm is really for. And how to get us out of here."

"Hah." Abigail tossed her head.

Emma tapped the heart tag. "See this?"

"What of it?"

"It's a heart, snapped in two."

"Clever," Abigail sneered. "You really do know something, after all."

Emma pressed on. "I was thinking of the separate halves before." She held up the heart by one of the halves, letting the other one dangle. "But the real point is that they are joined."

"So?"

Emma sighed. Abigail was being difficult. "The halves mean nothing by themselves. For the charm to work, you need them both."

"So?"

"I think it takes two people to make it work. In this case, me and you. We'll never get home on our own. Only if we help each other."

"I—help you? You must be mad!" Abigail cried, and lay back again.

"That does it." Emma raised the doll to the mirror. "Wabeno, I give up. It's your turn now." She rapped the doll smartly on the bureau top.

At the crack, Abigail came up, her shocked face turned toward the glass. A wisp of smoke appeared between them. It coiled about, then took shape, fleshing out into a face.

"Wabeno!" Just as Abigail had described him.

Abigail ran for the door.

The ancient face gazed impassively from the mirror. Emma stood transfixed in the old man's stare. Those eyes! Deep and dark, they were on her. *You called me,* they said. *So now I'm waiting.*

Emma did not feel the least afraid. She stood on tiptoe, leaning in toward the mirror. "I am right about all this, aren't I?" she asked quietly. "We're supposed to work together."

Wabeno stared back without a word.

The dollmaker was still waiting. For what? Emma glanced to Abigail at the door, hand still on the knob. For them to work his charm, of course.

101

"All right." Emma faced the old man squarely. "I'll speak first. I wish for Abigail to be back home with all my heart," she declared, then laid the doll in front of him. She turned to the door. "Now you, Abigail. Now you wish me home."

Abigail stayed put.

"Come on, Abigail," Emma urged, growing anxious. "Just give her a minute," she said, turning back to the glass. But Wabeno had disappeared.

Emma turned about. "Abigail, why didn't you speak?" she cried. "Now I have to call him back again."

Abigail took a faltering step into the room. "Emma?" she called, peering about. "Where are you?"

"Right here," Emma said, then groaned aloud. The charm had worked all right. Now Abigail could neither see nor hear her. "Abigail!" she shouted, but what was the use? Abigail was fully real again, leaving Emma behind. "I don't get it!" she yelled. "It's not supposed to work by halves! Only if we act together!"

Abigail was searching the room now, looking behind the curtains and under the bed. Didn't Abigail realize what had happened? Emma watched anxiously. "Hurry up and see then send me home. You do know how." Abigail didn't hear, of course. In desperation, Emma glanced to the doll on the dresser. Should she try to summon Wabeno again? Emma went to pick up the doll—and her hand passed right through it.

Noises sounded on the landing. The door crashed back and old Josiah stood puffing in the doorway. "Abigail? Abigail, *child!*"

Abigail leapt to her feet. "You *see* me, Grandpapa?"

"Oh, my dear." The old man seized her and hugged her tight. Keeping hold, he called over her shoulder. "Elizabeth! Ralph!"

Emma caught her breath. Now that Abigail understood what had happened, she'd surely speak.

Doors banged, and Abigail's mother rushed through in a flurry of nightclothes, Uncle Ralph on her heels. Helpless, Emma could only stand and watch their joyous reunion.

Suddenly, Elizabeth Bentley pulled back, holding her daughter at arm's length. "Abigail! Where have you been? Just look at your hair, your face! And those clothes! Where is your party dress?"

"Elizabeth," Josiah said mildly. "Give the child a chance."

Uncle Ralph spoke up. "Where did you go, though, Abigail? We were frantic. We had a search party out, you know."

"We—I saw." Abigail glanced about furtively. "We—I was here."

Emma listened, incredulous, as Abigail changed each *we* to *I*. She knows, Emma thought. She knows all right. And she's dumping me.

No one else seemed to have noticed Abigail's correction.

Josiah said, "If this was some jest, young lady, if you were hiding in the stables—"

"Oh, no, Grandpapa," Abigail said. She ran to the dresser and seized up the doll, passing Emma by a hair. "You'll never believe: I've been here all along, but couldn't let you know it."

Not true! thought Emma in a torment. Oh, how could she?

"I saw you run in here, Uncle Ralph," Abigail went on. "I followed you downstairs. When you all came in, I ran to you, Mama—and passed through you. I—thought I was a ghost," she added, shrinking into Emma's jacket.

"Passed through?" Abigail's mother snatched the doll from Abigail and tossed it onto the bed. "Oh, that Wabeno! Listen, you're safe now and very much alive!" She hugged Abigail close.

Emma watched, helpless, as Abigail soaked it up.

"What I'd like to know—" Uncle Ralph said.

Elizabeth Bentley raised a hand. "Later. Ralph,

have Hester boil a kettle for the tub. The child is filthy. She needs a wash and clean, decent clothes. When she's to rights, we can talk in the parlor where it's warm. Come on, Abigail, you may use my very best soap."

The bedroom cleared.

Left alone, Emma turned to the mirror. "What about me? When do I go home?" she murmured, hoping for Wabeno's face to reappear, but no such luck. Only Abigail can wish me home, she told herself. And right now, Abigail's still mad with me. Too mad even to admit that I exist.

A new thought came.

What if the spell worked both ways only if she and Abigail occupied the same space together? In that case—Emma gripped the dresser's edge, feeling dizzy. Even if Abigail did cool off and wish her home, the spell wouldn't work. And she was well and truly stuck: a ghost from the future doomed to haunt the Bentleys' past!

~*11*~

Downstairs, Josiah sat while Uncle Ralph paced the parlor rug. Crossing the chilly hall, Emma found Abigail with her mother in the kitchen. Emma breathed in the steamy warmth of the low-beamed room. Hester had dragged out a tin tub and set it before the stove, and was pouring in hot water from a large iron kettle. Emma rubbed her down-clad arms, feeling tired and gritty. She edged forward, the heat from the stove striking her cheeks. Except for this room and the area immediately around the parlor fire, the whole place was alive with icy drafts. If only they knew about central heating and insulation. Emma marveled that they hadn't all died of pneumonia already.

"Such strange clothes," Elizabeth Bentley said, stripping Emma's things off Abigail. She examined each piece curiously, then cast it aside.

Emma eyed the clothes pile, feeling slighted. "They aren't exactly rags, you know," she told them.

"You haven't told where you got these, Abigail," Mrs. Bentley went on. "Or where you left your new blue dress."

Abigail dibbled her toe in the tub, testing the water. Emma wriggled her toes inside her sneakers, aching to do the same.

"You were not in your room all the time, were you?" Abigail's mother said quietly. "Well?" she prompted, when Abigail did not reply.

Abigail stepped into the bath, sat down with a splash. "It was awful," she said, head bent, staring at the ripples. "I—I can't talk about it."

Awful? Emma folded her arms. What about the fun she'd had exploring Emma's room, and the bathroom? How she'd laughed at Emma's clowning?

"You poor darling," Abigail's mother said, taking up a cake of yellow soap. "Well, maybe later?"

Abigail nodded, looking around. "Yes," she said,

quickly. "Later." While Abigail splashed herself, her mother shook out Emma's clothes and folded them. "I'll have Hester take them over to the gatehouse tomorrow," she said. "The keeper's boys never have enough working clothes."

Emma puffed out in indignation. Working clothes, indeed!

"Hello, what's this?" Abigail's mother drew something from Emma's jacket pocket and laid it on her palm. "Oh, it's a tiny owl, reading a book. How exquisite. Oh," she went on, bending to look more closely. "There is writing on the cover. 'Alice Through the Looking Glass.' What a peculiar title. Who gave you this curio, Abigail?"

Abigail looked up, then glanced around guiltily. "I . . . found it, Mama."

"Found it?" Elizabeth Bentley crouched beside the bath. "Abigail, you must tell me: where did you find a thing as fine as this?"

Abigail made no move to speak.

"Abigail? Answer me," her mother commanded, her voice quite sharp now.

Abigail began to cry. "My head hurts, I feel faint," she wailed.

"I'll bet," Emma muttered. Surely Abigail's mother saw through the act? Or did Abigail often throw such scenes to get her way?

Abigail stood up now, her face tight set. *Definitely* still mad, Emma thought, her spirits sinking lower still. In that mood, Abigail would never wish her back.

Emma watched enviously as Abigail's mother toweled her daughter down, and slipped a thick white nightgown over her head. Emma wriggled her shoulders, her own skin tingling pleasurably at the sight. But she didn't envy Abigail as Elizabeth Bentley tugged a stiff, wire brush through the snarls of tangled hair. Abigail jerked her head away, squealing in protest, until the last knot was out. Quiet now, and looking sullen, Abigail sat while her mother twirled long white rags through the tamed hair. "So that's how they made ringlets," muttered Emma, absently shaking her own short wash-and-wear curls. "I'll bet they're torture to sleep in."

Still, the sight of Abigail and her mother sitting close together at the kitchen stove made Emma feel quite strange. It had been a while since her mom had barged in on Emma's bath time, not since that last fuss Emma had made. Now, if her mom should dare to poke her head around the bathroom door, Emma was ready to kick up such a stink in protest that she wasn't a baby anymore. This looked cozy, though. She watched wistfully as Abigail's mother hugged Abigail and breathed up the scent of her daughter's hair. "Mmmm," Elizabeth Bentley murmured, smiling fondly down. "You smell like my favorite tea rose. Come on, let's show them a clean girl."

Emma followed mother and daughter into the parlor, watched Josiah hand out cups of hot spice tea. Abigail sat holding audience, the center of her family's attention. Emma eyed the steaming cup in her hands, hoping Abigail would leave her some.

"Well, Abigail?" Josiah prompted.

Abigail looked up, her large dark eyes reflecting the firelight. "I do not want to talk," she said woodenly.

"The child is all in," Uncle Ralph said. "Come on, drink up, let's have you to bed, birthday girl."

"After she tells who gave her this," Elizabeth Bentley said, holding out her palm. On it, perched Emma's gift.

"Why, it's an owl," Ralph said.

"And a scholarly one." Josiah took it up and examined it closely, even the base. " 'Made in *Japan*'?" He looked up in astonishment. "Why, this is worth a ransom!"

A ransom? Emma frowned. She'd found it on sale in a five-and-ten. Some hot-shot merchant this guy was.

110

Abigail was crying again, quiet tears that slowly trickled down her cheeks, nicely calculated to squeeze the general sympathy.

"All right, young lady." Josiah set down the owl. "I see we'll get no more from you this night. Off to bed—we'll talk in the morning."

Uncle Ralph gathered Abigail in his arms and they all made for the stairs. Emma climbed after them, thinking hard. "Okay for Abigail," she muttered. "She's back home; clean, full of hot drink, with everybody fighting to tuck her in. What about me?" Emma had a flash of her own bed nestled cozily amid the packing boxes. "Wabeno, please," she begged, "give me one more chance."

Up in the cold bedroom, Abigail was under the covers, her family lined up alongside. Uncle Ralph took up Wabeno's doll and waved it in the air. "I'm leaving for Boston tomorrow first light, young lady." He looked to Josiah. "Alone, now the crisis is over, I hope?"

Josiah nodded.

"And I'll bring the birthday girl something else to make up," Ralph went on, turning back to Abigail. "What would you like?"

"Oh, Cassie, please!"

"Cassie?"

"A *real* doll," Abigail breathed, eyes shining.

"Pretty, with big blue eyes that open and close and hair that you can brush."

Uncle Ralph laughed. "You have named her already?" He bent to kiss her. "I guess she's what you wanted all along. Oh, well, forgive a foolish uncle, will you? I shall likely be gone before you awake, so I'll say good-bye now. As soon as I have put things right with Wabeno, I'll bring your Cassie, so don't fret, little one. Good-night."

Little one! thought Emma, outraged. *Hah!*

The grownups blew out the lamps, and left. In the chilly darkness, Emma heard a rustle as Abigail sat up again. "Emma? I know you're there," Abigail said softly. "And you can stay. I shan't wish you home, not ever. Deceitful wretch, you've got what you deserve."

Oh, boy. Emma listened in dismay. "Abigail?" she called. But Abigail slid down again and let out a long, luxurious sigh.

Another minute, and she'll be fast asleep, thought Emma, beside herself. She stood by the bed, thinking furiously. Come dawn, the doll would be gone, and with it her last chance to get back home.

Emma had to get Abigail's attention. But how? She tested the edge of Abigail's quilt and found it solid enough. She could yank off Abigail's covers, but what would be the point, when they couldn't talk to each other? Emma frowned, trying to think. Suddenly, she thought of a perfect way. But it would need light and writing stuff. Abigail's lamps were out. Had Hester turned out the house lamps yet?

Emma opened the bedroom door a crack. The hall lamp still burned. No sign of grownups. She crept down to the deserted parlor and searched for stationery, in vain. In any room of her house, she'd find a scribble pad and ball-point pen. So what to write with? Emma's gaze rested on the hearth. Charcoal! She scrabbled around in the cinders, found an ember of wood. Taking up a parlor lamp, she carried both back upstairs. Setting the lamp on Abigail's dresser, Emma took the charred wood firmly in her hand and tested it against the surface of the looking glass. The charcoal skidded, leaving not a trace. Emma pressed harder. The fragment crumbled, strewing bits of carbon over the dresser top. So much for that. Emma looked around, frustrated. Now what?

She eyed the lamp thoughtfully, the tall flame flickering in the drafts, the sooty smudges on the tall glass chimney, then broke out in a smile. Excitedly, Emma pulled down her coat sleeve to make a sort of oven mitt, lifted off the lamp's chimney, and carefully set it aside. Now she held the naked flame up close to the looking glass. The flame sputtered, coating the mirrored surface with a fine, black, sooty film.

Now to wake Abigail. Emma put the lamp down and moved to Abigail's bed. Then, taking the covers firmly, she yanked them to the floor.

Abigail sputtered and rolled over. "What—" She turned her head, saw the lamp burning on the dresser. Now she came bolt upright, looking around fearfully. "Who—who's there?"

"Who do you think?" Emma retorted. Abigail didn't hear, of course.

Abigail reached down, groping for her lost bed-clothes.

"Oh, no you don't!" Emma cried. She darted forward, seized the other end, and tugged. Abigail let go with a smothered squeal.

"Emma?" she called, fearfully.

"You bet!" Emma yelled. She jiggled the lamp on the dresser top, drawing Abigail's eye to the dancing light and the sooty patch above it. "Now." Emma braced herself. "Make it short and plain, and pray Abigail can make it out." She put a finger to the glass, and wrote:

WISH EMMA HOME

Abigail stared at the words appearing in the smoky patch, forming them silently with her lips.

Then, "No," she said, looking around. "I shan't."

Emma added:

"No," Abigail repeated defiantly, staring at the glass. "I already said. You deceived me. You were going to trap me in your time. Now you can stay here, in mine."

Emma gritted her teeth and wrote:

I GOT YOU HOME

"Who cares? I'm going back to sleep." Abigail blew out the lamp and climbed into bed.

Emma ran to pluck the covers off again, cracked her shins on the bed. Tears sprang at the pain. She slumped to the floor, rubbing her shin. Her one idea, used up.

It wasn't fair.

There came more rustling as Abigail settled deeper into the bed. Emma caught a faint whiff of camphor, like from the mothballs in her sweater drawer. Homesickness washed through. She saw her own room, littered with familiar treasures collected over many moves. Her room, her things, that told her who she was.

Emma clenched her fists. "I'm Emma Gibson,"

she declared loudly. "And I'm for real."

Light filtered in under Abigail's door, reflecting dully off the bureau glass. Emma stood stiffly and went to stand before it. She could just make out her letters etched in smoke. "Wish Emma home. Please. I got *you* home." How could Abigail have turned her down? Emma reached out, and drew a last appeal:

Now Emma climbed onto the foot of Abigail's bed, curled up, and lay, looking at the mirror. Steps sounded outside, the landing lamp went out. The steps retreated down the stairs again. Hester was going to bed. The air struck cold on Emma's cheeks. She shivered, shrinking inside her coat.

Darkness, silence, a distant crack of wood.

Abigail heaved a long sigh. Her breathing deepened and grew rhythmical, just as it was before, when Emma had slipped the fetish from her hand. Emma squeezed her eyes tight. Serve her right, just as Abigail had said. She'd been bad, she couldn't deny it. But not wholly so. Before she'd hidden the doll, she'd tried her best to help and comfort Abigail, and it had worked.

116

Maybe, she thought, trying to console herself. Maybe after a night's sleep, Abigail won't be so mad. Maybe in the morning she'll remember the good times, and how nice I was, and she'll change her mind.

Maybe . . .

~12~

Emma awoke in the gray light, lying curled up, knee to chin. Had someone called her name? She raised her head to find the bed empty, the covers thrown back.

She sat up. The room was empty, the bedroom door, ajar.

Emma scrambled from the bed, ran to the open doorway. She was almost there when Abigail came in, something cupped in her hands.

The owl!

"Emma, are you there?" Abigail looked around the room. "I hope—I'm almost sure you are." She crossed to the dresser and stood gazing up into the mirror. "What you tried to do to me was wrong, and when I think of how I might never have gotten home I still could almost faint! But, well, that doesn't make it right for me to do the same to you. Besides, we . . . did have fun. And I suppose one could get carried away. So . . . I've decided to forgive you, after all. See." Abigail reached out and with short, sharp strokes, joined the heart halves thus:

"And now I'm going to try to send you home with the same words you used last night." Abigail planted herself squarely before the glass and gripped the edge of the dresser. "I wish Emma home with all my heart," she declared.

Nothing happened.

"The doll," urged Emma. "You need the doll." If it isn't too late, she added to herself. Emma was just about to write *doll* on the glass when sounds came up from the front yard: the clop of hooves, the rattle of wheels.

"Oh, goodness! Uncle Ralph's leaving already?" Abigail raced to the window and hauled the heavy drapes aside. Emma followed, peering past her through the ripply panes. At the front porch stood a carriage and a pair of shiny black horses that snorted impatiently, tossing their manes and pawing the ground, jerking the carriage forward.

"Whoa!" A coachman came from under the porch, set down his whip, and grabbed their reins, talking in their ears. In the upstairs passage behind Emma, a door opened, closed, and light footsteps ran down the stair.

Uncle Ralph!

"Stop him, Abigail," urged Emma. "Quick—call him back!"

Down below, Uncle Ralph, swathed in cape and muffler, strode out toting two small carpet bags.

Abigail reached to raise the window sash and call, then stopped. "We don't want to rouse the whole house," she said, and ran out, her ringlet rags flapping, her nightgown billowing behind.

As Emma watched, her nose squashed to the pane, Uncle Ralph threw the bags into the carriage and climbed in, pulling the coach door to behind him. "Oh, come on, Abigail!" she whispered.

The coachman raised his whip, but even as he

brought it down, Abigail flew out from under the porch, waving wildly. The man halted, his whip in midair, while Abigail reached on tiptoe and rapped the coach window with her knuckles.

When Emma reached the landing, Uncle Ralph was halfway up the stairs, Abigail in his arms. He strode into the bedroom and set her down on the rumpled quilt. "Young lady!" he scolded. "What are you thinking of, running out into the cold! You'll catch your death." He pulled back the covers, gesturing her inside. "In, missie, before your mother has me whipped," he commanded, but Abigail grabbed his cape.

"Uncle Ralph—wait."

"What is this?" The young man looked puzzled.

Abigail put a finger to her lips. "A minute, please?" She ran to the doorway and, after peeping out both ways, closed it quietly.

"Good heavens, what's the mystery?" the young man demanded.

"I'll tell you in a while, Uncle Ralph." Abigail came back into the room. "First, where's the doll?"

Uncle Ralph looked surprised. "In my baggage, of course. Why?"

"Would you fetch it, just for a minute, *please?*"

Uncle Ralph shook his head vigorously. "Absolutely not, Abigail. Not after all the trouble we've had. Besides . . ." He lowered his voice, glancing to the door. "It's more than my life's worth."

"It's not yours that's at stake," Abigail said quickly. "But someone else's."

Uncle Ralph drew his brows together, looking greatly concerned. "My dear girl." He leaned closer, gazing earnestly into her face. "There's someone else connected with Wabeno's doll? Who?"

"The girl who gave me this." Abigail opened out her fist, revealing the owl. "If I tell you about her, will you fetch it then?"

Uncle Ralph nodded. "All right—but be quick." He went to the window and signaled the coachman to wait.

Abigail began her tale. Of how she'd tried to burn the doll. How everything had vanished, how Emma had found her standing in the ruins of the estate. How she'd seen the house in pieces, waiting to be shipped away.

"Wait, Abigail," Uncle Ralph said, raising a hand. "You're saying you went to the *future?*"

Abigail frowned. "You don't believe me?"

"I do, I do—go on," Uncle Ralph said quickly.

Abigail resumed, telling how she'd gone back to Emma's house.

Emma's face began to burn. Here it comes,

she thought. Abigail is going to roast me.

"... and I was so distressed. To comfort me, Emma gave me this owl."

"How kind," Uncle Ralph said. "She sounds like a fine person."

"Fine?" Abigail glanced past Uncle Ralph, quickly scanning the room. "Yes. Yes, she is. After all, she did get me home in the end."

"But?"

"Before that, she—" Abigail looked down, holding the owl with finger and thumb. "She played ... a very bad trick, and I was angry with her. So angry I forgot the good things and the fun we shared. We talked a lot, and she showed me marvelous things, you'd never believe! So now I want to send her home, and I'm going to need the doll."

Uncle Ralph looked around the room. "Send her home? You mean—she's still *here?* In this room?"

Abigail nodded. "I'm sure of it."

"Oh, my goodness. Wait here," said Uncle Ralph, and hurried out.

"Whoopee!" Emma thrust a fist into the air. *"Thanks, Abigail!"* she cried, exultantly.

Abigail paced to the window and back. "I only hope it's not too late," she said, into the glass.

Emma sobered up at once, recalling her thought that the spell might not work now. Even so, she was so glad to be on good terms again that she reached up to the mirror, and in what little space was left, wrote:

NEVER TOO LATE!
THANKS!
FRIENDS?

Abigail nodded. "Friends—forever. Oh, my goodness!" She put her hands to her face. "I still have your clothes, Emma. And you have mine. Let's wear them sometimes and remember each other. Won't that be grand?"

Uncle Ralph came in with the doll. He handed it over reluctantly. "Sure you know what you're doing?"

"Oh, yes, Uncle Ralph." Abigail took it, fingering the broken heart charm. She gazed all around the room, finishing up at the bureau, just about where Emma stood. "I wish we could say good-bye," she said.

"Me, too," Emma murmured.

Abigail raised the doll to the mirror and cleared her throat. "I wish Emma home with all my heart," she declared.

As she spoke, Uncle Ralph cried out, and there, in the glass, was Wabeno. He looked first to Emma, then to Abigail, and nodded.

Now Abigail cried, "Emma!" and Emma knew her friend could see her reflection, and, judging by the young man's face, so could Uncle Ralph!

Emma smiled at them both. "Thanks," she began, but even as Abigail whirled to face her, the room vanished, and Emma was left standing under a chill, dawn sky. Wind cut past the chimney corner, nicking Emma's ears, cutting the back of her legs. She stood for a moment, stiff as the chimney column. It had all been so quick!

Turning around, Emma glanced to the shrouded parlor up on the nearest rig. Only hours before, she'd stood on this very spot and watched the Bentley family gathered around that very hearth. And in the kitchen somewhere in back of that, she had watched Elizabeth Bentley bathe her daughter and brush out her matted hair.

Sad, to think that they were all long gone . . .

Emma moved off over the churned-up ground, then halted abruptly. In the early light, she could just make out twin sets of footprints going to and from the chimney. One, her own, made by the sneakers she wore. The other prints were smaller, narrower, with pointed toes. Abigail's party pumps still lay on Emma's floor, along with her party things.

Let's wear them sometimes and remember each other. . . .

Emma smiled. She'd never cram her flat feet into those shoes! But the dress would fit her. And the other stuff. When she got home, she'd stow them in among her private treasures until she got to Texas. And she'd keep them forever.

She trudged on slowly, tracing the footprints until, reaching firmer, drier ground, they vanished. For a moment, she lingered, gazing along the ragged tracks, back to the chimney. Tomorrow, when the rigs rolled out, those tracks would be wiped out. But not the memory of all that had happened.

She grinned, recalling the look of utter astonishment on Uncle Ralph's face. "I wonder what he made of me," she said aloud.

The Sunday papers were lying by the gate. Emma picked them up and headed for the side door. She'd take a shower, then maybe give her mom and dad a break and lay the table for brunch. After brunch, she'd call Kim. Ask how the movie was yesterday; no strings, no overtones. Then she'd casually suggest a bike ride in the afternoon.

And Kim might agree—maybe.

And if not?

"There's Texas—and this time, Abigail, I'll do it right," Emma promised. "Trust me!"

ABIGAIL FITCH, née Porterhouse-Bentley: 1836–1928

Daughter of Jonah Bentley (q.v.) and Elizabeth Porterhouse (q.v.). Married Boston plumbing merchant Benjamin Coates Fitch 1858, produced six children: Elizabeth, Josiah, Ralph, Emma, Mathilda, and Amos. Together with husband pioneered modern bathroom systems. Widowed in 1881, Abigail went on to found Fitch, Steele, & Adams, Inc., of which her grandson, Amos Bentley-Fitch Jr., is presently chairman. In 1891, Abigail acquired controlling interest in the company, and established a pioneer research-and-development department. In this facility, Abigail herself invented the revolutionary Boston Water Rocket Cistern, the first porcelain flush toilet prototype to be mass produced in the United States. It was on this invention alone that the family's multimillion-dollar plumbing empire was founded. After building her empire and consolidating it with strong head and iron hand, Abigail finally retired to the Bentley mansion in 1909. There, in the very bedroom in which she had stayed as a child, she died peacefully in her sleep in 1928.

GRACE CHETWIN's *Collidescope* was chosen as an ALA Best Book for Young Adults. Praising the novel, the *Washington Post Book World* said, "warmth and humor combine with thoughtfulness," and *ALA Booklist* called it "an entertaining and thought-provoking time travel tale."

Her most recent novel, *Child of the Air,* is set on a faraway planet beset by seasonal firestorms. There Mylanfyndra and her brother, Brevan, discover their secret gift. *School Library Journal* said, "Chetwin has created an unusual and interesting world in this novel, first portraying a small, insulated group with its customs and folklore and mistaken ideas about the rest of the world, then stepping back to view the wider world as it really is, with light and air and knowledge rushing in. . . ." *Kirkus Reviews* noted, "The charm here lies in Chetwin's ability to make a strange, mysterious world seem real," and *ALA Booklist* said, "the scenes of flying, or riding the wind currents, are breathtaking."

The author began writing when her daughters were in their late teens, to preserve some of the stories she'd told them when they were growing up. Her tales of Gom, the mountain boy who became a wizard, include *Gom on Windy Mountain, The Riddle and the Rune* (an *ALA Booklist* Editor's Choice), *The Crystal Stair,* and *The Starstone.*

Other fantasy adventures by the author include *On All Hallows' Eve* and *Out of the Dark World.*